Teen Health Resources

glencoe.com

New Student Edition Includes

- The latest health information
- Fitness Zone Handbook
- What Teens Think
- Health eSpotlight Videos
- Reading Skills Handbook

Cross-Curricular Activities

- Guide to Reading
- Building Academic Vocabulary
- Connect To… Science, Math and Language Arts
- Write About It

Online Learning Center

- Online Student Edition
- Chapter Summaries in English and Spanish
- Interactive Study Guides
- eFlashcards
- Building Health Skills
- Student Web Activities
- Career Corner
- Podcasts
- Study-to-Go

Meet the Authors

Mary H. Bronson, Ph.D., recently retired after teaching for 30 years in Texas public schools. Dr. Bronson taught health education in grades K–12, as well as health education methods classes at the undergraduate and graduate levels. As Health Education Specialist for the Dallas School District, Dr. Bronson developed and implemented a district-wide health education program. She has been honored as Texas Health Educator of the Year by the Texas Association for Health, Physical Education, Recreation, and Dance and selected Teacher of the Year twice, by her colleagues. Dr. Bronson has assisted school districts throughout the country in developing local health education programs. She is also the coauthor of the *Glencoe Health* textbook.

Betty M. Hubbard, Ed.D., C.H.E.S., has taught science and health education in grades 6–12, as well as undergraduate- and graduate-level courses. She is a professor at the University of Central Arkansas, where, in addition to teaching, she conducts in-service training for health education teachers in school districts throughout Arkansas. In 1991, Dr. Hubbard received the university's teaching excellence award. Her publications, grants, and presentations focus on research-based, comprehensive health instruction. Dr. Hubbard is a fellow of the American Association for Health Education and serves as the contributing editor for the Teaching Ideas feature of the *American Journal of Health Education.*

Michael J. Cleary, Ed.D., C.H.E.S., is a professor at Slippery Rock University where he teaches methods courses and supervises field experiences. Dr. Cleary taught health education at Evanston Township High School in Illinois and later served as the Lead Teacher Specialist at the McMillen Center for Health Education in Fort Wayne, Indiana. Dr. Cleary has published widely on curriculum development and assessment in K-12 and college health education. Dr. Cleary is also coauthor of the *Glencoe Health* textbook.

Contributing Authors

Dinah Zike, M.Ed., is an international curriculum consultant and inventor who has designed and developed educational products and three-dimensional, interactive graphic organizers for over thirty years. As president and founder of Dinah-Might Adventures, L.P., Dinah is author of over 100 award-winning educational publications. Dinah has a B.S. and an M.S. in educational curriculum and instruction from Texas A & M University. Dinah Zike's *Foldables*® are an exclusive feature of McGraw-Hill textbooks.

TIME® is the nation's leading news and information magazine. With over 80 years of experience, TIME® provides an authoritative voice in the analysis of the issues of the day, from politics to pop culture, from history-making decisions to healthy living. TIME® Learning Ventures brings the strength of TIME® and TIME® For Kids' editorial and photographic excellence to educational resources for school and home.

Printed in the United States of America.

Send all inquiries to:
Glencoe/McGraw-Hill
4400 Easton Commons
Columbus, OH 43219

ISBN: 978-0-07-877425-6   (Course 2 Student Text)
MHID: 0-07-877425-X   (Course 2 Student Text)

ISBN: 978-0-07-877426-3   (Course 2 Teacher Wraparound Edition)
MHID: 0-07-877426-8   (Course 2 Teacher Wraparound Edition)

7 8 9   QDB/QDB   12 11

Teen Health

COURSE 2

Mary H. Bronson, Ph.D.

Michael J. Cleary, Ed.D., C.H.E.S.

Betty M. Hubbard, Ed.D., C.H.E.S.

Contributing Authors
Dinah Zike, M.Ed.
TIME®

Glencoe

Health Consultants

Alia Antoon, M.D.
Chief of Pediatrics
Shriners Hospital for Children
Assistant Clinical Professor, Pediatrics
Harvard Medical School
Boston, Massachusetts

Elissa M. Barr, Ph.D., C.H.E.S.
Assistant Professor of Public Health
University of North Florida
Jacksonville, Florida

Beverly Bradley, Ph.D., R.N., C.H.E.S.
School Health Consultant
Retired Assistant Clinical Professor
University of California, San Diego
San Diego, California

Donna Breitenstein, Ed.D.
Professor and Coordinator, Health Education
Appalachian State University
Boone, North Carolina

Roberta L. Duyff, M.S., R.D., C.F.C.S.
Food and Nutrition Consultant/President
Duyff Associates
St. Louis, Missouri

Kristin Danielson Fink, M.A.
National Director
Community of Caring
Salt Lake City, Utah

Kathryn J. Gust, M.A.
Instructional Technology Specialist
Freedom High School
Morganton, North Carolina

Christine A. Hayashi, M.A. Ed., J.D.
Attorney at Law, Special Education Law
Adjunct Faculty, Educational Leadership
and Policy Studies Development
California State University, Northridge
Northridge, California

Michael E. Moore, M.A., LCSW
School Psychologist
Special Education Coordinator
Centerville/Abington Community Schools
Centerville, Indiana

Tinker D. Murray, Ph.D., FACSM
Professor of Health, Physical Education,
and Recreation
Texas State University
San Marcos, Texas

Don Rainey, M.S., C.S.C.S.
Director, Physical Fitness and Wellness
Texas State University
San Marcos, Texas

John Rohwer, Ed.D.
Professor of Health Education
Bethel University
St. Paul, Minnesota

Michael Rulon, M.S.
Instructional Coach
Health Instructor
Albuquerque Public Schools
Albuquerque, New Mexico

Robin Scarcella, Ph.D.
Director, Academic English/ESL
University of California, Irvine
Irvine, California

Diane Tanaka, M.D.
Assistant Professor of Clinical Pediatrics
Keek School of Medicine
Attending Physician
Division of Adolescent Medicine
University of Southern California
Los Angeles, California

Robert Wandberg, Ph.D.
Staff Development
St. Paul Public Schools
St. Paul, Minnesota

Reviewers

Neile Bennett
Health Educator
Pierce County Middle School
Blackshear, Georgia

Kathy Bowman-Harrow
Supervisor, Health Education
Orange County Public Schools
Orlando, Florida

David Bryant
Health/Physical Education
Athletic Director
Greene County Middle School
Snow Hill, North Carolina

Mary Capaforte
Healthful Living Teacher
Department Chair
Lufkin Road Middle School
Apex, North Carolina

Pamela Rizzo Connolly, M.E.
Curriculum Coordinator for Health
and Physical Education
North Catholic High School
Diocese of Pittsburgh
Pittsburgh, Pennsylvania

Jason S. Chandler
Physical Education/Health Teacher
Head Certified Athletic Trainer
Prince George County Public Schools
Prince George County, Virginia

Audrey Maria Diamond
Science Teacher
Ellis G. Arnall Middle School
Newnan, Georgia

Allison Duckworth, M.A.
Physical Education Teacher
Head Athletic Trainer
Freedom High School
Morganton, North Carolina

Valerie Hernandez, BSN, RN, M.S.
Registered Nurse/Health Educator
Escambia County School District
Pensacola, Florida

Andy Keyes
Health/Physical Education Teacher
Hastings Middle School
Upper Arlington, Ohio

April Lane
Health Teacher
Portland Middle School
Portland, Tennessee

Norma H. Lee, M.A.
Wellness Instructor
Jefferson County High School
Dandridge, Tennessee

Cindy Meyer
Health Educator
South Oldham Middle School
Crestwood, Kentucky

Bobby Jean Moore, M.A.T.
Health Education Specialist
Creekland Middle School
Lawrenceville, Georgia

Dale Mueller
Health/Physical Education Teacher
New Holstein School District
New Holstein, Wisconsin

Tammy Smith
Administrator
Tulsa Public Schools
Tulsa, Oklahoma

Joan Gilger Stear, M.Ed
Health Education Instructor
West Clermont Institute of Performing Arts
Glen Este High School
Cincinnati, Ohio

Stacia K. Tatum
Physical Education Teacher
Westridge Middle School
Orlando, Florida

Jeanne Title
County Coordinator
Office of Safety and Wellness
Napa County Office of Education
Napa, California

Lisa Ward
Health and Physical Education Teacher
Kernodle Middle School
Greensboro, North Carolina

Robert T. Wieselberg
Health Educator
Westridge Middle School
Orlando, Florida

FITNESSZONE Handbook xviii

CHAPTER 1

Understanding Health and Wellness

Lesson 1 **Your Total Health** 4

Lesson 2 **Skills for Building Health** 10

Health Skills Activity: A Physical Fitness Campaign 15

Lesson 3 **What Affects Your Health?** 18

Health Skills Activity: Evaluating Information in Ads 21

Lesson 4 **Health Risks and Your Behavior** 23

Building Health Skills: Making Healthy Choices *(Advocacy)* 28

HANDS-ON HEALTH: A Picture of Health 30

Chapter 1 Reading Review 31

Chapter 1 Assessment 32

Table of Contents

v

CHAPTER 2

Taking Charge of Your Health

Lesson 1   **Making Responsible Decisions**.................................... 36

Health Skills Activity: Is It Always Right to Help a Friend? 39

Lesson 2   **Setting and Reaching Your Goals** 42

Health Skills Activity: Setting a Physical Activity Goal 43

Lesson 3   **Building Good Character**.. 47

Health Skills Activity: Organizations to Get Involved With 50

Building Health Skills: Setting a Health Goal *(Goal Setting)* 52

HANDS-ON HEALTH: Read All About ... Your Big Decision............................ 54

Chapter 2 Reading Review 55

Chapter 2 Assessment.. 56

CHAPTER 3

Physical Activity and Fitness

Lesson 1   **Becoming Physically Fit** 60

Lesson 2   **Exploring Skeletal and Muscular Systems** 66

Lesson 3   **Exploring the Circulatory System**................................... 71

Lesson 4   **Creating Your Fitness Plan**.. 77

Health Skills Activity: Planning for Fitness 79

Lesson 5   **Weight Training and Sports** 84

Health Skills Activity: Mental Conditioning for Sports 89

Lesson 6   **Preventing Physical Activity Injuries**............................... 91

Health Skills Activity: Taking Safety Seriously 93

Building Health Skills: Which Sports to Choose? *(Decision Making)* 96

TIME **health news:** Meet Me at the Gym 98

Chapter 3 Reading Review 99

Chapter 3 Assessment.. 100

Nutrition

Lesson 1 **Nutrients for Good Health**.. 104

Lesson 2 **Creating a Healthy Eating Plan**... 111

Lesson 3 **Planning Healthful Meals**.. 116

Health Skills Activity: Eating Right When Eating Out 120

Lesson 4 **Digestion and Excretion**... 122

Lesson 5 **Body Image and Healthy Weight** 128

Lesson 6 **Maintaining a Healthy Weight** 131

Building Health Skills: Media Messages About Food
(*Analyzing Influences*) 136

HANDS-ON HEALTH: Keeping a Food Diary 138

Chapter 4 Reading Review 139

Chapter 4 Assessment 140

Mental and Emotional Health

Lesson 1 **What Is Mental and Emotional Health?** 144

Lesson 2 **Your Self-Concept and Self-Esteem** 149

Lesson 3 **Your Emotions** 153

Lesson 4 **Managing Stress** 156

Lesson 5 **Mental and Emotional Problems** 159

Lesson 6 **Help for Mental and Emotional Problems** 163

Health Skills Activity: Community Resources for Mental and
Emotional Problems 164

Building Health Skills: Dealing with Stress (*Stress Management*) 166

TIME **health news:** Stressed Out 168

Chapter 5 Reading Review 169

Chapter 5 Assessment 170

CHAPTER 6

Building Healthy Relationships

Lesson 1 **Building Communication Skills** 174

Lesson 2 **Understanding Family Relationships** 178

  Health Skills Activity: Communicating with Parents or Guardians............ 181

Lesson 3 **Your Friendships and Peer Pressure**..................................... 184

Lesson 4 **Abstinence and Refusal Skills** 189

  Health Skills Activity: Saying No to Risk Behaviors 193

Building Health Skills: Expressing Your Feelings *(Communication Skills)*...... 194

HANDS-ON HEALTH: One Story, Three Endings 196

Chapter 6 Reading Review 197

Chapter 6 Assessment 198

CHAPTER 7

Resolving Conflicts and Preventing Violence

Lesson 1 **Understanding Conflict** 202

Lesson 2 **Conflict-Resolution Skills** 206

Health Skills Activity: Settling a Disagreement 209

Lesson 3 **Preventing Violence** 211

Lesson 4 **Getting Help for Abuse** 217

Building Health Skills: Mediating a Conflict *(Conflict Resolution)* 222

TIME **health news:** Getting an Early Start on Peace 224

Chapter 7 Reading Review 225

Chapter 7 Assessment 226

CHAPTER 8

Tobacco

Lesson 1 How Tobacco Use Affects the Body 230

Health Skills Activity: Convincing Others Not to Smoke 234

Lesson 2 The Respiratory System 236

Lesson 3 Tobacco Use and Teens 242

Health Skills Activity: Quitting Tobacco Use 245

Lesson 4 Tobacco Use and Society 248

Health Skills Activity: Promoting a Tobacco-Free Community 250

Lesson 5 Saying No to Tobacco Use 252

Health Skills Activity: Refusing Tobacco 254

Building Health Skills: Media Messages About Tobacco
(Analyzing Influences) 256

HANDS-ON HEALTH: Inside Your Lungs 258

Chapter 8 Reading Review 259

Chapter 8 Assessment 260

Alcohol

Lesson 1 Alcohol Use and Abuse 264

Health Skills Activity: **Alcoholism** 269

Lesson 2 The Nervous System 272

Health Skills Activity: **Skateboard Safety** 276

Lesson 3 Alcohol Use and Teens 278

Health Skills Activity: **Dealing With Emotions** 280

Lesson 4 Alcohol Use and Society 282

Health Skills Activity: **Helping a Friend** 284

Lesson 5 Saying No to Alcohol Use 286

Health Skills Activity: **Encouraging Teens to Avoid Alcohol** 288

Building Health Skills: Saying No to Alcohol *(Refusal Skills)* 290

TIME **health news:** News About Teens and Alcohol Use 292

Chapter 9 Reading Review 293

Chapter 9 Assessment 294

Drugs

Lesson 1 **Drug Use and Abuse** 298

Health Skills Activity: **Taking Medicine** 299

Lesson 2 **Types of Drugs and Their Effects** 303

Health Skills Activity: **Drug Use and Pregnancy** 309

Lesson 3 **Drug Risks and Teens** 310

Health Skills Activity: **Campaign for a Drug-Free School** 314

Lesson 4 **Staying Drug Free** 316

Health Skills Activity: **Refusing Drugs** 319

Building Health Skills: Helping Others Say No to Drugs *(Advocacy)* 320

HANDS-ON HEALTH: Good News 322

Chapter 10 Reading Review 323

Chapter 10 Assessment 324

CHAPTER 11
Personal Health and Consumer Choices

Lesson 1 **Healthy Teeth, Skin, Hair, and Nails**... 328

Lesson 2 **Healthy Eyes and Ears** 334

Lesson 3 **Smart Consumer Choices** 340

Health Skills Activity: Choosing the Right Product 346

Lesson 4 **Using Medicines Safely** 347

Health Skills Activity: Scheduling a Dosage... 350

Lesson 5 **Choosing Health Care** 352

Building Health Skills: Glasses or Contact Lenses? *(Decision Making)* 356

TIME **health news:** Acne Facts.. 358

Chapter 11 Reading Review 359

Chapter 11 Assessment... 360

CHAPTER 12

Growing and Changing

Lesson 1 **Changes During Adolescence** 364

Health Skills Activity: Managing Anger 368

Lesson 2 **The Endocrine System** 370

Health Skills Activity: Managing Diabetes 372

Lesson 3 **The Male Reproductive System** 374

Health Skills Activity: How to Do a Testicular Self-Examination 377

Lesson 4 **The Female Reproductive System** 378

Health Skills Activity: Promoting Breast Self-Examinations 381

Lesson 5 **Heredity and Human Development** 383

Lesson 6 **The Life Cycle** 388

Health Skills Activity: Strategies for Reducing Stress 391

Building Health Skills: Using S.T.O.P. to Choose Abstinence
(Refusal Skills) 394

HANDS-ON HEALTH: Analyzing Inherited Traits 396

Chapter 12 Reading Review 397

Chapter 12 Assessment 398

Communicable Diseases

Lesson 1 **What Are Communicable Diseases?** 402

Health Skills Activity: Safe Drinking Water? 405

Lesson 2 **The Immune System** 407

Health Skills Activity: Keeping your Immune System Healthy 410

Lesson 3 **Common Communicable Diseases** 413

Lesson 4 **Preventing the Spread of Disease** 418

Health Skills Activity: Wash Your Hands! 420

Lesson 5 **Sexually Transmitted Diseases** 422

Health Skills Activity: Finding Information About STDs 425

Lesson 6 **HIV/AIDS** 427

Health Skills Activity: Media Messages About Sexual Activity 430

Building Health Skills: Finding the Facts About Disease
(Accessing Information) 432

TIME **health news:** Germ Survival Guide 434

Chapter 13 Reading Review 435

Chapter 13 Assessment 436

Noncommunicable Diseases

Lesson 1 **Allergies and Asthma** 440

Lesson 2 **Heart Disease** 446

　Health Skills Activity: What Ads Say About Fat 449

Lesson 3 **Cancer** 451

　Health Skills Activity: Promote Ways to Reduce Cancer Risk 457

Lesson 4 **Diabetes and Arthritis** 458

　Health Skills Activity: Juvenile Rheumatoid Arthritis 461

Building Health Skills: Lifelong Good Health Habits: Emily's Walk
　　　　　　　　　　(Goal Setting) 464

HANDS-ON HEALTH: Determining Lung Capacity 466

Chapter 14 Reading Review 467

Chapter 14 Assessment 468

CHAPTER 15

Personal Safety

Lesson 1 **Preventing Injury** 472

Lesson 2 **Staying Safe at Home** 475

Lesson 3 **Staying Safe Outdoors** 480

    Health Skills Activity: Preventing Drowning 483

Lesson 4 **Weather Emergencies and Natural Disasters** 486

    Health Skills Activity: Creating an Emergency Supplies Kit 491

Lesson 5 **Giving First Aid** 493

Building Health Skills: Safety at Home *(Practicing Healthful Behaviors)* 500

TIME **health news:** 10 Tips for Cyber Safety 502

Chapter 15 Reading Review 503

Chapter 15 Assessment 504

CHAPTER 16

The Environment and Your Health

Lesson 1 **How Pollution Affects Your Health** 508

Lesson 2 **Protecting the Environment** 513

    Health Skills Activity: Choosing Environment-Friendly Products 514

Building Health Skills: Finding Facts About the Environment
    (Accessing Information) 518

HANDS-ON HEALTH: Managing the Packaging 520

Chapter 16 Reading Review 521

Chapter 16 Assessment 522

Reading Skills Handbook 524

Glossary 534

Glosario 544

Index 556

Be Healthy and Active with

Teen Health

Physical activity and fitness are important to good health. Use the Fitness Zone Handbook and Glencoe's Online Fitness Zone to develop personal fitness.

Fitness Zone Handbook

The Fitness Zone Handbook on pages xviii to 1 can help you create a personal fitness plan to balance your activities and build your overall fitness level. You'll also learn about the elements of fitness and discover fun group activities.

FITNESS ZONE Handbook

Physical Fitness Plan

Everyone should have a fitness plan. A personal plan can help you get started in developing your physical fitness. If you are already active or even athletic, a physical fitness plan can help you balance your activities and maintain a healthy level of activity.

Planning a Routine

When you're ready to start a fitness routine, it may be tempting to exercise as hard as you can for as long as you can. However, that approach is likely to leave you discouraged and even injured. Instead, you should plan a fitness routine that will let your body adjust to activity. Work up to your fitness goals slowly. Gradually increase both the length of time you spend exercising and the number of times you exercise each week. For example, you might start by doing a fitness activity for just 5 minutes a day, 3 days a week. Increase the amount of time you exercise, to say 7 minutes the next week and to 10 minutes during the third week of your plan. When you are exercising 20 minutes, 3 days a week, you're ready to add a fourth day to your fitness routine. Eventually, you will be exercising for 20 to 30 minutes, 5 days a week.

Warming Up

There's more to a physical fitness plan than fitness activities. It's important to prepare your body for exercise. Preparation involves warm-up activities that will raise your body temperature and get your muscles ready for your fitness activity. Easy warm-up activities include walking, marching, and jogging, as well as basic calisthenics.

When you're developing your own fitness plan, you should include warm-ups in your schedule. As you increase the time you spend doing a fitness activity, you should also increase the time you spend warming up.

This chart shows how you can plan the time you spend on warm-ups and fitness activities.

Sample Physical Fitness Plan

DAY	Monday		Tuesday		Wednesday		Thursday		Friday	
WEEK	Warm Up	Activity	Warm Up	Activity	Warm Up	Activity	Warm Up	Activity	Warm Up	Activity
1	5 min	5 min	---	---	5 min	5 min	---	---	5 min	5 min
2	5 min	7 min	---	---	5 min	7 min	---	---	5 min	7 min
3	5 min	10 min	---	---	5 min	10 min	---	---	5 min	10 min
4	5 min	12 min	---	---	5 min	12 min	---	---	7 min	15 min
5	7 min	15 min	---	---	7 min	15 min	---	---	7 min	17 min
6	7 min	17 min	---	---	7 min	17 min	---	---	10 min	20 min
7	10 min	20 min	---	---	10 min	20 min	---	---	10 min	20 min
8	10 min	20 min	10 min	20 min	10 min	20 min	---	---	10 min	20 min
9	10 min	20 min	10 min	20 min	10 min	20 min	10 min	20 min	10 min	20 min

xviii Fitness Zone Handbook

Go Online

Get energized with Glencoe's Online Fitness Zone at *glencoe.com*

Fitness Zone Online is a multimedia resource that helps students find ways to be physically active each day.

The Nutrition and Physical Activity Resources include:

- Clipboard Energizer Activities
- Fitness Zone Videos
- Polar Heart Rate Monitor Activities
- Tips for Healthy Eating, Staying Active, and Preventing Injuries
- Links to additional Nutrition and Physical Activity Resources

Reading in the health classroom with
Teen Health

Preview the Lesson
Get a preview of what's coming by reading the lesson objectives in Focusing on the Main Ideas. You can also use this feature to prepare for quizzes and tests.

Review Key Terms
Complete the Building Vocabulary activity to become familiar with these terms before you read the lesson. Vocabulary terms are highlighted in yellow to make them easy to find.

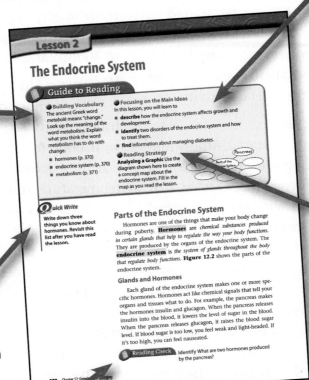

Strengthen Your Reading Skills
Complete the Reading Strategy activity to help you understand some of the information in the lesson.

Do the QuickWrite
This feature will help you start thinking about the information in the lesson.

Look at the Reading Checks
When you see a Reading Check, stop and answer the question to make sure that you understand what you have just read.

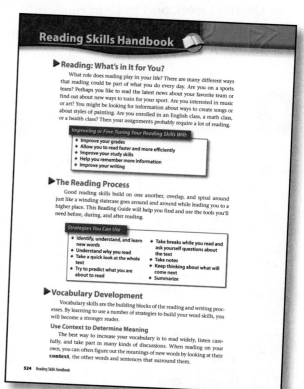

Reading Skills Handbook
The Reading Skills Handbook on pages 524-533 offers strategies to help you become a faster, more effective reader. Strong reading skills can help you improve your grades, study skills, and writing skills.

Physical Fitness Plan

Everyone should have a fitness plan. A personal plan can help you get started in developing your physical fitness. If you are already active or even athletic, a physical fitness plan can help you balance your activities and maintain a healthy level of activity.

Planning a Routine

When you're ready to start a fitness routine, it may be tempting to exercise as hard as you can for as long as you can. However, that approach is likely to leave you discouraged and even injured. Instead, you should plan a fitness routine that will let your body adjust to activity. Work up to your fitness goals slowly. Gradually increase both the length of time you spend exercising and the number of times you exercise each week. For example, you might start by doing a fitness activity for just 5 minutes a day, 3 days a week. Increase the amount of time you exercise, to say 7 minutes the next week and to 10 minutes during the third week of your plan. When you are exercising 20 minutes, 3 days a week, you're ready to add a fourth day to your fitness routine. Eventually, you will be exercising for 20 to 30 minutes, 5 days a week.

Warming Up

There's more to a physical fitness plan than fitness activities. It's important to prepare your body for exercise. Preparation involves warm-up activities that will raise your body temperature and get your muscles ready for your fitness activity. Easy warm-up activities include walking, marching, and jogging, as well as basic calisthenics.

When you're developing your own fitness plan, you should include warm-ups in your schedule. As you increase the time you spend doing a fitness activity, you should also increase the time you spend warming up.

This chart shows how you can plan the time you spend on warm-ups and fitness activities.

DAY	Monday		Tuesday		Wednesday		Thursday		Friday	
WEEK	Warm Up	Activity	Warm Up	Activity	Warm Up	Activity	Warm Up	Activity	Warm Up	Activity
1	5 min	5 min	---	---	5 min	5 min	---	---	5 min	5 min
2	5 min	7 min	---	---	5 min	7 min	---	---	5 min	7 min
3	5 min	10 min	---	---	5 min	10 min	---	---	5 min	10 min
4	5 min	12 min	---	---	5 min	12 min	---	---	5 min	12 min
5	7 min	15 min	---	---	7 min	15 min	---	---	7 min	15 min
6	7 min	17 min	---	---	7 min	17 min	---	---	7 min	17 min
7	10 min	20 min	---	---	10 min	20 min	---	---	10 min	20 min
8	10 min	20 min	10 min	20 min	10 min	20 min	---	---	10 min	20 min
9	10 min	20 min	10 min	20 min	10 min	20 min	10 min	20 min	10 min	20 min

Sample Physical Fitness Plan

Five Elements of Fitness

When you're making a plan for your own fitness program, you should keep the five elements of fitness in mind.

Cardiovascular endurance is the ability of the heart and lungs to function efficiently over time without getting tired. Activities that improve cardiovascular endurance involve non-stop movement of your whole body or of large muscle groups. Familiar examples are jogging, walking, running, bike riding, soccer, basketball, and swimming.

Muscle endurance is the ability of a muscle or a group of muscles to work non-stop without getting tired. Many activities that build cardiovascular endurance also build muscular endurance, such as jogging, walking, and bike riding.

Muscle strength is the ability of the muscle to produce force during an activity. You can make your muscles stronger by working them against some form of resistance, such as weights or gravity. Activities that can help you build muscle strength include push-ups, pull-ups, lifting weights, and running stairs.

Flexibility is the ability to move a body part freely, without pain. You can improve your flexibility by stretching gently before and after exercise.

Body composition is the amount of body fat a person has compared with the amount of lean mass, which is bone, muscle, and fluid. Generally, a healthy body is made up of more lean mass and less body fat. Body composition is a result of diet, exercise, and heredity.

On the next pages, you'll find ten different fitness activities for groups. They can help you develop all five elements of fitness, with an emphasis on cardiovascular endurance. They can also help you add variety and fun to your fitness plan.

Group Fitness Activities

Activity 1: Fitness Day

The exercises on this page should be completed with a teacher or other adult supervising the student. Correct form is important in order to reduce the risk of neck and back injuries.

Fitness Elements Muscle strength and endurance, flexibility

Equipment With a group of other students, make a set of exercise cards. Each card should name and illustrate an exercise. You can include some or all of the exercises shown here.

Formation Stand in two lines facing each other, or stand in a large circle.

Directions Take turns leading the group. The leader picks a card, stands in the center of the formation, and leads the group in the exercise on that card.

Reach for the Sky

Hold for a count of 10, rest, and repeat.

Plank

Hold for a count of 10, rest, and repeat.

Pointer

For each side, hold for a count of 10, rest, and repeat.

Open/Closed Pike

Hold for a count of 10, rest, and repeat.

Single Knee Hug

Hold for a count of 10, rest, and repeat.

Crab

Hold for a count of 10, rest, and repeat.

Flyer (half)

Raise legs. Hold for a count of 10, rest, and repeat.

Activity 2: Fitness Circuit

Fitness Elements Muscle strength and endurance, flexibility, and cardiovascular endurance

Equipment 2–4 jump ropes, 2–4 aerobic steps, signs or posters naming each station spread throughout the activity area (see diagram.)

Formation Set up stations as shown in the diagram. Form pairs, so that each student has a partner.

Directions With your partner, move through the stations: planks, jump rope, seated toe touches, sit-ups, push-ups, jumps in place, leg raises, jumping jacks, arm circles, step-ups. Each pair can start at any station. If your group is large, two pairs may use the same station. At each station, perform as many repetitions as you can in 30 seconds. After 30 seconds, have a teacher or a student volunteer signal the end of the time. With your partner, move in a clockwise direction to the next station.

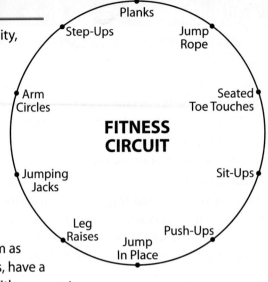

Activity 3: Multi-Ball Crab Soccer

Fitness Elements Muscle strength and endurance

Equipment 3–6 crab soccer balls or other large balls

Formation Mark a goal line at each end of the playing area, and divide the players into two teams. All the players on both teams get into the crab position and remain in that position throughout the game.

Directions Put the crab soccer balls in the middle of the playing area. Members of both teams kick the balls past the other team's goal line to score. Remember, all players have to stay in the crab position all the time. The game continues until all the balls have been scored.

Activity 4: Crab Relay

Fitness Elements Muscle strength and endurance

Equipment 4–5 flying disks

Formation Mark two lines 15–25 feet apart, depending on the fitness level of group members. One is the starting line, and the other is the turn-around line. Divide the group into four or five single-file lines behind the starting line. The first player in each group is in the crab position with a flying disk resting on his or her abdomen.

Directions Have a teacher or a student volunteer give a signal to start the relay. The first player in each line crab-walks to the turn-around line and back to the starting line. The players have to move in the crab position and must keep the disks on their abdomens. If the disk falls off, the player has to stop, pick the disk up, and place it back on his or her abdomen. When players return to the starting line, they hand their disks to the next player in line. The next player follows the same procedure. Continue playing until all the members of each team have participated. If you want to play again, reorganize the teams by having the first player in each line move to the team on his or her right.

Activity 5: Piranha River

Fitness Elements Cardiovascular endurance and flexibility

Equipment None

Formation Mark a line at each end of the activity area. One is the starting line and the other is the finish line. Mark two more lines, about ten feet apart, between the starting line and the finish line. The space between these two lines is the "river." Let two volunteers stand in the "river." They are the "piranhas." All the other players stand behind the starting line.

Directions Have a teacher or a student volunteer give the signal to begin. The players behind the starting line run down the river. As they run, the "piranhas" try to tag them. Players who reach the finish line without being tagged are safe. Players who are tagged stay in the "river" and become "helper piranhas." "Helper piranhas" must keep their feet in one place but can bend and stretch to tag the players running down the "river."

Activity 6: Partner Walk Tag

Fitness Element Cardiovascular endurance

Equipment None

Formation Form pairs, so that each player has a partner. With your partner, decide which one of you will begin as the tagger and which will begin as the walker.

Directions Have a teacher or a student volunteer give the signal to begin. If you are the tagger, chase and try to tag your partner. If you are the walker, walk to stay away from your partner. You must both walk at all times, not run. Once the tagger tags the walker, change roles with your partner. Continue until the teacher or student volunteer signals the end. You can vary this activity by hopping, skipping, or using another movement instead of walking.

Activity 7: Scarf Tag

Fitness Element Cardiovascular endurance

Equipment Scarves (one for each player)

Formation Each player should tuck one end of a scarf into the back of his or her waistband or into a rear pocket. Then players should scatter over the activity area.

Directions Have a teacher or a student volunteer give the signal to start. Each player moves throughout the activity area, trying to grab and pull out other players' scarves. Students who pull a scarf must say, "I got a scarf," bend down on one knee, and place the new scarf in their waistbands or pockets. They are "safe" while they are doing this. Players who lose their scarves continue playing, trying to capture other scarves. Players may pull only one scarf at a time. They may not hold onto their own scarves, and they may not push, pull, or grab other players. Play continues until the teacher or student volunteer gives the signal to stop.

Activity 8: Alien Invaders

Fitness Element Cardiovascular endurance

Equipment None

Formation Mark a goal line at each end of the playing area, and divide the players into two teams. One team is the "aliens," and the other team is the "soldiers." Form pairs, so that each player has a partner. Throughout the game, partners have to remain together, with their arms locked. All the players on the "aliens" team stand behind one goal line, and all the players on the "soldiers" team stand behind the other.

Directions The "aliens" stand with their backs to the playing area. The "soldiers" walk quietly toward the "aliens." When the "soldiers" are close to the "aliens," a teacher or student volunteer calls out "There are soldiers in your galaxy!" The "aliens" turn around and chase the "soldiers." All the "soldiers" who are tagged, or whose partners are tagged, become "aliens." "Soldiers" who reach their own goal line are safe.

Activity 9: Par Course

Fitness Elements Cardiovascular endurance, muscle strength and endurance

Equipment 4 jump ropes, 4 cones, signs or posters naming each station on the par course (See diagram.)

Formation: Set up stations as shown in the diagram. Mark each station with a cone and identify it with a sign or poster. Form groups of four.

Directions With the three other members of your group, start at one station on the course. Perform the activity identified there. Then jog to the next station, and perform that activity. Continue around the course until you have completed each activity at least once. If you're participating with a large class, you might work in two shifts, with half the groups completing the full par course and then giving the other groups a turn.

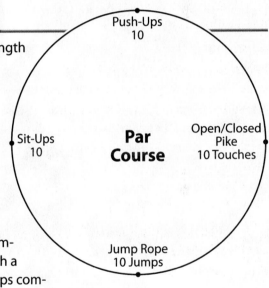

Activity 10: Intervals

Fitness Element Cardiovascular endurance

Equipment Whistle, 5-8 cones (optional)

Formation If possible, use a running track for this activity. If no track is available, use cones to mark a large circle on a gym floor or a field. All the players stand around the circle, not too close together, and all facing the same direction.

Directions Have a teacher or a student volunteer serve as the leader. The leader uses a whistle to signal how players should move. One blast on the whistle means walk, two blasts mean jog, and three blasts mean run. The leader varies the whistle commands, paying attention to the players' energy and to the temperature.

Understanding Health and Wellness

Chapter Preview

Lesson 1 Your Total Health 4

Lesson 2 Skills for Building
          Health 10

Lesson 3 What Affects Your
          Health? 18

Lesson 4 Health Risks and
          Your Behavior 23

Building Health Skills 28

Hands-on Health 30

Chapter Reading Review 31

Chapter Assessment 32

▲ Working with the Photo

Physical activity is an important part of your overall health. **How can being healthful make your day fun?**

Start-Up Activities

📖 **Before You Read**
What do you do to keep yourself healthy? Take the short health inventory below. Keep a record of your answers.

HEALTH INVENTORY

1. I get at least nine hours of sleep every night.
(a) always   (b) sometimes   (c) never

2. I am a good listener.
(a) always   (b) sometimes   (c) never

3. I try to fill my life with positive people and activities.
(a) always   (b) sometimes   (c) never

 **Study Organizer**

📖 **As You Read**   Make this Foldable® to record and organize what you learn in Lesson 1 about the three parts of health. Begin with two plain sheets of 8½″ × 11″ paper.

1 Line up one of the short edges of a sheet of paper with one of the long edges. Cut off the leftover rectangle.

2 Repeat Step 1 with the second sheet. You will now have two squares.

3 Stack the two squares and staple along the fold.

4 Title your Foldable® "Three Parts of Health." Label the inside page spreads *Physical, Mental/Emotional,* and *Social.*

Three Parts of Health

On the appropriate page of your Foldable® take notes on what you learn about each of the three parts of health, and give examples from your own life.

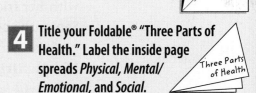

Go Online   Visit **glencoe.com** and use the eFlashcards to preview Chapter 1 vocabulary terms.

Your Total Health

Guide to Reading

● Building Vocabulary

Two of the words below have similar meanings. Write what you think are good definitions of each word. Make changes to the definitions as you read the lesson.

- health (p. 4)
- wellness (p. 7)
- mind-body connection (p. 8)

● Focusing on the Main Ideas

In this lesson you will be able to

- **identify** the three parts of health.
- **explain** the difference between health and wellness.
- **describe** how the mind and the body are connected.

● Reading Strategy

Finding the Main Idea Read the main headings in this lesson. For each heading, write one sentence that describes the main idea.

FOLDABLES | Study Organizer | Use the Foldable® on p. 3 as you read this lesson.

uick Write

Write a short paragraph describing how a person with "total health" might look and act. What might this person's lifestyle be like?

Three Parts of Good Health

Samantha eats plenty of fruits and vegetables each day. Three days a week, she runs two miles after school. However, some mornings she has a hard time getting up because she stayed up too late the night before. On those days, Samantha is cranky and argues with her friends. She is also too tired to pay attention in class. Is Samantha as healthy as she could be?

Like Samantha, your total health involves all the parts of your life. **Health** is *a combination of physical, mental/emotional, and social well-being.* These different parts affect each other throughout your life. They are like the sides of a triangle. You need all three sides to complete the triangle, and each side supports the other two sides to make up your total health. **Figure 1.1** shows the three sides of the health triangle.

Physical Health

One side of the health triangle is your physical health. Physical health involves the condition of your body. If you feel strong and have lots of energy, you probably have good physical health. Eating a well-balanced diet and doing plenty of physical activity, such as participating in a sport or individual fitness activities, are keys to good physical health. Getting plenty of sleep is also important. Most teens need about nine hours each night.

What else can you do to have good physical health? See your doctor and dentist for regular checkups. Brush your teeth every day and practice healthful hygiene habits. Always wear a safety belt when you ride in a vehicle. Wear proper protective gear when you are involved in physical activities. When you are at school, follow the safety rules. All of these actions are strategies for improving and maintaining personal health.

Some activities can harm physical health. You take chances with your health when you smoke cigarettes or use other forms of tobacco. Tobacco products can harm your mouth, heart, and lungs. Using alcohol or other drugs can harm your health, too. They can damage your liver, brain, and other organs. Taking unnecessary risks can also lead to accidents and injuries.

▼ FIGURE 1.1

THE HEALTH TRIANGLE

Your total health is made up of three parts, like a triangle. **Give an example of how physical, mental/emotional, and social health are interrelated during adolescence.**

PHYSICAL
MENTAL/EMOTIONAL
SOCIAL

Connect To... Science

Why Teens Need More Sleep

Scientific research suggests that teens need more sleep than other age groups. To be well rested, set up a regular sleep schedule that includes at least nine hours of sleep each night.

Use reliable resources from your home, school, and community to find out more information about the sleep needs of teens. Report your findings to the class.

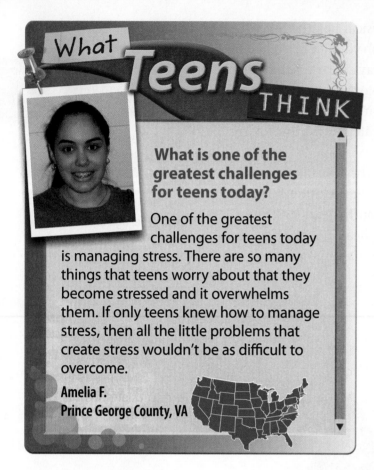

Academic Vocabulary

involves (in VOLVZ) *(verb)* includes. *Taking charge of your physical health involves eating healthful foods and exercising daily.*

Mental/Emotional Health

Another side of the health triangle is your mental/emotional health. Mental health refers to your ability to solve problems and handle the daily events of your life. When you have good mental health, you are able to see new ways of doing things. Emotional health **involves** feelings, such as happiness, sadness, and anger.

If you are mentally and emotionally healthy, you can face challenges in a positive yet realistic way. You are patient with yourself when you try to learn new subjects or new skills. You understand that everybody makes mistakes—including you! There is usually a "next time" when you can try to do better.

Taking action to reach your goals is another part of mental/emotional health. This can help you focus your energy and give you a sense of accomplishment. Making healthful choices, keeping promises, and taking responsibility for your actions also contribute to your mental/emotional health, because they help you to feel good about yourself. If you have good mental/emotional health, you feel in control of your life.

Reading Check **Recall** What is emotional health?

Social Health

Another part of the health triangle is your social health. Social health describes how you relate to people at home, at school, and everywhere else in your world. Strong friendships and warm family relationships are signs of good social health.

There are skills you can develop for building and maintaining relationships. Be friendly and open toward other people. Be supportive of family members and friends. Encourage them when they are learning new skills. Whenever you can, help them to reach their goals. Show friends and family members that you care about them and that they can count on you to be truthful and reliable. Be considerate and accept who they are. Listen carefully when they need someone to talk to. Follow through when you make promises.

Spending time with friends helps strengthen your social health. **Name two skills you can develop to build and maintain relationships.**

Sometimes, your opinions will differ from those of others. When you disagree, choose your words carefully. Pay attention to your tone of voice. You can disagree and express your opinions. However, you do not have to argue or show disrespect.

 **Reading Check** **Name** What are the three sides of the health triangle?

Your Overall Wellness

What is the difference between health and wellness? **Wellness** is *a state of well-being or balanced health over a longer period of time.*

Your health constantly changes. One day you might feel tired. Maybe you slept poorly. Maybe you pushed yourself too hard at sports practice. The very next day, you might feel well rested and full of energy. Your emotions change, too. You might feel sad one day but happy the next. Your overall health at any given time is a kind of snapshot of your physical, mental/emotional, and social health. Your overall wellness takes a longer view. It is the balance between the three sides of your health triangle over weeks and months.

How can you maintain overall wellness? You can practice good health habits and make smart health choices for your mind and body. The smart choices that you make every day can contribute to your wellness over your lifetime. When you practice positive health behaviors, you help to prevent injury, illness, disease, and other health problems.

Reading Check **Recall** What is wellness?

ACTIVITY

Go Online

Topic: Positive Health Behaviors

Visit **glencoe.com** for Student Web Activities on practicing positive health behaviors.

Activity: Using the information at the link above, list three positive health behaviors you could practice to stay healthy. Briefly explain how each one would benefit your health.

▶ Brushing your teeth regularly is a simple but important way to support your total health and wellness. **List three other activities that you can do regularly to maintain your health and wellness.**

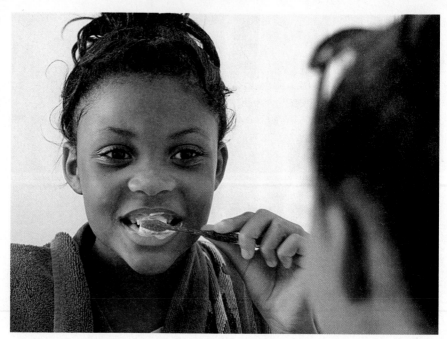

The Mind-Body Connection

Your emotions have a lot to do with your physical health. Think about an event in your own life that made you feel sad. How did you deal with this emotion? Sometimes people have a difficult time dealing with their emotions. This can have a negative effect on their physical health. For example, they might get headaches, backaches, upset stomachs, colds, the flu, or even more serious diseases. Why do you think this happens?

Your mind and body connect through your nervous system. This system includes thousands of miles of nerves. The nerves link your brain to every part of your body. Upsetting thoughts and feelings can affect the signals that go out from your brain to other parts of your body.

The **mind-body connection** is *how your emotions affect your physical and overall health and how your overall health affects your emotions.* It shows how important it is to keep the three sides of the health triangle in balance. If you become very sad or angry, or if you have other strong emotions, talk to someone. Sometimes just talking to a good friend helps. Sometimes you may be in a situation that requires the professional health services of a counselor or medical provider.

 **Reading Check** **Explain** How are your emotions and your physical and overall health interrelated?

To make sure that your physical, mental/emotional, and social health all work together in a positive way, practice the suggestions on the Healthful To-Do Lists in **Figure 1.2.**

Go Online

Visit **glencoe.com** and complete the Interactive Study Guide for Lesson 1.

HEALTHFUL TO-DO LISTS

Take responsibility for your personal health by keeping all three sides of your health triangle in balance. Which of the items on these lists do you already do? Which do you need to work on?

For My Mental/Emotional Health
1. Understand my strengths and weaknesses.
2. Express my feelings clearly and calmly.
3. Be patient with myself.
4. Accept helpful feedback and suggestions.
5. Find activities that I enjoy.
6. Be open to learning new skills and information.
7. Take responsibility for my actions.
8. Manage feelings in healthy ways.

For My Physical Health
1. Eat a well-balanced diet, including eating a healthy breakfast, every day.
2. Sleep at least nine hours each night.
3. Be physically active for at least 60 minutes each day.
4. Bathe and wash my hair regularly.
5. Brush my teeth at least twice a day.
6. Avoid using tobacco, alcohol, and other drugs.
7. Wear a safety belt when riding in a vehicle.
8. Visit the dentist and doctor for regular checkups.
9. Wear protective gear when I bike, skate, or ride a skateboard.

For My Social Health
1. Show that I respect and care for others.
2. Learn to disagree without arguing.
3. Learn to be a good listener.
4. Be open and friendly toward others.
5. Be loyal, dependable, and truthful.
6. Pay attention to the words I use when speaking to or about others.
7. Support my friends and family members.
8. Become close friends with at least one other person.

Lesson 1 Review

After You Read

Review this lesson for new terms, major headings, and Reading Checks.

What I Learned

1. *Vocabulary* Define *health*.

2. *Give Examples* List three activities that can contribute to your total health.

3. *Distinguish* What is the difference between health and wellness?

Thinking Critically

4. *Analyze* Reread the story of Samantha on page 4. What parts of her health triangle are out of balance? Suggest ways she could balance her health triangle.

5. *Describe* Name and describe at least three traits that you might find in a person who has good social health.

Applying Health Skills

6. *Goal Setting* Write down three strategies that you could use to improve and maintain your personal health. Choose one strategy from each side of the health triangle. Keep a journal for at least one week. Record what steps you took to carry out your plan.

Skills for Building Health

Guide to Reading

● Building Vocabulary
Each term below relates to a health skill. Write down each term. As you read the lesson, define each of the skills related to the term.

- reliable (p. 11)
- stress (p. 13)
- stress management (p. 13)
- interpersonal communication (p. 15)
- refusal skills (p. 16)
- conflict (p. 16)
- conflict-resolution skills (p. 16)
- advocacy (p. 17)

● Focusing on the Main Ideas
In this lesson you will be able to

- **identify** ten basic skills that you need for good overall health.
- **explain** why these skills are important.
- **describe** how to use these skills for total health and wellness.
- **apply** the health skill of advocacy to encourage teens to be physically active.

● Reading Strategy
Classifying Create a chart like the one shown here. As you read the lesson, list the health skills in the left column. In the right column, write ways in which each skill will benefit your health.

Health skill	Ways this skill will benefit my health
Accessing information	Will allow me to make informed choices about my health
Practicing Healthful Behaviors	Will allow me to stay well

Quick Write

Write a short paragraph describing a health decision that you made recently.

Learning Health Skills

Just as you learn sports, math, reading, and other kinds of skills, you can learn skills for taking care of your health. **Figure 1.3** lists ten different health skills that will be covered in detail in the following chapters. You will have the opportunity to practice each of these skills, and practicing them will help you master them. Using these skills will improve your health and overall wellness.

Accessing Information

A world of information is at your fingertips. Just pick up a newspaper or magazine. Turn on your television, radio, or computer. You can always learn more about whatever you are interested in. To make good choices for your health, you need good sources of information. You also need strong research skills.

Ten Building Blocks for Total Health

These ten skills will help you build lifelong health and wellness. Which part of the health triangle do you think communication skills benefit the most?

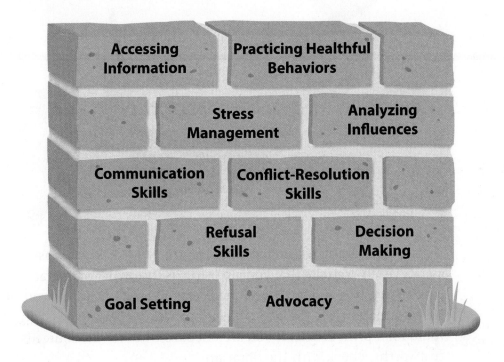

Sources of Information

Where can you find all this information? You can use resources from the home, school, and community to get valid health information. Your first source should be your parents, guardians, or other adults you trust. You can also use library resources.

You can find more facts about health and health-enhancing products or services through media sources such as television, radio, and the Internet. TV and radio interviews with health professionals can give you information about current scientific studies related to health. The Internet has up-to-the-minute information from government agencies, universities, and health care providers. Web sites that end in .gov and .edu are often the most reliable sites.

Getting health information is important, but so is analyzing whether that health information is valid, or reliable. **Reliable** means that the source is *trustworthy and dependable*. Try to learn something about the person or organization providing the information. For example, is the author of a health article an **expert** on the subject? Does he or she name scientific studies or other sources for the facts? To make sure the information is correct, try to find other books or articles that agree or disagree with the author.

Academic Vocabulary

expert (EK spert) *(noun)* a person who has a lot of knowledge in a specific subject. *Ms. Mendoza asked her neighbor to speak to our class because he is a fitness expert.*

▶ Making good decisions about your health begins with finding valid health information. Name two online sources that you can use to get valid health information.

If you are doing research on the Internet, check who owns or operates each Web site that you are using. Is the owner or operator a university, hospital, or government office? Find out who wrote the information for the site. Check out the author just as you would for a print article. If you are not sure whether the source is trustworthy, check with the librarian.

Reading Check **Define** What does *reliable* mean?

Self-Management

When you were younger, your parents and other adults decided what was best for your health. Now that you are older, you make many of these decisions for yourself. You take care of your personal health. You have a say in what you eat and when you sleep. You are developing your self-management skills. Two key self-management skills are practicing healthful behaviors and managing stress.

Practicing Healthful Behaviors

When you practice healthful behaviors, you start seeing benefits quickly. These benefits last as you grow and change. Exercise regularly, and your heart and muscles grow stronger. Eat healthful foods and drink plenty of water, and your body works more effectively. Get a good night's sleep, and you wake up with more energy. Practicing healthful behaviors can help you learn new skills, meet challenges, and enjoy life. Practicing positive health behaviors can also prevent injury, illness, disease, and other health problems.

Stress Management

Rashid was a good baseball player. When he played for fun with friends, he could hit, catch, and run the bases well. Before league games, however, Rashid often felt worried. He did not want to make a mistake. His worrying gave him a headache. His stomach got so upset he could hardly eat. These things made him play poorly. Rashid was showing signs of **stress,** *the body's response to real or imagined dangers and other life events.*

You will always have positive and negative stress in your life. Positive stress can be helpful. It can help you focus and take action. For example, you might study hard for a test so you will do well.

At times, however, stress can make you feel unsure of yourself. It can keep you from taking action or trying new things. This kind of stress is not helpful, as Rashid's story shows. This negative stress can hurt your physical health by making it hard to sleep or making your head or stomach hurt.

Stress is part of daily life. Learning strategies for dealing with stress is an important self-management skill. **Stress management** means *identifying sources of stress and learning how to handle them in ways that promote good mental/emotional health.*

 **Reading Check** **Define** What does *stress* mean?

Connect To...
Science

Stress Chemicals

When you feel stress, your body releases certain chemicals. One such chemical is adrenaline. Adrenaline makes your heart beat faster to pump more blood. It makes your lungs work harder to take in more oxygen. It also boosts the amount of sugar in your blood. This gives you more energy to deal with danger.

Research how adrenaline and other stress chemicals affect the body. Write a short paragraph about your findings.

◀ Preparing for a big test can be stressful. **Name two situations in your life that cause you stress.**

Smart Shopping

How can you be sure that a product is safe to use? You need to analyze whether the product's claims are valid. Read product labels carefully. Follow the directions and look for warnings. The U.S. Product Safety Commission warns buyers about unsafe products and their risks.

Research one of the latest U.S. Product Safety Commission's warnings. Share your findings with the class.

Analyzing Influences

Jonathan needed basketball shoes. He had finally saved enough money to buy a new pair. He did not want to waste his money, so he researched different brands. He wanted shoes that would fit well and last a long time. Jonathan found two brands that might work for him. He had seen ads on television for one of the brands featuring a major basketball star. The other brand was of high quality, but no sports star was promoting them. They cost less than the other brand and they were just as good. Even so, Jonathan's friends told him to buy the shoes worn by the star in the commercial.

Jonathan had to decide whether the more expensive shoes were worth buying. What might have affected his decision? First, he saw an ad for shoes that featured a basketball star. He also listened to his friends' opinions. Finally, Jonathan thought about which shoes he liked best.

Your decisions have to do with more than just knowing facts. They also have to do with your own values and beliefs. The opinions of your friends and family members, your culture, and messages from the media also affect your decisions. Understanding what influences you will help you make responsible choices in the future.

 Reading Check **Describe** What influences affect your decisions?

▶ Decisions that affect your health are often connected to personal taste: your likes and dislikes. **What information do you use to decide whether a food is healthful for you?**

Health Skills Activity

Advocacy

A Physical Fitness Campaign

You and some friends want to help teens in your community understand that physical activity benefits health. How can you influence your peers to make the positive choice of participating in regular physical activity? You have an idea: Make a comic strip showing that physical activity is healthy and fun.

With a Group

Create a comic strip that encourages teens to be physically active on a regular basis. Follow these steps:

1. Create a story line.
2. Develop characters. The characters can be people, talking objects like baseballs, or anything else that you can imagine.
3. As a group, discuss how to make your comic strip convincing and engaging.
4. Divide jobs, such as drawing and writing dialogue, among group members.
5. Present your completed comic strip to the rest of the class.

Communication Skills

How many people did you communicate with today? Did you tell someone how you were feeling? Did you listen to someone tell you about a new idea? Did you smile at a friend? Did someone smile at you? Your relationships with others depend on good communication skills. You must be able to speak well and listen carefully, too. Speaking skills help you express your ideas and feelings in healthful ways. Listening skills let you understand the messages other people send you. These skills are part of **interpersonal communication,** *the sharing of thoughts and feelings with other people.* Two of the most important communication skills are saying no when others want you to do something unhealthy and settling conflicts peacefully. By using these skills, you can handle difficult situations safely and fairly.

Communication skills involve more than speaking and listening. You send messages through the words you choose and how you say them, through your facial expressions, and even through your posture. When you communicate effectively, you can prevent misunderstandings. You can also support others when they need it.

▲ Refusal skills can help you avoid potentially harmful situations. **Name a situation in which a teen might need to use refusal skills.**

Refusal Skills

When you stand up for a decision you make, you also need to stand up for the values and beliefs behind that decision. This is especially true when you choose to avoid potentially harmful situations. **Refusal skills,** *ways to say no effectively,* are a great tool to use when you need to avoid behavior that is unhealthy, unsafe, or goes against your values and beliefs. Here are some ways to say no effectively:

- **Say no.** "No, I can't go with you today."
- **Tell why not.** "I would be breaking a promise."
- **Offer other ideas.** "What about tomorrow?"
- **Promptly leave** if you need to.

To say no effectively to behavior that you don't want to take part in, use the right body language and tone. For example, direct eye contact, a serious facial expression, and a firm but not angry tone of voice will communicate your message clearly.

Conflict-Resolution Skills

People have different wants, needs, and ways of looking at things. Sometimes this causes a **conflict,** or *a disagreement between people with opposing viewpoints, interests, or needs.* Conflict is a normal part of life. Dealing with conflict is an important part of social health. It takes good **conflict-resolution skills.** This means having *the ability to end a disagreement or keep it from becoming a larger conflict.*

People often disagree over how to spend time, spend money, or share resources. Here are some conflict-resolution tips:

- Take a time-out to let everyone calm down.
- Allow each person to tell his or her side of the story.
- Let each person ask questions of the other.
- Keep thinking of creative ways to resolve the conflict.

 **Reading Check** **Identify** What are refusal skills?

Decision Making and Goal Setting

The path to good health begins with good choices. These include the choice to eat nutritious foods and get enough sleep. Chapter 2 explains how to use the steps of the decision-making process to take responsibility for your physical, mental/emotional, and social health.

Learning how to set realistic goals is another step towards health and well-being. Maybe you want to run in a big race. Maybe you want to sharpen your skills in a sport so you can try out for the school team. In Chapter 2, you will find information that will help you develop your goal-setting skills.

Advocacy

You might know of unsafe or unhealthy conditions in your school or neighborhood. For example, each day you might pass a busy street corner without a stop sign. You might think that it's dangerous. When you care about an issue that could harm people's health, you work to improve it. Working to bring about a change involves the skill of advocacy. **Advocacy** is *taking action in support of a cause.* Advocates may write letters to newspaper editors to call for change. They may also collect signatures from people who support a cause and send the signatures to local government leaders.

Go Online

Visit **glencoe.com** and complete the Interactive Study Guide for Lesson 2.

 Reading Check   **Explain** What is advocacy?

Lesson 2 Review

 After You Read

Review this lesson for new terms, major headings, and Reading Checks.

What I Learned

1. *Vocabulary* Define *interpersonal communication.*

2. *Identify* Give two examples of self-management skills.

3. *Distinguish* What is the difference between stress and conflict?

4. *Give Examples* Name two activities that would allow you to be an advocate.

Thinking Critically

5. *Analyze* Why is it important to develop skills for finding reliable information?

6. *Describe* Name two refusal skills that can help you say no to activities that could harm your health.

Applying Health Skills

7. *Accessing Information* List three sources you could use to find valid information about nutrition. Explain why you think each source is or is not valid.

What Affects Your Health?

Guide to Reading

● Building Vocabulary
Three of the four terms below refer to types of influences on your health. Write down examples of each type of influence.

■ heredity (p. 18)
■ environment (p. 19)
■ cultural background (p. 21)
■ evaluate (p. 22)

● Focusing on the Main Ideas
In this lesson, you will be able to

■ **explain** why heredity is a health factor that you cannot control.

■ **explain** the role that environment plays in your total health.

■ **identify** internal and external influences that affect health choices.

■ **access** reliable information to evaluate an advertised product.

● Reading Strategy
Predicting Read the main headings and look at the figures in this lesson. Then write down three pieces of information that you think might be covered in the lesson. After you have completed the lesson, look back to see whether your predictions were correct.

Quick Write

List three influences that might affect your health.

Your Heredity

Many factors affect your health and wellness. You have control over some of these factors but not all. For example, you cannot control the color of your skin or eyes. You cannot control the shape of your nose or your ears. Heredity (huh·RED·i·tee) controls these and other physical traits, or parts of your appearance. **Heredity** is *the passing of traits from parents to their biological children.*

Genes are the basic units of heredity. They are made from a chemical called DNA, and they set the pattern for all of your physical traits. You inherited, or received, exactly half your genes from your father. You inherited the other half from your mother.

▶ Children look like their parents because of inherited traits. **Give two examples of inherited traits.**

Genes do more than determine traits such as hair and eye color. Genes control how every cell in your body works. Genes can affect your health in ways that you cannot control. For example, some genes can cause disease. It helps to be aware that you might have inherited genes that could increase your risk of developing a certain disease. That way, you can make better decisions about your health. For example, if you have a family history of heart disease, you can choose to eat a low-fat diet and exercise regularly to keep your heart healthy.

 Reading Check **Identify** What is heredity?

Your Environment

Think about where you live. Do you live in a city, a suburb, or a small town? Do you live in the country? Where you live is the physical part of your environment. **Environment** includes *all living and nonliving things around you.* Environment affects your personal health. **Figure 1.4** lists some of the parts of your environment.

▼ **FIGURE 1.4**

FACTORS OF YOUR ENVIRONMENT

People live in many different environments, including big cities and small towns. **What are two factors of your physical environment?**

Physical Environment
- Where you live
- Housing
- Climate
- Air and water quality

Social Environment
- Family
- Neighbors
- Educational opportunities
- Job opportunities

Health Officer

Health officers work for many departments of health at the local, state, and national level. They run programs that teach people how to live healthier lives. There will always be a need for health officers because people will always need information on maintaining good personal health. In order to prepare for a career as a health officer, you'll need to take science classes like biology and psychology.

What skills does a health officer need? Go to *Career Corner* at **glencoe.com** to find out.

Physical Environment

Your physical environment includes the home you live in, the school you go to, the air and water around you, and the climate. The climate is what the weather is like where you live. For example, some places have warm weather all year long. Other places have cold winters and warm summers.

Air and water quality are important parts of your physical environment. Breathing fresh air and drinking clean water are important for good health. Motor vehicles, factories, and power plants can all pollute the air. Air pollution can have negative effects on health. For example, polluted air can harm the health of teens with respiratory problems such as asthma. The quality of indoor air can be affected by whether family members smoke.

The water quality in cities is usually good because the drinking water is purified. Harmful pollutants are removed. Water in the country often comes from wells. Sometimes chemicals from farms pollute wells. Well water may need to be tested from time to time to ensure that the water is safe to drink.

Social Environment

Do you have brothers or sisters? Brothers, sisters, and other family members are all part of your social environment. Your social environment includes others in your life, such as friends, classmates, and neighbors. It also includes the services available to you, such as schools, health care, and recreation.

Does your community have places for recreation, such as parks and tennis or basketball courts? Recreation is as much a part of your social environment as schools and health care. Having places to play games and enjoy physical activities can have a positive effect on your overall health. Many communities have resources such as playgrounds and community centers where people can take part in different activities.

You may not be able to change your physical and social environments. However, you can recognize that there is a relationship between factors in these environments and your personal health. Understanding this relationship can help you develop strategies for improving and maintaining your personal health. For example, you probably can't change the fact that you live in a warm and sunny climate. You can, however, wear sunscreen to help protect your skin from the sun's harmful rays. You can't easily change the people who are your classmates, but you can choose which of them will be your close friends.

 **Reading Check**   **Describe** What makes up a person's social environment?

Health Skills Activity

Accessing Information

Evaluating Information in Ads

To make good health decisions, you must decide what is valid and what is not. Here are tips to help you evaluate information in ads.

- **Check the source.** What or who is the source of the information in the ad? Is the source reliable? Many ads do not give any source. Other ads list unclear sources such as "most doctors" or "leading athletes."

- **Consider claims the ads make.** Some ads make health claims about a product. How can you tell whether the claims are true? Look for facts that help prove whether the claims are true or misleading. Places to check the reliability of sources and claims in ads include your local library and Internet sites run by a government agency or university.

On Your Own

Choose a newspaper or magazine ad or TV commercial about a product that could affect your health. It could, for example, be about a food, drink, or cosmetic product. Find reliable sources of information and research the health benefits of the product. Present your findings to the class.

Your Health Choices

Your daily choices shape your health and wellness. These choices depend on many factors. Some factors are part of who you are. They include your likes, dislikes, feelings, and ways of thinking. Other factors are part of your physical and social environment. Your friends, family, trusted adults, and the media are some examples. Choices, unlike environment or heredity, are under your complete control. It's important to take responsibility for your personal health behaviors and choices.

▼ The celebration of Kwanzaa is a tradition in many African American families. **What are some other holiday celebrations from different cultural backgrounds?**

Influence of Family and Friends

Your family is one of the biggest influences on your life. It shapes your **cultural background,** or *the beliefs, customs, and traditions of a specific group of people.* Your family and its cultural background influence the holidays you celebrate, the foods you eat, and the activities you take part in. Your cultural background can also affect your health. Knowing how your lifestyle and family history relate to the cause or prevention of health problems can help you stay well.

Your friends can also influence your choices. This influence can be positive or negative. For example, a friend who listens to you and helps you find good solutions to problems is a positive influence. A friend who urges you to drink alcohol or try other risky behaviors is a negative influence. It is important to understand that peer pressure can influence healthful choices.

Influence of the Media

What do television, radio, movies, magazines, newspapers, books, billboards, and the Internet have in common? They all are forms of media.

The media are powerful sources of information. They can help you make wise health choices. However, you need to **evaluate,** or *determine the quality of,* everything you see, hear, or read. This is especially true of magazine ads and TV commercials. Their goal is to make you want to buy a product, whether or not it is good for your health. Knowing how to analyze health information, products, and services can help you make wise health choices.

 Reading Check **Identify** What are some influences on health choices?

Go Online

Visit **glencoe.com** and complete the Interactive Study Guide for Lesson 3.

Lesson 3 Review

After You Read

Review this lesson for new terms, major headings, and Reading Checks.

What I Learned

1. *Vocabulary* Define *evaluate.*

2. *List* Name two types of media that could influence your decisions.

3. *Identify* Name two factors that are part of the physical environment.

Thinking Critically

4. *Apply* Watch a TV commercial for a health-related product. What information does the commercial tell you about the product? Do you think the information is valid? Explain.

5. *Synthesize* What can a teen who has a family history of heart disease do to reduce the risk of getting the disease?

Applying Health Skills

6. *Analyzing Influences* For a week, identify as many influences on your health choices as you can. Label each influence as being positive or negative. Explain why you chose the labels you did.

Go Online For more Lesson Review Activities, go to **glencoe.com**.

Health Risks and Your Behavior

Guide to Reading

● Building Vocabulary
Two of the terms below are related to keeping you safe. Write down these words. As you read the lesson, write their definitions.

- risk (p. 23)
- risk behaviors (p. 24)
- consequences (p. 24)
- cumulative risk (p. 25)
- prevention (p. 26)
- abstinence (p. 27)

● Focusing on the Main Ideas
In this lesson you will be able to

- **describe** how risks and risk behaviors can affect your health.
- **explain** that risk behaviors have consequences.
- **identify** ways to avoid or reduce risk.

● Reading Strategy
Finding the Main Idea Read the main headings in this lesson. For each heading, write one sentence that describes the main idea.

Risk and Risk Behaviors

Some risk is a part of everyday life. A **risk** is *the chance that something harmful may happen to your health and wellness.* Some risks are easy to identify. For example, if you ride a bike without a helmet, you risk a head injury if you fall. Other risks are more hidden. For example, you might have a habit of snacking on high-fat foods. Eating these foods may lead to unhealthful weight gain and heart disease later in life.

**Quick Write**

Write about something you believe is a risky behavior. List the possible negative consequences of that behavior.

◀ Inline skating can be fun, but like all physical activities, it carries the risk of injury. **What steps have these teens taken to reduce their risk of injury while inline skating?**

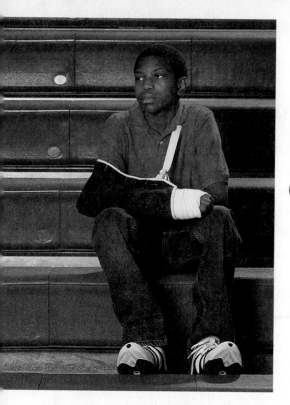

You cannot avoid every kind of risk. For example, if you play a sport, you risk injury. Wearing protective gear reduces the chance of injury but does not eliminate it completely. Risks that can be avoided often involve **risk behaviors,** which are *actions or choices that may harm you or others.* Smoking cigarettes is a risk behavior; riding in a car without wearing a safety belt is another.

 **Reading Check** **Identify** What are risk behaviors?

Risks and Consequences

Risk behaviors have consequences. **Consequences** are *the results of actions.* Some risks have consequences that may not be physically dangerous and may affect only you. If you choose not to study for a test, for example, you risk getting a low score on the test. Other risks can have serious consequences. For example, picking a fight at school can hurt both you and others.

 **Reading Check** **Identify** What are consequences?

▲ Physical injury can be a consequence of certain risk behaviors. **How might an injury affect mental/emotional and social health?**

Teens and Risks

Many teens know ways in which to reduce risks related to the health problems of adolescence. They know, for example, that using tobacco, alcohol, and other drugs are risk behaviors that have many serious effects on health and wellness.

Many teens also know how to compare the **benefits** and risks of activities to reduce risk to themselves. For example, they know that wearing a safety belt will help protect them in the event of a motor vehicle accident. Most middle-school students make sure to buckle up when riding in a vehicle. Teens also understand that regular exercise helps fight heart disease and other illnesses. Most teens try to be physically active. See **Figure 1.5** for more information on how teens choose behaviors that help them avoid risk and protect their health.

Academic Vocabulary

benefits (BEN uh fits) *(noun)* positive things. *One of the benefits of healthful eating is having enough energy to get through your day.*

How Risks Add Up

On its own, a risk may not seem that dangerous. The greater the number of risks, however, the greater the chances of negative consequences. For example, jogging on a busy street is one risk factor. Jogging on a busy street at night adds another risk factor. Jogging along a busy street at night during a rainstorm greatly increases the chances of serious injury. Or, eating a diet full of

MOST YOUNG PEOPLE CHOOSE TO AVOID RISKS AND PROTECT THEIR HEALTH

Most teens know ways in which to reduce risks related to the health problems of adolescence. What positive health behaviors do you practice to stay healthy?

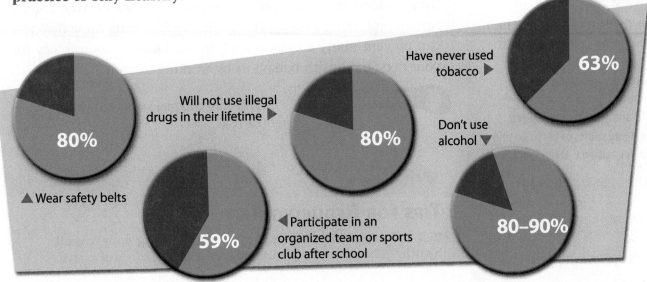

high-fat foods is one risk factor. Not getting regular exercise is another risk factor. These two risks combined greatly increase a person's chances of developing heart disease. *When one risk factor adds to another to increase danger,* it is called **cumulative risk.**

 **Identify** What is cumulative risk?

Is It Worth the Risk?

You travel to school and other places. You play sports or enjoy other physical activities. These activities offer you benefits. As with any activity, they also have some risks. Ask yourself, are the benefits greater than the risks? For example, are the benefits of playing a sport greater than the risk of getting hurt? Evaluate each risk before making a decision.

Check the facts before making decisions about risks. Study how likely it is that a risk behavior will have negative consequences. Research what healthful behaviors can reduce risks. The skill of accessing information can help you do this. For example, research has shown that wearing a safety belt when riding in a vehicle cuts the risk of serious injury in half in the event of a crash. When you know how much risk a behavior carries, you can decide whether it is worth doing.

How to Avoid or Reduce Risks

Practicing **prevention** means *taking steps to avoid something*. This is the best way to deal with avoidable risks. For example, wear a helmet when you ride a bike to help prevent head injury. Slow down on wet or icy pavement to help prevent a fall. Prevention also means watching out for possible dangers. When you know what dangers lie ahead, you can avoid them. See **Figure 1.6** for tips on protecting yourself from risks. By following these tips, you can prevent many accidents and injuries. Take responsibility for your personal health behaviors by working to reduce risks.

Reading Check

List What are two main ways to avoid or reduce risk?

▼ **FIGURE 1.6**

TIPS FOR REDUCING RISK

Risk-reducing behaviors are key to maintaining your overall health. **What other actions can you take to reduce risks?**

✓ Plan ahead.
✓ Think about consequences.
✓ Resist negative pressure from others.
✓ Stay away from risk takers.
✓ Pay attention to what you are doing.
✓ Know your limits.
✓ Be aware of dangers.

Risks and Your Total Health

Abstinence is *the conscious, active choice not to participate in high-risk behaviors.* If you choose not to smoke, you will reduce your risk of getting lung cancer. If you stay away from alcohol, illegal drugs, and sexual activity, you will avoid the many negative consequences of these risky behaviors.

By practicing abstinence from risk behaviors, you take an active role in caring for your health. This will benefit each part of your health triangle. Avoiding risk behaviors will help prevent illness and injuries, contributing to your physical health. When you take steps to reduce risks, you can feel good about making responsible health choices. This helps strengthen your mental/emotional health. In many cases, practicing abstinence from risk behaviors and reducing unavoidable risks can help keep others safe, too. This will benefit your social health.

Visit **glencoe.com** and complete the Interactive Study Guide for Lesson 4.

 **Explain** How can avoiding risk behaviors benefit your physical health?

Lesson 4 Review

 After You Read

Review this lesson for new terms, major headings, and Reading Checks.

What I Learned

1. *Vocabulary* Define *prevention* and use it in a sentence.

2. *Give Examples* Name three risk behaviors that can have negative health consequences.

3. *Explain* What does *abstinence* mean? Give an example of practicing abstinence.

4. *List* Name two or more risk factors that can create a cumulative risk.

Thinking Critically

5. *Hypothesize* Suppose two teens are riding their bikes on a busy street at night. One is wearing a helmet and the other is not. Describe the risks that both teens are taking. What possible consequences do these risks carry?

6. *Apply* Give an example of how prevention can help a person avoid a risk.

Applying Health Skills

7. *Refusal Skills* Suppose a peer asks you to participate in a high-risk behavior such as drinking alcohol. Write a dialogue between you and the peer in which you use refusal skills to say no to this risky behavior.

Accessing Information

Practicing Healthful Behaviors

Stress Management

Analyzing Influences

Communication Skills

Refusal Skills

Conflict Resolution

Decision Making

Goal Setting

Advocacy

What are Advocacy Skills?

Advocacy skills involve taking action in support of a cause. An advocate is someone who works to bring about a change.

Ways to Take Action

- Write letters to government leaders and newspaper editors.
- Collect signatures from people in your community.
- Organize activities in your school or neighborhood.
- Volunteer with a group that shares your feelings. If no group exists, start your own group.
- Contact local radio or television stations to see if they will give your cause airtime.

Making Healthy Choices

Follow the Model, Practice, and Apply steps to help you master this important health skill.

① Model

Read how Derek uses advocacy skills to convince his brother, Steve, to wear his safety belt while driving his car.

Derek's older brother, Steve, just got his driver's license. Derek asked Steve to drive him to his soccer game one Saturday morning. When they got in the car, Derek fastened his safety belt. Steve did not. He began to back the car out of the driveway.

Derek: Wait, Steve. You forgot to buckle your safety belt.

Steve: The soccer field isn't that far, so I don't need it.

Derek: That's what you think! It's no big deal to buckle up, you know. It can keep you from dying or getting really hurt if you get into an accident. I don't want to get hurt in an accident, and I don't want you to get hurt either.

Steve: You're right, Derek. I'll buckle up right now.

❷ Practice

Michael wants to use the skill of advocacy to convince his friend, Jose, to wear a helmet when he skateboards. Read the passage and then practice the skill of advocacy by completing the activity below.

A few days later, Jose and Michael got out their skateboards and headed over to the skate park. When they got there, Jose realized that he had forgotten to bring his helmet. He didn't feel like going home to get it. Michael knew that if Jose fell without a helmet, he could injure his head. Write a conversation showing how Michael could use the skill of advocacy to persuade Jose to make a healthy choice.

❸ Apply

Apply what you have learned about using advocacy skills by completing the activity below.

Think of a time when a friend or someone in your family engaged in a risk behavior. Write a sentence or two to describe the situation. Then write a letter persuading that person to make healthier choices [in the] future. In your letter, explain the consequences of the risk beha[vior.] Tell how changing the behavior will improve the person's hea[lth.]

Self-Check

- Did I describe a risk behavior and its consequences?
- Did I write a letter persuading that person to make a he[althy] choice in the future?

A Picture of Health

What does a healthy person look like?

Healthy people eat nutritious foods and participate in regular physical activity. They have the energy to do the work that they need to do, plus extra energy for fun. They use their time alone in useful ways. They can think clearly and learn new skills and information. They get along with others.

In this activity, you and your classmates will make a photo collage featuring people who display physical, mental/emotional, and social health.

What You Will Need

- Poster board
- Scissors
- Glue
- Old magazines
- Markers

What You Will Do

Your teacher will divide the class into small groups. He or she will hand out the materials to each group.

Look through the magazines for people demonstrating mental/emotional, and social health. Show a variety of ages.

3 Paste the cutout images on the poster board to create a photo collage. Title the collage "A Picture of Health."

Wrapping It Up

As a group, present your collage to the rest of the class. Explain to your classmates the images that show each side of the health triangle. Describe how physical, mental/emotional, and social health are related. If possible, display your collage in the classroom or in a school hallway.

Reading Review

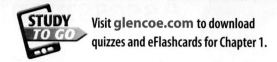
STUDY TO GO Visit glencoe.com to download quizzes and eFlashcards for Chapter 1.

FOLDABLES Study Organizer

Foldables® and Other Study Aids Take out the Foldable® that you created for Lesson 1 and any graphic organizers that you created for Lessons 1–4. Find a partner and quiz each other using these study aids.

Lesson 1 Your Total Health

Main Idea Your total health is made up of your physical, mental/emotional, and social health.

- Wellness is a state of well-being or balanced health over a longer period of time.
- The mind-body connection is a link between emotions and physical health.
- Eating healthy, getting enough sleep, and being physically active are a few ways to maintain good physical health.
- Being patient with yourself and others, understanding your strengths and weaknesses, and expressing your feelings in a calm way are a few ways to maintain good mental/emotional health.
- Showing respect for others, being a good listener, and supporting friends and family members are a few ways to maintain good social health.

Lesson 2 Skills for Building Health

Main Idea Health skills help you build lifelong health and wellness.

- Accessing information is the skill of knowing where and how to find reliable information.
- Practicing healthful behaviors and stress management are self-management skills.

- Analyzing influences means understanding how influences affect your choices.
- Communication skills include refusal skills and conflict resolution.
- Decision making involves a process for making good health choices.
- Goal setting includes setting a specific goal and creating a plan to achieve it.

Lesson 3 What Affects Your Health?

Main Idea Factors that affect your health include heredity, environment, and the choices you make.

- Your inherited traits are health factors that you cannot control.
- Your physical environment is the place where you live and the things around you.
- Influences on your health choices include family, friends, and the media.

Lesson 4 Health Risks and Your Behavior

Main Idea Risk behaviors have consequences that can affect your health and wellness.

- It is important to evaluate risks.
- A risk is the chance that something harmful may happen to your health and wellness.
- You can reduce risks to your health by avoiding alcohol, drugs, and tobacco; wearing a safety belt; and being physically active.
- Prevention means taking something.

 After You Read

HEALTH INVENTORY

Now that you have read the chapter, look back at your answers to the Health Inventory on the chapter opener. Is there anything that you should do differently?

Reviewing Vocabulary and Main Ideas

On a sheet of paper, write the numbers 1–4. After each number, write the term from the list that best completes each statement.

- mind-body connection
- wellness
- physical
- mental/emotional
- social

Lesson 1 Your Total Health

1. Your _____ health involves how you relate to others.

2. Powerful emotions might play a role in your catching a cold because of the _____.

3. A balanced health triangle helps to maintain _____.

4. _____ health can be improved by being physically active on a regular basis.

*Write the numbers 5–18. Write **True** or **False** for each statement below. If false, change the underlined word or phrase to make it true.*

Lesson 2 Skills for Building Health

5. Negative stress <u>can</u> cause physical problems, such as headaches.

Effective <u>refusal skills</u> include saying no ` unhealthy behaviors.

7. A reliable source has information based on <u>opinions</u>.

8. An example of <u>advocacy</u> is walking to raise money for cancer research.

9. Good listening skills are an important part of <u>goal setting</u>.

Lesson 3 What Affects Your Health?

10. Your cultural background <u>cannot</u> affect your health.

11. Your <u>physical</u> environment includes your family members.

12. Many of your physical traits are controlled by <u>heredity</u>.

13. Information from advertising needs to be <u>evaluated</u>.

14. Your personal likes and dislikes <u>can</u> influence the choices you make.

Lesson 4 Health Risks and Your Behavior

15. Wearing a safety belt greatly <u>reduces</u> the risk of injury in a motor vehicle accident.

16. The chance of negative consequences <u>decreases</u> as the number of risks increases.

17. Decisions about risks need to be based on <u>facts</u> rather than the opinions of other people.

18. One example of abstinence is <u>engaging</u> in sexual activity.

Thinking Critically

Using complete sentences, answer the following questions on a sheet of paper.

19. **Analyze** Identify the influences that affected your decision to buy a certain snack.

20. **Apply** Think about a health factor that you cannot control. What steps could you take to reduce the risk of that factor harming your health?

Write About It

21. **Narrative Writing** Write a story about a teen who needs to find valid information about allergies. In your story, show how the teen determines what sources are reliable.

ACTIVITY
↗ Applying Technology

Healthy Lifestyle Brochure

Use digital images in Microsoft Word® to create a brochure that encourages your peers to live a more healthy life. Follow the steps below to complete this project.

- Choose one of the three parts of the health triangle to focus on.
- Take digital pictures that represent the part of the health triangle that you have chosen.
- Scan the pictures into a new Word® document with a landscape view and three columns.
- In a few sentences, discuss what each picture says about your part of the health triangle.
- Edit your brochure. Make sure that you have used correct spelling, grammar and punctuation. Also, make sure that your brochure is colorful.
- Save your project.

Standardized Test Practice

Reading

Read the passage and then answer the questions.

Most people know how to keep from getting a cold or the flu. They stay away from people who are sick to reduce exposure to the cold or flu virus. However, many diseases are not caused by organisms. These are known as noncommunicable diseases. Noncommunicable diseases include cancer and heart disease. What causes these diseases? Heredity, diet, physical fitness, tobacco, and alcohol use are all possible factors.

> **TEST-TAKING TIP**
>
> Scan the passage and then read the questions. Go back to the passage to look for information related to the questions.

1. With which statement would the author most likely agree?
   - **A.** A healthy diet is only a small part of disease prevention.
   - **B.** There are many things that people can do to stay healthy.
   - **C.** Viruses cause the greatest number of noncommunicable diseases.
   - **D.** People should develop healthful habits only when they are at risk of disease.

2. What does *exposure* mean in this sentence? They stay away from people who are sick to reduce *exposure* to the cold or flu virus.
   - **A.** cold
   - **B.** risk of contact
   - **C.** relation
   - **D.** communicable

2 Taking Charge of Your Health

Chapter Preview

Lesson 1 Making Responsible
          Decisions 36

Lesson 2 Setting and Reaching
          Your Goals...........................42

Lesson 3 Building Good
          Character...........................47

Building Health Skills...........................52

Hands-on Health.....................................54

Chapter Reading Review.....................55

Chapter Assessment 56

▲ **Working with the Photo**

It is easy to take charge
of your health when you
choose friends who also
make healthful decisions.
**What healthful decisions
are these teens making?**

Start-Up Activities

Before You Read What do you already know about setting and achieving goals? Answer the Health eSpotlight question below and then watch the video. Keep a record of your answer.

Health eSpotlight

VIDEO

Taking Charge of Your Health:

Being organized is an important part of being successful at home, at school, and in life. How do you stay organized? What advice would you give to a friend who asked for help with managing his or her time?

Go to **glencoe.com** and watch the health video for Chapter 2. Then complete the activity provided with the online video.

FOLDABLES® Study Organizer

As You Read Make this Foldable® to help you organize what you learn about decision making in Lesson 1. Begin with a plain sheet of 11″ × 17″ paper.

1 Fold a sheet of paper in half the long way, then fold it in half again. This makes four rows.

3 Label the chart with the terms shown.

Decision Making	
Values	
Criteria	
H.E.L.P.	

2 Open and fold the short side on the left to make a 3″ column.

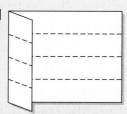

As you read Lesson 1, define and take notes on the terms listed in the chart.

 Online Visit **glencoe.com** and complete the Chapter 2 crossword puzzle.

Making Responsible Decisions

Guide to Reading

● **Building Vocabulary**
Write the terms below. As you come across them in the lesson, write the definitions next to each term.

■ decision making (p. 36)
■ values (p. 37)
■ ethical (p. 37)
■ criteria (p. 38)

● **Focusing on the Main Ideas**
In this lesson you will be able to

■ **explain** what decision making is and why it is important.
■ **describe** why values are important to decision making.
■ **demonstrate** how to use the six-step decision-making process to make a healthful choice.

● **Reading Strategy**
Analyzing a Graphic Take a look at Figure 2.3 on page 40. Use this figure to summarize the steps you would take to make a healthful decision.

 **FOLDABLES** Study Organizer Use the Foldable® on p. 35 as you read this lesson.

Quick Write

In a sentence or two, briefly describe a decision you made recently. List the steps you took when making that decision.

Decisions and Your Health

As you grow up, you take on more responsibility for yourself. One of the keys to being responsible is good **decision making,** *the process of making a choice or solving a problem.*

The choices and decisions you make can affect each part of your health triangle. For example, when you get enough sleep, you improve your physical health by having the energy for your activities. You affect your mental health by being able to focus on your schoolwork. And you affect your social health by being able to have more fun with your friends.

Some decisions may help you avoid harmful behaviors. Deciding never to use tobacco can have a lasting, positive effect on your health. Look at **Figure 2.1** on the next page. Use the list to help you understand some of the consequences of health-related decisions.

Good decision making comes from learning to analyze the validity of health information. If you take the time to analyze your decisions, you are less likely to make impulsive choices. It is also understanding the role that family, community, and cultural attitudes play when people make health-related decisions.

THINKING ABOUT CONSEQUENCES

You can make wiser choices if you first understand the consequences of a health-related decision. **What are two consequences of getting enough sleep?**

> **How will this decision affect my health?**
>
> **Will it affect the health of others? If so, how?**
>
> **Is the behavior I might choose harmful or illegal?**
>
> **How will my family feel about my decision?**
>
> **Does this decision fit with my values?**
>
> **How will this decision affect my goals?**

Decisions and Values

Your decisions show what's important to you. That's why it is important for your choices to be based on **values,** *the beliefs that guide the way a person lives.* Your values include your beliefs about what is right and wrong and what is most important to you.

Some values are generally shared by a group of people. These are known as core ethical values. **Ethical** means *choosing to take the right action.* Being honest and showing respect for others are examples of core ethical values. These values help you make decisions about right and wrong. They also help you maintain healthy relationships.

You also have personal values, which help you make decisions about what is important to you. For example, if you believe that it's important to keep parks clean, you might decide to spend time each week picking up trash in your local park.

Your values come from different sources. When you are young, you get most of them from your parents or guardians and other family members. They provide you with the moral foundation for the rest of your life. See **Figure 2.2** on the next page for more examples of how your values are formed.

Go Online

Topic: Stories That Share a Lesson

Visit **glencoe.com** for Student Web Activities where you can read stories and learn how to write stories that have a lesson to teach.

Activity: Using the information provided at the above link, write a story of your own that contains a lesson on values or ethics.

Reading Check

Describe How are core ethical values different from personal values?

SOME SOURCES OF VALUES

You learn values from many sources. **What are some values that might influence the decisions that you make?**

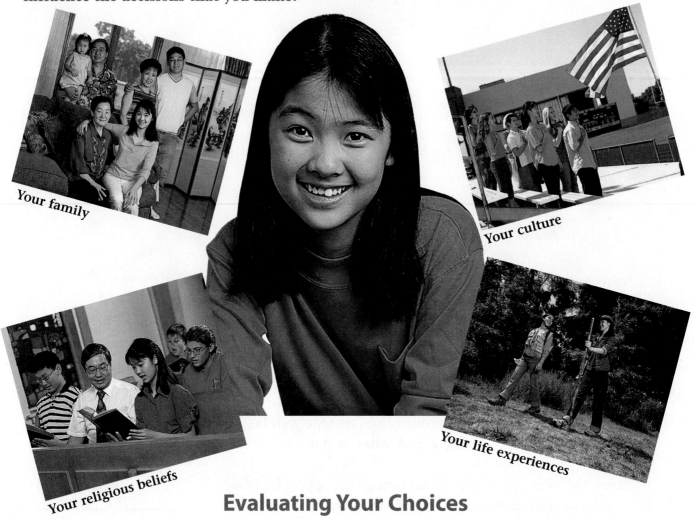

Your family

Your culture

Your religious beliefs

Your life experiences

Evaluating Your Choices

Your values help you evaluate your choices. Tyler's classmate Christopher told Tyler that he had a copy of the answers to a test. Tyler knew that he could easily get an A if he used the answers. He also knew that doing this would be dishonest. Tyler believed in honesty. He wasn't sure what to do and he didn't want to make an impulsive decision.

Values provide **criteria,** *standards on which to base decisions.* Criteria can help you evaluate the possible outcomes of your decision. Tyler used the H.E.L.P. criteria to decide what to do:

H (Healthful). What are the risks of cheating?

E (Ethical). Is cheating right, according to core ethical values?

L (Legal). Are there school rules against cheating on a test?

P (Parental Approval). Would my parents approve of cheating?

 Reading Check **Describe** How are criteria used in decision making?

Health Skills Activity

Decision Making

Is It Always Right to Help a Friend?

LaDonna had recently moved to a new school and was having a hard time making friends. Then she met Jason, who introduced her to many people at school. Thanks to him, LaDonna soon had many new friends.

Jason sat behind LaDonna in science class. One day, he asked LaDonna to let him copy answers from her test. LaDonna felt that she "owed" Jason for helping her. However, she also knew that cheating on a test is wrong. What should LaDonna do?

What Would You Do?

Apply the six steps of decision making to LaDonna's problem.

1. State the situation.
2. List the options.
3. Weigh the possible outcomes.
4. Consider your values.
5. Make a decision and act.
6. Evaluate the decision.

With a Partner

Role-play a scene in which LaDonna applies the steps of the decision-making process to keep from making an impulsive decision.

After using the H.E.L.P. criteria, Tyler saw that there were many negative consequences to cheating on the test. Cheating went against school rules and was not ethical. Tyler's parents would not approve of his cheating on a test. Tyler decided not to use the answers. He got an A and was proud that he earned his grade honestly. Tyler's values helped influence his decision not to cheat on the test.

Influences on Decisions

Sometimes you make decisions based on factual information. Other times, you make decisions because something else influences you. Your parents, friends, peers, and the media can also influence your decisions. For example, the other day

▲ These teens are tempted to take a swim even though a sign warns against it. **How would they use the H.E.L.P. criteria to make a responsible decision?**

THE SIX STEPS OF DECISION MAKING

When you apply the decision-making steps, you can make responsible decisions. **Why is it important to make a decision based on core ethical values?**

Emily has soccer practice at 3:30 P.M. Her friends want her to hang out with them instead. Emily loves soccer but also loves to spend time with her friends. Note how the six steps of the decision-making process can help her make a choice.

❶ **State the Situation.** What decision does Emily have to make? How much time does she have to make the decision? Emily has to decide whether to go to soccer practice or spend time with friends. She needs to make her decision by 3:30.

❷ **List the Options.** What are Emily's choices? Emily can go to practice today or she can skip practice and hang out with her friends.

❸ **Weigh the Possible Outcomes.** What are the consequences of each option? If Emily goes to practice today, she will be keeping her commitment to attend every practice. If Emily sees her friends today, her teammates and her coach will be disappointed, but her friends will be happy to see her.

❹ **Consider Your Values.** How does each option relate to Emily's values? Keeping commitments is important to Emily. She values her friends, but she committed to attending every soccer practice.

❺ **Make a Decision and Act.** What choice will Emily make? How will she follow through with her decision? Emily decides to attend practice because she made a commitment to her team and her coach. Emily explains her decision to her friends.

❻ **Evaluate the Decision.** What were the actual consequences of Emily's decision? Is she satisfied with the results? Emily is happy with her choice because she kept her commitment to her team and her coach. She practices for the upcoming game. Her friends are excited to spend time with her tomorrow.

Sue saw a TV ad that said a certain fruit drink gave you energy. She saw teens in the ad sipping the drink and then running energetically. Sue wanted to have more energy, so she added the name of the drink to her mom's grocery list.

The decision-making process can be broken down into six steps. These steps are shown in **Figure 2.3** on page 40. Applying these six steps can guide you through any decision that you need to make about an issue or problem. They can also help you avoid making impulsive decisions, or act without thinking.

At the store, Sue read the nutrition label on the bottle. She saw that the drink contained only 10 percent fruit juice. The rest was mainly sugar and water. Sue realized that the commercial did not give accurate information about the drink or its health benefits. The pictures of teens having fun influenced Sue's decision to try the drink.

 **Reading Check** **Analyze** What influences can affect your decisions?

Go Online
Visit **glencoe.com** and complete the Interactive Study Guide for Lesson 1.

Lesson 1 Review

 After You Read

Review this lesson for new terms, major headings, and Reading Checks.

What I Learned

1. *Vocabulary* Define *criteria*. Write a sentence that shows how criteria are important in decision making.

2. *Give Examples* Name three sources of values.

3. *Explain* What do the letters H.E.L.P. stand for?

4. *List* Name three possible influences on decisions.

5. *Identify* What are the six steps of decision making?

Thinking Critically

6. *Apply* Think back to a decision you made recently. What values influenced that decision?

7. *Analyze* Reread the story of Tyler on pages 38–39. Write a short paragraph explaining how he could have applied the steps of the decision-making process to help him make his choice.

Applying Health Skills

8. *Analyzing Influences* Suppose you have to make a health-related decision. Describe the decision you have to make. Then list three possible influences on that decision.

Lesson 2

Setting and Reaching Your Goals

Guide to Reading

● **Building Vocabulary**
Both terms listed below refer to goals. Write down the differences between the two terms.

■ long-term goal (p. 44)
■ short-term goal (p. 44)

● **Focusing on the Main Ideas**
In this lesson you will be able to

■ **explain** why it's important to set goals.
■ **distinguish** between the two different types of goals.
■ **create** a goal-setting plan to reach a health-related goal.

● **Reading Strategy**
Sequencing Review Figure 2.5 on page 46. Then list the steps of the goal-setting process in the correct order.

Quick Write

Write a brief description of a health goal that a teen might set.

Why Set Goals?

Omar got tired quickly in gym class and didn't feel very strong. He wanted to get in shape, but he wasn't sure how to begin. He had a brief talk with his older brother, Miguel. Miguel explained that the key to making changes in life is setting goals and working to reach them. Omar realized that he needed to set specific goals to improve his physical health.

Goal setting is a powerful tool, one that you can use to shape your future. Goals help you focus so that you can accomplish what you want in life. They can give you a sense of purpose and help you make good decisions. They can also help you measure your progress. In this way, goals become milestones along your journey of life. They can help you determine how far you have come and how far you want to go. Finally, reaching a goal can boost your self-confidence. This strengthens your mental/emotional health.

◄ This teen developed into a strong athlete. **What are two goals that this teen might have set to excel in this sport?**

Health Skills Activity

Goal Setting

Setting a Physical Activity Goal

Goal setting is one good strategy for improving and maintaining your personal health.

The President's Council on Physical Fitness and Sports recommends that teens participate in at least one hour of physical activity five days a week. Does that sound like a lot? Well, the good news is that you don't have to do it all at once. Here is an example of how to fit one hour of moderate to intense physical activity into your daily routine:

Inline skating after school with friends	20 minutes
Morning walk	15 minutes
Afternoon bike ride	25 minutes

You don't always have to take time out just to exercise. Instead, just do more of the physical activities that you already enjoy, such as dancing, biking, inline skating, skateboarding, swimming, and sports.

On Your Own

What are some physical activities that you enjoy but don't participate in very often? Choose one of these activities and set a goal to participate in it regularly. Use the goal-setting steps on page 45 to help you reach your goal.

Some goals you set may be easy to reach, while others may be more challenging. It's important that you set realistic goals. If you want to improve your grade in math, getting a better score on the next quiz is realistic. Getting an A for the whole year might be a lot harder. Thinking about your strengths and your limitations can help you decide what is realistic to achieve in a reasonable time period. Then you can start planning strategies for how you will reach your personal goal and improve your personal health. Reaching your goal can give you a sense of accomplishment.

Omar decided that a realistic goal for him would be to be able to run 2 miles without stopping. He also wanted to be able to do 50 push-ups. He could already run half a mile and do 10 push-ups, but he knew that he still had some work to do to reach these goals.

Careers for the 21st Century

Nurse Practitioner

Nurse practitioners are nurses who specialize in a variety of fields, such as family care, women's health, and elderly care. Nurse practitioners will always be in demand because they help people through all stages of life. In order to prepare for a career as a nurse, you should take courses in chemistry, biology, algebra, and English.

What skills does a nurse practitioner need? Go to *Career Corner* at glencoe.com to find out.

Academic Vocabulary

achieve (uh CHEEV) *(verb)* to get, complete, or accomplish. *If you achieve your goals you will feel very good about yourself.*

Often, setting a goal for one area in your life can lead to your accomplishing goals in other areas. For example, if your goal is learning to dance, you will also achieve fitness goals as well. Your overall sense of well-being can also benefit.

 **Reading Check** **Explain** How can reaching a goal strengthen mental/emotional health?

Long-Term Goals

Some goals take longer to achieve than others. A **long-term goal** is *a goal that you plan to reach over an extended period of time.* Omar's long-term goals were to do 50 push-ups and run 2 miles.

If the goal you set will likely take months or years to reach, it's a long-term goal. Learning to play the piano and making the soccer team are some examples of long-term goals. Becoming a teacher or a doctor is another example of a long-term goal.

Short-Term Goals

How do you reach a long-term goal? Usually by setting and meeting a number of short-term goals. A **short-term goal** is *a goal that you can achieve in a short length of time.*

To **achieve** his long-term goals, Omar set a few short-term goals. His first short-term goal was to run half a mile each day for one week. The next week he increased this goal to running three-quarters of a mile. He increased the distance each week until he could run 2 miles. Omar also set a similar short-term goal for push-ups. The first week, he would do 10 push-ups each day. The next week he would do 15 each day. He would increase the amount each week until he reached his goal of 50 push-ups.

Within three months, Omar had reached his long-term goal of doing 50 push-ups and running 2 miles. Take a look at **Figure 2.4** to see how short-term goals can help you reach a long-term goal.

Reading Check **Explain** What is a short-term goal?

Strategies for Attaining a Goal

Once you decide on your goal, you need to think of a plan or strategy to help you meet your goal. A goal-setting plan with a series of steps for you to take can be very effective. Creating and following a goal-setting plan will help you stay on track.

MILESTONES IN REACHING A LONG-TERM GOAL

Setting and meeting short-term goals helped this teen reach his long-term goal of getting an A in science. **How can reaching short-term goals improve mental/emotional health?**

Here are the steps of a goal-setting plan:

Step 1: Set a realistic goal and write it down.

Step 2: List the steps you need to take to reach that goal.

Step 3: Find others who can help and support you.

Step 4: Set checkpoints to evaluate your progress.

Step 5: Reward yourself after reaching the goal.

Read through the goal-setting plan shown in **Figure 2.5** on the following page. Notice how the plan helped a teen organize his time and activities so that he could keep moving toward reaching his goal.

Go Online

Visit **glencoe.com** and complete the Interactive Study Guide for Lesson 2.

 Reading Check **Identify** List the five goal-setting steps.

AN EFFECTIVE GOAL-SETTING PLAN

Making and following a goal-setting plan can help you meet a goal. Think of a goal to set. **What are some steps you could take to reach that goal?**

My Goal: Earn $400 to purchase a mountain bike and helmet

My Goal-Setting Plan:
Start a newspaper-delivery service
Make flyers to advertise my service
Deliver flyers to neighbors' houses
Deliver papers every day
Save all money earned

Sources of Help:
Jenna (can help me hand out flyers)
Mark (older brother)

Checkpoints:
By December: earn $125
By March: earn another $125
By June: earn another $150

Reward:
New mountain bike and helmet

Lesson 2 Review

 After You Read

Review this lesson for new terms, major headings, and Reading Checks.

What I Learned

1. *Vocabulary* Define *short-term goal* and *long-term goal.* Then use both terms in a sentence that shows the difference between them.

2. *Give Examples* List at least two steps in a goal-setting plan.

3. *Explain* How can short-term goals be used to reach long-term goals?

Thinking Critically

4. *Analyze* How are checkpoints useful in meeting a goal?

5. *Predict* How might priorities, changing abilities, and responsibilities influence setting health goals?

Applying Health Skills

6. *Goal Setting* Think of one goal that you would like to achieve. Then make a goal-setting plan for reaching it. Use the five goal-setting steps to create your plan.

Go Online For more Lesson Review Activities, go to **glencoe.com**.

Lesson 3

Building Good Character

Guide to Reading

Building Vocabulary
Write the terms below. As you come across them in the lesson, write the definitions next to each term.

- character (p. 47)
- integrity (p. 48)
- role model (p. 50)

Focusing on the Main Ideas
In this lesson you will be able to

- **explain** what character is.
- **identify** traits of good character.
- **describe** how to develop good character.
- **access** reliable information on community organizations where you can volunteer.

Reading Strategy
Skimming Look over the major and minor headings in this lesson. Then write a paragraph describing what you think this lesson will cover.

uick Write

Write a short description of a person who has been a positive role model for you.

What Is Character?

When Michael talks with friends, he listens to them. When he borrows money, he pays it back promptly. He keeps his promises and treats others with respect. When someone needs help, he offers a helping hand. Through his actions, Michael demonstrates the qualities of good character. **Character** is *the way a person thinks, feels, and acts.*

People with good character show certain qualities. They tend to be trustworthy, fair, responsible, respectful, caring, and good citizens. Having good character improves your relationships. You get along better with your friends and family. Being in strong friendships with people who like and trust you benefits your social health. Taking responsibility for doing your schoolwork benefits your

▶ Now that you're a teen, you can take on more responsibility. **What are some behaviors that show you are ready to handle more responsibility?**

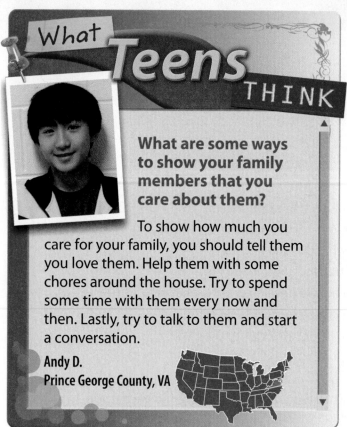

Academic Vocabulary

demonstrating (DEM uhn streyt ing) *(verb)* showing, describing, illustrating, or explaining. *Max enjoyed demonstrating how a volcano works at this year's science fair.*

mental/emotional health. Showing respect for yourself by eating healthfully and getting enough sleep benefits your physical health.

Traits of Good Character

Groups function best when each member demonstrates good character. You are probably a member of many groups, like a family, a sports team, or friends. In order for all members of a group to get along, they have to have good character traits. There are six basic traits of good character. The traits are described below and **Figure 2.6** on the next page shows the actions that demonstrate them.

Trustworthiness. Part of being trustworthy involves **integrity,** *being true to your ethical values.* When you have integrity, people know they can count on you to do the right thing.

Respect. Having respect means listening carefully and speaking kindly to others. You disagree without arguing and understand that others have the right to see situations differently. You show respect for yourself by practicing healthful behaviors and avoiding those that can be harmful. You respect your peers even when their abilities and skills differ from your own.

Responsibility. You take responsibility for everything you do. You accept credit when things go well and accept advice and feedback when they don't.

Fairness. When you are fair, you treat people equally and honestly. You are open-minded and willing to listen to other opinions.

Caring. Teens who are caring communicate consideration and acceptance of others. They listen to others' concerns and offer support and encouragement when needed.

Citizenship. Teens who obey rules and laws are responsible and are **demonstrating** citizenship. Citizenship is also doing what you can to help your school, community, and country. You protect the environment and encourage others to be good citizens, too. You accept the responsibilities and the privileges of being a citizen. You practice the skill of advocacy. Advocacy involves supporting causes you believe in, such as helping to prevent violence and making your community safe.

Reading Check

Identify What are two traits of good character?

SHOWING GOOD CHARACTER

You can see people demonstrate good character around you every day.
Name three examples of good character you saw in the last week.

Traits of Good Character	Major Qualities of Good Character	Examples of Good Character
Trustworthiness	Honest, truthful, can be counted on	Promptly returns borrowed items
Respect	Listens, disagrees without arguing	Listens carefully to others' concerns
Responsibility	Keeps promises, thinks before acting	Completes household tasks without being asked
Fairness	Treats people equally, open-minded, patient	Considers new ideas
Caring	Is kind, generous, compassionate, helpful	Helps younger students
Citizenship	Obeys rules and laws, practices advocacy	Follows school rules and helps others to follow them

What Shapes Your Character?

Unlike hair or eye color, you don't inherit character traits from your parents. You *choose* to be a person of good character. The choices you make are the building blocks of your character. However, many things can shape the development of your character.

Life Experiences

As a child, you learned good character traits from your parents or guardians. When your parents said, "Share your toys," you learned that being fair was important. When you heard, "Hey, that's cheating!" you understood that you should be honest, too.

You also learn character by how you are treated. If you are treated with kindness and respect, you can better understand how to practice these traits. As you grow older, you also learn about character from your teachers and coaches.

▼ Respecting the property of others is an example of good character. **What character trait is this teen demonstrating?**

Health Skills Activity

Accessing Information

Organizations to Get Involved With

Getting involved with activities that help others will help you build the character trait of good citizenship. Finding the right organization to support is the key to your success. Here is a list of some groups to get you started.

COMMUNITY IMPROVEMENT

Habitat for Humanity—Brings together volunteers to build affordable housing in communities.

Students Against Destructive Decisions (SADD)—Promotes ways to help teens avoid unhealthful behaviors.

Youth Volunteer Corps—Provides ways for young people to become volunteers.

ENVIRONMENT

Earth Day Network—Creates ways for teens to help the environment.

Global Response Youth Action—Provides ideas for protecting the environment.

LEADERSHIP TRAINING

Hugh O'Brian Youth Leadership—Conducts ethical-leadership training.

Boys & Girls Clubs of America—Runs leadership training courses.

MENTORING

Reading Is Fundamental—Provides teens with mentoring opportunities.

America's Promise—Provides resources for teens who want to become mentors.

With a Group

Work with a partner to choose three organizations that interest you. Use reliable online and print resources to research each of the organizations. Create a fact sheet on each organization and present your findings to the class.

You can also learn good character by being involved in activities that help others, such as tutoring younger children or volunteering with organizations that fight hunger and poverty.

Role Models

Watching how others behave is a way to learn good character traits. Your parents or guardians were probably your first role models. A **role model** *inspires you to think or act a certain way.* Other health role models include older siblings, teachers, coaches, doctors, police officers, and other community workers.

 **Reading Check** **Identify** What is a role model?

How to Develop Good Character

Developing good character requires effort. It involves thinking about what you say and how you act. Are your words and actions trustworthy? When you are honest, people know they can count on you. They can be confident in your ability to take on more responsibility. Do you speak respectfully to others? This shows other people that you care about them. How do you respond when someone wants to discuss a problem? You can show your good character by being a good listener. Do you help make your school or community a better place? When you see something wrong, you can show good character by speaking up about it.

Do you have any character traits you'd like to improve? When you discover a behavior or attitude in yourself that you would like to change, take action! Everyone has the potential to become a person of good character. People of good character not only strengthen their own total health, but also make the world a better place in which to live.

▲ These teens enjoy participating in activities that help others. It strengthens their character traits. **Name some volunteer opportunities in your community.**

Visit glencoe.com and complete the Interactive Study Guide for Lesson 3.

Lesson 3 Review

 After You Read

Review this lesson for new terms, major headings, and Reading Checks.

What I Learned

1. *Vocabulary* Define *character* and use it in a sentence.

2. *List* Name at least two examples of people who can be role models.

3. *Identify* What are two influences that can shape a person's character?

Thinking Critically

4. *Hypothesize* Think of an act of courage performed by someone you know or have heard or read about. What values do you think this person stood up for? What risks did the individual take in doing what he or she thought was right? How did this demonstration of good character benefit the community?

5. *Apply* What do you think is your strongest character trait, and why? Explain your answer in a brief paragraph.

Applying Health Skills

6. *Analyzing Influences* Who are your role models? Write down the names of three people whom you look up to. List the character traits that each role model demonstrates. Then describe the ways in which each one has influenced you.

Building Health Skills

Accessing Information

Practicing Healthful Behaviors

Stress Management

Analyzing Influences

Communication Skills

Refusal Skills

Conflict Resolution

Decision Making

Goal Setting

Advocacy

What Is Goal Setting?

Goal setting is a five-step plan for improving and maintaining your personal health. Some goals are easy to reach while others may be more challenging.

The Five Steps of the Goal-Setting Plan

- **Step 1:** Set a realistic goal and write it down.
- **Step 2:** List the steps that you need to take to reach the goal.
- **Step 3:** Find others, like family, friends, and teachers who can help and support you.
- **Step 4:** Set checkpoints along the way to evaluate your progress.
- **Step 5:** Reward yourself once you have reached your goal.

Setting a Health Goal

Follow the Model, Practice, and Apply steps to help you master this important health skill.

① Model

Read how Kayla uses goal-setting skills to get in shape and improve her basketball skills in time for tryouts.

Kayla wanted to try out for the basketball team. Tryouts were three months away. Kayla set a goal to get in shape and improve her skills in time for tryouts. She wrote down her goal: "Improve my basketball skills so I can make the team."

Next, Kayla listed the steps to reach this goal. These steps included being able to jog for 20 minutes without stopping and improving her passing skills. Kayla talked to the coach to find out how else she could prepare. She asked her friend Lauren, who also wanted to join the team, to practice with her.

Every day after school, Kayla and Lauren practiced basketball drills or went for a run. They made a schedule to track their progress and keep each other going. Both Kayla and Lauren did well in tryouts. To celebrate, they went out for pizza.

❷ Practice

Help Yoko use goal-setting skills by reading the passage and then answering the questions below.

Yoko has been feeling tired lately. Megan, however, always seems to have energy. At lunch, Yoko sees that Megan's meal is made up of a variety of healthful foods. Yoko realizes that she is eating a lot of empty-calorie foods that don't contain all of the nutrients her body needs.

Yoko sees that her food choices are affecting her energy level. What realistic health goal can she set to improve her energy level? Write down this goal. Use the remaining goal-setting steps to create a plan that will help Yoko achieve this goal.

❸ Apply

Apply what you have learned about goal setting by completing the activity below.

Choose one good character trait and set a health goal for yourself. Then create a tri-fold brochure that illustrates this goal. Use your goal as the title on the front of the brochure. On the inside of the brochure include: 1) a description of this character trait; 2) how reaching your goal will improve your health triangle; 3) a list of the steps you need to take to reach your goal; 4) the names of people who can help you reach your goal; 5) the checkpoints you'll use to evaluate your progress; and 6) your reward for reaching the goal. Use different fonts, graphics, or art to illustrate your brochure. Explain your brochure to the class.

Self-Check

- Does my title include a realistic goal?
- Does my brochure explain how the goal will improve my health triangle?
- Does my brochure show the steps of goal setting?

Building Health Skills

Read All About...Your Big Decision

Most stories in the newspaper follow the same pattern. They state the most important information first and add the details later. Reporters focus on the "5 W's and H" to describe an event: who, what, where, when, why, and how.

Teens make decisions every day, some large, some small. Think of a health-related decision that a teen might make. It could affect physical health, such as getting more sleep. It could affect mental/emotional health, such as communicating more honestly with family members. It could affect social health, such as trying out for the school play.

What You Will Need

- Paper
- Pen

 ### What You Will Do

1. Choose a health-related decision that a teen might make.

2. In class, spend 10 minutes writing down notes that include <u>what</u> the present situation is like, <u>who</u> will be affected by your decision, and <u>when</u> and <u>where</u> you will apply your decision. Explain <u>why</u> this decision is important. Weigh the outcomes and consider your values. Write <u>how</u> you will feel after practicing this decision regularly.

3. With this outline of ideas in front of you, write a newspaper story that has three paragraphs. The first paragraph will list the "W's and H." The second paragraph will tell when and where this will happen and give details of who will be affected. The third paragraph will explain why this decision is important.

4. Write a headline that announces the successful outcome of the decision. Volunteer to place your headline on a class bulletin board.

Wrapping It Up

Now that you've written the story and the headline, it's time to act on your decision. Place your newspaper article where you can look at it regularly. Use it to motivate yourself and guide your progress. Evaluate the decision. Have you been successful?

Reading Review

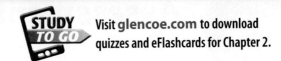
STUDY TO GO Visit glencoe.com to download quizzes and eFlashcards for Chapter 2.

FOLDABLES® Study Organizer

Foldables® and Other Study Aids
Take out the Foldable® that you created for Lesson 1 and any graphic organizers that you created for Lessons 1–3. Find a partner and quiz each other using these study aids.

Lesson 1 Making Responsible Decisions

Main Idea It is important to make wise, responsible decisions because you are responsible for your health.

- The decisions you make affect your health triangle.
- Your personal values come from a variety of sources, including your family, your religious beliefs, your culture, and your life experiences.
- Core ethical values are values shared by a group.
- Core ethical values and your personal values help you determine what is important to you.
- You can use the H.E.L.P. criteria to evaluate the possible outcomes of your choices.
- Your parents, friends, and peers can influence your decisions.
- There are six steps of decision making: state the situation, list the options, weigh the possible outcomes, consider your values, make a decision and act, and evaluate the decision.

Lesson 2 Setting and Reaching Your Goals

Main Idea In order to shape a successful future, it is important to set goals.

- Goals give you a sense of purpose and help you to make good decisions.
- Goal setting focuses your efforts and helps you measure your progress.
- The two types of goals are long-term and short-term. Long-term goals can take months and even years to achieve. Short-term goals don't take as long to complete.

Lesson 3 Building Good Character

Main Idea People who have good character are healthful and make the world a better place.

- Character is the way a person thinks, feels, and acts.
- A person who has good character is trustworthy, respectful, fair, and a good citizen.
- Role models are people who inspire you to think and act in a certain way.
- Developing good character takes effort.

After You Read

Health eSpotlight

VIDEO

Now that you have read the chapter, look back at your answers to the Health Quiz on the chapter opener. Would you change any of them? What would your answers be now?

Reviewing Vocabulary and Main Ideas

On a sheet of paper, write the numbers 1–3. After each number, write the term from the list that best completes each statement.

- decision making
- ethical
- criteria

Lesson 1 | Making Responsible Decisions

1. You can evaluate the possible outcomes of a decision by using _____.
2. Honesty and respect for others are two examples of core _____ values.
3. _____ is the process of making a choice or solving a problem.

On a sheet of paper, write the numbers 4–9. After each number, write the letter of the answer that best completes each statement.

Lesson 2 | Setting and Reaching Your Goals

4. An example of a long-term goal is
   a. eating a healthful breakfast today.
   b. graduating from college in four years.
   c. walking two blocks each day.
   d. passing a math test next week.

5. A common result of achieving a short-term goal is
   a. decreased loyalty.
   b. decreased character.
   c. increased frustration.
   d. increased self-confidence.

6. Eric wants to become a veterinarian, so he begins by volunteering at an animal shelter. Volunteering could be a
   a. short-term goal.
   b. long-term goal.
   c. character trait.
   d. conflict-resolution skill.

Lesson 3 | Building Good Character

7. Good character can be illustrated by
   a. favoring one person over another.
   b. respecting the opinions of others.
   c. refusing to obey school rules.

8. Actions, thoughts, and feelings are all part of a person's
   a. fairness.
   b. criteria.
   c. character.
   d. goals.

9. One action that would *not* demonstrate good character would be
   a. respecting your parents and teachers.
   b. treating everyone with kindness.
   c. volunteering in your community.
   d. borrowing a book and losing it.

56 Chapter 2: Taking Charge of Your Health

Go Online Visit glencoe.com and take the Online Quiz for Chapter 2.

Thinking Critically

Using complete sentences, answer the following questions on a sheet of paper.

10. **Analyze** List the six traits of good character. Next to each trait, give an example of how someone might demonstrate the trait.

11. **Predict** How can goal setting improve your physical health?

Write About It

12. **Expository Writing** Write directions of how you would find the latest research on the effects of using sunscreen. Include how to analyze whether this health information is valid.

ACTIVITY

↗ Applying Technology

Great Goals

You and a partner will use iMovie® to create a public service announcement video clip that encourages your peers to set goals and strive to achieve them. Follow the steps below to complete this project.

- Create a goal-setting plan. Make sure to include the five steps mentioned on page 45.
- Take digital photos of your partner as he or she completes each of the steps in the goal-setting plan.
- Open iMovie®. Click, drag, and drop your digital images into the *iMovie* clipboard.
- Add a title over a colored screen for each step of your goal-setting plan.
- Edit and save your project.

Standardized Test Practice

Reading

Read the passage and then answer the questions.

Most teens need about nine hours of sleep each night. When you don't get enough sleep, being tired is only one result. There are many other effects of not getting enough sleep. You may have trouble remembering things and not be able to think clearly. This is one reason why it is important to get enough sleep before a test. When you are tired, you also increase your chances of injuring yourself doing everyday activities. Your wellness can be affected, too, when you don't get enough sleep over long periods of time.

There are many reasons why you might not get enough sleep at night. These reasons can range from stress to too much caffeine. Sometimes distractions, like television, affect the amount of sleep you get. The decisions you make about how you spend your time can also affect how much sleep you get.

1. What does *effects* mean in this sentence from the passage?
   There are many other *effects* of not getting enough sleep.
   A. reasons
   B. ways
   C. results
   D. problems

2. Not getting enough sleep can best be described as a
   A. healthful behavior.
   B. health risk.
   C. distraction.
   D. healthful decision.

Chapter Preview

Lesson 1   Becoming Physically Fit....60

Lesson 2   Exploring Skeletal and
Muscular Systems..............66

Lesson 3   Exploring the
Circulatory System............71

Lesson 4   Creating Your
Fitness Plan......................77

Lesson 5   Weight Training
and Sports........................84

Lesson 6   Preventing Physical
Activity Injuries.................91

Building Health Skills..........................96

TIME health news 98

Chapter Reading Review 99

Chapter Assessment 100

▲ *Working with the Photo*

Being physically active improves your overall health. **How might the activity pictured here help these teens improve their health?**

Start-Up Activities

 Before You Read **What do you do to stay physically active?**
Take the short health inventory below. Keep a record of your answers.

HEALTH INVENTORY

1. I do 60 minutes of physical activity daily.
(a) always   (b) sometimes   (c) never

2. My daily physical activity includes an energetic 30-minute workout.
(a) always   (b) sometimes   (c) never

3. I wear the necessary safety gear when working out.
(a) always   (b) sometimes   (c) never

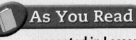 **Study Organizer**

As You Read   **Make this Foldable® to record the information presented in Lesson 1 about the elements of fitness.**

1 Begin with a plain sheet of 11″ × 17″ paper. Fold it into thirds along the short axis.

2 Open and fold the bottom edge up to form a pocket. Glue the edges.

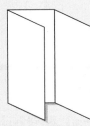

3 Label each pocket as shown. Place an index card or quarter sheet of notebook paper into each pocket.

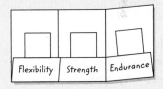

Write down key points on each of these elements of fitness on index cards or sheets of notebook paper cut into quarter sections. Store the cards in the appropriate pocket of your Foldable.

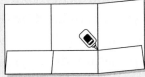 Visit **glencoe.com** and use the eFlashcards to preview Chapter 3 vocabulary terms.

Lesson 1

Becoming Physically Fit

📖 Guide to Reading

● Building Vocabulary
As you read this lesson, write down each new highlighted term and its definition.

- physical activity (p. 60)
- fitness (p. 60)
- exercise (p. 60)
- endurance (p. 62)
- muscle endurance (p. 62)
- cardiovascular endurance (p. 62)
- strength (p. 62)
- flexibility (p. 63)
- body composition (p. 63)
- aerobic exercise (p. 64)
- anaerobic exercise (p. 64)

● Focusing on the Main Ideas
In this lesson, you will be able to

- **discuss** the benefits of physical activity.
- **explain** how to increase your strength, endurance, and flexibility.
- **apply** advocacy skills to tell others about the benefits of fitness.
- **recognize** the influence of body composition on fitness.
- **measure** your fitness using fitness tests.

● Reading Strategy
Skimming Look over the lesson headings. Write a sentence or two describing what you think the lesson will contain.

FOLDABLES Study Organizer Use the Foldable® on p. 59 as you read this lesson.

List at least three physical activities you took part in this week. Which do you think does the most good for your health and why?

Physical Activity and Your Health

Your body is constantly on the move! You use it to climb stairs, carry books, and pedal your bike. These movements add up to lots of physical activity. **Physical activity** is *any movement that makes your body use extra energy.*

Being physically fit is a great strategy for improving and maintaining personal health through all stages of life. It's also a positive health behavior that can prevent many health problems. **Fitness** means *being able to handle physical work and play each day without getting overly tired.* If you exercise regularly, you will have lots of energy. **Exercise** is *planned physical activity done regularly to build or maintain one's fitness.* You can handle more activity in your day and not feel tired. Regular exercise also helps you develop skills to play sports.

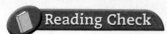 **Define** What is *physical activity*?

Benefits of Physical Activity

Physical activity can benefit your health in many ways, as **Figure 3.1** shows. For example, being active helps build and maintain your bones and muscles. It helps you manage your weight. It increases your strength and flexibility. It keeps your blood pressure at healthy levels and makes your heart and lungs work better. All these benefits help you enjoy life more fully. You have more energy. You move more freely and are more athletic. You also sleep better and are in less danger of developing certain diseases now and throughout all stages of life.

Have you ever noticed it just *feels good* to work out? You usually feel more relaxed or upbeat after playing a sport or going for a brisk walk. That's because an active lifestyle is good for your brain as well as your body. It improves the way you think and feel.

▼ FIGURE 3.1

PHYSICAL ACTIVITY HAS MANY BENEFITS

When you're active, you sleep better, have more chances to make friends, and think more clearly. **How else can physical activity benefit your health?**

Academic Vocabulary

element (EL uh ment) (noun) one of the parts of which something is made up, the state or place natural or suited to a person or thing. *One of the basic elements of geometry is a line.*

You have more self-confidence. You're also more mentally alert because more oxygen is going to your brain. Physical activity can help cut down on stress and give you a more easygoing attitude.

Being physically active can also give your social health a boost. When you sign up for sports teams at school or head outdoors to exercise, you're likely to meet more people. In a diverse society, physical activity can bring people together who share interests and goals. This leads to new friendships and helps you learn to work well with others. Getting along with others makes your school and community safer.

Reading Check

Recall Give one example of how physical activity benefits each side of your health triangle.

Elements of Physical Fitness

There are five **elements** of physical fitness: muscle endurance, cardiovascular endurance, strength, flexibility, and body composition. Learning about these elements will help you assess and improve your own fitness level.

Endurance

Endurance (en·DUR·uhnce) is *the ability to perform difficult physical activity without getting overly tired.* **Muscle endurance** is *the ability of a muscle to repeatedly use force over a period of time.* If you can run several miles and if your legs don't feel tired, your legs have muscle endurance. You can build your endurance if you spend more time doing a chosen exercise or physical activity.

Cardiovascular (kar·dee·oh·VASS·kyoo·luhr) **endurance** is *the measure of how well your heart and lungs work during moderate-to-vigorous physical activity or exercise.* If you are breathing so hard you can't speak in sentences, your activity is vigorous. If you can carry on a conversation, your activity level is light to moderate. Cardiovascular endurance is also a measure of how quickly your heartbeat and breathing return to normal after you stop exercising.

Strength

Strength is *the ability of your muscles to use force.* The amount of work your muscles can do is a measure of strength. By building muscle strength, you can improve your skills for sports and other activities. You also shape and tone your body. Lifting weights is one of the many ways to build and maintain muscle strength.

Flexibility

The ability to move joints fully and easily through a full range of motion is known as **flexibility.** You can increase your flexibility with regular, gentle stretches. When you become more flexible, you will be more agile, or able to change direction easily. You will also be less likely to get hurt as you exercise or play. **Figure 3.2** shows some ways to build not only flexibility, but also endurance and strength.

Body Composition

The last element of fitness is body composition. **Body composition** is *the proportions of fat, bone, muscle, and fluid that make up body weight.* A healthy body generally has more bone, muscle, and fluid than fat. Your body composition is the result of your eating habits, your level of physical activity, and genetics—the genes you inherited from your parents.

Effect of Body Composition on Fitness

You can improve your body composition by eating healthy foods and increasing your physical activity. If you exercise regularly, your body can gain muscle and lose fat. This helps you stay within a healthy weight range and helps to protect you against diseases like heart disease and cancer. Eating healthy foods and exercising also helps keep your cholesterol levels down. Cholesterol is a fatty substance in the blood that the body uses to build cells. High cholesterol levels can contribute to heart disease.

▼ FIGURE 3.2

EXERCISES FOR ENDURANCE, STRENGTH, AND FLEXIBILITY

Different exercises improve different elements of fitness. **Give examples of other exercises that can build endurance, strength, and flexibility.**

Endurance
Swimming is one way to build endurance.

Strength
Weight training is one way to build strength.

Flexibility
Stretching is one way to build flexibility.

Visit **glencoe.com** and complete the Interactive Study Guide for Lesson 1.

Types of Exercise

Whether they build endurance, strength, or flexibility, most physical activities and exercises can be described as aerobic or anaerobic. **Aerobic** (ah·ROH·bik) **exercise** is *rhythmic, moderate-to-vigorous activity that uses large amounts of oxygen and works the heart and lungs.* Dancing, running, swimming laps, and bicycling are examples of aerobic exercise. **Anaerobic exercise** is *intense physical activity that builds muscle but does not use large amounts of oxygen.* Lifting weights is one type of anaerobic exercise. Sprinting is another example of anaerobic exercise.

 **Compare and Contrast** What is the difference between aerobic and anaerobic exercise?

Measuring Your Fitness

Here are a few examples of common fitness tests that can help you measure your fitness level. **Figure 3.3** below shows typical results for teens your age. Compare your results with those in the chart.

- **Flexibility.** The Sit and Reach can help you measure your flexibility. Sit on the floor with your legs straight. Place a ruler between your feet with your heels at the end of the ruler. Keep your knees straight and slowly reach forward with both hands. How many inches past your toes can you reach?

 **FIGURE 3.3**

HEALTHY FITNESS ZONES

These fitness assessments can be used to measure your fitness level. Take these fitness tests and compare your results with the typical results for your age and gender. **Are there any areas of fitness that you need to work on?**

Healthy Fitness Zones for Ages 13 and 14			
Test	**Sex**	**Age 13**	**Age 14**
Curl-ups (# completed)	Boys	21–40	24–45
	Girls	18–32	18–32
1-mile run (in minutes and seconds)	Boys	10:00–7:30	9:30–7:00
	Girls	11:30–9:00	11:00–8:30
Modified Pull-ups (# completed)	Boys	8–22	9–25
	Girls	4–13	4–13
Push-ups (# completed)	Boys	12–25	14–30
	Girls	7–15	7–15
Sit and Reach (inches)	Boys	8	8
	Girls	10	10

- **Strength.** To test abdominal strength, do crunches for one minute. To test upper-body strength, do as many modified pull-ups or push-ups as you can in one minute.

- **Cardiovascular endurance.** You will need a 12-inch-high block or bench for this test. Before you start, take your pulse for 1 minute to determine your heart rate. Step up on the block, then step down. Repeat this stepping motion in a regular rhythm for 3 minutes. Take your pulse again for 1 minute. The more fit you are, the less your heart rate will increase.

- **Body composition.** The main method for measuring body composition is the skinfold test. This test involves pinching a fold of skin on the back of your upper arm and on the inside of your lower leg. Ask your physical education teacher for help with the skinfold test.

▲ Assess your fitness by seeing how long you can exercise before getting tired. Biking, for example, can measure cardiovascular endurance. **What other physical activities test cardiovascular endurance?**

 **Reading Check**

Explain What is one common fitness test you can use to measure your upper body strength?

Lesson 1 Review

 After You Read

Review this lesson for new terms, major headings, and Reading Checks.

What I Learned

1. *Restate* Name three ways that physical activity can benefit mental/emotional health.

2. *Vocabulary* Define *strength*.

3. *List* What are the five elements of fitness?

4. *Describe* What is body composition?

Thinking Critically

5. *Infer* Why might stretching help a person perform better at a sport?

6. *Evaluate* In a brief paragraph, describe your own thoughts and feelings about the benefits of being physically fit.

Applying Health Skills

7. *Goal Setting* Complete a personal fitness evaluation using the fitness tests provided in this lesson, or other tests recommended by your teacher. Use the results of your evaluation to set fitness goals. Develop a fitness program to help you reach your goals.

Exploring Skeletal and Muscular Systems

Guide to Reading

● **Building Vocabulary**
As you read this lesson, use each new highlighted term in a sentence. Write the sentences in your notebook.

- skeletal system (p. 66)
- joints (p. 66)
- tendons (p. 66)
- ligaments (p. 66)
- cartilage (p. 66)
- muscular system (p. 67)

● **Focusing on the Main Ideas**
In this lesson, you will be able to

- **discuss** the functions of the skeletal and muscular systems.
- **recognize** how bones and muscles work together.
- **describe** how to keep your bones and muscles healthy.

● **Reading Strategy**
Finding the Main Idea Look at the main headings in this lesson. For each heading, write a sentence that states the main idea.

Quick Write

Why do you think healthy bones are important to good health? Explain your ideas in a few sentences.

The Skeletal System

The **skeletal system** is *the framework of bones and other tissues that supports the body.* This system also protects your internal organs and helps you move. The 206 bones in your body make blood cells and store calcium and other minerals.

Joints are *the places where two or more bones meet.* Some joints allow the bones to move. Others, such as those in the skull, never move but protect organs instead. **Figure 3.4** on the following page shows the major bones in the skeletal system. It also describes the primary types of joints.

Several types of connecting tissue allow bones and muscles to work together as they move. **Tendons** are *a type of connecting tissue that joins muscles to bones and muscles to muscles.* Your Achilles tendon, for example, attaches your calf muscle to your heel bone. **Ligaments** are *a type of connecting tissue that holds bones to other bones at the joint.* Ligaments make it possible for your knees and ankles to work. **Cartilage** is *a strong, flexible tissue that allows joints to move easily, cushions bones, and supports soft tissues.* The tip of your nose contains cartilage. Cartilage also pads your knee joint.

Reading Check **Define** What are *ligaments?*

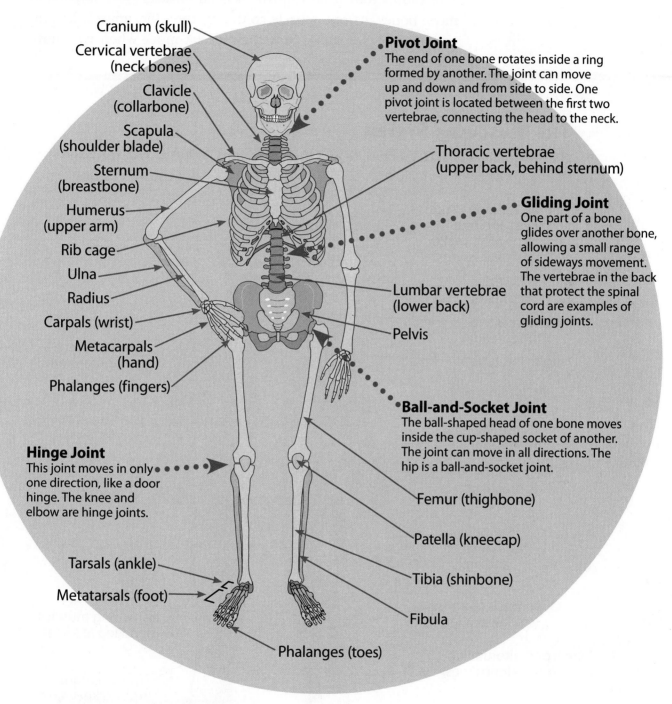

THE SKELETAL SYSTEM

Here are some of the major bones and joints of the skeletal system. **What type of joint are the vertebrae?**

Cranium (skull)

Cervical vertebrae (neck bones)

Clavicle (collarbone)

Scapula (shoulder blade)

Sternum (breastbone)

Humerus (upper arm)

Rib cage

Ulna

Radius

Carpals (wrist)

Metacarpals (hand)

Phalanges (fingers)

Pivot Joint
The end of one bone rotates inside a ring formed by another. The joint can move up and down and from side to side. One pivot joint is located between the first two vertebrae, connecting the head to the neck.

Thoracic vertebrae (upper back, behind sternum)

Gliding Joint
One part of a bone glides over another bone, allowing a small range of sideways movement. The vertebrae in the back that protect the spinal cord are examples of gliding joints.

Lumbar vertebrae (lower back)

Pelvis

Ball-and-Socket Joint
The ball-shaped head of one bone moves inside the cup-shaped socket of another. The joint can move in all directions. The hip is a ball-and-socket joint.

Hinge Joint
This joint moves in only one direction, like a door hinge. The knee and elbow are hinge joints.

Tarsals (ankle)

Metatarsals (foot)

Femur (thighbone)

Patella (kneecap)

Tibia (shinbone)

Fibula

Phalanges (toes)

The Muscular System

The human body has more than 600 muscles. The **muscular system** includes *tissues that move parts of the body and control the organs.* It provides the power and flexibility you need to move. The three main types of muscles are skeletal, smooth, and cardiac.

Figure 3.5 identifies skeletal muscles. These muscles are voluntary. That means you can control them. For example, imagine you want to turn your head. Your brain sends messages to muscles in your neck. In response, the neck muscles contract, or shorten. This causes your head to turn. Skeletal muscles work in pairs to move bones. As one muscle contracts, the other muscle lengthens. **Figure 3.6** shows how the muscles move when you move your arm.

▼ FIGURE 3.5

THE MUSCULAR SYSTEM

Here are the major skeletal muscles and their functions. **What is the function of the trapezius?**

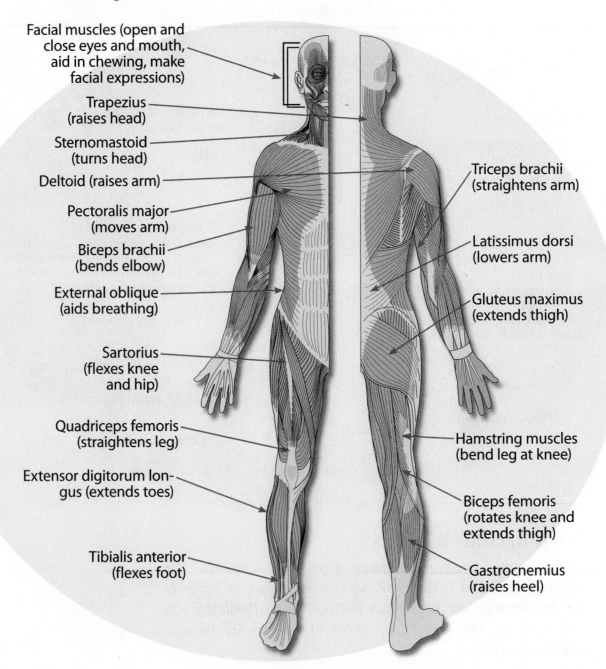

Facial muscles (open and close eyes and mouth, aid in chewing, make facial expressions)

Trapezius (raises head)

Sternomastoid (turns head)

Deltoid (raises arm)

Pectoralis major (moves arm)

Biceps brachii (bends elbow)

External oblique (aids breathing)

Sartorius (flexes knee and hip)

Quadriceps femoris (straightens leg)

Extensor digitorum longus (extends toes)

Tibialis anterior (flexes foot)

Triceps brachii (straightens arm)

Latissimus dorsi (lowers arm)

Gluteus maximus (extends thigh)

Hamstring muscles (bend leg at knee)

Biceps femoris (rotates knee and extends thigh)

Gastrocnemius (raises heel)

Your body's organs and blood vessels contain smooth muscles. These muscles are involuntary. That means they move without you consciously controlling their movement. The heart has its own special type of involuntary muscle called cardiac muscle.

Caring for Your Bones and Muscles

To keep your bones and muscles in good shape, stay physically active. Do flexibility exercises so you can move more easily and work out more safely. Choose physical activities that strengthen your muscles and bones. Also do activities that build cardiovascular endurance. Your heart and lungs will have more power.

"Stand up straight!" No doubt someone has told you this at least once in your life. It's good advice. Proper posture keeps bones, joints, and muscles in the right places. Just remember, good posture is not stiff posture. Sit and stand in a correct but relaxed way. Your lower back should be slightly curved. If you use a backpack, try not to overload it. Otherwise, you could strain your back.

ACTIVITY

Connect To... Science

Scoliosis

A person with scoliosis has a spine that curves sideways. No one knows what causes this curvature. Doctors usually find it in young people between the ages of 10 and 14. Your school may provide screening for scoliosis.

Use reliable sources to find out how doctors treat scoliosis. Report your findings to the class.

▼ FIGURE 3.6

PAIRED MOVEMENT

Pairs of muscles work together to move bones. They use opposite actions.
What muscles move when you bend your arm?

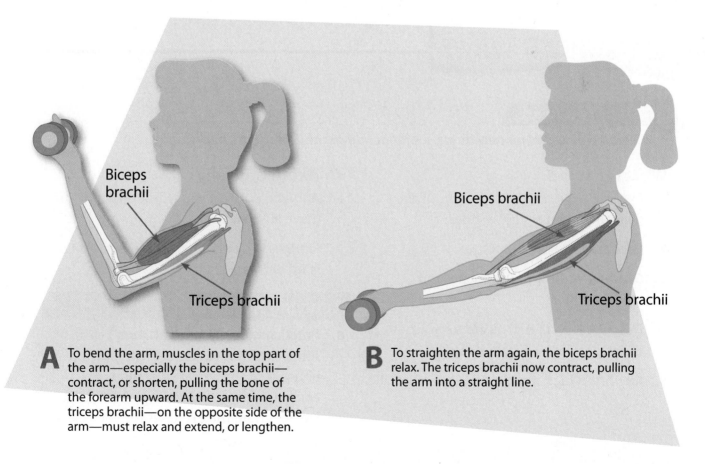

A To bend the arm, muscles in the top part of the arm—especially the biceps brachii—contract, or shorten, pulling the bone of the forearm upward. At the same time, the triceps brachii—on the opposite side of the arm—must relax and extend, or lengthen.

Biceps brachii

Triceps brachii

B To straighten the arm again, the biceps brachii relax. The triceps brachii now contract, pulling the arm into a straight line.

Biceps brachii

Triceps brachii

◀ From time to time, check to make sure you have good posture. **Why is having good posture important?**

When you lift heavy objects, keep your back straight. Bend your knees as you lift, and use your legs to do most of the work. If you get hurt, don't try to keep using the injured area. Visit a doctor or other professional health services right away.

Have you heard the saying "You are what you eat"? It's true. When you follow a healthful eating plan, your bones and muscles get the proper nutrients. Carbohydrates provide fuel for energy. Foods high in protein can help build muscle. Foods high in vitamin D, calcium, and other minerals help your bones grow and become stronger.

 Go Online

Visit **glencoe.com** and complete the Interactive Study Guide for Lesson 2.

Reading Check **Describe** How should you lift heavy objects to protect your skeletal and muscular systems?

Lesson 2 Review

 **After You Read**

Review this lesson for new terms, major headings, and Reading Checks.

What I Learned

1. *Explain* What are the functions of the skeletal and muscular systems?

2. *Vocabulary* Define *cartilage.*

3. *Distinguish* How do ligaments and tendons differ?

4. *Describe* How can you care for your skeletal and muscular systems?

5. *Identify* Which muscle turns your head?

Thinking Critically

6. *Analyze* Why do you think poor posture may cause backaches?

7. *Explain* Why do you think cardiac muscle is involuntary?

Applying Health Skills

8. *Practicing Healthful Behaviors* Learn some exercises to strengthen your bones. Ask a physical education teacher or other fitness expert for help. Demonstrate the exercises for your class.

Go Online For more Lesson Review Activities, go to **glencoe.com**.

Exploring the Circulatory System

Guide to Reading

● Building Vocabulary

Three of these terms are based on the word *circulari,* which means "to form a circle." How do you think the idea of a circle plays a part in their meanings?

- circulatory system (p. 71)
- arteries (p. 71)
- veins (p. 71)
- capillaries (p. 71)
- pulmonary circulation (p. 72)
- systemic circulation (p. 72)
- blood pressure (p. 73)
- plasma (p. 74)

● Focusing on the Main Ideas

In this lesson, you will be able to

- **identify** the functions of the circulatory system.
- **describe** how blood circulates through the body.
- **recognize** how to care for your circulatory system.

● Reading Strategy

Predict Look over the headings, figures, and captions in this lesson. Write a question you think this lesson will answer. After reading, look back to see if your question was answered.

Quick Write

Describe what kinds of physical activity might benefit your heart and blood vessels.

Your Heart and Blood Vessels

The **circulatory system** is *the group of organs and tissues that act as transfer stations carrying needed materials to cells and removing their waste products.* This system includes the heart, the blood vessels, and the blood itself. It is also called the cardiovascular system. *Cardio* refers to the heart, and *vascular* refers to the blood vessels. A healthy circulatory system is important to overall health.

The heart is a special muscle that serves as the center of the circulatory system. The heart pumps blood around the body through a network of blood vessels that is over 80,000 miles. The **arteries** are *blood vessels that carry blood away from the heart to various parts of the body.* The **veins** are *blood vessels that carry blood from all parts of the body back to the heart.* **Capillaries** are *tiny blood vessels that carry blood to and from almost all body cells and connect arteries and veins.*

 **Reading Check**   **Restate** Which type of blood vessels carry blood away from the heart?

The Process of Circulation

You cannot live more than a few minutes without oxygen. **Figure 3.7** shows how your heart and lungs work together to deliver oxygen to your body's cells. **Pulmonary circulation** takes place *when blood travels from the heart, through the lungs, and back to the heart.* (The word *pulmonary* refers to the lungs.) When blood travels this path, it gets rid of carbon dioxide. It also fills up with oxygen. Then systemic circulation begins. **Systemic** (sis·TEH·mik) **circulation** takes place *when oxygen-rich blood travels to all body tissues except the lungs.* At the same time, blood also delivers other nutrients to the cells and picks up waste products.

 **Reading Check** **Classify** What are the two types of circulation?

▼ **FIGURE 3.7**

PULMONARY AND SYSTEMIC CIRCULATION

In the pulmonary system, oxygen-rich blood exits the lungs, passes through the heart, and is pumped to the body tissues. In systemic circulation, this blood returns to the heart and is pumped to the lungs. **Where does the blood come from that enters the right atrium?**

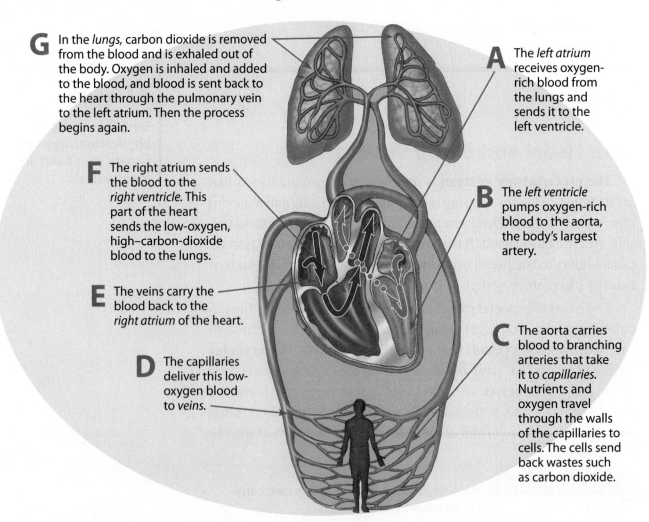

G In the *lungs,* carbon dioxide is removed from the blood and is exhaled out of the body. Oxygen is inhaled and added to the blood, and blood is sent back to the heart through the pulmonary vein to the left atrium. Then the process begins again.

F The right atrium sends the blood to the *right ventricle.* This part of the heart sends the low-oxygen, high–carbon-dioxide blood to the lungs.

E The veins carry the blood back to the *right atrium* of the heart.

D The capillaries deliver this low-oxygen blood to *veins.*

A The *left atrium* receives oxygen-rich blood from the lungs and sends it to the left ventricle.

B The *left ventricle* pumps oxygen-rich blood to the aorta, the body's largest artery.

C The aorta carries blood to branching arteries that take it to *capillaries.* Nutrients and oxygen travel through the walls of the capillaries to cells. The cells send back wastes such as carbon dioxide.

Blood Pressure

Have you ever had your blood pressure checked by a health care professional? **Blood pressure** is *the force of blood pushing against the walls of the blood vessels.* A certain amount of pressure is needed to make blood circulate. A medical provider takes two readings to measure blood pressure. He or she records the readings as two numbers, such as 110/70. The first number is the pressure read when the heart contracts and pumps blood into the arteries. It is called systolic (sih·STAHL·ik) pressure. The second number is the pressure read when the heart relaxes to refill with blood. It is called diastolic (di·uh·STAHL·ik) pressure.

▶ This teen is getting his blood pressure checked by a health care professional. **When was the last time you had your blood pressure checked?**

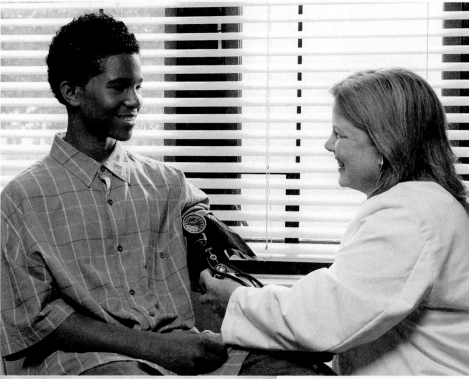

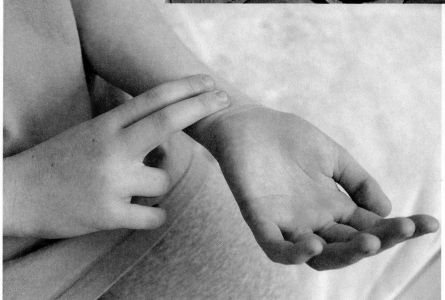

◀ A pulse registers the contractions of the heart as it pumps blood throughout the body. To feel your pulse, place two fingers on your wrist. **Why might a health care provider need to check a person's blood pressure?**

What Makes Up Your Blood?

Your blood has several parts, as shown in **Figure 3.8.** Each part carries out important functions. Blood supplies all parts of your body with materials needed to survive. It also helps fight off illness. **Plasma** (PLAZ·muh), *the yellowish, watery part of blood,* makes up over half its volume. The rest consists of red blood cells, white blood cells, and platelets.

▼ **FIGURE 3.8**

WHAT IS IN YOUR BLOOD?

Each part of the blood has a specific function. **How do platelets help when you have an injury?**

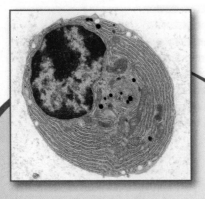

Plasma
The three types of blood cells are suspended in plasma, a liquid that carries nutrients to cells. It also carries hormones, which are chemicals that regulate body processes. In addition, plasma transports wastes to the lungs and kidneys for removal.

White Blood Cells
White blood cells fight infection in the body. Some white blood cells create substances that destroy foreign cells. Others find and devour disease-causing organisms.

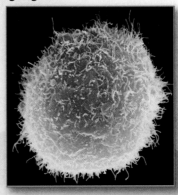

Platelets
Platelets are the smallest type of blood cell. Platelets help blood clot at the site of a wound.

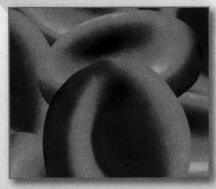

Red Blood Cells
Red blood cells, which look like little disks, carry oxygen from the lungs to all parts of the body.

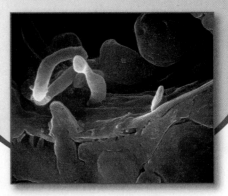

Blood Types

Red blood cells are one of four types: A, B, AB, or O. These four blood types are determined by the presence or absence of certain substances. Your blood type remains the same throughout your life. It is a result of blood factors from both of your parents.

Do you know your blood type? This information can be important. For example, a person may need blood from a donor during surgery. Doctors cannot use just any blood. Some blood types are compatible. This means that they can be safely mixed in one person's body. Others are not compatible. If incompatible blood types mix, the red blood cells in one type clump together and block the blood vessels. This can cause a person to be sick or even die. **Figure 3.9** shows which blood types can be safely combined.

People with type O-negative blood are called universal donors because their blood is compatible with all blood types.

Most people's blood contains a substance called an Rh factor, a type of protein. People who have Rh-factor in their blood are called Rh-positive. Rh-negative people do not have this substance in their blood. They can accept blood donations only from people who are Rh-negative. People with Rh-positive blood can receive blood from either Rh-positive or Rh-negative donors.

  **Reading Check** **List** What are the four blood types?

Connect To...
Science

Heart of the Matter

To get an idea of how hard your heart must work, try this experiment. You'll need a tennis ball and a watch or clock that displays seconds. Squeeze the ball 70 times over one minute's time: a little more than once per second. The pressure and strength you use to squeeze the ball are the same kind of pressure and strength your heart uses to pump blood.

▼ **FIGURE 3.9**

BLOOD TYPES AND COMPATIBILITY

Donated blood saves many lives each year. **Which blood type is compatible with all the others?**

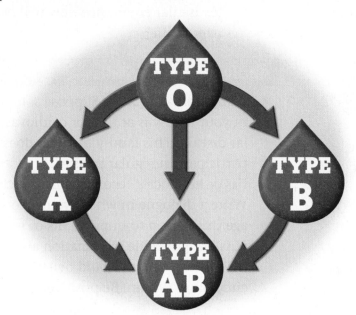

Caring for Your Circulatory System

Caring for your circulatory system now will help keep it healthy for life. Start by making aerobic activity a habit. It will improve your cardiovascular endurance, which helps your circulatory system. During aerobic activity, your heart, blood vessels, and blood step up the supply of oxygen and nutrients to your body. After several weeks of this, your heart can pump more blood each minute. Your muscle cells can use more oxygen.

Moderate-to-vigorous physical activity can help cut the amount of fatty materials in your blood. Your arteries will have less fatty buildup as a result. Regular physical activity also can help you stay at a healthy weight, which means the heart doesn't have to work as hard.

Be sure to follow a balanced food plan that is low in fats. It's also smart to develop strategies for managing stress. Stress can strain your heart and blood vessels. Avoid using tobacco as well. The nicotine in tobacco narrows the blood vessels, cutting down on the oxygen supply.

Visit **glencoe.com** and complete the Interactive Study Guide for Lesson 3.

Reading Check   **Restate** How does aerobic activity help the heart?

Lesson 3 Review

After You Read

Review this lesson for new terms, major headings, and Reading Checks.

What I Learned

1. *Identify* What is the function of the circulatory system?

2. *Vocabulary* Define *blood pressure*.

3. *Explain* Why can't certain blood types be combined?

4. *Distinguish* What is the difference between pulmonary and systemic circulation?

Thinking Critically

5. *Infer* Why do you think a blood pressure reading is part of a typical medical checkup?

6. *Apply* In what ways do you think building cardiovascular endurance now will benefit you later in life?

Applying Health Skills

7. *Communication Skills* Suppose someone in your family is at risk for cardiovascular disease. This family member doesn't participate in regular physical activity. His or her doctor recommends exercise. Write a dialogue in which you encourage this person to improve his or her fitness level. Include information about how these changes would benefit the circulatory system. Be positive.

 Go Online   For more Lesson Review Activities, go to **glencoe.com**.

Lesson 4

Creating Your Fitness Plan

Guide to Reading

● **Building Vocabulary**
Make flash cards with a term on one side and its meaning on the other. Use them with a classmate to learn the terms.

- warm-up (p. 80)
- cooldown (p. 81)
- frequency (p. 81)
- intensity (p. 81)
- target heart rate (p. 82)

● **Focusing on the Main Ideas**
In this lesson, you will be able to

- **list** factors to consider when developing a personal fitness program.
- **identify** the keys to a good workout.
- **calculate** your target heart rate range.
- **assess** your progress in meeting fitness goals.

● **Reading Strategy**
Drawing Conclusions List some factors that you think might be important to developing a personal fitness program. After you read the lesson, look back at your list to see if these factors were covered.

uick Write

List at least three ways you can fit more physical activity into your daily life.

Setting and Reaching Your Fitness Goals

Do you think you could use a little more physical activity in your life? Before you make changes, think about your goals. You may just want to feel better and think more clearly. Maybe you want to build your cardiovascular endurance. Perhaps you want to improve your skill in a chosen sport. Setting personal fitness goals can help you focus and stick with your plan. When you reach a goal, you'll feel great about getting there!

Where to begin? Start by asking your school's coach or physical education teacher to help you. He or she can measure your fitness level and suggest ways to improve it. Together, you can set realistic fitness goals. You should also speak with a medical professional. Let him or her know that you want to begin a fitness program. Ask whether it's safe for you to get started.

Try to work out for an hour each day. Spend about 30 minutes doing moderate activities. Take a speedy walk, mow the lawn, or play some fairly active sports. On most days, do 30 more minutes of harder activities. Choose aerobic exercises or very active sports. Include strength and flexibility exercises up to six times a week. The most important thing is for you to pick an activity you enjoy. Remember that fitness is a lifetime endeavor.

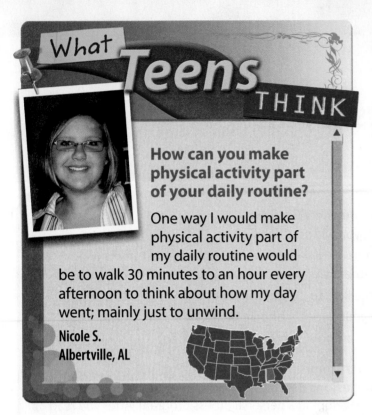

Think about your favorite physical activities. Do they require any special equipment? Exercise does not have to be expensive. Many community park districts run fitness centers. You can use their machines or take classes at a low cost. When and where will you exercise? If you would like to be in a group, you might sign up for volleyball or an aerobics class. If you would rather exercise alone, you might try jogging or bicycling. It makes sense to schedule activities you enjoy. That way, you will be more likely to actually do them.

Making Time for Fitness

List the activities you already do. Include gym classes and school sports. Also include any daily activity that gets you moving, like walking to and from school. Now list the activities you would like to add. Decide where they might fit into your schedule. Create a weekly plan that includes all your activities. Keep a chart or calendar to remind you of your schedule. Use a log to track how often you work out, what exercises you do, and how long each session lasts.

After two weeks or so, rethink your schedule. How is it working? Is it realistic? If you find yourself skipping activities, reschedule them for a different day or time. Be willing to make changes. Remember that your goals and needs may change as your fitness abilities improve. You may want to try a different activity. If you **vary** your program, you keep yourself from getting bored. Don't forget to have fun!

 **List** What should be included in a fitness log?

Working Out Safely

Getting hurt can take the fun out of any activity. You'll want to take steps to protect yourself and reduce your risk of injury before you begin a workout. Wear the right clothes. For most workouts, loose-fitting clothes are probably best. Make sure that running or walking shoes support your feet and don't give you blisters. If you're outside after dark, exercise with a parent, guardian, or trusted adult. Wear light colors and reflective gear so that drivers can see you.

Academic Vocabulary

vary (VEHR ee) *(verb)*
to give variety to, to be different, to show or undergo a change. *I vary the exercises I do each week.*

Health Skills Activity

Goal Setting

Planning for Fitness

Tiffany doesn't get much physical activity. She spends most of her free time playing computer games or reading. Yesterday, Tiffany told her friend Aleesha that she wouldn't be able to go to the local park for a picnic with their friends this weekend. Her parents were too busy to drive her, and she knew she would be too tired to walk or bike all the way. Tiffany wants to plan a physical-activity program so she will have more energy to do fun things. However, she doesn't know where to begin.

What Would You Do?

Help Tiffany come up with strategies for reaching a personal health goal of improving her fitness level. Use the five goal-setting steps.

Step 1 Set a specific goal and write it down.

Step 2 List the steps to reach your goal.

Step 3 Get help and support from others.

Step 4 Evaluate your progress by setting checkpoints.

Step 5 Reward yourself after you have reached your goal.

During cold weather, dress in several thin layers of clothing. As you warm up during exercise, you can peel off layers as needed. In hot weather, wear clothing that allows air to circulate and drink plenty of water. You might also need to occasionally drink specialty sports drinks that can help replace electrolytes you lose through sweating during longer workouts in hot weather. Cut your workout time if you get too hot. Use sunscreen with a sun protection factor of at least 15, and wear a hat and sunglasses.

For many activities, playing it safe means wearing protective equipment. Another way to play it safe is to work out with a friend. If you are running or jogging, stick to a path with a soft, even surface if you can. A dirt path is better than hard concrete. It will be easier on your muscles and joints. Be careful when working out at night or in an out-of-the-way place. Never go alone. If you plan to use an exercise machine such as a stair climber or treadmill, be sure you know how to use it. Ask a trained person to help you.

 **Reading Check**   **Describe** How should you dress for working out in hot weather?

Keys to a Good Workout

A workout is an exercise program that focuses on high-energy activity. It might include aerobic activities, moves to build strength or muscle endurance, or all of them combined. If your main activity is running, go biking or swimming, too. If your main activity is swimming, play volleyball or take a dance class.

Warm Up and Cool Down

Warm up your muscles before you begin a workout so they will be less likely to tear or get strained. A **warm-up** involves *gentle exercises that get heart muscles ready for moderate-to-vigorous activity.*

▼ FIGURE 3.10

WARMING UP AND COOLING DOWN

Warming up and cooling down are important parts of a safe workout.
What else can help ensure a safe workout?

Warm Up

- As you warm up, more blood flows to your muscles. They become more flexible. Your heart rate increases gradually and safely.
- Perform easy aerobic exercises.
- After you warm up, do a few easy stretches.
- Your warm-up should take about 10 minutes.

Light Stretches

- Light stretching after a warm-up helps loosen you up. Stretch only to the point where you feel a gentle pull.
- Hold the stretch for 30 seconds.
- To prevent injury, do not bounce or jerk.

Cool Down

- Cooling down brings your heart rate back down. It lowers body temperature and keeps your muscles flexible.
- Continue your workout movements, but at a slower pace.
- Cool down for about 10 minutes.
- Stretch again for 5 to 10 minutes.
- Afterward, drink plenty of water.

When your workout is finished, take time to cool down. The **cooldown** involves *gentle exercises that let the body adjust to ending a workout.* It allows your heartbeat, breathing, and blood pressure to return to normal. After the cooldown, stretch again to stay flexible. Drink water before, during, and after your workout. **Figure 3.10** shows you how to warm up and cool down.

Get Fit with F.I.T.T.

To be effective, a workout should follow the F.I.T.T. formula. F.I.T.T. stands for Frequency, Intensity, Time, and Type of activity. Keep these standards in mind as you plan your fitness program.

Frequency

Frequency refers to *the number of days you work out each week.* Frequency depends on your fitness goals. It also depends on the type of activity you plan to do, your schedule, and your current level of fitness. Are you just getting started in a fitness program? Then plan to work out three days a week. As your fitness level improves, increase the frequency of your workouts.

Intensity

Intensity refers to *how much energy you use when you work out.* How hard are you working? Begin slowly and increase the intensity a little at a time. If you work too hard too soon, you will tire quickly. You're also more likely to get injured. If you're able to talk while working out, you're probably working at the right level. If you are out of breath and can't talk, slow down.

 Reading Check Define What is *intensity*?

Time

Slowly increase how much time you spend at each workout session. If you're just starting out, aim for 20 minutes. Then gradually increase your workout time.

Keep in mind that you don't have to do your workout in one long session. If you're short on time, you can do some activity for 10 to 15 minutes at a time, two or three times throughout the day. Time spent working out adds up and still gives you beneficial results.

Type

What exercise is right for you? To answer this, think about the benefits that you want to gain. You will get the best benefits if you mix aerobic and anaerobic exercise. Spend more than half of your workout time doing aerobic activities. You could jog or bike. Finish up with anaerobic activities and stretching. The type of activities you choose should match your goals, schedule, and interests.

Connect To...
Language Arts

Reading for Inspiration

Check out a library book about a sports or fitness figure, such as Tiger Woods. Find out how the person became interested in his or her chosen activity.

How has this activity made his or her life better? What has he or she gained from it? Write a paragraph on your findings.

CALCULATE YOUR TARGET HEART RATE RANGE

If you know your target heart rate range, you can adjust your workout for the best results. Why is it important to know your target heart rate range?

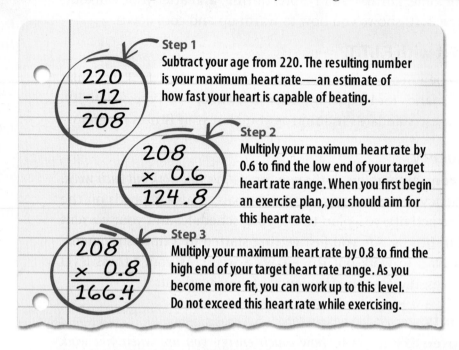

Step 1
Subtract your age from 220. The resulting number is your maximum heart rate—an estimate of how fast your heart is capable of beating.

$$\begin{array}{r} 220 \\ -\ 12 \\ \hline 208 \end{array}$$

Step 2
Multiply your maximum heart rate by 0.6 to find the low end of your target heart rate range. When you first begin an exercise plan, you should aim for this heart rate.

$$\begin{array}{r} 208 \\ \times\ 0.6 \\ \hline 124.8 \end{array}$$

Step 3
Multiply your maximum heart rate by 0.8 to find the high end of your target heart rate range. As you become more fit, you can work up to this level. Do not exceed this heart rate while exercising.

$$\begin{array}{r} 208 \\ \times\ 0.8 \\ \hline 166.4 \end{array}$$

Checking Your Heart Rate

You can monitor the intensity of your workout by checking your heart rate before, during, and after your workout. Before you begin your workout, take your resting heart rate. This is the number of times your heart beats per minute when you are relaxing. To check your heart rate, take your pulse for 10 seconds. Multiply this number by 6 to get your pulse rate for one minute. (To take your pulse, place the first two fingers of one hand on the inside of the other wrist. You can also place them on either side of your neck. Don't use your thumb, which has its own pulse.)

After you have worked out for a while, take your target heart rate. Your **target heart rate** is *the number of heartbeats per minute that you should aim for during moderate-to-vigorous aerobic activity to help your circulatory system the most.* **Figure 3.11** above explains how to calculate the range of your target heart rate. After you complete your workout, take your recovery heart rate. This measures how quickly your heart rate returns to normal right after you stop exercising. The higher your fitness level, the faster your heart rate drops.

 **Reading Check** **Explain** How is a pulse taken?

Go Online

Visit **glencoe.com** and complete the Interactive Study Guide for Lesson 4.

Tracking Your Progress

Are you happy with your fitness program? Is it giving you the results you want? After you've followed your weekly schedule for a while, check your fitness log. Compare early entries with later ones. Consider what you've done so far and what you still want to accomplish. Do you need to make some adjustments? Are you getting closer to your goal?

If you've been following your program for six to eight weeks, you should see some results. Your cardiovascular endurance may have increased, and you may feel stronger and more flexible. If you feel you haven't made much progress, think about why. Have you been keeping to your schedule? Did you set your goal too high? Maybe you need more time than you thought. If you're not sure what to do next, talk to your school's coach or physical education teacher.

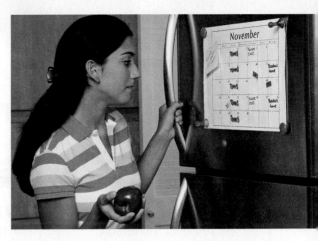

▲ Amy keeps a fitness log. She walks for 20 minutes in the park, three times a week. **What physical activities would you record in your fitness log?**

 **Reading Check** Describe What things will checking your fitness log tell you?

Lesson 4 Review

After You Read

Review this lesson for new terms, major headings, and Reading Checks.

What I Learned

1. *Vocabulary* Define *warm-up* and *cool down*.

2. *Describe* Why is it a good idea to see a health care provider before beginning a fitness program?

3. *Restate* How should you dress for working out in cold weather?

4. *Explain* Name and briefly describe each element of the F.I.T.T. formula.

5. *Identify* What are the keys to a good workout?

Thinking Critically

6. *Apply* Keiko is 12 years old and has begun an aerobics class. She wants to find out what her target heart rate range should be. What would you tell her to do?

7. *Justify* Why is it important to be flexible when planning a workout schedule?

Applying Health Skills

8. *Analyzing Influences* What is your favorite physical activity and why? Did friends or family spark your interest in this activity? Was it something you saw on television or in a magazine? Did social customs play a part? Explain your answer.

Weight Training and Sports

Guide to Reading

● Building Vocabulary

As you read this lesson, write down each new highlighted term and its definition.

- dehydration (p. 88)
- anabolic steroids (p. 88)
- conditioning (p. 90)
- overworking (p. 90)

● Focusing on the Main Ideas

In this lesson, you will be able to

- **recognize** the benefits of weight training.
- **discuss** the advantages of individual and team sports.
- **describe** various kinds of protective gear for sports.
- **identify** eating habits that can improve athletic performance.
- **recognize** why it is harmful to take drugs or supplements to improve sports performance.
- **practice** mental conditioning for sports.

● Reading Strategy

Predicting Look over the headings in this lesson. Then write a question that you think the lesson will answer. After reading, check to see if your question was answered.

Quick Write

Have you ever felt sore the day after you tried a new physical activity? Explain in a few sentences why you think this happened.

▶ This teen includes weight training as part of a fitness program. **What other types of activities should go into an overall fitness plan?**

Weight Training Basics

Weight training is a form of resistance training, which means that muscles must resist a force, such as gravity. Weight training does more than make you stronger. It also tones muscles, strengthens bones, and helps you manage your weight.

Learn how to use weights correctly. If you are just getting started, get help from a coach or physical education teacher. He or she can help design a program that fits your needs. Light weights or resistance bands, which look like large rubber bands, work best for beginners. Most people should wait until they are at least 15 years old or until their bodies are mature before trying to lift heavy weights.

If you want to succeed at fitness, start by setting a goal. Training for a particular sport might be different from training for overall fitness. You might want to concentrate part of your fitness training on lifting weights. If you do, be sure to lift the proper amount of weight. Try several different weights. A weight that tires your muscles after 10 to 12 repeated moves is about right. You only need to do one set to the point of muscle fatigue in order to benefit. When lifting that amount of weight becomes easy, you can move on to heavier weights. Always rest at least one full day between training days.

You might have heard that females who train with weights will develop large muscles. This is not true. Sports such as gymnastics and ice skating take a lot of strength. Lifting weights can help females build the strength to participate in sports and other physical activities they enjoy.

Sports for Fun and Wellness

Sports offer a great way to get fit. Some people are serious about sports and work hard to develop their skills. Others participate just for fun. Either way, participating in a sport is a positive health behavior that can help you increase your level of fitness. Muscular strength and endurance, flexibility, and body composition may also improve. Being fit can help you prevent health problems.

You'll get the most out of a sport that you enjoy. Take a moment to think about what sports you like the most. Do you like the excitement of competition? Do you like the challenge of mastering a skill? Even if you are not confident in your abilities, remember that practice will help you improve your skills and achieve consistency in sports or other physical activities.

Go Online

Topic: Fitness That Fits

Visit **glencoe.com** for Student Web Activities where you will learn how to choose a physical activity that's right for you.

Activity: Using the information provided at the link above, create a list and brief descriptions of six fitness activities that teens might enjoy.

◀ Ask yourself what you want to get out of playing a sport before you sign up for it. **What might be some reasons to sign up for swimming or track?**

Playing by the Rules

You can demonstrate good character by playing fair and showing good sportsmanship when playing a sport. Follow the rules, take turns, and share the credit when your team wins. Show that you are a good loser too by congratulating the other team if they win. When people play fair and show good sportsmanship, everyone can enjoy the game.

Think of three ways to show good sportsmanship when you are watching a game.

What Sports Type Are You?

There are plenty of individual sports to enjoy. For example you can swim, run, bike, hike, ski, surf, golf, play tennis, and horseback ride. You can do these sorts of activities by yourself or with others, whether or not you are part of a team. If you play individual sports, you can probably set your own schedule and pace. Unless you compete, you don't have to be compared to anyone else.

Volleyball, soccer, baseball, basketball, and field hockey are just a few popular team sports. Team sports are usually organized and have set rules. When playing a team sport, remember that not everyone on the team has the same level of skill. Show respect for individual differences. Encourage those with diverse backgrounds and abilities to join your team. Be sensitive to the feelings of others and don't criticize or put others down. Play fair, show good sportsmanship, and encourage each other. This will help you and your teammates have fun and get along better.

Reading Check **Compare and Contrast** How do individual sports differ from team sports?

Gearing Up for Sports

Protective gear is personal equipment you wear so you don't get injured. The type of protective gear you wear depends on the sport you play. Some sports, such as track, require special shoes to give you traction and support. Other sports, especially contact sports, require a helmet and elbow, knee, and shin protection. Males who play contact sports also need to wear an athletic cup to protect the groin area. **Figure 3.12** shows some important kinds of protective gear.

Reading Check **List** Name two pieces of equipment needed by teens who participate in contact sports.

► Both team sports and individual sports have benefits. **What are some benefits of each?**

PROTECTIVE EQUIPMENT FOR SPORTS

There are different pieces of protective gear for different sports. Which sports might require the use of some of the equipment pictured here?

 Mouth guards. These soft plastic shields protect your mouth, teeth, and tongue. Wear one for any sport where your mouth could be hit. Examples include baseball, football, and hockey. If you wear a retainer, take it out before you play.

 Face and throat protection. A face mask with a throat guard protects the face and throat from being hit by a ball or puck.

 Helmets. Always choose a helmet made for the sport you're playing. It should fit snugly but comfortably on your head. Be sure it doesn't tilt backward or forward. Never wear a cap under a helmet.

 Chest Protectors. A padded chest protector keeps the torso from being injured in sports such as baseball.

 Pads. Pads are used to protect bones and joints from fractures and bruises.

 Elbow, knee, wrist, and shin guards. Elbow and wrist guards can prevent arm and wrist fractures. Knee and shin guards can protect these areas during falls.

Eating Right for Sports

Your body burns a lot of energy when you play sports. You want to eat foods that provide the best fuel for your body. This may mean changing what and when you eat.

What You Eat

To get enough fuel for energy, eat a variety of foods each day. Follow guidelines for eating food from the major food groups. This will provide you with the nutrients and energy you need. If you play high-energy sports for long periods of time, you may need to eat more food. You will learn more about nutrition in Chapter 4.

The harder you play, the more you sweat! If you don't replace the water you lose dehydration occurs. **Dehydration** is *the excessive loss of water from the body.* It can cause muscle cramps and heatstroke. It can harm body systems. Drink water before, during, and after you play a sport. Don't wait until you're thirsty.

When You Eat

You know you have to eat right to enjoy physical activities. Did you know that *when* you eat is as important as *what* you eat? Here are some Do's and Don'ts to remember.

- Don't eat a heavy meal right before physical activity. Instead, eat a light snack one or two hours before. An apple, banana, glass of fruit juice, or a bagel are all good snack choices.

- Do drink enough fluids before you play. In general, drink about two cups (16 ounces) of water about two hours before. Then drink another two cups about 15 minutes before.

- Do drink water during the activity. Water helps control your body temperature and cools your muscles.

- Do drink water and other fluids after you play. Keep track of your weight before and after the event. For every pound lost, drink 2 cups of water.

- Don't forget to refuel. After the activity, eat a hearty, balanced meal.

 **Reading Check**

Identify How much water should you drink after you play a sport?

Avoiding Dangerous Substances

Athletes may be tempted to try substances to boost performance. Many of these substances are illegal and dangerous. Some harmful effects appear right away. Others show up later in life. Using these substances is a risk factor for many health problems.

Anabolic steroids (a·nuh·BAH·lik STAIR·oydz) are *substances that cause muscle tissue to develop at an abnormally high rate.* Steroids do have approved medical uses. Using steroids to improve athletic performance, however, is illegal.

Steroids can block teens' normal growth and development. They weaken tendons and bones, which may break more easily. Steroids can cause heart rate and blood pressure to become irregular. The risk of heart attack increases, as does the risk for brain and liver cancer. Acne is another common side effect. Steroid use can even cause changes in sexual characteristics. Females may grow facial hair. Males may develop breasts. Users may suffer from depression, irritability, anxiety, mistrust, mood swings, or sudden rage.

▲ Athletes need plenty of water before, during, and after an event. **Why do athletes need to make sure they drink enough fluids?**

Health Skills Activity

Practicing Healthful Behaviors

Mental Conditioning for Sports

Have you ever heard a sports figure say he or she was "in the zone"? This means that the mind and body are working together. Being in the zone is part of being successful at many sports. You are calm yet full of energy, challenged yet confident, focused yet able to trust your body's responses. Training your mind helps you get in the zone. It also helps you manage stress and use your abilities more effectively. Here are some tips that might help.

- Relax. Focus on enjoying the game, and don't worry about what might go wrong.
- Picture yourself doing everything correctly and with skill.
- Set some goals that relate to your personal best. They should have nothing to do with whether you win or lose a game.
- Think positively. Telling yourself "Don't miss that shot!" makes you freeze up. Instead, tell yourself, "I'm going to do well."

On Your Own

Think of a skill you would like to improve. Find a quiet spot, close your eyes, and picture yourself performing that skill correctly. Repeat this several times. Then perform the skill.

Some athletes have used a number of other substances to aid performance. Creatine is a compound naturally produced in the body and used by the body for short bursts of power. However, there is no proof that taking a creatine supplement improves sports performance. Creatine products can hurt your heart, kidneys, and liver. Other side effects include diarrhea, nausea, vomiting, and cramps.

Stimulants such as caffeine can make you feel more alert. They do so by making your central nervous system work harder. Your heart rate and blood pressure go up as a result. Stimulants have side effects that may actually hurt performance. They can make you nervous and crabby. You may have trouble concentrating. Even worse, you can develop an abnormal heart rhythm or other problems. Caffeine is not only in coffee and tea but also in some kinds of soda and sports drinks. Chocolate also contains a small amount of caffeine, although not as much as caffeinated drinks.

Visit glencoe.com and complete the Interactive Study Guide for Lesson 5.

 **Reading Check** **Restate** What are anabolic steroids?

Safety in Training

Training to get into shape for physical activity or a sport is called **conditioning.** Different activities require different types of conditioning. A speed skater, for example, needs strength, flexibility, and muscle endurance. Every conditioning program should be personalized to the individual. Age, body weight, and physical health should be factors when you begin a conditioning program. A long-distance runner needs cardiovascular endurance. An athlete also needs the right mental attitude to master his or her chosen sport. If you want to take part in a sport, have someone trained in sports suggest training exercises for the mental as well as the physical conditioning that is important for your sport.

Conditioning is good for you. However, too much of it can be harmful. **Overworking** means *conditioning too hard or too often without enough rest between sessions.* How do you know you are overworking? You might have an elevated resting heart rate. You might have trouble sleeping or get sick a lot. You may hurt the muscles you're trying to condition. Avoid overworking by taking a day off from conditioning every week. Switch off between heavy workouts and light ones.

 Taking time off from working out can help prevent overworking. **What are some signs of overworking?**

 Reading Check **Define** What is *overworking*?

Lesson 5 Review

After You Read

Review this lesson for new terms, major headings, and Reading Checks.

What I Learned

1. *Restate* What are the benefits of weight training?

2. *Identify* Name several advantages to playing team sports.

3. *Explain* Why should athletes eat a variety of foods each day?

4. *Vocabulary* Define *conditioning.*

Thinking Critically

5. *Infer* Why do you think you should avoid eating a heavy meal before playing sports?

6. *Predict* How might playing a sport throughout your life benefit your health?

Applying Health Skills

7. *Advocacy* Create a comic strip or write a short story that will encourage teens to eat right for sports.

 For more Lesson Review Activities, go to **glencoe.com.**

Lesson 6

Preventing Physical Activity Injuries

Guide to Reading

● Building Vocabulary
Use a medical dictionary or similar resource to find medical definitions of *sprain, tendonitis, dislocation,* and *fracture.* Rewrite the definitions in your own words.

- sprain (p. 92)
- tendonitis (p. 92)
- dislocation (p. 93)
- fracture (p. 93)
- stress fracture (p. 93)

● Focusing on the Main Ideas
In this lesson, you will be able to

- **list** tips for preventing physical activity injuries.
- **recognize** common injuries and their symptoms.
- **explain** the P.R.I.C.E. procedure for treating injuries.
- **apply** decision-making skills to situations involving safety when participating in physical activity.

● Reading Strategy
Finding the Main Idea Look at the major headings in this lesson. For each heading, write one sentence that states the main idea.

Tips for Injury Prevention

One way you know you've had a good workout is by what you feel. Your body feels pleasantly tired. You feel mentally energized and confident. You also know you've had a good workout because of what you *don't* feel. You don't feel hurt, dizzy, or sick to your stomach. Be smart and protect yourself when you exercise. Practice these injury-prevention strategies to maintain your personal health.

- Visit your doctor before you sign up for a sport.
- Be sure you're in good physical shape before you participate. Take some time to build endurance, strength, and flexibility.

▶ Be sure you read and understand the safety rules before you play or work out. **Why do you think it's important to report any injury to your coach or teacher and your parents or guardians?**

ⓠuick Write
In a short paragraph, briefly describe how you or someone you know recently got hurt as a result of physical activity.

▼ Physical activity injuries are a common cause of injury during the teen years. **How can you prevent injuries related to physical activity?**

- Do not try activities that are beyond your ability. Start slow and develop your abilities at a safe pace.

- Use the proper safety and protective equipment. See Chapter 15 for more information.

- Follow all safety rules during play and workouts.

- Warm up and do some light stretches before you begin.

- Cool down and stretch again after you finish your workout.

- Report any injury to your coach or teacher and to your parents or guardians.

- After an injury, don't return to playing sports or working out until a medical provider says you are well enough.

 **Reading Check** **Restate** Name two tips for injury prevention.

Common Injuries

Sports and recreational activities are a major cause of injury to teens. They are second only to car crashes. Positive health practices such as wearing the proper safety equipment can help prevent injuries. Some injuries, such as sore muscles, are considered minor. Others, such as bone injuries, are considered major.

Minor Injuries

Sore muscles are common when you are just beginning to work out or are trying a new activity. The soreness results from tiny tears in the muscle fibers. These injuries heal quickly. You can reduce or prevent soreness if you warm up, stretch, and cool down properly. Also, if you're not used to an activity, start slowly.

A muscle cramp is a pain caused by sudden tightening of the muscle. Muscles become cramped when they are overworked or dehydrated. Massaging and stretching the muscle can ease cramps. So can drinking water or specialty sports drinks.

Some injuries happen due to overwork. They include strains, sprains, and tendonitis. A strain is damage to a tendon or muscle from overstretching. A **sprain** is *an injury to the ligament connecting bones at a joint.* Sprains occur when a ligament is torn or stretched too far. Both strains and sprains can result in pain and swelling. Severe sprains need medical care. **Tendonitis** is *painful inflammation and swelling of a tendon caused by overuse.* Treatment often involves rest, medicine to reduce inflammation, and physical therapy. Proper warm-ups and stretches can reduce the risk of strains, sprains, and tendonitis.

Health Skills Activity

Decision Making

Taking Safety Seriously

Brian wants to get into bike racing. His parents bought him a bike for his birthday. They also bought a helmet, kneepads, and gloves. Brian read the instruction booklet for his bike. The booklet says that he should wear the safety equipment every time he rides. That's not what his friend Kevin says, though. Kevin says that Brian doesn't need to wear all that stuff if he's not actually racing. Brian wants to be safe, but he's wondering if Kevin is right. Brian must decide whether or not to follow the booklet's advice about wearing safety gear while bike racing.

What Would You Do?

Apply the six steps of the decision-making process to Brian's situation.

1. State the situation.
2. List the options.
3. Weigh the possible outcomes.
4. Consider your values.
5. Make a decision, and act.
6. Evaluate the decision.

Explain to the class how you arrived at your decision.

Major Injuries

A major injury is one that requires professional health services. A major injury often causes great pain. It may also cause numbness or make you feel dizzy.

A **dislocation** is *a major injury that happens when a bone is forced from its normal position within a joint.* Sometimes you may hear a popping noise at the same time. A doctor must push the bone back into position. The joint cannot be moved again until the tissues heal. A cast or sling over the joint holds it safely in place.

A **fracture** is *a break in a bone.* Sometimes you hear a cracking noise as the bone breaks. Fractures are often painful and may cause swelling. The bone has to be set by a doctor and may require a cast. The cast holds the bone in place until it heals. A **stress fracture** is *a small fracture caused by repeated strain on a bone.* For example, long-distance running could lead to a stress fracture. These fractures may be no more than a hairline crack and are usually less severe than other fractures.

Go Online

Visit **glencoe.com** and complete the Interactive Study Guide for Lesson 6.

Connect To... Math

Calculating SPF

How high should the SPF rating on your sunblock be? SPF is a measurement based on 15-minute increments. For example, an SPF of 8 means you can safely stay out for 8 times 15, or 120 minutes. Sunblock with a rating of *at least* 15 is suggested for most outdoor activities. It will protect you for up to 225 minutes. How many hours would that be?

▼ When going outside always use sunscreen on unprotected skin. **What is the lowest acceptable sun protection factor (SPF)?**

A concussion is a brain injury. It often results from a blow to the head. A concussion can cause swelling of the brain and even death. The person may feel dizzy or confused. Other signs include headache, loss of memory, or unconsciousness. Wearing a helmet is the best safeguard against concussions and other head injuries. It is always important to seek out professional health services if there is any possibility of a concussion.

Other Health Problems

Overworking your body can make you feel dizzy and out of breath. Know your limits and strategies for maintaining your personal health. Take breaks, especially during hot weather. Drink plenty of water and other fluids. Your body can overheat, which may lead to heat exhaustion or heatstroke. During heat exhaustion, a person's skin becomes cold and clammy. He or she may feel dizzy or nauseated. During heatstroke, a person's body temperature suddenly increases. He or she has trouble breathing and may collapse. Heatstroke can be deadly. If you think someone has it, get medical help right away.

If a person's body gets cold enough, its core temperature can drop dangerously low. Body systems begin to shut down. This condition is called hypothermia. A person with hypothermia may become confused and clumsy. Your body shivers when it needs heat. When this happens, warm yourself up. Get indoors. Wrap yourself in a blanket, or put on warmer clothes. Have a hot drink.

Skin can develop frostbite if it's exposed to severe cold and tissues freeze. Early signs of frostbite include whitening of the skin and a lack of feeling. If you think you have frostbite, get indoors right away and warm the exposed area with warm, not hot, water. Then get medical help.

A sunburn makes the skin red and sore, and it might even blister. Stay out of the sun during midday hours, when the sun's rays are strongest. Use a sunscreen with a sun protection factor (SPF) of *at least* 15. Put it on half an hour before you go outside. Cover your skin as much as possible before going outdoors, and wear a hat. Also wear sunglasses, because the sun's rays can hurt your eyes.

Reading Check **Identify** What are the symptoms of heat exhaustion?

The P.R.I.C.E. Procedure

Sometimes, even when you're careful, you get hurt anyway. A tough game or workout can leave you with scrapes and bruises. It can also leave you with aching muscles. When a muscle is stiff or feels painful, remember the word **P.R.I.C.E.** The letters stand for **p**rotect, **r**est, **i**ce, **c**ompress, and **e**levate. The sooner the treatment is applied, the better. You should:

- **P**rotect the injured part from further injury by keeping it still. Moving it may make the pain worse.

- **R**est the injured part.

- **I**ce the part using an ice pack.

- **C**ompress, or put pressure on, the part using a stretchy bandage. This will keep the injury from swelling. It will also help keep that part of your body motionless. Just be careful not to wrap the bandage too tightly, which can cut off blood flow.

- **E**levate the injured part above the level of the heart.

Remember to report any injury right away to a coach or teacher and your parents or guardians. They can decide if the injury needs the attention of professional health services.

▲ The P.R.I.C.E. procedure works for minor injuries resulting from physical activity. **What does P.R.I.C.E. stand for?**

Lesson 6 Review

 After You Read

Review this lesson for new terms, major headings, and Reading Checks.

What I Learned

1. *Vocabulary* Define *sprain*.

2. *Identify* What is frostbite? How is it treated?

3. *Explain* How can the P.R.I.C.E. procedure be used to treat minor injuries?

4. *Describe* What happens to your body during heatstroke?

Thinking Critically

5. *Infer* How would being in a cast for several weeks affect the muscles of a broken leg?

6. *Explain* Why is being in good physical condition before playing a sport an effective injury-prevention strategy?

Applying Health Skills

7. *Accessing Information* Use reliable print or online resources to find a news article about an athletic injury. Write a short summary of the article. Suggest ways the injury might have been prevented.

Building Health Skills

Accessing Information

Practicing Healthful Behaviors

Stress Management

Analyzing Influences

Communication Skills

Refusal Skills

Conflict Resolution

Decision Making

Goal Setting

Advocacy

What Steps Can You Take to Make Healthy Decisions?

The decision-making process can help you make healthy and responsible choices. The six steps of the decision-making process are as follows:

❶ State the situation.

❷ List the options.

❸ Weigh the possible outcomes.

❹ Consider your values.

❺ Make a decision and act.

❻ Evaluate the decision.

Which Sports to Choose?

Follow the Model, Practice, and Apply steps to help you master this important health skill.

❶ Model

Read how Jared uses the decision-making process to improve his physical fitness.

Jared wants to increase his cardiovascular endurance. He uses the decision-making steps to help him decide which activity to choose.

Step 1 State the situation. "I want to increase my cardiovascular endurance this summer."

Step 2 List the options. "I could swim laps, or play tennis."

Step 3 Weigh the possible outcomes. "Tennis is fun, but I need a partner to play. With swimming, I can set my own schedule."

Step 4 Consider values. "Swimming would be both comfortable and convenient."

Step 5 Make a decision and act. "I'll sign up for swimming."

Step 6 Evaluate the decision. "I can tell that my cardiovascular endurance is increasing."

② Practice

Read the passage and then practice decision making by answering the questions that follow.

Matt wants to increase his level of physical activity. He thinks about joining a softball team, jogging, or taking archery lessons. However, he also has homework and school activities to fit into his schedule.

1. What decision does Matt have to make?

2. What are Matt's options?

3. What outcomes could he expect from each of the sports he's considering? Which will maintain his endurance? Which would involve the company of friends?

4. What values might Matt need to consider?

5. Which sport would you advise him to choose?

6. Write a few sentences evaluating the decision you made for Matt.

③ Apply

Apply what you have learned about decision making by completing the activity below.

Think about how you might improve your own fitness level. Then write a one-page contract for yourself. At the top of your contract write a paragraph that explains 1) the element of fitness you want to improve and 2) how this decision will increase your health. Next, show how you would use the decision-making steps to make a change in your fitness.

Self-Check

- Does my paragraph explain an element of fitness and why I chose it?
- Did I use the six steps of the decision-making process to make a decision about how to improve my fitness level?

Whether they're headed to a local health club or another fitness center, growing numbers of teens are saying...

"Meet Me at the GYM!"

Victor Scotti wasn't feeling quite as fit as he wanted to be. So, like more and more fitness-conscious teens, he started going to a gym. Scotti showed up five times a week for circuit-training, which included a cardio workout, push-ups, crunches, and weight training. Now, Scotti says, "I've definitely gotten faster and a lot more limber."

Teens on the Move

Scotti is just one of a rapidly growing group of teens who regularly hit health clubs and gyms. There they lift weights, run on treadmills, and take spinning classes.

It was once thought that weight training could stunt growth by harming young developing bones. However, the American Academy of Pediatrics has determined that workouts, performed correctly, can benefit young people. So, with the number of overweight kids at an all-time high and teens wanting to train for organized team sports, health clubs are becoming popular places for young people to get active.

Be Your Best

There are many reasons why more and more teens are headed to a gym after school. Workouts serve as a way to reduce stress, and they are an option for students who are less interested in school team sports. In addition, growing

numbers of teens also use the clubs to improve their strength and agility on the basketball, tennis, and volleyball courts.

Mike DeMaria is director of a sports-performance academy in Mandeville, Louisiana. He oversees daily training for some 200 young people, including six girls' volleyball teams. Other teens organize routines on their own, sometimes even hiring a personal trainer. DeMaria says of the students, "They're very aware now that if they want to be the best they can be at their chosen sport, they have to be strong."

Some teens are discovering that working out can be an easy and enjoyable way to spend time with a parent. Rebecca Sernick asked her dad to teach her how to work out to help fight the weight gain that was affecting her performance on the softball team. Thanks to her dad's guidance, Rebecca lost 40 pounds and met her fitness goals. However, neither Rebecca nor her dad has any plan to stop their weekly workouts. It's just too much fun!

Reading Review

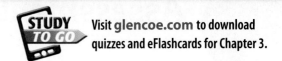

STUDY TO GO Visit glencoe.com to download quizzes and eFlashcards for Chapter 3.

FOLDABLES® Study Organizer

Foldables® and Other Study Aids Take out the Foldable® that you created for Lesson 1 and any graphic organizers that you created for Lessons 1–6. Find a partner and quiz each other using these study aids.

Lesson 1 Becoming Physically Fit

Main Idea Being physically fit will help you maintain good health for life.

- Physical activity will help you manage your weight, strengthen your heart and lungs, reduce stress, and help you meet new people.
- There are five elements of physical fitness: muscle endurance, cardiovascular endurance, strength, flexibility, and body composition.
- Aerobic exercise uses large amounts of oxygen and works the heart and lungs. Anaerobic exercise builds muscle but does not use large amounts of oxygen.

Lesson 2 Exploring Skeletal and Muscular Systems

Main Idea The skeletal and muscular systems work together to help your body move.

- There are three types of muscles: skeletal, smooth, and cardiac.
- Tendons, ligaments, and cartilage are connecting tissues that allow bones and muscles to work together as they move.
- Staying physically active can help keep your bones and muscles in good shape.

Lesson 3 Exploring the Circulatory System

Main Idea The circulatory system delivers nutrients to cells and carries away waste products.

- The heart pumps blood throughout the body.
- Blood travels through a network of blood vessels, including arteries, veins, and capillaries.

Lesson 4 Creating Your Fitness Plan

Main Idea A fitness plan will help you make physical activity part of your daily routine.

- F.I.T.T. stands for Frequency, Intensity, Time, and Type of activity.
- To monitor the intensity of your workout, check your resting heart rate, target heart rate, and recovery heart rate.

Lesson 5 Weight Training and Sports

Main Idea Weight training and playing sports will improve your physical fitness.

- Weight training improves strength and muscle tone, and helps manage weight.
- Avoid using dangerous substances, such as steroids, that can damage your health.

Lesson 6 Preventing Physical Activity Injuries

Main Idea Practicing injury-prevention strategies can help you avoid injuries during sports or other activities.

- Always wear appropriate protective gear for your sport or activity.
- The P.R.I.C.E. procedure can be used to treat minor injuries. P.R.I.C.E. stands for **p**rotect, **r**est, **i**ce, compress, and **e**levate.

Assessment

After You Read

HEALTH INVENTORY

Now that you have read the chapter, look back at your answers to the Health Inventory on the chapter opener. Is there anything that you should do differently?

Review Vocabulary and Main Ideas

On a sheet of paper, write the numbers 1–7. After each number, write the term from the list that best completes each statement.

- cardiovascular endurance
- flexibility
- aerobic exercise
- muscular system
- anaerobic exercise
- ligament
- cartilage

Lesson 1 **Becoming Physically Fit**

1. The rhythmic, moderate-to-vigorous activity that uses large amounts of oxygen and works the heart and lungs is known as _____.

2. Weight training is a type of _____.

3. The measure of how effectively your heart and lungs work during moderate-to-vigorous physical activity or exercise is called _____.

4. _____ is your ability to move joints fully and easily through a full range of motion.

Lesson 2 **Exploring Skeletal and Muscular Systems**

5. A _____ holds one bone to another at the joint.

6. _____ allows joints to move easily and cushions bones.

7. Tissues that move parts of the body and operate internal organs make up the _____.

*On a sheet of paper, write the numbers 8–14. Write **True** or **False** for each statement below. If the statement is false, change the underlined word or phrase to make it true.*

Lesson 3 **Exploring the Circulatory System**

8. <u>Veins</u> carry blood away from the heart.

9. <u>Pulmonary</u> circulation carries blood to the lungs.

Lesson 4 **Creating Your Fitness Plan**

10. As your fitness level improves, you <u>should not</u> change your goals.

11. Stretching should be done <u>before</u> a cardiovascular warm-up.

Lesson 5 **Weight Training and Sports**

12. Be sure to eat a <u>large meal</u> one or two hours before physical activity.

13. Anabolic steroids <u>cannot</u> be legally pre-scribed by a doctor to improve athletic performance.

Lesson 6 **Preventing Physical Activity Injuries**

14. Muscle <u>cramps</u> can be relieved by massaging the muscle.

Thinking Critically

Using complete sentences, answer the following questions on a sheet of paper.

15. Suggest A friend wants to join a sports team but is worried that she might get hurt. What advice would you give your friend to help her protect herself from injury?

16. Apply What would you tell someone who said that he doesn't participate in regular physical activity because he doesn't like team sports?

Write About It

17. Descriptive Writing Create a fitness plan that shows how you can be physically active for one hour, 5–6 days each week. Use a variety of activities in your plan and include both aerobic and anaerobic exercise. Remember, you can break your hour into 10–15 minute segments if you need to.

18. Personal Writing Write a journal entry about a fitness goal you would like to reach. What are some realistic steps that you could take to reach this goal?

Standardized Test Practice

Math

Answer the questions below.

1. Anita is starting an exercise program. She needs to figure out the low end of her target heart rate.

$$T = 0.6 (220 - a)$$

In the equation above, T represents the low end of the target heart rate range, and a represents Anita's age. Anita is twelve years old.

What is the heart rate Anita should aim for when starting her exercise program?

2. Anita's older sister Madeline has a target heart rate of 122 beats per minute. Her resting heart rate is 50 percent lower than her target heart rate. What is Madeline's resting heart rate?

A. 59

B. 60

C. 61

D. 62

Nutrition

Chapter Preview

Lesson 1 Nutrients for
Good Health......................104

Lesson 2 Creating a Healthy
Eating Plan...................... 111

Lesson 3 Planning Healthful
Meals...............................116

Lesson 4 Digestion and
Excretion 122

Lesson 5 Body Image and
Healthy Weight 128

Lesson 6 Maintaining a
Healthy Weight 131

Building Health Skills........................136

Hands-on Health 138

Chapter Reading Review..................139

Chapter Assessment 140

▲ **Working with the Photo**

Learning how to make healthy food choices helps you meet your nutritional needs. **What healthy foods do you like to eat?**

Start-Up Activities

Before You Read
Do you know how to create a healthy eating plan? Answer the Health eSpotlight question below and then watch the online video. Keep a record of your answer.

Health eSpotlight

Making Smart Food Choices

Do you know how to make healthy food choices? Where do you go to find reliable information about how much and what kind of food to put into your body?

Go to **glencoe.com** and watch the health video for Chapter 4. Then complete the activity provided with the online video.

FOLDABLES Study Organizer

As You Read Make this Foldable® to record what you learn about the types of nutrients in Lesson 1.

1 Begin with four plain sheets of 8½″ × 11″ paper. Place the sheets ½″ apart.

2 Roll up the bottom edges, stopping them ½″ from the top edges. This makes all tabs the same size.

3 Crease the paper to hold the tabs in place and staple along the fold.

4 Label the tabs as shown.

Record information on each type of nutrient and define key vocabulary terms under the appropriate tab.

Six Major Nutrients
Carbohydrates
Proteins
Fats
Vitamins
Minerals
Water
Vocabulary

Go Online Visit **glencoe.com** and complete the Health Inventory for Chapter 4.

Lesson 1

Nutrients for Good Health

 **Guide to Reading**

Building Vocabulary
Write each of the terms below. As you read this lesson, write the definition next to each term.

- nutrients (p. 104)
- carbohydrates (p. 105)
- fiber (p. 105)
- proteins (p. 105)
- fats (p. 105)
- saturated fats (p. 105)
- unsaturated fats (p. 105)
- cholesterol (p. 106)
- trans fatty acids (p. 106)
- vitamins (p. 106)
- minerals (p. 106)

Focusing on the Main Ideas
In this lesson you will be able to
- **list** the nutrient groups your body needs to be healthy.
- **discuss** the health benefits of good nutrition.
- **identify** nutrient-rich foods.
- **analyze** the information on a Nutrition Facts panel.

Reading Strategy
Predicting Quickly look over the headings in this lesson. Then write a few sentences describing what you think this lesson will be about.

FOLDABLES Study Organizer Use the Foldable® on p. 103 as you read this lesson.

Quick Write
List all the foods you ate yesterday. Underline those you think were the most nutritious.

What Nutrients Do You Need?

Just as a car needs fuel in order to run, your body needs the nutrients in food to perform the activities of daily life. **Nutrients** (NOO·tree·ents) are *substances in foods that your body needs to grow, have energy, and stay healthy.* The six types of nutrients are carbohydrates, proteins, fats, vitamins, minerals, and water. Each of these is explained in more detail below.

▶ Fortunately for pizza lovers, the food combinations in pizza contain varying amounts of the nutrient groups. **What are the nutrient groups?**

Carbohydrates

A baked potato, breads, and noodles all contain carbohydrates. Fruits and vegetables also contain carbohydrates. **Carbohydrates** are *the starches and sugars found in foods.* Your body uses carbohydrates as its main source of energy. When the energy from carbohydrates is not used right away, it is stored as body fat.

There are two kinds of carbohydrates: simple and complex. *Simple* carbohydrates are sugars. They occur naturally in foods like fruit, milk, and honey. Sugars may also be added when foods are processed. *Complex* carbohydrates are starches, which are made up of many sugars. Complex carbohydrates are found in foods such as potatoes, beans, and cereals. In order to use complex carbohydrates, the body must break them down into sugars.

Fiber is a *complex carbohydrate that the body cannot break down or use for energy.* Some fiber is found in the tough, coarse part of plant foods such as the bran in whole-grain wheat and oats.

Proteins

In order to grow and develop, your body needs **proteins** (PROH·teenz), *the nutrient group used to build and repair cells.* Proteins are made of compounds called amino (uh·MEE·noh) acids. Complete proteins contain all the essential, or necessary, amino acids and are found in meat, fish, eggs, dairy products, and soybeans. Essential amino acids are those your body cannot make. Most foods that come from plants are sources of incomplete proteins. They are called incomplete because, except for soybeans, they don't have enough of one or more of the essential amino acids. However, you can get all the needed amino acids by eating certain plant-based foods, such as beans and rice.

Fats

We hear about fats in the news, but what are they? **Fats** are *nutrients that promote normal growth, give you energy, and keep your skin healthy.* Fats help build and maintain your cell membranes. They also carry vitamins A, D, E, and K to all parts of the body.

Saturated fats are *fats that are usually solid at room temperature.* More of these types of fats are found in meat, poultry, butter, and many other dairy products. Many solid margarines also contain saturated fats. Over time, eating too much saturated fat can increase the risk of developing heart disease and other diseases. **Unsaturated fats** are *fats that are usually liquid at room temperature.* These fats are found mostly in plant-based foods such as olives, nuts, avocados, and vegetable oils. Over time, switching to mostly unsaturated fats and eating less total fat may lower the risk of diseases such as heart disease.

Connect To... Science

Building Bones

Your bones need to last your entire lifetime. One way to keep them strong is to make sure you get enough calcium. Eating too little calcium over a long time can lead to osteoporosis (ahs·tee·oh·poh·ROH·sihs), a thinning and weakening of the bones. This disease can cause bones to break easily later in life.

Use reliable sources to find out what other factors play a part in building strong, healthy bones.

You probably have heard of **cholesterol** (koh·LESS·tuh·rawl), *the waxy, fat-like substance that the body uses to build cells and make other substances.* Your body makes two kinds of cholesterol. HDL cholesterol is known as the "good" cholesterol because it protects against heart disease. LDL cholesterol is known as the "bad" cholesterol because it sticks to the walls of blood vessels, which can lead to heart disease. Eating a lot of saturated fats can raise blood levels of LDL cholesterol. Dietary sources of cholesterol include meat, some seafood, whole or reduced-fat milk, many cheeses, and butter. The body also makes some cholesterol.

Blood levels of LDL cholesterol can also rise if you eat too much trans fat, or trans fatty acids. **Trans fatty acids** are *a kind of fat formed when hydrogen is added to vegetable oil during processing.* This process turns the oil into a solid so that it can be used for such food products as stick margarine. It also keeps oils fresh longer. Trans fats were often found in snack foods, such as potato chips and crackers. However, many snack foods are now being made without trans fat.

Vitamins

Most of the foods you eat contain vitamins. **Vitamins** are *compounds that help to regulate body processes.* Some vitamins help your body fight disease, while others help your body produce energy.

Vitamins are either fat-soluble or water-soluble. Fat-soluble vitamins, such as A, D, E, and K, dissolve in fat and can be stored in the body. Water-soluble vitamins, such as vitamin C and the B vitamins, dissolve in water. Since your body can store only small amounts of them, it needs a fresh supply of water-soluble vitamins each day.

How can you be sure that you are getting enough vitamins? Eating a variety of foods helps. For example, you get vitamin D from fortified milk and eggs. Vitamins A and C are found in fruits and vegetables. Vitamins are often added to some processed foods, such as breakfast cereal.

Minerals

Minerals are also very important to your health. **Minerals** are *substances the body uses to form healthy bones and teeth, keep blood healthy, and keep the heart and other organs working properly.* Iron is a mineral that helps make red blood cells. You can get iron from meat, poultry, and beans. Calcium, magnesium, and phosphorus are minerals that help build your teeth and bones and keep

▼ Some fats remain solid at room temperature. Others are liquid at room temperature. **Which type of fat is solid at room temperature?**

them strong. Dairy products such as milk and cheese are good sources of these minerals. Potassium and sodium help maintain your body's fluid balance. Potassium is found in fruits such as bananas and cantaloupe, in fish, in many vegetables, and in meats such as chicken and turkey. Sodium is found in table salt and in many processed foods.

Water

Water is essential to every body function you have. In fact, a person can live for only about a week without it. Water carries nutrients to your cells, helps **regulate** your body temperature, and helps your body digest food and remove wastes. When you perspire heavily, you need to increase the amount of water you drink. Most foods contain water, but the best sources are plain water, milk, and juice. Sweetened iced tea, soda, and certain sports drinks are not good choices because they often contain a lot of added sugars and few, if any, other nutrients. Many also contain caffeine.

 **Reading Check** **Explain** What are minerals?

Guidelines for Good Nutrition

The U.S. Department of Agriculture (USDA) and the Department of Health and Human Services have developed the Dietary Guidelines for Americans to provide scientifically valid information about healthy eating and active living. These recommendations are meant for people ages two and up.

Make Smart Food Choices

What can you do to give your body the balanced nutrition it needs? You can start by eating a variety of nutritious foods every day. Eat more fruits; choose mostly whole fruit rather than drinking a lot of fruit juices. Whole fruit has more fiber. Vary your vegetables and eat more of them. Eat more leafy, dark-green vegetables, like broccoli and spinach. Orange vegetables, like carrots and sweet potatoes, are also high in nutrients. The more colorful your overall vegetable choices are, the greater the variety of nutrients they provide. At least half of the grains you eat should be whole grains. Try adding oatmeal, whole-wheat bread, and brown rice to your eating plan. Also, be sure to eat enough calcium-rich foods such as low-fat or fat-free milk, yogurt, or cheese. Eat a variety of protein-rich foods, such as fish, chicken, lean meats, eggs, nuts, seeds, and beans. Go easy on foods that are high in saturated fats, such as fatty meat and butter, and in trans fats, such as stick margarine. Eating too much of these foods can increase the risk

▲ The Dietary Guidelines give clear advice: balance your food choices with enough physical activity. **In what ways can you fit more physical activity into your life?**

Academic Vocabulary

regulate (reg u LAYT) *(verb)* to govern or direct according to rule; to fix the time, amount, degree, or rate of. *The doctor had to operate to regulate Mike's heartbeat after his heart attack.*

Reading Ingredient Lists

The terms on a food product's list of ingredients can be unfamiliar. Keep the following in mind, though: corn syrup, dextrose, and sucrose are all types of sugar. If they are among the first three items in a product's ingredient list, the amount of added sugar in it is likely to be high. Look at the ingredient list on one of your favorite snacks. If it has a lot of added sugar, consider choosing a more healthful snack.

of heart disease and stroke. When you eat meat, choose lean cuts and dishes that are baked, broiled, or grilled rather than fried.

Avoid Too Much Added Sugars and Salt

Some foods are high in added sugars. These foods are often low in other nutrients. They can fill you up, making you less likely to eat more healthful foods. They can also promote tooth decay. Calories from sugars that are not used by the body for energy are stored as body fat. This can lead to unhealthful weight gain. Foods that contain large amounts of added sugars include candy, non-diet soft drinks, and sugary desserts.

Eating too much salt and sodium can also cause problems for some people. Table salt contains sodium, a mineral that helps regulate blood pressure. Too much sodium can increase the risk of high blood pressure. You can avoid eating too much salt by cutting down on salty snacks and not sprinkling salt on your food at mealtimes. You can also use the information on food labels to choose foods lower in sodium.

Balance Food and Physical Activity

In Chapter 3 you learned that being physically fit is important to your health. Try to match how physically active you are with the amount of food you eat. To stay at a healthy weight, you need to eat just what your body requires for energy. To balance your weight with how much you eat, be sure to fit physical activity into your life. Aim for the recommended 60 minutes of moderate

▶ Foods like these are not only tasty, they can provide your body with many of the nutrients it needs. **Which of these healthful snacks do you enjoy?**

physical activity each day. You can break it up into 15-minute bursts of activity if you need to. You can participate in sports, ride a bike, or go inline skating with your friends. Walk up the stairs instead of using the elevator. Take a brisk walk instead of playing video games or watching television.

Reading Check **Explain** Why is it a good idea to limit your consumption of foods that are high in added sugars?

Getting the Nutrition Facts

Almost all packaged foods have a Nutrition Facts panel, which contains facts about the nutritional value of one label serving of the product. You can use these facts to help you make good choices about what foods to include in your eating plan.

Look at the Nutrition Facts panel in **Figure 4.1** below. It shows how large one label serving is and the number of calories

▼FIGURE 4.1

GETTING THE FACTS

The Nutrition Facts panel on a food package label gives you important information about a food's nutritional value. **How many calories does a label serving of this food contain?**

This section shows the suggested amounts of nutrients and food substances the average person should aim for each day. Your individual needs may be higher or lower.

The % Daily Value column helps you judge the amounts of the listed nutrients in one label serving of the product. The general guideline is that 20 percent or more is a lot and 5 percent or less isn't very much.

What is the total amount of fat in the product? How much of that fat is saturated? How much of that fat is trans fat?

The serving size is a reference amount. The amounts listed for calories, nutrients, and food substances are based on one label serving of the package's contents.

How many calories does one label serving contain? How many of those calories come from fat?

This shows the percentage of Daily Values for selected vitamins and minerals in one serving of the food.

Nutrition Facts

Serving Size: 2 bars (42g)
Servings Per Package: 1

Calories 180
Calories from Fat 60

Amount Per Serving: % Daily Value*	
Total Fat 6g	10%
Saturated Fat 0.5g	3%
Trans Fat 1.5g	2%
Cholesterol 0mg	0%
Sodium 160mg	7%
Total Carbohydrate 29g	10%
Dietary Fiber 2g	9%
Sugars 11g	
Protein 4g	

Vitamin A 40% • Vitamin C 0%
Calcium 0% • Iron 6%

*Percent Daily Values are based on a 2,000 calorie diet. Your daily values may be higher or lower depending on your calorie needs:

	Calories:	2,000	2,500
Total Fat	Less than	65g	80g
Saturated Fat	Less than	20g	25g
Cholesterol	Less than	300mg	300mg
Sodium	Less than	2,400mg	2,400mg
Total Carbohydrate		300g	375g
Dietary Fiber		25g	30g

it contains. Keep in mind that a package may contain more than one serving. If a package has two or more label servings and you eat the whole package, you're taking in twice the calories than are stated in the Nutrition Facts.

The label also shows percentages of Daily Value (DV) for key nutrients. These show how much one label serving of the food contributes in nutrient amounts to a 2000-calorie diet. Look for foods containing 20 percent or more of the vitamins, minerals, and fiber you need; 20 percent or more DV is high. Foods with 5 percent or less DV are low. Foods containing 5 percent or less of fat, cholesterol, and sodium are often healthy choices.

Finally, pay attention to food label claims on many packaged foods. Food labels often make health claims about food, such as "fat free" or "reduces your risk of heart disease." Do you ever wonder if you can trust those claims to be true? Actually, the Food and Drug Administration (FDA), a government agency, requires food companies to provide scientific evidence in order to print those claims on food labels. Even so, you should still read the claims carefully. Look on the Internet or ask an adult if you have trouble understanding what a claim means.

Visit glencoe.com and complete the Interactive Study Guide for Lesson 1.

Lesson 1 Review

 After You Read

Review this lesson for new terms, major headings, and Reading Checks.

What I Learned

1. *Vocabulary* What is *fiber*?

2. *Identify* Which nutrient group is preferred by the body as a source of energy?

3. *Explain* How do vitamins help your body?

4. *List* Name the six nutrient groups that your body needs to be healthy.

Thinking Critically

5. *Apply* Your friend eats a lot of snacks that are high in fat and added sugars. She also says she doesn't like fruits or vegetables. How could you influence your peer to make more healthful food choices?

6. *Infer* Why do you think the U.S. government requires a Nutrition Facts panel on packaged foods?

Applying Health Skills

7. *Practicing Healthful Behaviors* Study your school's weekly lunch menu. Find the most healthful food choices. Then make a plan to include these healthful choices in your daily eating plan.

Go Online For more Lesson Review Activities, go to glencoe.com.

Lesson 2

Creating a Healthy Eating Plan

Guide to Reading

Building Vocabulary
Write a sentence for each of the terms below. Trade papers with a classmate. Write the possible meanings of the terms based on the sentences.

- nutrition (p. 111)
- MyPyramid food guidance system (p. 112)
- calorie (p. 112)

Focusing on the Main Ideas
In this lesson you will be able to

- **use** the USDA's MyPyramid to make healthful food choices.
- **discuss** the factors that determine a person's nutrient needs.
- **identify** influences on food choices.

Reading Strategy
Organizing Information As you read the lesson, make a list of the five food groups. Next to each group, write down foods from that group that you might want to try.

Quick Write
Write a short paragraph explaining why variety is important in meals and snacks.

The USDA's MyPyramid

Nutrition (noo·TRIH·shuhn) is *the process of taking in food and using it for energy, growth, and good health.* Good nutrition allows your body to grow, have energy, and function in a healthy way. Eating the right amount of healthful food provides for the body's physical needs. Food is also used to satisfy your emotional and social needs. Eating healthful meals and snacks with friends and family can be fun.

◀ Trying new foods can help you find more foods to enjoy. **What food groups were represented in the lunch you ate yesterday?**

Lesson 2: Creating a Healthy Eating Plan **111**

MyPyramid—Steps to a Healthier You

MyPyramid suggests eating more whole grains, vegetables, and fruits. Name at least one of your favorite foods from each of those categories.

MyPyramid
STEPS TO A HEALTHIER YOU

GRAINS	VEGETABLES	FRUITS	MILK	MEAT & BEANS
Make half your grains whole	Vary your veggies	Focus on fruits	Get your calcium-rich foods	Go lean with protein

The USDA has created a useful tool to help you make healthful food choices. The **MyPyramid food guidance system** (**Figure 4.2**) is *a guide for developing a healthful eating plan*. The foods in its five groups can be combined in many different ways.

 **Reading Check** **Define** What is *nutrition*?

How to Meet Your Nutrient Needs

MyPyramid reminds you to be physically active every day, and to make healthy food choices. It groups foods into five food groups and a sixth group for oils. It also provides recommendations for how much to eat daily from each food group, based on how many calories you need each day. A **calorie** (KA·luh·ree) is *a unit of heat that measures the energy available in foods*. MyPyramid advice is based on your age, gender, and level of physical activity. For example, if you're very active, you may need more calories each day than someone who is less active. The two charts in **Figure 4.3** show how you can use the MyPyramid guidelines. First, determine your level of activity and find the suggested calorie needs. Then find the amount of food from each group needed to meet your nutrient needs. Meeting your nutrient needs promotes good health and helps prevent disease.

▼FIGURE 4.3A HOW MANY CALORIES DO YOU NEED?

Your Calorie Level	Sedentary Lifestyle	Moderately Active Lifestyle	Active Lifestyle
Females age 9–13	1600 calories per day	2000 calories per day	2200 calories per day
Males age 9–13	1800 calories per day	2000 calories per day	2600 calories per day

▼FIGURE 4.3B WHAT ARE YOUR FOOD GROUP NEEDS BASED ON CALORIES?

Your Calorie Level	1600	1800	2000	2200	2400	2600
Fruits	1.5 cups	1.5 cups	2 cups	2 cups	2 cups	2 cups
Vegetables	2 cups	2.5 cups	2.5 cups	3 cups	3 cups	3.5 cups
Grains	5 ounces	6 ounces	6 ounces	7 ounces	8 ounces	9 ounces
Meat and Beans	5 ounces	5 ounces	5.5 ounces	6 ounces	6.5 ounces	6.5 ounces
Milk	3 cups	3 cups	3 cups	3 cups	3 cups	3 cups
Oils	5 tsp.	5 tsp.	6 tsp.	6 tsp.	7 tsp.	8 tsp.
Extra Calories	132	195	267	290	362	410

Figure 4.3A Sedentary means that, in general, you just do the activities of daily life. A moderately active lifestyle means that you get at least 30 minutes per day of moderate physical activity, such as walking. An active lifestyle includes activity equivalent to walking three miles per day in addition to everyday activities. **What is the difference in calories needed between active and sedentary females?**

Figure 4.3B Depending on the foods you choose, you may have a small amount of extra calories to spend that are not needed to get your nutrient requirements. You can spend them on more foods from the food groups or on extras, such as beverages or candy. **How do you earn extra calories?**

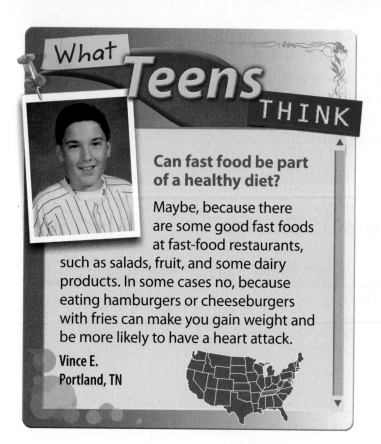

Eat a Variety of Foods

You can't get all the nutrients your body needs from just one food group. That's why it's important to eat a variety of foods from each group. Remember, many foods are combinations of ingredients from two or more food groups. A bowl of chicken vegetable soup, for example, has meat, vegetables, and sometimes grains.

Did you notice that some of the color stripes in MyPyramid are wider than others? The different sizes remind you to choose more foods from the food groups with the widest stripes. The colored stripes are also wider at the bottom of the pyramid than at the top. This is because every food group has foods that you should eat more often than others. These foods are at the bottom of the pyramid. For example, a baked sweet potato is an orange vegetable full of vitamins and minerals and would be at the bottom of the green stripe. French fries are also potatoes, but because they are fried and have a lot of fat, they would be near the top of the green stripe.

 **Reading Check** **Identify** Why are the colored stripes wider at the bottom of the pyramid than at the top?

▶ Messages from the media can influence your food choices. **How can messages from other sources influence your food choices?**

Influences on Food Choices

Your personal preferences affect the food choices you make. Most people like some foods more than others. The way a food looks, feels, smells, and tastes usually affects what you choose to eat. Other factors also play a part in your food choices. Your family's cultural traditions or ethnic background may influence what foods are served at your home. Peers also influence food choices. Have you ever decided to try a food because a friend liked it?

The agricultural products grown near where you live also affect which foods you eat. For example, many citrus fruits, such as oranges and grapefruits, are grown in Florida and Texas. Farmers' markets and farm stands during harvest season may offer these products. What kinds of food are grown in your area?

Messages from the media can influence which foods you eat. If you see a commercial for a new kind of pizza, does it make you want to try it? The cost and convenience of food are also factors. People short on time often select foods that are easy to prepare. The limited food choices available from many fast-food restaurants and vending machines can also affect what you choose to eat.

Visit **glencoe.com** and complete the Interactive Study Guide for Lesson 2.

Lesson 2 Review

 After You Read

Review this lesson for new terms, major headings, and Reading Checks.

What I Learned

1. *Vocabulary* Define *calorie*.

2. *Identify* List the five main food groups shown in MyPyramid.

3. *Explain* How much from the milk group does MyPyramid recommend for people ages 9 to 13?

4. *List* Name three factors that can influence your food choices.

Thinking Critically

5. *Hypothesize* What role might family, community, and cultural attitudes play in a teen's food choices?

6. *Analyze* How does choosing healthful foods show that you are taking responsibility for personal health behavior?

Applying Health Skills

7. *Advocacy* Using what you have learned so far, create an advertisement that influences peers to eat more fruits and vegetables. Think about your own likes and dislikes. What would convince you to make a change?

Lesson 3

Planning Healthful Meals

Guide to Reading

● **Building Vocabulary**
Look up the meaning of the word *dense* in a dictionary. Then write a definition of the term *nutrient-dense* in your own words.

■ nutrient dense (p. 119)

● **Focusing on the Main Ideas**
In this lesson, you will learn to

■ **plan** nutritious meals.
■ **describe** why eating a healthy breakfast is important.
■ **choose** healthful snacks.
■ **apply** accessing information skills to choosing healthful meals.

● **Reading Strategy**
Finding the Main Idea Take a look at the major headings in this lesson. For each heading, write one sentence that states the main idea.

Quick Write

In a short paragraph, describe your favorite breakfast. Do you think it's nutritious? Explain your answer.

Healthful Eating Habits

Healthful eating is a positive health behavior that can promote health and prevent disease. You'll get the proper amount of nutrients you need by eating a variety of foods from all of the food groups in the recommended amounts. **Figure 4.4** has some tips for healthful eating from the USDA. Each box lists a group of foods and suggestions for making healthful food choices.

Pay attention to the size of your portions whether you are eating at home or in a restaurant. You can use everyday objects to estimate portion sizes. For example, three ounces of meat is about the size of a deck of cards. One tablespoon of peanut butter is about the size of one nine-volt battery. One cup of raw vegetables is about the size of a baseball.

The best way to get the vitamins and minerals you need is with food. However, sometimes dietary restrictions can prevent you from getting the nutrients you need. In this situation, you may need to take a vitamin and mineral **supplement**. Always talk to your doctor before taking any supplements to make sure you really need them, and that you don't take too much. If you have food allergies be cautious! Supplements could contain ingredients that you could be allergic to. If you take a basic multivitamin,

Tips on Healthful Eating from the USDA

The USDA has suggestions for healthful eating. **Which groups of foods are included in a bowl of oatmeal made with low-fat milk and almonds on top?**

Connect To... Science

Dietary Supplements

Some people take large doses of vitamin and mineral supplements to be sure they're getting enough nutrients. However, large doses of some vitamins and minerals can be dangerous. For example, large doses of vitamin A can cause hair loss and turn the skin yellow.

Use school and community resources to find valid health information about a specific dietary supplement. Share your findings with the class.

Focus on fruits and vegetables.
- Make fruits and veggies half of what you eat at each meal.
- Eat more dark-green and yellow-orange veggies.
- Always have some fruit at breakfast.
- Keep baby carrots or other cut-up veggies on hand for snacks.

Make half your grains whole grains.
- Breakfast is a good time for eating whole grains. Have a bowl of hot oatmeal or ready-to-eat whole-grain cereal.
- Make sandwiches using whole-grain bread.
- Eat brown rice instead of white rice.

Get your calcium-rich foods.
- Drink your milk.
- For variety, include yogurt, smoothies, or cheeses.
- Make low-fat or fat-free milk part of your breakfast.

Choose healthful fats.
- Choose low-fat proteins.
- Eat foods such as nuts, walnuts, and almonds.
- Eat fish such as salmon or tuna twice a week.

Limit salt and added sugar.
- Check product labels for added salt and added sugar.

Academic Vocabulary

supplement (SUHP luh ment) *(noun)* something that supplies what is needed or makes an addition. *Sarah can't eat dairy products so she takes a calcium supplement to make sure she gets enough calcium.*

---

avoid brands that have higher than 100% of the Daily Value of any vitamin or mineral. Large doses of certain vitamins and minerals can cause serious health problems.

Begin the Day with a Healthful Breakfast

Your body continues to use energy while you sleep. By the time you wake up, you may have gone 10 to 12 hours without eating. Your body needs fuel. If you start your day with a healthful breakfast, you will have energy for later in the day. People who eat a healthful breakfast tend to feel less tired later in the day and find it easier to concentrate. It's also easier to maintain a healthy weight when you eat breakfast because you are less likely to overeat later.

▲ Breakfast on the go can still be healthful. **Which foods would you choose for breakfast on the go?**

What should you eat for breakfast? Choose foods that are high in complex carbohydrates and protein, such as a bowl of oatmeal with fruit and milk, or eggs with whole-wheat toast. However, you don't have to limit your choices to traditional breakfast foods. Why not try something different? Consider eating a bean burrito for breakfast. Beans are high in protein and fiber. Adding a glass of orange juice or a glass of low-fat milk will give you a good start for the day, too. Orange juice has vitamin C, and milk contains protein and calcium.

If you're running short on time in the morning, you can still eat a healthful breakfast. Just take it with you. Foods such as string cheese, a slice of whole-wheat bread, raisins, and a box of orange juice travel well and provide the fuel you need. Other good choices include a yogurt drink, an apple, and a whole-grain bagel.

Packing a Healthful Lunch

Each day when the lunch bell rings, you can have a nutritious and flavorful lunch. All it takes is a little planning. If you don't buy the school lunch, you can always pack your own. Should your lunch always contain a sandwich? No. There are many ways to add variety as well as nutrients to a packed lunch.

If you do want a sandwich, use whole-grain breads. These will give you more flavor and fiber. Consider a salad, too. You will boost the salad's vitamin and mineral content if you add raw spinach, tomatoes, cucumber, or even nuts or cheese. Many stores sell single-serving containers of low-fat or fat-free dressing that you can pack. Cheese sticks or yogurt add variety along with protein and calcium. A roll or cereal bar gives you some complex carbohydrates. Choose fresh fruit such as apples, grapes, or bananas for dessert. These fruits are delicious as well as easy to carry. Pack bottled water or unsweetened fruit juice instead of sugary soft drinks, or buy milk at school.

Finally, make sure you pack your lunch correctly so that your food doesn't spoil, which could make you ill. Read the food safety guidelines on pages 120–121 to learn more.

Smart Snacking

Snack foods such as potato chips and cookies may be tasty but they aren't the healthiest choices. These and many other snack foods are low in nutrients and high in added fat, sugar, or salt. There are better choices: snacks that are **nutrient dense.** This term refers to foods *having a high amount of nutrients relative to the number of calories.* How can you tell if a snack is nutrient dense? Use the Nutrition Facts on the package label to compare the nutrients and calories. Then you can find the most nutrient-dense snacks. Choose foods such as whole grains, nuts, yogurt, vegetables, and fruits.

For example, enjoy a fruit smoothie made with yogurt, bananas, and strawberries. Another good choice is a peanut butter sandwich with bananas on whole-wheat bread. A glass of tomato or vegetable juice along with baked tortilla chips also makes a healthful snack. Remember, if your school vending machines don't offer healthful snacks, pack your own.

Reading Check **Describe** Why are snack foods such as potato chips and cookies not the healthiest choices?

Go Online

Topic: Healthy Snacks

Visit **glencoe.com** for Student Web Activities to help you learn about the importance of eating healthy snacks and how to shop for them.

Activity: Using the information provided at the link above, compare three different brands of your favorite kind of snack and decide which is the most nutritious.

▲ Convenience foods can be healthful as well as portable.
Which healthful convenience foods do you enjoy?

Health Skills Activity

Accessing Information

Eating Right When Eating Out

Many people eat some of their meals at restaurants. Part of eating right is making nutrient-rich food choices when eating out. When ordering food, keep the Dietary Guidelines and MyPyramid in mind. Follow these strategies:

Pay attention to portion sizes. Many restaurants serve huge portions of food. You may want to eat only part of the meal and take the rest home to eat the next day.

Strive for balance. If you choose to eat the larger portion, eat a smaller meal later.

Think about what you order. Be aware that many restaurants add high-fat sauces or toppings to foods that may already be high in fat.

Order fewer foods with fats. Choose foods that are baked, grilled, or broiled rather than fried. You can also ask that sauces be served on the side.

Stay informed. Some restaurants make nutritional information available for items on their menus. Ask to see the information before you order.

On Your Own

Use reliable online or print resources to find nutritional information from a fast-food restaurant. Look for items that you might choose for a meal. Using the nutritional information, rate your choices based on what you have learned in this lesson. Note any changes you might make in your choices in the future. Present your ideas to the class.

Keeping Food Safe

When food is not handled, stored, or prepared properly, bacteria or other organisms can grow rapidly in the food. For example, food left out at a picnic on a warm day can be the source of a foodborne illness after an hour or so. To keep food safe, follow these steps.

Keep your hands, utensils, and surfaces clean. Always wash hands and utensils before handling food. Be especially careful after preparing raw meats, poultry, fish, and eggs. Use warm, soapy water to wash your hands and to clean utensils, cutting boards, and kitchen surfaces.

Separate raw, cooked, and ready-to-eat foods. Keep raw, cooked, and ready-to-eat products separate when you are preparing or storing them. If prepared or stored with raw foods, cooked and ready-to-eat foods can pick up harmful organisms. Use separate cutting boards for vegetables and meats and for cooked and uncooked foods, or wash the cutting board with hot soapy water in between.

Cook foods thoroughly. Use a food thermometer to make sure that foods are cooked to the proper temperature. Fish and meats such as beef and lamb should be cooked to at least 145 degrees. Ground beef should be cooked to 160 degrees. Poultry should be cooked to between 170 and 180 degrees. Be sure to reheat leftovers to at least 165 degrees.

Chill when necessary. Refrigerate foods that spoil easily such as meat, fish, chicken, and eggs. Frozen foods should be thawed out in the refrigerator rather than on a countertop. Put leftovers in the refrigerator right after a meal.

Serve safely. Keep hot foods hot and cold foods cold.

Follow directions. Read food labels and follow suggestions for cooking or refrigeration.

When in doubt, throw it out. Do not eat any food that you suspect has not been handled, cooked, or stored properly.

 Reading Check Explain What's the proper way to clean up after preparing raw meat for cooking?

 **G Online**
Visit **glencoe.com** and complete the Interactive Study Guide for Lesson 3.

Lesson 3 Review

 After You Read

Review this lesson for new terms, major headings, and Reading Checks.

What I Learned

1. *List* What are two foods that contain healthful fats?

2. *Vocabulary* Define *nutrient dense*. Give an example of a nutrient-dense snack.

3. *Give Examples* Suggest two nontraditional yet healthful breakfast foods.

4. *Explain.* Why is it important to keep raw, cooked, and ready-to-eat foods separate?

Thinking Critically

5. *Analyze* Why do you think it is often said that breakfast is the most important meal of the day?

6. *Apply* Yolanda packed a tuna sandwich and a carton of milk for lunch. Her lunch is in a paper bag, and she plans to store it in her school locker until she eats it. Do you think this is a safe practice? Explain why or why not.

Applying Health Skills

7. *Practicing Healthful Behaviors* Make a list of healthful breakfasts you could prepare when you're in a hurry. Include some foods that can be eaten on the way to school. Also, think of foods that you could prepare the night before so they're ready in the morning. Refer to your list each week for ideas.

Digestion and Excretion

Guide to Reading

● Building Vocabulary
As you read this lesson, write down each term below, along with its definition.

- digestion (p. 122)
- digestive system (p. 122)
- saliva (p. 122)
- enzyme (p. 122)
- small intestine (p. 123)
- colon (p. 124)
- pancreas (p. 124)
- liver (p. 124)
- excretion (p. 125)
- excretory system (p. 125)
- kidneys (p. 125)

● Focusing on the Main Ideas
In this lesson you will be able to

- **explain** the process of digestion.
- **discuss** how your body eliminates waste products.
- **explain** how to care for your digestive and excretory systems.

● Reading Strategy
Sequencing Take a look at Figures 4.5 and 4.6 in this lesson. Using these figures, briefly summarize the steps of digestion.

Quick Write

Write a paragraph describing what you know about the digestive system.

How Your Body Digests Food

Digestion (di·JES·chuhn) is *the process by which the body breaks down food into smaller pieces that can be absorbed by the blood and sent to each cell in your body.* It takes the body from 16 to 24 hours to digest food and remove waste products. Your **digestive system** is *the group of organs that work together to break down foods into substances that your cells can use.* As food is digested, chemical energy in the food is released.

Where Does Digestion Begin?

Digestion begins in your mouth. As you crush food with your teeth, saliva mixes with the food, as shown in **Figure 4.5. Saliva** (suh·LI·vah) is *a digestive juice produced by the salivary glands in your mouth.* Amylase (A·mih·laze), an enzyme in saliva, begins breaking down the carbohydrates in the food. It changes the starches into sugars. An **enzyme** (EN·zime) is *a substance that aids in the body's chemical reactions.* Saliva also moistens and softens the food, making it easier to swallow.

CHEWING AND SWALLOWING

The digestive process starts in your mouth. What role does saliva play in digestion?

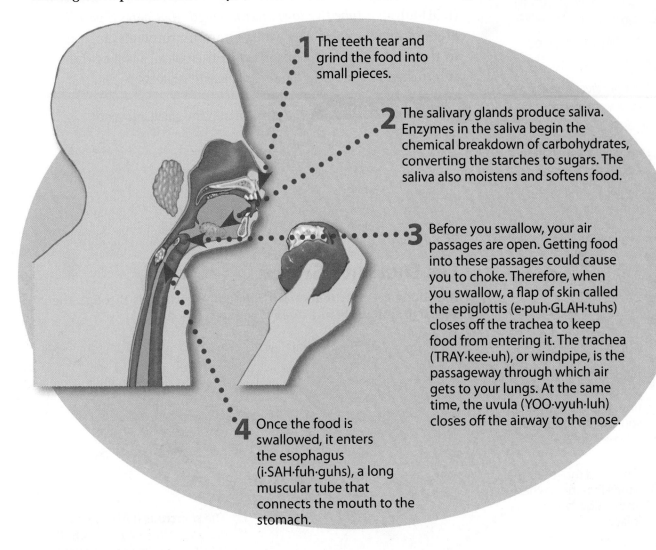

1 The teeth tear and grind the food into small pieces.

2 The salivary glands produce saliva. Enzymes in the saliva begin the chemical breakdown of carbohydrates, converting the starches to sugars. The saliva also moistens and softens food.

3 Before you swallow, your air passages are open. Getting food into these passages could cause you to choke. Therefore, when you swallow, a flap of skin called the epiglottis (e·puh·GLAH·tuhs) closes off the trachea to keep food from entering it. The trachea (TRAY·kee·uh), or windpipe, is the passageway through which air gets to your lungs. At the same time, the uvula (YOO·vyuh·luh) closes off the airway to the nose.

4 Once the food is swallowed, it enters the esophagus (i·SAH·fuh·guhs), a long muscular tube that connects the mouth to the stomach.

Your Digestive Organs

After you swallow food, it moves into your esophagus. The esophagus contracts and relaxes repeatedly to move the food along to the stomach (**Figure 4.6**). The strong muscles of the stomach churn, or mix, the food. The food then gets mixed with gastric juice, which is made up of acid and other enzymes. The food slowly gets turned into a thick, creamy mixture, and may remain in the stomach for up to four hours while this is happening. This mixture then passes into the small intestine.

The **small intestine** is *a coiled tube from 20 to 23 feet long, in which about 90 percent of digestion takes place.* Here, enzymes from the liver, the pancreas, and glands in the small intestine itself combine with the food mixture. Then villi (VILL·eye), finger-like projections in the wall of the small intestine, take in nutrients from

The Meanings of *Digest*

The word *digest* comes from a Latin word meaning "to separate."

Look up the word digest in a dictionary. What other meanings do you find? How are they related?

the food. Inside the villi are capillaries, which draw the nutrients into the bloodstream. The blood then carries them throughout the body.

Food that the body cannot digest then goes to the **colon** (KOH·luhn), *a tube five to six feet in length that plays a part in both digestion and excretion.* Any water, vitamins, minerals, and salts left in the food mixture are absorbed in the colon. Most of the water is returned to the body. The rest is waste material.

Reading Check **Identify** What is the small intestine?

▼ FIGURE 4.6

THE DIGESTIVE SYSTEM

Your body gets nutrients from the food that travels through the digestive system. **What does the pancreas do?**

1 Acid and enzymes in the stomach break down food until it looks like a thin soup, a mixture called chyme (KIME).

2 The food moves to the small intestine, where most digestion takes place.

3 The **liver** is *a digestive gland that secretes a substance called bile, which helps to digest fats.* In addition, the liver helps control the level of sugar in the blood, breaks down harmful substances such as alcohol, and stores some vitamins.

4 After the liver produces bile, it sends it to the gallbladder (GAWL·bla·duhr). The gallbladder stores the bile until it is needed in the small intestine.

5 The **pancreas** (PAN·kree·uhs) is *a gland that helps the small intestine by producing pancreatic juice, a blend of enzymes that breaks down proteins, carbohydrates, and fats.*

6 The walls of the small intestine are covered with villi, which absorb nutrients.

7 The colon absorbs any remaining water, vitamins, or salts contained in the food and stores the wastes until they are eliminated.

Removing Wastes

Materials from food that your body can't use need to be removed. **Excretion** (eks·KREE·shun) is *the process the body uses to get rid of waste.* The **excretory** (EKS·kru·toe·ree) **system** is *the group of organs that work together to remove wastes.* This system also controls the body's water levels. The main organs of the excretory system are the kidneys, bladder, and colon. Your skin and lungs also remove waste from your body. Your skin gets rid of some wastes when you sweat, and your lungs get rid of carbon dioxide when you breathe.

Study **Figure 4.7** below. It shows how liquid wastes are removed from the body in the form of urine, which contains mostly water and salts. Cell activity makes liquid waste. The **kidneys** are *organs that remove waste material, including salts, from the blood.* The kidneys also help in the production of red blood cells and the regulation of blood pressure. The bladder stores the urine until it is ready to be passed out of the body.

▼ FIGURE 4.7

ELIMINATING LIQUID WASTES

Many wastes are dissolved in liquid and excreted through the kidneys and bladder. What does urine contain?

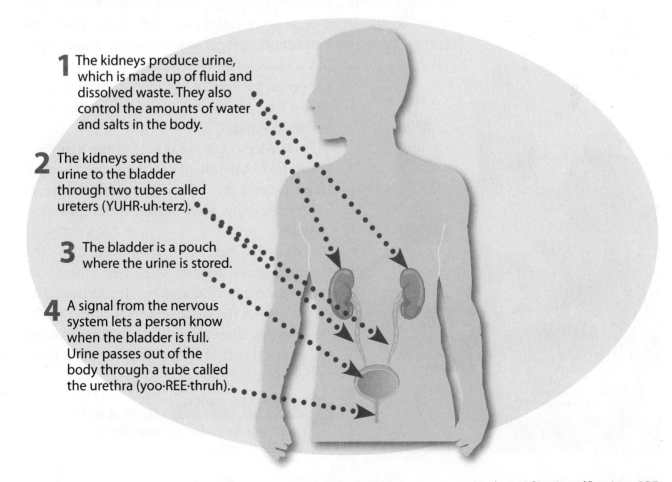

1 The kidneys produce urine, which is made up of fluid and dissolved waste. They also control the amounts of water and salts in the body.

2 The kidneys send the urine to the bladder through two tubes called ureters (YUHR·uh·terz).

3 The bladder is a pouch where the urine is stored.

4 A signal from the nervous system lets a person know when the bladder is full. Urine passes out of the body through a tube called the urethra (yoo·REE·thruh).

Your body's solid wastes are called feces (FEE·sees). They are stored in the colon until that organ becomes full. Then strong muscles in the wall of the colon begin to contract. This signal lets you know that the colon must be emptied. The feces are pushed out of the body through an opening called the anus. This completes the digestive and excretory processes. These two systems work together and influence each other to keep the body functioning properly.

Reading Check **Identify** What is the process the body uses to get rid of waste?

Caring for Your Digestive and Excretory Systems

What are some strategies for caring for your digestive and excretory systems? One way is to eat a balanced diet with low-fat, high-fiber foods. Eating a wide variety of fruits, vegetables, and whole grains will provide your body with the nutrients and fiber it needs. Fiber helps your digestive and excretory systems work properly. It's also a good idea to eat meals on a consistent schedule. This helps food move through your body at a steady pace.

Drinking enough water is another key to healthy digestive and excretory systems. Depending on age, gender, and other factors, 45 to 70 percent of your body weight is from water. This percentage shows how important water is to your health. Plain water and beverages such as unsweetened fruit juice and low-fat milk are good sources of this important nutrient. Soup and many fruits and vegetables also contain water.

Your teeth are important to the digestive process. To keep them healthy, brush them at least twice a day with a fluoride toothpaste and floss daily. Have dental checkups twice a year.

As with other body systems, your digestive and excretory systems work best when you get regular physical activity. Try to be active most days of the week. However, wait a while after eating a heavy meal before participating in physical activity. Your body needs a little time to digest some of your food.

▼ Enjoying these foods will provide your body with some of the water it needs. **Why is water important to the body?**

100% JUICE
No Sugar Added
APPLE

Reading Check **List** What are two strategies for caring for your digestive and excretory systems?

◀ This sandwich is made from whole-grain bread. Whole grains have more fiber, which benefits the digestive system. **Why is fiber important for good digestion?**

Visit glencoe.com and complete the Interactive Study Guide for Lesson 4.

Lesson 4 Review

 After You Read

Review this lesson for new terms, major headings, and Reading Checks.

What I Learned

1. *Vocabulary* Define *digestion*.

2. *List* Identify the major parts of the digestive system.

3. *Explain* What is the function of the kidneys?

4. *Describe* How can you take responsibility for caring for your digestive and excretory systems?

Critical Thinking

5. *Apply* Your friend Sherry doesn't like the taste of plain water. However, you know that drinking enough water is important for the digestive and excretory systems.

What might you say to Sherry to influence her to make a healthy choice to consume more water?

6. *Hypothesize* How do the digestive and excretory systems work together and influence each other?

Applying Health Skills

7. *Goal Setting* Make a list of actions you could take that would improve and maintain the health of your digestive and excretory systems. Choose one behavior from your list and develop goal-setting strategies to make this behavior part of your life.

Body Image and Healthy Weight

Guide to Reading

Building Vocabulary
Look up the word *image* in the dictionary. In a brief paragraph, discuss how you think this definition relates to the term *body image*.

- body image (p. 128)
- Body Mass Index (p. 129)

Focusing on the Main Ideas
In this lesson, you will be able to

- **explain** the concept of body image.
- **determine** your Body Mass Index.
- **state** the benefits of having a positive body image.

Reading Strategy
Predicting Look over the headings in this lesson. Then write a question that you think the lesson will answer. After reading, check to see if your question was answered.

Books on weight management are very popular. Why do you think this is so? Explain your ideas in a short paragraph.

Body Image

Your **body image** is *the way you see your body.* Body image can be influenced by many things. The attitudes of family and friends, as well as images from the media, affect how people see themselves.

Am I too thin? Do I need to lose weight? Many people ask themselves questions like these. Weight strongly affects a person's body image. Some people think they are too thin, while others believe they are too fat. Some wish they were more muscular or that their body had a different shape. People who are unhappy with their body may have a poor body image.

◀ Sometimes we wish we looked like someone else. **What effect might the popular media have on this teen's body image?**

People who have a poor body image may try to change their weight in extreme ways. This can damage their health and may even be life threatening.

 **Reading Check** **Explain** What can influence a person's body image?

How to Develop a Positive Body Image

The key to having a positive body image is to accept yourself and your body. How your body looks depends on your gender and the traits that you inherited from your parents. These factors are out of your control. Keep in mind, also, that very few people look like the people you see on television, in the movies, or in magazines. Don't compare yourself to these people. There is no one correct body shape or size.

Your growth stage affects your body shape, too. Many teens grow in spurts, and often they'll carry a few extra pounds for a while to prepare for the next spurt. They may suddenly grow taller and the extra body fat seems to disappear. Other teens may seem underweight because their bodies are using so much energy to grow.

If you need to lose or gain some weight in order to be healthier, set reasonable goals and do it slowly. Meet with a health care professional before you begin. Slowly add physical activity to your daily routine to help you maintain a healthy weight.

 **Reading Check** **Describe** What is the key to having a positive body image?

Finding Your Healthy Weight Range

You feel better when you maintain a healthy weight. A healthy weight can also help you avoid many serious health problems during all stages of life. What determines your healthy weight? Many factors, such as gender, age, height, inherited body type, and growth pattern, play a part. Your healthy weight is not a single weight on the scale but a range.

Body Mass Index

Is your weight within a healthy range? You can check by determining your Body Mass Index. The **Body Mass Index** (BMI) is *a method for assessing your body size by taking your height and weight into account.* **Figure 4.8** shows the BMI ranges for teen males and females. Checking the BMI chart for teens from time to time can help you track your growth pattern to determine if your weight is within a healthy range for your age.

Connect To... Math

Calculating BMI

You can use this formula to calculate your Body Mass Index.

1. Multiply your weight in pounds by 0.45.

2. Then multiply your height in inches by 0.025. Square the result.

3. Divide your answer in step 1 by the answer in step 2.

Calculate the BMI of a person who is 5'1" (61 inches) tall and weighs 95 pounds.

 **Go Online**

Visit **glencoe.com** and complete the Interactive Study Guide for Lesson 5.

BODY MASS INDEX RANGE

First calculate your Body Mass Index using the formula described in the Connect to Math on page 129. Then find your age on the graph. Trace an imaginary line from your age to your body mass index. See which range it falls into. **Why are age and height important factors in determining BMI?**

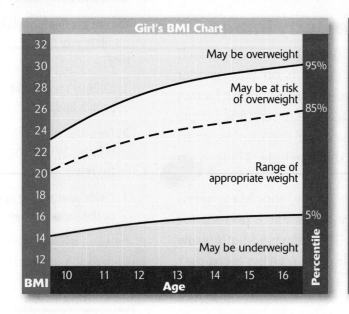

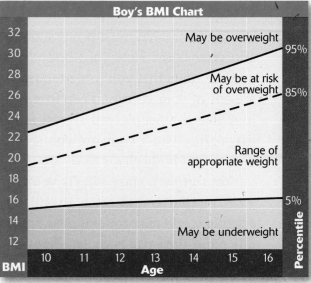

Lesson 5 Review

 After You Read

Review this lesson for new terms, major headings, and Reading Checks.

What I Learned

1. **Vocabulary** Define *Body Mass Index*.

2. **Explain** How might growth spurts affect a teen's weight?

3. **Identify** List the factors that help determine your healthy weight.

Thinking Critically

4. **Analyze** How can a positive body image contribute to mental/emotional health?

5. **Apply** Glenn has grown several inches this year, but hasn't gained weight. Now he feels self-conscious about being too thin. What would you tell Glenn to positively influence his body image?

Applying Health Skills

6. **Communication Skills** Write a short dialogue between you and a friend who has just been teased for being overweight. How would you help the friend manage his or her feelings and make healthful choices?

Go Online For more Lesson Review Activities, go to **glencoe.com**.

Maintaining a Healthy Weight

Guide to Reading

● **Building Vocabulary**
Many words in English have their roots in other languages. Look up the root language for *anorexia nervosa* and *bulimia nervosa*.

- eating disorders (p. 132)
- anorexia nervosa (p. 132)
- bulimia nervosa (p. 133)
- binge eating (p. 133)

● **Focusing on the Main Ideas**
In this lesson, you will be able to

- **state** the benefits of a healthy weight.
- **identify** common health risks related to weight.
- **discuss** the dangers of eating disorders.
- **list** tips for maintaining a healthy weight.

● **Reading Strategy**
Organizing Information
Using the diagram below as a guide, create a concept map that shows the benefits of a healthy weight.

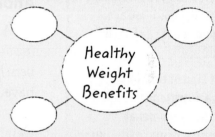

The Benefits of a Healthy Weight

Being within a healthy weight range is important for wellness. It can also help you have a positive body image. People who are overweight have a greater chance of developing serious health problems. Being overweight increases the risk of high blood pressure, cardiovascular disease, type 2 diabetes, and cancer later in life, but also in the teen years. Also, too much weight strains bones and muscles.

Being significantly underweight is also unhealthy. Teens who don't consume enough nutrients may grow and develop more slowly than they should. People who are underweight might not have enough stored body fat. This fat serves as a source of energy when the body doesn't get enough calories from food. Also, people who are underweight may feel tired and irritable and be unable to fight illness.

Your growth patterns may make you seem overweight or underweight for a period of time. This is usually normal. However, if you're not sure if your weight is within a healthy range, speak with a health care provider. Don't try to lose or gain weight unless the provider recommends it and helps you develop you a specific nutrition and physical activity plan.

Quick Write
Has a friend ever talked to you about his or her weight? Write a sentence or two that describes the concerns your friend expressed.

Eating Disorders

Sometimes a person becomes so concerned about weight and body image that he or she develops an eating disorder. **Eating disorders** are *extreme eating behaviors that can lead to serious illness or even death.* It is not known what causes eating disorders. However, people who feel bad about themselves or are depressed are more likely to develop an eating disorder. About 90 percent of the teens with eating disorders are female.

Eating disorders are serious and can adversely affect health. Often, people with eating disorders may deny that they have a problem. If you think that someone you know has an eating disorder, discuss this with an adult whom you trust. You can also help by being a friend and encouraging the person to ask for help. Eating disorders are situations requiring professional health services.

Anorexia Nervosa

Anorexia nervosa (a·nuh·REK·see·ah ner·VOH·sah) is *an eating disorder in which a person strongly fears gaining weight and starves herself or himself.* People with anorexia may feel as though they have to be very successful or be accepted by all people. Even if they are very slim, they believe they are overweight. To lose more weight, they eat very little and may exercise so much that it is unhealthy.

Eating very little prevents the body from getting enough nutrients. Bones may not develop properly, blood pressure may drop, and the heart may be damaged. People with anorexia may need to stay at a hospital or clinic to get treatment. They also need counseling.

▶ When you're healthy, you have the energy to do the things you enjoy. **Why might being underweight lead to a loss of energy?**

Clinics and counselors may offer support groups for teens with eating disorders. **Why might support groups be helpful to someone with an eating disorder?**

Bulimia Nervosa

Bulimia (boo·LEE·mee·ah) **nervosa** is *an eating disorder in which a person repeatedly eats large amounts of food and then purges.* There are several ways that people purge. One way is to throw up. Another way is to use laxatives. People with this disorder may be at a normal weight but still feel the need to go on an extreme diet. When they can't stay on the diet, they eat large amounts of food. Then, after eating, they purge. They may also try to burn the calories with constant exercise.

Bulimia not only robs the body of nutrients, but it can also harm many parts of the body. The colon, liver, heart, and kidneys may be damaged. Tooth enamel may wear off, because frequent vomiting exposes the teeth to stomach acids. The linings of the stomach and esophagus can also be damaged. The body may become dehydrated, meaning it does not have enough water to function properly. Bulimia is very serious. People with this disorder need help from a health care professional.

Binge Eating

Binge eating is *a disorder in which a person repeatedly eats too much food at one time.* It is also called compulsive overeating. Binge eaters often fast or diet to lose weight, but they do not purge. To fast means to not eat. Sometimes people will binge as a way to deal with depression or stress. As you might guess, binge eating can lead to serious weight gain. It can also lead to heart disease, diabetes, and some types of cancer. As with other eating disorders, people who are binge eaters usually need help from a counselor or other health care professional.

 **Reading Check** **Restate** What is an eating disorder?

ACTIVITY

Connect To... **Social Studies**

Food as a Symbol

In some cultures, being overweight can be a sign of success. It means that you have plenty of food to eat and that your family or group is probably well-off. Even when the hosts have little or no food to spare, important members of the community give food to their guests.

Are these two ideas popular in our culture? Give reasons for your opinion.

▲ To maintain a healthy weight, eat regular meals, choose snacks wisely, and be more physically active. **In what ways could planning ahead help with weight management?**

Calories and Weight

You know that taking extreme measures to lose weight can damage your health. So, what is a healthy way to manage your weight? The key is calories. You need to make sure that you don't take in more calories than you burn. Remember, as you digest food, your body converts food calories into energy. When you take in *more* calories than your body uses, it stores the extra calories as body fat. This makes you gain weight. If you eat *fewer* calories than you need, though, your body converts stored body fat into energy. This makes you lose weight.

Study **Figure 4.9.** It shows that if you eat 250 fewer calories than your body burns each day, you can lose one pound over two weeks. The same thing happens if, by exercising, you burn 250 more calories per day than your body uses. While 250 calories may not seem like very much, over time it can make a big difference in your weight.

Reading Check **Explain** What happens when you take in more calories than your body uses?

Tips for Maintaining a Healthy Weight

What can you do to stay at a healthy weight? In general, you need to balance the calories you eat with the calories your body uses. Choose healthful foods and stay physically active. If you need to gain weight, eat larger servings of nutrient-rich foods, and drink more milk or juice. If you need to lose weight, eat smaller

▼ **FIGURE 4.9**

THE WEIGHT-LOSS ENERGY EQUATION

To lose weight, you need to burn more calories than you take in by watching what you eat, exercising, or both. **How many calories are equal to a pound of body fat?**

1 pound = 3,500 calories
To lose 1 pound in two weeks:
- Eat 250 fewer calories a day.
  OR
- Burn 250 extra calories a day through physical activity.

$$\frac{250\ \text{calories}}{\text{day}} \times 14\ \text{days} = 3{,}500\ \text{calories}$$

servings. Also, take your time when you eat. Chew your food thoroughly. When you do these things, you give your stomach time to signal your brain that you are full.

Most teens should not diet to lose weight. Just because you are a little overweight does not mean you need to go on a diet. Instead, just let your body grow into your healthy weight. Boost your level of physical activity. Drink a lot of water and make time for regular meals. Rather than snacking a lot, try to eat only when you're hungry. It's easier to keep track of calories at set times. When you eat out choose foods that are broiled or baked rather than fried.

Also, avoid fad diets. Many of these diets allow you to eat only a few kinds of foods, such as grapefruit or high-protein foods. When you lose weight on a diet like this, you often gain it back as soon as you start eating other foods again. You also miss out on important nutrients. Instead, eat a variety of healthful foods, using MyPyramid as your guide. You may need to reduce the portion sizes or pick lower-calorie foods from the food groups. These are good strategies for maintaining a healthy weight.

Go Online

Visit **glencoe.com** and complete the **Interactive Study Guide** for Lesson 6.

Reading Check **Explain** Why is it best to eat slowly?

Lesson 6 Review

 After You Read

Review this lesson for new terms, major headings, and Reading Checks.

What I Learned

1. *Vocabulary* Define *anorexia nervosa*.

2. *Restate* Describe the symptoms of binge eating and how it can adversely affect health.

3. *Describe* What is a healthy way to manage your weight over time?

4. *Explain* Why is it better to avoid fad diets?

Thinking Critically

5. *Apply* How might family and friends help someone with an eating disorder?

6. *Infer* How can a teen "grow into" a healthy weight?

Applying Health Skills

7. *Communication Skills* Suppose you think a friend might have an eating disorder. Write that friend a letter giving her or him facts about the problem and suggesting that he or she get professional help.

Accessing Information

Practicing Healthful Behaviors

Stress Management

Analyzing Influences

Communication Skills

Refusal Skills

Conflict Resolution

Decision Making

Goal Setting

Advocacy

What Does Analyzing Influences Involve?

Analyzing Influences involves recognizing the factors that affect your health choices. These factors include:

- family and culture
- friends and peers
- messages from the media
- your likes, dislikes, values, and beliefs

Media Messages About Food

Follow the Model, Practice, and Apply steps to help you master this important health skill.

❶ Model

Read how Caitlin helps her younger sister, Jenny, recognize how the media influences her decision to try a new breakfast cereal.

Caitlin was watching television with her younger sister, Jenny. Suddenly, Jenny pointed to an ad for a new breakfast cereal. "I want Mom to get that for us!" she said. The ad was for a sugar-coated cereal shaped like cartoon characters. The characters bounced around to a song that made Jenny laugh. The ad made it look like eating the cereal would be really fun.

When the ad was over, Caitlin said, "Jenny, just because you like the ad doesn't mean the cereal is good for you." She explained to her that the cereal company just used the cartoon and music to make children want the food product. She also said, "Even though the cereal may taste good, it has a lot of added sugar that isn't good for you." Caitlin told Jenny that she should stick with the whole-grain cereal their mom always bought. Jenny realized that the sugar-coated cereal wasn't as appealing as the ad made it seem.

❷ Practice

Emily needs to use the skill of analyzing influences to make a decision at the grocery store. Read the passage and then practice analyzing influences by answering the questions that follow.

Emily and her mom were food shopping. In the store, a woman was offering free samples of breakfast bars. There was a TV on the table that ran an ad for the bars. In the ad, a man in a white doctor's coat talked about how nutritious the bars were. The ad also showed teens eating the bars while they laughed with their friends.

1. What influences might the ad appeal to?

2. What benefits did the ad seem to promise about the breakfast bars?

3. How could Emily use the food label to make a smart decision about the breakfast bars?

❸ Apply

Apply what you have learned about analyzing influences by completing the activity below.

Find an ad about a fast food item or a fast-food restaurant. Write a report describing the ad and the message it sends. Explain the internal and external influences the ad uses to persuade you to buy the food or to eat at the restaurant. Then give your opinion about whether eating the food would be part of a healthful diet. Support your opinion with facts about good nutrition.

Self-Check
- Did I explain the overall message of the ad?
- Did I describe the influences the commercial uses?
- Did I give my opinion and support it with facts?

Food Diary

Foods Eaten	Amount	Food Group
Monday		
Whole-grain cereal	2 cups	Grains
Carton of milk	1 cup	Milk
Turkey sandwich	2 ounces turkey	Meat and beans
on wheat bread	2 slices of bread	Grains
Baby carrots	1/2 cup	Vegetables
Orange juice	1/2 cup	Fruits

Keeping a Food Diary

In this chapter, you learned about making healthful food choices using MyPyramid. You can begin to make more healthful food choices by taking a look at what foods you typically eat each day. In this activity, you will keep a food diary for one week. This will help you compare your food choices to the recommendations provided by MyPyramid for a teen your age. That way you can see what changes, if any, you need to make.

What You Will Need

- pencil or pen
- ruler
- paper

What You Will Do

1. Make three vertical columns on your paper.
2. In the first column, list all the foods you eat for the next seven days. Be sure to include any snacks you have. Draw a horizontal line to show the end of each day. Use extra pages for your food diary as needed.
3. In the second column, write down the amount of each food you eat. Record the amount as a weight (such a ounces) or volume (such as cups).
4. In the third column, write down the name of the food group each food eaten belongs to. For example, a peanut butter sandwich would belong to the grains group, and the meat and beans group.
5. For each day, total up the amount eaten in each food group.

Wrapping It Up

1. How well does your list for each day match the recommendations for you from MyPyramid?
2. Did you eat foods from each food group? If not, which group is missing?
3. Was there too much from any food group? If so, which group?
4. How could you improve your food choices?

Reading Review

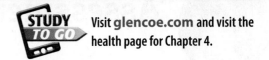

STUDY TO GO Visit glencoe.com and visit the health page for Chapter 4.

FOLDABLES® Study Organizer

Foldables® and Other Study Aids Take out the Foldable® that you created for Lesson 1 and any graphic organizers that you created for Lessons 1–6. Find a partner and quiz each other using these study aids.

Lesson 1 Nutrients for Good Health

Main Idea Good nutrition helps the body stay healthy and function well.

- Carbohydrates, proteins, fats, vitamins, minerals, and water are the six major nutrients.
- The Nutrition Facts panel on a food package gives you important information about the nutrients in that product.

Lesson 2 Creating a Healthy Eating Plan

Main Idea The Dietary Guidelines for Americans and MyPyramid can help you develop a healthy and active lifestyle.

- Your age, gender, and activity level affect your nutrient and calorie needs.
- The following factors can influence your food choices: personal preferences, family traditions and culture, friends, geography, cost, convenience, and media messages.

Lesson 3 Planning Healthful Meals

Main Idea Healthful eating habits can help your body get the nutrients it needs.

- It's important to start the day with a healthful breakfast.
- Foods that are nutrient-dense have a high amount of nutrients relative to the number of calories.

Lesson 4 Digestion and Excretion

Main Idea Through the process of digestion, your body breaks food down into energy.

- Waste products produced by digestion are removed by your excretory system.
- Drinking plenty of water will help keep the digestive and excretory systems healthy.

Lesson 5 Body Image and Healthy Weight

Main Idea Your body image is the way you see your body.

- Body image can be influenced by family, friends, the media, and how people see themselves.
- Someone with a positive body image accepts the body type that he or she has.
- The Body Mass Index (BMI) can tell you if your weight is within an appropriate range.

Lesson 6 Maintaining a Healthy Weight

Main Idea Maintaining a healthy weight will help prevent serious health problems.

- A person who is overly concerned about weight and body image may develop an eating disorder.
- Eating disorders threaten a person's health. They include anorexia nervosa, bulimia nervosa, and binge eating.
- You can maintain a healthy weight by choosing healthy foods and staying physically active.

Assessment

Health eSpotlight **VIDEO**

Now that you have read the chapter, look back at your answer to the Health eSpotlight question on the chapter opener. Have your ideas changed? What would your answer be now?

Reviewing Vocabulary and Main Ideas

On a sheet of paper, write the numbers 1–7. After each number, write the term from the list that best completes each statement.

- proteins
- trans fatty acids
- MyPyramid
- nutrient dense
- calories
- nutrition
- carbohydrates

Lesson 1 Nutrients for Good Health

1. Starches and sugars used by the body for energy are called _____.

2. _____ are made up of amino acids.

3. When oils are turned from a liquid to a solid during processing, _____ are formed.

Lesson 2 Creating a Healthy Eating Plan

4. An eating plan that has more _____ than your body can use results in weight gain.

5. _____ is the process of taking in food and using it for energy, growth, and good health.

6. _____ is a tool provided by the USDA to help you build a healthy eating plan.

Lesson 3 Planning Healthful Meals

7. Foods that are _____ have a high amount of nutrients relative to the number of calories.

*On a sheet of paper, write the numbers 8–15. Write **True** or **False** for each statement below. If the statement is false, change the underlined word or phrase to make it true.*

Lesson 4 Digestion and Excretion

8. Saliva is a digestive juice produced by the <u>liver</u>.

9. <u>Liquid</u> wastes are stored in the colon.

10. Dietary <u>fiber</u> helps food move through the digestive system.

Lesson 5 Body Image and Healthy Weight

11. The Body Mass Index is a way to assess your <u>level of physical activity</u>.

12. Your healthy weight is not a single weight but a <u>range</u> of weights.

13. A healthy body size <u>is not</u> the same for everyone.

Lesson 6 Maintaining a Healthy Weight

14. People with <u>anorexia nervosa</u> purge after eating.

15. <u>Binge eating</u> can lead to heart disease and diabetes.

Go Online Visit glencoe.com and take the Online Quiz for Chapter 4.

Thinking Critically

Using complete sentences, answer the following questions on a sheet of paper.

16. Hypothesize Why do you think weight lost on fad diets is usually regained?

17. Predict Describe the possible consequences for the rest of the body if the digestive system is not working properly.

Write About It

18. Persuasive Writing A local newspaper just printed an article about how the media do not have any influence on a person's body image. Decide whether you agree or disagree with the opinion in the article. Write a letter to the editor of the newspaper and state your reasons for agreeing or disagreeing with the article.

ACTIVITY
➚ Applying Technology

Healthy Hunts

Use PowerPoint® and the Internet to develop a WebQuest that shows how good nutrition is part of a healthy lifestyle.

- Use the following categories to make 30 PowerPoint® slides (5 slides per category): Nutrients, My Pyramid, Human Digestive System, Meal Planning, Body Image, and Healthy Weight.
- Create short, open-ended questions from the textbook and add to individual slides. Research additional information on each category, using Web sites that end in .gov or .edu, and insert a hyperlink onto each slide.
- Include brief background information in the *notes* section of each slide.
- Edit and save your work.

Standardized Test Practice

Reading

Read the paragraphs below and then answer the questions.

Most Americans consume too much fat. The Dietary Guidelines suggest that healthy people consume only 20 to 35 percent of their calories from fats. Most of these fats should be unsaturated. Many people, however, eat much more than that. If you look at the Nutrition Facts panel on a food package label, you will see what percentage of fat one label serving contributes to a 2000-calorie-a-day diet.

People lead busy lives and often depend on fast food when they are away from home or don't have time to prepare a meal. Unfortunately, many fast foods are very high in fat. One burger, for example, may contain more fat than a person should consume in an entire day. However, many fast-food restaurants offer more healthful options, such as salads. Just go easy on the dressing.

1. From the information in the first paragraph, the reader can conclude that the writer thinks Americans

   A. consume too little fat.

   B. consume too much fat.

   C. are poor cooks.

   D. care little about health.

2. Which of the following best describes the purpose of the second paragraph?

   A. To explain reasons why the body needs fats

   B. To rate fats according to health needs

   C. To suggest seeking alternatives to high-fat foods in fast-food restaurants

   D. To rate types of fast-food restaurants

What Is Mental and Emotional Health?

📖 Guide to Reading

● **Building Vocabulary**
As you read this lesson, write down each new highlighted term and its definition.

- mental and emotional health (p. 145)
- personality (p. 146)
- empathy (p. 147)
- resilience (p. 147)

● **Focusing on the Main Ideas**
In this lesson, you will be able to

- **identify** the signs of mental and emotional health.
- **explain** the three most important influences on your personality.
- **describe** resilience and how it affects mental and emotional health.
- **demonstrate** communication skills by showing empathy to others through active listening.

● **Reading Strategy**
Predicting Skim the headings, photos, and captions in this lesson. Write down three pieces of information you think will be covered in this lesson.

FOLDABLES Study Organizer Use the Foldable® on p. 143 as you read this lesson.

*Q*uick Write

Think about a time when you felt disappointed. Write down how you dealt with your feelings.

Understanding Mental and Emotional Health

Annie has three best friends. They spend hours Instant Messaging each other. She likes most of her classes at school, and her favorite subject is Spanish. She loves animals and wants to be a veterinarian. Annie often cracks jokes with her friends. Sometimes, though, she feels mad at the world and tapes a "Keep Out!" sign to her bedroom door. Like every teen, Annie has her ups and downs. She feels sad sometimes, but the feeling doesn't usually last. Annie knows that having these feelings is a normal part of being a teenager.

◄ Enjoying the company of others is a sign of mental and emotional health. **How can you tell that these teens like being with each other?**

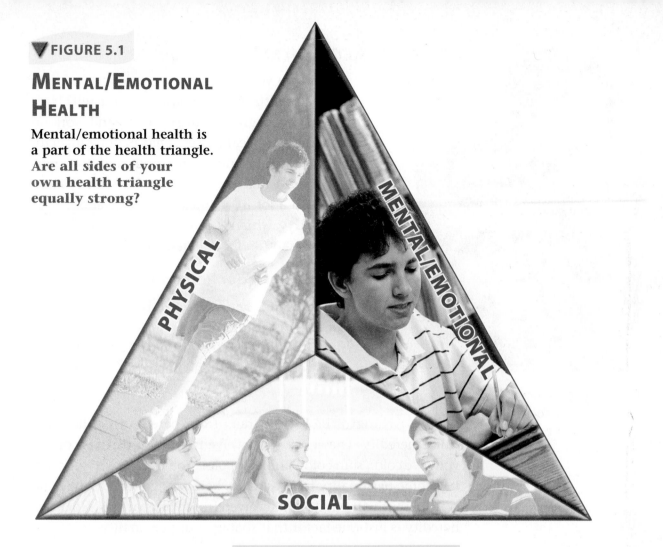

FIGURE 5.1

MENTAL/EMOTIONAL HEALTH

Mental/emotional health is a part of the health triangle. Are all sides of your own health triangle equally strong?

PHYSICAL

MENTAL/EMOTIONAL

SOCIAL

Annie shows many signs of **mental and emotional health**, *the ability to handle the stresses and changes of everyday life in a reasonable way.* She gets along well with others, has a positive outlook on the future, and a strong interest in school. Problems don't get her down for long. Having good mental and emotional health is an important part of **overall** health. **Figure 5.1** shows the health triangle you learned about in Chapter 1.

Where Mental and Emotional Health Begins

James rarely gets enough rest and has a poor diet. His physical needs are not being met, which makes it hard for him to be mentally and emotionally healthy. Meeting physical needs means getting enough food, water, rest, shelter, and a sense of safety.

Your social needs also influence your mental and emotional health. These include the need to give and receive love, to feel recognized, and to feel connected to people you trust. It is easier to deal with problems when you feel connected to others. Think of a time when you talked a problem over with a friend. You probably felt better afterward.

Academic Vocabulary

overall (OH ver awl) *(adjective)* including everything; total, complete. *If you want to maintain good overall health, you must balance all sides of your health triangle.*

Reading Check **Define** What is *mental and emotional health*?

▲ Showing love to family members is a social need. **What are two other social needs?**

Psychologist

A psychologist is a licensed mental health professional who helps people solve their problems in one-on-one or group counseling. There will always be a need for psychologists because people will always need help understanding their feelings. If you want to be a psychologist, you can take psychology classes that cover many topics like mental illness and family health.

What skills does a psychologist need? Go to *Career Corner* at glencoe.com to find out.

Accepting Who You Are

Accepting yourself is a key part of mental and emotional health. How do you accept yourself? First, you need to recognize your strengths and work on improving your weaknesses. That may be difficult for you to do right now, since you may not know yourself very well yet. If you're like most teens, you'll learn a lot in the next few years about your **personality,** which is *a combination of your feelings, likes, dislikes, attitudes, abilities, and habits.*

Influences on Your Personality

There is no one else exactly like you; your personality is unique. Many factors shape your personality. Three of the most important are heredity, environment, and behavior.

Heredity

The passing of biological traits from parents to children is called heredity. The genes you receive from your parents control your eye color, skin color, and hair color. You may also have inherited some personality traits, such as being outgoing. You have no control over what traits you received from your parents. However, heredity is just one factor that shapes your personality.

Environment

Your environment is your family and friends, your neighborhood, your school, and even the climate where you live. These play a big role in shaping your personality. For example, the people in Emily's family have a good sense of humor. They joke around a lot. Because of this, Emily learned how to be funny, and her friends enjoy her humor. Her personality might have turned out differently if she was raised in a different family.

Behavior

Your behavior is how you act. It's a big part of your personality. Of the three influences on personality, you have the most control over your behavior. Each day, you face choices about how to respond to events and people in your life. The actions you choose to take show how you feel about yourself or others. Your choices reflect your core ethical values and can help you improve your mental and emotional health. You can choose behaviors that develop qualities or skills that are important to you.

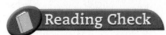 **Reading Check**   **Identify** What are the three main influences on your personality?

Signs of Mental and Emotional Health

Mental and emotional health often changes over time. Take Juan Carlos, for example. As a child, he moved from Mexico to the United States. Since he could not speak English, he felt different from his classmates and teachers for a long time. He also got poor grades. Over time, though, he learned to speak English, made friends, and began to do well in school. As these skills improved, so did Juan's mental and emotional health.

Like Juan Carlos, you can work to improve your mental and emotional health. When these inner qualities are strong, your outer life often shows it. Your relationships and activities give you more satisfaction. Here are some ways to build strong mental and emotional health:

- Have a good attitude and a positive outlook.
- Recognize your strengths and work on your weaknesses.
- Set realistic goals.
- Act responsibly.
- Be able to relax and have fun alone or in a group.
- Be aware of your feelings and express them in healthy ways.
- Practice empathy. **Empathy** involves *identifying with and sharing another person's feelings.*
- Accept constructive feedback and the messages people give you about yourself, without getting angry.

How to Build Resilience

Think about a rubber band. You can stretch it, but it almost always snaps back into shape. That's what being resilient is like. **Resilience** is *the ability to recover from problems or loss.* Resilience is an important part of mental and emotional health. It allows you to face challenges and move past them in a healthful way. When you get pulled out of shape by a problem or crisis, you bounce back. You recover and are healthy again. Most resilient teens believe that they can do something about their problems. They show persistence, flexibility, and strong self-confidence.

Go Online

Visit glencoe.com and complete the Interactive Study Guide for Lesson 1.

▼ Maya is good at showing empathy. **How is Maya showing empathy here?**

How can you be more resilient in response to life's ups and downs? Start by making positive choices for yourself. Strengthen your refusal skills. You will be better able to resist negative peer pressure. Take part in school activities that you feel can make a difference for you or others. Think carefully about situations, activities, and relationships in your life. Which ones help you feel more confident and in control? Resilient people often have strong relationships with family and friends. They may get extra support from good role models and a positive school climate.

 Reading Check **Define** What is *resilience*?

◀ Resilient teens focus on activities that help them feel more confident and in control. **How might this activity help build this teen's confidence?**

Lesson 1 Review

After You Read

Review this lesson for new terms, major headings, and Reading Checks.

What I Learned

1. *Vocabulary* What is *personality*?

2. *List* What are three ways to build mental and emotional health?

3. *Name* What is one environmental influence on your personality?

4. *Identify* What are two social needs that influence mental/emotional health?

5. *Explain* What are three ways a person might build resilience?

Thinking Critically

6. *Evaluate* Why do you think that showing empathy is a sign of mental/emotional health?

7. *Infer* Why might your mental/emotional health suffer if you don't practice healthful eating?

Applying Health Skills

8. *Analyzing Influences* What do you think has had the most influence on your personality: your heredity, environment, or behavior? Explain your answer.

 **Go Online** For more Lesson Review Activities, go to **glencoe.com.**

Your Self-Concept and Self-Esteem

Guide to Reading

● **Building Vocabulary**
Write a sentence using each of the terms below. Trade papers with a classmate. Write the possible meanings of the terms based on the sentences.

- self-concept (p. 149)
- self-esteem (p. 150)
- optimistic (p. 150)
- confidence (p. 151)

● **Focusing on the Main Ideas**
In this lesson, you will be able to

- **explain** what self-concept and self-esteem are.
- **describe** the benefits of high self-esteem.
- **identify** ways of improving self-esteem.

● **Reading Strategy**
Skimming Quickly look over the major and minor headings in this lesson. Then write a sentence or two describing what you think this lesson will be about.

Quick Write
Write a few sentences describing how self-confidence might benefit health.

Your Self-Concept

How would you describe yourself to someone who didn't know you? Your answer reveals a lot about your self-concept. Your **self-concept** is *the way you view yourself overall*. This mental picture includes how you see not only yourself physically but also your abilities and how you "fit in." Your self-concept includes the way you see yourself as a student, as a friend, and as a member of groups, such as a sports team. It is based on external input from others as well as internal thoughts and experiences.

◄ Having good self-esteem gives a person confidence to try new situations. **What do you notice about these teens that might suggest they have good self-esteem?**

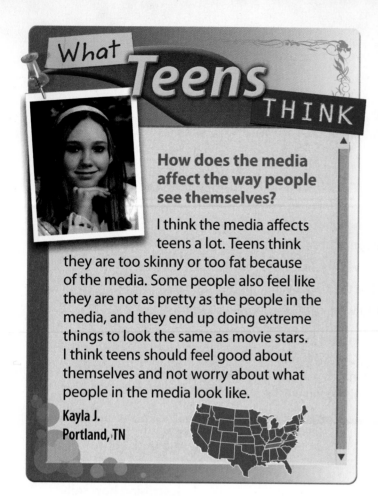

How does the media affect the way people see themselves?

I think the media affects teens a lot. Teens think they are too skinny or too fat because of the media. Some people also feel like they are not as pretty as the people in the media, and they end up doing extreme things to look the same as movie stars. I think teens should feel good about themselves and not worry about what people in the media look like.

Kayla J.
Portland, TN

Your Self-Esteem

Part of your self-concept is your **self-esteem,** *how you feel about yourself.* Do you like yourself? If so, then you probably have good self-esteem. Good self-esteem gives you a sense of pride in your accomplishments and helps you to be comfortable around others. People with high self-esteem respect themselves as well as other people. When you like yourself, others will like you because they will see how confident you are.

Reading Check **Compare** What is the difference between self-concept and self-esteem?

Influences on Self-Esteem

Many factors influence your self-esteem. One factor is the messages you get from family and friends. Supportive and loving family and friends build your self-esteem. Critical, hurtful messages from family and friends hurt your self-esteem.

The media also affects your self-esteem. Television, movies, the Internet, radio and magazines all tell you how you should look, what you should buy and how you should act. It is important to recognize that the media doesn't always present a true picture of life.

Your own attitude affects your self-esteem. If you think positive thoughts about yourself, you will build your self-esteem. If you think negative thoughts about yourself, you will lower your self-esteem. People with low self-esteem may think negative things about themselves no matter what nice things others say about them.

Benefits of Self-Esteem

Jared is **optimistic,** which means *having a positive attitude about the future.* Being optimistic is one of the benefits of having high self-esteem. Other benefits of high self-esteem include the following:

- Taking care of yourself, including your health and personal hygiene.

- Meeting new people and being with others. You are friendly and outgoing, which makes you fun to be around.

- Increased opportunities. You are willing to take on new challenges. You set goals for yourself and believe you can meet them.

- Having **confidence,** or *belief in your ability to do what you set out to do.* People with high self-esteem tend to think that they will succeed before they try a new activity. If they don't succeed at first, they keep at it until they do.

 Reading Check Define What is confidence?

Building Self-Esteem

Your self-esteem will change depending on how you view what happens to you. Everyone has low self-esteem sometimes. Here are some **strategies** you can use to build your self-esteem.

- **Set realistic goals.** These are goals that are reasonable to accomplish. Divide your larger goals into smaller goals. You can build on each smaller success to reach your overal goal.

- **Focus on what you are naturally good at.** Find something you like to do, such as a hobby, school activity, or sport. Work to improve your skills. Try to enjoy yourself, even when you make mistakes. This will help you develop more confidence as well as self-esteem.

- **Ask for help when you need it.** Recognize and accept when you might need help. This is especially true when you are learning something new. Find someone who can help guide you.

- **Accept that no one is perfect.** Everyone has different abilities. You may be better at writing or swimming than some of your friends. Recognize that there is always room for improvement. Identify your weaknesses without judging yourself and make a solid effort to improve them. If others give you constructive feedback, try to learn from it. Be proud of yourself when you succeed, but know that sometimes failure is out of your control. Mistakes can teach you what doesn't work and push you to grow.

Academic Vocabulary

strategies (STRAT i jeez) *(noun)* organized ways of achieving a certain goal or goals. *Ms. Rowe asked her students to come up with several strategies for researching their paper over the weekend.*

▶ Taking care of your physical health can boost your self-esteem. **What are two ways this teen's self-esteem might benefit from this activity?**

► Helping others can boost your self-esteem. How are these teens demonstrating self-esteem?

Visit **glencoe.com** and complete the Interactive Study Guide for Lesson 2.

• **Think positively.** Even when you're not entirely sure of yourself, a positive attitude can help you be more confident. Being positive also helps you relate better to others. You're likely to be more honest and honorable and to respect others' life experiences.

 Reading Check **List** Name two ways to build self-esteem.

Lesson 2 Review

 After You Read

Review this lesson for new terms, major headings, and Reading Checks.

What I Learned

1. **Vocabulary** What does *optimistic* mean?

2. **List** What are two benefits of high self-esteem?

3. **Explain** How can the media affect a person's self-esteem?

4. **Identify** What is an individual's self-concept based on?

5. **Explain** Why does thinking positively help to improve self-esteem?

Thinking Critically

6. **Evaluate** How can learning a new skill improve your self-esteem?

7. **Infer** Describe some character traits that people with high self-esteem have in common.

Applying Health Skills

8. **Communication Skills** Imagine that a friend of yours is feeling discouraged because he tried out for the school play but was not chosen. Write a letter of encouragement to your friend to boost his self-esteem.

Go Online For more Lesson Review Activities, go to **glencoe.com**.

Your Emotions

● **Building Vocabulary**
As you read this lesson, write down each new highlighted term and its definition.

■ emotions (p. 153)
■ mood swings (p. 153)

● **Focusing on the Main Ideas**
In this lesson, you will be able to

■ **recognize** different types of emotions.
■ **describe** how to handle difficult emotions.

● **Reading Strategy**
Predicting Look at the headings in this lesson, and write down three topics that you think will be covered in this lesson.

What Are Emotions?

People can experience and express a wide range of feelings. In fact, all of your life experiences go hand in hand with some kind of feeling, or emotion. **Emotions** are *feelings such as love, joy, or fear.* Your emotions affect all sides of your health triangle.

It's normal to experience many different emotions, sometimes in a short period of time. **Mood swings,** *frequent changes in emotional state,* are common in teens. These happen mainly because of physical changes in the body, such as changes in hormone levels, worries over the future, and concerns over relationships. Mood swings are a normal part of growing up.

Emotions are not always easy to recognize. You might not always know exactly what you're feeling or why. If you can identify your emotions, however, you can think of healthy strategies for dealing with them. The way you manage your emotions affects your mental and emotional health. How you manage your emotions also can affect those around you. Remember, emotions themselves are not positive or negative. It's how you cope with them that matters.

 **Reading Check** **Define** What are *mood swings*?

 **Q**uick Write
Write a few sentences describing an emotion that you think teens might have difficulty dealing with.

▼ Surprise is one of many common emotions. **What are some other common emotions?**

153

Types of Emotions

Common emotions include happiness, sadness, anger, fear, and grief. Everyone experiences these emotions.

Happiness makes people feel good. People often feel happy when their needs are met. People who feel happy tend to smile more often. They want to share this emotion with others.

Sadness is another basic emotion. You might feel sad when you lose something you care about or when you don't succeed at an activity you want to do. Sad feelings don't usually last very long, however, in people who are mentally and emotionally healthy.

Anger is a natural reaction to feeling threatened. It can be a warning signal. Anger can also help release tension. Sometimes, anger can make people act impulsively. This means that they act without thinking, which can make things worse. The key is to let anger pass.

Fear, like anger, can serve to protect us. However, it can also be unhealthy. It can make it difficult for you to take an active part in life. It is important to deal with fear healthfully so that it does not last too long.

Grief is a normal, healthy reaction to a loss. You might think it applies only to death, but you can also feel grief over other losses, such as the loss of a relationship.

There are five common stages of grief: *denial, anger, bargaining, depression,* and *acceptance.* Suppose your grandparent dies. At first, you may feel shock. You may even deny that the loss is real. Then you might feel angry. It's okay to be angry that the person you loved is no longer with you. You may try to make a "deal" to change things, saying, "I would give anything to have Grandma back." This brings sadness. Finally, you understand and accept that nothing will bring your grandmother back. This process allows you to start recovering from the loss.

 **Reading Check** **Identify** What emotions are healthy reactions to losing someone you care about?

Managing Your Emotions in Healthful Ways

Managing your emotions in healthful ways will help you avoid impulsive behavior. Suppose, for example, that you are angry with someone. Don't act impulsively by yelling or fighting. To deal with your anger in a healthful way, take time to cool down and think about what you want to say. Discuss the situation with someone you trust who is not involved. Then, calmly tell the person how you feel without placing blame.

Visit glencoe.com and complete the Interactive Study Guide for Lesson 3.

To cope with other strong feelings like sadness or fear, try writing in a journal, listening to music, or engaging in a hobby that you enjoy. Talk to a friend or trusted adult about how you feel.

Physical activity can also help you focus your energy so that you feel more capable of dealing with your feelings. Imagine a time and place when you felt safe and comfortable. Think about those positive feelings while you close your eyes and breathe deeply. Take time out to return to that safe and comfortable place whenever you need to cope with strong feelings.

 Reading Check   **Identify** What are some healthful ways to avoid impulsive behavior?

▲ There are many healthful ways to cope with strong feelings. **How is this teen dealing with her feelings?**

Lesson 3 Review

 After You Read

Review this lesson for new terms, major headings, and Reading Checks.

What I Learned

1. *Vocabulary* What are *emotions*?

2. *List* Which two emotions can serve to protect us?

3. *Explain* What are the stages of grief that most people experience?

4. *Analyze* How can physical activity help you deal with strong emotions?

Thinking Critically

5. *Apply* What strategies for dealing with anger do you think would work best for you? Why?

6. *Infer* How might expressing your feelings affect your social health?

Applying Health Skills

7. *Analyzing Influences* How do you think advertisements use people's emotions to sell products?

Managing Stress

Guide to Reading

● Building Vocabulary
Look up the meaning of the word *stress*. As you read the lesson, write down examples of how you think this definition relates to the other vocabulary terms.

- stress (p. 156)
- positive stress (p. 156)
- distress (p. 156)
- stressors (p. 157)
- fight-or-flight response (p. 157)
- adrenaline (p. 157)
- fatigue (p. 157)

● Focusing on the Main Ideas
In this lesson, you will be able to

- **recognize** sources of stress.
- **describe** the body's reaction to stress.
- **list** effective strategies to avoid and manage stress.

● Reading Strategy
Predicting Look over the major and minor headings in this lesson. List two topics that you think will be covered in the lesson.

Quick Write
Write a few sentences briefly describing a time when you felt stress. How did you manage your feelings?

▼ Getting up in front of others can be stressful for some people. **What are some other sources of stress for teens?**

What Is Stress?

Mario is worrying about his math test. He feels nervous and impatient. This is **stress,** *the body's response to real or imagined dangers or other life events.* Stress is an everyday experience, felt by all people at all ages. While you cannot get rid of all stress completely, you *can* learn to deal with it effectively.

Stress can be positive or negative. **Positive stress** is *stress that can help you reach your goals.* For example, you may feel positive stress when you try out for the school play or join a sports team. This stress makes you feel excited and ready to face a new challenge. **Distress,** or negative stress, is *stress that prevents you from doing what you need to do, or stress that causes you discomfort.* Getting into an argument with a friend may make you feel distressed. You may also feel distressed if you moved and had to make new friends at a new school.

Reading Check
Explain What is the difference between positive stress and distress?

156

What Are Stressors?

You're running behind on a school project. It's almost time for you to give your big speech. These situations are possible **stressors,** or *sources of stress*. Common events like being late for class or playing a solo during a concert may cause you to feel stress. More significant events that cause stress might include death, divorce, a move, a serious illness, or the loss of a friendship.

Different people find different situations stressful. For example, you may find it easy to make friends at a new school, while someone else may feel stressed about it.

 Reading Check **Define** What are *stressors*?

The Body's Response to Stress

Your body responds to all stressors by getting ready to act by either fighting the stressor or fleeing from it. *The body's way of responding to threats* is known as the **fight-or-flight response.** As your body prepares for action, it releases **adrenaline,** *a hormone that increases the level of sugar in the blood, giving your body extra energy.* Adrenaline also increases your heart rate and blood pressure. More blood flows to your brain and muscles, which tense for action. Your breathing gets faster, and your air passages expand so you can take in more air. Your senses sharpen, making you extra aware of your surroundings.

After a stressful situation, you may feel **fatigue,** or *tiredness*. This occurs because your body directed much of its energy into the fight-or-flight response. You can relieve fatigue by sleeping or resting, stretching, and breathing deeply.

Avoiding Stress

Sometimes you can avoid stressful situations. For example, your mornings might tend to be rushed. You can avoid this stress by planning ahead and getting up earlier. Other stressors result from exciting events that you don't want to avoid, such as performing in a piano recital. Still other stressors are unavoidable, such as taking a test or giving an oral report. You can deal with these types of stressors by being prepared and managing your time effectively. Give yourself some extra time in your schedule in case something happens that you didn't plan for. Don't overschedule yourself with too many activities and commitments.

 **Reading Check** **Name** What are two actions you can take to help avoid stress?

Go Online

Visit **glencoe.com** and complete the Interactive Study Guide for Lesson 4.

▼ There are many ways of coping with fatigue. **What are two other ways teens can handle their fatigue?**

Strategies for Managing Stress

Managing stress is a key part of mental/emotional health. **Figure 5.2** lists some strategies for managing stress.

HEALTHY STRATEGIES FOR MANAGING STRESS

Thoughts and actions determine how well you manage stress. How can thinking positively help manage stress?

Lesson 4 Review

 After You Read

Review this lesson for new terms, major headings, and Reading Checks.

What I Learned

1. **Vocabulary** Define *stress*.

2. **Describe** What is the *fight-or-flight response*?

3. **Give Examples** Give two examples of positive stress.

4. **Explain** What are three healthy strategies for managing stress?

Thinking Critically

5. **Analyze** Do you think life today is more stressful than it was for your parents? Why or why not?

6. **Hypothesize** Why might adrenaline have been more important to human survival in the past than it is today?

Applying Health Skills

7. **Advocacy** Write an article for the school newspaper in which you discuss common stressors in teens' lives. Suggest healthful ways for teens to relieve stress.

Go Online For more Lesson Review Activities, go to glencoe.com.

Mental and Emotional Problems

Guide to Reading

Building Vocabulary

As you read this lesson, write down each highlighted term and its definition.

- mental and emotional disorders (p. 159)
- anxiety disorder (p. 160)
- mood disorder (p. 161)
- suicide (p. 161)

Focusing on the Main Ideas

In this lesson, you will be able to

- **identify** several mental and emotional problems.
- **recognize** the warning signs of serious mental and emotional problems.
- **list** factors that contribute to the development of mental and emotional problems.

Reading Strategy

Finding the Main Idea Review each of the main headings in this lesson. Write one sentence describing what you think the main idea of the section will be.

*Q*uick Write

Some teens find it very hard to ask for help when they have problems. Is it easy for you to ask for help? In a paragraph, explain why or why not.

What Are Mental and Emotional Disorders?

Julie hadn't felt happy for a long time. She also had trouble sleeping and had lost interest in activities that she used to enjoy. Julie might be suffering from a mental and emotional disorder. **Mental and emotional disorders** are *illnesses that affect a person's thoughts, feelings, and behavior.*

Causes of Mental and Emotional Disorders

There are many causes of mental and emotional disorders. Physical factors include drug use, certain diseases, and accidental injuries to the brain. Heredity can also be a factor when there are problems with the levels of certain chemicals in the brain.

Other mental and emotional disorders do not have physical causes. They may come from repeated emotional stressors. If mental and emotional disorders are identified early, they can be treated so that they don't become lifelong problems.

Reading Check

Identify What are two physical causes of mental and emotional disorders?

Schizophrenia

Schizophrenia is an incurable mental and emotional disorder. People with this disorder may experience paranoia, the unrealistic fear that someone is trying to harm them. They may also have hallucinations, which are visions of people or objects that don't exist. With treatment, people with schizophrenia may be able to lead a normal life.

Research the possible causes of and treatments for schizophrenia. Write your findings in a brief paragraph.

Types of Mental and Emotional Disorders

There are many types of mental and emotional disorders, including anxiety disorders and mood disorders. All may be mild or severe.

Anxiety Disorders

Everyone feels anxious from time to time. However, someone with an **anxiety disorder** has *extreme fears of real or imaginary situations that get in the way of normal activities*. Below are some descriptions of different anxiety disorders.

Panic disorder

In panic disorder, people experience intense feelings of fear for a short time. Sometimes, there seems to be no reason for the feelings. During a panic attack, the body prepares for fight or flight, even during an ordinary situation such as waiting in line.

Phobias

A phobia is an exaggerated or unrealistic fear of something specific, such as tunnels, spiders, or public places. People with phobias may go out of the way to avoid an object or situation that they fear. Some phobias can interfere with normal, everyday activities.

Obsessive-compulsive disorder

People with obsessive-compulsive disorder (OCD) have unwanted thoughts that may not make sense. A person with OCD may feel that he or she *must* perform a certain activity, such as washing his or her hands several times. Doing these activities can make the anxiety go away for a short while, but it quickly returns.

Post-traumatic stress disorder

People experience post-traumatic stress disorder (PTSD) in reaction to a traumatic event, such as war or natural disaster. People with PTSD have bad memories of the event for a long time.

 Reading Check **Define** What is a *phobia*?

▶ Some people have an abnormal fear of heights. **How do you think a person with a phobia of heights would feel in this situation?**

Mood Disorders

It's normal for people to feel happy for a while, then later feel sad about something. However, a **mood disorder** is *a mental and emotional problem in which a person undergoes mood swings that seem extreme, inappropriate, or last a long time.* The following are some examples of mood disorders.

Depression

Depression is a mood disorder in which a person feels a strong sense of hopelessness, helplessness, worthlessness, guilt, and extreme sadness. These feelings can continue for weeks. A person who is depressed may lose interest in activities that used to be fun. If depressed people begin to feel hopeless, they may consider ending their lives.

Bipolar disorder

Also called manic depression, bipolar disorder involves extreme mood swings for no apparent reason. A person with bipolar disorder usually experiences alternating periods of excessive activity, called mania, and depression. During times of mania, the person has an unrealistic belief in his or her abilities. This can lead to poor judgment and even dangerous risk taking.

 **Reading Check** **Define** What is a *mood disorder*?

Signs of Mental and Emotional Problems

People suffering from a mental or emotional problem may show certain signs. For example, they may lose their appetite or fail to take care of their personal appearance. Others may have nightmares or have problems falling asleep. Some may hear voices that no one else can or think that others are trying to harm them. People who have long-lasting feelings of sadness may also have a mental or emotional disorder. Teens who experience any of these symptoms should seek help from a trusted adult right away.

What Is Suicide?

Suicide is *the act of killing oneself on purpose.* **Figure 5.3** lists some signs that a person might be thinking about suicide. If you notice any of these signs in someone you know, talk to a trusted adult right away. In the next lesson, you'll find out more about how and where to get help.

Topic: Lending a Helping Hand

Visit **glencoe.com** for Student Web Activities where you'll learn about organizations that train teens to be peer counselors.

Activity: Using the information provided at the link above, write a letter of introduction to one of the organizations detailing why you'd like to be a peer counselor.

▼ People with OCD may feel that they must constantly perform a certain activity, such as handwashing. **How might this person feel right after washing her hands?**

▼ FIGURE 5.3

WARNING SIGNS OF SUICIDE

These signs may indicate that a person is thinking about suicide. **What should you do if you suspect that someone is thinking about suicide?**

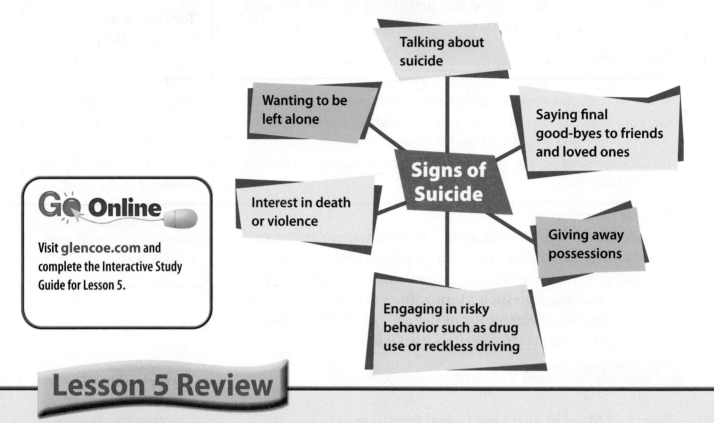

Talking about suicide

Wanting to be left alone

Saying final good-byes to friends and loved ones

Interest in death or violence

Signs of Suicide

Giving away possessions

Engaging in risky behavior such as drug use or reckless driving

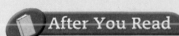

G⊙ Online

Visit **glencoe.com** and complete the Interactive Study Guide for Lesson 5.

Lesson 5 Review

📖 After You Read

Review this lesson for new terms, major headings, and Reading Checks.

What I Learned

1. *Vocabulary* What are *mental and emotional disorders*?

2. *Explain* What are three warning signs of suicide?

3. *Distinguish* What is the difference between a panic disorder and a phobia?

4. *Identify* What is one characteristic of bipolar disorder?

5. *List* What are two main types of mental and emotional disorders?

Thinking Critically

6. *Analyze* If you had a phobia about public places, how might this affect your social health?

7. *Explain* Why is getting treatment early for mental and emotional disorders so important?

Applying Health Skills

8. *Accessing Information* Use reliable online and print resources to find out more information about treatments for phobias. Write a one-page summary of your findings.

  For more Lesson Review Activities, go to **glencoe.com**.

Help for Mental and Emotional Problems

Guide to Reading

● Building Vocabulary
Write each term and its definition on a sheet of paper. Then write a paragraph using both.

■ resources (p. 165)
■ referral (p. 165)

● Focusing on the Main Ideas
In this lesson, you will be able to

■ **identify** treatment options available for mental and emotional disorders.
■ **list** resources available for help with mental and emotional disorders.
■ **explain** why treatment at an early stage is important.
■ **access** valid information to find resources to help people with mental and emotional disorders.

● Reading Strategy
Organizing Information As you read the lesson, list the different ways of treating mental and emotional problems.

**uick Write**

Think of a trusted adult whom you could talk to about a problem. Write a few sentences describing how that adult could help you.

Medical Treatments and Counseling

How are mental and emotional disorders treated? It depends on the cause and severity of the disorder. People with mental and emotional disorders receive counseling, which is also called therapy. This can include individual, group, and family therapy. Some disorders are also treated with medication. A few disorders may also require a hospital stay.

◀ In group therapy, people offer each other tips for coping with problems. **What do you think might be helpful about group therapy?**

Health Skills Activity

Accessing Information

Community Resources for Mental/Emotional Problems

One of the mental and emotional disorders you have read about in this chapter is obsessive-compulsive disorder (OCD). If you thought that someone you know suffered from OCD, would you know where to seek help? Would you be able to tell them what resources your community offers for counseling, therapy, treatment, or hospitalization? You could provide appropriate, helpful information by researching the topic using reliable sources such as the following:

- the Internet
- school and local libraries
- teachers
- health care professionals

On Your Own

Create a brochure that lists some community resources for treating OCD. Use several of the sources listed above for your research. Organize your information based on the types of resources and how each resource addresses the disorder. Include descriptions of the disorder as well as tips for how a person could help someone who needs information about treatment.

In individual therapy, a person with a problem talks to a mental health professional, such as a school counselor or school psychologist. The professional promises to keep the conversations private, unless the person being treated is in immediate danger or is talking about hurting someone else. The counselor tries to help the person deal with his or her problems.

In group therapy, people meet to discuss their problems and help each other. A mental health professional is there to guide the discussion. In family therapy, families learn how to help a family member with a mental or emotional disorder.

When to Get Help

Many people with mental and emotional disorders do not seek treatment. They may feel embarrassed or ashamed of their illness. They may not think that they need treatment. Others may not be aware that treatment is available. Some people just hope that the disorder will go away. However, mental and emotional disorders don't go away on their own. If left untreated, they can become more severe. Fortunately, help is available, and a person should seek help as soon as a disorder is recognized.

Go Online

Visit **glencoe.com** and complete the Interactive Study Guide for Lesson 6.

Where to Find Help

Aaron's mother had agoraphobia. She was afraid to leave the house, even for short periods of time. Aaron felt that she had a problem. However, he wasn't sure what it was or how to get help. When dealing with a serious problem, it's important to find valid resources. **Resources** are *places to get information, support, and advice.*

Resources might include a family member or friend, a health care professional, a religious leader, or a teacher. You can also call a crisis hotline. These hotline workers protect the privacy of callers. When you call a crisis hotline, the person who responds will not ask for your name. This makes it easier to discuss problems.

There are other ways of getting help. Many health care professionals can provide a referral. A **referral** is *a suggestion to seek help or information from another person or place.* No one should have to suffer with a mental or emotional problem alone. Many people have been treated for their problems and have gone on to lead normal lives.

▲ There are many resources available to help teens with mental and emotional problems. **Why is it important to get help right away?**

 Reading Check   **Define** What is a *referral*?

Lesson 6 Review

 After You Read

Review this lesson for new terms, major headings, and Reading Checks.

What I Learned

1. *Vocabulary* What is a *resource*?

2. *Analyze* Why might a person with a mental or emotional disorder fail to seek treatment?

3. *Identify* What are some differences between individual and group therapy?

4. *List* What are some resources a person could use to get help for a mental or emotional disorder?

Thinking Critically

5. *Infer* Why do you think someone might need to be hospitalized for treatment of a mental or emotional disorder?

6. *Evaluate* Dr. Gonzalez's patient, Dan, seemed extremely unhappy and talked about his wish for a pill that would make him sleep forever. He did not think life was worth living anymore. What should Dr. Gonzalez do with this information?

Applying Health Skills

7. *Advocacy* Create a poster about mental and emotional disorders. In your poster, address misconceptions that people have about these disorders as well as options for treating them.

Building Health Skills

- Accessing Information
- Practicing Healthful Behaviors
- **Stress Management**
- Analyzing Influences
- Communication Skills
- Refusal Skills
- Conflict Resolution
- Decision Making
- Goal Setting
- Advocacy

What Is Stress Management?

Stress Management includes activities and behaviors that help you deal with stress in a healthy way. When you experience stress, do one or more of the following:

- Get plenty of sleep.
- Think positive thoughts.
- Make time to relax.

- Be physically active.
- Talk to someone you trust.
- Manage your time wisely.

Dealing with Stress

Follow the Model, Practice, and Apply steps to help you master this important health skill.

1 Model

Read how Jessica uses stress-management skills to deal with her parents' divorce.

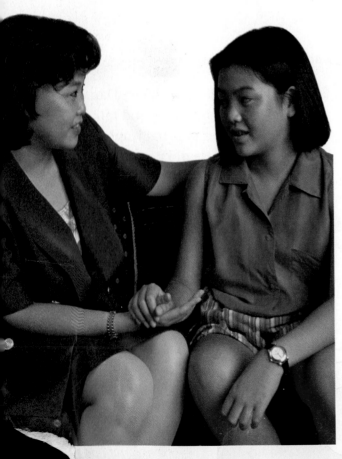

A year ago, Jessica's whole world turned upside down. Her grades started slipping and she wanted to sleep all the time. Jessica kept feeling worse and worse. Her younger brother, Matt, was upset, too. He couldn't focus during his basketball games. He was forgetful and snappy toward his friends.

Jessica knew that she had to deal with the problems she was having. First, she identified the cause of her stress. Jessica realized that her problems began when her parents divorced. She talked to her parents about how she felt and they went to see a family counselor together. Jessica said she was feeling angry and upset. The counselor told her that her feelings were normal. She also began having more discussions with Matt so that they could share how they were feeling. Jessica found that talking about the divorce made it easier to deal with. She also felt that talking with her brother made their relationship stronger. She became better able to adjust to the changes in her life.

❷ Practice

Use stress-management skills to help Nakita create a plan to manage her stress.

Nakita wants to do well in school, on the volleyball team, and in her music class. It seems that when she isn't worrying about one part of her life, she's worrying about another. Sometimes, she feels so much pressure that she doesn't even feel like eating. She also has trouble sleeping and doesn't feel like spending time with her friends. She knows this isn't healthy, but she's not sure what to do about it.

On a sheet of paper, identify what's causing Nakita's worries. Make a plan to help her by listing at least four activities that Nakita could do to manage the stress that she feels.

❸ Apply

Use what you have learned about stress management to complete the activity below.

Think about the stress in your life. When you share your thoughts with other students in your class, you can get ideas about healthful ways to deal with stress. In groups of three or four, discuss what causes stress in your life. Identify causes. Then describe ways that each of you manage stress. Discuss resources that teens can access for information, support, and advice. As a group, create a colorful brochure that explains four stressors for teens, and healthful strategies for coping. Identify resources that provide help for teens. Present your brochures to the class.

Self-Check

- Did we explain four stressors for teens?
- Did our brochure describe healthful ways to manage stress?
- Did our brochure identify resources for help?

Building Health Skills

STRESSED OUT

Everyone gets stressed from time to time. Here are some timely tips from teens on dealing with stress.

Q. How much stress is normal? It's hard for me to go even a day without stressing about a paper or who to hang out with.

A. Stress levels vary, so it's difficult to say what's "normal." Instead of thinking about how much is normal, think about what's making you stressed. If it's schoolwork, get a head start on papers and study for tests early. If it's about who to hang out with, spend time with the people who make you feel good.

Q. When I get stressed about school I always procrastinate. What's a better way to de-stress from my workload?

A. Find something that takes your mind off things for a while but still stimulates you enough so that afterward, you're ready to work hard. For some teens, it's writing in a journal. For others, it's running or playing the piano or dancing. Avoid lying on your bed, thinking about the work you're not doing.

Q. When I get stressed I yell at the people I love. How can I stop?

A. Remember that the people closest to you could actually help you through your stress. Try talking to them—they might have great advice. If it's too hard to control your temper, take some time to be by yourself, get calm, and then start talking.

Q. I couldn't handle all my honors classes last year, but I know colleges love APs and my parents want me to go to a good school. How can I explain that I can't do it all anymore?

A. Colleges like to see challenging courses, but they like you to do well in whatever classes you take. Tell your parents that your chances of getting into a good college are better if you're not so overwhelmed by your schoolwork that you can't keep your grades up. An easier workload will also give you time for the other things colleges look at, such as extracurriculars and community involvement. Plus, recognizing that you got in over your head shows you know yourself and have a good sense of responsibility. Your parents and the colleges will love that!

TELL US ABOUT IT!
What's your best trick for beating stress?

"I listen to music—it's great for getting mellow."

"I take a deep breath, stop doing whatever is stressing me out, and watch TV for a while."

"I sleep and try to forget about stuff."

"Kicking a soccer ball around, either by myself or with a friend, helps me calm down."

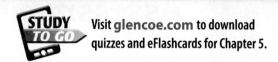
Visit **glencoe.com** to download quizzes and eFlashcards for Chapter 5.

Foldables® and Other Study Aids Take out the Foldable® that you created for Lesson 1 and any graphic organizers that you created for Lessons 1–6. Find a partner and quiz each other using these study aids.

Lesson 1 What Is Mental and Emotional Health?

Main Idea Mental and emotional health is the ability to handle the stresses and changes of everyday life in a reasonable way.

- Personality is the combination of feelings, likes, dislikes, attitudes, abilities, and habits.
- You can build strong mental and emotional health in many ways.
- Resilience is the ability to recover from problems or loss.

Lesson 2 Your Self-Concept and Self-Esteem

Main Idea Your self-concept is the way you view yourself overall.

- Your self-esteem is influenced by family, friends, the media, and your own attitudes and choices.
- Being optimistic means having a positive attitude about the future.
- There are many benefits to having high self-esteem.

Lesson 3 Your Emotions

Main Idea Managing your emotions in healthy ways is important to good mental/emotional health.

- Emotions are feelings like happiness, sadness, anger, joy, grief, and fear.
- Mood swings are frequent changes in emotional state.
- Physical activity is one of many ways to deal with your emotions.

Lesson 4 Managing Stress

Main Idea Stress is the body's response to real or imagined dangers or other life events.

- Positive stress is stress that can help you reach your goals.
- During a stressful situation, adrenaline provides an energy burst.
- There are many ways to manage stress.

Lesson 5 Mental and Emotional Problems

Main Idea Mental and emotional disorders are illnesses that affect thoughts, feelings, and behavior.

- Causes of mental and emotional problems include drug use, disease, brain injuries, emotional stressors, and heredity.
- Anxiety disorders and mood disorders are two types of mental and emotional disorders.

Lesson 6 Help for Mental and Emotional Problems

Main Idea There is help for mental and emotional problems.

- Therapy is group, individual, or family counseling.
- Some disorders are treated with medication.
- If left untreated, mental and emotional disorders can become more severe.

After You Read

HEALTH QUIZ

Now that you have read the chapter, look back at your answers to the Health Quiz on the chapter opener. Would you change any of them? What would your answers be now?

Reviewing Vocabulary and Main Ideas

On a sheet of paper, write the numbers 1–8. After each number, write the term from the list that best completes each statement.

- mood swings
- self-esteem
- personality
- emotions
- confidence
- resilience
- empathy
- optimistic

Lesson 1 — What Is Mental and Emotional Health?

1. The three most important factors that influence your _____ are heredity, environment, and behavior.

2. The ability to recover from problems or loss is _____.

3. The ability to identify and share another person's feelings is called _____.

Lesson 2 — Your Self-Concept and Self-Esteem

4. _____ is how you feel about yourself.

5. Belief in your ability to do what you set out to do is called _____.

6. Being _____ means having a positive attitude about the future.

Lesson 3 — Your Emotions

7. Frequent changes in emotional state are called _____.

8. _____ are feelings that include happiness, anger, and fear.

*On a sheet of paper, write the numbers 9–15. Write **True** or **False** for each statement below. If the statement is false, change the underlined word or phrase to make it true.*

Lesson 4 — Managing Stress

9. The chemical your body produces in response to a stressor is called <u>adrenaline</u>.

10. The tiredness that occurs after a stressful situation is called <u>depression</u>.

Lesson 5 — Mental and Emotional Problems

11. Illnesses that affect a person's thoughts, feelings, and behavior are known as <u>mental and emotional disorders</u>.

12. Obsessive-compulsive disorder is an example of an <u>anxiety disorder</u>.

13. <u>Schizophrenia</u> means killing oneself on purpose.

Lesson 6 — Help for Mental and Emotional Problems

14. When dealing with a mental or emotional problem, it's important to find reliable <u>resources</u>.

15. When a health care professional suggests that a person go somewhere else for help or information, this is known as <u>therapy</u>.

Go Online Visit glencoe.com and take the Online Quiz for Chapter 5.

Thinking Critically

Using complete sentences, answer the following questions on a sheet of paper.

16. Synthesize Why is being resilient important for mental and emotional health?

17. Explain Why might people who are often sad become sick more often?

Write About It

18. Narrative Writing Write a short story about a teen who is stressed out. Be sure to include what is causing stress in the teen's life and the healthful strategies that the teen uses to manage the stress.

19. Descriptive Writing Write a poem about the different activities you can do to increase your self-esteem. In your poem, include the benefits of having high self-esteem.

⚙ Applying Technology

Get Good Mental and Emotional Health

In pairs, use digital images and Comic Life to create a poster that will help your classmates and peers improve their mental and emotional health. Follow the directions below to complete your project.

- Take digital photos of teens who are doing activities that manage stress in a positive way.
- Open Comic Life and select a template.
- Upload the photos to your computer. Drag photos to the template.
- Select dialogue bubbles and add them to the photos on your template.
- Add a title to each bubble that identifies a positive or negative stressor. Add a few sentences that tell a positive way to deal with the stressor.
- Save your project.

Standardized Test Practice

Math

Use the chart to answer the questions.

Mental and Emotional Disorders in Young People	
Mental and emotional disorder	**Number of reported cases in the United States**
Anxiety disorders	As many as 1 in 10 young people
Depression	As many as 1 in 8 young people
Bipolar disorder	About 1 in 100 young people
Conduct disorder	As many as 1 in 10 young people
Eating disorders	1 in 100 to 200 teen females and a much smaller number of males
Schizophrenia	About 3 in 1,000 young people

1. What percentage of young people do *not* suffer from depression?

2. Of the disorders listed, which is the most common among young people?
- **A.** Anxiety disorders
- **B.** Conduct disorder
- **C.** Depression
- **D.** Eating disorders

3. What is the percentage of young people who have schizophrenia?

4. What is the percentage of young people who have bipolar disorder?

Chapter Preview

Lesson 1 Building
          Communication Skills 174

Lesson 2 Understanding Family
          Relationships 178

Lesson 3 Your Friendships and
          Peer Pressure 184

Lesson 4 Abstinence and
          Refusal Skills 189

Building Health Skills 194

Hands-on Health 196

Chapter Reading Review 197

Chapter Assessment 198

▲ *Working with the Photo*

Friendships play an important role in a teen's social health. What are some ways that friends can affect a teen's social health?

Start-Up Activities

Before You Read Do you know how to handle peer pressure? Answer the Health eSpotlight question below and then watch the online video. Keep a record of your answer.

Health eSpotlight

Healthy Peer Relationships

Learning how to recognize peer pressure will help you develop healthy peer relationships. If a friend encouraged you to do something you knew was wrong, how would you respond?

Go to **glencoe.com** and watch the health video for Chapter 6. Then complete the activity provided with the online video.

FOLDABLES Study Organizer

As You Read Make this Foldable® to help you organize what you learn about verbal and nonverbal communication in Lesson 1. Begin with a plain sheet of 8½″ × 11″ paper.

1 Fold the sheet of paper in half along the long axis.

3 Unfold and cut the top layer along both fold lines. This makes three tabs.

2 Turn the paper, and fold it into thirds.

4 Draw two overlapping ovals and label as shown.

Verbal   Communication   Nonverbal

Write down the definitions and examples of verbal and nonverbal communication under the appropriate tab. Under the middle tab, describe how both types of communication help to share feelings, thoughts, and information.

Go Online Visit **glencoe.com** and complete the Health Inventory for Chapter 6.

Building Communication Skills

Guide to Reading

● Building Vocabulary

As you read this lesson, write each new term and its definition in your notebook.

- communication (p. 174)
- verbal communication (p. 175)
- nonverbal communication (p. 175)
- body language (p. 175)
- tact (p. 176)

● Focusing on the Main Ideas

In this lesson, you will be able to

- **define** communication.
- **recognize** different ways of communicating.
- **list** ways of speaking clearly and listening carefully.
- **demonstrate** communication skills.

● Reading Strategy

Predicting Look at the main headings, figures, and captions before reading this lesson. Write a sentence or two to predict the kinds of information you might learn.

FOLDABLES Study Organizer Use the Foldable® on p. 173 as you read this lesson.

**uick Write**

Think of a time when a friend didn't understand what you were trying to say. Write two or three sentences that describe the situation.

What Is Communication?

Jenna just talked to Paul on the phone about a report for health class. Paul gave her some tips on finding the information she needed for her part of the report. Jenna and Paul communicated. **Communication** is *the exchange of information through the use of words or actions.*

Every communication needs three parts. The first is the sender. The second is the receiver. The third is the message. Communication depends on all three parts. The message must go from the sender to the receiver. The sender must make the message clear. The receiver must pay attention or the receiver might misunderstand. Then communication breaks down.

◀ Every communication requires a sender, a receiver, and a message. **What might prevent a message from getting through to a receiver?**

When you express yourself clearly and understand other people, you can communicate effectively. Healthy relationships have a lot to do with how you communicate. The better you communicate, the stronger your relationships are likely to be. Good communication skills can help you succeed in all parts of your life. Let's look at the two types of communication: verbal and nonverbal.

 **Reading Check** **List** What are the three parts of any communication?

Verbal Communication

Jenna and Paul used words to talk about their report. Their report will use words to express their ideas. These are examples of verbal communication. **Verbal communication** is *expressing feelings, thoughts, or experiences with words, either by speaking or writing.* This is the kind of communication people use most. Verbal communication lets you read a book, a magazine, an Internet site, or a street sign. It lets you keep in touch with people by phone, in person, and by writing letters and e-mail. It also lets you enjoy television, radio, and films.

Nonverbal Communication

You can send a clear message even when you don't say anything at all. When you smile, wave, or high-five a teammate after winning a relay race, you're using nonverbal communication. **Nonverbal communication** is *getting messages across without using words.* It uses **body language**—*postures, gestures, and facial expressions*—to send messages.

Body language is a powerful tool for nonverbal communication. It can give your words extra meaning. It can also send messages you're not aware of. If you feel calm and sure of yourself when speaking to a group, your body language will show it. For example, someone who feels disapproval might cross his or her arms or frown.

 **Reading Check** **Name** Give two examples of nonverbal communication.

▶ Body language is important in nonverbal communication. **What does the body language of these teens tell you?**

Connect To... Social Studies

Communication Across Cultures

Each culture has its own ways to communicate nonverbally. People of some cultures bow to show respect. People of other cultures feel that making direct eye contact during conversation is disrespectful. In the United States, people usually shake hands when they meet for the first time.

Research how nonverbal communication varies across cultures. Record your information in a chart. In your chart, include a description of each example and what it communicates.

▲ Being a good listener is part of communicating effectively. **How can you tell that one of these teens is demonstrating good listening skills?**

Go Online

Visit **glencoe.com** and complete the **Interactive Study Guide for Lesson 1.**

Communicating Effectively

Healthy relationships depend on good communication skills. For others to understand your message, it must be clear. Careful listening is also necessary for effective communication. It shows people that you are interested in what they wish to share.

Speaking Skills

When you express yourself clearly in words, people understand what you mean. Here are some tips for speaking effectively.

- Think about what you want to say.

- Use "I" messages to express your thoughts, feelings, needs, and expectations. For example, you might say, "The way I feel about writing the lab report is. . ." This keeps the focus on the message you are trying to get across.

- Use **tact,** *the sense of what to do or say to avoid offending others.* Avoid being rude or insulting.

- Make clear, simple statements. Be specific. Use examples when you express ideas or give suggestions.

Listening Skills

Effective communication also involves listening carefully. Here are some ways to be a good listener:

- Use body language to show you are listening carefully. Lean a bit toward the speaker. Look him or her directly in the eye. From time to time, nod and respond with facial expressions and other body movements.

- Take advantage of pauses in the conversation to offer encouragement. Use phrases such as "Really?" or "Tell me more about that." This shows that you are paying attention. It will also help the speaker feel comfortable about continuing to share.

- Do not interrupt. There may be times when you want the speaker to clarify a statement. Politely ask questions until you are sure you understand its meaning.

- When possible, mirror what you hear. Repeat or rephrase the speaker's thoughts and feelings as you understand them. Be sympathetic to show you understand how the speaker feels.

Writing Skills

You probably communicate in writing every day. You might write e-mails, text messages, or notes. Writing out your thoughts can have advantages. For example, you can make changes before you send your message. However, there are also challenges. If a written message isn't clear, the receiver can't always ask you what you meant. The person can't hear your tone of voice. He or she can't see your face or your body language. This can cause misunderstandings.

You can limit misunderstandings by working on your written communication skills. For starters, think about keeping a journal. You'll create a record of your experiences while you practice writing. Are there people you usually keep in touch with by phone? These might be family members or out-of-town friends. Why not send a letter or an extended e-mail message next time?

▲ E-mail and instant messaging are popular forms of communication. **How might electronic communication lead to confusion or misunderstandings?**

 Reading Check   **Explain** Why is it a good idea to use tact when speaking to others?

Lesson 1 Review

 **After You Read**

Review this lesson for new terms, major headings, and Reading Checks.

What I Learned

1. **Vocabulary** Define *communication*.

2. **Identify** What are the two types of communication?

3. **Give Examples** List two ways to show that you are listening carefully.

4. **Explain** Explain how body language plays a part in communication.

Thinking Critically

5. **Apply** Imagine you are having an emotional discussion with a friend. Each of your friend's comments begins with "You always. . ." or "You make me feel. . ." and other similar phrases. How would you react to hearing them?

6. **Synthesize** What are some nonverbal ways to show consideration for others?

Applying Health Skills

7. **Communication Skills** Using tact is an important skill. Imagine that a friend asked for your opinion about a jacket he or she was thinking of buying. You don't think the jacket looks good. How might you give your opinion honestly but tactfully?

Go Online   For more Lesson Review Activities, go to **glencoe.com**.

Lesson 1: Building Communication Skills   **177**

Lesson 2

Understanding Family Relationships

Guide to Reading

● Building Vocabulary
Write a definition for each term below. As you read this lesson, make changes to the definitions as needed.

- family (p. 178)
- nurture (p. 179)

● Focusing on the Main Ideas
In this lesson, you will be able to

- **describe** the family as the basic unit of society.
- **recognize** the functions of the family.
- **list** ways to improve family relationships.
- **identify** ways to cope with changes in the family.

● Reading Strategy
Skimming Look over the major and minor headings in this lesson. Skimming the lesson will give you an idea of what it is about.

Quick Write

Write two or three sentences that describe how family members might help each other when they face the challenge of moving.

Everyone Is Part of a Family

The **family** is *the basic unit of society and includes two or more people joined by blood, marriage, adoption, or a desire to support one another.*

Families give people a place to belong. Your family is part of a community, a state, and a country. Your family teaches you values, beliefs, and expectations.

Families can be large or small. People within them may have a number of different relationships. Some different types of families are listed below.

- A couple consists of two adults living together.

- A nuclear family consists of a husband and wife and their child or children.

- A blended family consists of one stepparent, one parent, and one or more children.

- A single-parent family consists of one parent and one or more children.

- An extended family consists of parents, children, and other family members (such as grandparents) living together.

 Reading Check **Identify** Name two types of families.

How Families Help Their Members

A family takes care of physical needs, providing food, water, and shelter for its members. A family also takes care of mental needs. It teaches its members life skills, answers questions, and helps expand knowledge. A family takes care of emotional needs, including love, trust, and security. Most of all, a family nurtures. To **nurture** means *to fulfill physical, mental/emotional, and social needs.* **Figure 6.1** shows examples of the ways a family nurtures its members.

As you grow up, your family helps you develop values and beliefs. These come from your family's way of life, traditions, culture, and religious beliefs. Your values and beliefs influence the decisions you make, even as an adult. They can influence the type of activities you participate in, the foods you eat, and the type of health care you choose. Your values and beliefs can even help you choose not to participate in risky behaviors, such as using tobacco, alcohol, or drugs.

 **Reading Check** **Name** What are the three kinds of needs that families meet?

▼ **FIGURE 6.1**

How Family Members Care for Each Other

Family members meet each other's needs. **What mental needs do families meet?**

Physical Needs Family members take care of each other with food, clothing, and shelter.

Mental Needs In a family, adults and children share knowledge, skills, and experience.

Emotional Needs Family members give each other love, acceptance, and support.

Social Needs Families teach their members how to get along with each other and with people outside the family.

▲ Family members have different roles and responsibilities. **Can you name some of the roles these family members might have?**

Academic Vocabulary

appreciate (uh PREE shee ayt) (verb) to be thankful for, to understand, to increase in value. *I appreciate your help with the science fair.*

Roles and Responsibilities

Every family member has one or more roles, such as parent, child, or sibling. There are responsibilities that come with each role. For example, parents are responsible for providing a place to live, food, and other basic needs for their children. Parents are also expected to teach their children and provide love and emotional support. Children have responsibilities, too. They are expected to cooperate and respect their parents. They may be expected to help with chores around the house. As a teen, your role may include helping younger siblings or grandparents.

As you get older, your roles and responsibilities will change as your family's needs change. You may take on new roles as an adult, such as spouse or parent. A person's role is always growing or changing depending on his or her age or stage of life.

Roles are very important to family life. They help families deal with the challenges of daily life. Sharing roles and responsibilities can help build strong family relationships.

Building Family Relationships

People in strong families feel connected. They enjoy spending time together. Below are some ways that families can strengthen their relationships.

- **Show appreciation for each other.** Families grow stronger when they show that they feel thankful for each other. A simple "Thank you" can show others you notice their efforts. You can also help them when they need it.

- **Support other family members.** Knowing that your family believes in you adds meaning to your successes. It also makes failure easier to handle. Show support for people in your family. Take part in events that are important to them. Help them when they need it.

- **Spend quality time together.** Set aside time for activities everyone enjoys. Spending mealtimes together can help families stay connected.

- **Communicate effectively.** Talking openly helps everyone resolve disagreements. It also helps develop trust and respect. Your discussions should not focus only on problems but on all topics important to people in your family.

Health Skills Activity

Communication Skills

Communicating with Parents or Guardians

Tyler has been dreaming of playing football for a while now. Tryouts for the local team are in two weeks. Tyler needs to talk to his parents first, but he is worried they will not understand how he feels about playing the sport. They want him to have enough time to do homework and study, and practices will take up a lot of time. Tyler is unsure about how to talk to his parents about playing football.

With a Group

Write a script showing how Tyler talks to his parents about playing football. Use the techniques below to effectively communicate ideas, thoughts, needs, and feelings. Role-play your conversation for the class.

- State clear reasons for your request.
- Use "I" messages.
- Use a respectful tone and stay calm.
- Use appropriate listening skills.
- Be willing to compromise.

- **Show responsibility.** Some families have charts showing who does certain household tasks each week. When it's your turn, do your job without being asked. When you share work equally in your family, you appreciate each other's efforts.

- **Show respect.** Speak to family members in a respectful tone of voice. Show respect for one another's differences. Don't tease or make fun of your siblings or other relatives. Respect each other's privacy and personal belongings, too. Don't borrow items without permission.

- **Follow family rules.** In your family, you may have rules for when to be home or when you need permission to do an activity. Many families also have rules about telephone, television, or computer use. Following the rules set by your parents or guardians helps build trust within your family.

 **Reading Check** **List** Give three examples of ways to keep family relationships strong.

DEVELOPING Good Character

Responsibility

Think of how you fit into your family. Are you a brother, a sister, a son, a daughter, a grandchild, a niece, or a nephew? What are your responsibilities to your family? How do you help others?

Make a list of words that you feel describe your family role and responsibilities. Survey family members. Ask them to choose words that describe you. How do the two lists compare?

POSITIVE WAYS TO COPE WITH CHANGE IN THE FAMILY

Changes that happen in a family affect all family members. **What are some serious changes that can affect families?**

CHANGE	POSITIVE WAYS TO COPE
Moving to a new home	Before the move, look at a map of your new neighborhood. Find your new house, your school, and nearby parks. When in a new neighborhood, try to meet other teens.
Separation, divorce, or remarriage of parents	Tell both parents you love them. Talk to them or to another trusted adult about how you feel. A separation or divorce is not your fault.
Job change or job loss	If the family needs to limit spending for a while, ask how you can help.
Birth or adoption of a new sibling	Spend time with your new sibling. Ask your parents how you can help. Imagine what your relationship might be like in the future.
Illness or injury	Show that you care about a sick or injured family member by spending time with him or her and asking how you can help.
Death, loss, and grief	Accept the ways family members express grief. Don't expect their ways of coping to be the same as yours. Pay extra attention to younger members of the family.

Go Online

Visit **glencoe.com** and complete the Interactive Study Guide for Lesson 2.

Coping with Change

Changes and challenges are a normal part of family life. During difficult changes, keeping up normal routines can help younger family members feel secure. Talking openly can help families decide how to best handle changes. Sometimes outside help is needed to deal with serious changes. Family members can go to counselors, health care workers, religious leaders, or people from law enforcement to get help. They may see legal advisors. **Figure 6.2** above lists some changes that can affect families. It also describes some positive strategies for coping with these changes.

Families Work Together

For most people, the family stands at the center of their lives. Children turn to family for learning, love, and security. They learn how to build relationships and stand on their own. As adults, people usually feel that building families is very important. People who enjoy healthy family relationships are more likely to enjoy healthy relationships with others.

 **Reading Check** **Identify** Name two ways families work together.

▶ Appreciating each other goes a long way toward building and maintaining good family relationships. **How can you show respect for members of your family?**

Lesson 2 Review

After You Read

Review this lesson for new terms, major headings, and Reading Checks.

What I Learned

1. *Vocabulary* Define *nurture*.

2. *Explain* What is the connection between family nurturing and the well-being of society?

3. *Give Examples* What are two ways to strengthen family relationships?

4. *Identify* Name two changes that a family might face.

Thinking Critically

5. *Apply* Describe three ways that a teen can support a family member in need.

6. *Infer* How might spending time with extended family members strengthen a teen's mental/emotional health?

Applying Health Skills

7. *Analyzing Influences* Think of a television show about a family. What kinds of relationships do the actors play out? Write a few sentences to describe this family. Do you think this TV family is realistic and healthy? Why or why not?

Your Friendships and Peer Pressure

Guide to Reading

● Building Vocabulary

As you read this lesson, write each new term and its definition in your notebook.

- friendship (p. 184)
- acquaintance (p. 184)
- compromise (p. 186)
- peers (p. 187)
- peer pressure (p. 187)
- assertive response (p. 187)

● Focusing on the Main Ideas

In this lesson, you will be able to

- **explain** why friends are important.
- **identify** the characteristics of a good friendship.
- **recognize** ways of keeping friendships strong.
- **describe** ways to resist negative peer pressure.

● Reading Strategy

Identifying Cause and Effect After reading this lesson, write a list of ways to build strong friendships.

Quick Write

Write a brief paragraph describing someone you know who is a good friend to others.

Friends Are Important

The family is one source from which children learn social skills. Friendships are another. A **friendship** is *a relationship with someone you know, trust, and regard with affection.* Your friends usually are people who live near you or who like the same things you do. Friends also have similar values. Strong friendships are a building block for social health.

Strong friendships take time to develop. Some people have only one close friend, while others have several. Some people have many acquaintances. An **acquaintance** is *someone you see occasionally or know casually.* In time, some of your acquaintances may become your close friends.

Having friends teaches you to communicate, work out problems, and compromise. You learn to give others support and to consider their feelings. Friendships also let you share your life, the good and the bad, with people who know you well.

◀ Having someone with you to share good times is one of the benefits of friendship. **What are some other benefits of friendship?**

Traits of a Good Friend

Some people confuse the terms *friend* and *acquaintance*. A friend is much more than an acquaintance. Friends are people you spend lots of time with and know very well. You value your friendships. In fact, they may be some of your most important relationships. Good friendships make you and your life better. People form friendships for many reasons. They may have common interests. They may live in the same neighborhood. Most friendships have the following qualities.

What Teens THINK

What makes a good friend?

A good friend is someone who listens and is always there when you need to talk. She or he also has to have the same interests. This is what I think makes a good friend.

Emily P.
Tucson, AZ

- **Trust.** Good friendships are based on honesty. Friends share their thoughts openly. You can also trust good friends to support you in tough times.

- **Caring.** True friends care about each other's well-being. A good friend will listen and try to understand how you feel. True friends recognize your strengths and help you build on them. They accept you as you are.

- **Respect.** Friends may not all share the same beliefs, but that's okay. Good friends respect each other's differences and treat each other as equals. They won't ask you to do anything that could hurt you or put you in danger. They won't expect you to act against your values.

- **Loyalty.** True friends stay together in good times and bad. They support each other and forgive mistakes. A loyal friend will not let others say untrue or mean things about you.

Reading Check **Identify** What are two traits of good friendship?

Building Friendships

Some people make friends easily, while others find it more difficult. Making new friends can be easier when you join groups who have interests similar to yours. Check out a sports team or a club. You are more likely to meet people who share your interests when you spend time doing activities that you like. **Figure 6.3** on the next page shows some ways to build friendships.

▼ FIGURE 6.3

BUILDING STRONG FRIENDSHIPS

One way to build strong friendships is to help friends when they need it. **Name two other ways to build strong friendships.**

Spend more time with your friends.

Identify problems and try to resolve them.

Communicate openly and honestly.

Be there when your friends need help.

Encourage your friends to go for their goals.

Careers for the 21st Century

Social Worker

Social workers help people deal with a wide range of problems, including family relationships, unemployment, and serious illness. As the population of the U.S. gets older, more social workers who specialize in helping older people will be needed. You can prepare for a career in social work by taking sociology, family & consumer science, and pschology courses.

What skills does a social worker need? Go to *Career Corner* at glencoe.com to find out.

Building and maintaining positive friendships is important. You can build stronger friendships through tolerance. *Tolerance* is the ability to accept other people as they are. This means that you are respectful of a person's individual differences, race, or culture. Tolerance will help you get along better with your friends and acquaintances.

Knowing When to Compromise

Being friends with someone does not guarantee that you will never have disagreements. You might even argue. Sometimes it is hard to find a solution. What do you do when this happens?

In most cases, you can choose to protect your friendship by working out your differences. When disagreements happen, friends are willing to compromise. **Compromise** is *when both sides in a conflict agree to give up something in order to reach a solution that satisfies everyone.* Friends may need to compromise on what to do when they are together or when they want others to join their social circle. They may need to find a way to meet in the middle when they disagree.

Compromise is the answer for many disagreements, but sometimes it is not the best choice. For example, you should never compromise when you would have to act against your values. You should not compromise when you might end up harming yourself or others. If a friend asks you to do something you know is unlawful or wrong, you should always be firm and say no.

 **Reading Check** **Define** What is compromise?

Peer Pressure

Most of your friends are probably your **peers,** *people close to you in age who are a lot like you.* Sometimes teens worry about what their friends think about them. Your friends' opinions can affect how you act. This is called **peer pressure,** *the influence that your peer group has on you.* Peer pressure can be negative or positive.

Negative Peer Pressure

Friends should not pressure you to do something that is unhealthy or unsafe, or that goes against your family's values. For example, friends should not pressure you to use tobacco, alcohol or other drugs. They should not ask to copy your homework or ask you to break the rules of your school or community. True friends will respect your choices.

Negative peer pressure can take many forms. Encouraging a person to act in a way that is harmful or illegal is one form of negative pressure. Other forms include bribes, dares, or threats. Negative peer pressure can also come in the form of teasing or name-calling. You can learn to recognize negative peer pressure by using the **H.E.L.P.** criteria. **H.E.L.P.** stands for **H**ealthful, **E**thical, **L**egal, and **P**arent approved. If what your friends are asking you to do doesn't fit the criteria, don't go along. **Figure 6.4** shows you some effective ways to resist negative peer pressure.

Visit glencoe.com and complete the Interactive Study Guide for Lesson 3.

▼ FIGURE 6.4

RESISTING NEGATIVE PEER PRESSURE

Resisting peer pressure is a skill you can learn. How can you handle negative peer pressure in your life?

▶ Avoid the Situation.
If you can tell that a situation might be unsafe or harmful, don't participate.

▶ Use assertive responses.
If your friends want to involve you in a dangerous situation, say no. Use an **assertive response.** This is *a response that declares your position strongly and confidently.*

▶ Focus on the issue.
If your friends make fun of you. Don't defend yourself or trade insults.

▶ Walk away.
It's best to talk things out with friends who try to pressure you. If someone becomes angry, walk away.

Positive Peer Pressure

Your friends give positive peer pressure when they suggest you do the right thing. They may encourage you to study more. They may advise you to work on a group project or become a volunteer. They may suggest you join the science club at school or ask you to welcome new people into the group. Friends can help you say no to risk behaviors, such as using tobacco. Positive peer pressure can be good for you. It can improve your health and safety and help you feel better about yourself.

 **Reading Check** **Explain** What is an assertive response?

◀ Your peers can have a positive influence on your health. **Give an example of positive peer pressure.**

Lesson 3 Review

 After You Read

Review this lesson for new terms, major headings, and Reading Checks.

What I Learned

1. *Vocabulary* Define *friendship*.

2. *Identify* What are three qualities of a good friend?

3. *List* Name three ways to build strong friendships.

4. *Distinguish* What is the difference between negative and positive peer pressure?

5. *Explain* When is it important to walk away from a situation in which you face negative peer pressure?

Thinking Critically

6. *Analyze* Why is tolerance important to a healthy society?

7. *Comparing and Contrasting* Explain the consequences that both positive and negative influences from a peer can have on a teen's life.

Applying Health Skills

8. *Analyzing Influences* Do you think adults experience as much pressure from their peers as teens do? Write a brief paragraph explaining why or why not.

 **Go Online** For more Lesson Review Activities, go to glencoe.com.

Abstinence and Refusal Skills

Guide to Reading

Building Vocabulary

As you read this lesson, write each new highlighted term, its definition, and an example.

- risk behaviors (p. 190)
- abstinence (p. 190)
- refusal skills (p. 192)

Focusing on the Main Ideas

In this lesson, you will be able to

- **identify** risk behaviors.
- **recognize** the benefits of abstaining from the use of tobacco, alcohol, and other drugs.
- **recognize** the benefits of practicing abstinence from sexual activity.
- **apply** refusal skills by using the S.T.O.P. formula.

Reading Strategy

Finding the Main Idea Review all the headings in this lesson. For each main heading, write one sentence that states what you think the main idea of the section will be.

Quick Write

Write a brief paragraph explaining why teens should avoid risk behaviors.

Acting Responsibly

Growing up means taking on more responsibility in all areas of life. Your parents recognize that you can make decisions for yourself and choose right from wrong. This additional responsibility also leads to more freedom. You might be allowed to go more places by yourself or with your friends.

Your responsibilities include taking care of your body and mind. How can you show responsibility for yourself? Some ways are simple, such as choosing healthy foods. Some are more challenging, such as staying away from risk behaviors.

◀ As you grow up, adults trust you with more responsibilities. **What kinds of responsibilities are associated with being a teen?**

Abstinence from Risk Behaviors

Risk is a part of life. You take a risk when you make a new friend or when you compete in a sporting event. Risks can be scary at times, but they are often worthwhile. As you get older, you will take risks when you choose a career, a place to live, and make other life decisions. These are positive risks that will help you grow.

Not all risks are worth taking, however. It just doesn't make sense to engage in risk behaviors that could put you or your health in danger. **Risk behaviors** are *actions or choices that may harm you or others.* Using tobacco, alcohol, or illegal drugs are risk behaviors. Other risk behaviors include engaging in sexual activity or breaking the law.

A teen's best response to risk behaviors is **abstinence,** which is *the conscious, active choice not to participate in high-risk behaviors.* By abstaining from risk behaviors, you can avoid serious negative consequences. For example, when teens abstain from sexual activity, they don't have to worry about unplanned pregnancy or exposure to sexually transmitted diseases.

Avoiding risk behaviors will benefit your physical, mental/emotional, and social health. **Figure 6.5** shows some of the benefits of practicing abstinence.

 **Reading Check**   **Identify** What are some risk behaviors that teens should avoid?

Abstinence from Tobacco, Alcohol, and Other Drugs

Abstaining from using tobacco, alcohol, and other drugs is the most healthful choice. It protects you from the dangers of using these substances. The dangers include:

- **Harm to your physical health.** Tobacco, alcohol, and other drugs can seriously affect your body and mind. Smoking is linked to heart and lung disease, including cancer. Alcohol and other drugs can harm the liver and nervous system.

- **Risk of becoming dependent.** If you start using tobacco, alcohol, or other drugs, you may not be able to quit without help from a health care professional.

▼ Teens can let others know they don't approve of risk behaviors in a variety of ways. **What might these teens hope to achieve through this event?**

FIGURE 6.5

BENEFITS OF ABSTINENCE FROM RISK BEHAVIORS

Practicing abstinence protects all areas of your health. **How does abstinence protect your social health?**

Risk Behavior	Benefits of Practicing Abstinence
Tobacco use	• Avoid becoming dependent • Reduce the risk of lung cancer and other diseases • Keep clothes, hair, and breath smelling fresh • Protect others from breathing tobacco smoke
Alcohol and other drug use	• Avoid becoming dependent • Protect the heart, liver, and nervous system • Stay focused on goals and dreams • Avoid legal consequences
Sexual activity	• Prevent STDs, including HIV/AIDS • Avoid unplanned pregnancy • Protect self-esteem and earn others' respect • Build better relationships

- **Having trouble with the law.** Society recognizes that alcohol and tobacco are not **appropriate** for young people. As a result, it is illegal to use tobacco if you are under 18 and illegal to use alcohol if you are under 21. Using certain drugs, such as marijuana or cocaine, is illegal for everyone. Having or using these illegal substances can lead to serious legal consequences.

- **Not reaching your goals.** Using tobacco, alcohol, or other drugs affects every area of your life and can threaten the goals you set for yourself. These risk behaviors can harm your physical health and hurt your performance in school. They can decrease your commitment to abstain from sexual activity. Your relationships can suffer, too.

You know how harmful these risk behaviors are for your health. The most healthful decision is to avoid them.

Abstinence from Sexual Activity

The decision to become sexually active requires maturity and responsibility. These character traits are still developing during the teen years. As a result, abstinence from sexual activity until marriage is the best choice for teens. By abstaining from sexual activity, teens can focus on building healthy relationships and fulfilling their dreams and goals.

Academic Vocabulary

appropriate (uh pro PREE uht) *(adj)* acceptable, agrees with some custom or rule, suitable for the purpose. *Reading or studying quietly is appropriate behavior in the library.*

G Online

Visit **glencoe.com** and complete the Interactive Study Guide for Lesson 4.

Abstinence from sexual activity is the only responsible choice for teens. Why? People who abstain from sexual activity until marriage never have to worry about unplanned pregnancy and the difficult decisions that go with it, such as adoption. They don't have to worry about sexually transmitted diseases (STDs). Abstinence until marriage is the only method that is completely effective in avoiding STDs and unplanned pregnancy.

Abstinence also gives teens freedom to get to know people without the pressure of engaging in sexual activity. They can develop appropriate feelings of love and trust without the emotional worries that come with sexual activity.

Practicing abstinence reflects respect for yourself and for others. If you want to show others you care for them, you can do so in healthful ways that don't involve sexual activity. You can offer support to others by talking to them, by listening to their opinions, or by hugging or holding hands to show affection.

 **Reading Check**

Describe Name two positive consequences of abstaining from sexual activity.

▼ There are many healthy ways to show affection and respect. **How are these teens showing their affection for each other?**

Developing Effective Refusal Skills

To avoid engaging in risk behaviors, you need to know and practice **refusal skills,** or *strategies that help you say no effectively.* Refusal skills are useful whenever you feel pressure to do something you do not want to do. The S.T.O.P. formula can help you remember four effective refusal skills.

- **S**ay no in a firm voice.
- **T**ell why not.
- **O**ffer another idea.
- **P**romptly leave.

When you say no, make sure your body language matches what you are saying. Offer brief but sensible reasons for your choice. Suggest an alternative activity that everyone can enjoy. If you have to, leave the scene. That immediately takes away someone's power to pressure you into something you do not want to do.

 **Reading Check**

Explain What does S.T.O.P. stand for?

Health Skills Activity

Refusal Skills

Saying No to Risk Behaviors

It's Saturday night and Zoe is at a party at a friend's house. At first it, seems like a fun party. However, Zoe soon realizes that her friend's parents are not home and some of the people who show up are older. She notices a lot of people smoking. She even sees a few bottles of beer around. Zoe decides this party is not for her. She calls her parents to pick her up. While she's waiting, someone offers her a cigarette.

What Would You Do?

Using the S.T.O.P. formula, write down what you would say to refuse the cigarette. The formula involves the following steps:

- Say no in a firm voice.
- Tell why not.
- Offer another idea.
- Promptly leave.

Lesson 4 Review

 After You Read

Review this lesson for new terms, major headings, and Reading Checks.

What I Learned

1. *Vocabulary* What is *abstinence*?

2. *Identify* Give two examples of risk behaviors.

3. *List* What are three benefits of not using alcohol?

4. *Describe* What are three benefits of abstaining from sexual activity until marriage?

5. *Explain* What are the four steps of the S.T.O.P. formula?

Thinking Critically

6. *Apply* Suppose one of your friends started smoking. What would you tell him in order to help him make a healthy choice?

7. *Analyze* Think of a risk behavior that could have long-term negative effects for a teen. Analyze what these effects might be. Explain the effects in a short paragraph.

Applying Health Skills

8. *Decision Making* Suppose a friend wants you to take part in a risk behavior. In a brief paragraph, apply the steps of the decision-making process to make a responsible choice in this situation.

Building Health Skills

Accessing Information

Practicing Healthful Behaviors

Stress Management

Analyzing Influences

Communication Skills

Refusal Skills

Conflict Resolution

Decision Making

Goal Setting

Advocacy

What Are Communication Skills?

Communication Skills involve learning how to effectively express yourself and understand others.

Speaking Skills

- Think before you speak.
- Use "I" messages.
- Be direct, but avoid being rude or insulting.
- Make eye contact, and use appropriate body language.

Listening Skills

- Use conversation encouragers.
- Pay attention.
- Show empathy.
- Avoid interrupting, but ask questions where appropriate.

Expressing Your Feelings

Follow the Model, Practice, and Apply steps to help you master this important health skill.

❶ Model

Read how Jasmine uses communication skills to work out a conflict with her friend, Holly.

Holly was disappointed that her babysitting job was canceled. She was counting on the money she would earn to buy a new CD. When Holly tried to tell Jasmine how disappointed she was, Jasmine just brushed her off. Holly was angry and avoided Jasmine for the rest of the day.

The next day, Jasmine used the communication skills she had learned to work things out with Holly. She found Holly and started the conversation with this "I" message. "I feel bad about not paying more attention to your problem. I know you were looking forward to buying that CD. *(shows empathy)* Did you find out why the babysitting job was canceled?" *(ask questions)* Jasmine listened while Holly explained and soon the girls were on good terms again.

❷ Practice

Kayla wants to use communication skills to show support for her brother, Alec. Read the passage and then practice communication skills by answering the questions that follow.

Kayla's younger brother Alec is upset about the low grade he received on his science paper. Kayla knows that Alec didn't spend much time working on the paper and is about to criticize him for it. Then she stops herself and decides to use better communication skills.

1. What should Kayla say and do in her conversation with Alec?
2. How can Kayla show empathy?
3. In what way is Kayla strengthening the relationships within her family?

❸ Apply

Apply what you have learned about using good communication skills by completing the activity below.

With a small group, brainstorm family situations that require good communication skills. Choose one of the situations and write a script showing behaviors, dialogue, and body language that demonstrate good communication skills. When you're finished, exchange scripts with another group. Read the group's script and label the communication skills that are used. Describe how the communication would contribute to the health of the family.

Self-Check
- Did we include evidence of good communication in our script?
- Did we correctly identify the communication skills used?
- Did my group describe how the communication would build healthy relationships in the family?

One Story, Three Endings

Conflicts happen because people have different wants, needs, and opinions. There are at least three ways to handle conflict: denial, confrontation, and problem solving. Denial is when people don't admit they are angry and don't talk about their feelings. Confrontation happens when the people are not willing to listen to each other or refuse to compromise. Problem solving occurs when people talk about the problem without insulting or blaming each other.

What You Will Need

- The story: Omar and Lou are playing basketball. Peter comes over and asks if he can play.

- Ending #1: Omar says, "Sure." Lou doesn't like Peter and would rather that he didn't play. Instead of saying anything, he just shrugs his shoulders and keeps playing, yet he doesn't try to do well. Peter asks him what's bothering him. Lou says, "Nothing."

- Ending #2: Omar says, "Sure." Lou claims that Peter always cheats and hogs the ball. Peter replies, "You don't want me to play because I'm better than you." Lou throws the basketball down and walks away.

- Ending #3: Omar says, "Sure." Lou says no because Peter always hogs the ball. Omar suggests they take turns and trade off after every three shots so no one will have to wait long. They all agree and start to play.

What You Will Do

1. Your teacher will divide the class into groups of three. In your group, read the story using the first ending. Then, answer these questions on a sheet of paper: Does this solution make someone angry? Who? Were the boys listening to each other? Did they understand each other's feelings?

2. Read the story again using the second ending and answer the same questions.

3. Read the story again using the third ending and answer the questions once more.

Wrapping It Up

You should be able to recognize the three conflict resolution styles in the three endings of the story. The best ending is when problem solving takes place.

Reading Review

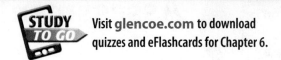

Visit glencoe.com to download quizzes and eFlashcards for Chapter 6.

FOLDABLES Study Organizer

Foldables® and Other Study Aids Take out the Foldable® that you created for Lesson 1 and any graphic organizers that you created for Lessons 1–4. Find a partner and quiz each other using these study aids.

Lesson 1 Building Communication Skills

Main Idea Good communication skills involve sending a clear message and listening carefully to messages from others.

- The two types of communication are verbal and nonverbal.
- To speak effectively you should use "I" messages, use tact, and be specific.
- To be a good listener, use body language to show interest, do not interrupt, and mirror what you hear.

Lesson 2 Understanding Family Relationships

Main Idea Families work together to meet the physical, mental/emotional, and social needs of each member.

- The family is the basic unit of society.
- Ways to build strong family relationships include showing appreciation, supporting each other, spending time together, communicating effectively, showing responsibility and respect, and following family rules.
- Talking openly can help families cope with changes.

Lesson 3 Your Friendships and Peer Pressure

Main Idea Building strong friendships is important to good social health.

- Good friendships have the qualities of trust, caring, respect, and loyalty.
- Positive peer pressure can influence you to make healthy choices. Negative peer pressure can influence you to act in a way that may be harmful or illegal.
- Resist negative peer pressure by avoiding harmful situations, walking away, or using assertive responses to say no.

Lesson 4 Abstinence and Refusal Skills

Main Idea Abstaining from risk behaviors, such as tobacco, alcohol, drug use, and sexual activity, is the healthy choice for teens.

- Abstaining from tobacco, alcohol, and drug use protects your physical health, protects you from legal consequences, and allows you to focus on your goals.
- Abstaining from sexual activity until marriage prevents unplanned pregnancy and STDs, including HIV/AIDS.
- Refusal skills, such as the S.T.O.P. strategy, can help you say no to risk behaviors.

After You Read

Health eSpotlight

VIDEO

Now that you have read the chapter, look back at your answer to the Health eSpotlight question on the chapter opener. Have your ideas changed? What would your answer be now?

Reviewing Vocabulary and Main Ideas

On a sheet of paper, write the numbers 1–5. After each number, write the term from the list that best completes each statement.

- tact
- family
- body language
- verbal communication
- nurture
- role
- compromise

Lesson 1 Building Communication Skills

1. Expressing your feelings, thoughts, and experiences in words, through speaking or writing, is _____.

2. _____ includes posture, gestures, and facial expressions that send messages.

3. Knowing what is appropriate to say is known as _____.

Lesson 2 Understanding Family Relationships

4. The _____ is the basic unit of society and includes two or more people brought together by blood, marriage, adoption, or a desire for mutual support.

5. To _____ is to fulfill physical, mental/emotional, and social needs.

*On a sheet of paper, write the numbers 6–16. Write **True** or **False** for each statement below. If the statement is false, change the underlined word or phrase to make it true.*

Lesson 3 Friendships and Peer Pressure

6. The influence that people your own age have on you is called <u>nurturing</u>.

7. You can use the <u>H.E.L.P.</u> criteria to resist negative peer pressure.

8. <u>Trust</u> is a trait of good friendships.

9. Friends urging you to come to a party where there might be alcohol is an example of <u>positive</u> peer pressure.

10. An <u>acquaintance</u> is someone you see occasionally or know casually.

11. <u>Tolerance</u> involves accepting others as they are.

Lesson 4 Abstinence and Refusal Skills

12. Teens should practice <u>abstinence</u> when it comes to risk behaviors.

13. Part of developing good <u>refusal skills</u> is learning how to apply the S.T.O.P. formula.

14. Using tobacco is a <u>risk behavior</u>.

15. A teen who practices abstinence from risk behaviors such as sexual activity or using tobacco, alcohol, or other drugs <u>will</u> experience negative legal consequences.

16. Tobacco, alcohol, and other drugs can <u>seriously affect</u> your mind and body.

Go Online Visit glencoe.com and take the Online Quiz for Chapter 6.

Thinking Critically

Using complete sentences, answer the following questions on a sheet of paper.

17. **Analyze** How do positive relationships affect your physical and mental/emotional health?

18. **Infer** What effect does abstaining from risk behaviors have on your relationships?

Write About It

19. **Descriptive Writing** Design a greeting card for someone who has had a positive influence on your life. Write a message for the inside of the card that includes specific examples of how that person has positively influenced your life.

20. **Narrative Writing** Write a skit that shows a situation in which a teen uses each step of the S.T.O.P. formula to refuse to participate in a risk behavior.

✈ Applying Technology

Relationships Made Real

Use a digital camera to create a PowerPoint® presentation that reflects a clear understanding of good communication skills. Follow the steps below to complete your project.

- Take 5-7 digital images of students on campus interacting with peers.
- Import the images into your photo software for later use.
- Write a script, using a dialogue format, to accompany each photograph taken. Be sure the dialogue uses both verbal and nonverbal communication.
- Open a new PowerPoint® project with 3-5 slides. Select the slide layout that has both an image and text box, side by side.
- Import one image onto each slide. Type dialogue text on each slide. Make sure your message is clearly delivered.
- Save your work.

Standardized Test Practice

Directions for Writing

Write an essay to persuade your principal to organize more after-school activities. Give some examples of activities you think would be worthwhile. Think of some benefits you feel these activities would have, and explain them in your essay. Use a respectful tone, but take a firm position.

TEST-TAKING TIP

Budget your time during an essay test. Read over all the essay questions and give yourself guidelines for how much time to spend answering each one.

Writing

You know that spending time with your friends builds stronger friendships. Strong friendships and positive peer pressure can add to your school success and your overall good health. You'd like to see your school offer more after-school activities. You think this is a good idea for several reasons: First, these activities would strengthen relationships between students. Second, parents would have a safe place for their children to go after school. Third, teens would have fun and improve their skills.

7 Resolving Conflicts and Preventing Violence

Chapter Preview

Lesson 1 Understanding Conflict 202

Lesson 2 Conflict-Resolution Skills.............................. 206

Lesson 3 Preventing Violence 211

Lesson 4 Getting Help for Abuse 217

Building Health Skills...................... 222

TIME health news 224

Chapter Reading Review................. 225

Chapter Assessment 226

▲ *Working with the Photo*

Bullying can happen to any student. **What can you do to prevent bullying at your school?**

Start-Up Activities

Before You Read What do you do to resolve conflicts? Take the short health survey below. Keep a record of your answers.

HEALTH INVENTORY

1. During conflict, I take time to calm down.
(a) always   (b) sometimes   (c) never

2. I try not to judge people by how they look.
(a) always   (b) sometimes   (c) never

3. I take steps to avoid violent situations.
(a) always   (b) sometimes   (c) never

FOLDABLES Study Organizer

As You Read Make this Foldable® to help you organize what you learn in Lesson 1 about the causes of conflict. Begin with a plain sheet of 11" × 17" paper.

1 Fold the sheet of paper into thirds along the short axis. This forms three columns.

2 Open the paper and refold into thirds along the long axis, then fold in half again lengthwise.

3 Unfold and draw lines along the folds.

4 Label the chart as shown.

Cause	Escalation	De-escalation
Argument		
Peer Pressure		
Revenge		
Prejudice		
Additional Notes		

As you read the lesson, fill in the chart with an example of a behavior that might escalate and de-escalate each type of conflict.

Go Online Visit **glencoe.com** and use the eFlashcards to preview Chapter 7 vocabulary terms.

Understanding Conflict

 Guide to Reading

● Building Vocabulary

As you read this lesson, write each new highlighted term and its definition in your notebook.

■ conflict (p. 202)

■ prejudice (p. 204)

● Focusing on the Main Ideas

In this lesson, you will be able to

■ **explain** the nature of conflict.

■ **identify** common causes of conflict.

■ **recognize** the signs of conflict.

■ **describe** types of conflicts at home and at school.

■ **discuss** when to avoid conflict.

● Reading Strategy

Organizing Information As you read this lesson, create an outline that shows the ways that disagreements can lead to conflict.

FOLDABLES Study Organizer Use the Foldable® on p. 201 as you read this lesson.

Q*uick Write*

List all the words that come to mind when you think of the word *conflict.*

The Nature of Conflict

Two teammates argue about who gets the ball. A brother and sister fight over the use of the computer. These are some common conflicts. A **conflict** is *a disagreement between people with opposing viewpoints, interests, or needs.* Conflicts happen to everyone. They are a normal part of life. They occur even in very close relationships. Resolving conflicts in a healthful way can prevent problems. Think of a conflict you've had recently. Did you handle it well?

Conflict can often be helpful. It can raise issues that need to be worked out. Conflict can be an opportunity for people to see the consequences of their behavior. They may see another side to the issues and use the process to help them create a healthful solution. If a conflict is handled peacefully, it can result in stronger relationships.

Conflict can hurt a relationship and even end in violence. It doesn't have to be this way. There is always a nonviolent solution to a conflict.

Reading Check **Define** What is a *conflict*?

What Causes Conflict?

Conflicts happen for many reasons. They often occur when one person has not met the expectations of another. Unmet needs, limited resources, and differences in values are other sources of conflict.

Arguments

Everyone has disagreements now and then. Many of them are easily settled. However, if disagreements are not settled, they can get out of hand and become arguments, or even fights. Some reasons teens argue include the following.

▲ Arguments can arise when people have different viewpoints. **What are two issues that may lead to arguments between teens?**

- **Property.** Teens may not respect one another's property. They may use others' possessions without asking permission. They may not take care of borrowed items properly.

- **Hurt feelings.** Teens may feel hurt when they are left out of activities. They may be jealous when a friend pays attention to someone else. Gossip, teasing, and insults can cause arguments when someone's feelings are hurt.

- **Territory.** Teens may feel that someone is trespassing on territory that they consider theirs.

Peer Pressure

Some conflicts are made worse when peers urge others to fight instead of resolving a conflict peacefully. When peer groups take sides, it makes it harder to find a peaceful solution. No one wins in these kinds of conflicts.

Revenge

People may want revenge when someone insults them, their family, or another group that they belong to. The problem with revenge, however, is that the other person may decide to get even as well. Soon the situation escalates, and the conflict worsens. This kind of behavior is common where there is gang activity. Unfortunately, revenge can lead to violence or even death.

Differences in Values

Your classmate Frank wants you to help him cheat on a math test. You don't believe in cheating, so you refuse. Now you and Frank have a conflict. Conflict can result when people have different values, which can be difficult to resolve. Differences based on **culture**, religion, and political views can also lead to conflicts.

Academic Vocabulary

culture (KUL cher) *(noun)* a group's way of life, including language, religion, values, and customs. *Every Saturday, Reiko and her friends study Japanese culture at the community center.*

School Counselor

School counselors help students deal with all kinds of issues, like problems with friends, peers, and family. They also help students select classes and plan for the future. There will always be a need for school counselors because students will always have questions or concerns about school or other challenges. If you want to be a school counselor, you should take courses in sociology and psychology.

What skills does a school counselor need? Go to *Career Corner* at **glencoe.com** to find out.

▼ Body language can be a sign that conflict is about to begin. **How can you tell that this teen doesn't agree with what her family is discussing?**

Prejudice

Prejudice, *a negative and unjustly formed opinion,* can also cause conflict. Prejudice is often directed against people of a different race, religion, or cultural group. It may also be directed against people who dress or speak differently, live in another town, or are rich or poor. When people refuse to accept others who are different from them, conflict can arise. However, when you show respect for people who are different from you, you develop healthy relationships and can avoid conflict.

 **Reading Check** **List** What are five causes of conflict?

Recognizing Signs of Conflict

The key to resolving conflict is to spot conflict early. The following are signs that show that conflict is about to begin.

- **Disagreement.** All conflict begins with some kind of disagreement. Be aware of any disagreements you have with others, since these can lead to a conflict.

- **Strong emotions.** Strong emotions arising over a disagreement is another sign that a conflict may soon begin. Maybe your friend never asks about your interests, and it makes you feel hurt or angry. Another warning sign is if you become very emotional as soon as you get into a disagreement.

- **Body language and behavior.** When you're in a disagreement, pay attention to your own body language and behavior as well as the other person's. Do you start to cross your arms or tighten your lips? Is the other person starting to ignore you? Is someone starting to raise his or her voice? These are signals that your disagreement has escalated.

Conflicts at Home and at School

Since teens spend most of their time with family, friends, and people at school, it is not surprising that home and school are where most teen conflicts occur. Teens may have disagreements with their parents or guardians about what each wants and expects. Teens may also have conflicts with siblings about how each person in the family is treated or how resources such as the family computer are shared.

At school, teens may have conflicts with other students, teachers, or school administrators. For example, teens who work together on school projects may feel that others are not doing their share of the work.

Avoiding Conflicts

Not every conflict is worth the time and effort to resolve. For example, suppose someone cuts in line ahead of you at the movie theater. You might choose to avoid this conflict because it's minor and you'll probably never see that person again.

Avoid getting in the middle of conflicts. Don't speak for someone in the conflict. Let each person speak for herself or himself. If a conflict starts to get worse, however, you can express your disapproval or suggest a positive solution.

It's important to avoid conflict when a situation becomes potentially harmful or unsafe. For example, if a conflict turns into a physical fight, leave the scene right away and get help from a trusted adult.

Go Online

Visit **glencoe.com** and complete the Interactive Study Guide for Lesson 1.

Reading Check **Explain** What are situations in which it is best to avoid a conflict?

Lesson 1 Review

 **After You Read**

Review this lesson for new terms, major headings, and Reading Checks.

What I Learned

1. *Explain* How can conflict be beneficial?

2. *List* What are three signs that a conflict is starting?

3. *Explain* Why do most conflicts for teens happen at home or school?

4. *Vocabulary* Define *prejudice*, and use the term in a sentence that shows its meaning.

5. *Identify* What are two reasons why teens argue?

Thinking Critically

6. *Apply* Peer pressure can make conflicts become violent. How can peer pressure also help prevent violence?

7. *Analyze* How can older siblings help younger siblings when they have a conflict with each other?

Applying Health Skills

8. *Analyzing Influences* How might movies and television misinform teens about the best ways to solve conflicts? Why do you think this could be so?

Conflict-Resolution Skills

Guide to Reading

Building Vocabulary

Write down your own definition for each of the words below. Then compare it to the definition that appears in the lesson.

- negotiation (p. 207)
- compromise (p. 207)
- collaborate (p. 207)
- mediation (p. 208)
- neutrality (p. 208)

Focusing on the Main Ideas

In this lesson, you will be able to

- **list** the steps in negotiation and mediation.
- **demonstrate** conflict-resolution skills.
- **identify** how conflict can lead to violence.

Reading Strategy

Identifying Cause and Effect As you read this lesson, list four behaviors that might indicate conflict is building toward violence.

Quick Write

Have you ever had a conflict with a friend that you were able to work out? Write a couple of sentences to describe what you did that made you successful.

Conflict-Resolution Strategies

Joe thinks that conflict is resolved when one person wins and the other loses. Joe is wrong. In fact, this belief can make conflict worse because one person is likely to feel cheated or angry. It's better to work out a solution in which everyone wins. This is known as a win-win solution. The people involved keep working on the conflict together and don't give up until they've reached an agreement that is acceptable to each person. As they discuss

▶ These teens are working through a disagreement. **What is the listening student doing to demonstrate that he is paying attention?**

the conflict, they may come up with solutions that make the situation even better than it was before the conflict. Two specific conflict-resolution strategies that work toward win-win solutions are negotiation and mediation.

Negotiation

In order to reach a win-win solution, everyone involved in an argument must negotiate. **Negotiation** is *the process of talking directly to the other person to resolve a conflict.* Two people meet face-to-face and share their feelings, their expectations, what they want, and why they want it in order to reach a solution.

Sometimes, negotiation involves a **compromise,** *when both sides in a conflict agree to give up something to reach a solution that will satisfy everyone.* Compromise works best in everyday disagreements about common matters like who gets to use the computer first or which movie to see at the theatre. You should never compromise your values; your sense of right and wrong; or your parents' rules, community laws, and school rules.

Like compromise, collaboration is another element of effective negotiation. When you **collaborate,** or *work together,* you build a relationship with another person as you work toward a common goal. Both sides have their needs met, but neither side gets exactly what they want. The T.A.L.K. strategy will help you remember the steps of conflict resolution through negotiation.

- **T**ake a time-out before you begin negotiating. Thirty minutes is enough time for everyone to calm down and control their emotions.

- **A**llow each person to tell his or her side of the story without being interrupted. Neither side should use angry words or gestures.

- **L**et each person ask questions of the other in a calm and polite way.

- **K**eep brainstorming until a fair solution is reached.

Negotiation usually works best if you talk to the other person privately. During negotiation, don't touch the other person, point a finger, call the person names, or yell. If you or the other person starts to get angry during negotiation, take a break. If the person

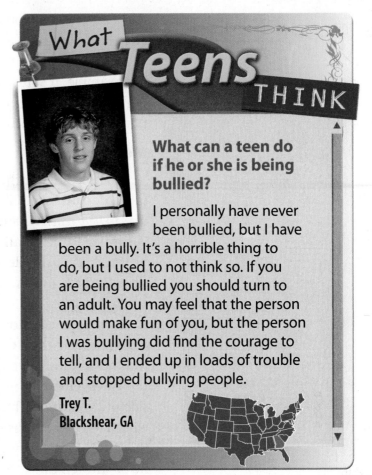

What **Teens** **THINK**

What can a teen do if he or she is being bullied?

I personally have never been bullied, but I have been a bully. It's a horrible thing to do, but I used to not think so. If you are being bullied you should turn to an adult. You may feel that the person would make fun of you, but the person I was bullying did find the courage to tell, and I ended up in loads of trouble and stopped bullying people.

Trey T.
Blackshear, GA

G **Online**

Topic: Creative Conflict Resolution

Visit **glencoe.com** for Student Web Activities where you can learn about how conflict can be handled effectively, as well as a creative way that teens are teaching conflict-resolution skills.

Activity: Using the information provided at the link above, write an outline for a skit about teens who resolve their conflict in a positive way.

threatens to hurt you or has a weapon, stop negotiation immediately, leave, and tell a trusted adult right away.

Also, remember that some issues are *not* open to negotiation. For example, if someone tries to persuade you to engage in bullying or to do something illegal, you do not need to negotiate. Say no, and leave the situation if necessary.

Mediation

The second conflict-resolution strategy you can use is mediation. **Mediation** is *resolving conflicts by using another person or persons to help reach a solution that is acceptable to both sides.* Mediation is similar to negotiation, except that a mediator is involved. He or she doesn't decide how to resolve the conflict but helps both sides find a solution. Mediators must have **neutrality,** *a promise not to take sides.*

In peer mediation programs, student mediators help other students solve their conflicts. First, the peer mediator determines that both sides agree to mediation. Then the mediator goes over the rules. One common rule is that each person tells his or her side of the story without being interrupted. The mediator restates what each person has said to make sure it is correct. The mediator then tries to identify what the conflict is and asks each person if he or she agrees.

 Reading Check **Define** What does *neutrality* mean?

▶ Negotiation is an important tool in conflict resolution. **How are these teens demonstrating that they know about negotiation?**

Health Skills Activity

Conflict Resolution

Settling a Disagreement

Tanisha and Chloe have been friends since elementary school. One Saturday, they agree to meet at the movies. Chloe shows up 30 minutes late. It's the third time in a row that Chloe's been late for something that they were going to do together. Because Tanisha waited, she missed the first part of the movie and is really angry about it. When Chloe arrives, Tanisha shouts, "Chloe, you're never on time! You ruin everything!"

What Would You Do?

Apply the steps of conflict resolution to Tanisha and Chloe's situation. Write a dialogue that shows them resolving their conflict peacefully.

- **T**ake a time-out of at least 30 minutes.
- **A**llow each person to tell his or her side uninterrupted.
- **L**et each person ask questions.
- **K**eep brainstorming to find a good solution.

The mediator looks for things that both people want. Maybe the students would like to remain friends. The mediator then asks each side to offer possible solutions. Once some solutions have been offered, each side comments on what might work. If an agreement is reached, the students in conflict write down what was agreed upon and both sign the document.

When Conflicts Get Out of Hand

The best time to resolve a conflict is in the early stages. If a disagreement is not managed well, it can escalate. Some conflicts that begin with a minor disagreement even become violent. **Figure 7.1** on page 210 lists some warning signs that a conflict might soon turn violent. Often, these warning signs appear because the teens in the conflict are getting angry and don't understand how to manage their emotions. By noticing these signs, you may be able to stop a conflict from escalating into violence.

 **Reading Check** **Give Examples** What are two warning signs that a conflict may become violent?

▼ **FIGURE 7.1**

NINE WARNING SIGNS OF BUILDING CONFLICT

Each of these signs is a clue that a conflict might be building toward violence. **What are some positive actions you could take if you see one of these signs?**

Visit glencoe.com and complete the Interactive Study Guide for Lesson 2.

Lesson 2 Review

 After You Read

Review this lesson for new terms, major headings, and Reading Checks.

What I Learned

1. *Explain* What is the difference between compromise and collaborate?

2. *Describe* What are the steps in the process of conflict resolution through negotiation?

3. *Vocabulary* Define *mediation*.

4. *Describe* Name four warning signs that conflict might be building toward violence.

Thinking Critically

5. *Analyze* What are some positive communication strategies for resolving conflict among teens at school?

6. *Synthesize* What might be the benefit of using a peer mediator rather than an adult mediator?

Applying Health Skills

7. *Conflict Resolution* Parker borrowed Ben's soccer shoes. When Parker returned them, they were dirty and a lace was broken. Ben wants Parker to clean the shoes and replace the lace, but Parker says that the shoes were dirty when he borrowed them. Use the T.A.L.K. strategy to help Ben and Parker resolve their conflict in a positive way.

Go Online For more Lesson Review Activities, go to **glencoe.com.**

Preventing Violence

Guide to Reading

● **Building Vocabulary**
After reading this lesson, write a paragraph using each vocabulary word.

- assault (p. 211)
- rape (p. 211)
- homicide (p. 211)
- gang (p. 212)
- bullying (p. 213)
- dating violence (p. 214)
- youth court (p. 215)

● **Focusing on the Main Ideas**
In this lesson, you will be able to

- **identify** causes of violence.
- **describe** what gangs are.
- **define** bullying.
- **analyze** dating violence.
- **develop** skills to protect against violence.

● **Reading Strategy**
Predicting Look over the major and minor headings in this lesson. Then write a brief paragraph describing the types of information that you think will be covered in this lesson.

Quick Write

What steps do you take to keep yourself safe? Write a short paragraph about these strategies.

Violence in Society

The news is filled with stories of violence. Many movies, videos, and computer games show violence. Violence is a major health problem in the United States.

The most common violent crime is **assault,** *an attack on another person in order to hurt him or her.* The attacker usually uses a weapon. The second most common crime is robbery, which is taking another person's property by force or the threat of force. **Rape** is *forced sexual intercourse.* **Homicide,** *a violent crime that results in the death of another person,* is the least common violent crime. This crime is also called murder.

Some teens use violence to get respect from their peers or demonstrate independence from adults. Some use it when they have too few choices and feel controlled by others. It is common for teens who have seen violence in their homes to use violence.

Factors That Contribute to Violence

People who commit violent acts may not have learned to deal with feelings such as anger in healthful ways. Other causes of violence include prejudice, the availability of weapons, peer pressure, and alcohol and other drugs.

MediaWatch

TV Violence

Many TV programs and movies show violence. Some experts say that this sends the message that violence is acceptable.

Keep a TV log for a week. Figure out how many of the shows you watch show violent acts. Report your findings to the class.

Prejudice is a negative and unjustly formed opinion of a particular group. It can lead to hate crimes. A hate crime is an illegal act committed against someone just because he or she is a member of a particular group. If people have easy access to weapons, including guns, they may be more likely to turn to violence.

Peer pressure can also lead to violence. Some teens get involved in violence because they want to be part of a group. Pressure from the group can cause teens to go against their values and do things they really don't want to do. The use of alcohol and other drugs can also lead to violence. In fact, almost half of all violent crimes are committed by people under the influence of alcohol or drugs.

Many teens who engage in violence have similar risk factors. These risk factors include:

- Engaging in risky behaviors
- Having parents who are violent
- Committing crimes when they were younger
- Seeing violence as an acceptable way to behave

Note, though, that many teens who have these risk factors are *not* violent. If teens are aware of these risk factors, it may help them to avoid conflict and violence.

 **Reading Check** **List** What are four causes of violence?

Gangs

A **gang** is *a group of young people who come together to take part in illegal activities.* Every day, gangs are responsible for people being hurt and even dying. Why do teens join gangs? Joining a gang may give teens a sense of being a part of something. It may make them feel more adult. Some teens think that joining a gang boosts their self-esteem. Other teens join gangs because they think the gang will protect them. Some join because a family member or friend joined a gang.

Here are some tips to keep you safe from gang violence:

- Don't join gangs or hang out with gang members.
- Don't wear gang-related colors or clothing.
- If gang members threaten you, stay calm and try not to show fear. Walk away calmly. Get help from police, school officials, or other trusted adults.

▼ These teens are demonstrating a positive response to gang activity. **What are some other ways the community can respond to gangs?**

Bullying

Have you ever been the victim of bullying? As a bystander, have you ever seen a bully pick on someone? **Bullying** is *a type of violence in which one person uses threats, taunts, or violence to intimidate another again and again.* There are different forms of bullying:

- **Physical bullying:** hitting, kicking, spitting, pushing, or taking personal belongings
- **Verbal bullying:** teasing, name-calling, or making threats
- **Psychological bullying:** spreading rumors, **isolating** a person, or threatening to use force

People who are bullied can be hurt physically and emotionally. These effects can be short-term or long-term. Help prevent bullying by treating others the way you want to be treated. As a bystander, if you see bullying, tell a trusted adult about it. **Figure 7.2** shows some ways you can respond to bullying situations.

 Reading Check **Identify** How can you respond to bullying as a bystander?

▼ FIGURE 7.2

HOW TO RESPOND TO BULLYING

Putting these tips to use can reduce your chances of being bullied. **How can these Do's and Don'ts help you avoid being bullied?**

Do's

- Do keep control of yourself.
- Do stay calm and speak softly.
- Do walk away if necessary.
- Do apologize if necessary.
- Do try to turn the other person's attention somewhere else.
- Do use your sense of humor.
- Do give the other person a way out.
- Do try to understand how the other person thinks or feels.
- Do tell an adult.

Don'ts

- Don't let your emotions get the better of you.
- Don't let the other person force you into a fight.
- Don't try to get even.
- Don't tease.
- Don't be hostile, rude, or sarcastic.
- Don't threaten or insult the person.

Dating Violence

Many people begin to date in their teens. Healthy dating relationships are built on respect. Avoid dating relationships that are not built on respect. *When a person uses violence in a dating relationship to control his or her partner,* this is known as **dating violence.** This violence can be physical, emotional, or psychological.

Why does dating violence occur? Many teens who use violence in dating have most likely learned this behavior. They may have seen violence in their own homes or been victims of abuse. They may have learned it from movies, music videos, video games, or other people. Teens who are just learning to date aren't always sure how to have a healthy dating relationship.

Warning signs of dating violence include feeling scared or threatened by a date, discovering that a date has a history of violence or alcohol or drug abuse, feeling bullied or put down in front of others, and learning that a date wants to control all the decisions in the relationship. If a dating relationship feels uncomfortable or has become violent, teen victims should tell a parent or other trusted adult right away.

 Reading Check **Define** What is *dating violence?*

Protect Yourself from Violence

There are many effective techniques for avoiding threatening situations that could lead to violence. **Figure 7.3** lists some ways to stay safe at home and away from home.

Reducing Violence at School

Schools use a variety of methods to help keep students safe. Some schools use dress codes or uniforms. Since all students are wearing similar clothes, it is harder to tell each student's economic situation. This can help make students feel "equal," and as a result, there may be less violence. Also, dress codes or uniforms make it harder for gang members to use clothing to show what gang they're in.

Some schools use security systems. Metal detectors, security cameras, and security guards help keep weapons out of schools. Sometimes student lockers may be searched.

◀ After-school programs are safe places where you can spend time with your friends. **What programs are available in your area?**

BEING SAFE ON THE STREET AND AT HOME

On the street or at home, there are ways you can protect yourself from becoming a victim of violence. **What other precautions could you take to stay safe?**

- Let your parents know where you are, your route home, and when to expect you.
- Don't walk by yourself, if possible. After dark, walk in well-lit areas. Don't walk in dark alleyways.
- If you think someone is following you, go into a public place, such as a store or a well-lit area where there are other people.
- When you are about to arrive home, have your keys out so you don't have to hunt for them.
- Don't accept rides from strangers, and don't hitchhike.

- When you're home, keep your doors and windows locked. Only open the door for someone you know, or not at all if your parents tell you not to answer the door.
- When you answer the phone or use the Internet, don't give out any personal information. Don't say that you are home alone.

Trained dogs are sometimes used to sniff out drugs and weapons. Schools may also have school resource officers assigned to them. They get to know students and help prevent problems.

Many schools educate students in conflict resolution. They also use peer mediation and youth court programs. In peer mediation, teens help other teens work through their conflicts. **Youth court** is *a special school program where teens decide punishments for other teens for bullying and other problem behaviors.*

Peers can influence other peers to make healthful choices. Students themselves sometimes start programs to reduce violence. Students Against Violence Everywhere (S.A.V.E.) is a program that teaches about alternatives to violence. The students put their ideas into action at school and in their community.

Reducing Violence in Communities

Community resources can play an important part in making neighborhoods safer. Some communities have created academic, recreational, or cultural after-school programs for teens. These programs can help teens feel safe and use their free time productively. Other communities have improved the lighting in parks and playgrounds. Brighter lights can discourage crime by making it more difficult to commit crimes without being seen. Members of a community may start a Neighborhood Watch Program, in which they learn to look for signs of trouble in the neighborhood. Communities may also put police officers on foot, bicycle, or horseback patrols.

 Reading Check **Identify** What are four ways that communities can reduce violence?

Go Online

Visit glencoe.com and complete the Interactive Study Guide for Lesson 3.

 After You Read

Review this lesson for new terms, major headings, and Reading Checks.

What I Learned

1. *List* What are four common violent crimes?

2. *Vocabulary* Define *gang*.

3. *Identify* What can you do to stay safe from gang violence?

4. *Explain* How can you help prevent bullying?

5. *Describe* What strategies should you use to keep yourself safe if you are walking home and you think you are being followed?

Thinking Critically

6. *Analyze* Maria and George are dating. Maria wants George to spend all his time with her and not to talk to other girls. Is this a sign of a healthy relationship?

7. *Apply* Imagine that you are home alone and two people you don't know come to the door. They tell you that their car broke down and ask if they can come in and use your phone. What should you do to avoid possible risks to your safety?

Applying Health Skills

8. *Goal Setting* Select one way you could help reduce bullying in your school. Use the goal-setting steps to make a plan to take part in this activity. See pages 44 and 45 in Chapter 2 to review the steps. Show your plan to your teacher. Follow your plan for a week, and write a paragraph about the experience.

Go Online For more Lesson Review Activities, go to glencoe.com.

Getting Help for Abuse

Guide to Reading

● **Building Vocabulary**
After you read this lesson, write one sentence for each vocabulary word below.

■ abuse (p. 217)
■ battery (p. 217)
■ neglect (p. 217)
■ sexual abuse (p. 218)

● **Focusing on the Main Ideas**
In this lesson, you will be able to

■ **define** abuse.
■ **explain** how abuse is never the fault of the victim.
■ **list** warning signs of abuse.
■ **identify** sources of help for abuse.

● **Reading Strategy**
Identifying Main Ideas Use the major and minor headings of this lesson to create an outline. As you read the lesson, write down the main points covered under each heading.

Quick Write

Think about adults whom you trust. Write one or two sentences that describe what makes them trustworthy.

What Is Abuse?

Abuse is *the physical, emotional, or mental mistreatment of another person*. Anyone can be a victim of abuse, and abuse is never the victim's fault. All abuse is wrong and is a serious crime. Professionals such as physicians, nurses, teachers, and school counselors are required by law to report suspected cases of abuse.

The Four Major Types of Abuse

There are four major types of abuse: physical, emotional, neglect, and sexual. Physical abuse causes serious injury and harm to a person's body. The most common form of physical abuse is **battery,** *the beating, hitting, or kicking of another person.*

Emotional abuse is repeated communication that makes another person feel worthless. The abuser sends this message through words or acts. Insults, harsh criticism, repeated threats, and teasing are all forms of emotional abuse. People who have been emotionally abused often feel helpless and bad about themselves. **Neglect** is *the failure to provide for the basic physical and emotional needs of a dependent.* Children need food, shelter, medical care, education, and supervision. Neglecting someone can be part of emotional abuse. If caregivers don't provide support for the people who depend on them, they may be guilty of neglect.

Sexual abuse is *sexual contact that is forced upon another person*. This contact may be touching, kissing, or sexual intercourse. Forcing a child to view or be photographed for sexual materials is also sexual abuse. The abuser is often someone whom the victim knows and trusts, such as a family member. People who have been sexually abused often feel responsible. Remember, however, that sexual abuse is *always* the abuser's fault. Talking to a trustworthy adult is the best way to stop sexual abuse and get help.

Warning Signs of Abuse

How can you tell if a person you know is being abused? A person who is being abused may have bruises or burns that he or she can't explain. The person may lose interest in school, and his or her grades may start to slip. Sometimes an abused person may have an uncared-for appearance. A person who had been outgoing and happy may now show extreme shyness, sadness, or fear. A victim of abuse may become unable to communicate or show aggressive behavior toward others. Abuse is very common. **Figure 7.4** shows **statistics** about abuse.

Reading Check List What are some warning signs of abuse?

Academic Vocabulary

statistics (stuh TIS tiks) *(noun)* information that is collected and analyzed for a purpose. *Vincent researched tobacco statistics so he could share with his friends just how dangerous smoking is.*

▼ **FIGURE 7.4**

ABUSE CAN HAPPEN TO ANYONE

Abuse can happen to people of all ages. Why do you think abuse is so high for people over age 65?

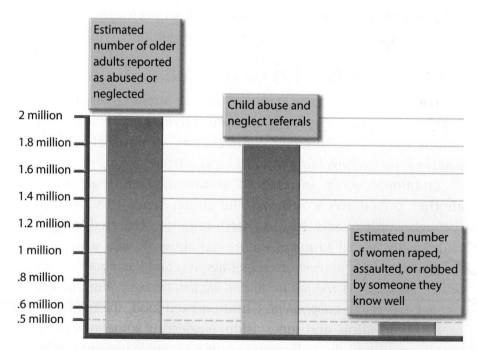

Sources: National Research Council on Elder Abuse, U.S. Department of Justice, U.S. Department of Health and Human Services.

FACTORS THAT MAY INCREASE THE RISK OF ABUSE

This chart presents some factors that can contribute to the risk of a person becoming abusive. **How can identifying and working to improve these situations help prevent abuse?**

Risk Factors for Abuse

All families have problems sometimes. Good communication skills can help families solve problems in healthful ways. When families don't know how to handle their problems in healthful ways, there is greater risk of abuse. Other factors may also increase the risk of abusive behavior. Some of these factors are listed in **Figure 7.5.**

 **Reading Check** **Explain** What skill can healthy families use to solve many of their problems?

Effects of Abuse

Gregory was abused when he was younger, and it caused him serious problems. His physical problems from the abuse needed medical attention. He soon ran away to try to escape the abuse. Sadly, he turned to crime to support himself and quickly became the victim of crime. Like many people who are abused, he experienced low self-esteem, high levels of stress, and emotional problems. If Gregory does not deal with these feelings, he may find himself in unhealthy relationships.

Why Victims Stay Silent

Unfortunately, many victims of abuse don't tell anyone about it, which stops them from getting the help they need. There are several reasons that victims of abuse stay silent. Some victims may think that no one will believe them. Other victims, especially children, sometimes think that if they report abuse, people will think they are lying or exaggerating. Victims of abuse may feel that it's a private matter. Victims also may mistakenly believe they deserve the abuse or that something they did caused the abuse.

Males may believe that they cannot or should not be abuse victims because they should be able to protect themselves. Abusers, however, usually have an advantage over their victims. Sometimes the abuser is stronger or older. Often, the abuser is in a position of power and trust.

Victims may be afraid to report abuse because they're worried that their abusers will seek revenge. Abusers often create this fear. They try to convince victims that the victim or the victim's family will be punished if he or she tells.

 **Reading Check** **Give Examples** What are two reasons that victims of abuse don't tell anyone?

▶ A crisis hotline can put abuse victims in touch with organizations that can help. **What is important to remember about the information someone may give to a crisis hotline?**

Finding Help for Abuse

An abused person should tell a parent or guardian or another trusted adult, such as a family friend, religious advisor, teacher, or school counselor. The victim should keep telling people until someone helps. He or she can also call a hotline for abuse victims. These crisis hotline numbers can be found in the phone book. A person who is trained to help victims of abuse will talk over the issues and offer helpful advice. Calls to abuse hotlines are anonymous. That means that the person who answers the call does not know who is calling.

Abusers, too, can get help, but they must take responsiblility for their behavior. They can take special classes that teach them how to avoid using violence and how to handle conflict peacefully. They can also take classes to help them learn more solid parenting skills.

 Reading Check **List** Name three sources of help for victims of abuse.

Visit glencoe.com and complete the Interactive Study Guide for Lesson 4.

Lesson 4 Review

After You Read

Review this lesson for new terms, major headings, and Reading Checks.

What I Learned

1. **Vocabulary** Define *abuse*.

2. **Describe** Name and describe the four major types of abuse.

3. **Give Examples** What are three warning signs of abuse?

4. **Identify** What are three factors that may increase the risk of abuse?

Thinking Critically

5. **Apply** Why do you think crisis hotlines assure callers that calls will be kept anonymous?

6. **Analyze** Are abusers always older than their victims? Explain your answer.

Applying Health Skills

7. **Communication Skills** Suppose you had a friend who was being abused. Write a dialogue in which you talk to your friend about getting help. How could you influence your friend to make a healthful choice? Include what your friend might say in response.

Building Health Skills

Accessing Information

Practicing Healthful Behaviors

Stress Management

Analyzing Influences

Communication Skills

Refusal Skills

Conflict Resolution

Decision Making

Goal Setting

Advocacy

What Is Conflict Resolution?

Conflict resolution is a strategy to help people work through a disagreement. If you have a conflict with someone, use the T.A.L.K. strategy to help you resolve your issue in a fair and peaceful way.

- **T**ake a time-out before you begin negotiating. Thirty minutes is enough time for everyone to calm down and control their emotions.
- **A**llow each person to tell his or her side of the story without being interrupted. Neither side should use angry words or gestures.
- **L**et each person ask questions of the other in a calm and polite way.
- **K**eep brainstorming until a fair solution is reached.

Mediating a Conflict

Follow the Model, Practice, and Apply steps to help you master this important health skill.

① Model

Read how Tara and Brandi use conflict-resolution skills to resolve their conflict.

Brandi and Tara had a conflict about a project they were working on in class. After class, Brandi called Tara "dumb and lazy" because she felt that Tara wasn't doing her share of the work. Then Tara started yelling at Brandi. Their teacher sent both students to the school counselor's office. The counselor encouraged the two teens to use the T.A.L.K. strategy to resolve their conflict.

First, they took half an hour to calm down and collect their thoughts. Brandi explained that Tara had not finished her part of the project. Tara said she felt angry that Brandi called her names. Both asked questions to make sure they understood the other's point of view. Then they brainstormed solutions. Finally, they reached a compromise. Brandi would apologize for insulting Tara, and Tara would complete the tasks that she had been assigned to do.

② Practice

Use conflict-resolution skills to help LeeAnne and David resolve their conflict.

LeeAnne and her brother, David, are doing their weekly chores one Saturday. They begin arguing about who should wash the dishes and who should vacuum the living room. David feels he always has to do the vacuuming because LeeAnne prefers washing the dishes. Write a dialogue between the two siblings in which they use the T.A.L.K. strategy to resolve their conflict. Share your dialogue with your classmates. Explain how you used compromise or collaboration in your dialogue.

③ Apply

Use what you have learned about conflict resolution to complete the activity below.

With a partner, brainstorm a list of common conflicts that two teens might be involved in. Choose one of these situations, and write a script showing how the characters use the T.A.L.K. strategy to resolve their conflict in a healthy way. Perform your skit for the class. After you have performed your skit, ask the class to point out each of the T.A.L.K. steps in your skit and explain how you showed compromise or collaboration.

Self-Check
- Did we choose a situation that would be a common conflict for teens?
- Does our script show how to use the T.A.L.K. strategy to resolve their conflict in a healthy way?
- Did we show compromise or collaboration in our skit?

Getting an Early Start on
PEACE

Some summer programs offer young people a chance to work toward international harmony.

Sometimes it can be hard for two people to resolve conflicts or misunderstandings between themselves. It can be even more difficult when citizens of two countries can't get along. Troubles between nations are a huge obstacle to achieving world peace. Some programs are now offering teens a way to promote peace and understanding between nations.

Seeds of Peace, started in 1993, holds a series of two-week peace camps each summer in Maine. American campers, ages 14 to 17, join with teens from such places as the Middle East, India, Pakistan, Greece, and Turkey to play sports together. The campers also spend time in sessions in which they learn how to listen to one another with respect and compassion. Says teen Liz Carlin, who attended Seeds, "Now I try to get as many perspectives as possible about current events."

NO MORE VIOLENCE

Global Children's Organization (G.C.O.) has sponsored similar camps in three regions of the world. The organization has brought together children who have suffered from violence in Bosnia, Croatia, and Serbia. Children caught in the conflicts of Ireland and Northern Ireland have also participated in G.C.O.'s camps. In Los Angeles, G.C.O.'s camps have helped refugee children from Iran, Afghanistan, and elsewhere, as well as neighborhoods affected by gang-related violence. "We teach children that conflict is inevitable, but violence isn't," says Judith Jenya, who founded G.C.O.

Kids learn to trust and respect one another during group activities at Seeds of Peace.

Teens who want a longer experience interacting with young people from other nations can go to the United World College (U.W.C.), which has 10 campuses around the globe. At the U.S. branch in New Mexico, 200 students ages 16 to 18 work toward a two-year diploma. In addition to academics, there are classes in nonviolent conflict resolution. The object, says Philip Geier, president of U.W.C.'s American campus, is "to create a global network of future decision makers." At the school, Israeli students joined Palestinian classmates in a presentation on the history of conflict in their homelands. "We...agreed on some topics and decided we would never agree on others," says Gadi Maayan, 17. Now, however, Maayan better understands other viewpoints.

Such encounters can be life changing for American teens, too. "I can no longer make stereotypical judgments about anyone," says Matt Farwell, a U.W.C. graduate. "I feel responsible for sharing what I learned with as many people as I can."

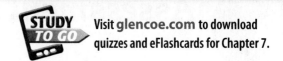

STUDY TO GO Visit **glencoe.com** to download quizzes and eFlashcards for Chapter 7.

FOLDABLES® Study Organizer

Foldables® and Other Study Aids Take out the Foldable® that you created for Lesson 1 and any graphic organizers that you created for Lessons 1–4. Find a partner and quiz each other using these study aids.

Lesson 1 Understanding Conflict

Main Idea It is important to know how to recognize conflicts and where they are most likely to happen.

- Conflict can often be helpful. It can raise issues that need to be worked out, help people to see the consequences of their behaviors, and help build stronger relationships.
- Causes of conflict include arguments, peer pressure, revenge, differences in values, and prejudice.
- The early warning signs of conflict are disagreement, strong emotions, and certain body language and behavior.

Lesson 2 Conflict-Resolution Skills

Main Idea There are several different ways to resolve conflicts.

- Negotiation is the process of talking directly to the other person to resolve a conflict.
- Compromise occurs when people in a conflict agree to give up something to reach a solution that will satisfy everyone.
- You can use the T.A.L.K. strategy to remember the process of negotiation.
- A mediator helps people in a conflict find a solution.

Lesson 3 Preventing Violence

Main Idea There are many ways to protect yourself from violence.

- Assault, robbery, rape, and homicide are common violent crimes.
- Teens are violent for many reasons, including wanting to be independent, to rebel, or because they have experienced or witnessed violence at home.
- You can help prevent bullying by refusing to take part in it, respecting yourself, treating others with respect, and walking away from fights.
- Dating violence occurs when a person uses violence to control his or her partner.

Lesson 4 Getting Help for Abuse

Main Idea There are many resources to help victims of abuse.

- Abuse is the physical, emotional, or mental mistreatment of another person.
- The four major types of abuse are physical abuse, emotional abuse, neglect, and sexual abuse.
- Abuse has serious short- and long-term consequences and is never the fault of the victim.
- Warning signs of abuse include unexplained bruises or burns, extreme shyness, sadness, or fear.
- Victims of abuse can get help from several sources, including parents, teachers, and school counselors.

After You Read

HEALTH INVENTORY

Now that you have read the chapter, look back at your answers to the Health Inventory on the chapter opener. Is there anything that you should do differently?

Reviewing Vocabulary and Main Ideas

On a sheet of paper, write the numbers 1–6. After each number, write the term from the list that best completes each statement.

- neutrality
- mediation
- compromise
- collaborate
- prejudice
- conflict

Lesson 1 Understanding Conflict

1. _____ is a disagreement between people with opposing viewpoints, interests, or needs.

2. _____ is a negative or unjustly formed opinion.

Lesson 2 Conflict-Resolution Skills

3. _____ involves resolving conflicts by using another person or persons to help reach a solution that is acceptable to both sides.

4. To be successful, a mediator must have _____, which means a promise not to take sides.

5. A _____ is when both sides in a conflict agree to give up something to reach a solution that will satisfy everyone.

6. When you work together, you _____.

Lesson 3 Preventing Violence

*On a sheet of paper, write the numbers 7–9. Write **True** or **False** for each statement below. If the statement is false, change the underlined word or phrase to make it true.*

7. <u>Assault</u> is a violent crime that results in the death of another person.

8. If gang members threaten you, <u>fight back</u>.

9. Bullying <u>cannot</u> be verbal.

Lesson 4 Getting Help for Abuse

On a sheet of paper, write the numbers 10–12. After each number, write the letter of the answer that best completes each statement.

10. Battery is a kind of
    a. emotional abuse.
    b. physical abuse.
    c. neglect.
    d. sexual abuse.

11. One risk factor for abuse is
    a. being abused as a child.
    b. knowing how to resolve conflicts peacefully.
    c. having emotional maturity.
    d. being able to handle daily stress.

12. A person who is being abused should *not*
    a. keep silent about the abuse.
    b. call a crisis hotline.
    c. tell a trusted adult.
    d. talk to a school counselor.

Go Online Visit **glencoe.com** and take the Online Quiz for Chapter 7.

Thinking Critically

Using complete sentences, answer the following questions on a sheet of paper.

13. **Analyze** How can being good at conflict resolution have positive benefits in your life?

14. **Compare and Contrast** How are negotiation and mediation similar? How are they different?

Write About It

15. **Descriptive Writing** Write a speech on positive communication strategies.

Applying Technology

Curing Conflicts

Using Garageband™ or Audacity®, you and a partner will write and record a 3–5 minute podcast dialogue, discussing conflict-resolution skills.

- Write a dialogue about two teens who need to resolve a conflict. Use the T.A.L.K. strategy to resolve their conflict.

- Open a new podcast project with two audio tracks; one for each of you to record your portion of the dialogue.

- Share your podcast using iTunes® or Windows Media®.

Standardized Test Practice

Reading

Read the passage and then answer the questions.

In the United States, it's illegal for any Web site to ask people under the age of 13 for personal information without parental permission. This law is for the safety of children. If you are 13 or older, make sure that you check out the Web site's privacy policy. Find out what they do with the personal information that they collect. Who is really asking for this information? Do you know who is receiving this information? Do they sell this information to other organizations? Will you start getting lots of junk mail?

1. What is the main purpose of the law described in the above passage?
   A. to prevent viruses from infecting computers
   B. to strengthen parental rights
   C. to protect young people by not allowing them to give out personal information without permission
   D. to track how many users are on any Web site

2. What would a Web site's privacy policy tell you?
   A. what they do with the information that they collect
   B. how to scan your computer for viruses
   C. how to block junk mail
   D. how to complain when someone sends you lots of junk mail

3. *Privacy policy* in this passage means
   A. a law passed by the U.S. government.
   B. how your family handles requests for information.
   C. the way that you would like to be treated.
   D. how the sponsor of a Web site handles issues on privacy.

Chapter Preview

Lesson 1 How Tobacco
Affects the Body..............230

Lesson 2 The Respiratory System..236

Lesson 3 Tobacco Use and Teens 242

Lesson 4 Tobacco Use and
Society 248

Lesson 5 Saying No to
Tobacco Use.......................252

Building Health Skills.........................256

Hands-on Health 258

Chapter Reading Review....................259

Chapter Assessment 260

▲ *Working with the Photo*

Most teens do not smoke. If you were offered tobacco, what would you say?

Start-Up Activities

Before You Read What do you already know about the effects of tobacco? Take the short quiz below. Keep a record of your answers.

HEALTH QUIZ Answer *True* or *False* for each of the following:

1. Secondhand smoke is not harmful.
2. Nicotine is a drug found in cigarettes.
3. If you have a habit of using tobacco, you can easily give it up.
4. Smokeless tobacco, or spit tobacco, is not as bad as cigarettes.
5. Cigarette smoke contains some of the same chemicals found in rat poison.

ANSWERS: 1. False; 2. True; 3. False; 4. False; 5. True

FOLDABLES Study Organizer

As You Read Follow the steps below to make this Foldable®. Use it to record what you learn in Lesson 1 about tobacco's effects on the respiratory system. Begin with a sheet of notebook paper.

1 Fold a sheet of paper in half so its long edges meet.

2 Cut a slit along every third line on the top sheet. Your Foldable™ now has 10 tabs.

3 Label the tabs as shown.

Tobacco
Nicotine
Tar
Carbon Monoxide
Cigarettes
Cigars
Pipes
Smokeless tobacco
Alveoli
Emphysema

Define key terms and record facts about tobacco's effects on the body.

Go Online Visit **glencoe.com** and complete the Chapter 8 crossword puzzle.

How Tobacco Affects the Body

Guide to Reading

● Building Vocabulary
As you read this lesson, write each term and its definition in your notebook.

- nicotine (p. 230)
- tar (p. 231)
- carbon monoxide (p. 231)
- alveoli (p. 234)
- emphysema (p. 234)

● Focusing on the Main Ideas
In this lesson you will be able to

- **identify** the harmful ingredients in tobacco smoke.
- **describe** how tobacco affects the body.
- **apply** the skill of advocacy to encourage someone to be tobacco free.

● Reading Strategy
Predicting Look over the headings in this lesson. Then write a question that you think the lesson will answer. After reading, check to see if your question was answered.

FOLDABLES Study Organizer Use the Foldable® on p. 229 as you read this lesson.

Quick Write

Write a few sentences to explain why you think tobacco use might be harmful.

Facts About Tobacco

A single puff of tobacco smoke contains more than 4,000 harmful chemicals! Most of those chemicals hurt your body's ability to work properly. Several of them can cause cancer in people who smoke. In the United States, more than 400,000 people die every year from smoking-related illnesses. Even if you aren't the one using tobacco, tobacco smoke can still be harmful.

What Is in Tobacco?

Natural tobacco contains harmful substances that are released when a person smokes or chews it. Tobacco companies add more harmful ingredients when they prepare tobacco to be sold. Some of the same ingredients you would find in cleaning products or pest poisons are added to tobacco products. Deciding not to take poisons into your body is a healthful decision.

Nicotine

One harmful substance found in tobacco is called nicotine. **Nicotine** is *an addictive, or habit-forming, drug found in tobacco.* Once you are addicted to nicotine, your body has a strong need, or craving, for it. As a result, you want to smoke again and again.

A person can become addicted to nicotine very quickly. Nicotine has other effects, too. It makes your heart beat faster and raises your blood pressure. It causes dizziness and an upset stomach and reduces the amount of oxygen your blood carries to the brain.

Tar

When tobacco burns, it produces tar. **Tar** is *a thick, dark liquid that forms when tobacco burns*. Tar coats the airways and the linings of the lungs. Lungs coated with tar can become diseased.

Carbon Monoxide

Tobacco smoke contains another substance called carbon monoxide. **Carbon monoxide** is *a colorless, odorless, poisonous gas produced when tobacco burns*. When carbon monoxide enters the body, it damages the brain and the heart by reducing the amount of oxygen available to these organs. Too much carbon monoxide can kill you.

Other Deadly Substances

Tobacco smoke and smokeless tobacco contain even more dangerous chemicals. For example, cyanide is a deadly poison. It is a common ingredient in pest-control products. Formaldehyde is a burning, stinging gas that is used as a preservative in the laboratory and also causes nasal cancer. Methyl ethyl ketone is used in solvents and harms the central nervous system. Polonium 210, an element known to cause cancer, is found in some tobacco products. These are only a few of the thousands of harmful ingredients contained in cigarettes and other forms of tobacco.

Reading Check   **Describe** What is the main harmful effect of nicotine?

◀ Tobacco products contain many harmful substances. Using tobacco puts people at risk for lung cancer and other health problems. **Name three harmful substances found in tobacco.**

▼ Tobacco contains many of the chemicals found in poisonous household products. **How can these chemicals damage your health?**

Forms of Tobacco

Tobacco companies harvest leaves from tobacco plants. They dry the leaves and prepare them for people to smoke or to chew. Tobacco products come in different forms. The most common ones are cigarettes, cigars, pipe tobacco, smokeless tobacco, clove cigarettes, and flavored tobacco.

Cigarettes

Cigarettes contain shredded tobacco leaves. They may also have filters. Tobacco companies claim that filters block some of the harmful chemicals found in cigarettes. However, filters do not remove enough chemicals to make cigarettes less dangerous. There is no such thing as a safe cigarette. Even if a tobacco user does not inhale the smoke, the smoke still can affect the person's health.

People can buy flavored cigarettes, which may taste and smell sweet. However, they have even more chemicals than regular cigarettes. Some people smoke clove cigarettes, which contain tobacco and ground spices called cloves. Others smoke flavored tobacco placed in water pipes called hookahs. Clove cigarettes and flavored tobacco are just as harmful as regular cigarettes because they contain the same substances that damage the body.

Cigars and Pipes

Cigars and pipes also contain shredded tobacco leaves. Cigar smoke contains up to 90 times more of the cancer-causing chemicals found in cigarette smoke. People who smoke cigars or pipes are more likely to develop mouth, tongue, or lip cancer than people who don't smoke.

Smokeless Tobacco

Smokeless tobacco comes in two forms: chewing tobacco and snuff. People often call chewing tobacco "dip" or "spit tobacco." Snuff tobacco can either be sniffed or chewed. Chemicals in chewing tobacco and snuff do not pass into the lungs. They are held in the mouth rather than inhaled as smoke. Nicotine is absorbed into the tissues and the bloodstream through the digestive tract.

Smokeless tobacco contains the same chemicals as cigarettes. Nicotine in smokeless tobacco has the same effects as nicotine in cigarettes. So smokeless tobacco is just as harmful and addictive as cigarettes.

 **Reading Check**   **Name** List two common forms of tobacco besides cigarettes.

Tobacco Affects Body Systems

When you smoke, your skin, breath, hair, and clothes smell like smoke. Tobacco use affects the senses of smell and taste. As a result, food doesn't smell or taste the same.

Tobacco use also has serious consequences. It is a risk factor that can cause diseases and other health problems. You have already learned that nicotine raises the heart rate and blood pressure. Smokers can't run as long or as fast as they did before they started smoking. They also get sick more often and tend to stay sick longer. Smoking tobacco can cause diseases in your mouth and lungs. It also affects your entire body. In fact, tobacco use damages each of the five main body systems. **Figure 8.1** lists some of the effects of tobacco on your body systems. Many of these problems and illnesses can be prevented if a person chooses the positive health behavior of staying tobacco free.

▼FIGURE 8.1

TOBACCO'S EFFECTS ON BODY SYSTEMS

Using tobacco harms many body systems, causing many health problems. **What does tobacco use do to the nervous system?**

Respiratory System	Digestive System	Nervous System	Excretory System	Circulatory System
Tobacco smoke damages the air sacs in the lungs. This damage can lead to a life-threatening disease that destroys these air sacs. Smokers are also between 12 and 22 times more likely than nonsmokers to develop lung cancer.	All forms of tobacco increase the risk of cavities and gum disease. Tobacco dulls the taste buds and can cause stomach ulcers. Tobacco use is linked to cancers of the mouth, throat, stomach, esophagus, and pancreas.	Tobacco use reduces the flow of oxygen to the brain, which can lead to a stroke.	Smokers have at least twice the risk of developing bladder cancer as nonsmokers. Smokeless tobacco can also put users at risk of developing bladder cancer.	Tobacco use is linked to heart disease. It increases the chances of a heart attack. Smoking also raises blood pressure and heart rate.

Health Skills Activity

Advocacy

Convincing Others Not to Smoke

Molly and her dad decided to spend their Saturday shopping at the mall. They took a break for lunch at the food court. During lunch, Molly tells her dad that she would like to help her aunt Kate quit smoking. Aunt Kate is Molly's favorite aunt, and Molly is concerned for her health. Molly's dad suggests that Molly have a talk with her aunt to influence her to make the healthful choice to quit smoking.

What Would You Do?

What would you say to Aunt Kate if you were in Molly's situation? Write a few sentences about what you would say. Use the following steps to help you:

- Have a clear, health-focused stand.
- Be ready to support your position with information.
- Remember your audience.
- Urge others to make healthful choices.

Respiratory System

Breathing in tobacco smoke affects your respiratory system. Tobacco smoke damages the **alveoli** (al·VEE·oh·lye), *the tiny air sacs in the lungs.* When this happens, your lungs are less able to supply oxygen to your body. In fact, damage to the alveoli can cause **emphysema**, *a disease that results in the destruction of the alveoli in the lungs.* When this disease affects a large part of the lungs, it can cause death.

Digestive System

Smoking can damage your digestive system. It can lead to mouth and stomach ulcers, which are painful, open sores. Smoking also harms teeth and gums, causing teeth to yellow and making it more likely that you will get cavities and gum disease.

Nervous System

Your brain needs oxygen. Tobacco smoke contains carbon monoxide, which can cut down the amount of oxygen that the blood can carry to the brain. Nicotine reaches the brain in only a few seconds and attaches to special receptors in brain cells. The brain **adapts** to nicotine by increasing the number of nicotine receptors. This causes tobacco users to need more tobacco.

Academic Vocabulary

adapts (uh DAPTS) (*verb*) adjusts; to get used to new conditions. *Brandon adapts to his new school by being friendly to other students and by joining the soccer team.*

Circulatory System

Smoking affects the circulatory or cardiovascular system, which includes the heart and blood vessels. As a person smokes, blood vessels constrict, or squeeze together. Over time, the blood vessels can harden. When this happens, the blood vessels cannot send enough blood and oxygen throughout the body. This increases the chances of a heart attack or stroke. People with hardened or clogged blood vessels have *coronary heart disease.* Smoking is a leading cause of this disease. Smoking also raises blood pressure and heart rate. Both side effects hurt the circulatory system.

Excretory System

Tobacco can harm your excretory system. Smokers and tobacco users are much more likely to develop bladder cancer than non-smokers. Chemicals in tobacco smoke are absorbed from the lungs and get into the blood. From the blood, the chemicals get into the kidneys and bladder. These chemicals damage the cells that line the inside of the bladder and increase the risk of cancer. Smoking tobacco is also a factor in the development of colorectal cancer, a cancer that affects the colon and the rectum.

 **Reading Check** **Explain** Describe how tobacco use affects the teeth.

Visit **glencoe.com** and complete the Interactive Study Guide for Lesson 1.

Lesson 1 Review

 After You Read

Review this lesson for new terms, major headings, and Reading Checks.

What I Learned

1. *Vocabulary* Define *tar.*

2. *Explain* Describe the ways in which smoking harms the body.

3. *Identify* Name five substances in tobacco smoke that are harmful to the body.

4. *List* Name three forms of tobacco.

Thinking Critically

5. *Hypothesize* How might you influence a peer to make the healthful choice to quit chewing tobacco?

6. *Analyze* Why do you think it is important for a teen to never try tobacco?

Applying Health Skills

7. *Accessing Information* Do research to find more information about the harmful effects of tobacco. Use health journals, magazines, and Web sites of national organizations to help you. Write a short report about the information you found.

The Respiratory System

Guide to Reading

Building Vocabulary
As you read this lesson, make flash cards for each new term.

- respiratory system (p. 236)
- trachea (p. 237)
- epiglottis (p. 237)
- bronchi (p. 237)
- lungs (p. 237)
- diaphragm (p. 237)

Focusing on the Main Ideas
In this lesson you will be able to

- **explain** why you need oxygen to live.
- **name** the parts of the respiratory system.
- **describe** the breathing process.
- **identify** problems of the respiratory system.

Reading Strategy
Sequencing As you read the lesson, summarize the steps of the breathing process.

Quick Write

Have you ever had a respiratory illness, like a cough or cold? Describe how you felt. Explain why you think a healthy respiratory system is important.

You Need Oxygen to Live

The body needs oxygen to work properly. Oxygen helps you perform all kinds of activities, like playing your favorite sport or talking to your friend on the phone. How does oxygen get into your body? You breathe it in. How does oxygen get to your cells? It travels through your respiratory system. Your **respiratory system** includes *the organs that supply your blood with oxygen*. Blood carries the oxygen to your whole body.

Parts of Your Respiratory System

The main parts of your respiratory system include the mouth and nose, the trachea, the lungs, and the diaphragm. **Figure 8.2** shows the respiratory system in more detail.

Air enters your body through your nose and mouth. *Cilia* (SIH·lee·uh) line the inside of your nose. These tiny, hair-like structures trap dirt and particles from the air you inhale before it travels to other parts of your respiratory system.

◀ Daily exercise is important to maintaining the health of your respiratory system. **How do you exercise every day?**

The **trachea** (TRAY·kee·uh) is *a passageway in your throat that takes air into and out of your lungs.* You may know the trachea as the windpipe. The **epiglottis** (eh·pi·GLAH·tis) is *a flap of tissue in the back of your mouth that keeps food out of your trachea.* It covers the trachea when you eat and uncovers it when you breathe.

As you breathe in, your body takes in oxygen. As you breathe out, your body rids itself of carbon dioxide. Carbon dioxide is a gas, just like oxygen. As your cells burn oxygen, they make carbon dioxide as a waste product. The exchange of oxygen and carbon dioxide happens in your lungs. The **bronchi** (BRAHNG·ky) are *two passageways that branch from the trachea, one to each lung.* Your **lungs** are *two large organs that exchange oxygen and carbon dioxide.* Your **diaphragm** (DY·uh·fram) is *a large, dome-shaped muscle below the lungs that **expands** and compresses the lungs, enabling breathing.*

 **Reading Check**   **Explain** What is the function of the diaphragm?

▼ **FIGURE 8.2**

PARTS OF THE RESPIRATORY SYSTEM

As you breathe, your lungs work with all the other parts of your respiratory system. Look at the diagram, and think about what happens when you cough. **Which parts of your respiratory system do you use when you cough?**

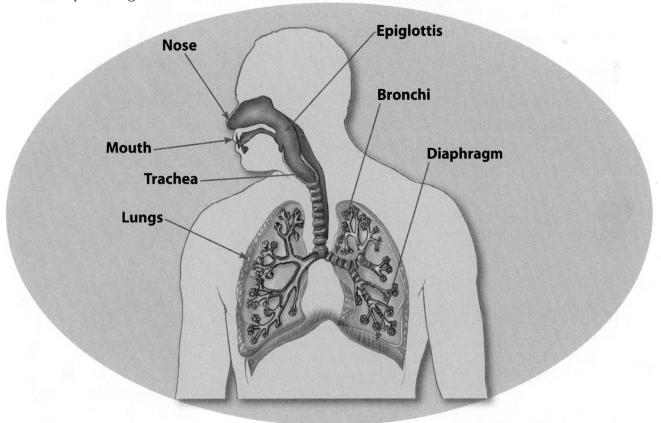

The Breathing Process

Three processes happen in your body when you breathe. First, you inhale, or breathe in air. The diaphragm, a muscle below the lungs, moves down and your chest expands, letting air into your lungs. Second, oxygen from the air passes out of your lungs and into your blood. At the same time, the oxygen replaces carbon dioxide. Third, you exhale, or breathe out air. Your diaphragm pushes up, forcing air and carbon dioxide out of your lungs. **Figure 8.3** shows the steps of the breathing process.

Reading Check **List** What are the three steps of the breathing process?

▼ FIGURE 8.3

HOW BREATHING WORKS

Your brain controls your respiratory system, so you breathe automatically. You don't have to think about breathing. **What chemical compound is contained in exhaled air?**

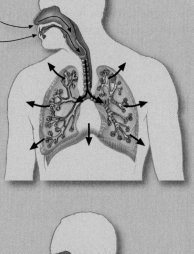

1 Inhaling. Your diaphragm moves down and your ribcage expands, creating more room in your chest. This causes air to flow into your body through the nose or mouth. The air then moves past the epiglottis and into the trachea and bronchi.

2 Inside Your Lungs. The bronchi divide into smaller passageways called bronchioles (BRAHNG·kee·ohlz). Air flows through the bronchioles into the alveoli, which are surrounded by capillaries. In the capillaries, oxygen moves from the air into the bloodstream, and carbon dioxide from the blood moves into the alveoli.

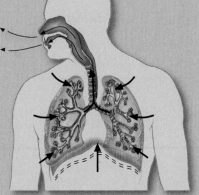

3 Exhaling. Your diaphragm moves up, and your ribs move in and down, pushing air out of your lungs. The air, now containing carbon dioxide, moves back through the bronchioles and bronchi, flows up the trachea, and out through the nose or mouth.

Problems of the Respiratory System

Tobacco use does not cause all the problems that can affect your respiratory system. However, it can make many of these problems worse. Tobacco smoke, chemicals, germs, and air pollution are harmful to your health because they can damage the many parts of your respiratory system. **Figure 8.4** lists some of the many problems tobacco can cause.

▼ FIGURE 8.4

DISEASES AND DISORDERS OF THE RESPIRATORY SYSTEM

People can take medicines to control some respiratory diseases, such as asthma. Without the right treatment, respiratory problems can become dangerous. Explain how using tobacco contributes to emphysema.

Disease or Disorder	Description	Treatment
Asthma	Disorder in which airways narrow; symptoms include wheezing or gasping, shortness of breath, coughing	Medication to relieve symptoms; avoiding activities or substances that trigger attacks
Cold/Flu	Illnesses caused by viruses; symptoms include fever, aches, cough, runny nose	Bed rest and liquids; vaccines can prevent some types of flu
Emphysema	Disease in which alveoli lose their ability to stretch; symptoms include extreme difficulty breathing; caused by smoking or severe and uncontrolled chronic asthma	No known cure; pure oxygen can make breathing easier
Lung Cancer	Uncontrolled growth of cells that reproduce abnormally in lungs; often caused by smoking	Surgery, radiation, chemotherapy; survival rates are very low
Mouth and Tongue Cancer	Uncontrolled growth of cells in the mouth and tongue; can cause growths called tumors that show on the cheeks and lips; almost always caused by tobacco use	Surgery, radiation, chemotherapy; survival rates are very low if it spreads
Pneumonia	Bacterial or viral disease that affects the lungs; symptoms include fever, breathing difficulty, chest pain	Antibiotics for bacterial type; bed rest for viral type
Tuberculosis	Bacterial disease that affects the lungs; symptoms include tiredness, cough; can be fatal	Antibiotics

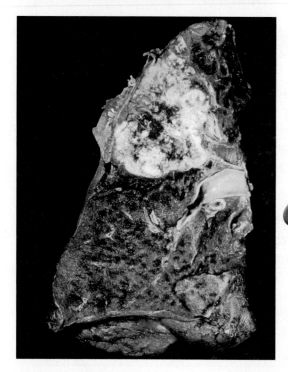

▲ The top photo is a healthy lung. The bottom photo is a cancerous lung. Healthy lungs provide oxygen to your body. **What happens to the cells in the lungs if they become cancerous?**

Respiratory Diseases

When did you last have a cold or the flu? These are two of the most common respiratory diseases. You usually get over a cold or the flu in a few days. However, smokers take much longer to get over a cold or the flu.

If your respiratory system is not healthy, you can develop chronic, or ongoing, disease, such as emphysema. Emphysema damages alveoli in the lungs. There is no cure for emphysema, but in most cases it can be prevented by not smoking tobacco.

Tobacco use can also aggravate or increase the symptoms of asthma. Asthma is a chronic respiratory disease that causes air passages to become narrow or blocked, making breathing difficult. People with asthma cough and gasp for air. They shouldn't smoke or be around smokers.

Some diseases of the respiratory system are inherited, such as cystic fibrosis (CF). A person with CF also has trouble breathing. The disease causes the lungs to make abnormally sticky mucus. A person with CF may feel like he or she cannot breathe at all. Smoking can also aggravate this condition.

 **Reading Check**   **Describe** What are the symptoms of cystic fibrosis?

Cancer

Smoking can cause cancer. Cancer is the uncontrolled growth of cells. Cancer can spread from one part of the body to another and attack healthy tissues and organs. All tobacco products contain substances that can cause cancer. Smoking can cause cancers of the mouth, throat, lung, kidney, and bladder. Lung cancer is the leading cause of death among people who smoke. Lung cancer is hard to diagnose and can spread quickly. A person who quits smoking can reduce the risk of developing cancer.

Smokeless tobacco can cause cancers of the mouth, head, and neck. Someone who uses smokeless tobacco has a higher risk of developing cancer than a smoker does. One-half to three-quarters of smokeless tobacco users develop mouth sores, or ulcers. These sores can disappear if the user quits. Quitting the use of smokeless tobacco reduces the risk of developing mouth cancer.

Tips for Taking Care of Your Respiratory System

Your whole body depends on a healthy respiratory system. The following positive health practices can help you keep it that way:

- Avoid tobacco use.
- Stay away from people who smoke. Don't go to places where the air is smoky.
- Take care of your body when you have a cold, the flu, or any other respiratory illness.
- Drink plenty of fluids.
- Take deep, full breaths often.
- Eat a healthful diet.
- Get outside and breathe fresh air.
- Pay attention to any allergy alerts, ozone alerts, and pollution alerts announced for your area.
- Be physically active on a regular basis.

 Reading Check **Name** List two ways you can care for your respiratory system.

 **G Online**

Visit **glencoe.com** and complete the Interactive Study Guide for Lesson 2.

Lesson 2 Review

After You Read

Review this lesson for new terms, major headings, and Reading Checks.

What I Learned

1. **Vocabulary** Define *trachea*.

2. **Explain** Why do you need oxygen to live?

3. **Identify** Name the different parts of the respiratory system.

4. **List** Name four respiratory illnesses.

Thinking Critically

5. **Describe** How might quitting smokeless tobacco use affect the health of the mouth?

6. **Analyze** Why is it important to take care of your respiratory system when you have a cold or the flu?

Applying Health Skills

7. **Communication Skills** Write a letter to a filmmaker. Ask the filmmaker to ban smoking scenes in movies. Explain why filmmakers should want to send out a tobacco-free message to everyone, especially children and teens. Use facts from this lesson in your letter.

Tobacco Use and Teens

Guide to Reading

Building Vocabulary
In your own words, use each new term in a sentence.
- addiction (p. 244)
- withdrawal (p. 244)
- psychological dependence (p. 244)
- physical dependence (p. 244)
- tolerance (p. 245)
- target audience (p. 246)
- product placement (p. 246)
- media literacy (p. 246)

Focusing on the Main Ideas
In this lesson you will be able to
- **identify** reasons why teens use tobacco.
- **explain** how a person can become addicted to nicotine.
- **apply** accessing-information skills to find health information on quitting tobacco use.
- **describe** how antismoking efforts are helping teens stay tobacco free.

Reading Strategy
Summarizing For each main heading in this lesson, make a flash card that captures the main points of the heading.

Quick Write

Do the ads you see on TV and in magazines affect your decisions? Write a few sentences about how advertising can influence a teen's choices.

▶ Each state has its own legal smoking age. Why do you think these signs are posted in stores that sell tobacco products?

Why Do Teens Begin Using Tobacco?

Most teens know that making the decision to avoid tobacco use is the way to stay healthy. They also know it's against the law for people under the age of 18 to buy tobacco. Still, teens try tobacco for many reasons. The good news is that the number of teen smokers has fallen over the years. A 2004 study found that 89 percent of middle school students don't smoke.

Reasons for Tobacco Use Among Teens

One of the main reasons teens may try tobacco is peer pressure. Teens may try tobacco even if they don't want to because they think they might lose their friends. Real friends will not pressure you to try an activity that is harmful to your health. It's important to choose friends who influence you to make healthful choices, like staying tobacco free.

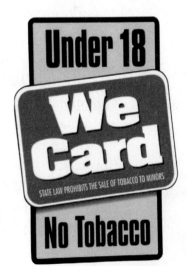

Under 18
We Card
STATE LAW PROHIBITS THE SALE OF TOBACCO TO MINORS
No Tobacco

WHY TEENS USE TOBACCO

Every day in America, 2,000 more young people start using tobacco. One-third of people who start using tobacco in their teens will die at a young age. **Reasons for using tobacco are listed below. Counter each by thinking of reasons not to use tobacco.**

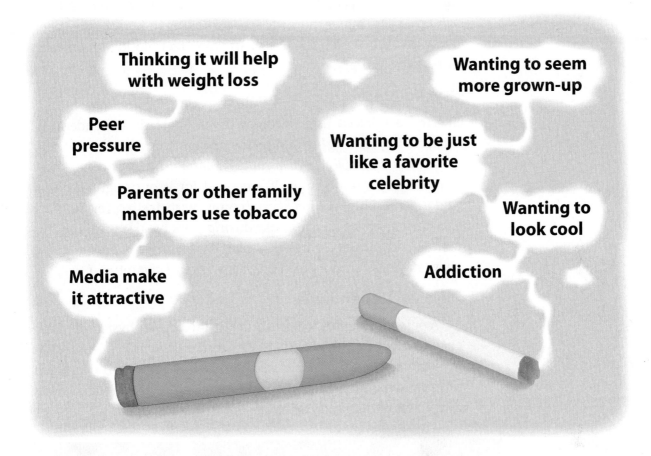

There are other reasons teens may try using tobacco. **Figure 8.5** names some of them. Some teens think using tobacco makes them seem cooler, older, or more mature. They also think smoking will help them feel more confident around others who smoke. Some teens may try tobacco simply because they've been told not to use it. They just want to rebel. Other teens are curious and want to try it for themselves. Teens often believe that they will not be harmed by tobacco use or that the health risks do not apply to them.

The media also play a part in teen tobacco use. Magazines, music videos, and movies show images of people using tobacco. Tobacco companies spend billions of dollars advertising their products. Ads are developed that appeal to teens. They show attractive-looking people using tobacco products.

 **Reading Check** **Identify** Name two reasons teens may consider trying tobacco.

Tobacco Addiction

As you learned in Lesson 1, tobacco contains nicotine. Nicotine is a drug that causes addiction. An **addiction** is *a mental or physical need for a drug or other substance*. Nicotine is as addictive as cocaine and heroin. Anyone who stops using nicotine goes through withdrawal. **Withdrawal** is *the unpleasant symptoms that someone experiences when he or she stops using an addictive substance*. During withdrawal from smoking, a person may sleep badly and crave nicotine. He or she may feel moody or nervous, or be extra hungry.

Psychological Dependence

First a tobacco user becomes psychologically dependent on tobacco. **Psychological dependence** is *a person's belief that he or she needs a drug to feel good or function normally*. Most people know that tobacco is dangerous. Their need for it outweighs the fear of danger as they connect tobacco use with feeling relaxed. For example, a person might smoke during work breaks. Breaking this connection means changing habits. For example, a person could chew sugarless gum instead of reaching for a cigarette.

Physical Dependence

A person who uses tobacco quickly develops a physical dependence to nicotine. **Physical dependence** is *an addiction in which the body develops a chemical need for a drug*. Teens can develop a physical dependence for nicotine much more easily than adults can. Their bodies and brains are not fully developed.

▶ Getting involved can help break a psychological dependence on tobacco. **Name two activities you could suggest to someone who wants to quit.**

500,000,000 people alive today will die from tobacco. NO LIE

The body's tolerance for nicotine also increases over time. **Tolerance** is *the body's need for larger and larger amounts of a drug to produce the same effect.* The body's need for nicotine causes a person to crave the tobacco product. Tobacco users must smoke or chew tobacco more often. They may constantly need to do something with their hands. They may have to keep something in their mouths all the time.

 **Reading Check** **Describe** Name some symptoms of nicotine withdrawal.

Tobacco Advertising

Tobacco companies spend millions of dollars a year to advertise their products. Colorful ads featuring happy, attractive people can make teens feel that it's fun or cool to use tobacco. Tobacco advertisements can strongly affect teens.

Targeting Teens

Tobacco companies see teens as a target audience. A **target audience** is *a group of people for which a product is intended.* Tobacco companies work hard to make their products appealing to teens. Companies may package their cigarettes in bright wrappers or use cartoon characters to sell their product.

Open any magazine and you will find a tobacco advertisement that shows young, attractive people having fun. Maybe they are dancing or playing sports. The tobacco companies want you to think that using their products is fun. They also want you to think that using tobacco makes you attractive.

Like many teens, you probably have favorite celebrities. You often see them wearing a particular brand of clothing or drinking a certain kind of soda. **Product placement** is *when a company pays to show its products in media being used by celebrities.* Tobacco companies pay to have celebrities use their products too. If your favorite celebrity smoked cigarettes, would you want to smoke too? By now, you know how harmful tobacco products are to your personal health.

Media literacy is *the ability to understand the goals of advertising and the media.* The goal of tobacco advertisements is to fool you into becoming a lifelong customer. However, if you are media literate, you will be able to ignore the ads. You will be able to analyze whether health information, products, and services are valid.

 **Reading Check**   **Describe** Explain how product placement can influence a teen to use tobacco.

Antismoking Efforts

Today, more than ever, both teens and adults are more informed about the dangers of tobacco. In fact, most teens want to stay healthy by avoiding tobacco use. As a result, most teens and adults are in favor of a tobacco-free society.

Legal Bans on Tobacco Ads

Tobacco advertising has more limits than ever before. In the United States, laws protect young people from tobacco advertising. For example, companies cannot place outdoor advertisements within 1,000 feet of schools and playgrounds. Tobacco companies cannot make or sell hats, T-shirts, and other items. Tobacco advertisements cannot appear on radio and television. This is why product placement in the media is such an important issue. This practice allows tobacco companies to sidestep the law. Finally, it is illegal to sell tobacco to anyone under age 18. In some states, the age is even higher.

Antismoking Ad Campaigns

Today, antismoking ads are helping to create awareness about the dangers of tobacco use. They want to send the message to people of every age that choosing to use tobacco is a risk behavior that has many negative short-term and long-term consequences. Smokers who see these ads recognize the dangers of tobacco and often try to quit or seek treatment as a result. Nonsmokers who see these ads recognize the benefits of remaining tobacco free.

 Reading Check **Describe** List some of the legal bans on tobacco ads.

 **Go Online**

Visit **glencoe.com** and complete the Interactive Study Guide for Lesson 3.

Lesson 3 Review

 After You Read

Review this lesson for new terms, major headings, and Reading Checks.

What I Learned

1. *Vocabulary* Define *product placement.*

2. *Identify* Name three reasons why teens use tobacco products.

3. *Explain* Describe how the media may encourage teens to use tobacco.

4. *Give Examples* List two ways in which tobacco companies target teens.

5. *Describe* Explain how antismoking ads help teens stay away from tobacco.

Thinking Critically

6. *Describe* How does physical tolerance affect how much a person smokes?

7. *Analyze* Explain what happens because of physical dependency on tobacco.

Applying Health Skills

8. *Refusal Skills* With a classmate, write a short play that shows a teen using the S.T.O.P. formula to say no to someone who offers him or her a cigarette.

Lesson 4

Tobacco Use and Society

Guide to Reading

● Building Vocabulary
As you read this lesson, write each new term and its definition in your notebook.

- secondhand smoke (p. 248)
- passive smokers (p. 248)
- mainstream smoke (p. 248)
- sidestream smoke (p. 248)

● Focusing on the Main Ideas
In this lesson, you will be able to

- **list** the effects of tobacco use on nonsmokers.
- **describe** the consequences of passive smoking.
- **explain** the rights of nonsmokers.
- **access** reliable information about groups that help promote a tobacco-free lifestyle.

● Reading Strategy
Finding the Main Idea Take a look at the major headings in this lesson. For each heading, write one sentence that states the main idea.

*Q*uick Write

How does tobacco smoke in the air harm nonsmokers? Write a few sentences that tell what you know about secondhand smoke.

Tobacco's Effects on Nonsmokers

Your environment affects your personal health. Even if you do not smoke, being around those who do can be harmful. When people smoke near you, you breathe their secondhand smoke. **Secondhand smoke** is *air that has been contaminated by tobacco smoke.* It is also called environmental tobacco smoke (ETS). When you are around secondhand smoke, you become a passive smoker. **Passive smokers** are *nonsmokers who breathe in secondhand smoke.*

Environmental Tobacco Smoke

Secondhand smoke comes in two forms. First is **mainstream smoke,** *the smoke that is inhaled and then exhaled by a smoker.* Second is **sidestream smoke,** *smoke that comes from the burning end of a cigarette, pipe, or cigar.* Sidestream smoke is especially dangerous. It contains twice as much tar and nicotine as does mainstream smoke.

Dangerous Contents of Secondhand Smoke

Secondhand smoke is filled with nicotine, carbon monoxide, and other harmful ingredients. The U.S. Environmental Protection Agency (EPA) has labeled secondhand smoke as a human carcinogen. This means it causes cancer.

Health Hazards to Adults, Children, and Unborn Babies

Imagine standing in a smoke-filled room for one hour. During that time, you would breathe in nicotine and carbon monoxide. In fact, it would be the same as smoking one cigarette.

Nonsmoking adults who regularly breathe secondhand smoke can get sick from it. They risk getting the same illnesses that affect smokers. This includes heart and lung diseases and respiratory problems. Each year, an **estimated** 53,000 people in the United States die as a result of passive smoking.

Secondhand smoke is especially harmful to children. When children are exposed to secondhand smoke, they are more likely to have respiratory and other problems, like allergies, asthma, ear infections, and heart problems.

Women who use tobacco while pregnant put their unborn children in serious danger. Their babies could die or they could have babies with low birth weight. The lower a baby's birth weight, the higher the chances that the baby will have health problems. Sudden infant death syndrome (SIDS) is linked to babies with mothers who smoked during or after pregnancy.

Reading Check **Identify** Name two health problems that secondhand smoke can cause in children.

Rights of Nonsmokers

You have the right to breathe air that is free of tobacco smoke. There are more smoke-free places than ever before. There are also more laws against secondhand smoke. As a nonsmoker, you have the right to protect yourself from secondhand smoke. You can ask people not to smoke around you. If a smoker is a guest in your house, you can ask the person to smoke outside. Talk to your parents about asking houseguests not to smoke in your house.

Smoke-Free Environments

Today, the number of smoke-free businesses and public spaces is on the rise. Most public places, including restaurants, do not allow people to smoke indoors. Some restaurants do not allow smoking indoors or out.

▼ Secondhand smoke is dangerous to everyone's health. **Why do you think smoke-free restaurants are healthier for customers and restaurant workers?**

Health Skills Activity

Accessing Information

Promoting a Tobacco-Free Community

Many groups work to help people live a tobacco-free lifestyle. As you learn more about what these groups do, you can share what you know with others who want to stay tobacco free. There are many ways to influence others to make the healthful choice not to smoke.

Do some research to find local organizations that promote being tobacco free. Interview people from three or four of these organizations. Ask them about the programs they sponsor and how they let people know about them. Discuss how to become a member. Get the organization's history.

With a Group

After collecting your information, organize a Tobacco-Free Health Fair to share what you have learned. Invite the people you interviewed to speak about their group and its programs at your Tobacco-Free Health Fair.

Legal Restrictions on Smoking

In the late 1980s, national laws went into effect to fight secondhand smoke. In 1989, smoking was outlawed on domestic airplane flights. Nearly all states also have laws that limit smoking. Employers have the legal right to ban smoking in their workplaces. Most employers now exercise this right.

Laws now control how tobacco companies package and sell cigarettes. Packages must have clear warning labels, or disclaimers. The disclaimers say that smoking is harmful. Cans of smokeless tobacco and tobacco ads must also have these disclaimers.

 **Reading Check**

Explain In what ways do laws control the sale and packaging of tobacco products?

SURGEON GENERAL'S WARNING: Smoking Causes Lung Cancer, Heart Disease, Emphysema, And May Complicate Pregnancy.

SURGEON GENERAL'S WARNING: Smoking By Pregnant Women May Result In Fetal Injury, Premature Birth, And Low Birth Weight.

◀ The U.S. government requires tobacco companies to label packages with these disclaimers. **Do you think that these labels keep people from smoking?**

Hidden Costs to Society

Tobacco products cost a lot of money. There are also hidden costs of tobacco use. Tobacco-related illnesses, such as lung cancer and emphysema, often require the person to be in the hospital. Hospital stays and treatments for these illnesses are very expensive. These preventable costs affect the health care system.

Tobacco Strains the Health Care System

People who use tobacco tend to need medical treatment more often than those who do not. If tobacco users have health insurance, it may help them pay some of the costs of their treatment. However, because health insurance companies face more costs to cover tobacco users, they charge tobacco users higher rates for their health insurance. If a tobacco user has no health insurance, the government helps cover the costs. This means that every U.S. family pays, too, as part of their taxes. It is estimated that taxpayers pay about $38 billion each year, whether or not they smoke.

Visit glencoe.com and complete the Interactive Study Guide for Lesson 4.

Reading Check **Describe** How can tobacco use affect how much people pay for health insurance?

Lesson 4 Review

After You Read

Review this lesson for new terms, major headings, and Reading Checks.

What I Learned

1. **Vocabulary** Define *sidestream smoke* and *mainstream smoke.*

2. **Explain** Describe the effects smoking can have on an unborn baby.

3. **Explain** Why do tobacco users pay more for health insurance?

4. **Explain** Why do nonsmokers have to pay to cover part of the cost of smokers' medical treatments?

Thinking Critically

5. **Analyze** How can laws to protect you from secondhand smoke help to protect your health?

6. **Apply** Imagine that you are sitting in the nonsmoking section of a restaurant. What would you do if the smoke from the smoking section bothered you?

Applying Health Skills

7. **Accessing Information** Research the latest restrictions on tobacco ads. Write a paragraph describing your findings.

Saying No to Tobacco Use

Guide to Reading

● Building Vocabulary
As you read this lesson, write this new term and its definition in your notebook.

- cold turkey (p. 255)

● Focusing on the Main Ideas
In this lesson, you will be able to

- **list** the reasons why it is good to be tobacco free.
- **practice** refusal skills to avoid tobacco use.
- **explain** how a person can get help to quit tobacco use.

● Reading Strategy
Outlining Before reading this lesson, make an outline using the heads as guidelines. Fill in your outline as you read.

Quick Write

What are your reasons for staying tobacco free? Write a few sentences describing why you say no to tobacco.

Tobacco Free: A Healthy Choice

Choosing not to use tobacco shows that you are taking responsibility for personal health behaviors. Choose to spend time with others who are tobacco free. That's another good strategy for improving and maintaining personal health. As a teen, you will probably be asked if you want to try tobacco. Be prepared for this possibility. Practice your refusal skills ahead of time. Take part in tobacco-free events in your community. Help others to be tobacco free.

 **Reading Check**

Explain How do you prepare yourself for when someone offers you a tobacco product?

Benefits of Being Tobacco Free

It's great to be tobacco free! There are many benefits to this safe behavior. To begin with, you'll be healthier. Look at the list below and at **Figure 8.6** to learn more.

- **Staying healthy.** People who smoke get sick more easily and more often than nonsmokers. They also stay sick longer than people who don't use tobacco.
- **Clear, healthy skin.** If you use tobacco, your skin cells are less able to take in oxygen and other nutrients, which leads to unhealthy skin.

- **Fresh breath.** Cigarettes and smokeless tobacco products cause bad breath.
- **Clean, fresh-smelling clothes and hair.** Smokers usually smell like smoke. Stinky cigarette odors cling to clothes and hair. It's hard to get rid of these odors.
- **Better sports performance.** People who use tobacco, especially smokers, don't do as well in sports. Nonsmokers make better athletes than smokers, partly because they have healthier respiratory systems.
- **Saving money.** Tobacco is expensive. The government keeps raising taxes on tobacco. That means costs will keep going up. Teens who do not buy tobacco have more money to spend on other things, like clothes and digital music.
- **Keeping the environment healthy.** Environmental tobacco smoke hurts everyone. By staying tobacco free, you are doing your part to keep the environment healthy. You also are protecting people who are part of your everyday life.

 Reading Check **Describe** Why are nonsmokers better athletes than smokers?

Topic: Taking Action Against Tobacco

Visit **glencoe.com** for Student Web Activities where you will learn why and how teens across the nation are speaking out against tobacco use.

Activity: Using information provided at the link above, draft an e-mail message entitled "The Top Ten Reasons I Choose Not to Smoke" that you and your friends can sign and e-mail to other teens.

▼ FIGURE 8.6

REASONS TO BE TOBACCO FREE

Reasons to be tobacco free really add up. **What are some other reasons to be tobacco free?**

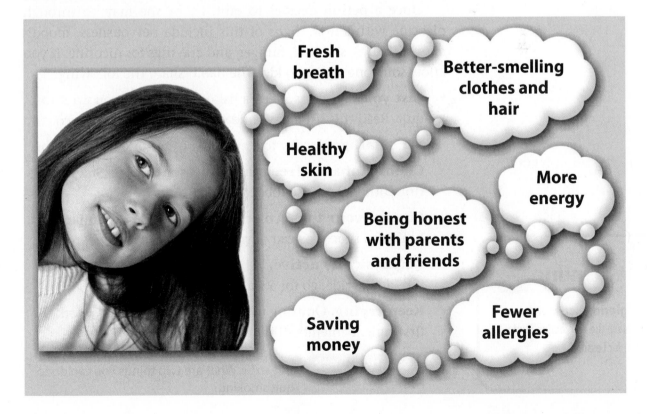

Fresh breath

Better-smelling clothes and hair

Healthy skin

More energy

Being honest with parents and friends

Saving money

Fewer allergies

Health Skills Activity

Refusal Skills

Refusing Tobacco

Sindhu and Andrea have been good friends since the third grade. Now that they are older, they go to different schools. Andrea spends much of her time with her new friends. One afternoon, Andrea and Sindhu meet after school. Andrea then offers Sindhu a cigarette. Sindhu wants to keep Andrea as a friend, but she does not want to smoke. What should she say to Andrea?

What Would You Do?

Role-play how Sindhu reacts to Andrea when Andrea asks her to have a cigarette. How can Sindhu use the S.T.O.P. formula in this situation?

- **S**ay no in a firm voice.
- **T**ell why not.
- **O**ffer another idea.
- **P**romptly leave.

You Can Quit

Once you start using tobacco, it's hard to stop. This is one of the best reasons to stay tobacco free. People who do smoke can quit if they really choose to. Many programs and support groups can help.

Once a person decides to quit, he or she may go through nicotine withdrawal. Signs of this include nervousness, moodiness, difficulty sleeping, hunger, and cravings for nicotine. If you know someone trying to kick the habit, share the following:

- **List your reasons.** Keep a list of the reasons you want to quit. Read this list every time you feel like using tobacco.

- **Set small goals.** Try to stay tobacco free one day at a time.

- **Choose tobacco-free places to spend time.** Stay away from others who use tobacco.

- **Change your tobacco-related habits.** For example, eat a healthful snack instead of smoking between meals.

- **Be physically active.** When you feel like using tobacco, take a bike ride, go for a walk, or jog.

- **Keep trying.** Quitting tobacco use doesn't always work the first time. Remember that each effort counts.

Go Online

Visit **glencoe.com** and complete the Interactive Study Guide for Lesson 5.

Reading Check **Describe** What are two things you can do to quit smoking?

Getting Help

Some people may choose to stop using tobacco **cold turkey.** This means *stopping all use of tobacco products immediately.* They will experience withdrawal symptoms that can last up to six months. Libraries, hospitals, and bookstores offer information if someone wants to quit on his or her own. Many organizations also help users quit. For example, users can find tips on quitting and support groups through the American Lung Association, the American Heart Association, and the American Cancer Society.

Resources for Quitting

Even some people who join a support group may fail to kick the habit. That's when professional health services can help. Doctors are able to prescribe medication to help tobacco users quit. There are also over-the-counter medications such as the nicotine patch or nicotine gum. All allow users to give up tobacco quickly while gradually stopping nicotine dependence.

 Reading Check **Name** List two organizations that can help a person stop using tobacco.

Connect To... **Math**

Personal Finances

Smoking is not only unhealthy, it's also an expensive habit. In some states, a pack of cigarettes costs as much as $7.00.

If a person smokes one pack a day, how much money would he or she spend on cigarettes in one year? What would you choose to buy with that amount of money?

Lesson 5 Review

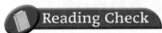 **After You Read**

Review this lesson for new terms, major headings, and Reading Checks.

What I Learned

1. *Vocabulary* Define *cold turkey.*

2. *Explain* Describe how you can help someone become tobacco free.

3. *Identify* List at least three benefits of being tobacco free.

4. *Explain* Describe how people who wish to stop using tobacco can get help.

Thinking Critically

5. *Analyze* Why is it easier never to start smoking?

6. *Apply* How would you influence a peer to make the healthful choice to quit smoking?

Applying Health Skills

7. *Goal Setting* Make a plan to help someone quit using tobacco. Include alternative activities the tobacco user can do when he or she experiences the urge to use tobacco.

Go Online For more Lesson Review Activities, go to glencoe.com.

Lesson 5: Saying No to Tobacco Use **255**

Accessing Information

Practicing Healthful Behaviors

Stress Management

Analyzing Influences

Communication Skills

Refusal Skills

Conflict Resolution

Decision Making

Goal Setting

Advocacy

What Does Analyzing Influences Involve?

Analyzing influences involves recognizing the factors that affect your health choices. These factors include:

- family and culture
- your friends and peers
- messages from the media
- your likes, dislikes, values, and beliefs

Media Messages About Tobacco

Follow the Model, Practice, and Apply steps to help you master this important health skill.

Model

Read about how Samantha uses the skill of analyzing influences to recognize how tobacco ads try to make smoking look appealing.

Samantha's health class has been studying how some media try to influence teens to smoke. Her teacher asked Samantha to analyze some newspaper ads for cigarettes. One of the ads was in the sports section. It showed several people having a good time watching a football game. Another ad showed a clear, blue lake with snow-topped mountains in the background.

Samantha saw that the first ad was trying to link good times with friends to tobacco use. The second ad was trying to show that smoking was refreshing and relaxing. Both ads were trying to influence people to buy their cigarettes.

❷ Practice

Read the dialogue below and then answer the questions that follow.

Lindsey and Robin were looking at a tobacco ad in a magazine.

Robin: This guy is so cute!

Lindsey: He's way cute! But you know why they picked this guy, right? It makes people think smoking is attractive.

Robin: I wasn't thinking about that. The advertisers are trying to make us think smoking is fun.

Lindsey: It's almost like the tobacco companies are trying to trick us into smoking.

Robin: Yes. They spend a lot of money trying to persuade people to smoke.

1. How do Lindsey and Robin think advertisers try to influence teens?

2. Why do advertisers spend so much money trying to influence teens?

❸ Apply

Use what you have learned about analyzing influences to complete the activity below.

Many magazines have tobacco ads. Look through magazines to find a tobacco ad. Write a brief report about the ad. Explain the message the ad is trying to send about smoking. Explain how this ad might influence a teen to smoke. What is the truthful message that tobacco ads *should* send to teens?

Self-Check

- Did I explain the message the ad sends about smoking?
- Did I tell how the ad might influence a teen?
- Did I explain the true message about smoking?

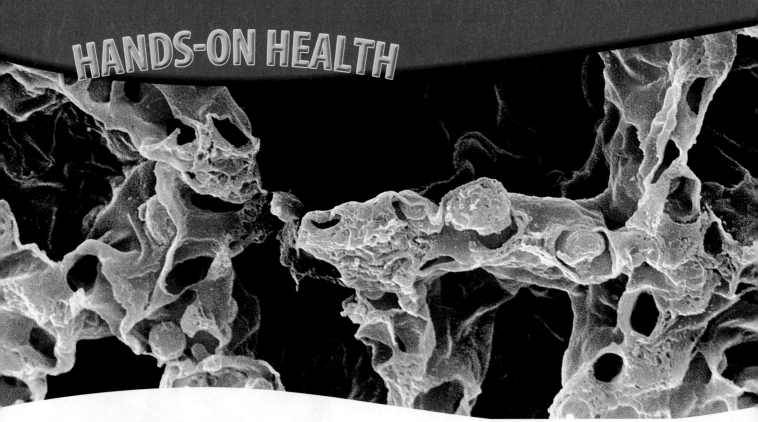

Inside Your Lungs

You've learned that smoking affects your lungs. Do you remember what's inside your lungs? Each lung contains millions of little sacs called alveoli. When you inhale, oxygen and anything else you breathe makes its way into these 600 million little sacs. Blood vessels surround the alveoli. They pick up oxygen from the alveoli and carry it to your cells. Smoking makes the alveoli less able to handle the oxygen your body needs.

What You Will Need

■ 64 sugar cubes
■ Cellophane tape
■ One sheet of graph paper

☀ ACTIVITY What You Will Do

1 Use the sugar cubes to make a square that is 4 cubes long, 4 wide, and 4 deep.

2 Use tape to hold these cubes together.

3 Use the graph paper to figure out how many paper squares can be covered by the large sugar rectangle.

4 Remove the tape and measure how many paper squares can be covered by a single cube. Remember to record all six sides.

5 Multiply this single cube measurement by 64.

Wrapping It Up

Which covers more graph paper squares: the large sugar rectangle or the 64 cubes? The cubes represent your alveoli. Just breathing in does not get oxygen to your body cells. It only gets it to your lungs. Alveoli pass oxygen to your blood. Dividing the lungs into many smaller sacs (alveoli) gets more oxygen to your blood faster. Warm-blooded animals like us need this trick. We need to get oxygen at a fast enough rate to perform all our activities.

Reading Review

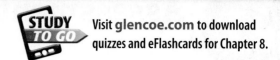

Visit **glencoe.com** to download quizzes and eFlashcards for Chapter 8.

FOLDABLES® Study Organizer

Foldables® and Other Study Aids Take out the Foldable® that you created for Lesson 1 and any graphic organizers that you created for Lessons 1–5. Find a partner and quiz each other using these study aids.

Lesson 1 How Tobacco Affects the Body

Main Idea All forms of tobacco have a negative effect on the body.

- There are more than 4,000 harmful chemicals in a single puff of tobacco smoke.
- Tobacco comes in many forms, including cigarettes, cigars, pipe tobacco, smokeless tobacco, clove cigarettes, and flavored tobacco.
- Several body systems are negatively affected by tobacco use.

Lesson 2 The Respiratory System

Main Idea Maintaining a healthy respiratory system is an important part of personal health.

- The respiratory system includes the mouth, nose, trachea, bronchi, lungs, and diaphragm.
- The three processes that happen in your body when you breathe are inhaling, sending oxygen into your blood to replace carbon dioxide, and exhaling.
- Diseases and disorders affected by tobacco include asthma; cold/flu; emphysema; lung, mouth, and tongue cancer; pneumonia; and tuberculosis.

Lesson 3 Tobacco Use and Teens

Main Idea Teens use tobacco for many reasons, including peer pressure and wanting to look cool.

- People who are addicted to tobacco have both a physical and a psychological dependence.
- Tobacco companies target teens with appealing advertisements and product placement.
- It is illegal to sell tobacco to anyone under age 18.

Lesson 4 Tobacco Use and Society

Main Idea Tobacco smoke harms both smokers and nonsmokers.

- Passive smokers are nonsmokers who breathe in secondhand smoke.
- Secondhand smoke causes cancer and is especially harmful to children.
- You have the right to breathe air that is free of tobacco smoke.

Lesson 5 Saying No to Tobacco Use

Main Idea Taking responsibility to be tobacco free is the best choice a teen can make for his or her health.

- There are many benefits to being tobacco free. They include staying healthy; having clear skin, fresh-smelling breath, hair and clothes; better sports performance; saving money; and a healthy environment.
- Quitting tobacco use isn't easy.
- If someone quits using tobacco immediately, it is called *cold turkey*.

Assessment

After You Read

HEALTH QUIZ
Now that you have read the chapter, review your answers to the Health Quiz on the chapter opener. Would you change any of them? What would your answers be now?

Reviewing Vocabulary and Main Ideas

On a sheet of paper, write the numbers 1–4. After each number, write the term from the list that best completes each statement.

- carbon monoxide
- trachea
- bronchi
- nicotine

Lesson 1 How Tobacco Affects the Body

1. A drug found in tobacco smoke that is extremely addictive is called _____.

2. The colorless, odorless, poisonous gas produced when tobacco burns is called _____.

Lesson 2 The Respiratory System

3. The _____ is the tube in your throat that takes air into and out of the lungs.

4. Two tubes that lead from the trachea to the lungs are called _____.

Lesson 3 Tobacco Use and Teens

*On a sheet of paper, write the numbers 5–7. Write **True** or **False** for each statement below. If the statement is false, change the underlined word or phrase to make it true.*

5. During <u>withdrawal</u> a person often feels worried, depressed, and crabby.

6. <u>Physical dependence</u> is when a person believes that he or she needs a drug to function normally.

7. Tolerance means needing <u>less</u> of a drug to feel its effect.

On a sheet of paper, write the numbers 8–11. After each number, write the letter of the answer that best completes each statement.

Lesson 4 Tobacco Use and Society

8. Passive smokers breathe in air
   a. that is clean, because secondhand smoke is harmless.
   b. that contains only carbon dioxide and oxygen.
   c. that contains nicotine and carbon monoxide.

9. Tobacco companies are required by law to
   a. advertise to attract teens.
   b. put disclaimers on all products.
   c. show people smoking in their ads.

Lesson 5 Saying No to Tobacco Use

10. When a person decides to quit, he or she can
    a. get help from a doctor.
    b. get help from an organization such as the American Cancer Society.
    c. use stress-relief techniques.
    d. all of the above.

11. One of the many benefits of being tobacco free is
    a. smoker's breath.
    b. reduced athletic performance.
    c. fresh-smelling hair and clothes.

Go Online Visit glencoe.com and take the Online Quiz for Chapter 8.

Thinking Critically

Using complete sentences, answer the following questions on a sheet of paper.

12. **Apply** Tobacco companies show only adults in their cigarette ads. Still, these ads are often aimed at teens. What about these ads do you think appeals to teens? Explain.

13. **Assess** What is the connection between research into passive smoking and environmental tobacco smoke and the rise of tobacco-free businesses, stores, and restaurants? Explain.

Write About It

14. **Expository Writing** Write an ad for your local newspaper about breaking the tobacco habit. Make sure to list two organizations that can provide tobacco users with support in their efforts to stop using tobacco. Be sure to include the benefits of being tobacco free.

Tobacco Tales

Using Microsoft Word®, you and your partner will create a chart that evaluates tobacco ads. Follow the steps below to complete this project.

- Cut five tobacco ads from magazines.
- Open a new Word® document with a portrait view.
- Build a table with five rows; one for each ad. Divide the rows into two columns. The left side of the row will have space to describe the ad. The right side of the row will have space for your analysis.
- Enter your descriptions of the ads.
- Enter your analysis of each ad. What are the messages of the ads? Think about the target audience.
- Save your project.

Standardized Test Practice

Math

Darrin knows he needs to stay tobacco free because he wants to join the track team. To join the team, he needs to improve the time it takes him to run a mile. He tracks his time on a weekly basis. See the chart below.

Week	Time to run 1 mile (min)
1	15
2	12
3	10
4	9

1. By what percent did Darrin improve his time from Week 1 to Week 2?
   - **A.** 25%
   - **B.** 30%
   - **C.** 15%
   - **D.** 20%

2. During which time did Darrin show a 33 percent improvement?
   - **A.** From Week 1 to Week 2
   - **B.** From Week 3 to Week 4
   - **C.** From Week 2 to Week 4
   - **D.** From Week 1 to Week 3

Alcohol

SOMETIMES IT TAKES A FAMILY OF
TO STOP A DRUNK DRIVER.

Chapter Preview

Lesson 1   Alcohol Use and Abuse ... 264

Lesson 2   The Nervous System 272

Lesson 3   Alcohol Use and Teens 278

Lesson 4   Alcohol Use and Society ..282

Lesson 5   Saying No to
           Alcohol Use 286

Building Health Skills...................... 290

TIME health news 292

Chapter Reading Review..................293

Chapter Assessment 294

▲ *Working with the Photo*

Thousands of people die each year in crashes related to drunk driving. Do you think billboard messages like this one help keep people from drinking and driving?

Start-Up Activities

 Before You Read What do you already know about alcohol use? Take the short quiz below. Keep a record of your answers.

HEALTH QUIZ Choose the best answer for each of the following questions:

1. It is legal to drink alcohol at age 17.
   a. always
   b. sometimes
   c. never

2. Alcohol affects the brain soon after it is consumed.
   a. always
   b. sometimes
   c. never

3. It is okay to get a ride with someone who has only had one drink.
   a. always
   b. sometimes
   c. never

4. At parties, teens should avoid alcohol.
   a. always
   b. sometimes
   c. never

ANSWERS: 1. c.; 2. a.; 3. c.; 4. a.

 FOLDABLES Study Organizer

 As You Read Make this Foldable® to help you organize the information on alcohol that's presented in Lesson 1. Begin with a plain sheet of 11" × 17" paper.

1 Fold the short sides of a sheet of paper inward so that they meet in the middle.

2 Fold the top to the bottom.

3 Unfold and cut along the inside fold lines to form four tabs.

4 Label the tabs as shown.

Under the appropriate tab, record what you learn about these four topics.

 **Online** Visit **glencoe.com** and complete the Chapter 9 crossword puzzle.

Alcohol Use and Abuse

Guide to Reading

● Building Vocabulary

As you read this lesson, make a flashcard for each new term.

- alcohol (p. 264)
- intoxicated (p. 265)
- blood alcohol concentration (p. 265)
- cirrhosis (p. 269)
- ulcer (p. 269)
- alcohol abuse (p. 270)
- alcoholism (p. 271)

● Focusing on the Main Ideas

In this lesson, you will be able to

- **identify** the dangers of using alcohol.
- **describe** the short-term effects of alcohol use.
- **explain** ways that alcohol use can damage body systems.
- **apply** accessing-information skills to find facts about alcohol abuse.

● Reading Strategy

Organizing Information Using the diagram below as a guide, create a chart that lists the reasons why using alcohol is dangerous.

Reasons	Why Using Alcohol is Dangerous
Reason 1	Alcohol can affect your control of your body.

FOLDABLES Study Organizer Use the Foldable® on p. 263 as you read this lesson.

Quick Write

Write a few sentences describing what you already know about alcohol.

Alcohol: What Is It?

Alcohol is a drug. In fact, it is one of the most widely used and abused drugs in the United States. **Alcohol** is *a drug created by a chemical reaction in some foods, especially fruits and grains.* Alcohol is addictive. It affects a person physically, mentally, emotionally, and socially. Alcohol use can greatly harm a person's health. It is against the law for any person under the age of 21 to purchase it.

▶ Alcohol abuse can lead to a wide range of physical, mental/emotional, and social problems. **Name two social problems caused by alcohol use.**

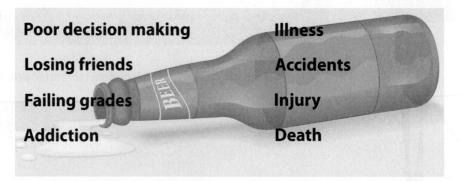

Poor decision making · Illness · Losing friends · Accidents · Failing grades · Injury · Addiction · Death

The Forms of Alcohol

By this point in your life, you have likely seen many TV commercials for alcohol. You may know that the three main forms of alcohol are beer, wine, and liquor. These drinks contain ethanol, a kind of alcohol that forms when the sugars from fruits, grains, or vegetables are fermented with yeast.

 **Reading Check** **Identify** What are the three main forms of alcohol?

The Dangers of Alcohol Use

Using alcohol is a dangerous behavior. It affects your ability to make good decisions and harms your physical health. Alcohol is a *depressant,* a drug that can slow down the activity of the brain and nervous system. A person may feel the effects of using alcohol right away. Judgment gets worse, making it more likely that a person will make bad decisions. Using alcohol can cause loss of control of motor skills, such as walking. If a person uses alcohol for a long time, he or she may develop many diseases. In fact, a person can die from drinking alcohol just once if he or she consumes too much in a short amount of time.

How Alcohol Affects Individuals

Not all people are affected by alcohol in the same way. A person is intoxicated (in·TAHK·suh·kay·tuhd) when he or she feels the effects of drinking alcohol. Being very **intoxicated** is also called *being drunk.* Some people can drink more alcohol than others before they become intoxicated. However, the amount of alcohol a person drinks is only one factor in understanding how drinking affects a person. **Figure 9.1** on the next page shows some other factors.

The more alcohol that is put into the body, the more the body is affected. The **blood alcohol concentration,** or BAC, is *the amount of alcohol in the blood.* A BAC of 0.10 percent means that there is 1 part alcohol per 1,000 parts of blood. Several factors determine a person's BAC, such as how much the person weighs, the amount of alcohol the person drank, and how much food is in the person's stomach.

Connect To... Science

Alcohol—A Depressant Drug

Alcohol is a kind of drug known as a depressant. What are some other depressants?

Do research to find out how alcohol acts as a depressant. Show what you learned in a pamphlet or on a poster.

▼ A 12-ounce bottle of beer contains about the same amount of alcohol as a 5-ounce glass of wine or 1.5 ounces of liquor. **Why might the same amount of alcohol affect two people differently?**

Liquor 1.5 oz. = Beer 12 oz. = Wine 5 oz.

ALCOHOL: DIFFERENT EFFECTS ON DIFFERENT PEOPLE

A person's body size helps determine how he or she will be affected by alcohol. **What are some other factors that explain how a person will be affected by alcohol?**

Factor	Description
Size and gender	Males can usually consume more alcohol before being affected by it than females. Also, the less a person weighs, the more easily and quickly he or she will be affected by alcohol.
Food in the stomach	If there is food in the stomach, the body will absorb the alcohol more slowly.
How fast a person drinks	Drinking quickly raises the level of alcohol in the blood because the body has less time to process it.
Other substances in the body	Drinking alcohol while taking certain medications and other drugs may have dangerous effects and can even be fatal.

In most states, a person is legally intoxicated when the BAC is greater than 0.08 percent, while in a few states, it is 0.01 percent. In most states, anyone under 21 is legally intoxicated if the BAC is greater than 0.02 percent. Police officers can measure the BAC in a person's body if they think that the person is driving drunk.

Over time, alcohol can damage the brain, heart, liver, and kidneys. It can also change how some medications act in the body. Consuming alcohol can also cause weight gain. It dehydrates the body, making your skin look older.

 Reading Check **Explain** What does *intoxicated* mean?

Short-Term Effects of Alcohol Use

Alcohol has both short- and long-term effects on the body. Some of the harmful short-term effects of alcohol are listed in **Figure 9.2.**

Alcohol Use and the Brain

Alcohol is absorbed into the bloodstream and reaches the brain almost as soon as it is consumed. Immediately, the brain and nervous system slow down. Even after only one drink, it becomes difficult to think. That's because alcohol blocks messages trying to get to the brain. After more drinks, it becomes harder to **concentrate** and remember. It is also hard to speak clearly or walk in a straight line. People who are drunk may also feel dizzy, have blurred vision, and lose their balance.

Academic Vocabulary

concentrate (KON suhn treyt) *(verb)* to focus on a thought; gather together; strengthen or thicken. *It is difficult for Reiko to concentrate on her homework because her neighbors are listening to loud music.*

Different parts of the brain have different functions. One part of the brain helps a person make decisions. When alcohol reaches that part of the brain, it becomes more difficult for the person to make good decisions. Because of this, a person who drinks alcohol can cause arguments, physical fights, and vehicle accidents. The person may also engage in risky behavior, such as using illegal drugs or engaging in sexual activity.

▼ FIGURE 9.2

How Alcohol Harms the Body

Alcohol has both short- and long-term effects on body systems. What effect does alcohol have on the blood vessels?

Brain
Immediate effects: Impaired judgment, reasoning, memory, and concentration; slowed reaction time; decreased coordination; slurred speech; distorted vision and hearing; reduced inhibitions; alcohol poisoning, causing unconsciousness and even death

Long-term effects: Brain cell destruction, nervous-system disorders, and memory loss

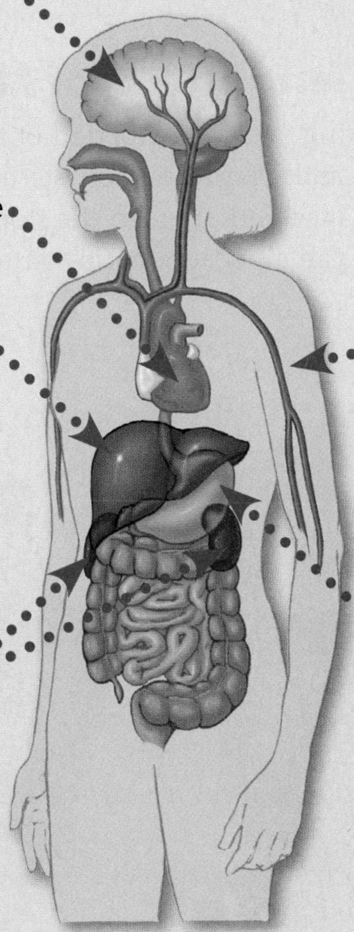

Heart
Immediate effects: Increased heart rate

Long-term effects: Irregular heartbeat; heart-muscle damage

Liver
Immediate effects: Processes of the liver, which filters out over 90% of the alcohol in the body, may become unbalanced

Long-term effects: Scarring and destruction of liver tissue and liver cancer, which can both cause death

Kidneys
Immediate effects: Increased urination, which can result in dehydration, headache, and dizziness

Long-term effects: Kidney failure resulting from high blood pressure

Blood Vessels
Immediate effects: Widened blood vessels, creating a false sense of warmth

Long-term effects: High blood pressure, stroke

Stomach
Immediate effects: Vomiting, which can lead to choking and death

Long-term effects: Ulcers (open sores) in the stomach lining; stomach cancer

Alcohol and the Heart

Alcohol affects the way the heart pumps blood through the body. It makes the blood vessels wider, bringing the blood closer to the surface of the skin. This makes the person drinking alcohol feel warm, even though his or her body temperature is actually dropping. Alcohol also slows down a person's heart rate.

Alcohol and the Liver and Kidneys

Short-term use of alcohol affects the liver and kidneys. The liver acts like a filter, taking alcohol from the bloodstream and removing it from the body. However, the liver can only do this for about half an ounce of alcohol each hour. The extra alcohol stays in the bloodstream and affects the body.

Alcohol causes the kidneys to make more urine. This can lead to dehydration, which is the loss of important body fluids. This is why people who drink too much often feel thirsty the next day.

 **Reading Check** **Identify** What is one short-term effect of alcohol on the kidneys?

Long-Term Effects of Alcohol Use

Drinking over a long period of time can lead to major health problems and even death. Long-term alcohol use can cause cirrhosis of the liver and ulcers in the stomach. Drinking alcohol while pregnant can also cause harm to the unborn child.

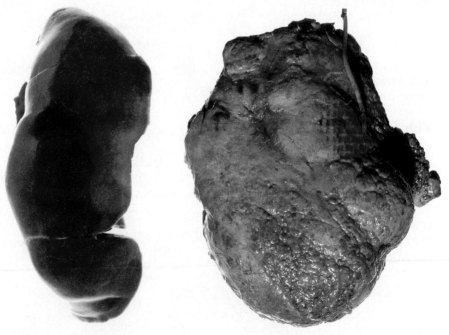

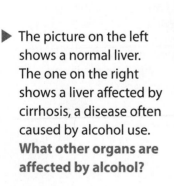 ▶ The picture on the left shows a normal liver. The one on the right shows a liver affected by cirrhosis, a disease often caused by alcohol use. **What other organs are affected by alcohol?**

Health Skills Activity

Accessing Information

Alcoholism

People who are addicted to alcohol are called alcoholics. There are various ways for alcoholics to get help for their addiction. To find valid information about overcoming alcoholism, follow these steps:

1. Research alcohol addiction.
2. Learn about local organizations that provide help to alcoholics.
3. Contact Alcoholics Anonymous (AA) and learn about their 12-step program for dealing with this addiction.

With a Group

Find out if your community has a chapter of Al-Anon or Alateen. These organizations support people whose friends or relatives have problems with alcohol. Al-Anon and Alateen can provide you with more information about alcoholism. Once you and your group have gathered your information, create a poster to present your findings to the class. As a class, organize an Alcoholism Awareness Day at your school. Put up your posters and hand out flyers containing the information you found about this disease and stating how people can get help for alcoholism.

Cirrhosis

Using alcohol can severely damage the liver. If used over a long period of time, it can cause **cirrhosis** (suh·ROH·suhs), which is *the scarring and destruction of liver tissue.* If a person keeps abusing alcohol, the normal liver cells turn into scar tissue. This scar tissue keeps blood from flowing normally through the liver. This can make it very difficult for the liver to carry out its important functions, which can cause serious health problems.

Symptoms of cirrhosis may include nausea, weight loss, yellowing of the eyes and skin, bleeding in the digestive system, itching, and swelling of the legs and feet. Although liver damage cannot be reversed, treatment can help prevent further damage and control the symptoms. In some cases where the damage to the liver is too severe, a liver transplant may be the only option.

Ulcers

When a person uses too much alcohol over time, the lining of the stomach becomes irritated. This causes ulcers to form. An **ulcer** (UHL·ser) is *an open sore in the stomach lining.* When an ulcer

▶ This support group was formed to help families of people who suffer from alcoholism. **What are some support groups for alcoholism in your area?**

Careers for the 21st Century

Substance Abuse Counselor

A substance abuse counselor helps individuals and families deal with substance abuse. Substance abuse can be alcohol or drug abuse or both. Counselors perform many activities, including diagnosing the addiction, managing treatment, counseling, and prevention strategies. If you want to be a substance abuse counselor, you should take classes in biology and psychology.

What skills does a substance abuse counselor need? Go to *Career Corner* **at glencoe.com to find out.**

forms, the acid in the stomach can damage the intestine or stomach tissue. It is very painful. Ulcers can be treated with medication. Ulcers left untreated can cause life-threatening problems.

Fetal Alcohol Syndrome

Even babies who aren't born yet can be harmed by alcohol. Suppose a pregnant female drinks alcohol. It goes through her bloodstream to the umbilical cord, the tube that brings blood and oxygen to her unborn baby. This can cause fetal alcohol syndrome (FAS). An FAS baby may have birth defects such as a small head and small brain. As these babies grow, they may also have major speech and learning problems.

Alcohol Is Addictive

Like many other drugs, alcohol is addictive. An addiction is a psychological or physical need for a drug or other substance. Over time, the need for alcohol may become so strong that a person may feel sick without it. Using alcohol becomes the most important part of that person's life. A person who is addicted to alcohol is called an *alcoholic*.

Alcohol Abuse

Alcohol abuse is *using alcohol in ways that are unhealthy, illegal, or both*. People may abuse alcohol because they are worried about something or because they feel insecure. They may also drink to deal with their problems. However, alcohol doesn't make the problems go away. Alcohol abuse can lead to a disease known as *alcoholism*.

Alcoholism

Alcoholism is *a disease in which a person has a physical and psychological need for alcohol.* It is a curable disease that requires treatment like counseling or even spending time in a hospital.

People may be alcoholics if they frequently drink alone or get drunk. Alcohol becomes more important to them than any other part of their lives—more important than family, friends, and work. In fact, alcoholics may stop participating in other activities just so they can drink. They often make excuses for drinking or refuse to admit how much they drink. Also, alcoholics may have blackouts, or periods when they cannot remember what they said or did while drinking. They might hurt themselves or hurt others.

Alcoholics can recover from their addiction. Organizations and support groups, such as Alcoholics Anonymous (AA), can help people who are addicted to alcohol. These groups can also help friends and families of alcoholics.

 Reading Check **Identify** What are two symptoms of alcoholism?

Visit **glencoe.com** and complete the Interactive Study Guide for Lesson 1.

 **Lesson 1 Review**

After You Read

Review this lesson for new terms, major headings, and Reading Checks.

What I Learned

1. *Vocabulary* Define *alcohol.*

2. *Identify* What is alcohol abuse?

3. *Explain* What are some short-term effects of alcohol on the body?

4. *Describe* What kinds of long-term damage can alcohol use cause?

Thinking Critically

5. *Evaluate* Explain how being addicted to alcohol can be harmful to your health.

6. *Analyze* Why is it risky for a pregnant female to drink alcohol?

Applying Health Skills

7. *Advocacy* Design a T-shirt that influences teens to lead an alcohol-free lifestyle. Use information about the short-term and long-term effects of alcohol to think of a catchy slogan and message that can be displayed on the T-shirt. What are some other facts you can add to your product to encourage teens to choose the positive health practice of being alcohol free?

The Nervous System

● Building Vocabulary
Write down each term below. As you come across it in your reading, write down the definition.

- neurons (p. 272)
- central nervous system (p. 272)
- peripheral nervous system (p. 272)
- brain (p. 273)
- spinal cord (p. 273)

● Focusing on the Main Ideas
In this lesson, you will be able to

- **list** the parts of the nervous system.
- **describe** problems of the nervous system.
- **explain** how you can keep your nervous system healthy.
- **practice** decision-making skills to protect the nervous system.

● Reading Strategy
Predicting Look at the headings in this lesson. Write a question that you think the lesson will answer. After reading, check to see if your question was answered.

Quick Write

Write a short paragraph describing how you can protect your nervous system.

The Control Center of the Body

Your nervous system is your body's control center. It carries messages back and forth between your brain and the rest of your body. It controls your senses: your ability to smell, touch, hear, taste, and see. It controls your breathing and the flow of blood throughout your body. It also controls your thoughts and movements. Your nervous system can be harmed or even permanently damaged by alcohol use.

Neurons are *cells that make up the nervous system.* Neurons are also called nerve cells. They send and receive messages to and from the brain. This information is sent in the form of tiny electrical charges. You can see how neurons communicate in **Figure 9.3.**

 **Reading Check** **Name** What is another name for neurons?

The Parts of the Nervous System

Your nervous system can be divided into two parts. The **central nervous system** (CNS) is made up of *the brain and the spinal cord.* The **peripheral nervous system** (PNS) is made up of *the nerves that connect the central nervous system to all parts of the body.*

NEURONS: YOUR MESSAGE CARRIERS

When you want to catch a ball, your neurons send messages to your muscles. **What might happen if your nervous system were not working properly?**

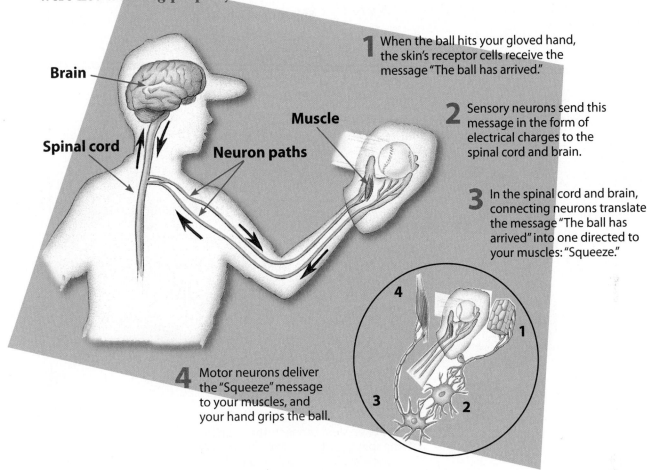

Brain

Spinal cord

Muscle

Neuron paths

1 When the ball hits your gloved hand, the skin's receptor cells receive the message "The ball has arrived."

2 Sensory neurons send this message in the form of electrical charges to the spinal cord and brain.

3 In the spinal cord and brain, connecting neurons translate the message "The ball has arrived" into one directed to your muscles: "Squeeze."

4 Motor neurons deliver the "Squeeze" message to your muscles, and your hand grips the ball.

Your brain is the most important part of these systems. The **brain** is *the command center, or coordinator, of the nervous system.* It receives information and sends messages to the other parts of the body. It works with the **spinal cord,** *a long bundle of neurons that sends messages to and from the brain and all parts of the body.* **Figure 9.4** shows the different parts of the nervous system.

 **Reading Check** **Describe** What is the function of the brain?

Problems of the Nervous System

The nervous system can become injured, or it may be affected by diseases and disorders.

Injuries

One of the most common causes of damage to the nervous system is physical injury. If you injure your head, neck, or back, it can be very harmful to your nervous system and your overall health.

YOUR NERVOUS SYSTEM

Your CNS is your brain and spinal cord. It controls heart rate, breathing, and digestion. Your PNS is all your other nerves. The nerves of your PNS link your CNS to your muscles. **What part of your CNS lets you ride a bicycle?**

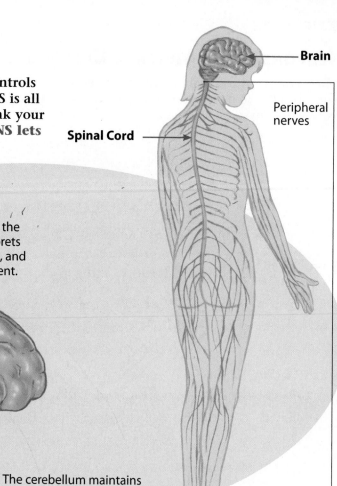

Brain

Peripheral nerves

Spinal Cord

A The cerebrum is the largest part of the brain. It processes thoughts, interprets information from the sense organs, and controls voluntary muscle movement.

B The cerebellum maintains balance and coordination.

C The brain stem connects the brain to the spinal cord. It controls involuntary muscle movement such as breathing.

Connect To... Science

Finding a Cure

Advances in science can help people who suffer from diseases such as multiple sclerosis (MS) and cerebral palsy. Many organizations work to help medical researchers find cures for these disorders.

Find out what these organizations do and how a person can help them. Report your findings to the class.

For example, a spinal cord injury can lead to paralysis. This means that a person loses feeling in, and often cannot move, some parts of the body. A brain injury can cause brain damage, loss of memory, and the loss of some physical abilities, such as being able to tie your shoes.

Disorders

There are also some medical disorders that can harm the nervous system. Multiple sclerosis, or MS, is a disorder that attacks the central nervous system. This disease damages the outer part of some nerves. Because of this, the nerves can't send messages properly. MS can cause problems with thinking and memory. Some people aren't able to walk because of MS. Another disease of the nervous system is cerebral palsy, which is caused by damage to the brain as it is growing. At this time, there is no cure for either of these diseases.

Alzheimer's disease, Parkinson's disease, and epilepsy also harm the nervous system. Alzheimer's disease, which normally affects older adults, harms the brain and causes a loss of memory. Alzheimer's eventually causes mental deterioration and death. People with Parkinson's disease often have shaking and stiffness of the arms and legs. Epilepsy is a nervous system disorder that occurs when the signals in the brain aren't sent in the normal way. A person with epilepsy experiences seizures, which are strong muscle twitches caused by abnormal electrical activity in the brain. A person having a seizure may lose control of his or her muscles, may not be able to speak for a short time, or may lose consciousness for a short time.

Infections

Some viruses cause illnesses that can harm the nervous system. Some examples are polio, rabies (RAY-beez), and meningitis (meh·nhn·JY·tuhs). Today, there are vaccines that help protect people from some of these illnesses. Other illnesses may be treated with medicine.

Alcohol and Drug Abuse

You know that alcohol can affect your brain. It can destroy millions of brain cells, which can never be replaced. Alcohol use can also affect your thinking and how your body moves. Other drugs can also harm your nervous system. Some drugs harm the part of the brain that helps control your heart rate, breathing, and sleeping. Other drugs affect the way your nervous system sends and receives messages. In fact, some drugs harm the nervous system so much that people using them may imagine objects or lights that aren't really there. This is called hallucinating.

Reading Check **Name** What are three viruses that can harm the nervous system?

▲ Mark has cerebral palsy, a nervous system disorder. He is an honor student and active in his community. **Name two other nervous system disorders.**

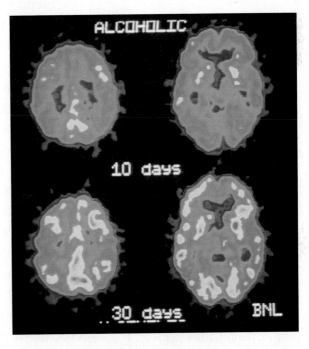

ALCOHOLIC

10 days

30 days   BNL

▲ Alcohol affects the activity of the brain, as this CAT scan shows. **What other substances or factors might affect brain activity?**

Health Skills Activity

Decision Making

Skateboard Safety

Jason is on his way home after picking up his skateboard from the repair shop. He does not have his helmet. He sees his friends Michael and Beth, who both have their skateboards. They ask Jason if he wants to skateboard with them. Jason wants to hang out with his friends, but he feels a lot safer when he wears his helmet. He's also thinking about his parents. He wants them to always know where he is and if he might be getting home late.

What Would You Do?

Suppose you were in Jason's situation. Use the six steps of the decision-making process to make a healthful choice.

1. State the situation.
2. List the options.
3. Weigh the possible outcomes.
4. Consider your values.
5. Make a decision and act on it.
6. Evaluate the decision.

Taking Care of Your Nervous System

Remember, your nervous system is your body's control center. Any damage to it can directly affect your other body systems. Therefore, it is very important to take good care of your nervous system.

One way to take care of your nervous system is to follow positive health practices by leading a healthy lifestyle. Be sure to eat nutritious foods and get enough rest. Also, do your best to protect yourself from disease. Even though you have already been vaccinated against some harmful diseases, you can take steps to avoid others. For example, to protect yourself from rabies, stay away from unfamiliar or wild animals.

If you participate in sports and other physical activities, it is important to protect yourself from physical injury. A good way to start is by wearing protective gear, such as a helmet, to protect your brain when skateboarding, in-line skating, riding a bicycle, or playing contact sports. If you enjoy indoor or outdoor water sports, never dive into shallow water. If you participate in gymnastics, make sure you always have someone to spot you. If you're thinking of adding weight lifting to your physical activities, be sure to protect your back and spinal cord by lifting properly.

Go Online

Visit glencoe.com and complete the Interactive Study Guide for Lesson 2.

These teens know that wearing a helmet is a good way to protect their nervous systems. **Name two other actions you can take to protect your nervous system.**

Another way to keep your nervous system safe is to follow basic safety rules. For example, follow the traffic laws when you are riding your bicycle. Wear your safety belt anytime you're in a car. You can also use positive health behaviors, such as deciding to never use alcohol or other drugs. Think about it: You need healthy brain cells for your whole life. Why damage them with alcohol and drug use? If you stay away from alcohol and drugs, you can protect yourself from permanent damage to your nervous system.

 Reading Check **Identify** What is one way you can prevent physical damage to your nervous system?

Lesson 2 Review

 After You Read

Review this lesson for new terms, major headings, and Reading Checks.

What I Learned

1. **Vocabulary** Define *neuron*.

2. **Name** List the two parts of the nervous system.

3. **Explain** Describe how multiple sclerosis affects the nervous system.

4. **Describe** How can alcohol damage the nervous system?

Thinking Critically

5. **Hypothesize** If the PNS stopped working, what would happen to the CNS?

6. **Apply** What decisions can you make to keep your nervous system healthy?

Applying Health Skills

7. **Accessing Information** Epilepsy is a nervous system disorder in which a person has seizures. During a seizure, the person may lose consciousness, twitch, and shake. Use library and Internet resources to investigate what happens in the brain of a person who has epilepsy. Write a paragraph describing what you find.

Lesson 3

Alcohol Use and Teens

Guide to Reading

● **Building Vocabulary**
In your notebook, use each term below in a sentence that shows its meaning.

■ binge drinking (p. 279)
■ minor (p. 281)

● **Focusing on the Main Ideas**
In this lesson, you will be able to

■ **describe** reasons why some teens may choose to use alcohol.
■ **explain** why alcohol is harmful to teens.
■ **demonstrate** positive ways to handle difficult emotions.

● **Reading Strategy**
Predicting Look at the main headings, figures, and captions before you read this lesson. Predict the kinds of information you might learn from the lesson. Write down three items you think might be covered in this lesson.

uick Write

Write a few sentences describing why you think a teen might choose to drink alcohol.

◀ Ads are designed to make products look fun and exciting. **What elements of this ad might encourage a teen to try alcohol?**

Why Do Some Teens Use Alcohol?

Studies show that most teens do not use alcohol. Then why do some teens try alcohol, even when they know it is harmful to their health and is also illegal? They may try alcohol for several reasons.

One reason is curiosity. Another is that they think it will make them more popular. Some teens think that alcohol use makes them feel relaxed or more grown-up. Others use it to feel some relief from confusing or painful emotions that they don't know how to handle.

Alcohol in the Media

In television commercials or movies, using alcohol is often made to look fun and exciting. You have likely seen a commercial for some type of alcoholic drink. The people who appear in the commercials look young and attractive. This is done on purpose. The companies that make alcohol don't want people to think about or see the negative effects of their product. Because of these media images, many teens feel that drinking alcohol is okay. They also think that by drinking alcohol, they will have fun and excitement in their lives, just like the people in the ads.

Peer Pressure

"I want to be cool, too," thinks Jim. He has decided to try alcohol, even though he doesn't really want to. He has given in to negative peer pressure, one of the main reasons why some teens use alcohol. Some teens may choose to drink in order to fit in or to not be embarrassed in front of their friends. Unfortunately, even one drink can be harmful to a teen's health. Teens run the risk of harming their health if they accept a drink. It is not always easy to say no, but negative peer pressure is not a good reason to choose alcohol.

Binge drinking

Many teens don't realize that using alcohol can kill them. Sometimes teens dare each other to drink a lot of alcohol as quickly as possible. **Binge drinking** is *the consumption of several alcoholic drinks in a short period of time.* Binge drinking is very dangerous. It can cause the body's systems to fail. The person may stop breathing, or his or her heart rate might fall to a dangerously low level. As you might expect, binge drinking may cause death.

 Reading Check   **Identify** What is binge drinking?

Why Is Alcohol Harmful to Teens?

You know that alcohol can be harmful to anyone. However, it is especially harmful to teens. Teens have to deal with many issues, such as the pressure to succeed and to fit in with others. They also have to learn to handle strong emotions. When teens use alcohol to deal with these issues, it only makes handling them harder. Using alcohol can also damage a teen's physical health. It can also lead to trouble with the law, which can affect a teen's future goals and dreams.

What Teens THINK

Why do you think some teens try alcohol?

Some teens might try alcohol out of curiosity or because of peer pressure. Some teens might try alcohol to relieve stress, which it doesn't.

Aaron B.
Centerville, IN

Health Skills Activity

Dealing with Emotions

Dealing with difficult emotions is part of life for a teen. Rather than using alcohol, teens can use the following strategies to deal with emotions in healthful ways.

- Get enough sleep. Being well rested can give you the energy you need to deal with difficult feelings and stress.
- Take some deep breaths. This can help you relax.
- Stay active. Physical activity can help you focus your energy and lower your stress level.
- Talk to someone you trust and respect about what you're feeling.

With a Group

Work with a group to make a brochure for your fellow classmates that describes positive ways to deal with difficult emotions. Be sure to point out the negative effects of using alcohol to deal with difficult emotions.

▼ Do you want to reach your goals? Avoid alcohol. **How can using alcohol affect a teen's performance in sports?**

Teens Are Still Growing

Teens' bodies are still growing and their brains are still developing. Alcohol can greatly harm the body and damage the brain. When teens use alcohol, their bodies do not grow and develop properly. They also run the risk of damaging their nervous systems.

Alcohol Can Affect Emotions

The teen years bring many emotional changes. Sometimes, teens have trouble dealing with their emotions. It is not always easy to handle anger, sadness, boredom, and other quickly changing emotions. Some teens may try alcohol, thinking it will help them deal with emotional changes. However, they will find out that alcohol may change how they feel for a little while, but it won't solve their problems.

Many people who use alcohol often feel bad about themselves. They often have trouble dealing with others. They don't understand that using alcohol to deal with emotions can be harmful, because people who drink are more likely to create bigger problems for themselves in the long run. Alcohol does not relieve stress. It disrupts sleep and can create even more stress. There are better ways for teens to deal with difficult feelings. One way is to talk to an adult they trust. Another way is to find effective strategies for managing stress.

Underage Drinking Is Illegal

Aside from being harmful, alcohol use is also illegal for minors. A **minor** is *a person under the age of adult rights and responsibilities*. Teens who use alcohol can get into trouble with the law. If they buy or are found with alcohol, they can be arrested and fined. A minor who is caught driving while intoxicated will lose his or her license. In many states, a teen will lose the privilege to get a license until he or she is 18 or older. Also, teens who drink are more likely to use other drugs or to commit crimes.

 Reading Check Name What are three legal consequences if a minor is found with alcohol?

▲ Using alcohol is not an effective strategy for dealing with difficult emotions. **What are some healthful strategies that teens can use to deal with difficult emotions?**

Go Online

Visit glencoe.com and complete the Interactive Study Guide for Lesson 3.

Lesson 3 Review

 **After You Read**

Review this lesson for new terms, major headings, and Reading Checks.

What I Learned

1. *Vocabulary* Define *minor*.

2. *List* Name two reasons why some teens choose to use alcohol.

3. *Explain* Why is using alcohol an unhealthful way to deal with difficult emotions?

4. *Describe* How does the media make alcohol use seem appealing?

Thinking Critically

5. *Apply* What's a healthful way for you to deal with your emotions? Give an example of a situation in which you would use this strategy to cope with a difficult emotion.

6. *Predict* How can using alcohol affect a teen's development?

Applying Health Skills

7. *Accessing Information* Do research to find some alcohol-free events that are taking place in your community. Make a list of these events and share the list with your classmates.

 **Go Online** For more Lesson Review Activities, go to **glencoe.com**.

Alcohol Use and Society

Guide to Reading

Building Vocabulary
In your notebook, use the term below in a sentence that shows its meaning.

- violence (p. 284)

Focusing on the Main Ideas
In this lesson, you will be able to

- **describe** how alcohol may affect the user's decisions.
- **explain** how using alcohol can affect a person's relationships.
- **describe** how using alcohol can lead to violence.
- **apply** decision-making skills to help someone get help for alcohol abuse.

Reading Strategy
Predicting Look over the headings in this lesson. Write a question that you think the lesson will answer. After reading, check to see if your question was answered.

**Quick Write**

Write a few sentences describing how alcohol can affect a person's behavior.

Other Risks of Alcohol Use

By now, you know how damaging alcohol use can be to your body and mind. However, alcohol can also harm other parts of your life, such as your schoolwork, your decision making, and your relationships.

Using alcohol is a behavor that is bad for your mental/emotional and social health. Teens who use alcohol are more likely to do poorly in school. They can be late or even miss school. Since they may have trouble paying attention in class, they may get failing grades. They may get suspended or expelled. Teens who use alcohol often may let their classmates or teammates down because of poor performance.

Alcohol Use Affects Decisions

Have you ever made a really poor decision, perhaps because you were tired or sad? When you're not in a good state

◀ This vehicle was involved in an alcohol-related crash. A drunk driver is not the only one who may be injured. **Who else might be injured as a result of a car crash?**

of mind, you can make a bad choice. That's how it is with alcohol: it can cause people to make some really bad decisions. A person under the influence of alcohol might take risks that he or she would not normally take. For example, a normally well-behaved teen under the influence of alcohol may decide to commit a crime. Another may choose to try other drugs. A person may engage in sexual activity, which can lead to unplanned pregnancy or a sexually transmitted disease. Teens may make poor choices like this when they use alcohol.

Fortunately, many schools have programs to help students to be alcohol, drug, and tobacco free. Students Against Destructive Decisions (SADD) **promotes** good decision making among teens. If you get involved with groups such as SADD, you can improve your decision-making skills.

Driving Drunk

One of the most dangerous problems with alcohol is drunk driving. It is very important for your safety that you not ride in a vehicle with a driver who has been using alcohol. A person who uses alcohol experiences a loss of coordination, concentration, and visual awareness. A drunk driver, however, often thinks that his or her abilities have not been affected. In reality, the person will not be able to drive safely, and the chances that he or she will be in an accident are very high. Driving drunk is extremely dangerous for both the driver and the passengers. It can end with a crash, which could result in serious injury or even death.

Alcohol Use Affects Relationships

Dave had been a dependable, happy, outgoing person, but after meeting a new student at school, he decided to try some alcohol. It was a bad choice. He started to drink more, and his personality began to change. He became irritable and moody. He argued more with his family. Most of his old friends no longer wanted to be around him because of his behavior. In time, almost all of Dave's relationships were harmed by his drinking.

Teens who use alcohol often find that they lose friends. Their interest in alcohol causes them to lose

Academic Vocabulary

promote (pruh MOHT) *(verb)* to advance, to contribute to the growth of, to present a product to a buyer for acceptance. *The students made posters to promote exercise during fitness month.*

▼ Using alcohol may lead to violence. **How can violence be avoided?**

Health Skills Activity

Decision Making

Helping a Friend

Katelyn and Lisa have been best friends for a long time. Lisa recently told Katelyn that her mom drinks alcohol nearly every day and sometimes becomes violent. She also told Katelyn that sometimes she gets very scared. Katelyn wonders what she should do to help Lisa.

What Would You Do?

Apply the six steps of the decision-making process to Katelyn's situation. With a partner, role-play what Katelyn would say to Lisa and how Lisa might respond.

1. State the situation.
2. List the options
3. Weigh the possible outcomes.
4. Consider your values.
5. Make a decision and act on it.
6. Evaluate the decision.

DEVELOPING Good Character

Citizenship

Students Against Destructive Decisions (SADD) helps people understand the harmful effects of alcohol on teens.

Do some research on SADD. Find out how you and your classmates can get involved with this organization. Then discuss your findings with your class.

interest in activities they used to enjoy, such as sports. These teens may end friendships or lie to cover up the alcohol abuse. Because they push away the people in their lives, people who abuse alcohol may become very lonely.

Alcohol Use and the Family

Family relationships can really be hurt by alcohol. Take Mara, for example. She lives with her parents and brothers, and she abuses alcohol. Can Mara be counted on to give emotional support to family members who need it? No. Does she keep her promises? Most of the time, she doesn't. Unfortunately, Mara's actions sometimes hurt other family members. She can be moody and unpredictable. Her whole family has suffered because of her alcohol abuse.

Alcohol Use and Violence

When a person uses alcohol to deal with emotions, he or she may suffer from mood swings. Often, these lead to **violence,** *an act of physical force resulting in injury or abuse.* People who become violent when they're using alcohol are often covering up difficult

◀ Teens who choose not to use alcohol usually have healthy family relationships. **Explain why a teen who abuses alcohol may have difficult relationships with family members.**

emotions, such as anger or extreme sadness. Professional health services or a support group can help these people deal with their anger or sadness. After getting this type of help, most people can deal with their feelings without using alcohol.

 Reading Check   **Describe** How can people who use alcohol to deal with their emotions get help?

Visit **glencoe.com** and complete the Interactive Study Guide for Lesson 4.

Lesson 4 Review

After You Read

Review this lesson for new terms, major headings, and Reading Checks.

What I Learned

1. *Describe* How can using alcohol affect a person's decisions?

2. *Explain* Describe why people who abuse alcohol often lose friends.

3. *Vocabulary* Define *violence*.

4. *Describe* How can alcohol use result in violence?

Thinking Critically

5. *Apply* Tracy is worried that her aunt might be abusing alcohol. What are two actions that Tracy could take?

6. *Evaluate* How might a teen's decision to use alcohol have negative long-term effects on his or her life?

Applying Health Skills

7. *Decision Making* Your friend Drew has been irritable and moody lately. One day, Drew asks you to help him get some alcohol. He tells you that he really needs it because he has been feeling upset and that only alcohol will make him feel better. Use the decision-making steps to help you make a responsible choice in this situation.

 Go Online   For more Lesson Review Activities, go to **glencoe.com**.

Lesson 4: Alcohol Use and Society   **285**

Lesson 5

Saying No to Alcohol Use

Guide to Reading

● Building Vocabulary
As you read this lesson, write down each new highlighted term and its definition.
- refusal skills (p. 286)
- withdrawal (p. 287)

● Focusing on the Main Ideas
In this lesson, you will be able to
- **identify** reasons not to use alcohol.
- **explain** how to get help for alcohol use.
- **apply** refusal skills to avoid alcohol use.
- **list** some alternatives to drinking alcohol.

● Reading Strategy
Finding the Main Idea
Look over the headings in this lesson. For each of the major headings, write one sentence that states the main idea.

Quick Write

Write a couple of sentences describing why it is important for teens to avoid alcohol use.

How to Say No to Alcohol Use

"I wanted to fit in with the group," many teens say when asked why they tried alcohol. It doesn't have to be that way. There are ways to deal with peer pressure. One way is to avoid situations where alcohol use may take place. If you find yourself in one of these situations, you can apply your refusal skills. **Refusal skills** are *strategies that help you say no effectively.* **Figure 9.5** shows some refusal skills you can use to say no to alcohol.

 Reading Check

Describe What is one strategy you can use to say no to alcohol?

▼ FIGURE 9.5

USING REFUSAL SKILLS

Here are some ways you can say no to using alcohol. **List two others.**

Say no firmly. Be direct and clearly state how you feel. Use direct eye contact and keep your statement short.

Tell why not. Use "I" messages to give your reasons. You can just say, "No thanks, I don't want to risk getting into trouble."

Offer another idea. Suggest an activity that does not involve alcohol.

Promptly leave. If you have to, just walk away.

Reasons to Refuse Alcohol

There are reasons for refusing alcohol. **Figure 9.6** lists some of the many benefits of making this healthful choice. When you choose not to use alcohol, you are showing respect for yourself and your body and looking ahead to a bright future. You are choosing to remain in control of who you are and what you do. You are also showing that you care about relationships with your family and friends. You are choosing to lead a healthy lifestyle.

Getting Help for Alcohol Abuse

Alcoholism is a difficult disease to overcome, but it can be done. Some alcoholics may try hiding or deny the problem. Others are afraid of going through **withdrawal,** *a series of painful physical and mental symptoms associated with recovery from an addictive substance.* You can get help for yourself, a friend, or a family member who has an alcohol problem. Speak with an adult you

▼ **FIGURE 9.6**

BENEFITS OF AVOIDING ALCOHOL

There are many benefits of avoiding alcohol use. **How can choosing to avoid alcohol have a positive effect on your future?**

Increased Self-Respect

High Self-Esteem

Good Friendships

Better Relationships with Your Family

Control Over Your Life

Maintaining a High Level of Wellness

A Bright Future

Health Skills Activity

Advocacy

Encouraging Teens to Avoid Alcohol

You know how important it is to be alcohol free. It is important to let other teens know, too. You can do this by organizing your own Be Alcohol Free campaign at school.

- Get together with a group of your classmates.
- Make a list of the top ten fun activities you like to do that don't involve alcohol or other drugs.
- Create a slogan and a logo for your campaign that encourage teens to be alcohol free.
- Use your ideas to make a poster, a bumper sticker, a brochure, or another type of handout.
- Role-play to create a skit that you can present to promote your cause.

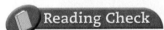

With a Group

Rehearse your skit, then present it to your class as part of your campaign. Hang your posters or share your handouts with other teens.

trust, such as a parent, teacher, religious leader, or school counselor. You can also ask for help from a support group or alcohol treatment center.

Reading Check **Identify** What is one place to find help for an alcohol problem?

◄ If you think someone you know may have a problem with alcohol, try talking to him or her. **How would you approach a friend who you think might have a problem with alcohol use?**

Healthy Alternatives

Alcohol use is never the answer. It is not going to solve any of your problems or make you feel any better. Many teens use alcohol because they're already having other problems. When you start to deal with whatever is causing your problems, you're on your way to avoiding alcohol abuse. It is normal for teens to go through some emotional difficulties. If you find that you need help dealing with your emotions, talk to someone you trust.

Instead of using alcohol, find a healthful way to spend your time. Do what interests you. Join a club or sports group at school. Volunteer at a local organization, such as a food bank or animal shelter. This can give you a sense of purpose and can make you feel good about yourself. Another idea is to start a hobby that you can share with your friends. Remember: using alcohol will *never* help you reach your goals.

▲ Volunteering is a positive way to spend your time. **What other activities can help teens avoid alcohol use?**

 **Reading Check**

Explain What can a teen do if he or she needs help dealing with problems?

 **Go Online**

Visit glencoe.com and complete the Interactive Study Guide for Lesson 5.

Lesson 5 Review

 After You Read

Review this lesson for new terms, major headings, and Reading Checks.

What I Learned

1. *Vocabulary* Define *withdrawal*.

2. *Identify* What are three benefits of avoiding alcohol use?

3. *Explain* Describe how a person can get help for an alcohol problem.

4. *Define* What is a refusal skill?

Thinking Critically

5. *Apply* What is the most important reason for a teen to be alcohol free?

6. *Hypothesize* How might you be affected if one of your close friends developed an alcohol problem? Explain your answer.

7. *Analyze* How can healthy alternatives prevent alcohol use?

Applying Health Skills

8. *Refusal Skills* Use the refusal-skill strategies you learned about in this lesson to write a dialogue in which you say no to someone who offers you an alcoholic drink.

Accessing Information
Practicing Healthful Behaviors
Stress Management
Analyzing Influences
Communication Skills
Refusal Skills
Conflict Resolution
Decision Making
Goal Setting
Advocacy

What Are Refusal Skills?

Refusal skills are strategies that help you say no effectively. If a peer asks you to engage in risky behavior, like drinking alcohol, remember the S.T.O.P. formula:

- **Say no firmly.** Be direct and clearly state how you feel. Use direct eye contact and keep your statement short.
- **Tell why not.** Use "I" messages to give your reasons. You can just say, "I don't want to risk getting into trouble."
- **Offer another idea.** Suggest an activity that does not involve alcohol.
- **Promptly leave.** If you have to, just walk away.

Saying No to Alcohol

Follow the Model, Practice, and Apply steps to help you master this important health skill.

❶ Model

Read how Maura uses the S.T.O.P. formula to resist peer pressure at a party.

Rosa and her friend Maura went to a party. When they got there, they saw that people were drinking alcohol. Maura used the S.T.O.P. strategy to say no to alcohol.

Maura: "What's going on?"

Dennis: "We're having fun. C'mon it's just beer."

- **S**ay no in a firm voice.

Maura: "No, I don't drink."

- **T**ell why not.

Maura: "I don't want the trouble that comes with drinking."

Dennis: "No one will find out."

- **O**ffer another idea.

Maura: "Come on, Rosa, let's go to a movie."

- **P**romptly leave.

Maura: "See you on Monday, Dennis."

❷ Practice

Help Ron use refusal skills by reading the scenario and answering the questions below.

Ron was hanging out with some classmates. He noticed that they were passing a bottle around. Someone offered him the bottle. Ron looked at the label and saw that it was a beer. Answer the following questions to identify how Ron could use the S.T.O.P. formula to refuse the offer of alcohol.

1. What could Ron say to resist peer pressure to drink?

2. What reasons could Ron give for why he doesn't want to drink the beer?

3. What could Ron offer as another activity?

4. What should Ron do if his friends keep insisting that he try the beer?

❸ Apply

Apply what you have learned about refusal skills and complete the activity below.

Working in small groups, brainstorm your "top five reasons to refuse" alcohol. Next, think of different situations in which a teen might be pressured to use alcohol. Write these on a sheet of paper. Choose one of the situations from the list. Write a skit in which a teen in that situation uses the S.T.O.P. formula to say no to alcohol. Include as many of your group's "top reasons to refuse" alcohol as you can in your skit. Perform your skit for the class.

Self-Check

- Did we choose a situation in which a teen might be pressured to use alcohol?

- Did we use the S.T.O.P. formula to refuse alcohol?

- Did the teen in our skit use our "top reasons" to refuse?

News About Teens and
ALCOHOL USE

Teen drinking is a serious problem, one that can cause harm to both the drinker and to others. Here is a round-up of three studies that prove the point.

Drinking Danger

A study from the University of Buffalo, New York, has some interesting findings about alcohol use among young people. Researchers surveyed the drinking habits of 2,200 Americans. They found that the younger their subjects were when they had their first drink, the more likely they were to abuse alcohol as adults. The scientists found that for every year earlier that a teen starts drinking alcohol, the chances of becoming a problem drinker increase by 12 percent. Researchers also discovered that people who begin drinking as teens are more likely to become seriously intoxicated during routine drinking episodes later in life.

The High Cost of Teen Drinking

According to a report from the National Academy of Sciences, drunken behavior and violent crimes that result from adolescent drinking cost the United States $53 billion a year. This includes $19 billion from traffic accidents alone. The academy made several recommendations to reduce these costs. These include cracking down on merchants who sell alcohol to kids, making alcohol use look less glamorous in movies, and increasing taxes on liquor.

Danger in the Passenger Seat

According to a study by the National Highway Traffic Safety Administration, 21 percent of teen drivers killed in car crashes were intoxicated. The study, however, suggests that the greater danger for teens is not drinking and driving but riding with a driver who has been drinking. A survey of 1,534 Californians ages 15 to 20 found that nearly 50 percent had ridden in a car with a drunk driver in the previous 12 months. The bottom line: Don't drink. Never get into a car with an intoxicated driver. And take away the car keys if someone wants to drive after drinking. You'll be doing yourself—and them—a life-saving favor.

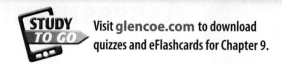

FOLDABLES Study Organizer

Foldables® and Other Study Aids Take out the Foldable® that you created for Lesson 1 and any graphic organizers that you created for Lessons 1–5. Find a partner and quiz each other using these study aids.

Lesson 1 Alcohol Use and Abuse

Main Idea Alcohol is a drug that can cause both short-term and long-term damage to your body.

- Alcohol is a depressant. It slows down activity in the brain and nervous system.
- In all states, it is illegal for anyone under the age of 21 to buy or drink alcohol.
- Several factors determine how drinking alcohol affects you: size and gender, the amount of food in your stomach, and how fast you drink.
- Alcoholism is a disease in which a person is addicted to alcohol.

Lesson 2 The Nervous System

Main Idea The nervous system is your body's control center.

- The central nervous system includes the brain and spinal cord.
- The peripheral nervous system includes the nerves that connect the central nervous system to the rest of the body.
- Injuries to the nervous system include brain damage and paralysis, and loss of bodily functions.
- Alcohol and drug use can severely damage the nervous system.

Lesson 3 Alcohol Use and Teens

Main Idea Alcohol use is harmful to teens because teens' bodies are still growing, their brains are still developing, and they are going through many emotional changes.

- Television or movies often make using alcohol look fun and exciting.
- Binge drinking is the consumption of several alcoholic drinks in a short period of time. A person can die from binge drinking.
- Teens may choose to use alcohol for many reasons, including peer pressure and curiosity.

Lesson 4 Alcohol Use and Society

Main Idea Alcohol use affects the individual, their friends and family, and society.

- Alcohol affects a person's judgment and ability to make good decisions.
- Abusing alcohol can harm a person's relationships with family and friends.

Lesson 5 Saying No to Alcohol Use

Main Idea Saying no to alcohol use means that you respect yourself.

- Refusal skills are strategies that can help you say no to alcohol.
- People addicted to alcohol go through withdrawal when they stop using it.
- Alternatives to alcohol use include doing volunteer work or developing a hobby.

Assessment

HEALTH QUIZ

Now that you have read the chapter, look back at your answers to the Health Quiz on the chapter opener. Would you change any of them? What would your answers be now?

Reviewing Vocabulary and Main Ideas

On a sheet of paper, write the numbers 1–8. After each number, write the term from the list that best completes each statement.

- intoxicated
- cirrhosis
- alcoholism
- blood alcohol concentration
- alcohol
- alcohol abuse
- depressant
- ulcer

Lesson 1 Alcohol Use and Abuse

1. _____ is a drug created by a chemical reaction in some foods, especially fruits and grains.

2. _____ is a disease in which a person has a physical and psychological need for alcohol.

3. The amount of alcohol in the blood is also known as the _____.

4. A(n) _____ is an open sore in the lining of the stomach.

5. _____ is using alcohol in ways that are unhealthy or illegal.

6. A person who is drunk is _____.

7. A(n) _____ is a drug that slows the brain and the nervous system.

8. _____ is the scarring and destruction of liver tissue.

Lesson 2 The Nervous System

*On a sheet of paper, write the numbers 9–10. Write **True** or **False** for each statement below. If the statement is false, change the underlined word to make it true.*

9. Your nervous system is made up of <u>neurons.</u>

10. The <u>peripheral</u> nervous system is made up of the brain and spinal cord.

On a sheet of paper, write the numbers 11–13. After each number, write the letter of the answer that best completes each statement.

Lesson 3 Alcohol Use and Teens

11. Reasons why teens should avoid alcohol include the following:
    a. Alcohol is a harmful way of dealing with emotions.
    b. Underage drinking is illegal.
    c. All of the above

Lesson 4 Alcohol Use and Society

12. Alcohol can affect a teen's life because
    a. it can help a teen at school.
    b. it can make teens take dangerous risks.
    c. All of the above

Lesson 5 Saying No to Alcohol Use

13. A healthy alternative to drinking alcohol is
    a. doing other drugs.
    b. doing volunteer work.
    c. offering alcohol to someone else.

Go Online   Visit glencoe.com and take the Online Quiz for Chapter 9.

Thinking Critically

Using complete sentences, answer the following questions on a sheet of paper.

14. **Interpret** How can binge drinking lead to death? In what way is this connected to blood alcohol concentration?

15. **Evaluate** Explain how avoiding alcohol can have a positive effect. Be certain to include physical, emotional, and social effects.

Write About It

16. **Expository Writing** Write a short advertisement encouraging teens to be alcohol free. Be sure to include ways to say no to negative peer influences and stay alcohol free.

↗ Applying Technology

Alcohol Podcast

With a partner, use Garage Band™ or Audacity® to record a podcast about alcohol use and refusal skills. Follow the steps below to complete this project.

- Using the textbook as a guide, write a 3–5 minute dialogue that discusses and defines alcohol use.
- Include facts about the effects of alcohol, teens and alcohol use, alcohol use and society, and refusal skills.
- Open a new podcast project with two audio tracks; one for each of you.
- Record your audio tracks. Add lead-in music.
- Edit for content and clarity.
- Save your project and make sure that it is accessible on iTunes®.

Standardized Test Practice

Rachel's Writing Plan

Rachel made the following concept map to organize her ideas for a paper. Review her concept map and then answer questions 1–3.

1. Under which subtopic should details about the three types of alcohol be placed?
   - **A.** Dangers of Alcohol
   - **B.** Alcohol Abuse
   - **C.** Forms of Alcohol
   - **D.** Effects of Alcohol

2. Which detail below supports the subtopic "Dangers of Alcohol"?
   - **A.** Binge drinking may lead to death.
   - **B.** Alcohol is found in three forms: beer, liquor, and wine.
   - **C.** It is illegal for anyone under the age of 21 to use alcohol.
   - **D.** Alcoholism can be treated.

3. Based on this writing plan, what type of paper is Rachel planning to write?
   - **A.** a persuasive essay to convince adults not to drink alcohol
   - **B.** a paper that describes alcohol use and abuse
   - **C.** a paper that discusses the physical effects of alcohol
   - **D.** none of the above

FRIENDS DON'T LET FRIENDS DO DRUGS

Chapter Preview

Lesson 1   Drug Use and Abuse..........298

Lesson 2   Types of Drugs and
           Their Effects......................303

Lesson 3   Drug Risks and Teens.......310

Lesson 4   Staying Drug Free.............316

Building Health Skills.........................320

Hands-on Health..................................322

Chapter Reading Review....................323

Chapter Assessment............................324

▲ *Working with the Photo*

Spreading the word about the dangers of drug use helps others avoid drugs. **What are some ways to spread the word about the dangers of drug use?**

Start-Up Activities

Before You Read Do you know the risks associated with using illegal drugs? Answer the Health eSpotlight question below and then watch the online video. Keep a record of your answer.

Health eSpotlight

Choosing to Be Drug Free

Club drugs are a dangerous group of street drugs that can cause blackouts, memory loss, and even death. If you were offered a club drug at a dance, with the promise that it will make you "feel great," how would you respond?

Go to **glencoe.com** and watch the health video for Chapter 10. Then complete the activity provided with the online video.

FOLDABLES® Study Organizer

As You Read Make this Foldable® to help you organize the main ideas on drug use and abuse in Lesson 2. Begin with four circles of paper: one large (8" across), one medium (7" across), and two small (each 2½" across).

1 Fold the medium circle in half. Glue the top half onto the large circle, making sure that the bottoms of the two circles are aligned. This will create a tab from the unglued part of the medium circle.

2 Fold the two small circles in half. Glue the top half of each circle onto the bottom half of the medium circle. This will create two more tabs.

3 Label as shown.

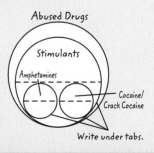

Abused Drugs

Stimulants

Amphetamines

Cocaine/ Crack Cocaine

Write under tabs.

Under the appropriate tab, define key terms and record information on abused drugs.

**Online** Visit **glencoe.com** and complete the Health Inventory for Chapter 10.

Drug Use and Abuse

Guide to Reading

● Building Vocabulary

List each term below in your notebook. As you come across it in your reading, write the definition.

- drug (p. 298)
- over-the-counter (p. 299)
- drug misuse (p. 300)
- drug abuse (p. 300)

● Focusing on the Main Ideas

In this lesson, you will be able to

- **define** *drug*.
- **describe** drug abuse.
- **identify** risks associated with drug use.
- **apply** the decision-making steps to make a healthful choice about taking medicine.

● Reading Strategy

Make an Outline Using the main heads in this lesson, make an outline of the lesson. As you read, fill in your outline with details.

List two illegal drugs. Then list two drugs that are legal.

What Is a Drug?

You've heard the word *drug* many times before. You may also have been offered drugs by a peer. So what *is* a drug? A **drug** is *a substance other than food that changes the structure or function of the body or mind.* Some drugs can be very harmful to your health. Other drugs can save your life or the life of someone you love. It is important to know the difference between a helpful drug and a harmful drug.

▶ When you avoid drugs, you can apply your talents and skills in many ways. **Give an example of a talent or skill you can develop because you avoid drugs.**

Health Skills Activity

Decision Making

Taking Medicine

Katie runs track. Because of all the training she does, Katie often has sore muscles. She takes an over-the-counter pain reliever for her sore muscles, but lately it hasn't been helping. What should Katie do?

What Would You Do?

Use the six steps of the decision-making process to determine what you would do if you were in Katie's position.

1. State the situation.

2. List the options.

3. Weigh the possible outcomes.

4. Consider your values.

5. Make a decision and act on it.

6. Evaluate the decision.

Drugs as Medicine

Medicines are drugs. Medicines prevent or cure illnesses or treat their symptoms. Some medicines are available **"over-the-counter"** (OTC), which means that they are *found on the shelves of local pharmacy or grocery stores.* Anyone can buy them there. Then there are prescription medicines. These can be legally obtained only with a doctor's written permission. You will learn more about the proper use of OTC and prescription medicines in Chapter 11.

Drug Use

You need to be careful about using *all* drugs, including the ones prescribed by your doctor. Even helpful medicines and pain relievers found at your local drugstore can be harmful if they are used incorrectly. Some people combine drugs. That is, they use several different drugs at once. Doing this without a doctor's permission can be very dangerous. Drugs can interact with each other and cause harmful reactions inside the body. No drugs or medicines should ever be taken by anyone other than the person for whom they were prescribed.

Drug Misuse and Abuse

When you hear the term *drug abuse,* you may think only of the use of illegal drugs. Many drugs are illegal for a good reason: they can be extremely harmful or addictive. However, any kind of drug can be misused or abused. **Drug misuse** means *taking or using medicine in a way that is not intended.* Misuse of a drug may involve taking too much of the drug or taking a medication prescribed for someone else. For example, Brian has allergies. To relieve his symptoms, he takes medicine prescribed for a friend. This is drug misuse. It can be very harmful to misuse drugs. Misuse of medicine can lead to drug abuse.

Drug abuse is *intentionally using drugs in a way that is unhealthful or illegal.* When people take illegal drugs, such as marijuana or heroin, they are abusing drugs. When people intentionally use **legal** drugs for nonmedical purposes, they are also engaging in drug abuse.

Recent studies show that fewer people nowadays are using illegal drugs, but more are misusing prescription drugs. However, even prescription medicines, such as those used to treat problems like attention-deficit/hyperactivity disorder (ADHD), are dangerous if taken by someone other than the person they were prescribed for. You put your health at great risk if you take medicine that is not prescribed for you by a doctor. Misusing or abusing any type of drug can damage your body and lead to allergic reactions, illness, or even death.

 **Reading Check** Explain What is drug abuse?

Academic Vocabulary

legal (LEE guhl) *(adj)*
allowed by the law.
When your city sets a curfew for minors, it means that it is not legal for you to be outside of your house past a certain time.

▶ Drug addiction is a very serious problem that can cause many health risks. It can require medical intervention. **Name two places in your area where people can get information and help for avoiding drugs.**

Recognizing the Risks

Serious illness and death are just two of the possible consequences of drug misuse or abuse. Others include damage to your mental/emotional and social health. Misusing or abusing drugs can negatively affect all parts of the health triangle.

Risks to Physical Health

Drugs can do a lot of harm to the body. Drugs are especially dangerous for teens because their bodies are still growing and developing. The brain and nervous system don't work properly under the influence of drugs. Drugs may make a person feel nauseated or confused. They may make a person lose control of his or her ability to walk or talk. They can also cause memory loss, seizures, coma, or even death. If a drug user drives while taking drugs, he or she is putting other people at risk, too.

Drug Addiction

Many drug users feel like they can't stop taking drugs. A drug addiction is a dependency on a chemical substance that is very difficult and painful to quit. A person who becomes addicted to drugs often has a hard time stopping his or her drug use. These people may need help from others. Addiction is considered a disease. Anyone affected by it should seek help from a health professional.

Risks to Mental/Emotional Health

The consequences of drug abuse are very serious. Some people may use drugs to cope with uncomfortable feelings. This kind of drug use puts their mental/emotional health at risk. Drug abuse weakens a person's ability to think and learn, even though the person may not realize it at the time. Drug users often have low self-esteem and have trouble relating to others. They often experience depression, anxiety, and confusion.

Drug abusers may feel that by using drugs, they will be able to solve their problems, but drugs only cover up the problems. Drug abuse can even cause new problems. It is important to find a healthful way of dealing with problems rather than using drugs.

What Teens THINK

How can a teen avoid being pressured to use drugs?

One effective way would be to choose your friends wisely. It would be better to hang out with people who don't do drugs instead of being around people who do because there's always a chance you can be asked to join in, especially if you are easily influenced.

Alexis H.
Atlantic City, NJ

Risks to Social Health

Are you interested in keeping your relationships with your friends and family strong? Then stay away from drugs. Drug use can harm your relationships. Drug users often have a difficult time dealing with others, even those closest to them.

Drug abuse can change a person's personality. It can cause mood swings and sometimes even lead to violence. Drug abusers often lose touch with what they are really feeling. Someone addicted to drugs will start to think only of his or her need for the drug. Teens who abuse drugs may lose touch with their families. They often don't respect or care for their families. A drug abuser's actions affect the whole family.

Teens who abuse drugs can also lose their friends. Some may end their friendships and lie to friends to cover up their addictions. In time, having the drug becomes more important than having strong relationships. Stay friends with people who are drug free. This is a good way to build strong friendships.

 Reading Check

Explain Why do people who abuse drugs risk straining their relationships?

Go Online

Visit **glencoe.com** and complete the Interactive Study Guide for Lesson 1.

Lesson 1 Review

 **After You Read**

Review this lesson for new terms, major headings, and Reading Checks.

What I Learned

1. *Vocabulary* Define *drug misuse.*

2. *Explain* How can medicines be harmful?

3. *Identify* Name three ways drug abuse affects mental/emotional health.

4. *List* Name three effects drugs can have on a person's physical health.

5. *Describe* How could using illegal drugs negatively affect your social health?

Thinking Critically

6. *Evaluate* What is the difference between using drugs as medicine and abusing drugs?

7. *Analyze* How might pain relievers be misused or abused?

Applying Health Skills

8. *Accessing Information* Use the Internet to research one common OTC drug. Describe its purpose, its possible side effects, and any possible dangerous combinations with other medicines. Share your findings with the class.

Go Online For more Lesson Review Activities, go to **glencoe.com**.

Types of Drugs and Their Effects

Guide to Reading

● **Building Vocabulary**
Write a sentence that describes the meaning of each new term in your own words.

- tolerance (p. 303)
- overdose (p. 303)
- stimulant (p. 304)
- amphetamines (p. 304)
- depressants (p. 305)
- club drugs (p. 306)
- narcotics (p. 307)
- hallucinogens (p. 307)
- inhalants (p. 308)

● **Focusing on the Main Ideas**
In this lesson, you will be able to

- **explain** how different drugs affect the body.
- **identify** the dangers of different drugs.
- **describe** the effects of drugs on an unborn baby.
- **access** reliable information on drug use and pregnancy.

● **Reading Strategy**
Predicting Look over the headings in this lesson. Write a question that you think the lesson will answer. After reading, check to see if your question was answered.

 Use the Foldable® on p. 297 as you read this lesson.

Quick Write

List two illegal drugs you know about. Then briefly describe how these two drugs are harmful to health.

Drug Use and the Body

Jaron and Mei-Ling have colds. They are taking the same cold medicine. When Mei-Ling takes it, her stuffy nose goes away and she feels much better. Jaron, though, can't sleep because of the medicine. All drugs affect the body in some way, but the same drug can affect people differently.

Some drugs are more harmful than others. When a person uses a drug over time, he or she can develop a tolerance to the drug. **Tolerance** is *the body's need for larger and larger amounts of a drug to produce the same effect.* People can also overdose on a drug. **Overdose** is *taking more of a drug than the body can tolerate.*

Types of Drugs

There are many different types of drugs, including stimulants, depressants, club drugs, narcotics, and hallucinogens. All of them can be harmful to your physical, mental/emotional, and social health. Reduce your risks and avoid health problems by avoiding these harmful substances.

▲ Using drugs can harm the body and weaken athletic skills. **How do you think drug use might affect a teen's ability to run?**

Connect To...
Science

Caffeine

Caffeine is a stimulant found in foods and drinks such as chocolate, coffee, tea, and some soft drinks.

Research how caffeine affects the human body. Is caffeine addictive? Describe your findings in a paragraph.

Stimulants

Have you ever had a soda near bedtime and then couldn't fall asleep? Chances are you drank a soda that had caffeine in it. Caffeine is found in coffee and some soft drinks and energy drinks. Caffeine is a **stimulant,** *a drug that speeds up the body's functions.* For example, stimulants speed up heart and breathing rates and raise blood pressure. In addition to these physical effects, stimulants affect a person's mental/emotional health by giving a false sense of energy, well-being, confidence, and power. In time, these effects wear off, and the user often feels exhausted and irritable.

Amphetamines (am·FEH·tuh·meenz) are *strong stimulant drugs that speed up the nervous system.* Amphetamines are sometimes prescribed to treat certain medical conditions, such as attention deficit disorder (ADD) or attention-deficit-hyperactivity disorder (ADHD). These drugs are often called "speed." They come in different forms that may be swallowed, inhaled, smoked, or injected. You may have heard of the drug "crystal meth." This is the street name for methamphetamine (meth·am·FEH·tuh·meen), an extremely addictive drug that can cause a person's heart to suddenly stop working. The misuse or abuse of any amphetamine can lead to serious health effects, including death.

Cocaine is an illegal stimulant made from the coca plant. Cocaine is inhaled through the nose, smoked, or injected into the veins. It is also known as "blow," "snow," or "coke." On first use, it produces a brief feeling of well-being and even confidence. The feeling soon wears off, and the user may feel anxious. Crack is a concentrated form of cocaine that is smoked. After smoking it, a user may feel more alert and even energetic. As with cocaine, the stimulant effect of crack soon wears off.

Figure 10.1 describes what happens when someone first takes a stimulant and how the drug may make him or her feel. It also explains what happens when the drug wears off.

Now think about this frightening fact: a person can become addicted to a drug like cocaine or crack after using it *just a few times.* Once addicted, the person can no longer function without the drug. He or she needs more and more of the drug to feel better. These drugs can eventually lead to heart attack and death.

Reading Check **Define** What is a *stimulant?*

FIGURE 10.1

EFFECTS OF STIMULANTS AND DEPRESSANTS

Stimulants and depressants have serious physical and mental/emotional effects. **How is a depressant different from a stimulant?**

Effects/Possibility of Addiction	Stimulants	Depressants
Physical effects	Speed up body functions, such as heart rate, breathing rate, and blood pressure	Slow down body functions, such as coordination
Mental/emotional effects	False sense of energy, well-being, confidence, and power	False sense of well-being through reduced anxiety and relaxation
Effects when the drugs wear off	Exhaustion and mental imbalance	Depression, mood swings
Addictive?	Yes	Yes

Depressants

While stimulants speed up body processes, **depressants** (di·PREH·suhntz) are *drugs that slow down the body's functions and reactions, including heart and breathing rates.* Depressants work by slowing down a person's motor skills and coordination. They can **affect** a person mentally and emotionally by giving a false sense of well-being through reduced anxiety and relaxation. When they wear off, the user may experience mood swings and depression.

Most depressants come in tablet or capsule form. Depressants are legal when prescribed by a doctor to treat certain conditions. For example, doctors sometimes prescribe tranquilizers (TRANG·kwuh·ly·zurz) and barbiturates (bar·BIH·chuh·ruhtz) to treat people who suffer from anxiety. Alcohol is also a depressant. It is legal for people who are 21 or older to purchase it. Misuse and abuse of depressants can lead to coma or even death. If a person has both depressants and alcohol in his or her body at the same time, it can also lead to coma and death. Figure 10.1 above describes the physical and mental/emotional effects of depressants. It also explains the effects when these drugs wear off.

Academic Vocabulary

affect (uh FEKT) *(verb)* causes change or influences. *Julio was deeply affected by the music his son played at the school recital.*

 **Reading Check** **Describe** What are some dangers of using depressants?

Marijuana

You may have heard about "pot" or "weed." These are some names for marijuana (mar·uh·WAHN·uh), a drug made from the dried leaves and flowers of the hemp plant, *Cannabis sativa.* This drug is usually smoked.

▲ Think of all the ways you can have fun without using drugs. **What are some drug-free activities that you and your friends enjoy?**

Marijuana affects people differently. It acts as a depressant for some people. For others, it acts as a stimulant. Some people may see or hear things that are not really there. They may feel relaxed or talkative. Some people affected by marijuana may giggle a lot. They may experience memory loss, forgetting what was just said or done. Their eyes may become bloodshot, and they may feel confused, shaky, or fearful.

Marijuana harms the body. If used over a long period of time, it causes many of the same problems that smoking tobacco causes, such as lung damage. It can lower testosterone levels in males and reduce the number of sperm the body makes. It may cause females to have irregular periods.

 **Reading Check**

Explain How does marijuana affect males and females differently?

Club Drugs

Another type of drug is the club drug. **Club drugs** are *illegal drugs that are found mostly in nightclubs or at all-night dance parties called raves.* These drugs are often used to make people feel more relaxed. Some club drugs include Ecstasy, or X; rohypnol; and ketamine. Rohypnol is known as the date-rape drug, or "roofies," and ketamine is also known as "special K." These drugs often are made in home laboratories and mixed with other harmful chemicals. This means that a person who uses club drugs never knows what exactly is in them.

Dangers of Club Drugs

Just taking a club drug one time can damage the body. A person using Ecstasy may experience tingly skin or clenched jaws. The drug increases the heart rate and body temperature, which can damage a person's organs. Also, Ecstasy can make a person feel anxious and paranoid. These feelings may last long after the drug wears off.

Rohypnol makes a person's blood pressure drop. The user feels dizzy and very sleepy. It also causes blackouts and memory loss. When slipped into the drink of an unsuspecting person, it can cause a loss of consciousness. The person won't remember what happened. This is why rohypnol is often used to commit date rape. It is a serious crime to use such drugs to commit rape.

Ketamine, an anesthetic, can be deadly if abused. It causes hallucinations, and people who use it often have memory loss. An overdose of ketamine can cause a person to stop breathing. Many teens have died this way.

 **Reading Check** **Explain** Why is rohypnol often used as a date-rape drug?

Narcotics and Hallucinogens

Narcotics are highly addictive drugs. **Narcotics** are *drugs that get rid of pain and dull the senses.* Morphine and codeine, which are both used as medicine, are narcotics. Like all narcotics, they are very addictive.

Heroin is a narcotic that is usually injected, giving users an instant "high," or a feeling of happiness. This feeling does not last, however. As it wears off, the user experiences nausea, stomach cramps, and vomiting. Heroin is highly addictive, and the withdrawal symptoms are very painful. It is easy for people to soon need larger amounts of the drug to feel its effects. It's also very easy to overdose on heroin. Many users die this way. Another risk of injecting heroin is contracting HIV, the virus that causes AIDS. Some heroin users share needles, which means they can expose each other to HIV and other serious blood-borne viruses.

Hallucinogens are *drugs that distort moods, thoughts, and senses.* These drugs may create imaginary images in the user's mind. People who use hallucinogens may become disoriented or confused and less sensitive to pain. They may also become violent.

Connect To...

Language Arts

Drug Use and Depression

Drug users may suffer from *depression,* a state of being sad or having feelings of hopelessness. This term comes from the Latin word *deprimere,* which means "to press down."

How does the meaning of the Latin word *deprimere* relate to the definition of *depression*? How do you think the meaning of the word *depression* relates to drug use? Write a paragraph describing your ideas.

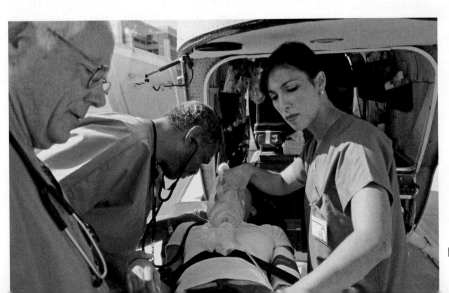

◄ Drug abuse often leads to overdose, and overdose can cause death. **Why do you think a person might overdose on a drug?**

Visit **glencoe.com** and complete the Interactive Study Guide for Lesson 2.

Inhalants

Some preteens and younger teens use **inhalants,** *the vapors of chemicals that are sniffed or inhaled to get a "high."* Where do they get these chemicals? Most come from household products that are not meant to be taken into the body. Many inhalants have dangerous poisons. Breathing inhalants can cause nausea, dizziness, mental confusion, and loss of motor skills. When the drug is inhaled, the poisons go straight to the brain, where they can cause permanent damage or even death. You should never inhale anything that is not meant to be inhaled.

Steroids

You may have heard about athletes using drugs to try to play better. They might try *steroids,* drugs that are either human hormones or similar to hormones found in the human body. The steroids naturally found in the body help it grow and develop. The steroids that people take usually contain artificial male hormones. This makes muscles grow faster and larger.

Steroid use is dangerous and causes serious health problems. People who use steriods may have a problem controlling their anger. This is often called "'roid rage." In males, steroids may cause the testicles to shrink and stunt the body's overall growth. In females, steroids can affect the production of estrogen, an important female hormone. This can result in a deeper voice, excess facial hair, and a masculine-looking body. In both males and females, steroid use can increase the risk of heart disease, high blood pressure, strokes, cancer, sterility, hair loss, and severe acne. The drugs may also cause depression, as well as liver and kidney damage.

The Effects of Drugs on Unborn Babies

Babies don't take drugs, or do they? If a pregnant female takes drugs, the drugs can hurt her unborn baby. Pregnant females who use drugs, alcohol, or tobacco often give birth to low-weight babies. These babies may also have brain problems, because the drugs interfered with the baby's development. Also, pregnant females who inject drugs and become infected with HIV from a shared needle can pass the virus on to their unborn babies.

▼ Babies can be seriously harmed by their mother's drug use. **Why do you think a mother's drug use could put an unborn baby at risk of low birth weight and other disabilities?**

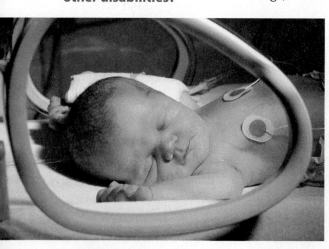

Explain How can an unborn baby contract HIV?

Health Skills Activity

Accessing Information

Drug Use and Pregnancy

Pregnant females who use drugs can seriously harm their unborn babies. Use home, school, and community resources to find out more about how pregnant females who use drugs can get help.

- Research drug or substance abuse. Find specific information about help for pregnant females who suffer from substance abuse.
- Contact the Substance Abuse and Mental Health Services Administration (SAMHSA) or the National Institute on Drug Abuse (NIDA) and learn about how they can help with substance abuse.

On Your Own

Find out if your community has a local organization that helps people, including pregnant females, who have substance abuse problems. Report your findings to the class.

Lesson 2 Review

After You Read

Review this lesson for new terms, major headings, and Reading Checks.

What I Learned

1. *Vocabulary* Define *tolerance*.

2. *Describe* How does using marijuana affect the body?

3. *Explain* What can using rohypnol do to a person's memory?

4. *Describe* What kinds of effects can drugs have on an unborn baby?

Thinking Critically

5. *Analyze* How might hallucinogens cause a person to act violently?

6. *Synthesize* Heroin is extremely addictive. How does this make overdosing on heroin more likely?

Applying Health Skills

7. *Refusal Skills* Research how marijuana affects a person's ability to drive a car. Use this information to write a short skit about a teen who refuses to ride in a car driven by someone who is using marijuana.

Drug Risks and Teens

Guide to Reading

● Building Vocabulary
Before you read this lesson, make a flash card for each new term and its definition.

- drug-free zone (p. 314)
- drug possession (p. 315)
- probation (p. 315)

● Focusing on the Main Ideas
In this lesson, you will be able to

- **describe** reasons drug use is harmful to teens.
- **explain** how drug use may lead to crime.
- **advocate** for drug-free schools.

● Reading Strategy
Finding the Main Idea Copy each main heading in the lesson. For each heading, write one sentence that states the main idea.

uick Write

Write a short paragraph describing why you think drug use may be harmful for teens.

Why Do Some Teens Use Drugs?

Megan wants to be cool like her older sister. She smokes pot. Blake says that he wants to feel accepted by his peers. He drinks alcohol. Wendy wants to escape her emotional problems. She uses Ecstasy. Teens may start using drugs for many reasons.

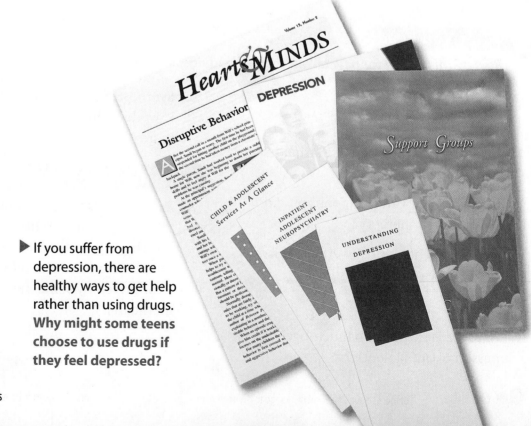

▶ If you suffer from depression, there are healthy ways to get help rather than using drugs. **Why might some teens choose to use drugs if they feel depressed?**

Peer Pressure

When his friends offered Jim marijuana, he knew he didn't want to smoke it. Yet he found it hard to say no to his friends. Saying no to drugs is easier, however, once you're aware of the dangers of drug use. You can pass up the drugs that may be offered to you when you remember the harmful effects that they have on the body and mind. Instead of using drugs, you can resist peer pressure and engage in healthful activities. These positive health behaviors show that you respect yourself. You will learn more about resisting peer pressure on page 317.

Drug Use in the Media

The handsome man snorts cocaine and smiles. Later in the movie, he drives a fast sports car. The movie never shows, however, all the problems he has to deal with because of his drug use. Many TV shows and movies glamorize drug use. All of these images send teens the message that drug use is harmless. They make it look exciting and even safe. You rarely see people struggling with addiction, going to jail, dealing with withdrawal, and hurting their family relationships.

Remember, though, that the media also give solid information about drugs. Television reports and magazine articles often provide a lot of valid information about how drugs can negatively affect the brain and body. This information can help teens stay drug free.

 **Reading Check** **Explain** How does the media glamorize drug use?

MediaWatch

Antidrug Campaigns

What do you know about the antidrug programs that are available? Groups such as D.A.R.E. (Drug Abuse Resistance Education) and the Partnership for a Drug-Free America help spread the message about avoiding drug use.

Do some research to find out more about these and other antidrug campaigns. Write a brief paragraph describing your findings.

◄ Spending time with friends or participating in community-service activities are two good ways to stay away from drugs. **Why do you think a teen might have difficulty saying no to drug use?**

Why Are Drugs Harmful to Teens?

Drugs can be very harmful to anyone who uses them. Teens, though, are especially at risk when they choose to use drugs.

Drug Use Harms Growth and Development

So why are drugs especially harmful to teens? One reason is that teens' bodies and brains are still developing. **Figure 10.2** lists how using drugs can harm the body. Drugs can affect the long-term development of many body systems. They can reduce your motor skills, or the ability to move your muscles in normal ways. Simple tasks such as writing, speaking, or walking can be affected. What's worse, this type of damage can often be permanent. Also, drugs trick the brain into thinking that the body needs them to **function** properly. Over time, the body may need more and more of the drug to function.

Academic Vocabulary

function (FUNK shun) *(verb)* to work or operate. *Eating a healthful breakfast in the morning helps your body function well for the rest of the day.*

▼ FIGURE 10.2

DRUG USE AFFECTS GROWING TEENS

This chart shows how drug abuse seriously affects teens. **Name two reasons why drug use is especially harmful to teens.**

In males, drug use can negatively affect:

- height
- weight
- male hormone levels
- testicle size and function
- muscle mass and development
- the age at which voice gets lower
- the age at which body and facial hair increases

In females, drug use can negatively affect:

- height
- weight
- onset of first menstrual cycle
- regularity of periods
- breast development
- function of ovaries
- pregnancy
- the health of unborn babies

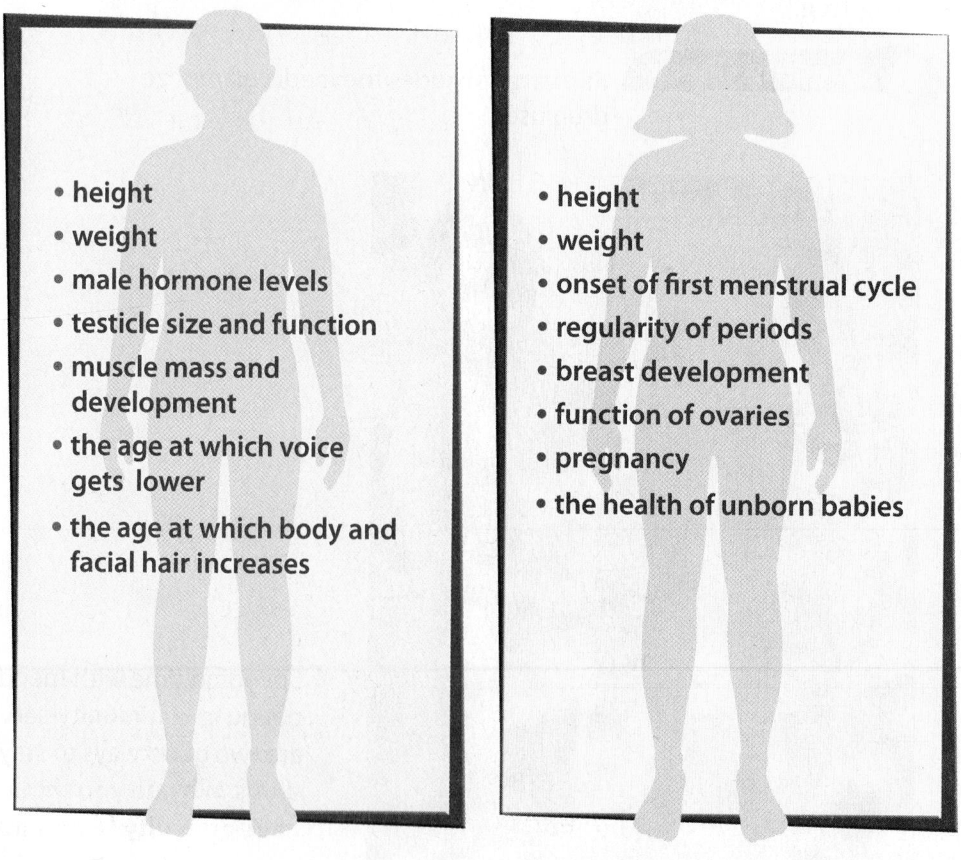

Drug Use Harms Mental/Emotional Health

Gwen has been smoking marijuana lately. She finds that she can't concentrate like she used to. Also, she can't stay focused when trying to complete a task. Gwen has found out the truth about drug use: it can affect a person's ability to learn and think. She also sees that drug use could be affecting her long-term goals for success.

David was feeling a little down. He decided to take drugs to feel better. He thought that this was a good way to deal with his emotional problems. Emotional changes, though, are a part of growing up. Using drugs at this point in your life is dangerous because it keeps you from learning to handle difficult emotions in healthful ways, which will help you to mature. Using drugs affects how you handle situations. Drug use often leads to making poor decisions and using bad judgment. It can make you act violently or put yourself in danger. When you use drugs to deal with your emotions, it not only puts both you and other people at risk but also stops the emotional growth that will help you become a healthy adult.

Drugs Are Illegal

Breaking the law is a risky behavior and is not the right thing to do. Most drug use is illegal and dangerous. Federal and state laws say that dangerous and addictive drugs may not be used or sold. Some drugs, such as morphine and codeine, are illegal except in certain medical situations. Other drugs, such as heroin and crack, are always illegal, no matter how they are used. People who are caught with these drugs or selling them can be arrested and may go to jail.

 Reading Check **Describe** How can drug use affect a person's emotional health?

ACTIVITY
Careers for the 21st Century

Paramedic

A paramedic is a medical professional who provides emergency care to injured people at the scene of an accident. There will always be a need for paramedics because accidents and other emergencies occur every day. To prepare for a career as a paramedic you should take courses like anatomy and physiology to learn about the human body.

What skills does a paramedic need? Go to *Career Corner* at **glencoe.com** to find out.

◀ Selling or just having illegal drugs can result in serious legal consequences. **What is one legal consequence of using illegal drugs?**

Health Skills Activity

Advocacy

Campaign for a Drug-Free School

Find out more about your school's drug policy. Create your own drug-free campaign by distributing information about your school's rules on drugs, alcohol, and tobacco.

- Create posters and pamphlets that outline your school's drug policy.
- Provide information describing why remaining drug free is the most healthful choice for teens.
- Tell students how they can report drug use to a teacher or school counselor.

With a Group

Write a contract that encourages your fellow students to lead a drug-free lifestyle. Make several copies of the contract and hand them out to students. Ask students to voluntarily sign a contract to help promote a drug-free school.

Drug Use Creates Problems at School

Richard is in the eighth grade. He abuses drugs and has problems at school. Not only does he miss school often, he does poorly because he can't pay attention. Because he was caught with drugs, he may not participate in school activities—and he has lost his chance to learn new skills. The lesson is clear: teens who abuse drugs often hurt their chances of reaching their long-term goals.

Today, most schools have made themselves drug-free zones. A **drug-free zone** is *a 1,000-yard distance around a school where anyone caught with drugs can be arrested.* Anyone of any age caught with illegal drugs within the drug-free zone can be arrested and go to jail. Students caught using drugs or being under the influence of any drugs can be suspended and even expelled from school.

▼ Friends can be an important influence during the teen years. **How can friends help you stay drug free?**

Reading Check **Describe** What are two ways that a teen may experience problems at school because he or she is abusing drugs?

Drug Use and the Law

The legal consequences of drug use are one of the many negative effects of this harmful behavior. When someone is caught using illegal drugs, the legal consequences are very serious. Teens can be arrested for possession of drugs. **Drug possession** is *when a person has or keeps illegal drugs.* Teens can be arrested or spend time in a detention center, and they as well as their parents may be fined. Teens can also get a criminal record.

Some teens are sentenced to **probation,** *a set period of time during which a person who has been arrested must check in regularly with a court officer.* A person who fails to check in with the court officer during probation may face even stronger punishment.

Drug Use and Crime

There is a connection between drug use and crime. People addicted to drugs often build up a greater tolerance to the drug. This means the person needs more of the drug to get the same feeling. Very often, the person may steal the drugs or steal money to buy the drugs. Stealing can lead to violence and accidents, and this increases the chances of being caught and put in jail.

 Reading Check **Explain** How can drug abuse lead to crime?

 **Go Online**

Visit **glencoe.com** and complete the Interactive Study Guide for Lesson 3.

Lesson 3 Review

 After You Read

Review this lesson for new terms, major headings, and Reading Checks.

What I Learned

1. *Vocabulary* Define *probation.*

2. *List* What are two reasons why some teens might choose to use drugs?

3. *Explain* How can the use of drugs affect a teen's body?

4. *Describe* How can drug use affect a person's mental health?

Thinking Critically

5. *Analyze* What is the difference between using a drug such as codeine illegally and using the drug legally?

6. *Synthesize* Why do you think using drugs to deal with difficult feelings could be harmful to a teen's emotional health?

Applying Health Skills

7. *Goal Setting* Identify some short-term and long-term goals you have set for yourself, such as college or a career. In a brief paragraph, explain the effects that drug use could have on these plans for the future.

Staying Drug Free

Guide to Reading

● Building Vocabulary

As you read this lesson, write down each new highlighted term and its definition.

- alternative (p. 317)
- assertive (p. 318)

● Focusing on the Main Ideas

In this lesson, you will be able to

- **describe** some reasons to be drug free.
- **identify** alternatives to drug use.
- **practice** refusal skills to stay drug free.

● Reading Strategy

Mapping Concepts Using the main heads in this lesson and the partially completed concept map shown below, draw a concept map of the topics presented. As you read this lesson, complete your concept map with ways to avoid drugs.

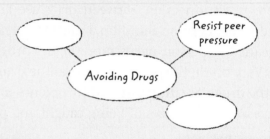

Quick Write

Describe a situation in which you had to use refusal skills. How could you apply what you learned in that situation to refuse drugs?

▶ Helping out in your community, perhaps by teaching others about the dangers of drugs, is one way to stay drug free. **What local groups would you like to become involved in?**

Reasons to Avoid Drugs

You'll make a lot of decisions in the course of your life. Choosing to avoid illegal drugs and avoiding the improper use of legal drugs are the most healthful and important decisions you'll ever make. If you keep drug abuse out of your life, you have a much greater chance of reaching your goals. There are many good reasons to avoid drugs. Here are just a few.

- When you avoid drugs, you show respect for yourself. You show that you care for yourself and your health.

- When you avoid drugs, you plan for your future. You look ahead to a healthy and more mature future.

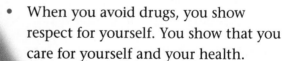

- When you avoid drugs, you stay in control. Choosing not to use drugs will help you stay in control and act more responsibly.
- When you avoid drugs, you respect the law. By avoiding drug use, you are obeying the law and being a good citizen.

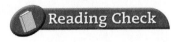 **Reading Check** **Name** What are two reasons for avoiding drugs?

Alternatives to Drug Use

You don't need to use drugs to have fun. You can choose positive behaviors as alternatives to using drugs. An **alternative** is *another way of thinking or acting.* You and your friends can participate in activities that do not involve drugs, such as sports or clubs. You can explore a new hobby, learn to play music, or be part of a play. You can paint or learn how to make sculptures and pottery. You can go to a state or national park to explore nature. You can volunteer for an organization that you are interested in. You can also choose to teach others about the dangers of drug use.

Remember that you always have alternatives to drug use. It is especially important to remember this when you are having a hard time dealing with your feelings. Deal with your problems and issues rather than covering them up with drug use. Talk with a trusted adult or a counselor about what is bothering you. This is the mature way to handle problems. Using drugs is just taking the easy way out, and the problem will return just as soon as the drug wears off.

 **Reading Check** **Identify** What are two alternatives to drug use?

How to Refuse Drugs

Sooner or later, you'll probably be pressured to try drugs. You need to be ready to handle this situation in the right way.

Resisting Peer Pressure

You no doubt hear the phrase "peer pressure" a lot. Remember, your peers are people who are your age and who are similar to you in many ways. Most important, your peers are the people most likely to pressure you to use drugs. When they pressure you, remember your reasons for choosing to be drug free.

Go Online

Topic: Speak Out About Drugs

Visit **glencoe.com** for Student Web Activities to learn about the dangers of drug use.

Activity: Using the information provided at the link above, create a public service announcement about the dangers of drug use and how to stay drug free.

▼ Resisting peer pressure involves knowing communication strategies for avoiding harmful behaviors like drug use. **What are some of your reasons for not using drugs?**

It's important to remember that you are not alone when you choose to say no to drugs. Others will be making the same wise choice. Choosing to spend time with friends who do not use drugs is one of the most important decisions you can make. When you resist peer pressure to use drugs, you are protecting your health and your future.

Refusal Skills

You've been told to resist peer pressure, but how do you do it? You use refusal skills. Refusal skills are effective **strategies** for saying no to harmful behaviors. Some strategies work better than others depending on the situation, so it is important to know the strategies that work for you. It's often not enough to just say no. You need to say it with your body language and attitude, too. Be **assertive,** or *willing to stand up for yourself in a firm but positive way.* Speak in a firm voice while you're standing up straight. This positive communication strategy will tell others that you mean what you say.

It's a good idea to practice your refusal skills. This will make you better at using them. **Figure 10.3** provides some strategies for saying no to unhealthful behaviors. You can practice using these strategies by role-playing situations with a group of friends that you trust.

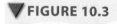

Visit **glencoe.com** and complete the Interactive Study Guide for Lesson 4.

 **Reading Check** **Explain** What does *assertive* mean?

▼ **FIGURE 10.3**

STRATEGIES FOR STAYING DRUG FREE

Below are some effective strategies for refusing drugs to maintain your personal health. Why is using the right body language a positive communication strategy for avoiding harmful behaviors such as drug use?

Use the S.T.O.P. formula.	• **S**ay no in a firm voice. • **T**ell why not. • **O**ffer other ideas. • **P**romptly leave.
Take your time.	• If you have to speak slowly or stall in order to collect your thoughts, do so. • Take all the time you need in order to be firm in what you are saying.
Be direct.	• State how you feel as simply as possible. • Keep your statements short and clear.
Use the right body language.	• Make sure your body language helps you get your point across. • Stand up straight and make eye contact.
Don't apologize.	• Stick up for what you believe. • You don't need to make excuses or apologize for your decisions.
Walk away.	• If you cannot get your point across, you still have the right to leave. • Don't be afraid to do so.

Health Skills Activity

Refusal Skills

Refusing Drugs

Tyler has noticed that his best friend, Jonathan, has become a little distant. Jonathan recently changed schools, so Tyler doesn't see him every day anymore. Tyler knows that Jonathan has met some new friends at his new school. When they get together, Tyler notices that Jonathan doesn't seem interested and has trouble following the conversation.

One day, Tyler meets up with Jonathan and some of his new friends. Jonathan's new friends suggest that everyone go back to Jonathan's house to smoke marijuana. Tyler wants to keep Jonathan as a friend, but he doesn't want to use drugs. What should Tyler do?

What Would You Do?

Apply the S.T.O.P. formula to Tyler's situation.

- **S**ay no in a firm voice.
- **T**ell why not.
- **O**ffer other ideas.
- **P**romptly leave.

Lesson 4 Review

 After You Read

Review this lesson for new terms, major headings, and Reading Checks.

What I Learned

1. *Vocabulary* Define *alternative*.

2. *List* Name three reasons not to use drugs.

3. *Describe* What are two alternatives to drug use? Describe how these alternatives could make a teen less likely to use drugs.

4. *Explain* What is the S.T.O.P. formula? How can it allow you to stay drug free?

Thinking Critically

5. *Analyze* How can being prepared help you refuse drugs?

6. *Apply* What is the most important reason for you to stay drug free?

Applying Health Skills

7. *Advocacy* What advice would you give a friend who has trouble saying no to her peers when they pressure her to use drugs?

Building Health Skills

Accessing Information
Practicing Healthful Behaviors
Stress Management
Analyzing Influences
Communication Skills
Refusal Skills
Conflict Resolution
Decision Making
Goal Setting
Advocacy

What Is Advocacy?

Advocacy involves taking action in support of a cause. An advocate is someone who works to bring about change.

Ways to Take Action

- Write letters to government leaders, and magazine and newspaper editors.
- Collect signatures from people in your community.
- Organize activities in your school or neighborhood.
- Volunteer with a group that shares your feelings. If no group exists, start your own group.
- Contact local radio or television stations to see if they will give your cause airtime.

Helping Others Say No to Drugs

Follow the Model, Practice, and Apply steps to help you master this important health skill.

❶ Model

Read how Carlos and his class used the skill of advocacy by contributing to the Say No to Drugs campaign at their school.

In health class, Carlos studied ways teens can say no to drugs. His teacher, Mr. Johnson, explained how to start a Say No to Drugs campaign to encourage teens in their school to be drug free. He suggested they start by thinking of themselves as advocates.

Mr. Johnson directed the class to gather information on the physical, mental/emotional, and social dangers of drug use and the benefits of being drug free. Then the class created colorful posters to display during the Say No to Drugs campaign at school.

❷ Practice

Help Sarita and Delanie develop a Say No to Drugs program.

On the way home from school, Sarita thought about ways to help young people stay drug free. She asked her mom to help her think of ideas. "Why don't you create a presentation for younger kids?" her mom suggested. Sarita asked her friend Delanie to help her with the project. Answer the following questions to help Sarita and Delanie develop their program.

1. How can Sarita and Delanie make their stand on drug use clear in the program?

2. What physical, mental/emotional, and social risks should they talk about?

3. How can they persuade younger students to stay drug free?

❸ Apply

Use what you have learned about advocacy skills to complete the activity below.

In small groups, use your advocacy skills to create a public service announcement (PSA) to help teens stay drug free. In your announcement, include the risks of drug use. Also include the most important reasons to stay drug free. Be as persuasive as you can to encourage fellow students to choose to be drug free.

Self-Check

- Does our PSA explain the risks of drug use?
- Does our PSA contain the most important reasons for staying drug free?
- Is our PSA persuasive?

Good News

Newspaper stories often focus on teens who abuse drugs and alcohol. These stories emphasize negative behaviors instead of positive ones. What if newspapers did the opposite and wrote stories about all the teens who make positive choices? What if a newspaper headline stated the high percentage of young people who have never used illegal substances? What if the stories also explained why these students make good choices? Write that story!

What You Will Need

- Paper
- Pencil or pen
- A partner to work with

What You Will Do

1 Choose one of the following statistics from The Monitoring the Future Study conducted by the University of Michigan:

- 60% of eighth graders have never used alcohol.
- 80% of eighth graders report never having been drunk.
- 98% of eighth graders have never used Ecstasy.
- 98% of eighth graders have never used steroids.

2 Write a headline that shows the percentage of students who avoid these illegal activities.

3 Write a story that gives reasons why you think these students avoid the substance stated in your headline.

Wrapping It Up

Use the headline and story you wrote to create a newspaper-style handout, then distribute it to the rest of the class. Ask the other students to think about this: When you avoid the risky behavior of drug use, you are doing what most other teens do. Know that you have a lot of company when it comes to staying drug free.

Reading Review

STUDY TO GO Visit **glencoe.com** to download quizzes and eFlashcards for Chapter 10.

FOLDABLES® Study Organizer

Foldables® and Other Study Aids Take out the Foldable® that you created for Lesson 2 and any graphic organizers that you created for Lessons 1–5. Find a partner and quiz each other using these study aids.

Lesson 1 Drug Use and Abuse

Main Idea Drug misuse and abuse can seriously harm your health triangle.

- A drug is a substance other than food that changes the structure or function of the body or mind.
- Medicines are drugs and can either be purchased over-the-counter (at a pharmacy or grocery store) or prescribed by your doctor.
- Drug misuse is taking a drug in a way that is not intended.
- Drug addiction means that a person is dependent on a drug that is very hard to quit.

Lesson 2 Types of Drugs and Their Effects

Main Idea Drugs can harm your body in many ways.

- The same drugs can affect people differently.
- Tolerance is the body's need for larger and larger amounts of a drug to produce the same effect.
- An overdose is taking more of a drug than the body can tolerate.

- Types of drugs include stimulants, depressants, club drugs, narcotics, hallucinogens, inhalants, and steroids.
- If a pregnant woman takes drugs, the drugs can hurt her unborn child.

Lesson 3 Drug Risks and Teens

Main Idea Drugs are especially harmful to teens because their bodies are still growing.

- Media messages that glamorize drug use can encourage teens to use drugs.
- Drug use often leads to making poor decisions, bad judgment, and violence.
- Drug possession and drug use are illegal.
- A drug-free zone is a 1,000-yard distance around a school where anyone caught with drugs will be arrested.

Lesson 4 Staying Drug Free

Main Idea Avoiding drugs means that you have self-respect, want a bright future, are responsible, are in control, and are a good citizen.

- Alternatives to drug abuse include playing sports, joining after-school clubs, volunteer work, and taking music or art lessons.
- Use refusal skills to resist peer pressure to use drugs.
- Be assertive when you say no drugs.

Assessment

Now that you have read the chapter, look back at your answer to the Health eSpotlight question on the chapter opener. Have your ideas changed? What would your answer be now?

Reviewing Vocabulary and Main Ideas

On a sheet of paper, write the numbers 1–6. After each number, write the term from the list that best completes each statement.

- drug
- depressant
- club drugs
- amphetamines
- tolerance
- overdose

Lesson 1 Drug Use and Abuse

1. A _____ is a drug that slows down the body's functions.

2. _____ are illegal drugs that are often used at all-night parties called raves.

3. Strong stimulant drugs that speed up the nervous system are _____.

4. A substance other than food that changes the way your body works is a _____.

Lesson 2 Types of Drugs and Their Effects

5. Taking more of a drug than your body can stand is called a(n) _____.

6. _____ is the body's need for larger and larger amounts of a drug to produce the same effect.

On a sheet of paper, write the numbers 7–10. After each number, write the letter of the answer that best completes each statement.

Lesson 3 Drug Risks and Teens

7. Because a teen's body is still developing,

   a. drug use can interfere with brain development.

   b. drug use can help a teen manage his or her weight.

   c. a teen cannot develop an addiction to drugs.

   d. None of the above

8. Misuse of drugs includes

   a. ignoring the directions on medicine given to you by a doctor.

   b. using someone else's prescription medicine.

   c. using a medicine in a way that is not intended.

   d. All of the above

Lesson 4 Staying Drug Free

9. The best way to say no to drugs is to

   a. be unprepared to say no.

   b. apologize for wanting to avoid drugs.

   c. avoid people who use drugs and avoid places where drugs are available.

   d. have friends that use drugs.

10. Participating in community activities

    a. takes up too much time to be worth it.

    b. is one healthy alternative to drug use.

    c. is an unhealthy alternative to drug use.

    d. None of the above

Go Online Visit glencoe.com and take the Online Quiz for Chapter 10.

Thinking Critically

Using complete sentences, answer the following questions on a sheet of paper.

11. **Hypothesize** Why might someone ignore the risks of drug use?

12. **Explain** How can avoiding drugs support a teen's decision to avoid sexual activity?

Write About It

13. **Narrative Writing** Write a story about a teen athlete who is considering using steroids.

14. **Expository Writing** Write a paragraph describing how a teen can use positive peer pressure to influence others to avoid using drugs.

✦ Applying Technology

Say No to Drugs Puppet Show

You and a partner will create and film a puppet show using iMovie® that teaches young children how to say no to drugs. Follow the steps below to complete this project.

- Create puppets out of old socks or paper bags. Use a variety of materials like markers, glitter, and buttons.
- Write a five-minute dialogue for your puppets. Make sure to include each step from the S.T.O.P. formula.
- Use a digital recorder to film the puppet show. Import your video into *iMovie*®.
- Edit your video. Make sure that the vocabulary you use is age-appropriate for younger students.
- Save your project.

Standardized Test Practice

Reading

Read the two paragraphs and then answer the questions.

Heroin is a narcotic, a type of drug that relieves pain and dulls the senses. Heroin is a highly addictive drug, and withdrawal from heroin is extremely painful. Heroin is usually injected, and it gives users a sense of *euphoria*. This feeling of joy is short-lived, however. Very soon, the user suffers from withdrawal.

The symptoms of heroin withdrawal are so painful that most users need professional help to quit. The user must go through a detoxification process. This process may be drug free or it may include the use of legal doses of other drugs that relieve the symptoms of withdrawal. One of the drugs used in heroin detoxification is called methadone, a *synthetic* drug not found in nature. It delays the feelings and cravings that users experience during withdrawal.

1. In the first paragraph, *euphoria* means
   A. a feeling of sadness.
   B. a feeling of joy.
   C. a period of confusion.
   D. None of the above

2. What is the main idea of the second paragraph?
   A. Withdrawal from heroin is painful and difficult.
   B. Heroin can be used only by injection.
   C. Heroin is an extremely addictive narcotic.
   D. All of the above

3. In the second paragraph, *synthetic* means
   A. helpful.
   B. not found in nature.
   C. effective.
   D. healthful.

Chapter Preview

Lesson 1   Healthy Teeth, Skin, Hair, and Nails............................328

Lesson 2   Healthy Eyes and Ears 334

Lesson 3   Smart Consumer Choices 340

Lesson 4   Using Medicines Safely....347

Lesson 5   Choosing Health Care 352

Building Health Skills.......................356

TIME health news 358

Chapter Reading Review...................359

Chapter Assessment 360

▲ *Working with the Photo*

You make many choices about your health each day. **Name one type of personal health care product that a teen might use.**

Start-Up Activities

Before You Read What do you do to take care of your personal health? Find out by taking the short health inventory on this page. Keep a record of your answers.

HEALTH INVENTORY

1. I brush my teeth twice a day.
(a) always   (b) sometimes   (c) never

2. I apply sunscreen before going outdoors.
(a) always   (b) sometimes   (c) never

3. I make sure to have plenty of light when reading or doing homework.
(a) always   (b) sometimes   (c) never

FOLDABLES Study Organizer

As You Read Make this Foldable® to help you organize information on personal care presented in Lesson 1. Begin with a plain sheet of 11" × 17" paper.

1 Fold the short edges of the paper inward so that they meet in the middle.

2 Fold the top edge down to meet the bottom edge.

3 Unfold and cut along the inside fold lines to form four tabs.

4 Label the tabs as shown.

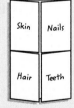

Skin | Nails
Hair | Teeth

Record what you learn about the form, function, and care of teeth, skin, hair, and nails under the appropriate tab.

G⊙ Online Visit **glencoe.com** and complete the Health Inventory for Chapter 11.

Healthy Teeth, Skin, Hair, and Nails

Guide to Reading

Building Vocabulary
The prefix *epi-* means "above" and the root *derma* means "skin." Choose two terms from the list below that you think describe two layers of skin. Identify which layer is the outermost layer of skin. Add formal definitions for these terms to your notes as you read the lesson.

- fluoride (p. 329)
- plaque (p. 329)
- tartar (p. 329)
- pores (p. 330)
- dermis (p. 330)
- epidermis (p. 330)
- hair follicles (p. 330)
- ultraviolet (UV) rays (p. 331)
- melanin (p. 331)
- acne (p. 332)
- dandruff (p. 333)

Focusing on the Main Ideas
In this lesson, you will be able to

- **explain** how to keep your teeth and gums healthy.
- **describe** ways to clean and protect your skin.
- **identify** how to care for your hair and nails.

Reading Strategy
Organizing Information As you read the lesson, write down the functions of each body part discussed.

 **Study Organizer** Use the Foldable® on p. 327 as you read this lesson.

Quick Write

Write down three reasons why personal hygiene is an important part of health.

Healthy Teeth

Healthy teeth give you a great-looking smile. Teeth do more than help you look good, though. You need them to chew your food for digestion. You also need healthy teeth to speak clearly. Each tooth has a root that goes into your jawbone. Roots are surrounded by pink flesh called gums. The top of the tooth is the crown, which is covered with a layer of hard, white enamel.

Your teeth and gums need to last a lifetime. It makes sense to take good care of them. Limit sugary foods and soft drinks, and brush and floss often. Fruits, vegetables, and calcium-rich foods such as milk and yogurt will help you avoid tooth decay and prevent gum disease.

Tooth Care

The keys to having healthy teeth and gums are proper brushing and flossing. Brush after every meal (or at least twice a day) with toothpaste and a soft-bristled toothbrush. Rinse with warm water or with mouthwash. Use dental floss daily to remove anything caught between your teeth, such as bits of food your toothbrush can't reach. Flossing also keeps gums healthy and prevents gum disease. **Figure 11.1** shows the right way to brush and floss.

Be sure to use a toothpaste or mouthwash that contains fluoride. **Fluoride** is *a chemical that helps prevent tooth decay.* In many areas, fluoride is added to tap water.

Tooth Decay

Brushing and flossing also remove plaque. **Plaque** is *a thin, sticky film that builds up on teeth and leads to tooth decay.* Bacteria in plaque feed on the carbohydrates—sugars and starches—in the foods you eat. These bacteria produce acids that can break down tooth enamel leading to tooth decay and holes, or cavities.

Plaque also causes tartar. **Tartar** is *hardened plaque that hurts gum health.* You can't just brush away tartar. A dentist or dental hygienist must remove it with special tools that clean and polish surfaces of the teeth.

 Reading Check **Compare** How does plaque differ from tartar?

 **FIGURE 11.1**

BRUSHING AND FLOSSING THE RIGHT WAY

Brushing and flossing regularly helps prevent tooth decay and other health problems. How else can you improve the health of your teeth?

How to Brush
Be sure to brush your teeth for at least two minutes—30 seconds for each area of your mouth.

Brush the outer surfaces of your upper and lower teeth. Use a combination of up-and-down strokes and circular strokes.

Thoroughly brush all chewing surfaces with a soft-bristle brush to protect your gums.

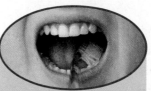

Brush the inside surfaces of your upper and lower teeth.

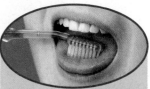

Brush your tongue and rinse your mouth.

How to Floss

Take about 18 inches of floss and wrap each end around the middle finger of each hand.

Grip the floss firmly between your thumb and forefinger.

Slide the floss back and forth between teeth toward the gum line until it touches the gum line.

Curve the floss around the sides of each tooth. Keep sliding the floss back and forth gently as you move it up and down.

Healthy Skin

When you think of an organ, you might think of something like your heart or your stomach. You might overlook your body's largest organ, which doesn't lie beneath your skin—it *is* your skin! **Figure 11.2** shows the different layers that make up the skin.

Your skin has many jobs. It gives you a sense of touch and of temperature. Skin is the first line of defense against infection. It keeps germs from getting into the body. When you sweat, your skin gets rid of water and salts and cools your body. The blood vessels in your skin allow your body to control its temperature. Finally, your skin uses energy from sunlight to make vitamin D, which helps keep your bones and teeth healthy.

▼ **FIGURE 11.2**

PARTS OF THE SKIN

Each layer of the skin has a different function. **What layer of the skin has structures that keep the skin from drying out?**

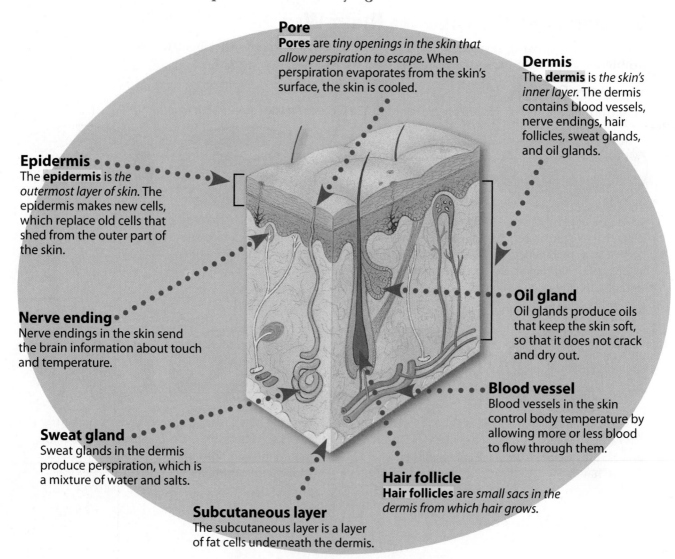

Pore
Pores are *tiny openings in the skin that allow perspiration to escape.* When perspiration evaporates from the skin's surface, the skin is cooled.

Dermis
The **dermis** is *the skin's inner layer.* The dermis contains blood vessels, nerve endings, hair follicles, sweat glands, and oil glands.

Epidermis
The **epidermis** is *the outermost layer of skin.* The epidermis makes new cells, which replace old cells that shed from the outer part of the skin.

Nerve ending
Nerve endings in the skin send the brain information about touch and temperature.

Sweat gland
Sweat glands in the dermis produce perspiration, which is a mixture of water and salts.

Oil gland
Oil glands produce oils that keep the skin soft, so that it does not crack and dry out.

Blood vessel
Blood vessels in the skin control body temperature by allowing more or less blood to flow through them.

Hair follicle
Hair follicles are *small sacs in the dermis from which hair grows.*

Subcutaneous layer
The subcutaneous layer is a layer of fat cells underneath the dermis.

Skin Care

Keeping your skin healthy can help you feel, look, and smell good. Try these tips for taking care of your skin:

- Take a bath or shower every day. Use soap to wash away dirt, sweat, oils, and bacteria that collect on your skin.

- Moisturize dry skin with lotion. Dry or cracked skin can itch or become irritated.

- Limit time spent in the sun, and avoid tanning beds. When you go outdoors, wear sunscreen to protect your skin from the sun's rays.

- Avoid tattoos and piercings. Permanent body decoration can put you at risk for disease and scarring.

Sun Damage

Factors in the environment can affect your personal health. The sun gives off **ultraviolet (UV) rays,** *an invisible form of radiation that can enter skin cells and change their structure.* Sunburn happens when UV rays damage skin cells. You might think soaking up lots of UV rays will give you a nice tan, but it will also wrinkle your skin. Even worse, too much time in the sun increases the risk of skin cancer. Be smart; protect yourself from UV rays by limiting your sun exposure and by using sunscreen.

Special cells in the epidermis make **melanin,** *the substance that gives skin its color.* Darker skin has more melanin than paler skin. Melanin can block some, but not all, UV rays from reaching the lower layers of skin.

Being outdoors in the sun isn't the only way you can be exposed to UV rays. What about indoor tanning beds? Many people use them to stay tan year-round. Tanning beds also give off UV rays. They can damage the skin, lead to skin cancer, and hurt the eyes and immune system. The healthful choice is to stay out of tanning beds.

▶ Ultraviolet rays from the sun can harm skin cells. **How can you protect yourself from ultraviolet rays and reduce your risks for developing skin cancer?**

Connect To... Science

The Dangers of Body Decoration

Tattoos and piercings are created with needles or equipment that leave a pattern of permanent dye in the skin or punch holes in the skin. Dirty equipment and needles can spread serious infections such as HIV and hepatitis. Even with sterile needles, a tattoo or piercing can cause scarring.

Write a story about a teen whose friend wants to get a tattoo. In the story, show how the main character positively influences his or her friend to make a healthful choice about body decoration.

UV Index

11+	**Levels 11 and higher:** Extremely high risk. Avoid the sun between 10 A.M. and 4 P.M. Use sunscreen with an SPF of 15 or higher, and wear protective clothing and sunglasses.
10 9 8	**Levels 8 through 10:** Very high risk. Avoid the sun between 10 A.M. and 4 P.M. Use sunscreen with an SPF of 15 or higher. Wear protective clothing and sunglasses.
7 6	**Levels 6 and 7:** High risk. Cover up, wear a hat with a wide brim, and use sunscreen with an SPF of 15 or higher.
5 4	**Levels 3 through 5:** Moderate risk. Stay in the shade around midday.
3 <2	**Level 2 or below:** Low risk. Wear sunglasses on bright days, cover up, and use sunscreen.

How Acne Forms

Whiteheads, blackheads, and pimples are all forms of acne that commonly affect teens. What structure in the skin becomes clogged to form acne?

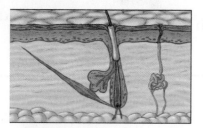

Whiteheads
A whitehead forms when a pore gets plugged up with the skin's natural oils and dead skin cells.

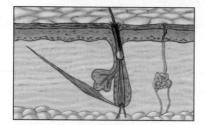

Blackheads
When a whitehead reacts to the air and darkens, it becomes a blackhead.

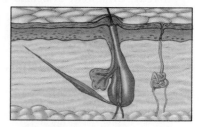

Pimples
A clogged follicle can burst, which lets in bacteria. The follicle becomes infected and a pimple forms.

Acne

Did you ever wake up on an important day, only to see a huge pimple? One skin problem experienced by many teens and some adults is acne. **Acne** is *a skin condition caused by active oil glands that clog hair follicles.* The openings of these hair follicles onto the skin are called pores. Bacteria gathers in the clogged pores, making them swell up. If you have a bad case of acne, you may need to see a dermatologist, a doctor who specializes in problems of the skin.

Figure 11.3 shows how acne forms. If you get acne, don't pick at it or try to pop the clogged pores. In fact, try not to touch your skin at all. Instead, wash the area with a mild soap and warm water. Be gentle, and don't scrub too hard. Washing helps remove the dirt, oil, sweat, or makeup that can cause pores to clog.

> **Reading Check** **Identify** What is acne?

Topic: Acne from A to Z

Visit glencoe.com for Student Web Activities where you can get the facts about the causes of and treatments for acne.

Activity: Using the information provided at the link above, create a fact sheet that contains information on acne myths and facts as well as acne treatments.

Healthy Hair and Hair Care

You might spend a lot of time and money to give your hair "life" and "body." Hair grows from hair follicles in the scalp. The scalp is the skin beneath the hair on your head. Your hair contains a protein called keratin. Keratin gives hair strength and allows it to bend without breaking.

Caring for your hair keeps your scalp from getting irritated. Brushing your hair daily removes dirt from your hair and scalp. It also spreads oils throughout your hair. These natural oils help keep hair healthy and whole. Wash your hair with shampoo to clean away dirt and extra oil, leaving it looking and smelling clean.

Hair and Scalp Problems

One common problem with the hair and scalp is dandruff. **Dandruff** is *a condition that results when too many dead skin cells flake off the outer layer of the scalp.* Dandruff can happen due to certain skin diseases. It can also result from a fungus. Using a special dandruff shampoo can help control and prevent dandruff.

Head lice can also cause problems for the hair and scalp. Head lice are tiny insects that live and feed on strands of hair and can make a person's scalp itch. Anyone can get head lice. They spread when people share combs, brushes, hats, or other personal items. You can use a special shampoo to treat head lice.

 Reading Check Identify What protein is found in hair and nails?

Healthy Nails and Nail Care

Nails protect sensitive fingertips and the tips of toes. To care for your nails, wash your hands regularly. Use hand lotion to keep nails and skin moist. Clip nails to keep them trimmed and neat. Use a nail file to smooth any rough edges on your nails so they won't catch on objects and rip. Don't bite, tear, or pick at your nails. The same goes for your cuticles, the thin layers of skin-like tissue at the base of each nail. Otherwise, germs can invade the weakened tissue and infect it.

Visit **glencoe.com** and complete the Interactive Study Guide for Lesson 1.

Lesson 1 Review

 After You Read

Review this lesson for new terms, major headings, and Reading Checks.

What I Learned

1. *Describe* Name two healthful behaviors that keep your teeth and gums healthy.

2. *Give Examples* Describe three functions of the skin.

3. *Vocabulary* Define *dandruff.* Describe how to treat it.

4. *Identify* What are ultraviolet rays?

Thinking Critically

5. *Analyze* How can the foods you eat affect the health of your teeth and gums?

6. *Apply* What can you do to care for your nails and cuticles?

Applying Health Skills

7. *Practicing Healthful Behaviors* Tisha's friends have invited her to join them at the beach. They plan on lying out in the sun to tan. How can Tisha protect her skin from the sun's UV rays?

Lesson 2

Healthy Eyes and Ears

Guide to Reading

● **Building Vocabulary**
As you read the lesson, write down each highlighted term and its definition.

- optometrist (p. 336)
- ophthalmologist (p. 336)
- cataract (p. 336)
- glaucoma (p. 336)
- astigmatism (p. 337)
- tinnitus (p. 338)
- deafness (p. 338)
- decibel (p. 338)

● **Focusing on the Main Ideas**
In this lesson, you will be able to

- **identify** ways to keep your eyes healthy.
- **explain** why people wear glasses or contact lenses.
- **describe** ways to care for your ears.

● **Reading Strategy**
Organizing Information As you read the lesson, create a chart that describes the functions of each body part discussed in the lesson and how to care for it.

Body Part	Function	Care
Eyes		
Ears		

Quick Write

Make a list of five ways you have used your sense of hearing today. How would these activities be different if you could not hear very well?

Healthy Eyes

Like a camera, your eyes focus light in order to give your brain a picture of the world around you. Eyes allow you to see shapes, colors, and motion. Each part of the eye plays an important role in how you see. **Figure 11.4** shows the parts of the eye and explains how each one works.

Eye Care

Your eyes need light to see. However, too much light can hurt them. The sun can be very hard on your eyes. For example, you should never look directly at the sun. In addition, UV rays can damage eye cells. You can solve this problem by wearing sunglasses that block UV rays.

Sitting too close to the television can cause eyestrain and headaches. Sit at least 6 feet away. If you get eyestrain while sitting at a computer, change the monitor position to cut down on the glare. Reading in dim light can also cause eyestrain. To reduce your risk for eyestrain and to protect your eyes, be sure you have adequate lighting while you read, work, or watch TV.

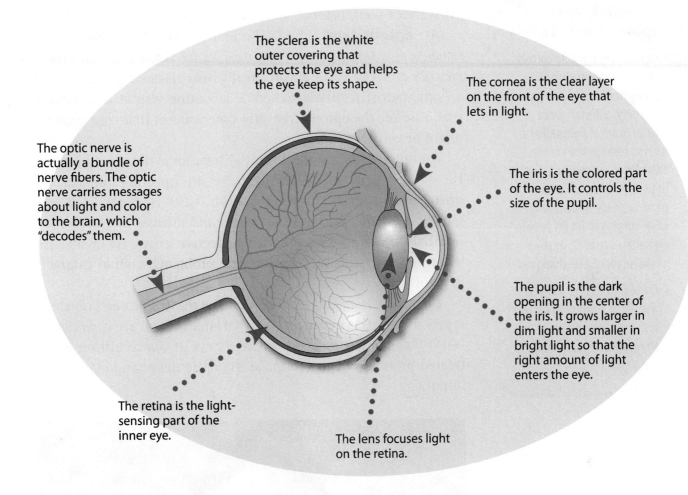

PARTS OF THE EYE

Here are some of the major structures in the human eye. Through what opening does light enter the inner part of the eye?

The sclera is the white outer covering that protects the eye and helps the eye keep its shape.

The cornea is the clear layer on the front of the eye that lets in light.

The optic nerve is actually a bundle of nerve fibers. The optic nerve carries messages about light and color to the brain, which "decodes" them.

The iris is the colored part of the eye. It controls the size of the pupil.

The pupil is the dark opening in the center of the iris. It grows larger in dim light and smaller in bright light so that the right amount of light enters the eye.

The retina is the light-sensing part of the inner eye.

The lens focuses light on the retina.

In many ways, your eyes are more delicate than your skin. Protect your eyes when you are doing yard work, handling power tools, or playing sports that involve flying objects. Wear glasses or goggles designed for these activities. Wear goggles when you work with strong chemicals, too. These chemicals could splash into your eyes. Chemical gases in the air or tiny bits of other material could blow into your eyes. Even small particles and dust can scratch your cornea and cause painful injury.

Don't rub your eyes if something gets in them. Don't use your hand to remove whatever is bothering them. Instead, flush particles out with clean water or eyedrops.

Diseases such as conjunctivitis, or pinkeye, can bother your eyes and make them very red. If your eyes feel painful for more than a short time, see a doctor right away. Also see a doctor if you have watery or crusty eyes.

Connect To...
Science

Correcting Vision Problems with Lasers

Laser surgery can help correct vision problems such as nearsightedness. In this type of surgery, a doctor uses a special beam of light called a laser to reshape the cornea. This allows the cornea to focus light differently so that a person can see more clearly. Laser surgery is not for people under the age of 20, as their vision might still be changing.

Do research to find out more about laser surgery to correct vision problems. Prepare a one-page report of your findings.

Eye Examinations

Do you have trouble reading tiny print on a page? Does the writing on the chalkboard look blurry or fuzzy if you sit in the back of the room? If you answered yes, you might need corrective lenses: glasses or contacts. You can find out by having an optometrist check your vision.

An **optometrist** (ahp·TAH·muh·trist) is *a health care professional who is trained to examine the eyes for vision problems and to prescribe corrective lenses.* If you already wear glasses or contacts, visit an optometrist regularly. Schedule a routine visit at least once a year. Also see the optometrist any time you feel that your eyesight might be getting worse.

An optometrist might do initial tests for serious eye diseases. He or she may then send you to an ophthalmologist. An **ophthalmologist** (ahf·thahl·MAH·luh·jist) is *a physician who specializes in the structure, functions, and diseases of the eye.* An ophthalmologist fits people with corrective lenses. He or she also identifies and treats more serious eye problems, such as cataracts or glaucoma.

Cataract is *an eye condition in which the lens becomes cloudy as a person ages.* **Glaucoma** (glah·COH·mah) is *an eye condition in which fluid pressure builds up inside the eye.* If the condition is not treated promptly, it can damage the optic nerve and even cause blindness.

▲ Some activities put you at risk for splashing harmful chemicals into your eyes. **What activities might put you at risk for this?**

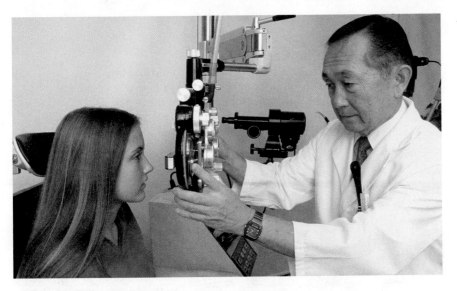

◄ An optometrist can tell you if you need vision correction. **What are some signs that you may need to see a vision specialist for corrective lenses?**

Correcting Your Vision

Vision specialists often treat people who are nearsighted, farsighted, or have astigmatism. A nearsighted person can clearly see objects only if they are up close. A farsighted person can clearly see objects only if they are at a distance. Many people become farsighted as they get older. They may need reading glasses to see objects up close. **Astigmatism** (uh·STIG·muh·tiz·uhm) is *an eye condition in which images appear wavy or blurry.* Corrective glasses or contact lenses can help people with all three of these vision problems. Contact lenses are clear plastic lenses placed directly in the eyes. They rest on top of the corneas.

 **Reading Check** **Explain** What are three types of vision problems?

Academic Vocabulary

vision (VIZH uhn) *(noun)* the act or power or seeing, sight. *Looking through another person's glasses can make your vision blurry.*

Healthy Ears

You probably know that your ears let you hear sound. Did you know that your ears also give you your sense of balance? **Figure 11.5** explains how ears control your senses of hearing and balance.

Ear Care

To care for your ears, wash and dry them regularly. Your ears produce earwax, which helps trap dirt and carry it out of the ear opening, or auditory canal. Use a wet washcloth to wipe off dirt and earwax on the outside of your ears. Do not insert anything inside your auditory canal. If you get water in your ears, use special ear drops to help dry out the water and prevent an infection. Protect your ears from the cold by wearing a hat or scarf that covers your ears, or earmuffs. See a doctor if any parts of your ears hurt or become infected.

PARTS OF THE EAR

Here are some of the major parts of the human ear. What are two major functions of the ear?

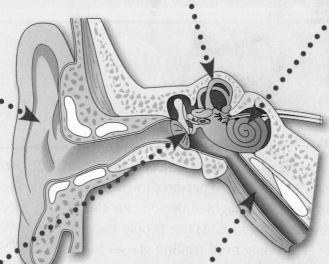

Semicircular Canals
The semicircular canals are filled with fluid and tiny hair cells. When your body moves, the fluid in the canals moves. This moves the hair cells. These hair cells send messages through nerves to the brain, helping your body keep its balance.

Outer Ear
The outer ear is shaped like a cup. It acts like a funnel to collect and send sound waves through the outer auditory canal.

Inner Ear
The bones of the middle ear cause vibrations in the fluid in the cochlea. The cochlea is a snail-shaped organ within the inner ear. Tiny hair cells in the cochlea vibrate in response to the fluid movement. They send electrical messages to the auditory nerve. These messages travel to the brain, which identifies the sound.

Middle Ear
In the middle ear, sound waves make the eardrum vibrate. In turn, vibrations in the eardrum make three tiny bones vibrate. They are called the hammer, the anvil, and the stirrup.

Eustachian Tube
The eustachian tube connects the inside of your throat to your inner ear. The tube keeps air pressure equal on both sides of the eardrum. If you feel pressure inside your ears, it's because there is uneven pressure around your eardrum. You can swallow to get rid of this feeling. This allows air to travel through the eustachian tube. The extra air equalizes the air pressure in your ear.

Hearing Damage

When it comes to caring for your ears, the best action you can take is to protect against hearing loss. Common hearing problems include tinnitus and deafness. **Tinnitus** is *a constant ringing in the ears.* You can get tinnitus from listening to loud music and from certain diseases.

Deafness is *a condition in which someone has difficulty hearing sounds or has complete hearing loss.* People can be born deaf or lose hearing later in life. Loud sounds most often cause hearing loss. *The unit for measuring the loudness of sound* is called a **decibel.** Normal conversation is about 60 decibels. Noises above 90 decibels can permanently damage the hair cells in the inner ear.

To protect your hearing, keep the volume down when listening to music. Wear earplugs when you are near loud sounds.

Describe How can you protect your ears from the effects of loud sounds?

Music at a rock concert might be 140 decibels or louder. Earplugs let you enjoy loud music without damaging your hearing. **What other activities might damage your hearing?**

Visit **glencoe.com** and complete the Interactive Study Guide for Lesson 2.

Lesson 2 Review

After You Read

Review this lesson for new terms, major headings, and Reading Checks.

What I Learned

1. *Vocabulary* What is the difference between an *optometrist* and an *ophthalmologist*?

2. *Identify* What roles do hair cells play in hearing and balance?

3. *Explain* What happens when sound waves reach your outer ear?

Thinking Critically

4. *Analyze* Janet plays on the soccer team. She is nearsighted and needs to correct her vision. What type of vision correction do you think might be best for Janet? Explain your reasoning.

5. *Evaluate* A woodshop produces noise that reaches 100 decibels. Should you wear earplugs to reduce the risks of injury to your ears while working in a woodshop? Explain your reasoning.

Applying Health Skills

6. *Practicing Healthful Behaviors* Imagine that you are packing for a backpacking trip in the mountains. The weather will be sunny but very cold. What kind of gear or clothing would you pack to protect your eyes and ears?

Lesson 3

Smart Consumer Choices

Guide to Reading

Building Vocabulary
Read each of the words below. If the word is familiar, write down what you think it means. If it's not, guess at its meaning using word clues. For example, the word *infomercial* is a combination of the words *information* and *commercial*.

- consumer (p. 340)
- advertisement (p. 341)
- fraud (p. 342)
- endorsement (p. 342)
- infomercials (p. 342)
- comparison shopping (p. 343)
- generic products (p. 343)
- warranty (p. 344)

Focusing on the Main Ideas
In this lesson, you will be able to

- **explain** what it means to be a consumer.
- **describe** what influences your buying decisions.
- **evaluate** media messages about consumer choices.
- **apply** accessing-information skills when making a consumer choice.

Reading Strategy
Predicting Look at the main headings, figures, and captions before you read this lesson. Predict the kinds of information you might learn from the lesson. After you have read the lesson, look back to see if your predictions were correct.

 **Quick Write**

List two products you buy regularly. Now list two services you pay for regularly. How often do you make each type of purchase? How do you decide which product or service you want?

Being a Responsible Consumer

A **consumer** is *a person who buys products and services.* You are a consumer when you buy products like a snack or a movie ticket. You are also a consumer when you pay for services such as a haircut.

▶ You make consumer choices all the time. What types of consumer choices can affect your health?

Most times, you can choose among products and services to buy. For example, when you shop for shampoo, many brands fill the store shelves. They have different prices and are designed to target different areas of your personal health. **Figure 11.6** discusses factors that might affect consumer choices. Be smart about which products and services you choose.

 **Reading Check** **Describe** What are two situations in which you are a consumer?

Advertising

You face choices every day about how to spend your money. One strong influence on what you choose to buy is advertising. An **advertisement** is *a message designed to influence consumers to buy a product or service.* It describes why the product might be good for you. Always remember, though, that advertisers spend billions of dollars to sell products and services. As a result, they may not explain a product's drawbacks or how it compares to competing products.

▼ FIGURE 11.6

INFLUENCES ON CONSUMER CHOICES

Teens often tell their friends about products and services they have bought and liked. **How can your friends' buying tips help you make a wise purchase?**

Personal Factors	You buy many products based on your personal interests and tastes. You may have had good or bad experiences with certain brands or products in the past.
Family Background	You might choose certain products or services because your family members always have, or because of cultural preferences.
Peers	Your friends may tell you to try certain products or brands. They may also tell you some are a waste of money. These opinions may affect your consumer choices.
Cost	Sometimes you make a consumer choice based on how much a product or service costs.
Salespeople	Salespeople often suggest certain products once you explain what you are looking for or what you need.
Advertising	Advertisers use many approaches to sell their products.

Evaluating Advertising

It helps to be able to judge an advertiser's claim. Before you decide to make a purchase based on an ad, ask yourself a few questions. Does the ad present facts or opinions? Does the product seem too good to be true? It might be fraudulent. **Fraud** is *a calculated effort to trick or fool others.*

Selling medicines that have not been proven to work is a form of *medical quackery,* or health fraud. These medicines may offer fast or painless cures, but they can be noneffective or harmful. They can even keep a person from getting the medical treatment they really need. Talk to a health care professional or other adult if you are unsure about a medicine or other health care product.

Types of Advertising

Companies use different techniques to sell products. Some ads focus on people's wish to be noticed. These ads claim that a brand name or designer product will make you popular.

Some ads suggest that a product will make you successful or beautiful, like the people shown in the ad. Many ads include celebrity endorsements. An **endorsement** is *a statement of approval.* Often, advertisers will pay actors or athletes large amounts of money to endorse a product.

Some ads show a group of teens having fun. These ads suggest that other teens use the product, so you should, too. It also sends the message that you'll have good times if you use the product.

Ads called **infomercials** are *long television commercials whose main purpose seems to be to present information rather than to sell a product.* An infomercial may look like a news story or even a TV show. However, an infomercial is really an ad. It always features some sort of product.

 **Reading Check**

Explain How might a celebrity endorsement affect what you buy?

Think Before You Buy

So how can you be a smart shopper? Take some time to make an informed decision. **Figure 11.7** lists some questions to consider before buying a product or service. The Health Skills Activity on page 346 will help you become an intelligent health consumer.

Comparison Shopping

One way to make smart purchases is to comparison shop. **Comparison shopping** is *collecting information, comparing products, evaluating their benefits, and choosing products with the best value.* Different brands may differ in features, quality, or price. Some products may even have generic varieties.

Generic products are *products sold in plain packages at lower prices than brand-name products.* Many generic products have the same ingredients and produce the same results as similar brand-name products. Before buying, read the label and compare the ingredients to those found in a similar product. Make sure the generic variety has the same amount of active ingredient found in the brand-name product. This can help you determine whether the product will be as effective as the brand-name product.

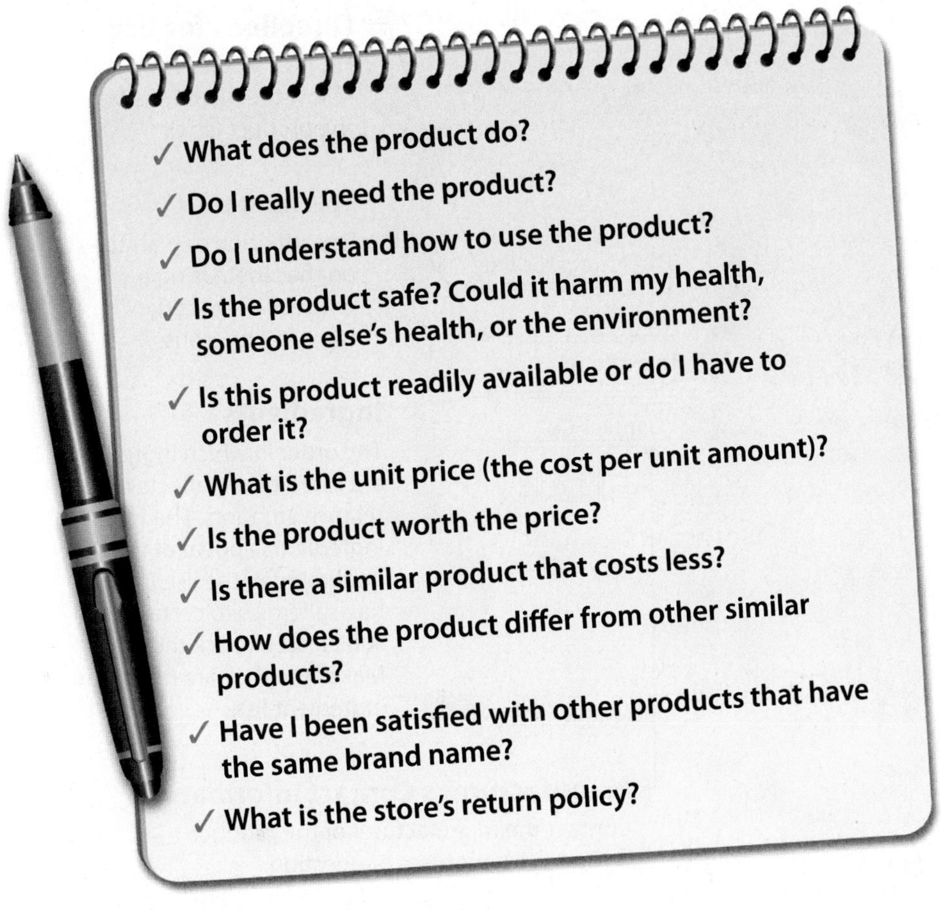

▼ FIGURE 11.7

SHOULD I MAKE THIS PURCHASE?

Before you make a purchase, ask yourself several questions to help you make a healthful choice. **Where can you find answers to consumer questions?**

✓ What does the product do?

✓ Do I really need the product?

✓ Do I understand how to use the product?

✓ Is the product safe? Could it harm my health, someone else's health, or the environment?

✓ Is this product readily available or do I have to order it?

✓ What is the unit price (the cost per unit amount)?

✓ Is the product worth the price?

✓ Is there a similar product that costs less?

✓ How does the product differ from other similar products?

✓ Have I been satisfied with other products that have the same brand name?

✓ What is the store's return policy?

Some products come with a warranty. A **warranty** is *a company's or a store's written agreement to repair a product or refund your money if the product does not function properly.* Warranties may include certain services and not others. If you have to pay for a warranty, read the fine print to help you decide if it's worth paying for.

Reading Product Labels

One way to learn about a product is to read the product label. By law, labels for foods, medicines, and many health products must include certain kinds of information. Product labels can also help you compare similar products. Don't be fooled by fancy packaging with catchy phrases. It's designed to make you want to buy the product. Take a look at **Figure 11.8.** It tells you the kinds of information you can find on a product label.

▼ FIGURE 11.8

WHAT A LABEL TELLS YOU

Be sure to read a product's label before you purchase or use the product. **What kinds of information are found on a product's label?**

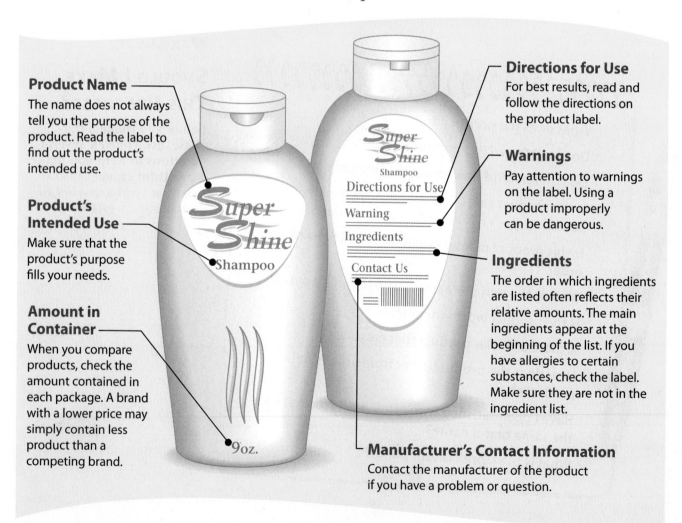

Product Name
The name does not always tell you the purpose of the product. Read the label to find out the product's intended use.

Product's Intended Use
Make sure that the product's purpose fills your needs.

Amount in Container
When you compare products, check the amount contained in each package. A brand with a lower price may simply contain less product than a competing brand.

Directions for Use
For best results, read and follow the directions on the product label.

Warnings
Pay attention to warnings on the label. Using a product improperly can be dangerous.

Ingredients
The order in which ingredients are listed often reflects their relative amounts. The main ingredients appear at the beginning of the list. If you have allergies to certain substances, check the label. Make sure they are not in the ingredient list.

Manufacturer's Contact Information
Contact the manufacturer of the product if you have a problem or question.

Protecting Your Consumer Rights

Even when you are a smart shopper, you may still have problems with your purchase. A product can turn out to be faulty, broken, or noneffective. A service may not be what you expected.

Your first action is to return to the business where you made the purchase. They may be able to exchange the product, refund your money, or help you understand the warranty. If they cannot help you, you can contact the manufacturer or service provider. They may be able to help you replace or repair what you bought, or refund the cost of the service.

It helps to be organized when resolving a problem related to a product or service. Have a copy of your original purchase receipt. Write down the product serial number and/or the name of the salesperson who helped you. Also write a complete description of the problem. Your consumer rights are shown in **Figure 11.9.** This figure also lists community resources that you can access to get additional help for problems with products and services.

 Reading Check Sequence What steps can you take if you buy a faulty product?

Go Online

Visit **glencoe.com** and complete the Interactive Study Guide for Lesson 3.

 **FIGURE 11.9**

CONSUMER RIGHTS

You have many rights as a consumer. **How can you be active in protecting your consumer rights?**

The following is a list of your rights as a consumer.	
You have the right to safety.	Products should not harm your health.
You have the right to be informed.	Product labels and advertising should not be fraudulent.
You have the right to choose.	There should be a variety of products at competitive prices.
You have the right to be heard.	Government laws should address consumer issues and problems.

You may be unhappy with how a company responds to a problem. If so, you can get help from many organizations. The following organizations work to protect consumer rights.	
Consumer advocates	The Consumers Union and other consumer groups help consumers settle problems.
The Better Business Bureau	This business organization and others handle consumer complaints against local companies and small businesses.
Government agencies	Agencies such as the Food and Drug Administration and the Consumer Product Safety Commission set standards and uphold laws that protect consumer rights.
Small-claims court	Judges in these state courts rule on legal arguments between consumers and businesses.

Health Skills Activity

Accessing Information

Choosing the Right Product

When you plan to buy a health-related product or service, learn as much as you can about it. A poor decision can cost you money or even harm your health. Here are some ways to research all your options before buying.

- Compare labels.
- Do research at the library or on the Internet.
- Talk to others. Get advice from friends and family, as well as from experts.

With a Group

Choose a health care product or service. Make a list of at least ten questions about the product or service that you would like answered. Find at least four different brands of the product or four different service providers. Do research to answer the questions on your list. Which product or service would you choose?

Lesson 3 Review

 After You Read

Review this lesson for new terms, major headings, and Reading Checks.

What I Learned

1. **Vocabulary** Define *fraud*.

2. **List** Name three of your rights as a consumer.

3. **Contrast** How does an endorsement differ from an infomercial?

Thinking Critically

4. **Analyze** Lotion A costs 20 cents per ounce. Lotion B costs $3.20 for 15 ounces. Compare the costs of these health products in order to assess which is the better value.

5. **Apply** The label for Product A lists the following ingredients: 98 percent isopropyl alcohol and boric acid. Product B contains isopropyl alcohol and 4 percent boric acid. The active ingredient is isopropyl alcohol. Which product has a greater percentage of the active ingredient?

Applying Health Skills

6. **Decision Making** Imagine that you buy an electric toothbrush from a local store. When you first try to brush your teeth, it doesn't work properly. Using the decision-making steps on page 40, show how you would handle the situation.

Go Online For more Lesson Review Activities, go to glencoe.com.

Using Medicines Safely

Guide to Reading

● **Building Vocabulary**
As you read this lesson, write down each new highlighted term and its definition.

- medicine (p. 347)
- prescription medicine (p. 348)
- pharmacist (p. 348)
- over-the-counter (OTC) medicine (p. 348)
- side effect (p. 349)

● **Focusing on the Main Ideas**
In this lesson, you will be able to

- **identify** different types of medicines.
- **describe** the proper use of medicines.
- **explain** how to avoid misusing medicines.
- **practice** good decision-making skills when using medicines.

● **Reading Strategy**
Identifying Cause-and-Effect Look at the headings in this lesson. List three ways that medicines can help you. Then list three ways that medicines might harm you if used improperly.

**uick Write**

Write about a time when you took medicine prescribed by a doctor because you were ill.

Drugs and Medicines

If you feel a cold or cough coming on, you might head to the drugstore to buy medicine. Remember that a drug is a substance other than food that changes the structure or function of the body or mind. A **medicine** is *a drug that prevents or cures an illness or eases its symptoms.* Medicines can help your body in many ways. **Figure 11.10** on page 348 gives some examples.

◄ You make important consumer choices when you buy medicine. **How can choosing the wrong kind of medicine affect your health?**

Types of Medicines

There are two main types of medicines: prescription medicines and over-the-counter medicines. A **prescription medicine** is *a medicine that can be obtained legally only with a doctor's written permission.* When you go to the doctor, he or she may order, or prescribe, medicine. Your doctor will write out instructions that explain how much medicine you should take and how often you should take it. You can fill this prescription at a pharmacy. A **pharmacist** is *a person trained to prepare and distribute medicines.* **Figure 11.11** shows a prescription medicine label.

An **over-the-counter (OTC) medicine** is *a medicine that you can buy without a doctor's permission.* Over-the-counter medicines are products found in grocery and drugstores. They commonly include pain relievers and cold medications. Always be careful when you use OTC medicines. Follow the directions on the label. If you have questions, contact your doctor or pharmacist. Both OTC and prescription medicines can cause serious problems if you don't use them properly.

Reading Check **Identify** What is an OTC medicine?

▼ FIGURE 11.10

WHAT MEDICINES DO

Medicines keep people healthy in many ways. How can medicines contribute to good health?

Prevent disease. Medicines called vaccines protect against diseases that can spread from person to person. When you have been vaccinated, your body can make substances that will fight off the germs that cause a disease.

Relieve pain. Aspirin, ibuprofen, and acetaminophen are three types of medicines that help reduce pain and fever. Aspirin can also reduce swelling.

Kill germs. Medicines called antibiotics kill disease-causing bacteria. Antibiotics should be used with caution because improper use can lead to the development of antibiotic-resistant bacteria. If that happens, when you really need an antibiotic, it might not be able to stop an infection.

Treat conditions and diseases. Some conditions and diseases can be treated with medicines. For example, people with diabetes take insulin to control the disease. People with allergies can take antihistamines to treat allergy symptoms.

PRESCRIPTION MEDICINE LABEL

Your doctor or pharmacist can help you understand a prescription medicine label. What types of information can you find on a prescription medicine label?

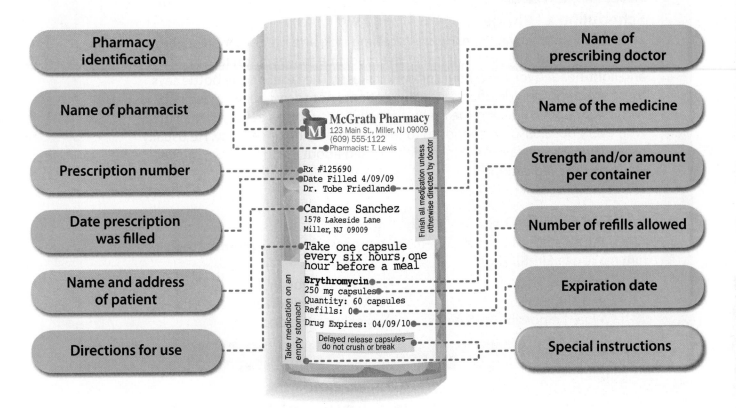

Pharmacy identification

Name of pharmacist

Prescription number

Date prescription was filled

Name and address of patient

Directions for use

Name of prescribing doctor

Name of the medicine

Strength and/or amount per container

Number of refills allowed

Expiration date

Special instructions

McGrath Pharmacy
123 Main St., Miller, NJ 09009
(609) 555-1122
Pharmacist: T. Lewis

Rx #125690
Date Filled 4/09/09
Dr. Tobe Friedland

Candace Sanchez
1578 Lakeside Lane
Miller, NJ 09009

Take one capsule every six hours, one hour before a meal

Erythromycin
250 mg capsules
Quantity: 60 capsules
Refills: 0
Drug Expires: 04/09/10

Delayed release capsules—do not crush or break

Finish all medication unless otherwise directed by doctor

Take medication on an empty stomach

Guidelines for Safe Use of Medicines

Medicines can fight disease, but if you don't use them properly, they can hurt you. One way this happens is through side effects. A **side effect** is *a reaction to a medicine other than the one intended.* Some side effects are simply unpleasant. For example, a medicine might make you feel thirsty or sick to your stomach. A more serious side effect is an allergic reaction, which may require immediate medical attention from professional health services. Other side effects are dangerous because they might lead to injury. For example, medicines might make you sleepy or dizzy.

You can avoid some side effects if you follow the instructions from your doctor and pharmacist and always inform your doctor of any known allergies to medicines. Read the label on any kind of medicine you use. It explains when and how to take the medicine. Some medicines cannot be taken together. Also, some activities are dangerous when you take certain medicines. Ask your doctor or pharmacist if you don't understand the label.

 **Reading Check** **Identify** Name one example of a side effect.

Health Skills Activity

Scheduling a Dosage

Jason is on summer vacation. He starts feeling sick, and his doctor prescribes medicine for him. The problem is that the medicine makes Jason feel sleepy and light-headed for a few hours after he takes it. The label on the bottle says these are common side effects. It warns patients not to use heavy machinery within four hours of taking the medication. It also suggests eating a small meal with every dose. Jason is supposed to take the medicine once a day. He usually mows lawns every day after lunch. He's worried about using the lawn mower while on the medication.

What Would You Do?

Apply the six steps of the decision-making process to Jason's problem to help him make a healthful choice.

1. State the situation.
2. List the options.
3. Weigh the possible outcomes.
4. Consider your values.
5. Make a decision and act on it.
6. Evaluate the decision.

Misuse and Abuse of Medicines

Medicines are drugs. If misused, they can be as harmful as illegal drugs. They can cause addiction, injury, and even death. If you misuse medicines when you're young, you can have health problems later in life. For example, your liver or kidneys might fail. Certain medicines can also be very dangerous to unborn babies, newborns, or young children. A woman who is pregnant or plans to become pregnant should talk to a doctor before she takes any medicine. **Figure 11.12** lists some ways to avoid problems when using medicines.

 **Reading Check** **Compare** How are medicines and illegal drugs similar?

◀ Some medications have to be taken at certain times of the day. **How can you remember when to take a medication?**

TIPS FOR USING MEDICINES CORRECTLY

You can use medicines properly by following these guidelines. **What are some resources you can use if you do not understand how to take a medicine?**

- Follow label instructions or directions from your doctor or pharmacist.

- Take the correct dosage or amount set by your doctor or pharmacist.

- Do not take the medicine for any length of time longer or shorter than your doctor tells you to. Even after you feel better, some medicines continue to work to prevent a second infection. If you don't feel well after you finish your medication, see your doctor.

- Do not take any medicine after the expiration date.

- Do not give your prescription medicines to other people or take other people's medications.

- Keep all medicines out of the reach of children.

- If you take too much medicine or have an allergic reaction to a medicine, see a doctor right away.

Visit **glencoe.com** and complete the Interactive Study Guide for Lesson 4.

Lesson 4 Review

 After You Read

Review this lesson for new terms, major headings, and Reading Checks.

What I Learned

1. *Contrast* How do prescription medicines differ from over-the-counter medicines?

2. *Vocabulary* Define *side effect*.

3. *Give Examples* Name three ways you can avoid side effects.

Thinking Critically

4. *Analyze* A certain medication makes you feel dizzy and affects your balance. What activities should you avoid while you are taking that medicine?

5. *Apply* Latrice's doctor gave her a six-day prescription of an antibiotic for her sore throat. After only three days, all of her symptoms are gone. Should Latrice continue taking the antibiotic? Explain why or why not.

Applying Health Skills

6. *Refusal Skills* Min's friend has offered her some of her prescription medication just to try it out. What are some ways that Min could refuse the offer?

Choosing Health Care

● **Building Vocabulary**

Think about the terms *HMO, PPO,* and *POS*. Write the definitions of each term. Then rewrite the definitions to include the words that each of their abbreviations stands for.

- primary care provider (p. 353)
- specialist (p. 353)
- health insurance (p. 354)
- managed care plans (p. 354)
- health maintenance organization (HMO) (p. 354)
- preferred provider organization (PPO) (p. 355)
- point-of-service (POS) plan (p. 355)

● **Focusing on the Main Ideas**

In this lesson, you will be able to

- **describe** the goals of health care.
- **identify** the types of health care providers and facilities.
- **explain** the types of insurance that help pay for health care.

● **Reading Strategy**

Comparing and Contrasting As you read this lesson, make a chart to compare and contrast the three different types of managed care plans.

 **Quick Write**

Imagine that you are choosing a health care specialist for an injury or disease. Make a list of questions you might ask him or her about your health.

The Goals of Health Care

What would you do if you got the flu or broke a bone while playing sports? You would visit a doctor. The doctor can help you feel better. He or she can also treat you to prevent further infection or injury.

The goals of health care are to prevent disease and injury as well as cure them. Visit a doctor once a year as part of your health care routine. During these visits, the doctor will examine you to see if you have any conditions that might lead to disease or injury. He or she might also talk to you about any problems that you may

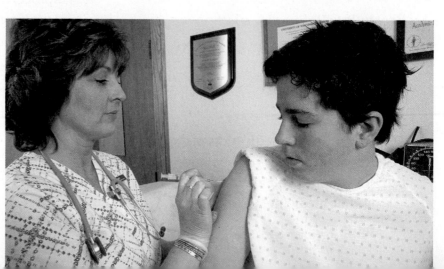

▶ Patients often receive vaccines and other forms of preventive care from primary care providers. **How does a primary care provider differ from a specialist?**

have. You might talk about how well you sleep, or how nutritious your eating plan is. The doctor might ask you how much physical activity you get on a daily basis. During a checkup, you might also receive care to prevent disease. For example, you might get your vaccinations updated.

Health Care Providers

Doctors are not the only **professionals** who can help you care for your health. Pharmacists, nurses, health educators, counselors, mental health specialists, dentists, and nutritionists also provide health care services. Health care providers are any professionals who help prevent and treat injury and illness.

A **primary care provider** is *a health care professional who provides checkups and general care*. Examples of primary care providers include your family physician or a nurse practitioner. A primary care provider might send you to a specialist. A **specialist** is *a health care professional trained to treat a special category of patients or specific health problems*. **Figure 11.13** lists several specialists and their areas of specialty.

 **Reading Check** **Name** Give examples of three specialists and a problem that each one might treat.

Academic Vocabulary

professional (pruh FESH uhn uhl) *(noun)* a person who trains for and practices a particular career. *John's dad is a business professional who helps companies create Web sites.*

▼ FIGURE 11.13

TYPES OF MEDICAL SPECIALISTS

There are many different kinds of medical specialists. What type of specialist would you see if you had blurred vision?

Below is a list of medical specialists and descriptions of their specialties.	
Allergists	treat people with allergies and asthma
Cardiologists	specialize in heart and circulatory system problems
Dermatologists	specialize in skin disorders
Gynecologists	specialize in problems of the female reproductive system
Ophthalmologists	specialize in disorders of the eye
Orthopedists	specialize in bone, joint, and muscle problems
Pediatricians	treat infants, children, and young teens
Plastic surgeons	perform plastic surgery to repair injuries or improve appearance
Psychiatrists	specialize in mental and emotional problems
Urologists	specialize in kidney, bladder, and urinary problems
Orthodontists	specialize in straightening the teeth

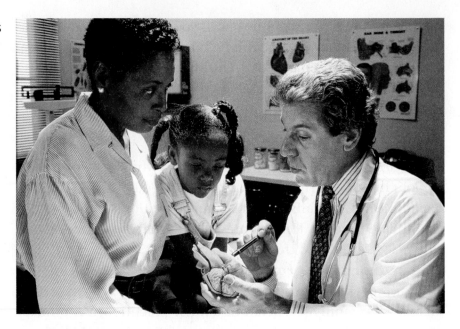

▶ Health care professionals work to help people stay healthy. **What are the goals of health care?**

Health Care in Your Community

Where you go for health care depends on your individual needs. In your community, you'll find doctors, dentists, and other health care professionals. You will also find a range of other health services provided by the government or other community agencies. These include the public health department, fire department, police, family resource centers, hospitals, and pharmacies. Other resources include nonprofit organizations, such as the American Heart Association and the American Cancer Society.

Health Insurance

Health care can be very expensive, especially in the case of serious disease or injury. Health insurance can help pay for health care costs. **Health insurance** is *a plan in which a person pays a set fee to an insurance company in return for the company's agreement to pay some or all medical expenses when needed.* There are several different types of health insurance plans. Each one covers health-related expenses differently. It is important to learn about the types of health insurance plans available before choosing the one that is right for you.

Private Health Care Plans

Managed care plans are *health insurance plans that emphasize preventative medicine and work to control the cost and maintain the quality of health care.* These include the following. A **health maintenance organization (HMO)** is *a health insurance plan that contracts with selected physicians and specialists to provide medical services.* HMO members pay a fixed monthly rate.

A **preferred provider organization (PPO)** is *a health insurance plan that allows its members to select a physician who participates in the plan for a reduced cost or to visit the physician of their choice.* PPO members who use their own doctors must pay full price for services until a certain amount of money has been paid. A **point-of-service (POS) plan** is *a health insurance plan that combines the features of HMOs and PPOs.* Members can see participating physicians at a reduced cost or see nonparticipating physicians for a higher cost.

Government Public Health Care Programs

The government has passed health care laws at the federal, state, and local levels that protect people who use and deliver health care services. Public health departments regulate how clean restaurants and other businesses must be to operate safely. Some government programs provide health information to the community. Others offer free or low-cost health care.

Visit **glencoe.com** and complete the Interactive Study Guide for Lesson 5.

Lesson 5 Review

 After You Read

Review this lesson for new terms, major headings, and Reading Checks.

What I Learned

1. *Vocabulary* Define *primary care provider.*

2. *Identify* What kind of managed care plan offers a fixed monthly payment but limits which health care providers it covers?

3. *Give Examples* What kinds of services do government health care programs provide?

Thinking Critically

4. *Apply* How might seeing a health care provider for regular checkups keep a person's medical costs down?

5. *Analyze* Compare and contrast the similarities and differences of an HMO, PPO, and POS plan.

6. *Synthesize* How can understanding the coverage limits of different health care plans help you choose the best plan for yourself?

7. *Analyze* Why are community health resources and organizations important to healthful living?

Applying Health Skills

8. *Accessing Information* Charles and his family have moved to a new town. His parents have asked him to find out about health services in their community. What resources can Charles use to find out what health services are offered in his community?

Go Online For more Lesson Review Activities, go to **glencoe.com**.

Lesson 5: Choosing Health Care **355**

Building Health Skills

Accessing Information
Practicing Healthful Behaviors
Stress Management
Analyzing Influences
Communication Skills
Refusal Skills
Conflict Resolution
Decision Making
Goal Setting
Advocacy

What Steps Can You Take to Make Healthy Decisions?

The decision-making process can help you make healthy and responsible choices. The six steps of the decision-making process are as follows:

- State the situation.
- List the options.
- Weigh the possible outcomes.
- Consider your values.
- Make a decision and act on it.
- Evaluate the decision.

Glasses or Contact Lenses?

Follow the Model, Practice, and Apply steps to help you master this important health skill.

① Model

Read how Diana uses the decision-making process to help her decide whether or not to try contact lenses.

Diana wears glasses. She recently joined the volleyball team and wonders if she should get contact lenses instead. Here are the steps that Diana used to make the decision.

Step 1 State the situation: "Wearing glasses bothers me while I'm playing volleyball."

Step 2 List the options: "I could get contact lenses or sports glasses."

Step 3 Weigh the possible outcomes: "If I get contact lenses, I can concentrate on playing volleyball. If I get sports glasses, I won't have to get used to wearing contact lenses."

Step 4 Consider your values: "Contact lenses can be expensive."

Step 5 Make a decision and act on it: After talking to the optometrist, Diana decided to try contact lenses.

Step 6 Evaluate the decision: "I am looking forward to my first volleyball game of the season and not having to worry about my glasses."

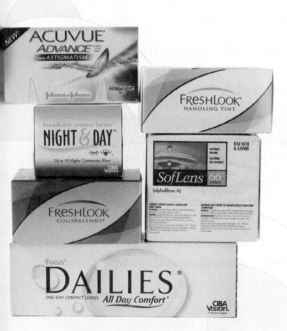

❷ Practice

Read the passage and then practice the decision-making process by answering the questions that follow.

Amanda has noticed that some girls in her school have a tan all year long. She knows that they go to a tanning salon in her neighborhood. Amanda thinks she would look good with a tan but has heard that tanning beds can be unhealthy.

1. What decision does Amanda have to make?
2. What are her options?
3. What outcomes could she expect from each of the choices she's considering?
4. Which values might Amanda need to consider?
5. What advice would you give Amanda?
6. Write a few sentences evaluating the decision you advised Amanda to make.

❸ Apply

Apply what you have learned about decision making by completing the activity below.

Pick a hygiene- or health-related item you might want to buy. It might be a tooth whitener, self-tanning lotion, or sunglasses. Then select two different brands or types of that item. Using the decision-making steps, decide which of the two brands or types you would want to buy. Copy the six decision-making steps on a sheet of paper. Next to each step, explain what you did as you completed that step. At the bottom of your paper, describe how the decision will improve your health.

Self-Check

- Did I pick a hygiene- or health-related item that I might want to buy?
- Did I use the six decision-making steps to make a choice?
- Did I describe how the decision will improve my health?

ACNE FACTS

Got questions about your skin? We've got answers!

Q: What is acne?

A: Acne is the term for blemishes—such as pimples and blackheads—that occur on the face, neck, chest, back, and upper arms. Dermatologist James Fulton Jr. divides acne into four grades: Grade I is the mildest form, with an equal mix of blackheads and whiteheads. With Grade II, there is an increase in whiteheads. Grade III involves inflamed pimples along with whiteheads and blackheads. Grade IV is the most severe, with large cysts (often red or purple in color), pimples, and, yes, more whiteheads and blackheads.

Q: What causes acne?

A: Acne is mainly caused by the hormonal changes of puberty. Hormones stimulate certain glands to produce more oil. This oil combines with dead skin cells in the pores and becomes acne. While stress alone isn't enough to cause acne, it may aggravate already problematic skin.

Q: Is acne hereditary?

A: Yes and no. Thanks to genetics, some people are more likely to get acne, but it's not the only factor.

Q: Why do my nose and chin have so many little black bumps? Are they blackheads or just pores?

A: Most likely they're blackheads—a combination of dead skin cells and oil. A pore is where the hair follicle comes out of the skin. A blackhead is a plug in that pore.

Q: Does eating empty-calorie foods give you more acne?

A: Diet is not the major factor in acne that it was once thought to be. Foods such as pizza, french fries, and chocolate are not to blame for acne. The oils you eat have nothing to do with the oil that the glands in your skin produce.

LABEL CHECK

When treating acne with over-the-counter products, look for these powerful ingredients:

1. Benzoyl peroxide
2. Salicylic acid
3. Sulfur
4. Retinol
5. Glycolic acid

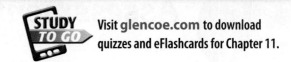

STUDY TO GO Visit glencoe.com to download quizzes and eFlashcards for Chapter 11.

FOLDABLES Study Organizer

Foldables® and Other Study Aids Take out the Foldable® that you created for Lesson 1 and any graphic organizers that you created for Lessons 1–5. Find a partner and quiz each other using these study aids.

Lesson 1 Healthy Teeth, Skin, Hair, and Nails

Main Idea Taking care of your personal health includes caring for your teeth, skin, hair, nails, eyes, and ears.

- To care for your teeth and gums, brush and floss daily and see a dentist regularly.
- Wash your skin daily and use a sunscreen to protect it.
- Washing and brushing your hair regularly will help keep it healthy.
- Both your hair and nails contain a protein called keratin. Keratin gives these structures their strength and flexibility.

Lesson 2 Healthy Eyes and Ears

Main Idea Caring for your eyes and ears will help keep them healthy.

- Avoid eyestrain by wearing sunglasses outdoors, sitting at least six feet from the television, and using adequate lighting while reading and doing homework.
- Your ears let you hear sound and give you a sense of balance.
- Protect your hearing by keeping the volume down when listening to music and wearing earplugs when near loud sounds.

Lesson 3 Smart Consumer Choices

Main Idea Knowing how to evaluate products and services will help you become a smart consumer.

- A consumer is a person who buys products and services.
- It's important to evaluate advertising claims before buying a product or service.
- Comparison shopping can help you make an informed decision.

Lesson 4 Using Medicines Safely

Main Idea Medicines can contribute to good health when used properly.

- A prescription medicine can only be used with a doctor's written permission.
- An over-the-counter (OTC) medicine can be used without a doctor's permission.
- Using medicines improperly can cause harmful side effects.

Lesson 5 Choosing Health Care

Main Idea The goals of health care are to prevent and treat disease and injury.

- A primary care provider provides checkups and general care. A specialist treats specific diseases.
- Most communities offer a wide range of health care resources and services.
- Health insurance helps people pay for health care costs.

Reviewing Vocabulary and Main Ideas

On a sheet of paper, write the numbers 1–9. After each number, write the term from the list that best completes each statement.

- consumer
- melanin
- advertisement
- acne
- astigmatism
- fraud
- fluoride
- tinnitus
- cataract

Lesson 1 Healthy Teeth, Skin, Hair, and Nails

1. _____ is a chemical that helps prevent tooth decay.
2. Skin gets its color from _____.
3. _____ is a skin condition caused by active oil glands that clog hair follicles.

Lesson 2 Healthy Eyes and Ears

4. An eye condition in which the lens becomes cloudy as a person ages is called _____.
5. _____ is an eye condition in which images of objects appear wavy or blurry.
6. A condition in which there is a constant ringing in the ears is called _____.

Lesson 3 Smart Consumer Choices

7. An infomercial is a type of _____ shown on television.
8. When an ad contains deliberate trickery, the advertisers are guilty of _____.
9. The rights to safety, to be informed, to choose, and to be heard are all _____ rights.

*On a sheet of paper, write the numbers 10–15. Write **True** or **False** for each statement below. If the statement is false, change the underlined word or phrase to make it true.*

Lesson 4 Using Medicines Safely

10. You must get a doctor's permission in order to take an <u>OTC medicine</u>.
11. A <u>pharmacist</u> is a person trained to prepare and dispense prescription medicines.
12. Drowsiness and nausea are examples of <u>side effects</u> that you could have from taking medicine.

Lesson 5 Choosing Health Care

13. A <u>specialist</u> is a health care professional who provides checkups and general care.
14. A <u>cardiologist</u> is a kind of health care specialist who treats eye disorders.
15. HMOs, PPOs, and POS plans are all types of <u>managed care</u> plans.

Go Online Visit glencoe.com and take the Online Quiz for Chapter 11.

Thinking Critically

Using complete sentences, answer the following questions on a sheet of paper.

16. **Interpret** How do government requirements for drug labels protect your consumer rights?

17. **Apply** A prescription medicine causes Damien to feel nauseated. What should Damien do?

Write About It

18. **Descriptive Writing** A new brand of underarm deodorant causes your skin to break out in a rash. Write a detailed plan you could follow to help you find the cause of the rash.

19. **Expository Writing** Write a letter to your friend who has just moved to a new town. Describe how your friend might get information to help him or her choose a new primary care physician.

Applying Technology

Personal Health

Using Microsoft Word®, create a poster to showcase the variety of choices available to help foster good personal hygiene.

- Open a new Microsoft Word® project with a landscape view and insert a table with 2 columns and 6 rows.

- Add the captions: *Teeth*, *Skin*, *Hair*, *Eyes*, and *Ears*, by clicking Insert- Picture-WordArt. Adjust the caption font size to 16 and drag them to the top of your poster.

- Using either Clip Art or digital media files, insert an image for each section of your poster. Highlight the image and drag the corner toward the center to size.

- Place your cursor in the box and add details under each caption on how to care for that part of your personal health.

- To remove outside lines of the table, click on Toolbar view–Formatting–Tables and charts. Then select the border button that reflects the desired highlighting: grid outside, grid all boxes, or no grid at all.

Standardized Test Practice

Writing

Read the prompts below. On a separate sheet of paper, write an essay that addresses each prompt. Use information from the chapter to support your writing.

1. A person is experiencing deafness due to problems with his inner ear. Explain how a person with healthy ears is able to hear. Be sure to describe the role that hair cells play in hearing. Then, predict how damage to hair cells could cause deafness.

2. Imagine that you have a company that makes sunscreen. How would you convince buyers to choose your product? Write a script for a television or radio advertisement that sells your product. What health concerns could you address in your advertising?

TEST-TAKING TIP

Find out how much time you have to write your essay. Plan to spend part of that time at the beginning of the test organizing your thoughts and writing a rough outline. Plan to spend another part of that time at the end revising your essay and checking for errors in spelling and grammar.

Chapter Preview

Lesson 1   Changes During
           Adolescence 364

Lesson 2   The Endocrine System 370

Lesson 3   The Male Reproductive
           System 374

Lesson 4   The Female Reproductive
           System 378

Lesson 5   Heredity and Human
           Development 383

Lesson 6   The Life Cycle 388

Building Health Skills 394

Hands-on Health 396

Chapter Reading Review 397

Chapter Assessment 398

▲ *Working with the Photo*

Siblings often look similar to each other. **What physical traits do you share with other members of your family?**

Start-Up Activities

 Before You Read What do you know about how people grow and change? Take the short quiz below. Keep a record of your answers.

HEALTH QUIZ Choose the best answer for each of the following:

1. When children go through puberty, they experience emotional changes.
    (a) always   (b) sometimes   (c) never

2. It is important to care for the reproductive system even if you don't plan to have children.
    (a) always   (b) sometimes   (c) never

3. Members of the same family look alike.
    (a) always   (b) sometimes   (c) never

ANSWERS: 1. a; 2. a; 3. b.

FOLDABLES Study Organizer

 As You Read Make this Foldable® to help you organize what you learn in Lesson 1 about the changes of adolescence. Begin with a plain sheet of 8½" × 11" paper.

1 Fold the sheet of paper along the long axis, leaving a 2" tab along the side.

2 Turn the paper and fold it into thirds.

3 Unfold and cut the top layer along both fold lines. This makes three tabs.

4 Label the tabs as shown.

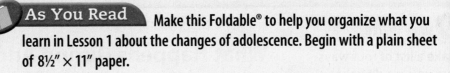
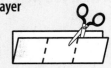

ADOLESCENCE

Physical Growth | Mental/ Emotional Growth | Social Growth

As you read the lesson, record what you learn about the changes of adolescence.

Go Online Visit **glencoe.com** and complete the Chapter 12 crossword puzzle.

Changes During Adolescence

Guide to Reading

● Building Vocabulary
Write definitions of the vocabulary terms below in your own words. As you read the lesson, revise or add to your definitions.

- adolescence (p. 364)
- puberty (p. 365)

● Focusing on the Main Ideas
In this lesson, you will learn to

- **identify** the physical, mental, emotional, and social changes that occur during adolescence.
- **describe** healthy ways of expressing your emotions.
- **develop** ways to manage strong emotions.

● Reading Strategy
Predicting Skim the headings, photos, and captions in this lesson. Write down three pieces of information you think will be covered in this lesson.

FOLDABLES Study Organizer Use the Foldable® on p. 363 as you read this lesson.

Quick Write

Make a list of four ways that you are different now than you were five years ago.

What Happens During Adolescence?

You grew rapidly as a child. You got taller, you outgrew your clothing and shoes, and before you knew it, you were almost a teen.

During your teen years, your body will continue to grow and change. So will your interests. This is a normal part of **adolescence,** *the stage of life between childhood and adulthood, usually beginning somewhere between the ages of 11 and 15.* During adolescence, you experience many physical, mental, emotional, and social changes. These changes prepare you to be an adult.

Reading Check **Define** What is *adolescence?*

▶ Many people become more interested in sports during the teen years. **Which activities that you enjoy now do you think you will enjoy throughout your life?**

Physical Growth

Gary has grown taller and speaks in a deeper voice than he used to. These physical changes are a sign that he is going through the development stage called puberty. **Puberty** is *the time when you develop physical characteristics of adults of your own gender.* During puberty, males' and females' bodies begin to change. These changes are a normal part of becoming a healthy adult. **Figure 12.1** describes how male and female bodies change during puberty.

Teens go through puberty at different rates. Your body may change faster or slower than your friends' and peers' bodies. Most females start puberty between the ages of 8 and 13. Most males start between the ages of 9 and 14.

With so many changes happening at different times for different people, teens can vary widely in shape and size. You don't need to be worried about these differences. Accept them; that's how puberty is. You may be developing physically at a different rate than your friends and peers, but just remember that all teens are going through similar mental, emotional, and social changes.

▼FIGURE 12.1

YOUR CHANGING BODY

Your body goes through many physical changes during puberty. **What is one change that happens to both males and females during puberty?**

MALES	FEMALES
Male hormone production increases.	Female hormone production increases.
Sudden, rapid growth occurs.	Sudden, rapid growth occurs.
All permanent teeth come into place.	All permanent teeth come into place.
Acne may appear.	Acne may appear.
Underarm hair appears.	Underarm hair appears.
Pubic hair appears.	Pubic hair appears.
Perspiration increases.	Perspiration increases.
External genitals grow.	Uterus and ovaries enlarge.
Shoulders broaden.	Breasts develop.
Muscles develop.	Hips become wider.
Sperm production starts.	Body fat increases.
Facial hair appears.	Ovulation occurs.
Larynx gets larger, and voice deepens.	Menstruation starts.

Connect To... Science

Depression

It's common for teens to feel sad from time to time. For some teens, however, these feelings may be a sign of depression. Signs of depression include long periods of sadness, sleeping or eating problems, and an inability to enjoy favorite activities. Depression can be treated.

Use reliable resources to research two types of treatments for depression. Make a list of the benefits of each.

Try not to compare yourself with other teens. If a person hasn't started growing or is not going through the same stage that you are, there is nothing wrong with him or her, or you. Every teen develops at a rate that is just right for him or her.

Mental Growth

It's not just your body that changes during adolescence. You also change mentally and emotionally. That's partly because as your brain grows, its ability increases to do complex reasoning and problem solving. You learn to be more responsible for your actions. You begin to make more decisions on your own and see the consequences of those decisions. You are able to work independently for various periods of time.

You start to think in a more complex way during adolescence. Soon, your opinions about social issues and politics may start to change. That's because you start to understand that many questions don't have simple answers. Also, you begin to see that other people have different points of view from your own. You start to make decisions based on your values and beliefs. Like the physical changes that teens experience, these mental and emotional changes happen at different rates, too.

Reading Check **Describe** What two tasks does the brain become more capable of performing during adolescence?

▼ Friends become very important during adolescence. **What qualities do you look for in a friend?**

Emotional Growth

Carlos is acting a little different these days. He gets mad at his mother very quickly and doesn't want to listen to her. Carlos' mother doesn't get too upset, though. She knows that this behavior is normal for people during adolescence.

Like Carlos, you will likely experience a lot of emotional changes during adolescence. You might start to feel differently about your peers, your parents, and other adults. You might become closer to your friends and feel less connected to your parents. In time, you may begin to experience a physical attraction toward another person. Being attracted to someone and feeling close to him or her emotionally is an important part of healthy adult relationships. All these new feelings, however, can be difficult to handle. Just know that as you mature, you will learn to manage your emotions in a positive way.

Expressing Emotions

During adolescence, you may feel many different emotions in a short period of time. For example, in one day, you may feel angry, sad, happy, scared, and excited. You don't need to worry because mood swings like this are a normal part of adolescence.

When you try to manage many strong feelings at once, it can feel overwhelming. You might feel like lashing out at others or keeping your feelings hidden. Neither of these approaches is the best way to handle strong emotions.

Instead, you need some healthy ways to express your feelings. There are many ways to do this. You can write in a journal, draw, or play music. Some people think about their problems while exercising or participating in a hobby. You can also get help by talking with your friends, a sibling, your parents, a counselor, or another adult you trust.

▶ Talking to someone you trust can help you cope with strong feelings. **What are two other healthful ways to express your emotions?**

Health Skills Activity

Stress Management

Managing Anger

You're very focused studying for an important math test. Then your younger sister interrupts you with questions about her homework. An interruption is the last thing you need right now. You feel angry, but you know that yelling at your sister isn't likely to make you feel better. When you're feeling a strong emotion such as anger or frustration, it can be hard to know how to react.

One thing you can always do when you feel really angry is to take a moment to cool off. In your mind, try making a list of what makes you angry. The math test and interruptions might be at the top of the list right now. Then think about what other factors might be stressing you out enough to make you angry. Make a plan to relieve some of those stresses. It often helps to deal with your problems one at a time.

On Your Own

Create a list of situations that make you angry. Then think about some ways to relieve stress in your life. Make a weekly plan that helps keep you better prepared to handle problems without getting angry.

Social Growth

Adolescence is a time to find out more about yourself and those around you. Many teens participate in different social activities such as volunteer groups, sports teams, or special-interest clubs. Do any of these interest you? Your interests have changed since you were a child. They may change again as you become an adult.

The social growth experienced as a teen is very important. It can help you find your place in society. The social connections that you make as a teen can help you develop friendships, find job opportunities, and get emotional support. These connections also shape your values and help you discover who you are.

During adolescence, you may begin spending more time with friends. Friends can influence many of the decisions you make as a teen. It is important to choose friends who will support and influence you in a positive way. This will help you make good choices during your teen years.

 **Reading Check**

List Name three types of social organizations available to teens.

▲ What's important to you? Being involved in social activities can help you answer this question. **What activities might help you develop socially?**

Visit glencoe.com and complete the Interactive Study Guide for Lesson 1.

Lesson 1 Review

After You Read

Review this lesson for new terms, major headings, and Reading Checks.

What I Learned

1. *Identify* Name three ways that females' and males' bodies change during puberty.

2. *Vocabulary* Define *puberty*.

3. *Give Examples* Give three examples of how to express strong emotions in a healthy way.

4. *Identify* Identify two ways teens grow emotionally during adolescence.

Thinking Critically

5. *Analyze* How can after-school activities help you discover who you will be as an adult?

6. *Analyze* Teens face a lot of challenges. Which do you think are hardest, and why?

Applying Health Skills

7. *Practicing Healthful Behaviors* Travis has been having trouble in math class. To relieve stress, he often goes running in his neighborhood. He has considered joining the track team, but he worries that he isn't fast enough. He also doesn't have a lot of extra time. Travis knows that the members of the track team often help each other with their homework. What advice would you give Travis? Explain your reasoning.

The Endocrine System

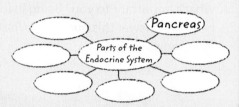

uick Write

Parts of the Endocrine System

Hormones are one of the things that make your body change during puberty. **Hormones** are *chemical substances produced in certain glands that help to regulate the way your body functions.* They are produced by the organs of the endocrine system. The **endocrine system** is *the system of glands throughout the body that regulate body functions.* **Figure 12.2** shows the parts of the endocrine system.

Glands and Hormones

Each gland of the endocrine system makes one or more specific hormones. Hormones act like chemical signals that tell your organs and tissues what to do. For example, the pancreas makes the hormones insulin and glucagon. When the pancreas releases insulin into the blood, it lowers the level of sugar in the blood. When the pancreas releases glucagon, it raises the blood sugar level. If blood sugar is too low, you feel weak and light-headed. If it's too high, you can feel nauseated.

Reading Check   **Identify** What are two hormones produced by the pancreas?

FIGURE 12.2

PARTS OF THE ENDOCRINE SYSTEM

The endocrine system controls many of the changes that happen during puberty. **What does the pituitary gland do?**

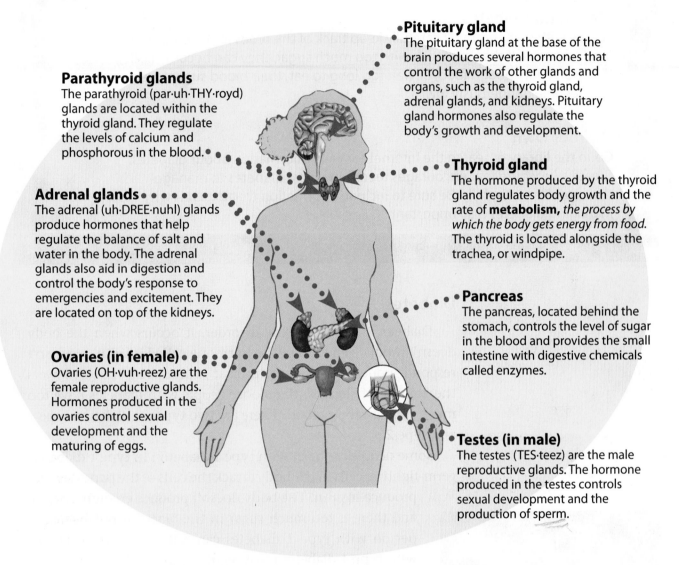

Pituitary gland
The pituitary gland at the base of the brain produces several hormones that control the work of other glands and organs, such as the thyroid gland, adrenal glands, and kidneys. Pituitary gland hormones also regulate the body's growth and development.

Parathyroid glands
The parathyroid (par·uh·THY·royd) glands are located within the thyroid gland. They regulate the levels of calcium and phosphorous in the blood.

Thyroid gland
The hormone produced by the thyroid gland regulates body growth and the rate of **metabolism,** *the process by which the body gets energy from food.* The thyroid is located alongside the trachea, or windpipe.

Adrenal glands
The adrenal (uh·DREE·nuhl) glands produce hormones that help regulate the balance of salt and water in the body. The adrenal glands also aid in digestion and control the body's response to emergencies and excitement. They are located on top of the kidneys.

Pancreas
The pancreas, located behind the stomach, controls the level of sugar in the blood and provides the small intestine with digestive chemicals called enzymes.

Ovaries (in female)
Ovaries (OH·vuh·reez) are the female reproductive glands. Hormones produced in the ovaries control sexual development and the maturing of eggs.

Testes (in male)
The testes (TES·teez) are the male reproductive glands. The hormone produced in the testes controls sexual development and the production of sperm.

One major role of the endocrine system is to control the body's metabolism. **Metabolism** is *the process by which the body gets energy from food.* It is regulated by hormones made by the thyroid gland.

Diseases of the Endocrine System

Remember, some organs are controlled by endocrine glands. These organs can't do their job unless they receive the hormones they need. If there are problems with one or more glands in the endocrine system, these organs don't function properly. Diseases of the endocrine system can develop when either too much or too little of a hormone is produced.

Health Skills Activity

Diabetes

Diabetes is an endocrine disorder. It occurs when the body doesn't produce enough of the hormone called insulin or doesn't respond properly to the insulin that is produced. Insulin lowers the amount of sugar in the blood. People with diabetes have too much sugar in their blood. There are two types of diabetes: type 1 and type 2.

Some people are born with type 1 diabetes. In type 1 diabetes, germ-fighting cells in the body attack the cells of the pancreas that produce insulin. The body doesn't produce enough insulin, and there is too much sugar in the blood. If not treated, a person with type 1 diabetes can fall into a coma. People with type 1 diabetes must regularly inject themselves with insulin to keep their blood sugar at the right level.

People with type 2 diabetes produce a normal amount of insulin, but their bodies can't use it well. This kind of diabetes often develops in adulthood, but people of all ages, including children, can develop it. It's more common in people who are overweight. People with this disorder may feel tired a lot and often sick to their stomachs. They may

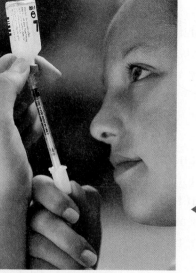

◄ This teen, like others with type 1 diabetes, has learned to monitor her blood sugar and give herself insulin injections. **Why do people with diabetes have to be careful of what they eat?**

also have infections and wounds that do not heal. People with type 2 diabetes have to carefully control their diets and engage in regular physical activity. They also sometimes need medication.

If diabetes is not managed well, there can be long-term harmful effects. People may suffer from poor circulation, nerve damage, heart disease, kidney failure, or blindness. Poor circulation and nerve damage can result in the need to amputate, or remove through surgery, a body part such as a toe, foot, or leg.

Thyroid Diseases

Metabolism can be affected by diseases of the thyroid gland. If the gland doesn't make enough hormones to regulate metabolism, a person can develop a condition called hypothyroidism. A person with hypothyroidism may feel tired and cold, have dry skin, and gain extra weight. In teens, hypothyroidism can also delay growth. Fortunately, hypothyroidism can be treated with a thyroid replacement hormone.

Hyperthyroidism is the opposite of hypothyroidism. In hyperthyroidism, the thyroid produces *too many* hormones. This leads to a very high metabolism. A high metabolism can lead to sweating, excessive eating, weight loss, tremors, and muscle weakness. Hyperthyroidism can be treated with medication.

 Reading Check Explain What is hyperthyroidism?

Visit **glencoe.com** and complete the Interactive Study Guide for Lesson 2.

Lesson 2 Review

 After You Read

Review this lesson for new terms, major headings, and Reading Checks.

What I Learned

1. *Vocabulary* What is *metabolism?*

2. *List* What are three functions of the hormones produced by the thyroid gland?

3. *Explain* How are type 1 and type 2 diabetes usually treated?

4. *Explain* How is hypothyroidism treated?

Thinking Critically

5. *Infer* Why might a disease that affects an endocrine gland have effects on other parts of the body?

6. *Apply* Some drugs are synthetic, or artificial, hormones. Why is it necessary to consult a doctor before taking this kind of medication to treat a disease?

Applying Health Skills

7. *Communication Skills* Imagine that your friend has diabetes. You notice that your friend is not managing the condition properly. What advice would you give him or her?

Lesson 3

The Male Reproductive System

Guide to Reading

● Building Vocabulary
Write each of the terms below. As you read this lesson, write the definition next to each term.

- reproduction (p. 374)
- reproductive system (p. 374)
- sperm (p. 375)
- testes (p. 375)
- semen (p. 375)

● Focusing on the Main Ideas
In this lesson, you will learn to

- **describe** the function of the male reproductive system.
- **identify** the organs and structures of the male reproductive system.
- **identify** common problems of the male reproductive system.
- **explain** how to care for the male reproductive system.
- **identify** ways of detecting testicular cancer.

● Reading Strategy
Sequencing Take a look at Figure 12.3. Using this figure, trace the path of sperm from where they are produced to the outside of the body. Make a list of the structures that sperm pass through.

Quick Write

Do you plan to have children when you become an adult? How do you picture your family life when you are older?

Reproduction

All forms of life on earth reproduce. **Reproduction** is *the process by which living organisms produce others of their own kind.* Each human results from the joining of two cells that come from the reproductive systems of a female and a male. The **reproductive system** consists of *the body organs and structures that make it possible to produce children.*

Reading Check **Define** What is the *reproductive system*?

▶ The male and female reproductive systems make it possible for people to have children. **What process allows living things to produce others of their own kind?**

Parts of the Male Reproductive System

The male reproductive system's main job is to produce sperm. **Sperm** are *male reproductive cells*. Each sperm can join with a female reproductive cell and make another human.

The **testes** are *the pair of glands that produce sperm*. The testes are located in the scrotum. The scrotum keeps the testes at the right temperature to produce sperm. Sperm leave the testes and travel to the urethra.

Semen (SEE·muhn) is *a mixture of sperm and fluids that protect sperm and carry them through the tubes of the male reproductive system*. The semen is released from the urethra through the penis. The body's release of semen is called ejaculation (i·ja·kyuh·LAY·shun). There are 3 to 4 million sperm cells in each ejaculation. The parts of the male reproductive system are shown in **Figure 12.3**.

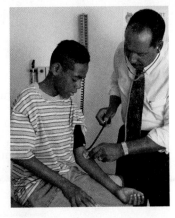

▲ Visit a doctor for a yearly checkup to prevent health problems. **What are some issues that a male might discuss with a health care provider?**

▼ **FIGURE 12.3**

PARTS OF THE MALE REPRODUCTIVE SYSTEM

Each part of the male reproductive system has a job to do. What part produces sperm?

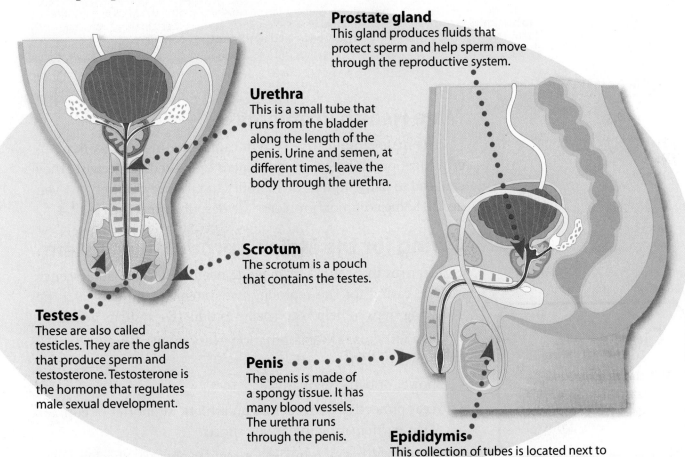

Prostate gland
This gland produces fluids that protect sperm and help sperm move through the reproductive system.

Urethra
This is a small tube that runs from the bladder along the length of the penis. Urine and semen, at different times, leave the body through the urethra.

Scrotum
The scrotum is a pouch that contains the testes.

Testes
These are also called testicles. They are the glands that produce sperm and testosterone. Testosterone is the hormone that regulates male sexual development.

Penis
The penis is made of a spongy tissue. It has many blood vessels. The urethra runs through the penis.

Epididymis
This collection of tubes is located next to the testes. Mature sperm are stored here.

▼ FIGURE 12.4

PROBLEMS OF THE MALE REPRODUCTIVE SYSTEM

An inguinal hernia can form when a male strains his abdominal muscles. **How can an inguinal hernia be repaired?**

Inguinal hernia
The intestines are held in place by a layer of muscles. Sometimes these muscles have a weak spot due to muscle strain or other injuries. A part of the intestine may push through the weak spot into the scrotum or into the area above the inner thigh. This is called an inguinal hernia. A hernia can be treated through surgery.

Testicular cancer
Cancer is the uncontrolled growth of abnormal cells. A lump or swelling of the testicles, and pain or tenderness in the testicles, abdomen, or groin, may be signs of testicular cancer. It is the most common cancer of males aged 14 to 34. If it is detected early enough, many of the serious complications can be prevented.

Testicular torsion
Within the scrotum, the testicles are held in place by a structure called the spermatic cord. Sometimes, the cord becomes twisted around a testicle. Blood flow is cut off to the testicle, causing pain, swelling, or tenderness. Immediate treatment is necessary.

Prostate cancer
The tissue of the prostate gland can become cancerous. This condition is more common in older men. This cancer can be treated through surgery, radiation treatment, or chemotherapy.

Sterility
Males who produce no sperm are sterile. Sterility can be caused by untreated STDs or exposure to pesticides, lead, or dangerous amounts of radiation, such as X rays. Certain drugs can also cause sterility. Some types of sterility can be treated by medications or surgery.

Male Health Problems

The male reproductive system can sometimes not work properly. Most problems can be prevented or treated. Otherwise, they can lead to pain, injury, the inability to produce children, or even death. Some common problems are described in **Figure 12.4.**

Caring for the Male Reproductive System

Changes in health and hygiene needs related to adolescence include caring for the reproductive system. Males can take the following steps to help keep their reproductive systems healthy.

- Do a testicular self-examination every month after a warm shower or bath.

- Shower or bathe regularly.

- Wear protective gear, such as an athletic supporter or cup, when participating in contact sports.

- Visit a health care provider for regular physical checkups.

Go Online

Visit glencoe.com and complete the Interactive Study Guide for Lesson 3.

Health Skills Activity

Practicing Healthful Behaviors

How to Do a Testicular Self-Examination

When a male goes for his yearly physical checkup, the doctor will usually examine him for testicular cancer. This can help detect the disease before it becomes very serious or difficult to treat. Testicular cancer can grow and spread very quickly if it is not detected. So it is important for males to do a testicular self-examination every month.

On Your Own

Go to the library or use the Internet to find instructions for how to do a testicular self-examination. Write out the instructions. Make a list of at least four signs of testicular cancer to watch out for. Then write two questions that a male might have for a health care provider about testicular self-examinations.

Lesson 3 Review

 After You Read

Review this lesson for new terms, major headings, and Reading Checks.

What I Learned

1. *Vocabulary* Define *reproduction*.

2. *List* What are four problems of the male reproductive system?

3. *Name* What are two types of gear that protect the reproductive system of a male athlete?

4. *Explain* How do regular visits to the doctor help prevent male reproductive problems?

Thinking Critically

5. *Evaluate* Why is it important to take care of the male reproductive system?

6. *Apply* Tim has noticed a swelling in one of his testes. He is uncomfortable discussing this problem with his parents, but it is not going away. What steps should Tim take to prevent a serious problem?

Applying Health Skills

7. *Accessing Information* Some teens and adults use anabolic steroids to change the shape of their body or improve athletic performance. Use the Internet to find valid information about anabolic steroids. Include the information that you find in an informative brochure that warns against the use of these illegal substances.

The Female Reproductive System

Guide to Reading

● **Building Vocabulary**
The uterus is also called the womb. The word *womb* can mean "a protective space." Relate this meaning to the definition in the text.

■ ovaries (p. 378)
■ uterus (p. 378)
■ ovulation (p. 379)
■ menstruation (p. 379)
■ fertilization (p. 380)
■ gynecologist (p. 382)

● **Focusing on the Main Ideas**
In this lesson, you will learn to

■ **describe** the functions of the female reproductive system.
■ **identify** the organs and structures of the female reproductive system.
■ **explain** how to care for the female reproductive system.
■ **apply** the skill of advocacy to promote breast self-examinations.

● **Reading Strategy**
Predicting Before you read this lesson, take a look at the major headings, figures, and photo captions. Then write down two questions that you think might be answered by reading this lesson.

**uick Write**

Why is it important to know about the reproductive system?

Parts of the Female Reproductive System

The female reproduction system has three main functions: to produce egg cells, to create a new life, and to give birth. Eggs are the female reproductive cells. The **ovaries** are *the female endocrine glands that release mature eggs and produce the hormones estrogen and progesterone.* These hormones control female sexual development and the other organs in the female reproductive system.

The female reproductive system also includes the uterus. The **uterus** is *a pear-shaped organ, located within the pelvis, in which the developing baby is nourished and protected.* **Figure 12.5** lists the parts of the female reproductive system and describes what they do.

The Menstrual Cycle

You may have heard of a female having a "period." This refers to her menstrual **cycle**. The menstrual cycle is the series of events that prepares the female reproductive system for reproduction. Menstrual cycles begin when a female's hormone production increases and she reaches full puberty. Most complete menstrual cycles last about 28 days. However, the length of a menstrual cycle varies from female to female. For the first year or two, menstrual cycles are often irregular.

Academic Vocabulary

cycle (SY kel) *(noun)* a period of time taken up by a series of events or actions that repeat themselves regularly and in the same order. *The police detectives looked at the cycle of events that led to Mark's death.*

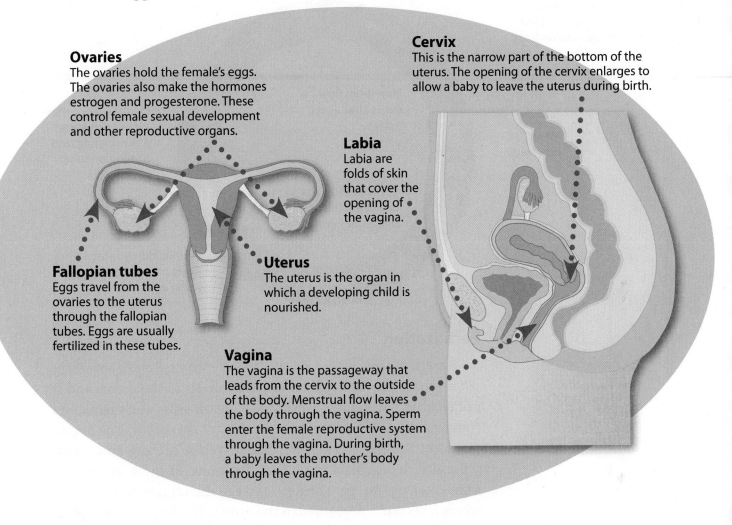

PARTS OF THE FEMALE REPRODUCTIVE SYSTEM

This diagram shows the parts of the female reproductive system.
Where are eggs stored?

Ovaries
The ovaries hold the female's eggs. The ovaries also make the hormones estrogen and progesterone. These control female sexual development and other reproductive organs.

Cervix
This is the narrow part of the bottom of the uterus. The opening of the cervix enlarges to allow a baby to leave the uterus during birth.

Labia
Labia are folds of skin that cover the opening of the vagina.

Fallopian tubes
Eggs travel from the ovaries to the uterus through the fallopian tubes. Eggs are usually fertilized in these tubes.

Uterus
The uterus is the organ in which a developing child is nourished.

Vagina
The vagina is the passageway that leads from the cervix to the outside of the body. Menstrual flow leaves the body through the vagina. Sperm enter the female reproductive system through the vagina. During birth, a baby leaves the mother's body through the vagina.

In the first stage of the menstrual cycle, hormones cause the lining of the uterus to build up with a cushion of blood, tissue, and fluid. Next, the level of the hormone estrogen reaches its highest point during the cycle. This causes **ovulation,** *the process by which the ovaries release mature eggs, usually one each menstrual cycle.* The egg is released from the ovary. It travels through the fallopian tube toward the uterus.

If the egg is not fertilized, the lining of the uterus begins to break down. **Menstruation** is *the flow from the body of blood, tissues, and fluids that results from the breakdown of the lining of the uterus.* The period of time in which menstruation takes place is called the menstrual period. It can last from two to seven days. After menstruation, the cycle begins again. The lining of the uterus once again begins to thicken. A complete menstrual cycle is shown in **Figure 12.6** on page 380.

FIGURE 12.6

THE MENSTRUAL CYCLE

The menstrual cycle ranges from 25–30 days. This can differ for some females, especially during the first two years of menstruation. **How long does a menstrual period usually last?**

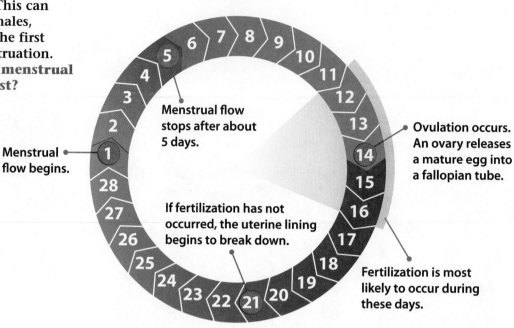

Menstrual flow begins.

Menstrual flow stops after about 5 days.

If fertilization has not occurred, the uterine lining begins to break down.

Ovulation occurs. An ovary releases a mature egg into a fallopian tube.

Fertilization is most likely to occur during these days.

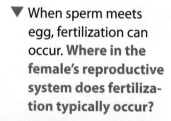

▼ When sperm meets egg, fertilization can occur. **Where in the female's reproductive system does fertilization typically occur?**

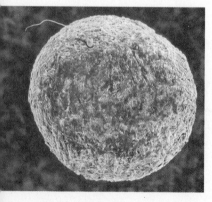

Fertilization

Fertilization is *the joining of a male sperm cell and a female egg cell to form a fertilized egg.* An egg that travels to the uterus and is not fertilized eventually dissolves. If sperm enter the vagina and travel to the fallopian tubes shortly after ovulation, one sperm can meet the egg cell and fertilize it. When the egg and sperm cell unite, the egg develops a film that prevents more sperm cells from entering the egg. The fertilized egg then travels to the uterus where it becomes implanted in the lining. The female is now pregnant. She does not menstruate or ovulate again until after the pregnancy is over. Inside the uterus the fertilized egg begins to grow. It is nourished and protected by the lining of the uterus. Eventually, the fertilized egg develops into a baby.

Female Health Problems

Many problems can affect the female reproductive system. Fortunately, many of them can be prevented and treated. Here are some common problems and their treatment.

• A **yeast infection** is an infection of the vagina. It is caused by changes in the amounts of bacteria and fungi that normally live in the vagina. As a result, the female experiences itching as well as a discharge. The infection is usually brought on by hormone changes, certain medicines, and tight clothing. It can be treated with medicine.

Advocacy

Promoting Breast Self-Examinations

Doctors usually examine a female's breasts for lumps or signs of breast cancer. Breast cancer can grow and spread very quickly if not detected early. Females can detect signs of cancer by doing a breast self-examination every month. It should be done about seven days after menstruation.

On Your Own

Go to the library or use the Internet to find instructions for how to do a breast self-examination. Make a brochure that features these instructions. In your brochure, include a list of at least four signs of breast cancer to watch out for.

- **Vaginitis** is an infection of the vagina. The female may have itching, discharge, and sometimes pain. Vaginitis is treated with medication.

- **Toxic shock syndrome** (TSS) is a rare bacterial infection. Some studies show that it can be caused by using a single tampon for more than 24 hours. TSS can lead to death if it is not treated. Signs of TSS include high fever, a rash, and vomiting. TSS can be prevented. Females who use tampons must read the directions that come with the package and follow them very carefully. A female should change her tampon every four to six hours.

- **Cancer** can occur in the breasts, ovaries, uterus, and cervix. It is caused by uncontrolled cell growth in the tissues of these organs. Early detection is the best way to prevent the serious complications of cancer. This is done by having regular health screenings. Many kinds of cancer can be treated through surgery, radiation, or chemotherapy. Fortunately, cancer involving the reproductive system is rare among teens.

- **Sterility** is the inability to produce children. Sterility can be caused by many factors, including untreated STDs and hormone imbalances caused by stress, diet, and overexertion, as well as aging. Some types of sterility can be treated by medicine or surgery. Infertility is a reduced ability to produce children. It can be caused by some of the same factors that cause sterility, including untreated STDs.

▼ By keeping track of her menstrual cycle, a female can better monitor her health. **How long is a typical menstrual cycle?**

Caring for the Female Reproductive System

Here are some steps females can take to keep their reproductive systems healthy.

- Do a breast self-examination every month.

- Shower or bathe daily.

- Keep track of your menstrual cycle. It may be irregular for the first year or two. If a menstrual period is missed for several months, or if there is severe pain or a very heavy menstrual flow, see a doctor.

- See a health care provider if you experience premenstrual syndrome (PMS). PMS occurs just before menstruation. It can include headaches, breast tenderness, fatigue, irritability, acne, and abdominal cramps.

- Visit a gynecologist for regular checkups. A **gynecologist** is *a doctor who specializes in the female reproductive system.*

 Reading Check List What are four ways to care for the female reproductive system?

Go Online

Visit **glencoe.com** and complete the Interactive Study Guide for Lesson 4.

Lesson 4 Review

After You Read

Review this lesson for new terms, major headings, and Reading Checks.

What I Learned

1. **Vocabulary** Define *fertilization*.

2. **Explain** What happens to the lining of the uterus if fertilization does not occur after ovulation?

3. **List** What are the three functions of the female reproductive system?

4. **Explain** Where does the egg go after ovulation has occurred?

Thinking Critically

5. **Synthesize** What parts of the female reproductive system are also part of the endocrine system? What hormones do they produce?

6. **Analyze** How does fertilization affect the menstrual cycle?

Applying Health Skills

7. **Communication Skills** Molly is 18 years old and not sexually active. She feels that she does not have time to go to a gynecologist and that since she isn't sexually active, she doesn't have to worry about her reproductive system. How would you explain to Molly why it is important that she have a yearly checkup? What health concerns might she prevent by visiting a gynecologist?

Go Online For more Lesson Review Activities, go to **glencoe.com**.

Heredity and Human Development

📖 Guide to Reading

🔴 Building Vocabulary
Both *embryo* and *fetus* are used to describe a human being before it is born. Use a dictionary to find out the difference in meaning between these two terms.

- chromosomes (p. 383)
- genes (p. 383)
- cell (p. 384)
- tissue (p. 384)
- organ (p. 384)
- body system (p. 384)
- embryo (p. 384)
- fetus (p. 384)

🔴 Focusing on the Main Ideas
In this lesson, you will learn to

- **explain** how humans inherit certain characteristics.
- **identify** the basic unit of life.
- **describe** how a fetus develops.
- **identify** ways an expectant mother can care for her developing fetus.

🔴 Reading Strategy
Analyzing a Graphic Using the diagram shown here, create a concept map about the different levels of body structure. As you read the lesson, fill in the concept map.

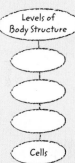

Levels of Body Structure

Cells

🅠 Quick Write
Do you know people who look like their family members? Which traits do they have in common?

Heredity

Tina looks very much like her mother. Frank looks a little like his mom and a little like his dad. These similarities occur because genetic material is passed from parent to child. When a sperm and an egg unite, the newly fertilized egg has a complete set of chromosomes. **Chromosomes,** located in the cell's nucleus, are *threadlike structures that carry genes.* **Genes** are *the basic units of heredity.* They carry the codes for inherited traits.

A sperm has 23 chromosomes, and an egg also has 23 chromosomes. The fertilized egg contains 46 chromosomes, half from the mother and half from the father. This is shown in **Figure 12.7** on page 384.

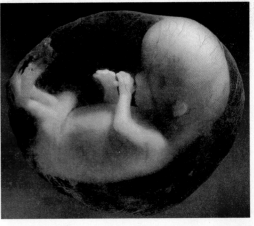

▶ A zygote becomes an embryo and then a fetus. **When is an embryo first called a fetus?**

COMBINING CHROMOSOMES

Each sperm contains 23 chromosomes, as does each egg. How many chromosomes does a cell in a fertilized egg have?

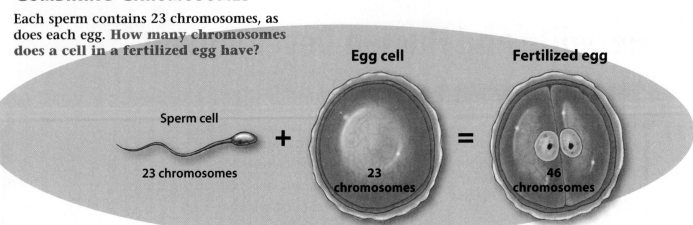

Sperm cell

23 chromosomes

+

Egg cell

23 chromosomes

=

Fertilized egg

46 chromosomes

Careers for the 21st Century

Biological Scientist

Biological scientists study living organisms and their relationship to their environment. Some biological scientists work in the growing field of biotechnology. They study the genetic material in cells to learn about inherited traits and diseases, such as cancer and obesity. You can prepare for a career as a biological scientist by taking classes in biology and chemistry.

What other fields would a biological scientist work in? Go to *Career Corner* at **glencoe.com** to find out.

Fertilization and Human Development

A **cell** is *the basic unit of life*. Humans are made of millions of cells. A fertilized egg, however, is just one single cell. How, then, does a single cell become a person made of many cells? Soon after fertilization, the fertilized egg begins to divide and multiply. Soon, an organism made up of many cells is formed.

As the organism continues to develop, its cells form more and more complex body parts. Groups of cells make up tissues. A **tissue** is *a group of similar cells that do a particular job*. Tissues then make up organs. An **organ** is *a body part made up of different tissues joined to perform a particular function*. Eventually, an entire body system is formed. A **body system** is *a group of organs that work together to carry out related tasks*.

Cells, tissues, organs, and body systems are different levels of organization in the body. Cells are the most basic level of organization. Body systems are the most complex. The different levels of organization in the body are shown in **Figure 12.8.**

Development of the Fetus

A fertilized egg is first called a zygote. The zygote divides to form two cells about 24 hours after fertilization. Then these cells divide, forming more cells. After about a week, the zygote attaches itself to the lining of the uterus. After another week, the zygote is called an embryo. An **embryo** is *the developing organism from two weeks until the end of the eighth week of development*. Each time one of an embryo's cells divides, it produces two cells. The number of cells continues to multiply as the embryo develops. After the eighth week, the human embryo is called a fetus. A **fetus** is *the developing organism from the end of the eighth week until birth*. About

▼ **FIGURE 12.8**

BUILDING BODY SYSTEMS

One fertilized egg cell will eventually develop into a complete human being with body systems that work together. **How are cells, tissues, organs, and body systems related?**

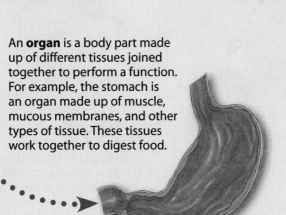

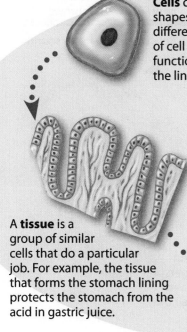

Cells come in different shapes and perform different tasks. Each type of cell has a particular function. This cell is from the lining of the stomach.

A **body system** is a group of organs that work together to carry out related tasks. The digestive system is the body system shown here.

An **organ** is a body part made up of different tissues joined together to perform a function. For example, the stomach is an organ made up of muscle, mucous membranes, and other types of tissue. These tissues work together to digest food.

A **tissue** is a group of similar cells that do a particular job. For example, the tissue that forms the stomach lining protects the stomach from the acid in gastric juice.

nine full months after fertilization, birth takes place. During this nine-month period, the fetus develops the **complex** body systems needed for survival. The stages the fetus goes through are shown in **Figure 12.9,** on page 386.

The fetus gets nutrients and oxygen from its mother through the umbilical (uhm·BI·li·kuhl) cord. This is a tube that attaches to the abdomen of the fetus. At birth, the umbilical cord is cut.

Academic Vocabulary

complex (kuhm PLEKS) *(adjective)* complicated. *The teacher had a complex method for determining each student's grade on the science project.*

 Reading Check

Compare How does an embryo differ from a fetus?

Care During Pregnancy

An expectant mother can do many things to create a healthy environment for her growing fetus. Since the fetus is inside her body, all the mother's health choices can also affect its health. Expectant mothers should practice these positive health behaviors.

- **Eat healthful foods.** The fetus gets its nourishment directly from its mother. Eating nutritious foods will greatly benefit the health of both the mother and the fetus.

STAGES OF FETAL DEVELOPMENT

This diagram shows the stages of development a fetus goes through.
When does a fetus develop eyebrows and fingernails?

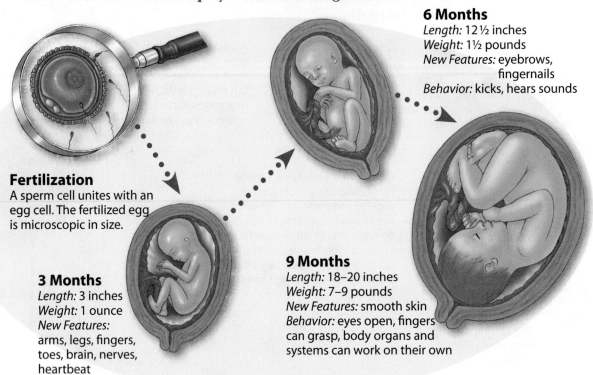

Fertilization
A sperm cell unites with an egg cell. The fertilized egg is microscopic in size.

6 Months
Length: 12½ inches
Weight: 1½ pounds
New Features: eyebrows, fingernails
Behavior: kicks, hears sounds

3 Months
Length: 3 inches
Weight: 1 ounce
New Features: arms, legs, fingers, toes, brain, nerves, heartbeat
Behavior: begins to move

9 Months
Length: 18–20 inches
Weight: 7–9 pounds
New Features: smooth skin
Behavior: eyes open, fingers can grasp, body organs and systems can work on their own

- **Have regular checkups.** The doctor will monitor both the mother's health and the fetus's development. An expectant mother should also take prenatal vitamins as recommended by the doctor.

- **Beware of infections.** Some diseases are very dangerous to the fetus. For example, rubella (also called German measles) and some sexually transmitted diseases can cause problems.

- **Don't use tobacco.** Smoking, chewing tobacco, and breathing secondhand smoke can be harmful to the fetus.

- **Don't drink alcohol.** This can cause a fetus to develop fetal alcohol syndrome (FAS) or fetal alcohol effects. Sometimes the problems are mild, such as having a small size at birth. At other times, they are severe. The child may have brain damage, mental retardation, learning disabilities, or emotional problems.

- **Don't take any unnecessary drugs.** Any medicine or illegal drug can affect the growth and development of a fetus. A pregnant female should take medication only if absolutely necessary and only as instructed by her doctor. She should also avoid all illegal drugs.

Go Online

Visit **glencoe.com** and complete the Interactive Study Guide for Lesson 5.

Parenthood

Parenthood involves making a lifelong commitment to another person. There are personal, social, and legal responsibilities associated with parenthood. Parents are responsible for providing physical care, such as a place to live, food, clothing, and medical care. Parents must also meet their children's emotional needs. Children need love, attention, and guidance. They also need to learn social skills, or how to get along with others. Parents should be good role models for their children. They should demonstrate good character traits, such as fairness, trust, caring, and respect.

▶ An expectant mother gives her baby solid nourishment by eating a healthful diet. **How is eating healthfully important to a pregnant female and her baby?**

Lesson 5 Review

 After You Read

Review this lesson for new terms, major headings, and Reading Checks.

What I Learned

1. *Vocabulary* Define *chromosomes*.

2. *Identify* List four levels of body organization from most complex to most basic.

3. *Describe* Describe the development of a human from the point of fertilization to birth.

4. *List* What are four ways that a pregnant female can care for her developing baby?

Thinking Critically

5. *Apply* A test of Ling's fetus shows that its cells each have one more chromosome than normal human cells. How many chromosomes does each of the fetus's cells have?

6. *Analyze* Using the information given in Figure 12.9, calculate the weight that the developing fetus gains at each three-month stage. During which stage does it gain the most weight?

Applying Health Skills

7. *Analyzing Influences* Imagine that your aunt is going to have a baby. Both she and her husband smoke cigarettes. However, your aunt has decided to quit during her pregnancy. Your uncle says he doesn't need to quit. What information or advice might you give your aunt and uncle?

G **Online** For more Lesson Review Activities, go to glencoe.com.

The Life Cycle

 **Guide to Reading**

● Building Vocabulary
Look up the meaning of the word *toddle*. Write a sentence to explain why you think it is used to describe toddlers.

- infancy (p. 389)
- toddler (p. 389)
- preschooler (p. 389)

● Focusing on the Main Ideas
In this lesson, you will learn to

- **describe** the stages of life.
- **identify** the ways in which adolescence will prepare you for adulthood.
- **list** ways to reduce stress in your life.

● Reading Strategy
Organizing Information As you read this lesson, make a list of events that happen at different stages of the life cycle.

*Q*uick Write

Describe a time that you or someone you know played with a baby or helped care for one. What could the baby do without your help? What did you have to help the baby do?

The Stages of Life

A fetus develops and changes over the nine months of pregnancy. It develops certain behaviors at different times. When the fetus is fully developed, the mother feels strong contractions. These help push the baby out of her body. After birth, the baby will continue to develop certain behaviors during different stages of life. These different stages that people go through in life are all part of the human life cycle.

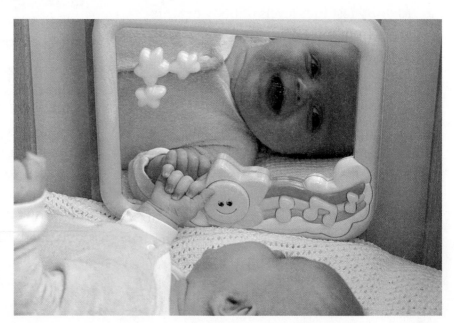

▶ Babies learn to interact with their surrounding world. **Why might it be important to provide infants with a variety of toys?**

Infancy

Infancy is *the first year of life after birth.* At this time, a baby grows rapidly in weight and in size. In fact, the baby's weight triples, and the size increases by half. Infants begin to observe the world around them. They do this by watching, touching, tasting, and listening. Soon, the baby learns to respond to those nearby. He or she may start to smile and make sounds. The baby learns to reach for objects and crawl.

By the end of infancy, babies can recognize some words and may even say a few of them. Within a year, they learn to sit up by themselves and can often pull themselves up into a standing position.

Childhood

Next, a child becomes a toddler. A **toddler** is *a child between the ages of one and three.* While toddlers continue to grow in weight and size, they don't do so as rapidly as when they were infants. They learn to do many activities. They can feed themselves, scribble on paper, and use the toilet. Their language skills begin to develop, and they begin to talk to others. Also, they become very physically active. They can walk, run, and climb on their own. Toddlers are very curious, and they learn quickly.

The toddler soon becomes a **preschooler,** *a child between ages three and five.* Preschoolers begin to develop complex physical skills. For example, they can use a paintbrush, button their clothes, and ride a tricycle. Their mental skills develop, too, and they enjoy using their imagination. They like to pretend and to imitate others. Preschoolers learn how to follow rules and how to express their needs. They also start to make friends.

The period between ages 6 and 11 is called late childhood. In this period, physical growth continues, and children become stronger and more coordinated. They enter school and continue to develop their social skills. They make friends and participate in social activities. Overall, they learn to do many things on their own and need less and less adult supervision.

Adolescence

The next stage is called adolescence. This period, usually between the ages of 12 and 18, brings rapid growth and development. The many physical changes that occur help prepare the body for

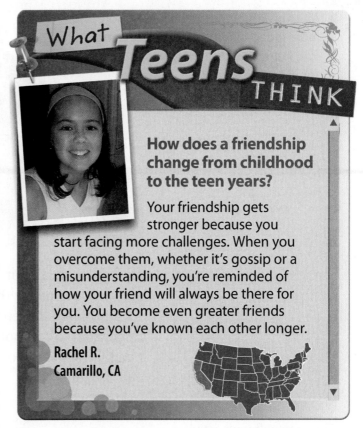

What Teens THINK

How does a friendship change from childhood to the teen years?

Your friendship gets stronger because you start facing more challenges. When you overcome them, whether it's gossip or a misunderstanding, you're reminded of how your friend will always be there for you. You become even greater friends because you've known each other longer.

Rachel R.
Camarillo, CA

As Amy gets older, she becomes more and more independent. **How do the things you learn as a child help prepare you for life as an adult?**

reproduction. The mental, emotional, and social changes help prepare a person for the challenges of adulthood.

During adolescence, teens begin to take on more and more responsibilities in both their households and in their communities. Many of the choices they make will help shape the paths they take as adults.

Adulthood

At about age 19, the stage called young adulthood begins. At this time, physical growth slows significantly, but young adults continue to grow mentally, emotionally, and socially. Many young adults become independent. They often live on their own and begin their careers. Many develop deeper relationships with others, marry, and have children.

Then comes what is called middle age. Adults in their thirties, forties, and fifties continue to strengthen their careers, relationships, and families. During these years, most adults focus on their jobs and children. Some take classes to learn new skills.

Try some different activities. They can often help you discover what you enjoy. **How can hobbies improve your health?**

After middle age, adults begin to show signs of physical aging. Some people in their mid-sixties and older may decide to retire. Despite showing signs of aging, many people continue to be very physically active, often long into their retirement years. They may travel, enjoy new hobbies, and become more involved in their communities. Exercise is important at all stages of life. Exercise helps prevent disease and other health problems, allowing you to do the things you like to do.

In time, though, a person's body systems begin to weaken, and he or she eventually dies. Death is the final part of the human life cycle. It is important to see dying as a natural part of the life cycle.

Reading Check

Explain When can you see signs of an adult's physical aging?

Health Skills Activity

Preparing for Adulthood

How are adolescence and adulthood connected? The physical, mental, emotional, and social growth you make during adolescence prepares you for adulthood. You learn to make important decisions that can affect your health. In fact, many of the decisions you make as an adolescent will affect you long into your adulthood.

Reducing Risk

Do you want to lead a long and healthy life? Then consider the consequences of your day-to-day actions. These guidelines can help you stay safe and healthy.

- **Protect yourself from injury.** Stay safe at home and at school. Always wear a safety belt when riding in a vehicle. Wear protective gear when participating in sports. Do the same if you ever have to work with dangerous chemicals or machines. Know how to protect yourself if there's a fire or other emergency.

- **Choose a healthy lifestyle.** Be sure to eat a nutritious diet. Get plenty of physical activity. Figure out the best way for you to manage stress, and get enough

▼ Buckle up! Do what you can to stay safe and healthy. **In what ways can you reduce risk in your daily life?**

▼ People develop strong relationships in adulthood. **What kind of social changes can happen to someone as he or she becomes an adult?**

sleep and rest. All of these things will reduce your risk of developing many diseases later in life, such as heart disease and cancer.

- **Don't use drugs.** Be wise when it comes to using medicines. Stay drug free so you can protect your health. Do your best to avoid social situations in which drugs might be offered to you. Remember, drugs can permanently damage your body and mind.

- **Avoid tobacco and alcohol.** Smoking cigarettes, chewing tobacco, and inhaling secondhand tobacco smoke can cause many serious health problems, including cancer. Using alcohol can cause you to make poor decisions. It can also slow your reflexes. These effects can have many negative, even deadly, consequences. Continued use of alcohol can damage your liver and digestive system.

- **Avoid sexual activity.** By choosing to avoid sexual activity until marriage, you can prevent an unplanned pregnancy and sexually transmitted diseases, including HIV. These can damage your physical health and may even cause death. Practicing abstinence from sexual activity will also protect you from the many difficult emotional and social consequences associated with sexual activity.

 **Reading Check**

Explain How does practicing abstinence from sexual activity benefit your health?

Moving Toward the Future

The teen years are a time of growth and development—physically, mentally, emotionally, and socially. The experiences you have and the knowledge you gain as a teen will help you meet the challenges of adulthood. During adolescence, you explore who you are and find out what's important to you. You become more independent in your thoughts and feelings. As you discover how to solve problems and make important decisions, you will learn to take responsibility for your actions. You'll also learn that effort, ability, and chance are factors in your future success and failures. The teen years are a time to discover what makes you a unique individual.

During your teen years, your relationships with other people will mature, and you'll develop a greater interest in your community and the world. You'll also begin to make plans for what you want to do as an adult. An interest or hobby that you have now could develop into a rewarding career. So make the most of your teen years by caring for your personal health and preparing for your future.

Go Online

Visit **glencoe.com** and complete the Interactive Study Guide for Lesson 6.

Lesson 6 Review

 After You Read

Review this lesson for new terms, major headings, and Reading Checks.

What I Learned

1. *Vocabulary* Define *infancy,* and use it in a sentence.

2. *List* Identify four choices you can make to reduce risk in your life.

3. *Give Examples* In what ways do your teen years prepare you for adult life?

4. *Explain* How does death relate to the human life cycle?

Thinking Critically

5. *Apply* Brent is feeling pressure to engage in sexual activity with his girlfriend. What would you say to Brent to encourage him to make the healthful choice of abstaining from sexual activity?

6. *Infer* How do a teen's responsibilities at school prepare him or her for adulthood?

Applying Health Skills

7. *Accessing Information* Make a list of three careers that might interest you. Do research to find out what kind of education, training, or experience you would need to have a job in each career. Then identify at least two activities you could do as a teen to prepare for each career.

Building Health Skills

Accessing Information

Practicing Healthful Behaviors

Stress Management

Analyzing Influences

Communication Skills

Refusal Skills

Conflict Resolution

Decision Making

Goal Setting

Advocacy

What Are Refusal Skills?

Refusal skills are strategies that help you say no effectively. If a peer asks you to engage in risky behavior, like sexual activity, remember the S.T.O.P. formula:

- **Say no firmly.** Be direct and clearly state how you feel. Use direct eye contact and keep your statement short.
- **Tell why not.** Use "I" messages to give your reasons.
- **Offer another idea.** Suggest an activity that does not involve sexual activity.
- **Promptly leave.** If you have to, just walk away.

Using S.T.O.P. to Choose Abstinence

Follow the Model, Practice, and Apply steps to help you master this important health skill.

❶ Model

Read how Felisha uses the S.T.O.P. strategy to say no to an uncomfortable situation.

Felisha and Darnell just started dating. One day, Darnell invited Felisha to his house to watch a movie. When she arrived, she discovered that they were alone.

DARNELL: "I thought it would be nice if we were by ourselves."

FELISHA: "No, I won't stay here if your mom or dad isn't home." **(Say no firmly)**

FELISHA: "My parents wouldn't want me to be alone with you." **(Tell why not)**

FELISHA: "Why don't we go to my house and watch the movie?" **(Offer another idea)**

DARNELL: "Your parents won't find out."

FELISHA: "I'm going home." **(Promptly leave)**

❷ Practice

Dan and his friends need to use refusal skills to say no to tobacco. Read the following passage and then practice refusal skills by answering the questions that follow.

Dan and Laura were hanging out with friends after school. Laura offered everyone a cigarette.

1. Why might Dan and the other teens want to avoid this risky behavior?

2. Write a dialogue that shows how the teens apply the S.T.O.P. strategy to avoid this risky behavior.

❸ Apply

Apply what you have learned about refusal skills by completing the activity below.

In small groups, brainstorm situations in which a teen would need to use refusal skills to avoid a risky behavior. Choose one idea and write a brief description of the situation. Descriptions should include the following:

1. The circumstances that put the teen in danger of engaging in a risky behavior.

2. The teen's reasons for wanting to abstain from the risky behavior.

Based on your description, write a scene showing how the teen uses the S.T.O.P. strategy to avoid the risky behavior. If time permits, role-play your scenario for the class.

Self-Check

- Did we describe a risky situation that a teen would need to avoid?

- Did we give reasons for the teen to avoid the behavior?

- Did our scene show how the teen uses S.T.O.P. to avoid the risky behavior?

Building Health Skills

Analyzing Inherited Traits

You might have a chin just like your mother's. Your brother's eyes might look just like your father's. Do all family members have the same features? How about hair color, eye color, or the ability to play the guitar? Which traits are caused by heredity? Which are influenced by one's environment?

Believe it or not, even the food you like can result from inherited traits. Some people enjoy or dislike certain foods because they are influenced by family or friends. However, scientists have shown that some people taste a chemical in broccoli that is bitter and others don't taste it at all. The ability to taste the chemical is genetic. Knowing whether a feature is the result of genes, your environment, or a little bit of both might require some serious investigation.

What You Will Need

- Salt substitute (sold in grocery stores)
- Cotton swabs
- Paper cups of water

What You Will Do

1. Your teacher will hand out the materials to each student and will write the headings "Tasters" and "Non-tasters" on the board.

2. Put a small amount of salt substitute on your tongue, and record if it tastes bitter. If you wish, take a sip of water afterward.

3. When called upon, add your reaction under one of the two headings on the board.

4. After all the students have recorded their reactions, the class will calculate the percentage of "tasters" by dividing the number of "tasters" by the number of students who participated in the activity.

Wrapping It Up

Seventy-five percent of the population has the dominant gene that makes them "tasters." How does your class compare? Do you think age makes a difference? Does gender make a difference? What other factors might influence this test?

Reading Review

STUDY TO GO Visit **glencoe.com** to download quizzes and eFlashcards for Chapter 12.

FOLDABLES Study Organizer

Foldables® and Other Study Aids Take out the Foldable® that you created for Lesson 1 and any graphic organizers that you created for Lessons 1–6. Find a partner and quiz each other using these study aids.

Lesson 1 Changes During Adolescence

Main Idea The physical, mental, emotional, and social changes of adolescence prepare you for adulthood.

- Teens go through puberty at different rates.
- During adolescence, teens begin to form their own opinions and beliefs.

Lesson 2 The Endocrine System

Main Idea The endocrine system is made up of glands that regulate body functions.

- Endocrine glands include the thyroid gland, parathyroid glands, adrenal glands, ovaries, pituitary gland, pancreas, and testes.
- One major role of the endocrine system is to regulate metabolism.

Lesson 3 The Male Reproductive System

Main Idea The main function of the male reproductive system is to produce sperm.

- When a sperm cell fertilizes a female's egg cell, a new life is formed.
- Problems of the male reproductive system include inguinal hernia, prostate and testicular cancers, testicular torsion, and sterility.

Lesson 4 The Female Reproductive System

Main Idea The main functions of the female reproduction system are to produce egg cells, to create a new life, and to give birth.

- The menstrual cycle prepares a woman for reproduction.
- Problems of the female reproductive system include yeast infections, vaginitis, toxic shock syndrome, cancer, sterility, and infertility.

Lesson 5 Heredity and Human Development

Main Idea When an egg cell is fertilized, inherited traits are passed from parent to child through chromosomes.

- The body is organized into cells, tissues, organs, and body systems.
- A fertilized egg, or zygote, becomes an embryo, then a fetus.
- An expectant mother should eat healthy foods and have regular checkups. She should also avoid tobacco, alcohol, and other drugs.

Lesson 6 The Life Cycle

Main Idea The stages of life are infancy, childhood, adolescence, and adulthood.

- Exercise can help prevent diseases and other health problems at all stages of life.
- To protect your health, avoid injury; choose a healthy lifestyle; avoid tobacco, alcohol, and other drugs; and practice abstinence.

Assessment

 After You Read

HEALTH QUIZ

Now that you have read the chapter, look back at your answers to the Health Quiz on the chapter opener. What would your answers be now?

Reviewing Vocabulary and Main Ideas

On a sheet of paper, write the numbers 1–6. After each number, write the term from the list that best completes each statement.

- puberty
- reproduction
- testes
- adolescence
- hormones
- metabolism

Lesson 1 Changes During Adolescence

1. The stage of life between childhood and adulthood is _____.

2. _____ is the time when a person develops the physical characteristics of his or her gender.

Lesson 2 The Endocrine System

3. Progesterone, estrogen, and testosterone are examples of _____.

4. _____ is the process by which the body gets energy from food.

Lesson 3 The Male Reproductive System

5. Without the process of _____, humans could not produce children.

6. The pair of endocrine glands that produce sperm are the _____.

Lesson 4 The Female Reproductive System

On a sheet of paper, write the numbers 7–8. After each number, write the letter of the answer that best completes each statement.

7. _____ takes place once about every 28 days in females.
   a. metabolism
   b. hormones
   c. ovulation
   d. puberty

8. The joining of a male sperm cell and a female egg cell to form a zygote is called _____.
   a. fertilization
   b. puberty
   c. fetus
   d. ovulation

*On a sheet of paper, write the numbers 9–12. Write **True** or **False** for each statement below. If the statement is false, change the underlined word or phrase to make it true.*

Lesson 5 Heredity and Human Development

9. A fetus differs from an embryo in that a fetus is <u>less</u> than 8 weeks old.

10. A <u>tissue</u> is a group of similar cells that do a particular job.

Lesson 6 The Life Cycle

11. A <u>toddler</u> is a child in the stage of life that occurs right after infancy.

12. A child between ages three and five is a <u>toddler</u>.

Go Online Visit glencoe.com and take the Online Quiz for Chapter 12.

Thinking Critically

Using complete sentences, answer the following questions on a sheet of paper.

13. **Synthesize** How might the endocrine system affect other body systems? Give three examples.

14. **Summarize** Describe the paths that a sperm cell and an egg cell take before fertilization. Describe the path that the fertilized egg takes once fertilization has occurred.

Write About It

15. **Persuasive Writing** A friend wants to go to a party where there will be drugs and alcohol. Write a dialogue in which you tell your friend about the dangers of alcohol and drug use and encourage him or her to avoid the party.

Applying Technology

Growth and Change

Use the textbook and medical resources to develop a PowerPoint® presentation that reflects a clear understanding of the changes teens go through during adolescence. Follow the steps below to complete your project.

- Create charts and add clip-art to illustrate the mental, emotional, physical, and social changes experienced during adolescence.
- Create text to support each illustration.
- Open a new PowerPoint® project with 8–10 slides. Select the slide layout that has both an image and text box.
- Import one image onto each slide, and insert text where applicable.
- Edit for clarity and punctuation.
- Save your work.

Standardized Test Practice

Writing

Read the prompts below. On a separate sheet of paper, write an essay that addresses each prompt. Use information from the chapter to support your writing.

1. Imagine that you have been given a group assignment at school. It requires several hours of work each week for a month. One of your group members said that his house can be the meeting place for the group. His parents smoke, however, and at the first meeting, the secondhand smoke irritates your lungs. It also makes your clothes smell. How does this situation introduce risk in your life? Write an essay that describes how you might reduce that risk while still completing the group assignment. Give at least three solutions to the problem.

2. When a person reaches puberty, his or her reproductive system develops the ability to produce a child. However, he or she is not ready to be a parent. Explain why an adolescent is unable to care for a child. What steps can an adolescent take to reduce the risk of becoming a teen parent?

TEST-TAKING TIP

Find out how much time you have to write your essay. Use this time wisely. Spend some of the time at the beginning of the test organizing your thoughts and planning out your essay. Save some time at the end of the test so you can revise and review your essay.

13 Communicable Diseases

Chapter Preview

Lesson 1 What Are Communicable
Diseases? 402

Lesson 2 The Immune System 407

Lesson 3 Common Communicable
Diseases 413

Lesson 4 Preventing the Spread
of Disease 418

Lesson 5 Sexually Transmitted
Diseases 422

Lesson 6 HIV/AIDS 427

Building Health Skills 432

TIME health news 434

Chapter Reading Review 435

Chapter Assessment 436

▲ *Working with the Photo*

Staying home and getting rest when you are sick helps you limit the number of people who are exposed to your illness. **What are some other ways to prevent the spread of disease?**

Start-Up Activities

What do you already know about how some diseases spread? Take the short quiz below. Keep a record of your answers.

HEALTH QUIZ Choose the best answer for each of the following:

1. Covering your mouth when you cough
   a. is dangerous for your lungs.
   b. prevents pathogens from spreading.
   c. kills germs.
2. Strep throat is caused by
   a. a virus.
   b. a bacterium.
   c. eating the wrong food.
3. A good way to avoid getting sick is
   a. washing your hands often.
   b. shaking hands with someone who is sick.
   c. sharing other people's food.

ANSWERS: 1. b; 2. b; 3. a.

FOLDABLES Study Organizer

As You Read Make this Foldable® to help you record the main ideas about the causes of communicable diseases. Begin with a plain sheet of 8½″ × 11″ paper.

1 Fold the sheet of paper along the long axis, leaving a ½″ tab along the side.

2 Turn the paper. Fold in half, then fold in half again.

3 Unfold and cut the top layer along the three fold lines. This makes four tabs.

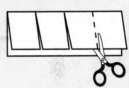

4 Label as shown.

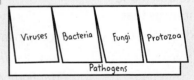

Under the appropriate tab, summarize what you learn about each type of pathogen.

 Online Visit **glencoe.com** and complete the Chapter 13 crossword puzzle.

What Are Communicable Diseases?

Quick Write

How do people catch colds? Write down one or two sentences that explain your answer.

Germs and Disease

You wake up feeling tired. Your nose is stuffy. Your throat is sore. You have a cold. A cold is one kind of disease. A **disease** is *any condition that interferes with the normal or proper functioning of the body or mind.* Diseases such as colds are called communicable diseases. A **communicable disease** is *a disease that can be spread to a person from another person, an animal, or an object.*

Communicable diseases are caused by germs. **Germs** are *organisms that are so small they can only be seen through a microscope.* The environment is filled with many types of germs. *Germs that cause diseases* are called **pathogens.** An **infection** is *a condition that happens when pathogens enter the body, multiply, and cause harm.* When the body cannot fight off an infection, a disease develops. **Figure 13.1** shows some kinds of pathogens and lists the diseases they cause.

PATHOGENS AND THE DISEASES THEY CAUSE

Communicable diseases are all caused by pathogens. According to the chart, what common diseases do fungi cause?

Pathogens	Diseases
Viruses	Colds, chicken pox, influenza, measles, mononucleosis, mumps, hepatitis, herpes, HPV, HIV, yellow fever, polio, rabies, viral pneumonia
Bacteria	Pinkeye, whooping cough, strep throat, tuberculosis, Lyme disease, most foodborne illnesses, diphtheria, bacterial pneumonia, cholera, gonorrhea
Fungi	Athlete's foot, ringworm
Protozoa	Dysentery, malaria, trichomoniasis

Kinds of Pathogens

There are four basic kinds of pathogens: viruses, bacteria, fungi, and protozoa. **Viruses** (VY·ruh·suhz) are *the smallest and simplest pathogens*. Viruses are not alive. They are usually made of genetic material and protein. Viruses cause upper respiratory infections and many other types of diseases.

Bacteria are *simple one-celled organisms*. Bacteria exist in every environment on earth. Most kinds of bacteria are not only harmless but actually helpful. Helpful bacteria live in your digestive system and help break down food. Other bacteria live on your skin and prevent harmful bacteria from infecting you. Harmful bacteria cause diseases such as strep throat and pneumonia.

Fungi (FUHN·jy) are *organisms that are more complex than bacteria but cannot make their own food*. Molds, yeast, and mushrooms are examples of fungi. Fungi thrive in warm, moist environments. Most fungi are harmless, but some can cause disease. For instance, a fungus causes athlete's foot.

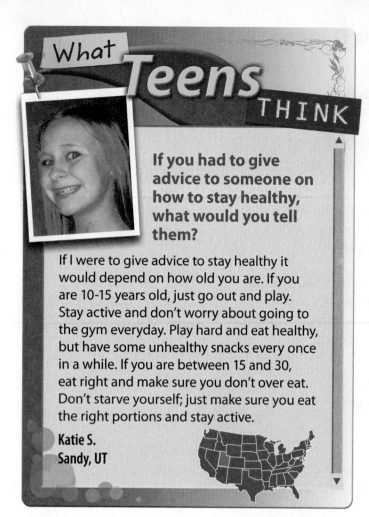
Protozoa (proh·tuh·ZOH·uh) are *one-celled organisms that are more complex than bacteria*. Although many protozoa are harmless, some can cause serious diseases. For example, one type of protozoa causes malaria. This disease can be transferred to people through mosquito bites.

How Pathogens Spread

Communicable diseases spread when a person gets infected by pathogens from another person, an animal, or an object. Most pathogens are spread in one of the following ways.

Direct contact with others

Some pathogens spread directly from one person to another. For example, a person with pinkeye might wipe his or her eye with a hand. If that hand touches your hand, and you touch your eye, you could get pinkeye. Washing your hands often with soap helps stop the spread of these pathogens.

Indirect contact with others

Some pathogens can spread from person to person without direct contact. When you have a cold or sore throat and you sneeze or cough, you can send pathogens into the air. Anyone breathing this air can become infected with the pathogen. Using tissues to cover your mouth and nose when you sneeze or cough can keep these pathogens from spreading.

Pathogens can also spread when people share drinking glasses, eating utensils, and other personal items. Always wash glasses, cups, and eating utensils with warm, soapy water before using them. Never share eating utensils, cups, drinking glasses, or personal items, such as toothbrushes or razors, with others.

Contact with someone else's blood

Some pathogens, such as the human immunodeficiency virus (HIV), which causes Acquired Immunodeficiency Syndrome (AIDS), can spread when blood from an infected person comes in contact with someone else's blood. This can happen when someone injects drugs using a needle that someone else has used. Unclean needles and tools used for tattooing and piercing can also spread pathogens. In some cases, pathogens can spread when the blood

Health Skills Activity

Accessing Information

Safe Drinking Water?

You turn on the faucet and water comes out of the tap into your glass. How does water get to your sink? Typically, it takes a long trip with several stops, where it's made safe for you to drink. The Environmental Protection Agency sets safe drinking water standards for the whole country. It enforces these standards through the Safe Drinking Water Act. State and local governments make sure cities and towns meet these standards. They must make sure the water you have in your home is safe to drink.

With a Group

In a group, research the journey water makes before it comes out of your tap. Where is drinking water stored in your community? Who makes sure that the water is safe? How is the water treated to make it clean? If possible, visit a water treatment plant. Present your findings in an oral report.

---

from an infected person touches the broken skin of a noninfected person. When a person donates blood, it is carefully screened for all pathogens before it is given to a person who needs it.

Sexual contact

Some pathogens are spread through sexual contact. You will learn more about these pathogens and the diseases they cause in Lessons 5 and 6.

Contact with contaminated food and water

Rare meat may taste good, but it may not be healthy for you. Undercooked meat may still contain bacteria that can make you sick. Illnesses people get from pathogens in food are called *foodborne illnesses*. To prevent foodborne illnesses, you must carefully prepare food before you eat it. You should properly store food that can spoil, such as dairy products and meat. Always wash fruits and vegetables. Handle meat, poultry, eggs, and fish carefully, and cook these foods thoroughly. Cleaning up is also very important. First, wash all knives and surfaces that meat, poultry, and fish have touched. Then mix one tablespoon of bleach into one gallon of warm water. Use it to wipe down all knives and cutting boards to kill germs. Even tap water can become contaminated in times of emergency.

Visit glencoe.com and complete the Interactive Study Guide for Lesson 1.

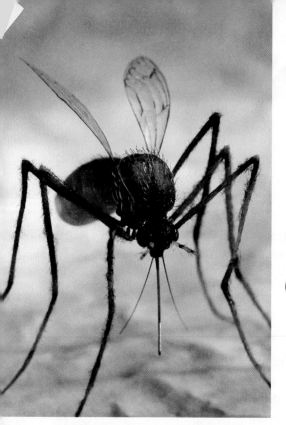

Some pathogens are spread through contaminated water. Never drink water directly from lakes and rivers. Most towns and cities must purify their water to make it safe to drink.

Contact with animals or insects

Animals and insects can spread pathogens. For example, animals that carry the rabies virus can infect other animals and humans if they bite them. A deer tick's bite can spread the virus that causes Lyme disease. Mosquitoes infected with the West Nile virus can spread that virus to birds, horses, and humans.

Reading Check Explain What are six ways that communicable diseases can be spread?

◀ Mosquitoes can infect humans with the West Nile virus. Controlling mosquito populations is one way to help control the spread of the West Nile virus. **What other ways can communities help prevent the spread of diseases spread by animals?**

Lesson 1 Review

 After You Read

Review this lesson for new terms, major headings, and Reading Checks.

What I Learned

1. **Vocabulary** Define *communicable disease* and *pathogen*. Write a sentence using both terms.

2. **Identify** What is an infection?

3. **Give Examples** What are three kinds of pathogens? Give an example of a disease caused by each kind.

4. **Explain** Why is it important to clean kitchen cutting boards carefully?

Thinking Critically

5. **Analyze** How does keeping insect populations down help keep people healthy?

6. **Apply** Aaron wants a drink of water. He finds a plastic cup on the table but does not know if it has been used or not. Should Aaron use the cup? Explain your answer.

Applying Health Skills

7. **Goal Setting** List three ways that you can prevent the spread of pathogens. Use the goal-setting steps on page 45 to create a plan, and write a paragraph describing the results.

 **Online** For more Lesson Review Activities, go to **glencoe.com**.

The Immune System

Guide to Reading

● **Building Vocabulary**
As you read this lesson, write each new term and its definition in a list. Write a second list that groups related terms together. For example, you might group "lymphatic system" and "lymphocytes." Compare your groups with the groups that other classmates made.

■ immune system (p. 407)
■ inflammation (p. 408)
■ lymphatic system (p. 409)
■ lymphocytes (p. 409)
■ antigens (p. 410)
■ antibodies (p. 410)
■ immunity (p. 412)
■ vaccine (p. 412)

● **Reading Strategy**
Sequencing As you read this lesson, create an outline that shows the steps of the immune system's response to an infection.

● **Focusing on the Main Ideas**
In this lesson, you will be able to

■ **describe** the function of the immune system.
■ **explain** how antibodies protect the body.
■ **describe** how you can develop immunity to a disease.
■ **practice** behaviors to keep your immune system healthy.

Keeping Pathogens Out

You can't escape pathogens; they are everywhere! Pathogens are in the air you breathe, in the water you drink, and on every surface you touch. You can pick them up on your skin when you come in contact with a person who has an infection. You can even catch them from insects. And yet, there is nothing to be afraid of. After all, you aren't sick all of the time, are you? This is because your body protects you. It can block, trap, or break down most pathogens before they make you sick. Your body uses five major barriers to block pathogens. These barriers are shown in **Figure 13.2.** They are: tears, saliva, skin, mucous membranes, and stomach acid.

These five barriers are your body's first line of defense. If a pathogen gets past the barriers, your body's immune system goes to work. Your **immune** (ih·MYOON) **system** is *a combination of body defenses made up of the cells, tissues, and organs that fight pathogens in the body.* Your immune system has two responses: the nonspecific **response** and the specific response.

**uick Write**

What are some functions of your skin? Write your ideas in a sentence or two.

Academic Vocabulary

response (ree SPONS) *(noun)* the act of responding or reacting to a change in the environment. *Greg's family couldn't wait to see his response to winning the art contest.*

Reading Check List What are the five barriers that keep pathogens out of your body?

▼ FIGURE 13.2 THE FIVE MAJOR BARRIERS

Your body has barriers that keep pathogens out. Which barrier protects your body from pathogens that might land on your arm?

Tears

Tears cover and protect the eye from dust and pathogens. As tears flow, they carry foreign material away from the eye.

Saliva

Saliva contains chemicals that kill pathogens in your mouth.

Skin

Skin provides a protective surface that keeps pathogens from entering your blood. If you get a cut or scrape, pathogens might get through this barrier.

Mucous Membranes

Mucous membranes are the soft skin that line the nose, mouth, eyes, and other body openings. They are coated in a fluid called mucus (MYOO·kuhs). Mucus traps pathogens. When you cough, sneeze, or clear your throat, your body rids itself of mucus.

Stomach Acid

Stomach acid kills many of the pathogens that make it past the saliva and mucous membranes of your mouth.

The Immune System's Nonspecific Response

When you get a splinter in your finger, dirt and pathogens on the splinter also enter your system. Your body responds with a nonspecific immune response. This is called nonspecific because it is the same no matter what foreign matter enters the body.

You may have noticed that the skin around a splinter soon becomes swollen and red. This is known as inflammation. **Inflammation** is *the body's response to injury or disease, resulting in a condition of swelling, pain, heat, and redness.*

Why does the area become inflamed? After the splinter breaks the skin, circulation to the area slows down. Fluids trapped in the area leak into the surrounding tissues. White blood cells called phagocytes (FAY·guh·sytes) surround the pathogens and destroy them. **Figure 13.3** shows how a phagocyte works.

Your body has other nonspecific immune responses as well. When you have an infection, the body begins producing a protein called interferon (in·ter·FEER·ahn). Interferon boosts the body's immune system to help stop viruses from multiplying. A fever is another nonspecific immune response. When your body temperature rises, it's harder for pathogens to reproduce.

Reading Check   **Explain** How does your immune system react when a splinter gets under your skin?

HOW A PHAGOCYTE DESTROYS A PATHOGEN

A phagocyte destroys a pathogen by surrounding it and breaking it down.
What other responses does the body have to pathogens?

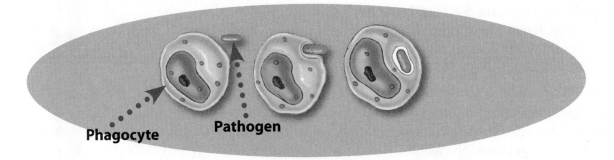

Phagocyte   **Pathogen**

The Immune System's Specific Response

Sometimes pathogens get past the body's nonspecific immune response. When this happens, the immune system's second response takes action. This is called the *specific response*. Each specific response attacks a particular pathogen and its poisons. Your immune system can recognize pathogens it has dealt with before. Once your immune system has created a specific response, those response cells remain in your body. When the pathogen attacks again, the cells recognize it. They go to work right away to fight it. So the second response is much faster than the first.

The Lymphatic System

The **lymphatic system** is *a secondary circulatory system that helps the body fight pathogens and maintains its fluid balance.* The fluid circulating in the lymphatic system is called lymph (LIMF). Macrophages (MA·kruh·fay·juhz) are also found in the lymph. Like phagocytes, macrophages surround and destroy foreign substances in the body. After they have destroyed the foreign substance, they help the lymphocytes identify it. **Lymphocytes** (LIM·fuh·sytes) are *special white blood cells in the blood and lymphatic system.*

There are three main kinds of lymphocytes: B cells, T cells, and NK cells. B cells and T cells are named for where the body makes them. B cells form in the bone marrow, and T cells form in the thymus gland. NK stands for "natural killer" cells. NK cells attack cancers and viruses.

▼ When you were born, you could already resist some diseases because of immunity passed to you from your mother. Now, the vaccines you receive help protect you from many communicable diseases. **If you've had a chicken pox vaccine, why is it likely you will not get that disease?**

Health Skills Activity

Practicing Healthful Behaviors

Keeping Your Immune System Healthy

You can play an active role in keeping your immune system healthy. A healthy immune system means that your body will be better able to fight off infection. Follow these tips to help keep your immune system in top condition.

- Get regular exercise.
- Eat plenty of vitamin-rich fruits, vegetables, and whole grains. Make sure that you get enough calcium-rich foods. Go easy on high-fat and sugary snacks. Eating healthy is one of the best ways to keep from getting sick.
- Learn strategies for managing stress. Reducing stress in your life can help your immune system fight off pathogens more successfully.
- Get enough sleep. Teens need about nine hours a night. Rest strengthens the body's defenses and reduces your chances of becoming ill.

With a Group

Use library or online resources to find articles that explain how vitamins and minerals can affect the immune system. Create a chart that describes at least five vitamins and minerals that strengthen the immune system. List foods that are rich in these vitamins and minerals.

Antigens and Antibodies

All three types of lymphocytes are activated when the body recognizes a part of a pathogen known as an antigen. **Antigens** (AN·ti·genz) are *substances that send the immune system into action.* For example, substances on the surface of a bacterium can be antigens. Blood cells of a different blood type than your own have different antigens on their surfaces.

Your body reacts to antigens by making more B cells and T cells. Some of the B cells make antibodies. **Antibodies** are *specific proteins that attach to antigens, keeping them from harming the body.* B cells produce specific antibodies to fight a particular type of antigen. Some of the new B cells and T cells don't react to the first encounter with a pathogen. They wait to react if the same kind of pathogen invades the body again. These cells are called memory B cells and memory T cells. A complete explanation of the immune response is found in **Figure 13.4.**

410 Chapter 13: Communicable Diseases

The Immune System's Specific Response to Infection

Many different kinds of cells in your immune system work together to fight invading pathogens. **What is the purpose of memory B and T cells?**

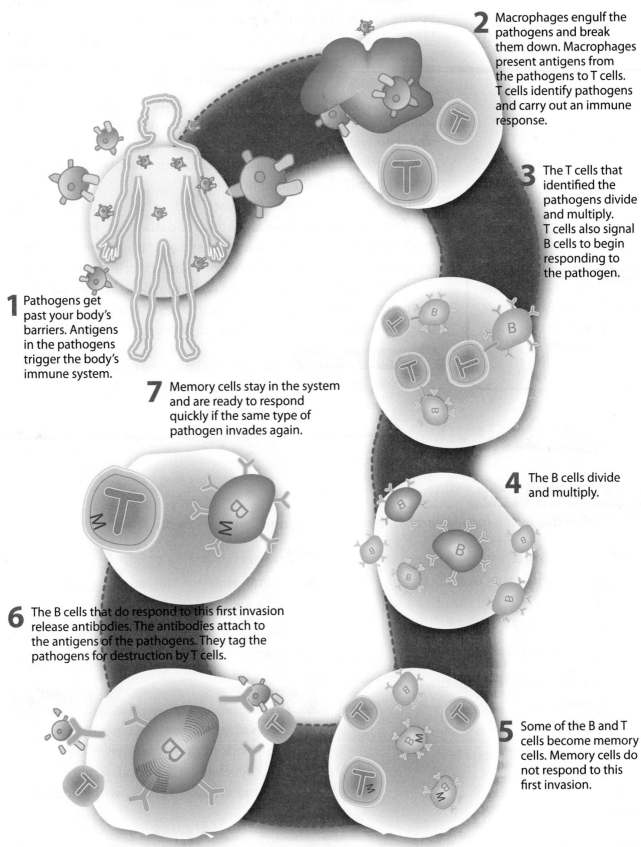

1 Pathogens get past your body's barriers. Antigens in the pathogens trigger the body's immune system.

2 Macrophages engulf the pathogens and break them down. Macrophages present antigens from the pathogens to T cells. T cells identify pathogens and carry out an immune response.

3 The T cells that identified the pathogens divide and multiply. T cells also signal B cells to begin responding to the pathogen.

4 The B cells divide and multiply.

5 Some of the B and T cells become memory cells. Memory cells do not respond to this first invasion.

6 The B cells that do respond to this first invasion release antibodies. The antibodies attach to the antigens of the pathogens. They tag the pathogens for destruction by T cells.

7 Memory cells stay in the system and are ready to respond quickly if the same type of pathogen invades again.

Immunity

Immunity is *the ability to resist the pathogens that cause a particular disease*. Healthy mothers pass immunity to their babies during pregnancy and through breastfeeding after birth. These immunities last for a few months. At that time, the baby's immune system can begin fighting pathogens on its own.

Your body also builds immunity when it responds to pathogens and when you get certain diseases. When your body encounters an antigen, it produces memory B cells and T cells. Scientists learned many years ago how to help the immune system prepare memory cells for specific diseases without making a person sick. A **vaccine** (vak·SEEN) is *a preparation of dead or weakened pathogens that is introduced into the body to cause an immune response*. This process is called immunization.

Immunization works because dead or weakened pathogens have the same antigens as live or active pathogens. However, they can't make you sick. Your immune system "learns" what a harmless pathogen looks like. It creates memory cells in response to the vaccine. If your body should meet the harmful version of the pathogen, the memory cells attack it. There are vaccines for many diseases, such as polio, measles, chicken pox, and tetanus.

 Reading Check Explain How do babies fight pathogens before they can respond to pathogens on their own?

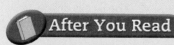
Visit **glencoe.com** and complete the Interactive Study Guide for Lesson 2.

Lesson 2 Review

After You Read

Review this lesson for new terms, major headings, and Reading Checks.

What I Learned

1. *Vocabulary* Define *immune system*. Name three kinds of blood cells that are part of the immune system.

2. *Restate* What is immunity?

3. *Describe* Briefly explain the steps of the immune system's specific response to infection.

4. *Apply* How can a fever help fight infection?

Thinking Critically

5. *Explain* How are antigens and antibodies like a lock and key?

6. *Analyze* Why is stomach acid considered a barrier to foreign objects?

Applying Health Skills

7. *Accessing Information* Research the two kinds of polio vaccines. Find out who developed each kind, when each became available, and how they differ.

 For more Lesson Review Activities, go to **glencoe.com**.

Common Communicable Diseases

Guide to Reading

Building Vocabulary
Write each term and its definition on a sheet of paper. Then write a paragraph that uses all the new terms.

- influenza (p. 414)
- contagious period (p. 414)
- mononucleosis (p. 415)
- hepatitis (p. 415)
- tuberculosis (p. 416)
- pneumonia (p. 416)
- strep throat (p. 416)

Focusing on the Main Ideas
In this lesson, you will be able to

- **distinguish** the differences between a cold and the flu.
- **identify** some common communicable diseases.

Reading Strategy
Predicting Look at the headings in each lesson, and predict what will be covered in the lesson. List your predictions on a sheet of paper. After you have read the lesson, look back at your list to see if your predictions were correct.

Quick Write

Write down the names of three common diseases. What are the symptoms of each disease?

Colds

A communicable disease that strikes just about everyone is the common cold. You've probably had one and know the symptoms: a runny nose, a sore throat, and sneezing. Colds spread by both direct and indirect contact.

Why can't your doctor give you a vaccine to protect you against a cold? There are too many viruses, hundreds of them, that cause colds. In fact, every cold you have had was probably caused by a different strain of virus. Developing vaccines for that many different viruses is very difficult. Besides, scientists believe that almost half of the viruses that cause colds have not yet even been identified. So it looks like the common cold will be common for years to come!

Reading Check  **Explain** Why is it difficult to create a vaccine against the common cold?

▶ In Japan, people who are ill wear masks to prevent spreading germs. **How can you help prevent spreading cold viruses to other people?**

▲ Some people should get flu shots before each flu season including people 65 and older and anyone with a weakened immune system. **Why does the flu vaccine change every year?**

The Flu

Another common communicable disease is influenza, or the flu. **Influenza** is *a communicable disease characterized by fever, chills, fatigue, headache, muscle aches, and respiratory symptoms.* Flu symptoms usually affect you more quickly and more seriously than cold symptoms do. The flu can be spread through both direct and indirect contact. Most cases of the flu are reported from December through March, which is why that time is called "the flu season."

Flu viruses differ from the ones that cause colds. Each year, certain strains of the flu virus spread faster and are stronger than previous years. Scientists meet every year to figure out which strains will spread fastest during the next flu season. This planning allows them to make vaccines for the upcoming flu season. Some types of flu can be dangerous. Just after World War I, an outbreak of the flu killed about 20 million people throughout the world, including over 600,000 people in the United States. Scientists today worry that new strains of the flu virus, such as the avian flu, could also be deadly to large numbers of people.

Reading Check **Define** What is *influenza*?

Chicken Pox, Measles, and Mumps

Chicken pox, measles, and mumps are all contagious diseases caused by viruses. Every contagious disease has a contagious period. The **contagious period** is *the length of time that a particular disease can be spread from person to person.* Often, the contagious period includes a length of time before the infected person begins to show symptoms. Chicken pox, measles, and mumps all have well-defined contagious periods.

- **Chicken pox** is contagious for about a week before symptoms appear. Common symptoms of chicken pox include a rash, fever, and aching muscles. The rash shows up as small, red, itchy bumps on the skin. It may even appear inside the mouth and throat. The bumps develop into blisters. When the blisters dry up, chicken pox is not contagious anymore. The vaccine for chicken pox became available in 1995. Before then, almost all children got chicken pox. Now, about 80 percent of all U.S. children are vaccinated against chicken pox. The disease is much less common.

- **Measles** involves a rash, fever, and head and body aches. The contagious period starts a few days before symptoms

Connect To...
Social Studies

Diseases and History

Many diseases have shaped the course of history. For example, when early explorers arrived in North and South America, they brought European diseases such as smallpox and measles. The native people had no resistance to these new diseases. The pathogens spread quickly and killed many of them.

Research a disease that changed the course of history. Write a brief report on your findings.

begin. It lasts until about five days after that. Measles is a very dangerous disease. Around the world, over 1 million children die each year from measles. Over 90 percent of the children in the United States are vaccinated against measles, so fewer people get the disease now.

- **Mumps** causes a fever, headache, and swollen salivary glands. The contagious period for mumps starts about a week before symptoms begin. It lasts for about nine days after that point. Over 90 percent of the children in the United States are vaccinated against mumps. As a result, mumps is much less common than it used to be.

Fortunately, chicken pox, measles, and mumps are under control in the United States. Children routinely get vaccinated for each of these diseases. This protects them against these diseases.

Reading Check **Explain** Why are measles, mumps, and chicken pox much less common in the United States than they used to be?

Other Communicable Diseases

Many other communicable diseases are common around the world. The United States has good medical care and clean living conditions. As a result, people here are better protected from many of these diseases. However, some communicable diseases are still quite common here. Mononucleosis, hepatitis, tuberculosis, pneumonia, and strep throat are some of the communicable diseases that are common in the United States.

Mononucleosis

Mononucleosis (MAH·noh·nook·klee·OH·sis), or mono, is *a viral disease characterized by a severe sore throat and swelling of the lymph glands in the neck and around the throat area.* Symptoms may also include fatigue, loss of appetite, fever, and headache. Often called "the kissing disease," mono is spread when a person comes in contact with the saliva of an infected person. Contaminated eating utensils and drinking glasses can also spread the disease.

Hepatitis

Hepatitis (hep·uh·TY·tis) is *a viral disease characterized by an inflammation of the liver and yellowing of the skin and the whites of the eyes.* Other symptoms include

▼ When you cough, cover your mouth to prevent your saliva from escaping into the air. Saliva can carry pathogens that cause diseases such as pneumonia and strep throat. **What are two other ways that pathogens spread?**

weakness, fatigue, loss of appetite, fever, headaches, and sore throat. There are three common strains of hepatitis: A, B, and C. A different virus causes each strain.

Hepatitis A is common in areas with poor sanitation. It spreads among people when infected human wastes contaminate the food or water. When someone eats or drinks food or water that is contaminated, that person can become infected. People can also become infected if they have open wounds exposed to contaminated water.

Hepatitis B and C can permanently damage the liver and can lead to cirrhosis and liver cancer. They are most commonly spread through contact with contaminated blood or other contaminated body fluids. For example, hepatitis B and C can be spread when drug users share needles or through sexual contact. There are vaccines for hepatitis A and B. There are medications that can help treat hepatitis C.

Tuberculosis

Tuberculosis (too·ber·kyuh·LOH·sis), or TB, is *a bacterial disease that usually affects the lungs.* Symptoms include cough, fatigue, night sweats, fever, and weight loss. TB is spread through the air. When a person with TB coughs or sneezes, he or she sends infected droplets into the air. Another person then breathes them in. It is possible for a person to carry the bacteria that cause TB without showing symptoms. Even though these infected people do not get sick, they can spread the disease. Because of this, health care providers often test people to be sure they do not carry TB.

Reading Check

Describe Why are healthy people tested for TB?

Pneumonia

Pneumonia is *a serious inflammation of the lungs.* Symptoms include fever, cough, chills, and difficulty breathing. Either a virus or bacterium can cause pneumonia. Pneumonia can be spread through direct or indirect contact with an infected person. Bacterial pneumonia can be treated with antibiotics. People with pneumonia need rest and plenty of fluids. People who already have other diseases or who have weakened immune systems are at greater risk of getting pneumonia.

Strep Throat

Strep throat is *a sore throat caused by streptococcal bacteria.* Symptoms of strep throat include a red and painful throat, fever, and swollen lymph nodes in the neck. People who have strep throat may also experience headache, nausea, and vomiting. Strep throat is spread through direct or indirect contact with an infected person. Like many other diseases, strep throat is commonly spread through direct contact or when infected people breathe or cough droplets into the air. Medical professionals can diagnose strep throat by testing bacteria taken from an infected person's throat.

If you have a sore throat, tell a parent or guardian. The same goes for if you have a fever. You may have strep throat, and you will need to be treated. Since bacteria cause strep throat, you can take antibiotics for it. All cases of strep throat need medical attention. Left untreated, a person with strep throat can develop more serious problems. One example is rheumatic fever, a condition that can damage the heart. Another example, called nephritis, can damage the kidneys.

 Reading Check **Name** What are two symptoms of strep throat?

Visit **glencoe.com** and complete the Interactive Study Guide for Lesson 3.

Lesson 3 Review

 **After You Read**

Review this lesson for new terms, major headings, and Reading Checks.

What I Learned

1. *Vocabulary* Define *contagious period*.

2. *Give Examples* Name three childhood diseases that used to be common but are now under control in the United States.

3. *List* What are the symptoms of influenza?

4. *Explain* How is tuberculosis spread?

5. *Analyze* Why is it important to get treatment for communicable diseases like strep throat?

Thinking Critically

6. *Analyze* A study by the Aviation Health Institute shows that people who ride in a plane are seven times more likely to catch a cold than people who do not ride in an airplane during the same period. Suggest a reason for the difference. How might someone lower this risk?

7. *Evaluate* You see an ad on the Internet for a product that claims to cure the common cold. How can you analyze whether the ad is valid?

Applying Health Skills

8. *Practicing Healthful Behaviors* Write a short article about the importance of covering your mouth when you sneeze or cough and washing your hands frequently with soap. How can positive health behaviors like these help control the spread of disease?

Preventing the Spread of Disease

Guide to Reading

Building Vocabulary
In your own words, write a definition of *hygiene*.

■ hygiene (p. 418)

Focusing on the Main Ideas
In this lesson, you will be able to

■ **describe** how to protect yourself against pathogens.

■ **explain** how to avoid spreading pathogens to others when you are sick.

■ **identify** habits that can help you stay healthy.

■ **practice** a positive health behavior to prevent the spread of disease.

Reading Strategy
Finding the Main Idea Look at the main headings in this lesson. For each heading, write one sentence that explains the main idea.

uick Write

Write two ways that washing your hands with soap helps keep you and others healthy.

Keeping Pathogens from Spreading

By now, you understand that you can't avoid pathogens. However, you can develop good habits to protect yourself from them. Good personal **hygiene,** or *cleanliness,* helps limit the number of pathogens you encounter. Eating foods that are good for you, getting exercise, and sleeping well all help your body fight pathogens. Keeping your environment clean keeps the number of pathogens down, too.

▶ Wash dishes right after use to keep pathogens from growing on plates and eating utensils. **Why is it important to use warm, soapy water?**

Protecting Yourself from Pathogens

To keep yourself from getting sick, follow these guidelines:

- Avoid close contact with people who have a communicable disease, especially if they are still contagious.

- Never share eating utensils, cups, glasses, toothbrushes, or any other personal items.

- Wash your hands thoroughly and often, especially before you prepare and eat food. Use plenty of warm, soapy water. Remember to wash your hands after you use the bathroom, play with pets, visit a sick person, or touch garbage or any other source of pathogens.

- Keep your fingers and hands away from your mouth, nose, and eyes. Don't bite your nails.

- Handle and prepare food safely. This is especially important for meat, poultry, and fish. Wash vegetables and fruits and cook meat thoroughly.

- Wipe counters thoroughly. Use paper towels and spray disinfectants. Using sponges and cloths repeatedly can actually spread more germs than it removes.

- Empty the trash often. Keep trash cans clean.

- Keep pets clean and healthy. Clean up after your pet.

▼ Keeping yourself and your environment clean is one way to stay safe and healthy. **How might emptying out the trash often help keep you healthy?**

Reading Check **Identify** When should you remember to wash your hands?

Protecting Others from Pathogens

When you're sick, help protect the people around you. Think ahead, and take these safety measures.

- If you feel sick, tell a parent or guardian. This person can help you get the medical help you need as soon as possible. If you are sick at school, tell a teacher or the school nurse as soon as you can. Early treatment helps keep your condition from getting worse. It also limits the number of people who are exposed to whatever is making you sick.

- If you are ill, stay home from school and other public places. You don't want to expose others to your illness. Avoid close contact with others, too. Wash your hands often.

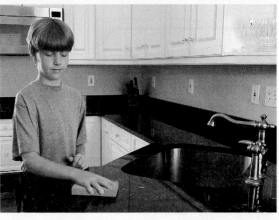

Health Skills Activity

Practicing Healthful Behaviors

Wash Your Hands!

Every time you rub your eyes, touch your face, or cut your finger, you risk exposing your body to pathogens. One of the best ways to block pathogens from entering your body is to keep your hands clean. You may think you do a good job of this. However, if you just splash water on your hands and wipe them on a towel, you aren't doing enough. This simple action isn't enough to kill pathogens.

Here's how to wash your hands the right way.

1. Wet your hands with warm water and apply soap.
2. Rub your hands together vigorously. Scrub all parts of your hands for 30 seconds or more.
3. Rinse your hands well. If you are using a public restroom, use a paper towel to turn the water off.
4. Dry your hands using a clean towel or a paper towel. If you are using a public restroom, use the paper towel you dried your hands with to open the door when you leave. (This will help you avoid getting any pathogens from the doorknob on your clean hands.)

With a Group

Without looking at a clock, pretend to wash your hands for what you think is at least 30 seconds. Have another member of the group time you. Create a graph showing how well each member of the group estimated the time.

G Online

Visit **glencoe.com** and complete the Interactive Study Guide for Lesson 4.

- Cover your mouth and nose when you sneeze. Turn your head away from others when you cough and sneeze, too. Use a tissue only once, and throw it away in a proper place. What if you don't have a tissue? Sneeze or cough into the crook of your elbow rather than your hand. You'll be less likely to spread germs to items you touch.

- If a medical professional has told you to take medicine, follow the directions on the label exactly. Take all the medicine you are supposed to take. Don't stop taking a medicine because you feel better. If you do, it might be too soon. You could get sick again.

Explain When you are sick, why should you tell your parents or guardians right away?

A Healthful Lifestyle

The more healthful choices you make, the more likely that you will stay well. Here are some positive health practices that you can develop.

- Eat a balanced diet.

- Bathe or shower regularly using soap and shampoo.

- Avoid all tobacco products, alcohol, and other drugs.

- Get 8–9 hours of sleep every day.

- Rest when you are sick.

- Ask a parent or guardian to make sure that your immunizations are up to date.

- Learn to manage stress. Too much stress can weaken your immune system.

- Visit the doctor regularly for routine checkups. Follow any advice your doctor gives you.

▲ You make choices every day that affect your health. Choosing a healthful diet can help keep your immune system strong. **What other choices can you make that will help keep you healthy?**

 **Reading Check**

Identify Name five healthful habits that can help you stay well.

Lesson 4 Review

 After You Read

Review this lesson for new terms, major headings, and Reading Checks.

What I Learned

1. *Vocabulary* Define *hygiene,* and use the term in a sentence.

2. *Describe* How can staying home when you are sick help keep others healthy?

3. *Identify* What are three strategies for protecting yourself from pathogens?

Thinking Critically

4. *Explain* Why do you think you should keep your trash can clean?

5. *Apply* Turtles and other reptiles carry salmonella. This bacteria often makes people sick if they ingest it. What would be a good way to make sure you don't get sick from your friend's pet turtle?

Applying Health Skills

6. *Practicing Healthful Behaviors* Carlos wakes up with a scratchy throat and a stuffy nose. His friends are expecting him to play in the soccer game after school, and Carlos doesn't want to let them down. What should Carlos do?

Lesson 5

Sexually Transmitted Diseases

Guide to Reading

● Building Vocabulary
Write down each term below. As you come across it in your reading, write the definition.

- sexually transmitted diseases (p. 422)
- chlamydia (p. 423)
- genital warts (p. 423)
- genital herpes (p. 423)
- trichomoniasis (p. 424)
- gonorrhea (p. 424)
- syphilis (p. 424)
- hepatitis B (p. 425)

● Focusing on the Main Ideas
In this lesson, you will be able to

- **identify** common sexually transmitted diseases.
- **explain** how to protect yourself from sexually transmitted diseases.
- **access** valid information about sexually transmitted diseases.

● Reading Strategy
Organizing Information Create a three-column table like the one shown below. As you read the lesson, write the names of the sexually transmitted diseases that you read about in the first column. In the next column, write down the symptoms and effects of the diseases. In the last column, write down how to prevent the sexually transmitted diseases.

STD	Symptoms and Effects	Prevention

uick Write

Write down one or two facts you know about sexually transmitted diseases.

What Are Sexually Transmitted Diseases?

Sexually transmitted diseases (STDs) are *infections that are spread from person to person through sexual contact*. STDs are also called sexually transmitted infections (STIs). In this lesson, you will learn more about STDs, their causes, and how to prevent them. **Figure 13.5** tells you some important facts about STDs.

Common STDs

STDs include a wide range of diseases. All these are passed on to partners who engage in sexual activity. All affect both men and women. The good news about STDs is that they are completely preventable. The bad news is that most STDs are found in young people, ages 15-24. Some common STDs are described on the next pages.

THE STD FACT FILE

When you know the facts about STDs, you have the power to avoid them.
What is the best way to avoid getting STDs?

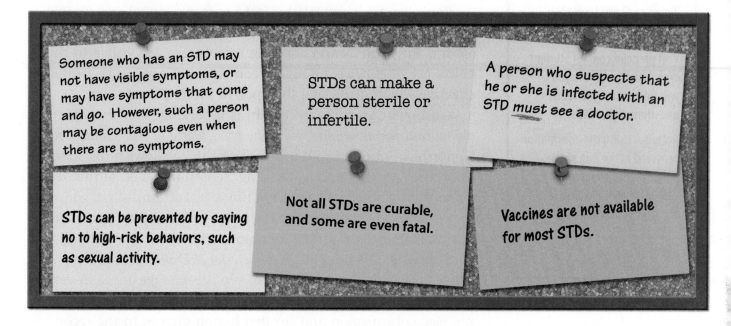

Someone who has an STD may not have visible symptoms, or may have symptoms that come and go. However, such a person may be contagious even when there are no symptoms.

STDs can make a person sterile or infertile.

A person who suspects that he or she is infected with an STD must see a doctor.

STDs can be prevented by saying no to high-risk behaviors, such as sexual activity.

Not all STDs are curable, and some are even fatal.

Vaccines are not available for most STDs.

Chlamydia (kluh·MI·dee·uh) is *a bacterial STD that may affect the reproductive organs, urethra, and anus.* Chlamydia is often referred to as a "silent" disease because in many cases there are no symptoms; a person can have it and not know that he or she does. When symptoms do occur, they can include genital discharge and pain when urinating. Left untreated, chlamydia can cause other infections in the body and infertility. Chlamydia can be treated with antibiotics.

Genital warts are *growths or bumps in the genital area caused by certain types of human papillomavirus (HPV).* HPV infections are the most common type of STD in the United States. Like chlamydia, HPV is often a silent disease, causing no obvious symptoms until many years after the **initial** infection. The warts can be treated, but there is no cure for the HPV infection itself. Some strains of HPV are linked to the development of cervical cancer. A vaccine has been developed to protect females against these strains of the HPV virus.

Genital herpes (HER·peez) is *a viral STD that produces painful blisters on the genital area.* Herpes often does not cause any obvious symptoms for many years. Some people have periodic outbreaks of painful blisters or sores. Even when the symptoms go away, the virus remains in the body. Other symptoms include pain in the lower genital area and genital discharge. There is no known cure for genital herpes, but medication can reduce the frequency of outbreaks.

Academic Vocabulary

initial (in ISH ul) *(adjective)* the beginning or first. *Sometimes there are no symptoms in the initial stages of certain diseases.*

▼ Millions of cases of STDs occur each year in the United States. **What can be done to stop the spread of these diseases?**

Trichomoniasis (TREE·koh·moh·NI·ah·sis) is *an STD caused by the protozoan* Trichomonas vaginalis. The disease may be silent, but symptoms can include vaginal discharge, discomfort during urination, and irritation or itching in the genital area. Trichomoniasis can be treated and cured with medications.

Pubic lice are insects that infect a person's genital area. People sometimes call pubic lice "crabs." Symptoms include itching around the genitals and crawling insects that are visible to the naked eye. Pubic lice are highly contagious. They can be treated effectively with medicated shampoo or prescription lotion.

Gonorrhea (gahn·uh·REE·uh) is *a bacterial STD that affects the mucous membranes of the body, particularly in the genital area.* Gonorrhea symptoms often include a thick yellowish discharge from the genitals and a burning sensation when urinating. Gonorrhea can be treated with antibiotics. Left untreated, gonorrhea can infect other parts of the body, including the joints and heart. It can also cause fertility problems.

Syphilis (SIH·fuh·luhs) is *a bacterial STD that can affect many parts of the body.* The symptoms of syphilis change as the disease progresses. Symptoms of the first stage include painless sores at the place of infection and swollen lymph glands. In the second stage, the bacteria can cause a severe rash. During late stages of syphilis, the bacteria move throughout the body. They can cause damage to many body organs, including the brain. Untreated disease can eventually cause mental disorders, heart problems, blindness, and death. If diagnosed and treated in the first or second stage, syphilis can be cured with antibiotics.

KNOWLEDGE

PREVENTS HIV. FIGHTS AIDS. CURES HOPELESSNESS.

KNOW HIV▸AIDS

Health Skills Activity

Accessing Information

Finding Information About STDs

How can you find valid information about diseases or medical conditions? First, talk to your parents, guardians, or family doctor about any medical concerns you have. You can also learn more about a disease by doing your own research. Medical journals and scientific publications have strict rules about the information they publish. They are valid sources of information.

Finding valid health information on the Internet is a little trickier. Be sure that the source of any information you find online is an expert on the subject you are reading about. A good place to start is the information found at the Centers for Disease Control and Prevention and the National Institutes of Health.

On Your Own

Research one of the STDs from this lesson. Find out more about the symptoms, effects, and any treatments for the disease. Prepare a short report on your findings.

Hepatitis B is *a disease caused by the hepatitis B virus that affects the liver.* It can be transmitted by sexual contact or through contaminated needles. There is a vaccine available for hepatitis B.

Human immunodeficiency virus (HIV) infection is an STD covered in Lesson 6. There is no cure for HIV infection.

Anyone who has had sexual contact with another person may have an STD and not know it. The only sure way to avoid getting an STD is to practice abstinence from sexual activity.

Abstinence from Sexual Activity

You cannot tell by looking at people if they have an STD. The only 100 percent effective way to avoid STDs is to abstain from sexual activity. Often, the media send the message that sexual activity is exciting, yet there is no mention of the risks. Engaging in sexual activity before marriage puts teens at risk for STDs and unplanned pregnancy. It can lead to social and emotional problems. Refusal skills can help teens avoid being pressured to take part in sexual activity.

It's normal to have sexual feelings when you are a teen. Talking about these feelings with a parent, guardian, or other trusted adult can help you deal with them. It also helps you understand your family's values and what your parents expect of you.

► Being a responsible teen involves upholding the values of your family. **How does abstinence from sexual activity show that you are responsible?**

Visit **glencoe.com** and complete the Interactive Study Guide for Lesson 5.

This doesn't mean you have to hide feelings of affection for others. You can share these feelings in ways that don't risk your health or compromise values. Appropriate ways for teens to show affection include holding hands and giving small gifts. Practicing abstinence pays off in many ways. You can be sure that your relationships are built on shared interests and trust, rather than on sexual attraction.

By practicing abstinence from sexual activity until marriage, you protect yourself against unplanned pregnancy and STDs. You get to know someone in a way that goes beyond physical attraction. You show respect for the wishes of your family. You can remain committed to your long-term goals, such as education, career, and family.

Lesson 5 Review

 After You Read

Review this lesson for new terms, major headings, and Reading Checks.

What I Learned

1. *Vocabulary* Define *sexually transmitted disease.*

2. *Explain* Why are some STDs referred to as "silent" diseases?

3. *List* What are two consequences of untreated chlamydia?

4. *Apply* What is the best way to avoid STDs?

5. *Explain* What are some appropriate ways for teens to show affection?

Thinking Critically

6. *Analyze* How do values influence a person's decision to practice sexual abstinence until marriage?

Applying Health Skills

7. *Advocacy* Create a pamphlet that warns teens of the dangers of STDs. In your pamphlet, explain that many STDs cause harm without showing symptoms for a long time. Also discuss how sexual abstinence keeps teens safe and healthy.

Go Online For more Lesson Review Activities, go to **glencoe.com**.

Lesson 6

HIV/AIDS

Guide to Reading

● **Building Vocabulary**
Explain the relationship between the two vocabulary terms below.

- HIV (human immunodeficiency virus) (p. 427)
- AIDS (acquired immunodeficiency syndrome) (p. 427)

● **Focusing on the Main Ideas**
In this lesson, you will be abe to·

- **explain** how people become infected with HIV and develop AIDS.
- **explain** what is being done to fight AIDS.
- **analyze** how media messages about sexual activity might influence teens.
- **describe** how to protect yourself from HIV/AIDS.

● **Reading Strategy**
Identifying Problems and Solutions After reading this lesson, identify how HIV is transmitted and what can be done to prevent the spread of HIV.

uick Write

Write a response to this question: What would happen if the cells that control your immune responses began to be destroyed?

What Are HIV and AIDS?

HIV (human immunodeficiency virus) is *the virus that causes AIDS.* **AIDS (acquired immunodeficiency syndrome)** is *a disease that interferes with the body's ability to fight infection.* In Lesson 2, you learned how the immune system fights disease. You learned that T cells coordinate the body's response to infections. HIV is especially dangerous because it attacks and kills T cells. As a result, the immune system cannot fight HIV or any other infection. HIV does not kill all the T cells immediately. An infected person can have the virus for years without showing any signs or symptoms. Nevertheless, once a person is infected with HIV, the virus begins damaging the person's immune system. Infected people can also spread the disease to others. **Figure 13.6** details how HIV attacks the immune system.

The Spread of HIV

HIV is not transmitted through casual contact. It is transmitted in one of the following ways:

- **Having any form of sexual intercourse with an infected person.** The most common way that HIV spreads from one person to another is through sexual intercourse. HIV circulates in the bloodstream and in other body fluids, such as semen and vaginal fluid. When people have sexual

HOW HIV ATTACKS THE BODY

HIV cripples the immune system by killing the T cells that control immune responses. What kinds of diseases eventually harm people who have AIDS?

1 The virus enters the body through the mucous membranes or a break in the skin. HIV invades a host cell, a T cell, using the cell's resources to make copies of itself. When that T cell is activated, it will start producing more of the virus instead of performing T cell functions. Eventually, the host cells are destroyed.

KEY

🦠 HIV

Ⓣ T cell

🌀 Pathogens

2 These viruses infect other T cells and multiply. These infected T cells are destroyed, and more copies of the virus are released.

3 More and more T cells are infected and destroyed. Without T cells to control the immune response, the body loses its ability to fight diseases and infections.

intercourse, the virus can be transmitted from one person to the other. The virus circulates in a person's body even before it destroys the immune system. Many people who are infected with HIV do not know they have the virus. Even so, they can still infect other people. *Abstinence from sexual activity is the only sure way to protect yourself against this method of transmission.*

- **Using a contaminated needle.** A single drop of blood left on a needle can contain enough HIV to infect someone. Never inject yourself with any illegal drugs. Contaminated needles used for tattooing and body piercing can also **transmit** the virus. People with diabetes and others who need to use needles should do so strictly under the care of a medical professional.

- **Other modes of transmission.** A pregnant female can transmit HIV to her child during delivery or through breast milk. Expectant mothers with HIV can take medicine to help reduce the chances of transmission during pregnancy and delivery. Before HIV was known to be the cause of AIDS, people sometimes became infected with HIV during blood transfusions. Since 1985, all blood is carefully screened for HIV. The United States blood supply is considered to be extremely safe.

Academic Vocabulary

transmit (TRANS mit) *(verb)* to spread or transfer from one person or place to another. *Sneezing or coughing without covering your mouth can transmit germs to people nearby.*

How HIV Is NOT Spread

HIV is a dangerous virus, but it is NOT spread through casual contact. You cannot get HIV or AIDS in any of the following ways.

- swimming in a pool with an infected person
- sharing utensils with an infected person
- breathing the air near an infected person
- donating blood
- being bitten by a mosquito that has bitten an infected person
- hugging or shaking hands with an infected person
- using the same shower, bathtub, or toilet as an infected person
- sharing sports equipment with an infected person

You don't have to avoid people with HIV and AIDS. In fact, people with HIV and AIDS deserve the same respect, kindness, and consideration you give to everyone you meet.

 **Reading Check** **List** What are some ways that HIV cannot be transmitted?

ACTIVITY
DEVELOPING
Good Character

Caring

Practicing abstinence from sexual activity until marriage and avoiding illegal drug use, especially the use of injectable drugs, will help protect you from HIV infection.

How does avoiding these risk behaviors show that you care about yourself and others? Write your answer in a brief paragraph.

Fighting AIDS

Around the world, HIV infection and AIDS remain a huge problem. In Africa, for example, millions of adults have died from AIDS. As a result, millions of children do not have parents. In the United States, more than 14,000 people die every year from AIDS. In many countries around the world, scientists and educators work to prevent HIV infection by teaching as many people as they can about the disease.

▼ The AIDS quilt is a memorial to people who have died of AIDS. Each square represents one person who died from the disease. **What can you learn from seeing the AIDS quilt?**

Health Skills Activity

Analyzing Influences

Media Messages About Sexual Activity

Teens have many influences in their lives. Families, friends, movies, music, books, magazines, and the Internet all influence what teens think and how they act. Popular cultural messages often glamorize sexual activity. They may lead teens to believe that sexual activity is an acceptable way to express affection. However, sexual activity also exposes teens to STDs, including HIV. Try to recognize the messages aimed at you so that you can make positive health choices for yourself.

In a Group

Review some magazines aimed at teens. Find ads that show teens together. What kinds of behaviors are the ads suggesting? Are the suggested behaviors healthful ones? Do the ads seem to encourage sexual activity for teens? Make a list of the messages you find in ads. Then make a list of messages that would be more positive and healthful for teens.

With the development of safe and effective drugs, people with HIV are now able to live longer and healthier lives. These drugs are not a cure for HIV. They work together to slow the progress of the disease by preventing HIV from reproducing. However, many of these drugs have side effects and are very expensive. There is also some evidence that some drugs are losing their ability to treat HIV. As HIV is exposed to the new drugs, the virus is changing in ways that make the drugs ineffective.

Scientists are also working on a vaccine against HIV. However, their progress has been very slow. Because there are several forms of HIV, vaccines that work on one form might not work on another. A single vaccine that protects people against HIV is possible, but it will likely take many more years to develop.

Battling HIV infection is difficult and expensive. That's why scientists and educators work very hard to help people keep from becoming infected in the first place. The best weapon in the fight against HIV and AIDS so far has been knowledge. When people learn how HIV is spread, they can take steps to avoid getting it.

Visit glencoe.com and complete the Interactive Study Guide for Lesson 6.

Explain Why has progress on developing an HIV vaccine been slow?

Abstinence and HIV

AIDS is a disease that still has no cure. You are protecting yourself against HIV infection when you abstain from sexual activity until marriage and avoid sharing needles.

People who inject illegal drugs face many risks. They risk the dangers of the drugs they inject. Also, they risk exposing themselves to diseases. People who share needles expose themselves to any diseases that the other people who have used that needle may have.

Similarly, when people engage in sexual activity, they are exposing themselves to any STDs that their partner may have. The more sexual partners a person has, the more likely it is that the person will become infected with an STD such as HIV.

The only 100 percent sure way to avoid getting HIV is to avoid contact with sources of this virus. This means abstaining from sexual activity until marriage and avoiding injecting drugs and sharing needles. If you are pressured to use injectable drugs or engage in sexual activity, talk to your parents, guardians, or a trusted adult. Use your refusal skills. Stay away from people who encourage you to make dangerous choices. Abstinence from sexual activity is the responsible choice for teens. It could save your life.

▲ Abstinence from sexual activity helps protect you from HIV and other STDs, as well as many other problems. It also lets you spend more enjoyable and safe times with friends. **What are three activities that are fun and safe for you?**

Lesson 6 Review

 After You Read

Review this lesson for new terms, major headings, and Reading Checks.

What I Learned

1. *Vocabulary* Define *HIV* and *AIDS*.

2. *Identify* How is AIDS related to HIV?

3. *Give Examples* People are often mistaken about how HIV is transmitted. Name four ways HIV is not transmitted.

4. *Describe* What happens to T cells that are infected with HIV?

Thinking Critically

5. *Analyze* Why is HIV an especially dangerous virus?

6. *Apply* Many people who have HIV do not know that they are infected with the virus. How can this be?

Applying Health Skills

7. *Advocacy* Create a pamphlet that shows teens how to protect themselves against HIV infection.

Building Health Skills

Accessing Information

Practicing Healthful Behaviors

Stress Management

Analyzing Influences

Communication Skills

Refusal Skills

Conflict Resolution

Decision Making

Goal Setting

Advocacy

What Does Accessing Information Involve?

Accessing information involves finding reliable information to make healthy choices. When looking at a source of information, ask yourself these questions:

- Is it scientific?
- Does it give more than one point of view?
- Does it agree with other sources?
- Is it trying to sell something?

Finding the Facts About Disease

Follow the Model, Practice, and Apply steps to help you master this important health skill.

❶ Model

Read how Eric uses the skill of accessing information to prepare for a camping trip.

Eric's family planned to rent a cottage in one of the national parks for vacation. A week before they left, Eric saw a news program about flooding in the area. The program explained that water supplies had become contaminated. It did not say whether or not people needed to take special safety measures.

Eric went to the park's Web site and learned about the pathogens found in the water. Next, he checked out a medical site and two government sites that gave information about the pathogens. He learned that boiling the water for three minutes would kill the pathogens. When his family left for the park, they felt confident that they would be safe on their trip.

❷ Practice

Trevor wants to find reliable information about colds. Read the passage below and then practice the skill of accessing information by answering the questions that follow.

When Trevor's sister caught a cold, the entire family was careful about not spreading germs. Trevor told his friend Randy not to come over until his sister was better. However, Randy told him not to worry. A cold was not contagious after the first three days. Trevor wondered if Randy was a reliable source of information.

1. Do you think Randy's information was accurate? Why or why not?

2. What is Randy trying to accomplish by what he told Trevor?

3. Locate three sources that Trevor can use to find reliable information about colds.

❸ Apply

Apply what you have learned about accessing reliable information by completing the activity below.

Find out how flu vaccines are created and how well they work. Use at least three different sources of information to research this topic. These sources might include magazines, newspapers, books, printed materials, the Internet, and trusted adults. Analyze whether each source is valid. Then write a one-page report on your findings. In your report, explain what you found out about flu vaccines. Also, tell why you think your sources are accurate.

Self-Check

- Did I use at least three different sources of information?
- Did I write a one-page report on my findings?
- Did I explain why I believe each source is accurate?

Building
Health Skills

The good news: Few germs actually cause great harm. The bad news: The ones that do can be really dangerous—even deadly. Here's how to stay healthy.

GERM SURVIVAL GUIDE

The word *germs* refers to a wide range of organisms, including bacteria, viruses, and fungi. Luckily, the helpful germs in your body outnumber the bad ones. They perform many important tasks, such as helping your intestines to digest food. However, there are also germs that can cause stomachaches, colds, or more serious diseases. The tips below can help protect you from those microscopic bad guys.

Wash your hands—often. Be sure to suds up before preparing food or eating it, after using the bathroom, and after sneezing or coughing into your hands. Wash for a full 30 seconds—about as long as it takes to sing "Happy Birthday" twice.

Take good care of yourself. The healthier you are, the better chance you have of fighting off bad germs. Get enough sleep, drink plenty of water, eat a variety of fruits and vegetables, and exercise regularly. In addition, stay away from tobacco use: It weakens the body's natural defenses.

Avoid touching your nose and eyes. Most people tend to do so more than 20 times a day, but the nose and eyes are the spots where cold viruses and other germs usually enter the body.

Cover up cuts with a bandage. Dab on a little antibacterial ointment while you're at it, or use a bandage that has antibiotic ointment built in. This will help protect and heal an open wound, another place germs can enter the body.

Carry alcohol-based hand sanitizers in your school bag. They work faster than soap and kill bacteria more efficiently, without encouraging antibacterial-resistant germ strains.

Keep pets healthy. Cats and dogs can carry germs that are easily transmitted to humans. Make sure your pets' immunizations are up-to-date and that the animals are groomed regularly. Wash your hands after touching pets.

CHAPTER 13

Reading Review

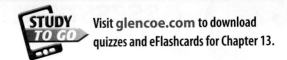

FOLDABLES Study Organizer

Foldables® and Other Study Aids Take out the Foldable® you created for Lesson 1 and any graphic organizers that you created for Lessons 1–6. Find a partner and quiz each other using these study aids.

Lesson 1 What Are Communicable Diseases?

Main Idea Communicable diseases are diseases that can spread from one person to another.

- Communicable diseases are caused by pathogens, such as viruses, bacteria, fungi, and protozoa.

Lesson 2 The Immune System

Main Idea The immune system has two responses to pathogens that invade the body: the nonspecific response and the specific response.

- Tears, saliva, skin, mucous membranes, and stomach acid are barriers that help keep pathogens out of your body.

Lesson 3 Common Communicable Diseases

Main Idea Common communicable diseases include colds, the flu, chicken pox, measles, mumps, mononucleosis, hepatitis, tuberculosis, pneumonia, and strep throat.

- Viruses cause both colds and the flu. They have similar symptoms, but a case of the flu is more severe.

- Every communicable disease has a contagious period, a period of time that a disease can be spread from person to person.

Lesson 4 Preventing the Spread of Disease

Main Idea Practicing good personal hygiene and other healthful behaviors can protect you from pathogens.

- Staying home and taking care of yourself when you have a communicable disease can help keep you from spreading pathogens to others.

Lesson 5 Sexually Transmitted Diseases

Main Idea Sexually transmitted diseases (STDs) are infections spread through sexual contact.

- Common STDs include chlamydia, genital warts, genital herpes, trichomoniasis, gonorrhea, syphilis, and hepatitis B.

- Abstinence from sexual activity until marriage is the best way to avoid STDs.

Lesson 6 HIV/AIDS

Main Idea HIV causes acquired immunodeficiency syndrome (AIDS), a deadly disease that interferes with the body's immune system.

- HIV is transmitted mostly through sexual intercourse and sharing needles. It is not transmitted through casual contact such as hugging or shaking hands.

- Treatments are available to help manage an HIV infection, but there is no cure.

Assessment

 After You Read

HEALTH QUIZ

Now that you have read the chapter, review your answers to the Health Quiz on the chapter opener. Have any of them changed? What are your answers now?

Reviewing Vocabulary and Main Ideas

On a sheet of paper, write the numbers 1–7. After each number, write the term from the list that best completes each statement.

- bacteria
- immune system
- lymphatic system
- influenza
- hepatitis
- viruses
- vaccine
- contagious period

Lesson 1 What Are Communicable Diseases?

1. The smallest and simplest pathogens are called _____.

2. _____ are simple one-celled organisms.

Lesson 2 The Immune System

3. The _____ is a combination of body defenses made up of the cells, tissues, and organs that fight pathogens.

4. The _____ is a second circulatory system that helps the body fight pathogens and maintain its fluid balance.

5. A preparation of dead or weakened pathogens that is introduced into the body to cause an immune response is called a _____.

Lesson 3 Common Communicable Diseases

6. Most cases of _____ are reported from December through March.

7. The _____ of a disease is the length of time that a particular disease can be spread from person to person.

Lesson 4 Preventing the Spread of Disease

On a sheet of paper, write the number 8 and write the letter of the answer that best completes the statement.

8. Hygiene is another word for _____.

   a. cleanliness.

   b. antibodies.

   c. antigens.

*On a sheet of paper, write the numbers 9–14. Write **True** or **False** for each statement below. If the statement is false, change the underlined word or phrase to make it true.*

Lesson 5 Sexually Transmitted Diseases

9. <u>Abstinence from</u> sexual activity is the best way to avoid getting an STD.

10. Chlamydia <u>cannot</u> be treated.

11. If left untreated, syphilis is <u>fatal</u>.

Lesson 6 HIV/AIDS

12. HIV is the virus that causes <u>hepatitis</u>.

13. People <u>can</u> become infected with HIV from sharing eating utensils.

14. A vaccine for HIV <u>is</u> currently available.

Go Online Visit glencoe.com and take the Online Quiz for Chapter 13.

Thinking Critically

Using complete sentences, answer the following questions on a sheet of paper.

15. **Inferring** Many people who have AIDS actually die of pneumonia. Why do other diseases kill people who have AIDS?

16. **Interpret** Sometimes, after you get a vaccination, you also get a "booster shot" years later. A booster shot is another dose of the vaccine. Why do you think you might need a booster shot?

Write About It

17. **Expository Writing** Write an article about STDs for the school paper. Explain how people become infected.

~ Applying Technology

Communicable Diseases

Using PowerPoint®, create data cards that share your understanding of communicable diseases and how they are spread.

- Working in pairs or triads, open a new PowerPoint® project and name it.
- Create 14 slides using the following categories (2 slides per category): *Communicable Diseases, Pathogens, Colds/Flu, STDs, HIV/AIDS, Immune System,* and *Preventing the Spread of Disease.*
- Add short open-ended questions and answers to each slide.
- Include brief background information in the *notes* section of each slide.
- Use the game format to review the individual slides and test students' knowledge of communicable diseases.

Standardized Test Practice

Reading

Read the passage to answer the questions.

During the Middle Ages, the bubonic plague killed many people in a short period of time. The pathogen for the plague is a bacterium called *Yersinia pestis.* The bacteria lived inside fleas. The fleas lived on rats. The fleas infected the rats by biting them. Uninfected fleas that bit infected rats could also become infected. Fleas jumped from rat to rat and spread the plague quickly. When a rat got the plague, it died. As the disease swept through the rat populations in cities, many rats died off. As rats became scarce, more and more infected fleas began living on and biting humans. People became hosts for the plague. From the years 1347 to 1350, the plague killed one-third of the population of Europe.

1. What is the main point of the passage?
   A. to explain how bacteria kill fleas
   B. to explain how the population of Europe became so low
   C. to explain how to prevent the plague from killing people
   D. to explain how the plague killed so many people so quickly

2. What does *pathogen* mean in this sentence from the passage?
   The pathogen for the plague is a bacterium called *Yersinia pestis.*
   A. disease-causing germ
   B. disease symptom
   C. name of disease
   D. route of infection

TEST-TAKING TIP

When questions ask for the main point of the passage, reread the first and last sentences of the passage. Authors often put the most important information in the first and last sentences.

Chapter Preview

Lesson 1 Allergies and Asthma 440

Lesson 2 Heart Disease 446

Lesson 3 Cancer 451

Lesson 4 Diabetes and Arthritis.....458

Building Health Skills........................ 464

Hands-on Health 466

Chapter Reading Review.................. 467

Chapter Assessment 468

▲ *Working with the Photo*

A disabled person can lead a happy, active life. **What activities do you think this person enjoys doing?**

Start-Up Activities

📖 **Before You Read** What do you do to prevent disease? Take the short health survey below. Keep a record of your answers.

HEALTH INVENTORY

1. I participate in physical activity that helps my heart.
(a) always   (b) sometimes   (c) never

2. I apply sunscreen before going outdoors.
(a) always   (b) sometimes   (c) never

3. I eat a variety of fruits and vegetables each day.
(a) always   (b) sometimes   (c) never

FOLDABLES® Study Organizer

📖 **As You Read** Make this Foldable® to help you organize what you learn about allergies and asthma. Begin with a plain sheet of 11" × 17" paper.

1 Fold a sheet of paper in half along the short axis, then fold in half again. This forms four columns.

3 Unfold and draw lines along the folds.

2 Open the paper and refold it into thirds along the long axis. This forms three rows.

4 Label the chart as shown.

Noncomm. Diseases	Causes	Effects	Treatment
Allergies			
Asthma			

Fill out the chart as you read lesson 1.

G͡e Online   Visit **glencoe.com** and use the eFlashcards to preview Chapter 14 vocabulary terms.

Allergies and Asthma

📖 **Guide to Reading**

● **Building Vocabulary**
As you read this lesson, write each new highlighted term and its definition.

- noncommunicable disease (p. 440)
- chronic (p. 440)
- allergy (p.441)
- allergens (p. 441)
- pollen (p. 441)
- histamines (p. 442)
- antihistamines (p. 443)
- asthma (p. 443)
- bronchodilators (p. 445)

● **Focusing on the Main Ideas**
In this lesson, you will be able to

- **identify** causes of noncommunicable diseases.
- **describe** what allergies are and how they are treated.
- **describe** what asthma is and how it is treated.
- **practice** healthful behaviors to manage asthma.

● **Reading Strategy**
Skimming Look over all the headings of the lesson. Looking over the major and minor headings will give you an idea of what the lesson is about. Write down three main ideas of the lesson that you learned from skimming the headings.

FOLDABLES Study Organizer Use the Foldable® on p. 439 as you read this lesson.

**uick Write**

Write a sentence or two describing some of the symptoms of allergies.

What Are Noncommunicable Diseases?

When Jenna is at her friend Tracy's house, her eyes get red and itchy and she starts to sneeze. Why? Jenna is allergic to Tracy's cat. An allergy is one example of a **noncommunicable disease,** *a disease that cannot be spread from person to person.* Some noncommunicable diseases are chronic. **Chronic** diseases are *present continuously on and off over a long period of time.*

Causes of Noncommunicable Diseases

Some noncommunicable diseases, such as rheumatoid arthritis and Alzheimer's disease, have no known cause. However, scientists do know what causes many noncommunicable diseases.

People may be born with some diseases. Hereditary factors cause some diseases including cystic fibrosis and sickle cell anemia. Babies may be born with other diseases that result from problems before or during birth.

People may choose unhealthful behaviors. For example, smoking causes most cases of lung cancer. Eating high-fat foods is linked to many cases of heart disease.

The environment can cause some diseases or make others worse. For example, air pollution is an environmental factor linked to disease. Breathing polluted air can worsen respiratory problems such as asthma, emphysema, bronchitis, and even lung cancer.

 **Reading Check** **Identify** Name three causes of noncommunicable diseases.

What Are Allergies?

Your immune system keeps you healthy as it helps your body fight off foreign substances. However, some people's immune systems react to fairly harmless substances. These reactions are allergic responses. An **allergy** is *an extreme sensitivity to a substance.* Between 40 million and 50 million Americans are affected by allergies.

Substances that cause allergic responses are called **allergens.** For example, people who are allergic to ragweed are allergic to the tiny pollen grains from the ragweed plant. **Pollen** is *a powdery substance released by the flowers of some plants.* **Figure 14.1** shows some common allergens.

▲ When smog is especially heavy, people with asthma or other respiratory conditions should limit their time and activities outdoors. **What other environmental factors can cause disease?**

▼ **FIGURE 14.1**

COMMON ALLERGENS

Many different substances can be allergens. Some are easier to avoid than others. **How could you avoid each of these allergens?**

Pollen

Insect bites or stings

Food

Plants such as poison ivy

Allergic Reactions

When you are allergic to something, your immune system reacts quickly. It thinks that your body is under attack! In order to protect your body, your immune system produces antibodies to the allergen. Antibodies are a special kind of protein that locks onto cells. Antibodies cause certain cells in the body to release **histamines** (HIS·tuh·meenz), *the chemicals that the immune cells release to draw more blood and lymph to the area affected by the allergen.* Histamines cause the symptoms of the allergic reaction. When you are exposed to the same allergen again, the same antibody response will occur. You'll have an allergic reaction every time you come into contact with that allergen.

Allergic reactions can be mild, like sneezing or a runny nose. Although they are uncomfortable, they are harmless. Other allergic reactions such as swelling of the throat can be life threatening. **Figure 14.2** shows some common allergic reactions. Learning how to control your allergies will help you avoid or reduce the symptoms of allergic reactions.

▼ FIGURE 14.2

COMMON ALLERGIC REACTIONS

Common allergic reactions vary depending on the allergen. Different people may also react differently to the same allergen. Which of the allergic reactions listed here do you think is the most serious?

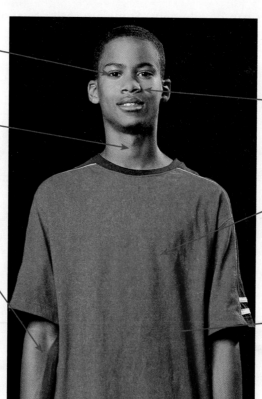

Eyes can be red, watery, and itchy.

Throat can become irritated and swollen. With severe swelling the throat can close shut.

Skin can become irritated and break out in a rash or hives (itchy bumps).

Nose can be runny and irritated. Sneezing is common.

Respiratory system can become irritated. May lead to coughing and difficulty breathing.

Digestive system can be upset. Cramping, stomach pains, and diarrhea are common.

Managing Allergies

There are three basic steps to control allergies.

- **Avoid the allergen.** For example, if you know you are allergic to poison ivy, learn what it looks like and stay away from it. Wear long sleeves and pants if you go into the woods. If you have a food allergy, check the ingredient labels on food products. When you go to restaurants, ask about the ingredients of menu items you want to order. Nut allergies are dangerous because they often cause severe reactions. People with allergies to peanuts or other nuts need to be especially careful about what they eat or come into contact with.

- **Take medication.** Some allergens such as dust and pollen are nearly impossible to avoid. People with these allergies often take medicines to help reduce the symptoms. These medicines are known as **antihistamines,** *medicines that reduce the production of histamines.*

- **Get injections.** Sometimes a long-term series of injections can help people overcome allergies. The injections contain a tiny amount of the allergen. They can gradually desensitize the immune system to the allergen.

 **Reading Check** **Describe** What are three ways to manage allergies?

Connect To... Science

Epinephrine

People who are at risk for severe allergic reactions such as bee stings or severe food allergies, often carry allergy medicine with them. The medicine may come in syringes preloaded with a substance called epinephrine (eh·pin·EFF·rihn).

Use the Internet to research epinephrine. What is it? How does it help people with severe allergic reactions? Report your findings to the class.

What Is Asthma?

Asthma is *a chronic inflammatory disorder of the airways that causes air passages to become narrow or blocked, making breathing difficult.* Asthma is a growing problem in many countries. In the United States, more than 20 million people are reported to have asthma. More than 6 million of these asthma sufferers are people under the age of 18. Many substances and conditions can cause an asthma attack. Common triggers include:

- allergens such as mold, dust, pollen, and pets.
- physical activity.
- air pollutants such as paint and gas fumes, cigarette smoke, industrial smoke, and smog.
- infections of the respiratory system, such as colds and the flu.
- dramatic weather changes, especially when the air becomes colder.
- rapid breathing, which often happens under stress, when laughing, or when crying.

HOW AN ASTHMA ATTACK AFFECTS THE AIRWAYS

An asthma attack makes breathing more difficult. Airways become narrower and clogged with mucus. **What are some symptoms of an asthma attack?**

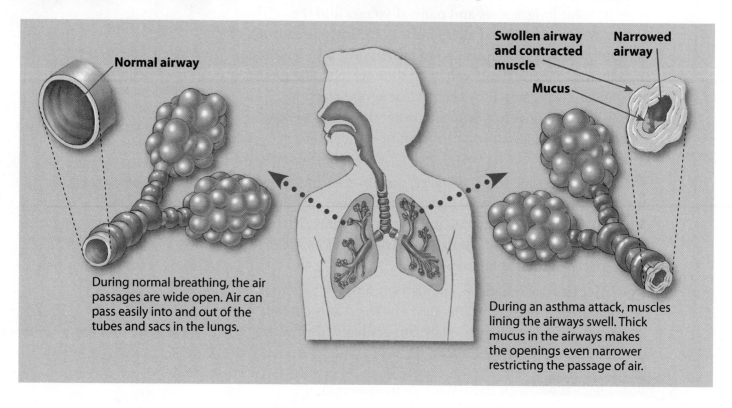

Normal airway

Swollen airway and contracted muscle

Narrowed airway

Mucus

During normal breathing, the air passages are wide open. Air can pass easily into and out of the tubes and sacs in the lungs.

During an asthma attack, muscles lining the airways swell. Thick mucus in the airways makes the openings even narrower restricting the passage of air.

An Asthma Attack

What are the symptoms of an asthma attack? A person may wheeze, cough, or feel short of breath during an attack. Symptoms can also include tightness or fullness in the chest. **Figure 14.3** above shows how an asthma attack affects the airways.

 **Reading Check** **Define** What is *asthma*?

Academic Vocabulary

monitor (MON i ter) *(verb)* to watch or pay attention to. *Calvin's mom has to monitor her blood sugar because she has diabetes.*

 **Go Online**

Visit glencoe.com and complete the Interactive Study Guide for Lesson 1.

Managing Asthma

People with asthma must take an active role in managing their condition. They can choose positive behaviors that will help them learn to avoid or control attacks. Examples include:

- **Monitor the condition.** People with asthma must pay attention to the early signs of an attack. That way, they can act quickly if they sense an attack coming. They also can track their long-term lung capacity, or ability to take in air. An instrument called an airflow meter measures lung capacity. When used regularly, an airflow meter helps people know when their airways are narrowing.

- **Manage the environment.** For example, if dust and mold trigger your asthma, reduce them in your environment. It helps to keep floors, bedding, and pets clean.

- **Manage stress.** Stress is a major cause of asthma attacks. Panicking during an attack can make it even worse. Relaxing and staying calm can help those with asthma avoid attacks. Relaxing will help even during an attack.

- **Take medication.** Two kinds of medicines can treat asthma: relievers and controllers. Relievers help reduce symptoms during an asthma attack. **Bronchodilators** (brahng·koh·DY·lay·turhz) are *reliever medications that relax muscles around the air passages.* People usually use an inhaler to take a bronchodilator. This small device sends medicine directly to the respiratory system. Controller medicines are taken daily, and help prevent attacks by making airways less sensitive to asthma triggers.

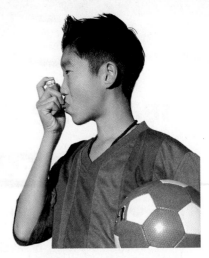

▲ Many people with asthma carry inhalers containing bronchodilators. These medicines ease breathing. **How does keeping their environment clean help people with asthma breathe easier?**

 **Describe** How can a person with asthma manage his or her condition?

Lesson 1 Review

 After You Read

Review this lesson for new terms, major headings, and Reading Checks.

What I Learned

1. *Vocabulary* Define *noncommunicable disease* and use it in a sentence that shows its meaning.

2. *Give Examples* What are examples of two diseases that a person may be born with?

3. *Describe* What are the symptoms of an asthma attack?

4. *Identify* List four common types of allergens.

5. *Explain* What is the difference between relievers and controllers as treatments for asthma?

Thinking Critically

6. *Hypothesize* Why do you think it's important for people with food allergies to be careful when eating out?

7. *Synthesize* What tools help people who have asthma manage their disease?

Applying Health Skills

8. *Communication Skills* Adrian wants to join the soccer team. He does not want anyone to know he has asthma. Write a short letter to Adrian telling him why you think he should make a healthful decision to tell his coach and his teammates that he has asthma.

Go Online For more Lesson Review Activities, go to glencoe.com.

Lesson 1: Allergies and Asthma **445**

Heart Disease

Quick Write

Write down three ways to keep your heart healthy.

What Is Cardiovascular Disease?

Cardiovascular or heart disease is any condition that reduces the strength or function of the heart and blood vessels. Common forms include high blood pressure and hardening of the arteries. According to the American Heart Association, 13 million people in the United States have heart disease. Almost half a million people a year die from this condition. Heart disease leads to 38 percent of all deaths in the United States. Sometimes heart disease is due to heredity. However, most heart disease is related to lifestyle. People who smoke, get very little exercise, or have other unhealthy habits are more at risk for developing the disease.

Types of Coronary Heart Disease

Your heart is a muscle that pumps blood through your body. Because your heart is a muscle, it needs oxygen just like all your other organs. Coronary arteries on the surface of your heart supply it with oxygen-rich blood. Veins on your heart take oxygen-poor blood away. When the arteries are clear, the blood flows freely. When the coronary arteries are blocked, blood does not flow as well. At this point, coronary artery disease begins to develop.

Arteriosclerosis (ar·tir·ee·oh·skluh·ROH·sis) is *a group of disorders that cause a thickening and hardening of the arteries.* **Atherosclerosis** (a·thuh·roh·skluh·ROH·sis), a form of arteriosclerosis, is *a condition that occurs when fatty substances build up on the inner lining of the arteries.* When this buildup collects inside arteries, it takes up space needed for blood to flow through. **Figure 14.4** shows the difference between a healthy artery and a blocked artery. If the coronary arteries become blocked with too much buildup, the heart may not get enough oxygen.

A Heart Attack

If the heart does not get enough oxygen, a heart attack is likely. A **heart attack** *occurs when the blood supply to the heart slows or stops and the heart muscle is damaged.* **Figure 14.5** shows what happens during a heart attack. For males, symptoms include pain or pressure in the chest, or pain in the arms, jaw, back, or abdomen. Males may also be short of breath, have cold skin, throw up, feel tightness in the chest, or pass out. Females are more likely than males to also experience pain in the back or jaw.

▼ **FIGURE 14.4**

ATHEROSCLEROSIS

The muscle tissue of the heart gets blood from the coronary arteries. Blocked arteries prevent the heart from getting all the blood it needs. **What happens when part of the heart does not get enough blood?**

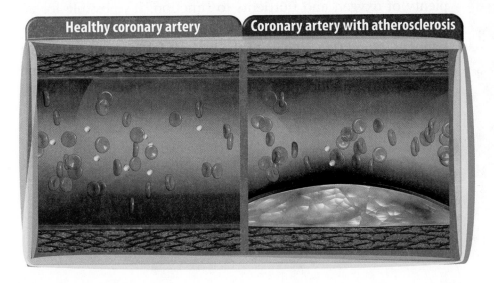

Healthy coronary artery | Coronary artery with atherosclerosis

A HEART ATTACK

During a heart attack, a coronary artery becomes blocked. As a result, part of the heart dies because it does not get enough oxygen from the blood. **What are the symptoms of a heart attack?**

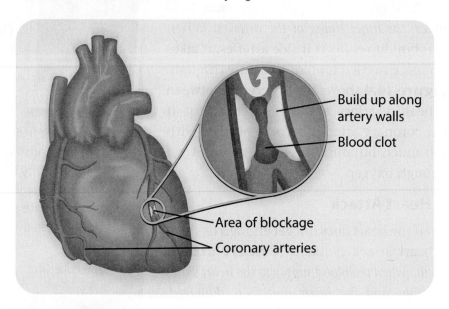

Build up along artery walls

Blood clot

Area of blockage

Coronary arteries

▼ Regular physical activity is a positive behavior that strengthens the heart. It can help people with hypertension reduce their need for medication. **What kinds of physical activities strengthen the heart?**

Other Problems of the Circulatory System

Blood pushes against the walls of the blood vessels as it flows through them. One of the most common forms of heart disease is high blood pressure. High blood pressure, or **hypertension,** is *a disease in which the pressure of the blood on the walls of the blood vessels stays at a level that is higher than normal.* Hypertension can lead to a heart attack or a stroke. People with hypertension can manage the condition by following a healthful eating plan, exercising regularly, avoiding stress, and taking medicine if needed.

A **stroke** is *a serious condition that occurs when an artery of the brain breaks or becomes blocked.* Like the heart, the brain needs plenty of oxygen and nutrients to function. It's possible for an artery to leak or develop a thick mass called a clot. When this happens, blood flow to part of the brain is interrupted. That part of the brain is damaged as a result. The effects of a stroke depend on what part of the brain is damaged. A person who has had a stroke may have trouble moving or speaking.

Reading Check **Identify** What are two causes of strokes?

Health Skills Activity

Analyzing Influences

What Ads Say About Fat

Many ads try to sell you foods high in saturated fats or trans fats. Some also feature foods that are "heart healthy." Find one print or television ad for a high-fat food and one for a heart-healthy food. Analyze the ads. What about the design of the ad makes the foods appealing? What language do they use? What do advertisers want you to believe about eating the food? How do these ads affect you?

With a Group

Think of a fast-food meal that has at least one item high in trans fats or saturated fats. Create a warning label for this fast-food meal. It should include facts about the dangers of eating a diet high in saturated fats and trans fats.

Preventing Heart Disease

To keep your heart and circulatory system healthy, follow these tips:

- **Eat healthful foods.** Choose plenty of fresh fruits and vegetables, whole grains, and lean sources of proteins.

- **Limit the amount of cholesterol, trans fats, and saturated fats that you eat.** Foods high in cholesterol, saturated fats, and trans fats are linked to cardiovascular disease such as atherosclerosis.

- **Participate in regular physical activity.** Regular physical activity makes your heart stronger.

- **Maintain a healthy weight.** Your heart works best if your weight is within a healthy range. Talk to a healthcare provider about the range that is best for you.

- **Manage stress.** Learning to relax will help you keep your blood pressure within a healthy range.

- **Stay tobacco free.** Chemicals in tobacco can cause heart disease, heart attacks, hypertension, and strokes. Staying tobacco free will help you avoid all of these problems.

- **Stay alcohol free.** Alcohol has been linked to high blood pressure and heart failure. Staying alcohol free helps you avoid these problems.

Connect To... Science

Trans Fats

Consuming too many trans fats is linked to high cholesterol levels and heart disease. Trans fats are produced when hydrogen is added to liquid vegetable oil to make it a solid. Packaged baked goods often contain trans fats.

Why do you think the Food and Drug Administration requires that packaged foods list the amounts of trans fats they contain?

Treating Heart Disease

Health care providers can usually treat heart disease with the following methods:

- **Angioplasty** (AN·je·uh·plas·tee) is *a surgical procedure in which an instrument with a tiny balloon, drill bit, or laser attached is inserted into a blocked artery to clear a blockage.* With the balloon method, doctors inflate the tiny balloon until it pushes the blockage up and against the artery wall. Lasers or drill bits cut or burn away the blockage.

- **Medications** can break up blood clots that may block arteries. They can also lower cholesterol levels.

- **Pacemakers** and implantable defibrillators are electronic devices placed inside the chest. A pacemaker sends electrical signals helping the heart beat regularly. An implantable defibrillator starts the heart beating when it has stopped.

- **Bypass surgery** creates new pathways for the blood. When a person has a blocked coronary artery, surgeons use a healthy blood vessel from another part of the body to set up a new route for blood to flow around the blockage.

- **Heart transplants** completely replace a damaged heart with a healthy heart from someone who has just died.

 Go Online

Visit **glencoe.com** and complete the Interactive Study Guide for Lesson 2 .

 Reading Check **List** What are two ways to treat heart disease?

 **Lesson 2 Review**

 **After You Read**

Review this lesson for new terms, major headings, and Reading Checks.

What I Learned

1. *Vocabulary* Define *arteriosclerosis* and *atherosclerosis.*

2. *Explain* What is angioplasty?

3. *Describe* What are the symptoms of a heart attack in females?

Thinking Critically

4. *Hypothesize* How is hypertension similar to putting too much air in a balloon?

5. *Synthesize* Why do you think that medical professionals focus on preventing heart disease even though there are so many treatments for it?

Applying Health Skills

6. *Practicing Healthy Behaviors* John wants to develop an eating plan to keep his heart healthy. What can John do to eat better?

 Go Online For more Lesson Review Activities, go to **glencoe.com.**

Cancer

Guide to Reading

● **Building Vocabulary**
As you read this lesson, write each new highlighted term and its definition on separate cards. With a partner, take turns matching each term to its definition.

- cancer (p. 451)
- tumor (p. 451)
- benign (p. 452)
- malignant (p. 452)
- risk factors (p. 452)
- carcinogen (p. 453)
- biopsy (p. 455)
- radiation therapy (p. 456)
- chemotherapy (p. 456)

● **Focusing on the Main Ideas**
In this lesson, you will be able to

- **identify** what cancer is.
- **give** examples of different kinds of cancer.
- **identify** some causes of cancer.
- **describe** how to reduce the risk of developing cancer.
- **explain** the ways that cancer is treated.
- **advocate** for ways to reduce cancer risk.

● **Reading Strategy**
Predicting Look over the headings of the lesson. Write down two questions you have that you hope the lesson will answer. When you are done reading, look back at your questions to see if they were answered.

 **Quick Write**

Write a sentence or two explaining why people need to apply sunscreen before going outdoors.

What Is Cancer?

Cancer is *a disease that occurs when abnormal cells multiply out of control.* Cancer is actually a collective term for more than 100 different diseases. Any tissue in the body can become cancerous. While doctors can successfully treat many cancers, it is still the second leading killer in the United States. Only heart disease kills more Americans each year.

How does cancer develop? The adult human body contains more than 100 trillion cells. These cells constantly divide to make more cells so the body can grow and repair itself. Most of the body's cells are normal at any given time. However, even in healthy bodies, some cells become abnormal. Your body's immune system usually destroys these cells. However, some abnormal cells can survive and begin to divide.

Some of these abnormal cells grow in clumps called tumors. A **tumor** (TOO·mer) is *a group of abnormal cells that form a mass.* Tumors are either benign (bi·NYN) or malignant (muh·LIG·nuht).

COMMON TYPES OF CANCER

This chart lists some of the most common types of cancer. Why do you think people with lymphoma usually struggle with other diseases, too?

Form of Cancer	Important Facts
Skin cancer	The most common kind of cancer, usually caused by exposure to sunlight.
Breast cancer	Most often diagnosed in women over age 50 but can strike younger women as well as men.
Reproductive organ cancers	Cancers that affect the testicles and prostate gland in men, and the ovaries, cervix, and uterus in women.
Lung cancer	Closely tied to smoking; causes more cancer deaths in the United States than any other type of cancer.
Colon and rectal cancers	Affect the large intestine and rectum; better screening tests and early detection have reduced the number of cases of these kinds of cancer.
Leukemia	Causes cancerous white blood cells to multiply; these abnormal white blood cells interfere with the immune response of healthy white blood cells.
Lymphoma	Cancer of the tissues in the lymph system; can weaken the immune system, leaving the body unable to fight infections.

Benign tumors are *not cancerous* and do not spread. **Malignant** tumors are *cancerous*. They may multiply out of control and sometimes they also spread to other parts of the body.

Types of Cancer

Almost any tissue in the body can become cancerous. Some types of cancer are more common than others. **Figure 14.6** lists and describes some of the most common types of cancer. Skin cancer tops the list. More than a million new cases of skin cancer are reported every year in the United States. They make up about half of all the cancer cases reported. Luckily, most cases of skin cancer are highly curable if detected early and treated appropriately.

Lung cancer is the deadliest form of cancer. It kills an estimated 163,000 people per year. In 2005, about one of every three people who died from cancer had lung cancer. The good news is that this number has been falling in recent years.

Risk Factors and Causes of Cancer

Some types of cancers develop for unknown reasons. However, doctors have identified specific risk factors for certain types of cancer. **Risk factors** are *characteristics or behaviors that increase the likelihood of developing a medical disorder or disease.*

Risk factors for cancers can include inherited traits, age, behavior choices, and environmental factors. For example, a high-fat, low-fiber diet may be a risk factor for developing colon and rectal cancers.

Some types of cancer have well-known causes. For example, asbestos is a mineral that once was used in construction and manufacturing. Breathing asbestos dust can cause lung cancer. Asbestos is a carcinogen (kar·SI·nuh·juhn). A **carcinogen** is *a substance that can cause cancer.* According to the American Cancer Society, about 90 chemicals are known carcinogens for humans. However, not all carcinogens are chemicals. For example, UV rays from the sun can cause skin cancer.

Reading Check **Identify** What are two carcinogens and the cancers they cause?

▲ Most cells divide at a controlled rate. Cancer cells divide at an uncontrolled rate. **The cells on top are healthy. Those below are cancerous cells. If these cells form a tumor, is the tumor benign or malignant?**

Reducing the Risk of Cancer

Anyone can get cancer, but you can protect yourself from some types of the disease. Staying tobacco free can greatly reduce your risk of developing lung cancer. Here are some more tips on how to reduce your cancer risk.

- **Eat well and exercise.** Many cancers, such as colon and rectal cancers, may be linked to diet. Eating well and staying fit can help you avoid these cancers.

- **Limit sun exposure.** UV rays from the sun can cause cancer. To protect yourself from UV rays, avoid being in the sun between 10:00 A.M. and 4:00 P.M. That's when the sun's rays are the strongest. If you need to be outdoors during this time, apply a sunscreen with an SPF of at least 15 before you go outdoors. Also, wear a hat that shades your neck and the tops of your ears. You should also avoid tanning beds. They give off UV rays that can lead to skin cancer and damage the immune system.

- **Perform self-examinations.** Females should perform a breast self-exam once a month. Males should perform a testicular self-exam once a month. Ask your health care provider about the correct way to perform these exams.

If you notice any unusual lumps, see a health care provider right away. Also, check all moles and other skin growths frequently. See a health care provider immediately if you notice any changes in them. Take a look at **Figure 14.7** to learn what to look for in moles.

- **Know the seven warning signs of cancer.** These signs are listed in **Figure 14.8.** The American Cancer Society has identified seven possible signs of cancer. The first letter of each sign spells the word CAUTION. You play the most important role in early cancer detection. If you notice any of the warning signs, tell a parent, guardian, or health care professional right away.

Reading Check **Explain** What do the letters in CAUTION stand for?

▲ It's important to apply sunscreen before going out in the sun. **What other steps can you take to protect your skin from the sun's rays?**

▼ FIGURE 14.7

CHECK YOUR ABCDS

One way to prevent skin cancer is to check moles regularly. Follow the American Cancer Society's ABCDs. Check moles for asymmetry, border irregularity, color, and diameter. Any suspicious moles should be checked by a dermatologist right away. **What is another way to reduce the risk of skin cancer?**

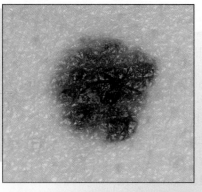

Asymmetry One side of a mole looks different from the other side.

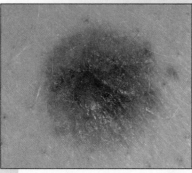

Border irregularity The edges are jagged or blurred.

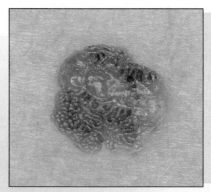

Color The color is not uniform, or the same, throughout. If a mole is tan and brown, black, or red and white, have it checked.

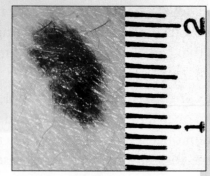

Diameter The diameter is greater than 6 millimeters (about the size of a pencil eraser). A growth that has expanded to this size over time should be checked.

THE SEVEN WARNING SIGNS OF CANCER

Knowing the warning signs of cancer can help you **detect** cancer in its early stages. **Why is early detection helpful in treating cancer?**

Academic Vocabulary

detect (dee TEKT) *(verb)* to discover or catch. *Olympic athletes are often given a drug test to detect illegal drugs in their bodies.*

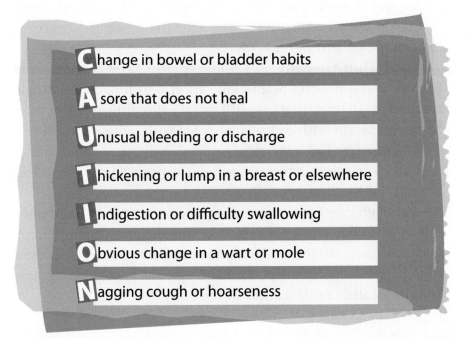

C hange in bowel or bladder habits

A sore that does not heal

U nusual bleeding or discharge

T hickening or lump in a breast or elsewhere

I ndigestion or difficulty swallowing

O bvious change in a wart or mole

N agging cough or hoarseness

Diagnosing Cancer

Health care professionals use many methods to detect cancer. Some are very simple. For example, a doctor might spot a group of skin cells that don't look normal. He or she might feel a lump where the tissue should be soft. Health care professionals also use more involved methods. They can use X rays and other scanning equipment to look for unusual cell formations. If tissue shows a suspicious lump or formation, it usually undergoes a biopsy. A **biopsy** is *the removal of a sample of tissue from a person for examination.*

The tissue from a biopsy goes to a lab for careful examination to see if the cells are cancerous. If they are, technicians will do other tests to learn more about the cancer. Together, a team of health care providers and the patient can decide on a plan for treatment.

Reading Check Explain How is a biopsy used to help diagnose cancer?

▼ Health care professionals sometimes use X rays to look for signs of cancer. **How do X rays and other scanning tools help doctors detect more cases of cancer than they could without these tools?**

Treating Cancer

The most common cancer treatments include surgery, radiation therapy, and chemotherapy. Cancer patients usually receive at least two of these treatments and sometimes all three.

Surgery is used to treat some cancers, including breast, lung, and colon cancers. Surgery is most effective when the cancer is isolated in one part of the body.

Radiation therapy uses *X rays or other forms of radiation to kill cancer cells*. It works best to kill cancer cells limited to a single area and to kill those that may still remain after surgery. More than half of all people with cancer are treated with radiation therapy.

Chemotherapy is *the use of powerful medicines to destroy cancer cells*. Doctors use this therapy to fight cancers that have spread beyond one location or occur throughout the body.

Although cancer treatments are improving, all of them have side effects. Side effects of radiation therapy and chemotherapy include nausea, fatigue, and temporary hair loss. Side effects differ from person to person depending on age, the type of treatment, and the location of the cancer in the body.

Reading Check

Explain What treatment is commonly used for a cancer that has spread?

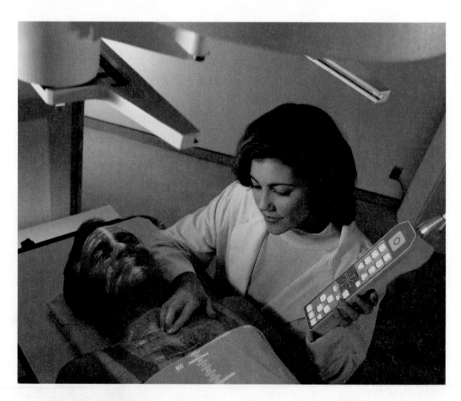

▲ Radiation therapy is one way to treat some types of cancer. During radiation therapy, special machines direct powerful rays at groups of cancer cells. The radiation kills the cells. **What are two other ways to treat cancer?**

Visit glencoe.com and complete the Interactive Study Guide for Lesson 3.

Health Skills Activity

Advocacy

Promote Ways to Reduce Cancer Risk

You can reduce the risk of getting certain cancers. Decisions you make now can help you reduce your risk of developing cancer later in life. Use reliable online and print sources to research how to help prevent certain types of cancer. Here is a head start:

- Lung cancer—stay tobacco free.
- Skin cancer—limit exposure to UV rays from the sun.
- Colon and rectal cancers—eat a diet rich in whole grains, fruits, and vegetables.

With a Group

Write and illustrate a booklet or create a computer slide show on ways to reduce cancer risks. Give your resource a catchy name, slogan, and logo. Share your booklet or slide show with the class.

Lesson 3 Review

After You Read

Review this lesson for new terms, major headings, and Reading Checks.

What I Learned

1. *Vocabulary* Define *cancer*.

2. *Give Examples* What are three types of cancer?

3. *Identify* Name three tools for diagnosing cancer.

4. *Describe* What is radiation therapy?

Thinking Critically

5. *Synthesize* Moles get larger when the skin cells in the mole divide. Why do you think moles larger than 6 millimeters might be a warning sign of cancer?

6. *Apply* Why are people who work in outdoor jobs at higher risk of skin cancer than people who work indoors?

Applying Health Skills

7. *Communication Skills* Write an editorial for the school newspaper on the importance of detecting cancer early. In your editorial, include information about the seven warning signs of cancer.

 Go Online For more Lesson Review Activities, go to **glencoe.com**.

Lesson 4

Diabetes and Arthritis

Guide to Reading

● Building Vocabulary
Write down each of the terms below. As you read this lesson, write the definition next to each term.

- diabetes (p. 458)
- insulin (p. 458)
- arthritis (p. 461)
- osteoarthritis (p. 462)
- rheumatoid arthritis (p. 462)

● Focusing on the Main Ideas
In this lesson, you will be able to

- **describe** what diabetes is and how it is treated.
- **describe** what arthritis is and how it is treated.
- **access** information to find out about juvenile rheumatoid arthritis.

● Reading Strategy
Organizing information Create a table like the one shown below. As you read the lesson, fill in the table with information about the different types of diabetes and arthritis.

Disorders	Important facts
Type 1 diabetes	Often begins in childhood.
Type 2 diabetes	
Rheumatoid arthritis	
Juvenile rheumatoid arthritis	
Osteoarthritis	

Quick Write

Write down two facts you know about diabetes.

What Is Diabetes?

Diabetes mellitus (dy·uh·BEE·teez MEH·luh·tuhs), or **diabetes,** is *a disease that prevents the body from converting food into energy.* Your body breaks down the food you eat to get the energy it contains. To do so, it turns food into a form of sugar called glucose. Your body then uses the glucose for energy.

After your body digests food, glucose levels in the bloodstream rise. Some of the glucose begins to enter cells with the help of a hormone in your body called *insulin*. **Insulin** (IN·suh·lin) is *a protein made in the pancreas that regulates the level of glucose in the blood.* Some people who have diabetes do not have enough natural insulin. As a result, glucose cannot get into cells. Other people make enough insulin, but the insulin does not do its job properly. In both cases, the glucose remains in the blood. This leads to many health problems. If left unmanaged, diabetes can cause diseases such as kidney disorders, blindness, and heart disease.

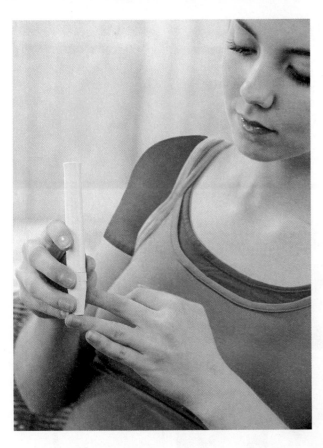

It is important for young people with type 1 diabetes to learn how to manage their condition. **Why is it helpful for young people with diabetes to take responsibility for managing their disease?**

The two main types of diabetes are known as type 1 and type 2 diabetes. Type 1 diabetes most often begins in childhood, but it can sometimes begin in adulthood. Researchers believe that in type 1 diabetes, the body's immune system attacks and kills the cells in the pancreas that make insulin. Without insulin, the body cannot control how much glucose is in the bloodstream. Between 5 and 10 percent of people with diabetes have type 1.

Between 90 and 95 percent of people with diabetes have type 2 diabetes. In type 2 diabetes, the body doesn't make enough insulin or the body's cells can't effectively use the insulin that is produced. This kind of diabetes most often begins in adulthood. However, it occurs more and more in today's children and teens. Type 2 diabetes is closely linked to poor food choices, lack of physical activity, and being overweight. Children and teens who are very overweight are at a higher risk of developing diabetes.

 **Identify** What is the most common form of diabetes?

Managing Diabetes

All people with diabetes must deal with it as part of their daily lives. People with type 1 diabetes usually need to have injections of insulin or to receive insulin from an insulin pump attached to their bodies. Young people who have type 1 diabetes can learn

Topic: Coping with Health Challenges

Visit **glencoe.com** for Student Web Activities where you will learn about a variety of noncommunicable diseases and how they are treated.

Activity: Using the information provided at the link above, choose one disease and create a pamphlet that discusses symptoms, treatments, and resources for teens who want to learn more.

▼ FIGURE 14.9

MANAGING DIABETES

There is no cure for diabetes, so people who have it must make sure they manage the condition carefully. This includes keeping track of blood glucose levels. **What are some of the dangers of untreated diabetes?**

Healthful Eating Plan

A healthful eating plan can help keep blood glucose levels within a healthy range.

Weight Management

Regular physical activity helps people with diabetes maintain a healthy weight.

Insulin

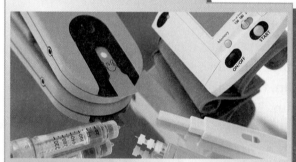

People with type 1 diabetes and some people with type 2 diabetes receive insulin through a syringe or pump.

Medical Care

People with diabetes need to be under the care of a medical professional.

to take charge of their health. People who have type 2 diabetes may also need insulin or other medications. Many of them, however, can control their disease by practicing healthful habits. They can eat nutritious foods, watch their weight, and be active. **Figure 14.9** decribes strategies that people with diabetes can use to manage the condition.

 **Reading Check** **Describe** How do people manage diabetes?

Health Skills Activity

What Is Arthritis?

Arthritis (ar·THRY·tus) is *a disease of the joints marked by painful swelling and stiffness.* More than 40 million people in the United States have arthritis.

You may think of arthritis as a disease that strikes older adults, but even children can develop it. There are two main types of arthritis: osteoarthritis (ahs·tee·oh·ar·THRY·tus) and rheumatoid (ROO·muh·toyd) arthritis. When rheumatoid arthritis affects a young person, it's called juvenile rheumatoid arthritis (JRA).

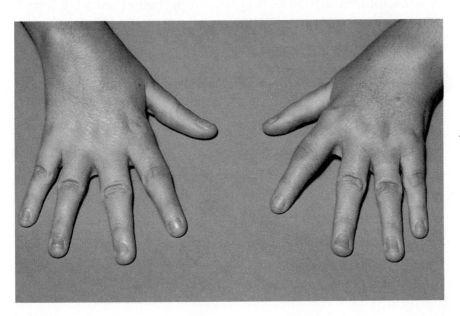

◄ This teen has juvenile rheumatoid arthritis. The condition can make it difficult for a person to use his or her arms, legs, and hands. **What are the symptoms of JRA?**

Osteoarthritis

Osteoarthritis is *a chronic disease that is common in older adults and results from a breakdown in cartilage in the joints.* Osteoarthritis is the most common form of arthritis. Osteoarthritis develops as a result of wear and tear on the joints, such as those of the knees and hips. The hard, slippery tissue in the joints between the bones is called *cartilage.* When cartilage in a joint wears down, the bones in the joints rub against each other. This rubbing causes pain, swelling, and morning stiffness. Risk factors include age, genetic factors, and extra weight.

Rheumatoid Arthritis

Rheumatoid arthritis is *a chronic disease characterized by pain, inflammation, swelling, and stiffness of the joints.* Rheumatoid arthritis is usually more serious and disabling than osteoarthritis. People develop rheumatoid arthritis when their immune systems attack healthy joint tissue. These attacks damage joint tissue and cause painful swelling. Rheumatoid arthritis can affect any joint, including those in the hands, elbows, shoulders, hips, and feet. Symptoms include soreness, joint stiffness and pain, aches, and fatigue.

Juvenile Rheumatoid Arthritis (JRA)

JRA is the most common form of arthritis in young people. JRA appears most often in young people between the ages of 6 months and 16 years. Early symptoms include swelling and pain in the joints. The skin covering the joints may be red and warm to the touch. Children with JRA also typically get rashes and high fevers. Many children with JRA continue to have arthritis as adults. Some children with JRA, however, get better after puberty.

 **Reading Check** **Name** What are two kinds of arthritis?

Managing Arthritis

There is no cure for arthritis, but people with arthritis can learn to manage the disease. They usually work with health care professionals to develop a plan to reduce the symptoms of arthritis. Many plans involve a combination of the following:

- **Physical activity and rest.** People with arthritis suffer less if they balance rest with low-impact physical activity. Rest helps handle fatigue that comes with the disease.

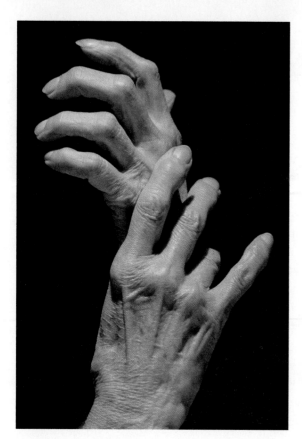

▲ You can see the effects of osteoarthritis in this older person's hands. Joints swell because the cartilage in the joints breaks down. **How can physical activity help people with osteoarthritis?**

Physical activity reduces swelling in the joints and allows joints to bend more easily.

- **Maintain a healthy weight.** Maintaining a healthy weight reduces stress on arthritic joints in the knees and feet.
- **Joint protection.** People can wear braces and splints to support arthritic joints. This equipment wraps around the joint and holds it steady.
- **Heat and cold treatments.** Hot baths ease the pain of some kinds of arthritis. Cold treatments can help reduce the swelling.
- **Medication.** Medicine can help slow the progress of some kinds of arthritis. OTC medicines and prescription medicines can also help ease the pain and swelling of arthritic joints.
- **Massage.** A trained massage therapist can help some arthritis patients by gently massaging affected areas. This helps to relax the joints and increase blood flow to sore areas.
- **Surgery and joint replacement.** In extreme cases, surgeons can operate to repair a joint or correct its position. They may even replace the damaged joint with an artificial one.

Visit glencoe.com and complete the Interactive Study Guide for Lesson 4.

Reading Check Explain How do physical activity and rest help people who have arthritis?

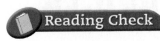

Lesson 4 Review

After You Read

Review this lesson for new terms, major headings, and Reading Checks.

What I Learned

1. *Vocabulary* What is *diabetes?*

2. *Describe* What practices can some people with type 2 diabetes use to manage their disease without medication?

3. *Describe* What happens to a person's joints when osteoarthritis develops?

Thinking Critically

4. *Synthesize* How are rheumatoid arthritis and type 1 diabetes similar?

5. *Hypothesize* What are two ways that staying physically active helps people with arthritis?

Applying Health Skills

6. *Practicing Healthful Behaviors* You can protect yourself from type 2 diabetes by staying physically active. List your favorite physical activities. Include everyday activities such as walking to school, as well as sports. Try to participate in one of these activities at least three times per week.

Go Online For more Lesson Review Activities, go to glencoe.com.

Lesson 4: Diabetes and Arthritis **463**

Accessing Information

Practicing Healthful Behaviors

Stress Management

Analyzing Influences

Communication Skills

Refusal Skills

Conflict Resolution

Decision Making

Goal Setting

Advocacy

What Is Goal Setting?

Goal setting is a five-step plan for improving and maintaining your personal health. Some goals are easy to reach while others may be more challenging.

The 5 Steps of the Goal-Setting Plan

- **Step 1:** Choose a realistic goal and write it down.
- **Step 2:** List the steps that you need to take to reach the goal.
- **Step 3:** Find others, like family, friends, and teachers who can help and support you.
- **Step 4:** Set checkpoints along the way to evaluate your progress.
- **Step 5:** Reward yourself once you have reached your goal.

Lifelong Good Health Habits: Emily's Walk

Follow the Model, Practice, and Apply steps to help you master this important health skill.

❶ Model

Read how Emily uses goal setting to get ready for a diabetes walkathon.

Emily wants to take part in a 10-mile walkathon to support diabetes research. Read the steps Emily took to reach this goal.

1. On a sheet of paper Emily wrote, "Walk 10 miles in the diabetes walkathon."
2. To reach this goal, Emily talked to her physical education teacher to outline a walk program. She also located a safe place to walk near her home.
3. Emily asked her friend to walk with her 3 times a week and also during the walkathon.
4. Each time Emily walked, she recorded her progress on a calendar.
5. After the walkathon, the girls wore their walkathon tee shirts to school to show their friends.

② Practice

Read about Greg and practice goal setting by answering the questions below.

Greg knew that eating healthful foods could prevent heart disease later in life. He also knew that the chips and cookies he snacked on each day were not a healthy choice. He wanted to snack on healthier foods.

1. What is Greg's goal?
2. What are the steps Greg needs to take to reach his goal?
3. Who can help Greg reach his goal?
4. How can he evaluate his progress?
5. How can he reward himself for reaching his goal?

③ Apply

Use what you have learned about goal setting to complete the activity below.

Choose a health goal that can reduce your risk of getting a noncommunicable disease. Then create a one-page plan to post in your room as a reminder of how to achieve this goal. Write down your goal at the top of your plan and list everything you would need to be successful. Show who might help you and state how you will know whether or not you are making progress toward reaching your goal. At the bottom of the page, tell how you will reward yourself.

Self-Check

- Did I choose a goal that will reduce my risk of getting a noncommunicable disease?
- Did I include all of the goal-setting steps in my plan?

Determining Lung Capacity

In this activity, you will work with a partner to measure the air capacity of your lungs, or their ability to take in air. Then you will graph the results so that you can see how air capacity is related to body size.

What You Will Need

- Round balloon for every student
- String
- Ruler
- Graph paper
- Strip of paper on the wall that is longer than the tallest student in class and that is marked in inches

What You Will Do

1. Your teacher will hand out the materials and divide the class into pairs.

2. Stretch the balloon several times to loosen the rubber. Take a deep breath and then exhale all of that air into the balloon to blow it up as far as you can.

3. Your partner will wrap the string around the widest part of the balloon, then measure the length of string with a ruler. This measurement is the balloon's diameter. Record this number.

4. Switch places with your partner and repeat steps 2 and 3.

5. Go to the measuring strip on the wall and determine your height in inches.

6. Make a graph on a sheet of paper. Mark the vertical (y) axis in inches or centimeters for balloon diameter. Mark the horizontal (x) axis in inches or centimeters for height.

7. Plot the results from steps 2 and 3 on the graph.

Wrapping It Up

The average adult is able to exhale about 4.5 liters, or 8.4 pints, of air. A well-trained athlete may be able to exhale 6.5 liters, or 12 pints, of air. Did you find a relationship between height and lung capacity? How would smoking affect lung capacity? How do you think lung capacity changes during an asthma attack?

Reading Review

STUDY TO GO 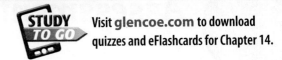 Visit **glencoe.com** to download quizzes and eFlashcards for Chapter 14.

FOLDABLES Study Organizer

Foldables® and Other Study Aids Take out the Foldable® you created for Lesson 1 and any graphic organizers that you created for Lessons 1–4. Find a partner and quiz each other using these study aids.

Lesson 1 | Allergies and Asthma

Main Idea Allergies and asthma are two kinds of noncommunicable diseases.

- Noncommunicable diseases are diseases that cannot be spread from one person to another.
- Heredity, unhealthful behaviors, and the environment can all cause noncommunicable diseases.
- Different people may react differently to the same allergen.
- Asthma is a chronic respiratory disease that narrows or blocks air passages and makes breathing difficult.

Lesson 2 | Heart Disease

Main Idea Heart disease is any condition that reduces the strength or function of the heart.

- There are two types of coronary artery disease: arteriosclerosis and atherosclerosis.
- If the heart does not get enough oxygen, a heart attack is likely.
- Stroke and hypertension are circulatory problems.
- Strategies for preventing heart disease include getting regular physical activity, eating healthful foods, and staying tobacco free.

- Health care professionals can treat heart disease with angioplasty, medication, surgery, pacemakers, or transplants.

Lesson 3 | Cancer

Main Idea Cancer is a noncommunicable disease that occurs when abnormal cells multiply out of control.

- Almost any tissue in the body can become cancerous.
- Risk factors for cancer include inherited traits, behavior choices, and environmental factors.
- People can cut the risk of cancer by staying tobacco free, avoiding UV rays, and knowing the seven warning signs of cancer.

Lesson 4 | Diabetes and Arthritis

Main Idea Type 1 diabetes and juvenile rheumatoid arthritis often begin in childhood.

- Diabetes is a disease that prevents the body from converting food into energy.
- There are two main types of diabetes: type 1 and type 2. Both types need management, including medicine, diet, and exercise.
- Arthritis is a disease of the joints marked by painful swelling and stiffness.
- Arthritis can be managed with physical activity, rest, weight control, joint protection, heat and cold treatments, medication, massage, and surgery.

CHAPTER 14 Assessment

 After You Read

HEALTH INVENTORY

Now that you have read the chapter, look back at your answers to the Health Inventory on the chapter opener. Is there anything that you should do differently?

Reviewing Vocabulary and Main Ideas

On a sheet of paper, write the numbers 1–9. After each number, write the term from the list below that best completes each statement.

- allergen
- asthma
- atherosclerosis
- chronic
- hypertension
- heart attack
- benign
- carcinogen
- tumor

Lesson 1 Allergies and Asthma

1. A _____ disease is one that is present on and off over a period of time.

2. Anything that causes an allergic response in people is a(n) _____.

3. _____ is a condition that makes breathing difficult.

Lesson 2 Heart Disease

4. A _____ can happen if the heart does not get enough oxygen-rich blood.

5. A condition in which a fatty substance builds up on the inner lining of the arteries is called _____.

6. When someone's blood pressure stays at a level that is higher than normal, that person has _____.

Lesson 3 Cancer

7. A _____ is a clump of abnormal cells.

8. A tumor that is not cancerous is _____.

9. A _____ is a substance that causes cancer.

Lesson 4 Diabetes and Arthritis

*On a sheet of paper, write the numbers 10–12. Write **True** or **False** for each statement below. If the statement is false, change the underlined word or phrase to make it true.*

10. <u>Arthritis</u> is a disease that prevents the body from converting food into energy.

11. <u>Type 2</u> diabetes is the most common form of the disease.

12. <u>Being active</u> helps control diabetes.

On a sheet of paper, write the numbers 13 and 14. After each number, write the letter of the answer that best completes each statement.

13. Wear and tear on the joints causes
    a. osteoarthritis.
    b. rheumatoid arthritis.
    c. juvenile rheumatoid arthritis.
    d. all of the above

14. Treatments for arthritis include
    a. insulin
    b. radiation
    c. heat and cold treatments
    d. none of the above

Go Online Visit glencoe.com and take the Online Quiz for Chapter 14.

Thinking Critically

Using complete sentences, answer the following questions on a sheet of paper.

15. **Apply** Why might playing the piano help people with arthritis in their hands?

16. **Hypothesize** Why do people with pollen allergies often have fewer symptoms in winter?

Write About It

17. **Expository Writing** Write an article for your school newspaper about the connection between weight and arthritis symptoms. Be sure that your article explains how a person's weight can affect the joints in the knees and feet. Explain the benefits of maintaining a healthy weight.

⚡ Applying Technology

Noncommunicable Diseases

Using Comic Life or Microsoft Word®, you and a partner will create a poster on one of the following topics: allergic reactions, asthma, arteriosclerosis, or cancer.

■ Choose a topic and locate images or take digital photos that reflect your topic and what you want to say about it.

■ Arrange your images on your poster. Add dialogue bubbles for each image. In a few sentences, explain what is going on in the picture and how it relates to your topic.

■ Include local resources that can help people deal with the noncommunicable disease that your group has chosen.

■ Edit for correct spelling, grammar, and accuracy of information.

■ Save your project.

Standardized Test Practice

Math

Use the table to answer the questions.

Acute Lymphoblastic Leukemia (A.L.L.) is a disease that affects the white blood cells. The table below shows the survival rates of children with this disease.

Survival rates for children with A.L.L.	
Year	Percentage of patients surviving at least 5 years
1965	5
2000	85

TEST-TAKING TIP

When trying to find trends in data from a chart, sometimes it helps to quickly sketch a line graph of the data.

1. What is a TRUE statement about A.L.L.?
   A. A greater percentage of patients with A.L.L. survived in 1965 than in 2000.
   B. A greater percentage of patients with A.L.L. survived in 2000 than in 1965.
   C. Five patients with A.L.L. survived for at least five years in 1965.
   D. 85 patients with A.L.L. survived for at least five years in 2000.

2. Suppose that 3500 people were diagnosed with A.L.L. in 1965 and that the same number were diagnosed in 2000. How many more patients would survive in 2000?
   A. 2,075
   B. 2,550
   C. 2,800
   D. 2,975

Chapter Preview

Lesson 1 Preventing Injury............ 472

Lesson 2 Staying Safe at Home...... 475

Lesson 3 Staying Safe Outdoors 480

Lesson 4 Weather Emergencies
and Natural Disasters......486

Lesson 5 Giving First Aid 493

Building Health Skills....................... 500

TIME health news 502

Chapter Reading Review...................503

Chapter Assessment 504

▲ *Working with the Photo*

Performing activities safely allows you to spend less time dealing with problems and more time having fun. **What is this teen doing to avoid injury?**

Start-Up Activities

Before You Read Do you know how to recognize dangerous situations? Answer the Health eSpotlight question below and then watch the online video. Keep a record of your answer.

VIDEO

Health eSpotlight

Personal Safety

Recognizing a dangerous situation and staying out of harm's way isn't always easy. Have you ever had to make quick decisions to stay safe? Could the situation have been avoided? Explain your answer in detail.

Go to **glencoe.com** and watch the health video for Chapter 15. Then complete the activity provided with the online video.

FOLDABLES Study Organizer

As You Read Make this Foldable® to organize what you learn in Lesson 1 about the causes and prevention of an accident chain. Begin with three plain sheets of 8½" × 11" paper.

1 Collect three sheets of paper and place them 1" apart.

2 Fold up the bottom edges, stopping them 1" from the top edges. This makes all the tabs the same size.

3 Crease the paper to hold the tabs in place. Staple along the fold.

4 Turn and label the tabs as shown.

The Accident Chain

1. The Situation
2. The Unsafe Habit
3. The Unsafe Action
4. The Accident
5. The Result

Under the appropriate tab, write down what you learn about each link in the accident chain.

Go Online Visit **glencoe.com** and complete the Health Inventory for Chapter 15.

Preventing Injury

Guide to Reading

● Building Vocabulary
Write each term below. As you read the lesson, write the definition of each term.

- safety conscious (p. 473)
- hazards (p. 473)
- accidental injuries (p. 473)

● Focusing on the Main Ideas
In this lesson, you will learn to

- **explain** what it means to be safety conscious.
- **identify** causes of accidental injuries.
- **describe** how to prevent accidental injuries.

● Reading Strategy
Skimming Look over all the headings in this lesson. For each heading, write a sentence describing what information you think will be covered in that section.

 FOLDABLES Study Organizer Use the Foldable® on p. 471 as you read this lesson.

*Q*uick Write
What are some examples of accidental injuries that people experience? Write down two or three examples.

Safety First

"Buckle up!" "Look both ways before you cross the street!" You've probably been hearing warnings like these for as long as you can remember. You might have helped teach these safe habits to a younger brother or sister. Accidents do happen, but you can prevent many of them. When you stay safe and avoid accidents, you help yourself and those around you stay healthy.

You might not think serious accidents can happen to you. However, the National Safety Council reports that about 85,000 people die from accidental injuries every year. The highest number of teen deaths occur in auto accidents. Other safety risks for teens include drowning, bicycle injuries, and burns.

◀ Keeping books and other items off the stairs can help prevent accidental injuries. **What are accidental injuries?**

THE ACCIDENT CHAIN

Many accidents can be avoided. You may find yourself getting into patterns that lead to accidents. If so, you can change your habits. **What habits could Tony change to help him avoid accidents?**

1. The Situation Tony has overslept. He wakes up in a panic. The bus is coming in 15 minutes.

2. The Unsafe Habit Tony didn't put his books away from the night before. He just left them on the floor.

3. The Unsafe Action Without looking where he is going, Tony runs to the bathroom to wash up.

4. The Accident Tony trips over his books and falls down.

5. The Result When Tony falls, he sprains his wrist. He misses his bus and is in a lot of pain.

The first step in staying safe is to be safety conscious. To be **safety conscious** means *being aware that safety is important and being careful to act in a safe manner.* It is easier to prevent injuries than to treat them. Think ahead. Pay attention to your surroundings. Look for hazards around you. **Hazards** are *potential sources of danger.* Avoid or fix possible hazards. For example, water spilled on the floor is a hazard. If you see a spill on the floor, clean it up. Keep your environment safe to help prevent accidental injuries. **Accidental injuries** are *injuries caused by unexpected events.*

You can also be safety conscious by resisting negative peer pressure. Take responsibility for your own safety. Do what you think is right even if it goes against what your friends might want you to do.

 **Identify** What is the first step in preventing accidents?

How Accidental Injuries Happen

Safety-conscious people are less likely to have accidents. Accidents usually happen when people stop being safety conscious and become careless. Think back to the last accident you had. You can probably see the accident chain that led up to it. **Figure 15.1** shows what an accident chain looks like.

 **Explain** Why do accidents usually happen?

DEVELOPING

Good Character

Responsibility

When you put your belongings in their proper place, they're not in the way, so they're less likely to cause accidents. Putting away clothes and equipment also helps cut down on clutter.

What else can you do to help prevent accidents?

Breaking the Accident Chain

Tony's accident did not have to happen. Look at the links in Tony's accident chain. Breaking just one link would have kept Tony from being injured.

- **Change the Situation.** Tony could have gotten up earlier. He could have set his alarm for a reasonable time. He could have asked a family member to wake him if he overslept.

- **Change the Unsafe Habit.** Tony could have put his books on a bookshelf or in his book bag.

- **Change the Unsafe Action.** Tony could have paid attention to where he was going. He could have slowed down and watched his step. Being safety conscious might have kept Tony from tripping and falling.

By changing the situation, the unsafe habit, or the unsafe action, Tony could have prevented his accident. By becoming more safety conscious, Tony can take responsibility for preventing accidents in the future.

Visit **glencoe.com** and complete the Interactive Study Guide for Lesson 1.

 Reading Check

Explain What changes can break the accident chain?

Lesson 1 Review

 After You Read

Review this lesson for new terms, major headings, and Reading Checks.

What I Learned

1. *Vocabulary* Define *hazard,* and use it in a sentence that shows its meaning.

2. *Identify* What are the five links in the accident chain?

3. *Give Examples* What are three ways to break the accident chain?

Thinking Critically

4. *Analyze* Describe how rain can make riding a bike hazardous.

5. *Apply* Beth has always had a bookshelf on the wall next to her bed. Now that she is taller, the bookshelf has become a problem. In fact, this year Beth has bumped her head on the shelf three times. What should she do to be safer?

Applying Health Skills

6. *Decision Making* Oscar sees a small pile of sticks left on the sidewalk in front of his house. He knows someone might trip on the sticks. Still, he didn't put them there, so he's not sure if he should move them. Use the decision-making steps on page 40 to help Oscar decide what to do.

 For more Lesson Review Activities, go to **glencoe.com**.

Staying Safe at Home

● **Building Vocabulary**
As you read this lesson, write each new highlighted term and its definition. Then write a short paragraph that uses all four terms.

- flammable (p. 475)
- electrical overload (p. 475)
- smoke alarm (p. 476)
- fire extinguisher (p. 476)

● **Focusing on the Main Ideas**
In this lesson, you will be able to

- **explain** how to protect yourself and others from fires.
- **identify** ways to prevent accidental injuries at home.

● **Reading Strategy**
Sequencing As you read this lesson, write down the sequence of actions that can help you stay safe in a fire.

**uick Write**

What is the first thing that you should do if you think the building you are in is on fire? Write a sentence or two describing the action you would take.

Fire Safety

Fires happen in more than 370,000 homes in the United States each year, killing more than 3,300 people. Fires often involve materials that are **flammable,** or *able to catch fire easily.* These materials may catch fire due to a spark, an open flame, or a burning object such as a lighted cigarette. Other fires start from **electrical overload,** *a dangerous situation in which too much electric current flows along a single circuit.* See **Figure 15.2** on page 476 for some common causes of fires.

Reading Check **Identify** What is one cause of home fires?

Preventing Fires

Here's a list of actions you can take to prevent fires:

- Keep stoves and ovens clean. Keep flammable materials away from burners.

- Never let a smoker toss a cigarette into a trash can before making sure it is completely extinguished. You can also remind people not to smoke in bed.

- Store matches and lighters out of the reach of children. Never play with matches or lighters. Don't leave candles burning unattended.

CAUSES OF FIRES IN THE HOME

Fires in the home usually result from one of the situations described here. Almost all people killed in fires are children and older adults. **Why do you think that children and older adults are the most likely to die in house fires?**

Careless cooking. Spattered grease and oil can cause kitchen fires. Unattended cooking pots can spill onto burners or in the oven.

Careless smoking. Cigarettes can start fires if people leave them unattended or fall asleep while they are still burning. Cigarettes can also start fires if people toss them into the trash when they are still burning.

Incorrect storage of flammable materials. Examples of flammable materials are paint, chemicals, oil, rags, and newspapers.

Damaged electrical systems or electrical overload. Fires can start due to too much current flowing through overloaded circuits. Shredded wires or torn cords can also lead to fires. Broken appliances can cause fires as well.

Gas leaks. Gas lines can leak and catch fire. Natural gas is odorless and colorless, so it has an additive that makes it smell. If you smell gas, first get out of the house, then call 911.

- Check appliances regularly for loose or damaged cords. Never pull on the cord to unplug an appliance. Never run cords under rugs or carpets. If you notice worn or shredded cords, tell an adult about them.

Being Prepared in Case of Fire

The earlier you receive warning of a fire, the better your chances of getting out of the building safely. A **smoke alarm** is *a device that sounds an alarm when it senses smoke.* Every level of a house should have smoke alarms. Smoke alarms are especially useful when you are sleeping and might not notice the early signs of a fire. As a result, you should install them as close to sleeping areas and bedrooms as possible. Test smoke alarms every month. If batteries power them, put in fresh batteries at least once a year.

Water will put out fires in which paper, wood, or cloth is burning. However, you should never use water to put out a fire that involves grease, oil, or electricity. That will actually make the fire worse. Instead, use a **fire extinguisher,** *a device that sprays chemicals that put out fires.* Every home should have a fire extinguisher. Read the fire extinguisher's directions, and make sure that you know how to use it properly.

Academic Vocabulary

device (dee VYS) *(noun)* a machine or piece of equipment designed to perform a task. *Alex was using a remote control device to turn on the television.*

Create a fire escape plan with your family. Most fires happen at night, so be sure to know escape routes from each bedroom. Choose a meeting point outside where everyone can gather in the event of a fire. Practice the escape plan with your family every six months. **Figure 15.3** on the next page shows what to do if a fire happens in your home.

 **Reading Check** **Recall** What type of fires cannot be put out with water?

Preventing Injuries at Home

Other dangers at home include falls, poisonings, electrical shocks, and gun accidents. Help prevent these unsafe situations by being safety conscious.

Preventing Falls

Most falls in the home occur in the kitchen, the bathroom, or on the stairs. These safety rules can help you prevent falls.

- **Safety in the kitchen.** Clean up spills right away. Use a stepstool, not a chair, to get items that are out of reach.
- **Safety in the bathroom.** Put a nonskid mat near the tub or shower. Use rugs that have a rubber backing to prevent the rug from slipping. Keep personal products in plastic bottles.
- **Safety on the stairs.** Keep staircases well lit and clear of all objects. Apply nonslip treads to slippery stairs. Make sure handrails are secure and stable. If small children live in the house, put gates at the top and bottom of the stairs.

Preventing Poisonings

Many common household products are poisonous. To help keep the people in your home safe from poisoning, never call a child's medicine or vitamins "candy." Be sure that all medicines are in bottles with childproof caps. Make sure that labels on containers of household products are clearly marked, and keep them out of children's reach.

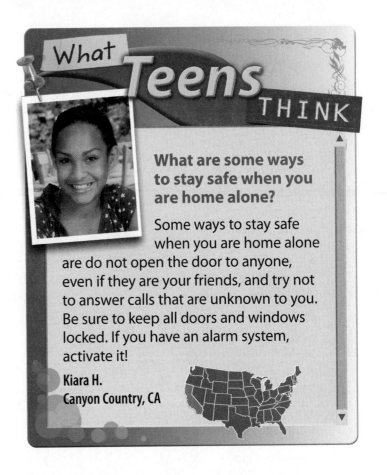

What Teens THINK

What are some ways to stay safe when you are home alone?

Some ways to stay safe when you are home alone are do not open the door to anyone, even if they are your friends, and try not to answer calls that are unknown to you. Be sure to keep all doors and windows locked. If you have an alarm system, activate it!

Kiara H.
Canyon Country, CA

 **Online**

Visit glencoe.com and complete the Interactive Study Guide for Lesson 2.

WHAT TO DO IN CASE OF FIRE

If you are in a fire, you need to know what to do to escape safely. Memorizing these tips can help you to stay safe. **Why should you get outside first and then call 911?**

1 If possible, leave quickly. Get out of the building before calling 911 or the fire department.

2 Before opening a closed door, feel it to see if it is hot. If it is hot, do not open it. There may be flames just outside the door.

3 If you must exit through smoke, crawl along the floor. Smoke and hot air rise, so it is important to stay as low as possible. The air you breathe will be cleaner. The smoke will not be as likely to overcome you.

4 If you can't get out, stay in the room with the door closed. Roll up a blanket or towel and put it across the bottom of the door to keep out smoke. If there is a telephone in the room, call 911 or the fire department. If possible, open the window and yell for help.

5 If your clothing catches fire, stop, drop, and roll. Rolling on the ground will smother the flames. Never run; the rush of air will fan the flames.

6 Once outside, go to the prearranged meeting point. Let everyone know that you are safe. Then someone should call 911 or the fire department. Never go back into a burning building.

Preventing Electrical Shocks

Improper use of electrical appliances or outlets can cause dangerous electrical shocks. To prevent electrical shocks, never use an electrical appliance around water or if you are wet. Unplug small appliances such as hair dryers when they are not in use. To unplug electrical appliances, gently pull the plug, not the cord. In homes with small children, cover unused outlets with plastic outlet protectors.

Gun Safety

If you are in a house where someone keeps a gun, observe all gun safety rules. In many states it is illegal for most teens to own a gun. If you find a gun, do not touch it. Call a parent, guardian, or other trusted adult immediately. Always treat a gun as if it were loaded. Never play with a gun or point it at someone. If you know that someone at school is carrying a gun or any other weapon, tell a school authority right away.

▲ Some schools have metal detectors to help keep guns and other weapons out of schools. **Whom should you tell if you think that a student has brought a weapon to school?**

Lesson 2 Review

 After You Read

Review this lesson for new terms, major headings, and Reading Checks.

What I Learned

1. *Vocabulary* Define *flammable*.

2. *Describe* How can you be prepared for a fire that might happen in your home?

3. *Identify* List three strategies for preventing poisoning.

4. *Give Examples* How can you help keep stairways safe?

Thinking Critically

5. *Synthesize* Explain why it is important to follow rules against bringing a weapon to school and what you should do if you think a classmate has a weapon.

6. *Analyze* Why is it a bad idea to call medicine "candy" to get children to take it?

Applying Health Skills

7. *Refusal Skills* Mark wants to see the hunting rifle that Juan's dad just bought. The rifle is in a locked case, but Juan knows where the key is. How could Juan refuse Mark's request?

Go Online For more Lesson Review Activities, go to glencoe.com.

Lesson 2: Staying Safe at Home **479**

Staying Safe Outdoors

● Building Vocabulary

Many words in English have their roots in other languages. Look up the root language of *pedestrian*.

■ pedestrian (p. 480)

● Reading Strategy

Compare and Contrast Create a chart like the one shown here. As you read this lesson, use the chart to note the similarities and differences between pedestrian and bicycle safety.

● Focusing on the Main Ideas

In this lesson, you will be able to

■ **describe** how to stay safe on the roads.

■ **describe** how to stay safe in your neighborhood.

■ **identify** ways to stay safe in hot and cold weather.

■ **access** valid information about drowning prevention.

■ **describe** how to be safe in and around water.

■ **explain** safety measures for hiking and camping.

	Helmet		
Pedestrian safety			
Bicycle safety	Yes		

Quick Write

Write down three actions you take to stay safe when participating in outdoor activities.

Safety on Foot

Ever since you learned to walk, you have been a pedestrian. A **pedestrian** is *a person who travels on foot*. Safety is important for pedestrians. Start by paying attention to what is happening around you. Follow these rules to become a safer pedestrian.

• Walk on sidewalks when you can or walk on the side of the road facing oncoming traffic.

• Cross in crosswalks when they are available.

• Look both ways several times before crossing, and keep looking and listening for oncoming cars.

◄ Always look both ways before crossing a street. **Why is it dangerous to cross a busy street wearing headphones?**

- If you cross in front of a stopped vehicle, be sure the driver can see you. Make eye contact with him or her before stepping in front of the vehicle.

- If you walk at night, take a well-lit route. Wear light-colored or reflective clothing.

- Do not talk on a cell phone or wear headphones as you walk. Be aware of your surroundings.

 **Reading Check**   **Explain** If no sidewalk is available, which side of the road should you walk on?

Safety on Wheels

Always play it safe when riding a bike, skateboard, or scooter or going in-line skating. Wear a helmet when you take part in these activities. A helmet can protect you from serious head injury if you fall. When using in-line skates, scooters, and skateboards, your gear should also include wrist guards, elbow and knee pads, and light gloves. Make sure your clothing fits well and does not interfere with your activities. Always follow your community's rules on where you can ride your skateboard or scooter. If you are skating, learn how to stop and fall safely.

Before you ride a bike, check the seat and handlebars to make sure they are secure. Test the wheels to see if they spin freely. The tires should be fully inflated, and they should have a large amount of tread. Reflectors on a bike help drivers see you. In some states, all bikes must have them. If you ride at night, your bike should also have a light. Finally, make sure your bike is the right size for you.

Stay alert when you ride. Obey all traffic laws. Ride a bike *with* the flow of traffic. When you ride in a group, ride single file, not side by side. Learn hand signals, and use them before you turn. Avoid riding in bad weather, and keep your speed under control.

 **Reading Check**   **Describe** How do you ride a bike safely?

Safety in Vehicles

Motor vehicle crashes are the leading cause of death for children ages 2 to 14. To be a safety-conscious passenger, wear a safety belt whenever you ride in a vehicle. Safety belts help keep you in your seat if your vehicle gets into a crash. Many cars have air bags, too. Air bags

▼ Helmets, pads, and other safety equipment can help protect you when you bike, skate, or ride a scooter or skateboard. **What is the most important piece of safety equipment to wear while riding a scooter?**

▲ Everyone riding in a car needs to be buckled up. Younger children must be in a car seat. **Why are children safest in the back seat?**

can help keep people in the front seats from colliding with the steering wheel and dashboard. However, the force of air bags can hurt small children. The safest place for children to ride is in the back seat. Infants and small children should ride in an appropriate car seat or booster seat until they are large enough to use a safety belt.

If you take the bus to school, don't bother the bus driver while he or she is driving. Don't get up while the bus is moving or put your arms out the window. When you get off the bus, make sure the bus driver and all drivers of the vehicles around the bus can see you clearly. Don't cross behind the bus. If you are in a bus during an emergency, cooperate with the driver so that you and everyone else on the bus will remain safe.

Describe What should you do to be safe when you are riding in a school bus?

Neighborhood Safety

Violence is physical force used to harm people or damage property. Here are some strategies to help you protect yourself from violence in your neighborhood.

- **Avoid potential trouble.** Don't travel alone at night or go into an area that you know is unsafe. Tell a parent or guardian where you are going. Explain who will be with you and when you will be home. Walk in well-lit places. Leave expensive items at home and carry identification. Also carry a cell phone, money, or a calling card for a pay phone, along with the number of someone you can call for help.

- **Be aware.** Notice the people around you and what they are doing. Move away from anyone who makes you feel uncomfortable.

- **Get help.** If someone tries to touch you or hurt you, scream and get away any way you can. Run to the nearest public or safe place. Find someone who can help you. Call 911. Explain the details of what happened to anyone who can help.

Identify What are two things you can do to stay safe in your neighborhood?

Health Skills Activity

Accessing Information

Preventing Drowning

Use library and Internet resources to research drowning and how it can be prevented. Take notes on what you learn. With your teacher, invite a water safety instructor to visit your class. Have the instructor explain ways to avoid drowning in both warm and cold water.

On Your Own

Create a video or poster that shows and describes the different drowning-prevention techniques for warm and cold water.

Safety at Play

Chances are, you like to spend time outdoors. To stay safe, follow these tips:

- **Take a buddy or two.** When you spend time outdoors, be sure you are with at least one other person. If something happens to you and you are with a group, one friend can stay with you and another friend can go for help.

- **Stay aware.** Learn the signs of weather emergencies. When necessary, move quickly to shelter.

- **Know your limits.** Don't take on more than you can handle. For example, if you are a beginning swimmer, don't try to swim a long distance.

- **Use good judgment.** Plan ahead. Make sure you have the equipment you need and that what you are doing is safe. If you're unsure, ask a trusted adult.

- **Warm up and cool down.** This will help prevent injuries. Stretch after your warm-up and cooldown.

Hot Weather Safety Tips

Your body can overheat when you are active outdoors in hot weather. If you feel dizzy, out of breath, or have a headache, take a break. Keep cool by drinking plenty of water. Rest in the shade when you can. Overworking your body in the heat can lead to two dangerous conditions: heat exhaustion and heatstroke. Signs of heat exhaustion can include cold, clammy skin, dizziness, or nausea. Signs of heatstroke can include an increase in body

Go Online

Visit **glencoe.com** and complete the Interactive Study Guide for Lesson 3.

temperature, difficulty breathing, and a loss of consciousness. Heatstroke can be deadly. If someone shows signs of heatstroke, get medical help right away.

Cold Weather Safety Tips

Cold weather can be dangerous if your body or parts of your body get too cold. When you are active outside in cold weather, dress in layers. Wear a hat, warm footwear, and gloves or mittens. Anyone who starts to feel very cold or shiver should go inside and get warm.

Water Safety

Always think about safety when you are in and around water. **Figure 15.4** lists tips for staying safe in and around water.

Hiking and Camping Safety

Following the tips in **Figure 15.5** will help you stay safe while hiking and camping.

▲ It's important to drink enough liquid when you play or exercise outside. **What are two other ways to stay cool when you're outside?**

▼ FIGURE 15.4

TIPS FOR WATER SAFETY

Taking a swimming and water safety course from a trained instructor is the most important step you can take toward being safe in and around water. **List two other water safety tips.**

- Follow all posted safety rules.

- Swim only when a lifeguard or other trusted adult is present.

- Swim with a buddy.

- Monitor yourself. Don't swim if you are tired or cold, or if you have been out in the sun for too long.

- Look around your environment often. Watch for signs of storms. If you are swimming when a storm begins, get out of the water right away.

- Never swim in water with strong currents.

- Dive only in areas that are marked as safe for diving. The American Red Cross suggests that water be at least nine feet deep for diving or jumping. Never dive into unfamiliar water or into above-ground pools.

- If you are responsible for children, take extra care. Don't let them near the water unless there is a trained lifeguard on duty. Accidents can happen even in small wading pools.

HIKING AND CAMPING SAFETY

Safe hiking and camping takes planning. Why is it important to let people know where you're going hiking and when you plan to return?

- **Never camp or hike alone.** Make sure family members know your schedule and your route. Carry a cell phone or long-range walkie-talkie if you can.

- **Dress properly.** Be aware of the weather and dress accordingly. If you are hiking up a mountain, know that the weather may change as you change altitude. Wear sturdy footwear. Before you hike in any shoes or boots, break them in to avoid getting blisters.

- **Check your equipment.** Take along a supply of fresh water, a first-aid kit, and a flashlight with extra batteries.

- **Know where you are.** Learn how to read a compass and carry one. Carry a map of the area in which you will be hiking or camping.

- **Know the plants and animals.** Learn to recognize the dangerous plants and animals in your area so that you can avoid them. For example, learn what poison ivy and poison oak look like. To avoid insect bites and stings, tuck your pant legs into your socks and apply insect repellent.

- **Use fire responsibly.** Learn the proper way to build a campfire. Put out all campfires completely before you go to sleep or leave the campsite. To do so, soak the campfires with water or cover them completely with sand or dirt.

Lesson 3 Review

After You Read

Review this lesson for new terms, major headings, and Reading Checks.

What I Learned

1. *Vocabulary* What is a *pedestrian*?

2. *Identify* What are the signs of heatstroke?

3. *Describe* How can you dive safely?

4. *Give Examples* Name three items to take along when hiking.

Thinking Critically

5. *Apply* While Jordan is visiting his friend Mario, he loses track of the time. When he leaves Mario's house to walk home, it's dark. What would you advise Jordan to do?

6. *Analyze* Why should you cross in front of a school bus and not behind it?

Applying Health Skills

7. *Advocacy* Create a poster that displays the dangerous plants in your area. Show plants such as poison ivy or poison oak as well as plants that are poisonous if eaten. Post a phone number to call if someone has eaten a poisonous plant.

Lesson 4

Weather Emergencies and Natural Disasters

Guide to Reading

● **Building Vocabulary**

As you read this lesson, write each new highlighted term and its definition on separate index cards. Practice matching the definition to the term.

- weather emergencies (p. 486)
- tornado (p. 487)
- hurricane (p. 488)
- blizzard (p. 488)
- hypothermia (p. 489)
- earthquake (p. 490)
- aftershocks (p. 490)

● **Focusing on the Main Ideas**

In this lesson, you will be able to

- **describe** the different types of weather emergencies and natural disasters.
- **list** safety measures to take during a weather emergency or natural disaster.
- **practice** healthful behaviors by preparing an emergency supplies kit.

● **Reading Strategy**

Predicting Skim the headings, figures, photos, and captions in this lesson. Then jot down two questions that you think might be answered in the lesson.

Quick Write

What is one kind of weather emergency that is common in your area? List two things you could do to stay safe during that emergency.

What Are Weather Emergencies?

Weather events make the news on a fairly regular basis. Reports from around the world tell of disasters that destroy property and even take lives. These events often happen with little warning. People cannot prevent them. **Weather emergencies** are *dangerous situations brought on by changes in the atmosphere*. Weather emergencies are natural events. Examples include thunderstorms, tornadoes, hurricanes, and blizzards.

The National Weather Service (NWS) works to track the progress of storms. The NWS sends out bulletins to the public. The bulletins keep people informed about possible weather emergencies. This helps keep people and communities safe. Storm bulletins may involve watches or warnings. A storm watch indicates that a storm is likely to develop. A storm warning indicates that a severe storm has already developed and a weather emergency is happening. As a result, people in the area are in danger. If your area is under a storm warning, turn on the television or radio. Follow the instructions of the NWS and local officials.

Technology has helped scientists who watch the weather. Satellites gather data very quickly and feed it into powerful computers. Computers can also help predict the paths of storms. Television and the Internet can warn the public of danger very quickly. These early warnings give people more time to plan and stay safe.

Tornadoes

Tornadoes are a type of weather emergency. A **tornado** is *a whirling, funnel-shaped windstorm that drops from storm clouds to the ground.* Tornadoes can happen all over the United States. However, states in the Midwest and those nearest the Gulf of Mexico experience more tornadoes than other states do. In fact, this region is often called "Tornado Alley."

Tornadoes typically happen in the summer. They can be up to a mile wide. Most tornadoes move at about 25 to 40 miles per hour, although some speed along as fast as 60 miles per hour. **Figure 15.6** explains the conditions that lead to a tornado.

▼ FIGURE 15.6

HOW A TORNADO FORMS

Tornadoes can occur during a storm if two air masses collide and begin to spin. **What should you do if you are inside a building during a tornado?**

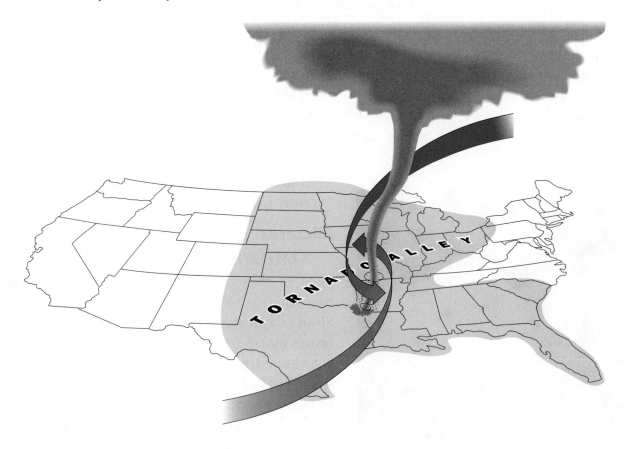

If a tornado watch is issued for your area, listen to the radio for updates. Decide where you will take shelter if you need to protect yourself. If a tornado warning is issued for your area, get to this shelter right away.

- **Where to go.** You are safest underground in a cellar or basement. If you cannot go underground, take shelter in a windowless room or hallway. If you are outdoors, lie in a ditch or flat on the ground. Stay away from trees, cars, and anything that could fall on you.

- **What to do.** Cover yourself with whatever protection you can find. If you are in the basement, try to get under a workbench. If you are in a room with furniture, stay under a heavy table. Lying in a bathtub under a cushion, mattress, or blanket may also offer good protection. Stay where you are. The storm will pass quickly.

Hurricanes

A **hurricane** is *a strong windstorm with driving rain that forms over the sea.* Each hurricane has a center, or eye, where the weather conditions are calm. A circular cloud mass swirls around the eye. This swirling mass gives the hurricane its high winds. The faster the air mass swirls, the more powerful the hurricane.

Most hurricanes happen in the late summer or early fall. Unlike tornadoes, hurricanes form and move slowly. As a result, scientists can estimate when and where a hurricane will hit land. This gives people time to plan ahead. Take these steps to stay safe in a hurricane.

- Board up windows and doors. Bring inside items such as furniture and bikes that wind could smash into houses.

- Evacuate, or leave the area, immediately if the NWS tells you to do so.

- If no evacuation is called for, stay indoors away from windows and doors.

Blizzards

A **blizzard** is *a very heavy snowstorm with winds up to 45 miles per hour.* Blizzards can last from an hour or two to several days. During a blizzard, always stay inside. The driving snow that a blizzard brings makes it very hard to see anything. People who leave their houses during blizzards can lose their sense of direction easily. They may get lost. In fact, a person may not be able to find his or her own home, even if it is only a few yards away.

▼ This is an image taken of a hurricane. **Give one example of how technology has affected predictions of weather emergencies.**

If you are outside when a blizzard begins, find shelter as soon as possible. Get inside and stay inside. One danger in a blizzard is hypothermia. **Hypothermia** is *a sudden and dangerous drop in body temperature.* Hypothermia can shut down your body's systems, so they stop functioning properly. It can even lead to death. To prevent hypothermia, keep your head, face, and body covered and warm. If you're in a car, pull over to the side of the road. Stay in the car, and turn on its flashers.

▲ The cold weather, high winds, and snowfall of a blizzard can be dangerous. **Why is hypothermia a danger for someone caught outside in a blizzard?**

Thunderstorms and Lightning

Lightning is a dramatic and dangerous side effect of thunderstorms. Florida leads the United States in the number of lightning strikes that happen each year. It is also the leading state for the number of people killed by lightning. How can you protect yourself during thunderstorms? If possible, stay inside or seek shelter as soon as possible. Unplug electrical appliances and computers. Be prepared for a power loss. Also, avoid using telephones or running water during a storm with lightning. If you are caught outdoors when lightning is striking, crouch low to the ground. Keep away from electrical poles and wires, tall trees, water, and metal objects.

 Reading Check   **Describe** What should you do if you are caught outside when lightning is striking?

What Are Natural Disasters?

A natural disaster is an event caused by nature that results in widespread damage. Natural disasters include floods and earthquakes. Plan ahead so you can stay safe if a natural disaster strikes. Keep some basic supplies on hand such as fresh water, a radio, a flashlight, batteries, blankets, canned food, a can opener, and a first-aid kit.

Floods

Of natural disasters, only floods kill more people than lightning strikes. Flash floods are the most dangerous of all. Flash-flood waters rise very quickly and are surprisingly powerful. Two feet of moving water has enough force to sweep away cars. More water than that can carry away trucks and houses.

► Water in motion is a very powerful force. It can wash away cars, trucks, and even buildings. Never try to cross water in a flood. **Why should you never try to cross water that is flooding across a road?**

If the NWS issues a flood watch for your area, follow their warning instructions. Take your emergency kit, and go to the highest place in your home. Listen to a battery-powered radio for a flood warning. If a flood warning is issued and you are told to evacuate, do so immediately. The following tips can help you survive a flood:

- Head for higher ground. The home of a relative or neighbor who lives outside the warning area on higher ground is a good choice.

- Never walk, swim, ride a bike, or drive a car through flooding water. You could be swept away, drown, or be electrocuted.

- Drink only bottled water. Floodwater is easily polluted by garbage and other waste.

- If you have evacuated the area, return home only after you are told it is safe for you to do so.

- Once you return home, throw away contaminated food. Disinfect everything that has come into contact with the floodwater.

Earthquakes

An **earthquake** is *a shifting of the earth's plates, resulting in a shaking of the earth's surface.* An earthquake happens when a large piece of the earth's crust actually moves. Earthquakes usually involve more than a single event. A large quake typically is followed by a series of aftershocks. **Aftershocks** are *smaller earthquakes, as the earth readjusts after the main earthquake.*

Health Skills Activity

Practicing Healthful Behaviors

Creating an Emergency Supplies Kit

During an emergency or disaster, an emergency supplies kit can save your life. Your kit should include enough supplies to last your family for three days. If you have to evacuate your home, take these supplies plus sturdy walking shoes, money, and any necessary prescription medicines.

- **Gallon jugs of fresh water.** Allow one gallon of fresh water per person per day.
- **Canned food.** Select food that can be eaten with little or no preparation.
- **Can opener and eating utensils.**
- **First-aid kit.** Include bandages and any needed prescription medicines, along with doses and instructions for taking the medicine.
- **Small battery-powered or crank-powered radio.**
- **Flashlight.**
- **Spare batteries for the flashlight and radio.**

On Your Own

Create your own emergency supplies kit with all the appropriate safety supplies. Prepare a personal and family emergency plan to follow in case of an emergency.

Scientists still can't predict earthquakes very accurately. However, they can measure how strong earthquakes are when they happen. Scientists use the Richter scale to measure the strength of all but the very largest earthquakes. The Richter scale rates the magnitude, or force, of ground motion during an earthquake. An earthquake that measures 1 on this scale is slight. One that measures a 2 is 10 times stronger than 1. Likewise, one that measures a 3 is 10 times stronger than 2, and so on. Many small earthquakes happen every month. The most destructive earthquakes have a magnitude of 7 or more on the Richter scale. They are much less common. Scientists have never recorded an earthquake that measures more than about 9 on the Richter scale. **Figure 15.7** describes how you can protect yourself during an earthquake.

Visit glencoe.com and complete the Interactive Study Guide for Lesson 4.

Reading Check

Apply How many times stronger is an earthquake that measures 2 on the Richter scale than an earthquake that measures 1?

PROTECTING YOURSELF DURING AN EARTHQUAKE

During an earthquake, stay clear of falling objects. Why do you think standing in a doorway could help keep you safe during an earthquake?

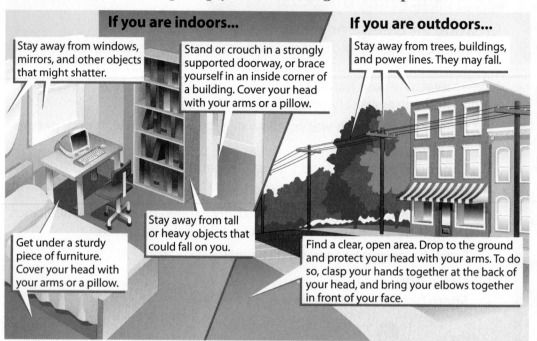

Lesson 4 Review

 After You Read

Review this lesson for new terms, major headings, and Reading Checks.

What I Learned

1. *Vocabulary* What is an *earthquake*?

2. *Describe* What are two risks of being outside in a blizzard?

3. *Identify* What time of year do most hurricanes happen?

4. *Give Examples* Name four items that should be part of an emergency supplies kit.

5. *Explain* What regions of the United States are likely to experience tornadoes?

Thinking Critically

6. *Infer* Why do you think aftershocks are sometimes more deadly than the initial earthquake?

7. *Apply* You are playing soccer in a field, and you see a flash of lightning from an approaching thunderstorm. What should you do?

Applying Health Skills

8. *Practicing Healthful Behaviors* Peter's family lives in Tornado Alley. What can Peter do to be safety conscious about tornadoes?

Go Online For more Lesson Review Activities, go to glencoe.com.

Giving First Aid

Guide to Reading

● Building Vocabulary

Fold a piece of paper in half lengthwise. As you read this lesson, write each new highlighted term on one side of the fold, and write the definition on the other. Then fold the paper to quiz yourself on the definitions.

- first aid (p. 493)
- cardiopulmonary resuscitation (CPR) (p. 494)
- rescue breathing (p. 494)
- abdominal thrusts (p. 496)
- chest thrusts (p. 497)
- first-degree burn (p. 498)
- second-degree burn (p. 498)
- third-degree burn (p. 498)
- fracture (p. 498)
- dislocation (p. 498)

● Focusing on the Main Ideas

In this lesson, you will be able to

- **list** steps to take in an emergency.
- **describe** how to perform CPR.
- **describe** ways to help a person who is choking.
- **explain** how to stop severe bleeding.
- **describe** how to treat burns.
- **describe** treatments for fractures, sprains, and bruises.
- **practice** healthful behaviors to avoid burns.

● Reading Strategy

Predicting Read the main headings, and look at the figures in this lesson. Then write down three pieces of information that you think might be covered in the lesson. After you have completed the lesson, look back to see whether your predictions were correct.

Quick Write

Write a couple of sentences describing how you would treat a minor burn.

Emergency Situations

In emergency situations, time is often critical. Acting quickly and correctly can save someone's life. When an emergency happens, call 911 or the emergency number in your area. Give your name, location, and reason for calling. Explain the condition of the injured person. Describe what help he or she has already received. If you cannot call, have someone else call right away.

Knowing basic first aid may help you deal with some emergencies while you wait for help to arrive. **First aid** is *the immediate care given to someone who becomes injured or ill until regular medical care can be provided.* Anyone who has received first aid should be taken to a medical provider as soon as possible.

Explain What information should you give when calling 911 or another emergency number?

Taking Universal Precautions

To protect yourself and the victim when giving first aid, follow *universal precautions*. These are steps you can take to minimize contact with blood and other body fluids, which can contain viruses. Whenever possible, wear gloves when giving first aid to a victim. Avoid touching any object that was in contact with the victim's blood. Wear a face mask or use a mouthpiece, if one is available, when giving a victim rescue breaths. Always wash your hands immediately after giving first aid.

Restoring Breathing and Heartbeat

All organs, including the brain, need oxygen-rich blood to work properly. If the heart stops beating, the flow of blood to the brain stops, too. When the brain stops functioning, breathing also stops. In this situation, check to see if the victim can respond before taking action. Tap the victim and shout, "Are you OK?" If there is no response, call 911. A trained person should then begin **cardiopulmonary resuscitation** (or CPR), *a first-aid procedure to restore breathing and circulation.* The first steps of CPR involve checking the victim's airway and rescue breathing. **Rescue breathing** is *a first-aid procedure where someone forces air into the lungs of a person who cannot breathe on his or her own.* The steps needed to perform rescue breathing are shown below in **Figure 15.8.**

▼ FIGURE 15.8

RESCUE BREATHING

CPR begins with checking the airway and rescue breathing. Why do you need to make sure that the airway is cleared before performing rescue breaths?

Before performing rescue breathing, check to see if the victim is breathing. Tilt the victim's head back and lift the chin. Look, listen, and feel for normal breathing for 5 to 10 seconds. Signs of normal breathing include

- seeing the person's chest rise and fall.
- hearing breathing sounds, including wheezing or gurgling.
- feeling air moving out of the person's mouth or nose.

If you cannot detect signs of breathing, begin rescue breathing. Follow these steps:
1. Pinch the victim's nose shut with your thumb and forefinger. With your other hand, tilt the victim's chin upward to open the airway.
2. If you have a sterile breathing mask available, place it securely over the victim's mouth and nose. Then take a breath and place your mouth over the opening in the

mask. If you do not have a mask, take a breath and place your mouth over the victim's mouth, forming a tight seal.
3. Exhale for one second and watch to see if the victim's chest rises.
4. Remove your mouth from the person's mouth and take another breath. Allow the victim's chest to fall, and feel the air escape. Then give the victim a second breath.

PERFORMING THE CPR CYCLES

Performing CPR correctly involves switching between rescue breaths and chest compressions. When performing CPR on an adult, how many chest compressions should you perform before giving two rescue breaths?

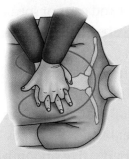  

1 To perform chest compressions, kneel next to the victim's chest. Find a spot on the center of the chest. Place the heel of one hand on that point. Place your other hand on top of the one you just put into position. Interlock your fingers with the fingers of the other hand. Raise your fingers so they do not touch the person's chest.

2 Kneel over the victim so that your shoulders are directly over your hands. Be sure your elbows are locked. Press straight down quickly and firmly at a rate of about 100 compressions per minute. Allow the victim's chest to spring back between compressions. After every 30 compressions, give the victim two rescue breaths.

3 After performing 30 compressions, give two more rescue breaths. Repeat the cycle of 30 compressions and two breaths until the victim breathes, coughs, or moves, or until professional rescuers arrive to take over.

The basic cycle of CPR involves switching between rescue breaths and chest compressions. For adults and children over the age of 12, alternate two rescue breaths with 30 chest compressions. This cycle is illustrated above in **Figure 15.9.** If you are planning to babysit, contact the American Red Cross for training in CPR for young children and infants.

Automated External Defibrillators (AEDs)

When a person's heart stops beating, an automated external defibrillator (AED) can help restore the heartbeat. This electronic device sends a quick jolt of electricity to the heart through the chest to make the heart start beating again. More and more public places keep AEDs on hand. Anyone can receive training on how to use them. In this way, more lives can be saved.

 **Explain** What does an AED do?

How to Help Someone Who Is Choking

Choking results when a person's airway becomes blocked. Signs of choking include grabbing at the throat and neck, coughing, gagging, wheezing, or turning blue in the face. If someone appears to be choking but can cry, speak, or cough forcefully, do not try to give first aid. Air is still able to pass to the lungs. However, if the choking person makes no sound and cannot speak or cough, give first aid immediately. A person can die from choking within minutes.

For an adult or child who is choking, give the person five back blows. To perform back blows, stand slightly behind the person. Place one arm diagonally across the chest and lean the person forward. Strike the person between the shoulder blades five times. If the back blows do not dislodge the object, give five abdominal thrusts. **Abdominal thrusts** are *quick inward and upward pulls into the diaphragm to force an obstruction out of the airway.* **Figure 15.10** shows how to perform abdominal thrusts.

▼ FIGURE 15.10

FIRST AID FOR CHOKING

Follow these steps to help a person who is choking. Why do you think chest thrusts are used to help a choking infant?

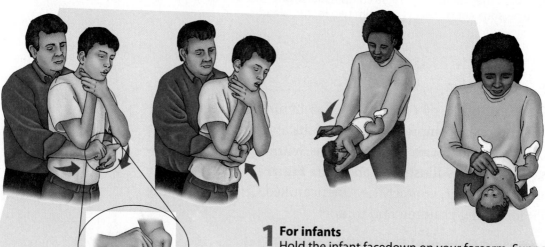

1 For adults and children Place the thumb side of your fist against the person's abdomen, just above the navel. Grasp your fist with your other hand.

2 Give quick, inward and upward thrusts. Give five abdominal thrusts and then five back blows until the person coughs up the object. If the person becomes unconscious, call 911 or the local emergency number. Begin CPR.

1 For infants
Hold the infant facedown on your forearm. Support the child's head and neck with your hand. Point the head downward so that it is lower than the chest. With the heel of your free hand, give the child five blows between the shoulder blades. If the child doesn't cough up the object, move on to chest thrusts (step 2).

2 Turn the infant over onto his or her back. Support the head with one hand. With two or three fingers, press into the middle of the child's breastbone—directly between and just below the nipples—five times. Repeat chest thrusts until the object comes out or the infant begins to breathe, cry, or cough. Make sure a health care professional checks the infant. If the infant becomes unconscious, call 911.

If an infant is choking, hold the infant face down along your forearm. You can use your thigh for support. Hit the area on the infant's back between the shoulder blades five times with the heel of your other hand. Then turn the infant over and perform chest thrusts. **Chest thrusts** are *quick presses into the middle of the breastbone to force an obstruction out of the airway.* Figure 15.10 shows how to help an infant who is choking.

If you start to choke and there's no one around, use your fist and hand to perform abdominal thrusts on yourself. If this does not work right away, do abdominal thrusts on a low railing or the back of a chair, as shown in the photo on this page.

 **Identify** When does a person need first aid for choking?

How to Stop Severe Bleeding

Severe bleeding can be a life-threatening emergency. Blood loss prevents oxygen from getting to the body's organs. If possible, put on sterile gloves before helping someone who is bleeding. Avoid touching anyone else's blood. The blood may contain viruses or other pathogens that can make you sick. If the victim has a wound that is bleeding severely or needs other medical help, call 911 before taking action. Wash the wound with mild soap and water to remove dirt and debris. Then follow these steps to control the bleeding:

- If possible, raise the wounded body part above the level of the heart.
- Cover the wound with sterile gauze or a clean cloth.
- Press the palm of your hand firmly against the gauze. Apply steady pressure to the wound for five minutes, or until help arrives. Do not stop to check the wound; you may interrupt the clotting of the blood.
- If blood soaks through the gauze, do not remove it. Instead, add another gauze pad on top of the first and continue to apply pressure.
- Once the bleeding slows or stops, secure the pad firmly in place with a bandage or strips of gauze or other material. The pad should be snug, but not so tight that you cannot feel the victim's pulse.
- Stay with the victim until help arrives.

 **Explain** What should you do if the cloth you have used to cover a wound is soaked with blood?

▲ If abdominal thrusts with your hands fail, try using a low railing or a chair. **Why is it important to remove objects blocking the airway as soon as possible?**

G Online

Topic: First-Aid Skills

Visit **glencoe.com** for Student Web Activities where you can find out more about first-aid techniques, and how and where to learn them.

Activity: Using the information provided at the link above, make an emergency checklist card that list steps to take in a medical emergency, has space to write local emergency numbers and gives the name of organizations to contact about taking first-aid classes.

Burns

Being safety conscious can help you avoid burns. For example, never play with matches or fire. Handle hot foods carefully. Avoid making the water too hot in the shower. Sunburns can be serious, too. Protect yourself by wearing sunscreen, staying covered, and limiting time in the sun.

If you do get burned, make sure the burn gets treated. The following is a list of the different types of burns and ways to treat them.

A first-degree burn, or superficial burn, is *a burn in which only the outer layer of skin has burned and turned red.* To treat this type of burn, flush the burned area with cold water for at least 20 minutes. Do not use ice. Then loosely wrap the burn in a clean, dry dressing. Most sunburns are first-degree burns.

A second-degree burn, or partial-thickness burn, is *a moderately serious burn in which the burned area blisters.* To treat this type of burn, flush the burned area with cold water (not ice) for at least 20 minutes. Elevate the burned area. Loosely wrap the cooled burn in a clean, dry dressing. Do not pop blisters or peel loose skin.

A third-degree burn, or full-thickness burn, is *a very serious burn in which all the layers of skin are damaged.* These burns usually result from fire, electricity, or chemicals. Third-degree burns require immediate medical attention. Call 911 or another emergency number immediately. Do not try to remove burned clothing. Reduce the heat on the affected area and then cover with a clean cloth. Only a medical professional should treat full-thickness burns.

Describe How should you first treat all first- and second-degree burns?

Treating Other Emergencies

Other common injuries include broken bones, dislocations, sprains, bruises, and animal and insect bites.

Broken bones and dislocations. *A break in a bone* is called a **fracture.** Fractures usually happen along the length of a bone. However, problems can also develop where bones meet at a joint. A **dislocation** is *a major injury that happens when a bone is forced from its normal position within a joint.* For example, a dislocation happens if your upper arm bone is pulled out of your shoulder socket. Moving a broken bone or dislocated joint could cause further injury. For both fractures and dislocations, call for help at once. While you wait for help, keep the victim still. Once a trained medical professional arrives, he or she can then immobilize the fracture or dislocation.

Visit **glencoe.com** and complete the Interactive Study Guide for Lesson 5.

Sprains and bruises. To treat these types of injuries, keep the victim still. Then use the P.R.I.C.E. formula that you learned about in Chapter 3: **P**rotect the injured part, **R**est the injured part, **I**ce the injured part using an ice pack with a towel between the skin and the ice (be sure to remove it every 15–20 minutes so that it does not become too cold), **C**ompress the part with a bandage, and **E**levate the part above the level of the heart. Remember to report any injury to a coach or teacher, as well as a parent or guardian.

Insect and Animal Bites. Insect bites and stings can be painful but are not usually dangerous unless the person is allergic to the venom of the insect. If an allergic person has been stung, get medical help immediately. For all other bites and stings follow these steps:

- Remove the stinger by scraping it off with a firm, straight-edged object. Do not use tweezers.

- Wash the site thoroughly with mild soap and water.

- Apply ice (wrapped in a cloth) to the site for ten minutes to reduce pain and swelling. Alternate ten minutes on and off.

To treat animal bites, wash the bite with soap and water. Apply pressure to stop any bleeding. Apply antibiotic ointment and a sterile dressing. For any bite that has broken the skin, contact your doctor.

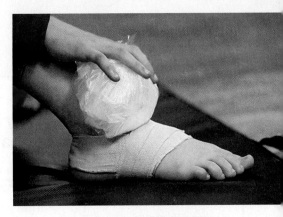

▲ Ice helps slow swelling after a sprain. **How can you reduce the risk of sprains during physical activity?**

Lesson 5 Review

 After You Read

Review this lesson for new terms, major headings, and Reading Checks.

What I Learned

1. ***Vocabulary*** What is the difference between a *fracture* and a *dislocation*?

2. ***Describe*** What are the steps of CPR?

3. ***Give Examples*** What kinds of accidents can cause third-degree burns?

4. ***Explain*** What can you do if you are choking and there is no one around to help?

Thinking Critically

5. ***Apply*** Why should medical professionals always wear gloves when they help someone who is bleeding?

6. ***Infer*** Why can you infer that a person who cannot speak or cry is choking?

Applying Health Skills

7. ***Advocacy*** Create a brochure that explains the steps of CPR. Also explain why it's important to know CPR.

Accessing Information

Practicing Healthful Behaviors

Stress Management

Analyzing Influences

Communication Skills

Refusal Skills

Conflict Resolution

Decision Making

Goal Setting

Advocacy

Why is it Important to Practice Healthful Behaviors?

When you practice healthful behaviors you take specific actions to stay healthy and avoid risky behaviors. This will help you prevent injury, illness, disease, and other health problems. The following behaviors will help you make a safer place.

- Make home safety checks.
- Plan for safety emergencies.
- Share safety plans with family members.

Safety at Home

Follow the Model, Practice, and Apply steps to help you master this important health skill.

❶ Model

Read how Matt practices healthful behaviors by conducting a safety check of his home to identify potential hazards.

Matt's grandmother was coming for a visit. Matt's father wanted to be sure she would stay safe during her visit. He asked Matt to help develop a safety plan. Matt did a safety check of the rooms and stairways. He made a list of possible hazards and solutions. Look at the safety plan Matt made.

Safety Plan

Room	Hazard	Solution
Kitchen	Slippery floor mat in front of sink	Remove the floor mat.
Bathroom	Slippery bathtub	Buy and place a mat in the tub.
Stairway	Loose handrail (missing screws)	Replace screws.

Matt and his dad worked together to make the repairs. Thanks to Matt's help, his grandmother enjoyed a safe visit.

② Practice

Andrew works with his parents to create a fire escape plan for their home. Read the passage below and then practice healthful behaviors by answering the questions that follow.

In health class, Andrew learned about how to safely escape fires. He suggested to his parents that they come up with a fire safety plan for their home. Andrew's parents asked him to develop the plan for their family. Look at the floor plan of Andrew's house and answer the following questions.

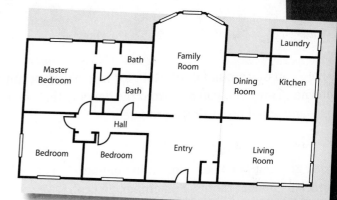

1. What are the escape options they should consider?

2. What action should they take if an escape route is blocked?

3. How can they ensure that all family members are familiar with the plan?

③ Apply

Apply what you have learned about safety by completing the activity below.

Create a fire escape plan for your home. First, draw a floor plan of your house or apartment. Then show the escape routes from each room and a meeting point outside. Present your plan to a classmate and explain common causes of fires in homes. Take your plan home and practice it with your family.

Self-Check
- Did I draw a floor plan and show escape routes?
- Did I have a meeting point outside?
- Did I explain causes of fires in homes?

The Internet is like any tool. You've got to use it right to stay safe.

10 Tips for CYBER SAFETY

There's no way around it. Whether for schoolwork or fun, it's almost impossible to avoid using the Internet. However, you *can* avoid the dangers that might be lurking online. Just follow these 10 easy tips—and you'll be surfing more safely.

1. No sharing!

Don't give out personal information online, especially in chat rooms. Remember, you can't actually see the people in chat rooms. Some may not be telling the truth about themselves.

2. Get permission.

Make sure to get the okay from a trusted adult before heading online—and especially before filling out any forms on the Internet.

3. NEVER meet in person.

Never agree to meet in person someone you've "met" online. This is extremely dangerous.

4. Don't send photos to strangers online.

In addition, be sure to get permission from a trusted adult before sending photos to friends.

5. Look before you link.

Some sites are not intended for you. To avoid them, don't click on links that are sent in e-mails from strangers.

6. Be careful of what you download.

Unless a site has a solid reputation, don't use it to download applications. The applications could come with viruses and spyware attached.

7. Keep your passwords private.

Your passwords are types of protection. Never reveal them to people online.

8. Watch out for viruses.

If you open an attachment from a stranger, you might be inviting a virus into your computer. Be sure to run a virus scan before opening any attachments—even if you know the sender. He or she could be passing along a virus without even knowing it.

9. Turn on your filter.

Search engines and browsers have a filter function that can block information that's not meant for you. Check out the "preferences" tab to set it up.

10. Talk to a trusted adult.

Feeling uncomfortable or scared about something that happened online? Tell a trusted adult about it immediately.

15 Reading Review

Visit glencoe.com to download quizzes and eFlashcards for Chapter 15.

FOLDABLES® Study Organizer

Foldables® and Other Study Aids Take out the Foldable® that you created for Lesson 1 and any graphic organizers that you created for Lessons 1–5. Find a partner and quiz each other using these study aids.

Lesson 1 Preventing Injury

Main Idea Being safety conscious means being aware that safety is important and acting safely.

- Eliminating hazards in your environment will help you prevent accidental injuries.
- Breaking the accident chain involves changing the situation, the unsafe habit, or the unsafe action.

Lesson 2 Staying Safe at Home

Main Idea Staying safe while at home involves taking action to prevent fires, injuries, and gun-related accidents.

- Smoke alarms and fire extinguishers help keep homes safe.
- Falls in the kitchen, bathroom, and stairway are common injuries in the home.
- Always treat as gun as if it were loaded. Never play with a gun or point it at someone.

Lesson 3 Staying Safe Outdoors

Main Idea Wearing appropriate clothing and safety gear can help you stay safe when participating in outdoor activities.

- Safety on foot requires being an alert pedestrian.
- Safety in vehicles includes wearing a safety belt and not distracting the driver.

- Safety in the neighborhood includes avoiding trouble and being aware of danger.

Lesson 4 Weather Emergencies and Natural Disasters

Main Idea Weather emergencies include tornadoes, hurricanes, blizzards, and thunderstorms. Natural disasters include floods and earthquakes.

- Weather emergencies are dangerous situations brought on by changes in the atmosphere.
- Natural disasters are dramatic events caused by earth's processes.
- You can protect yourself in weather emergencies and natural disasters by following any instructions issued by authorities and by being prepared.

Lesson 5 Giving First Aid

Main Idea First aid is the immediate care given to someone who becomes injured or ill until regular medical care can be provided.

- CPR is the first aid for someone whose heart has stopped beating.
- Abdominal thrusts can help save someone who is choking.
- To control bleeding, apply a cloth and direct pressure to the wound and elevate the wound, if possible.
- Flush all burns with cold water for at least 20 minutes. Major burns require medical attention as soon as possible.
- Use the P.R.I.C.E. formula to help victims of sprains and bruises. P.R.I.C.E. stands for **P**rotect, **R**est, **I**ce, **C**ompress, and **E**levate.

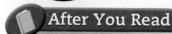

After You Read

Health eSpotlight

VIDEO

Now that you have read the chapter, look back at your answer to the Health eSpotlight question on the chapter opener. Have your ideas changed? What would your answer be now?

Reviewing Vocabulary and Main Ideas

On a sheet of paper, write the numbers 1–6. After each number, write the term from the list that best completes each statement.

- safety conscious
- accidental injuries
- hazard
- flammable
- smoke alarm
- fire extinguisher

Lesson 1 Preventing Injury

1. _____ are injuries caused by unexpected events.

2. Anything that is a potential source of danger is a _____.

3. If you are _____, you are aware that safety is important.

Lesson 2 Staying Safe at Home

4. A _____ can be used to put out a grease fire.

5. Materials that are _____ are able to catch fire easily.

6. A _____ can warn you that there is a fire in the house.

*On a sheet of paper, write the numbers 7–12. Write **True** or **False** for each statement below. If the statement is false, change the underlined word or phrase to make it true.*

Lesson 3 Staying Safe Outdoors

7. People who travel <u>by car</u> are pedestrians.

8. When you ride your bike, ride <u>with</u> the flow of traffic.

9. To stay safe in cold weather, dress in <u>layers</u>.

Lesson 4 Weather Emergencies and Natural Disasters

10. More people die from <u>earthquakes</u> than from any other natural disaster or weather emergency.

11. The center of a hurricane is called the <u>eye</u>.

12. Tornado Alley includes the <u>East Coast</u> region of the United States.

Lesson 5 Giving First Aid

On a sheet of paper, write the numbers 13 and 14. After each number, write the letter of the answer that best completes each statement.

13. The most serious kind of burn is a
    a. first-degree burn.
    b. second-degree burn.
    c. third-degree burn.

14. Chest thrusts
    a. are used with infants who are choking.
    b. are used with adults who are choking.
    c. are used to stop severe bleeding.

Go Online Visit glencoe.com and take the Online Quiz for Chapter 15.

Thinking Critically

Using complete sentences, answer the following questions on a sheet of paper.

15. **Interpret** When you are hiking, why are you safer with two friends rather than just one friend?

16. **Analyze** You are riding your bike and it starts to rain. You are two miles from home. You see lightning and the rain is getting heavier. You are approaching a fire station, a strip mall, and a neighborhood. What would you do?

Write About It

17. **Expository Writing** Research the kinds of weather emergencies that are most likely to strike in your area. Learn what you can do to protect yourself from each one. Record this information on a sheet of paper.

Applying Technology

Simple Safety

Use Microsoft Word® to create a personal safety cube illustrating how to practice safe behaviors. Follow the steps below to complete your project.

- Working in pairs or groups of three, create a new Microsoft Word® document.
- With Draw Tools form a 3" box. Copy and paste to form a net with 3 across and 4 down.
- Select one safety topic from the text, such as accident prevention, fire safety, gun safety, or water safety, for each side of the cube. Write 2–3 sentences on how to plan ahead and stay safe for each topic.
- Click, drag, and drop digital images from the media files on the right side into each box.
- Make sure your information is accurate and useful for teens.
- Edit for clarity and punctuation.
- Print and cut out. Fold and form your personal safety cube with suggestions on how to plan ahead and stay safe.

Standardized Test Practice

Writing

Read the paragraph below. Write a short essay about other places that you think automatic external defibrillators should be placed to save people who are having heart attacks. Explain your choices.

CPR can save lives, but public access to automatic external defibrillators (AEDs) can save even more. AEDs are machines that detect an irregular or missing heartbeat. In response, they send an electric shock through the chest. This restarts the heart. Every hospital has AEDs. Now, some cities are beginning to place them in more public locations.

They are training people to use them. One city trained police to use AEDs, where every police car carried one of these machines. In that city, the survival rate for people having heart attacks went from 28 percent to 40 percent. Many airports and airplanes have AEDs that have already saved people's lives. The more AEDs that are available, the more lives that can be saved.

TEST-TAKING TIP

When identifying persuasive facts, first eliminate all statements that are not facts.

Chapter Preview

Lesson 1 How Pollution Affects
          Your Health 508

Lesson 2 Protecting the
          Environment.....................513

Building Health Skills.........................518

Hands-on Health 520

Chapter Reading Review...................521

Chapter Assessment 522

▲ *Working with the Photo*

Picking up trash is one way to keep the environment clean. **How do you keep the environment clean in your neighborhood?**

506

Start-Up Activities

HEALTH QUIZ Choose the best answer for each of the following:

1. Fossil fuels include
   a. wind power and solar power.
   b. nuclear power and hydroelectric power.
   c. coal and natural gas.

2. What gas high in the atmosphere protects you from the sun's harmful rays?
   a. nitrogen
   b. carbon dioxide
   c. ozone

3. The three Rs of conservation are reduce, reuse, and
   a. repair.
   b. recycle.
   c. remember.

ANSWERS: 1. c; 2. c; 3. b.

FOLDABLES Study Organizer

As You Read Make this Foldable® to record what you learn in Lesson 1 about the causes and effects of air pollution. Begin with a plain sheet of 8½" × 11" paper or a sheet of notebook paper.

1 Fold the sheet of paper from top to bottom, leaving a 2" tab at the bottom.

2 Fold in half from side to side.

3 Unfold the paper once. Cut along the center fold line of the top layer only. This makes two tabs.

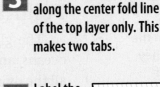

4 Label the tabs as shown.

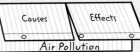

Causes   Effects
Air Pollution

Under the appropriate tab, take notes on the causes and effects of air pollution.

Go Online Visit glencoe.com and complete the Chapter 16 crossword puzzle.

How Pollution Affects Your Health

Guide to Reading

● **Building Vocabulary**
As you read this lesson,
write each new highlighted
term and its definition.

■ pollution (p. 508)

■ fossil fuels (p. 508)

■ acid rain (p. 509)

■ ozone (p. 509)

■ smog (p. 509)

■ groundwater (p. 510)

■ sewage (p. 510)

■ landfills (p. 510)

■ biodegradable (p. 511)

■ hazardous wastes (p. 511)

● **Focusing on the Main Ideas**
In this lesson, you will be able to
■ **describe** the causes and effects of pollution.
■ **identify** which hazardous products may be in your home.

● **Reading Strategy**

Organizing Information Write down all the main headings
and subheadings in this lesson. Use these headings to create
an outline as you read the lesson.

FOLDABLES Study Organizer Use the Foldable® on p. 507 as you
read this lesson.

Quick Write

Which household
products do you
think could harm the
environment if they
were disposed of
improperly? List these
on a sheet of paper.

Pollution and the Environment

The global environment includes forests, mountains, rivers,
oceans, and all living things on earth. Your environment includes
all the living and nonliving things around you. Sometimes people
act in ways that harm the environment. The result is **pollution,**
dirty or harmful substances in the environment. Pollution harms
the environment, can harm your health, and is often ugly. So
it's important for each person to do his or her part to keep the
environment clean.

Reading Check **Identify** What is pollution?

Air Pollution

Most air pollution comes from the burning of fossil fuels.
Fossil fuels are *the oil, coal, and natural gas that are used to provide
energy.* The energy from fossil fuels provides heat for homes and
electricity to power factories, towns, and cities. Fossil fuels also
power most motor vehicles.

Acid Rain

When fossil fuels burn, they **release** gases into the atmosphere. Chemicals in these gases mix with moisture in the air to form **acid rain,** which is *rain that is more acidic than normal rain.* Over time, acid rain can harm plants and even whole forests. It can contaminate freshwater supplies and harm aquatic life, too. Acid rain can even eat away at rock and stone.

Smog

Fossil fuels create other gases when they burn. Some of these gases are changed by heat and sunlight into ozone. **Ozone** is *a gas made of three oxygen atoms.* High up in the atmosphere, ozone occurs naturally and helps protect you from the sun's harmful rays.

Closer to ground level, ozone mixes with other gases to form smog. **Smog** is *a yellow-brown haze that forms when sunlight reacts with air pollution.* Ozone and smog can cause health problems or aggravate existing health problems. For example, people who have bronchitis, asthma, or emphysema have a very hard time breathing when smog is in the air. Many cities issue warnings on days when there is too much smog or ozone in the air. On such days, people sensitive to smog or ozone should limit the time they spend outside.

The Ozone Layer

The naturally occurring layer of ozone in the upper atmosphere shields the earth from the sun's harmful UV rays. In the 1970s, scientists discovered that the ozone layer was breaking down. Chemicals such as the propellants used in aerosol cans, emissions from automobiles, and the chemical that keeps refrigerators and air conditioners cool were damaging the ozone layer. Without the protection of this layer of gas, people are more likely to develop skin cancer and eye damage. That's why it's especially important to protect yourself from the sun's rays with sunscreen and sunglasses. Today, many countries are working to help restore the ozone layer by banning the use of the chemicals that damage it. You can do your part by using products that won't cause more damage to the ozone layer.

Reading Check List What are two types of air pollution?

Academic Vocabulary

release (ree LEES) *(verb)* to free or to let go. *Mario was released from the hospital only after the doctor made sure that his leg was not broken.*

▼ Acid rain can eat away at stone. **How are acid rain and smog related?**

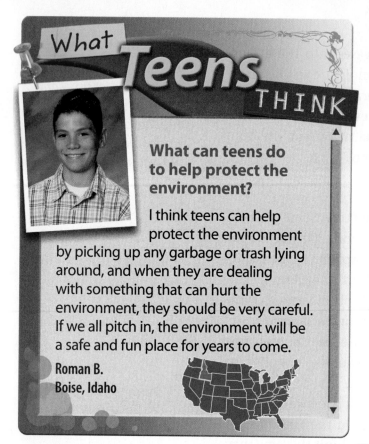

Careers for the 21st Century

Environmental Engineer

Environmental engineers are engineers who apply science and engineering principles to solve environmental problems. Finding ways to solve environmental problems is an ongoing challenge. In order to prepare for a career as an environmental engineer, you should take biology and chemistry classes.

What skills does an environmental engineer need? Go to *Career Corner* at glencoe.com to find out.

Water Pollution

Water pollution is a widespread problem. Forty percent of all the nation's rivers, lakes, streams, and oceans are too polluted to use for swimming, fishing, or drinking. Drinking water comes from sources both above and below the earth's surface. Lakes, rivers, and streams are sources of water above the earth. **Groundwater** is *water that collects under the earth's surface.* Water is dangerous to drink if it becomes polluted.

There are many sources of water pollution. **Sewage** is *human waste, garbage, detergents, and other household wastes washed down drains and toilets.* Sewage can spread diseases such as hepatitis A, typhoid fever, dysentery, and cholera. Factories are another source of water pollution. They can produce industrial waste or cause oil spills. Some factories dump chemical waste into water sources even though it is against the law.

Most of the pollution found in water comes from chemicals like fertilizers and pesticides used on farms or even on your front lawn. The oil that drips from your family car can also pollute water. When the oil mixes with water, it can sink into the earth or run into a stream. Eventually, the polluted water will end up in the ocean where it will hurt all kinds of sea life.

Reading Check

Explain What is the biggest source of water pollution?

Solid Waste

Land may also become polluted. Many of the items we use in daily life are made of plastic and metal. When they are thrown away, these materials take a long time to break down, if they ever do. Much of this solid waste goes into **landfills**—*huge, specially designed pits where waste materials are dumped and buried.* Landfills may have walls or linings of clay or plastic so that water flowing through the landfill does not carry chemicals or other material into water supplies. In time, all landfills get filled up. When this happens, they are capped and sealed. A new landfill is made somewhere else.

Oil spills drop 37 million gallons of oil into the oceans yearly. Yet 363 million gallons of oil go in the oceans from oil changes done at home. **How much more oil comes from oil changes than from oil spills?**

Biodegradable Wastes

Not all solid waste ends up in landfills. Many discarded items are **biodegradable,** or *easily broken down in the environment.* For example, food waste, paper, and wood all break down naturally. Some people set up a compost pile, a place where biodegradable wastes can break down naturally and turn into fertilizer. Leaves, grass, shredded newspaper, and some food wastes are items that can be composted.

 **Reading Check** Define What does *biodegradable* mean?

Hazardous Wastes

Some wastes are hazardous to the health of all living things. These wastes should never go into a landfill. **Hazardous wastes** are *human-made liquid, solid, sludge, or radioactive wastes that may endanger human health or the environment.* Some examples of hazardous wastes are dangerous industrial chemicals, asbestos, radioactive materials, and some medical wastes. Hazardous substances from our homes include: motor oil, paint, insecticides, nail polish remover, antifreeze, bleach, and drain cleaner. Batteries, computers, and air conditioners also contain hazardous wastes.

Because hazardous wastes are dangerous to all living things and the environment, they need to be disposed of properly. Most are stored in facilities where they will not be released into the environment. If you need to dispose of household hazardous waste, contact your local health department or environmental agency.

► Even computers need to be disposed of properly or they can harm the environment. **What other household products need to be disposed of as hazardous waste?**

Visit **glencoe.com** and complete the Interactive Study Guide for Lesson 1.

They will explain how to get rid of it safely. Many communities have drop-off centers to collect household hazardous waste. Never put household hazardous wastes in the regular trash.

Lesson 1 Review

After You Read

Review this lesson for new terms, major headings, and Reading Checks.

What I Learned

1. *Vocabulary* Define *hazardous wastes*.

2. *Explain* Describe how groundwater can become polluted.

3. *List* What are three items that can go into a compost pile? What do these items have in common?

4. *Identify* How is smog formed?

Thinking Critically

5. *Analyze* What is the difference between ozone in the upper atmosphere and ozone nearer to ground level?

6. *Synthesize* Your older brother wants to pour a bottle of antifreeze down the drain. What would you say to encourage him to protect the environment and his health?

Applying Health Skills

7. *Advocacy* Create text and a logo for a sticker that people could put on cabinets that contain household products. The sticker should list common items that are household hazardous waste materials. It should also have space for a local hazardous waste information phone number.

Go Online For more Lesson Review Activities, go to glencoe.com.

Protecting the Environment

Guide to Reading

● **Building Vocabulary**
Write a sentence using each of these terms: *recycle, nonrenewable resources,* and *conservation.* Trade papers with a classmate. Write the possible meanings of the terms based on the sentences.

■ Environmental Protection Agency (p. 513)

■ Occupational Safety and Health Administration (p. 513)

■ recycle (p. 515)

■ nonrenewable resources (p. 516)

■ conservation (p. 516)

● **Focusing on the Main Ideas**
In this lesson, you will be able to

■ **identify** what you can do to keep air and water clean.

■ **describe** how you can reduce solid wastes.

■ **describe** ways in which you can conserve energy and water.

■ **demonstrate** decision-making skills to choose environment-friendly products.

● **Reading Strategy**
Predicting Quickly skim this lesson, writing down all the major headings. Next to each heading, write down what you think the most important point of that section would be.

Quick Write
Write down three ways you can use less water.

You Can Help Reduce Pollution

We can all do our part to help reduce pollution, and in turn, protect our health. When we work together as a community, we can do even more. All around the world, many local and national governments are working together to help stop pollution.

The **Environmental Protection Agency** (EPA) is *an agency of the U.S. government that is dedicated to protecting the environment.* The **Occupational Safety and Health Administration** (OSHA) is *a branch of the U.S. Department of Labor that protects American workers.* OSHA makes sure that work environments are safe and are free of hazardous materials.

◄ Whenever you can, ride a bike rather than in a motor vehicle. It's better for the environment. **What health benefits do you gain from riding a bike?**

Health Skills Activity

Decision Making

Choosing Environment-Friendly Products

Gus, a seventh grader, has a snack when he gets home from school every day. His favorite snack is prepackaged, single-serving crackers and cheese. This snack comes in a plastic tray. It has a plastic knife, crackers, and cheese; all of the items are wrapped in plastic. Gus's sister sees the snack and asks Gus if he can think of another way to have crackers and cheese that doesn't produce so much trash every day.

What Would You Do?

Use the six steps of the decision-making process to help Gus figure out some options that would produce less trash.

1. State the situation.
2. List the options.
3. Weigh the possible outcomes.
4. Consider your values.
5. Make a decision and act on it.
6. Evaluate the decision.

Go Online

Topic: Being Proactive about the Environment

Visit glencoe.com for Student Web Activities where you can learn about different ways to help the environment.

Activity: Using the information provided at the link above, create a "You Can Make a Difference" e-mail urging teens to help protect the environment and listing Web sites where they can find out how.

Helping to Reduce Air Pollution

Reducing air pollution can help keep you and your community safe. Here are some strategies to help reduce air pollution in your community.

- **Carpool or take public transportation.** When you share rides, you burn less fuel. That helps cut down on pollution.

- **Ride your bike or walk to nearby activities.** When you ride a bike or walk rather than ride in a vehicle, you save fuel and reduce pollution.

- **Stay tobacco free.** Tobacco smoke is not only unhealthy for people who smoke, it pollutes the air.

- **Plant trees and other plants.** Plants convert carbon dioxide to oxygen, making the air clean.

Helping to Reduce Solid Waste

The key to reducing solid waste is simple: create as little of it as you can. You can do this by following the three Rs: reduce, reuse, and recycle. **Figure 16.1** shows how using the three Rs can help reduce solid waste.

 Reading Check **List** What are some ways to reduce solid waste?

REDUCE, REUSE, RECYCLE

When you follow the three Rs, you reduce the amount of material that goes into landfills. **How does this help the environment?**

Reuse objects.
Think of other ways to use items you would otherwise throw away. You can buy reusable food containers. Reuse plastic grocery bags as trash bags or to clean up after pets. Donate unwanted clothes to charity rather than throwing them out.

Reduce waste. Cut down on the amount of trash you throw away. Use baskets or cloth bags to carry groceries home. Avoid using paper plates and plastic cups, knives, forks, or spoons. Buy products in bulk to reduce the amount of packaging you throw away and buy items that have less packaging.

Recycle. To **recycle** means *to change items in some way so that they can be used again.* Find out how recycling works in your community. Learn which items can be recycled and how these items are collected. When you buy products made from recycled materials, you are continuing to help the environment.

Helping to Reduce Water Pollution

Everyone needs clean drinking water that is free from disease-causing organisms and harmful **chemicals.** Clean water is important for aquatic plants and animals. The industries and farms that use water to produce the foods and beverages we eat and drink need clean water. We also need clean water for water recreation activities. To help keep water clean, follow these tips.

- Pick up pet waste from public areas to reduce toxic runoff.
- Use environment-friendly soaps, detergents, and cleaners.
- Pick up any litter that is not hazardous.
- Dispose of chemicals properly. Never pour them into a drain.

Academic Vocabulary

chemicals (KEM i kuhlz) *(noun)* substances that can be transformed or broken down using chemistry. *Bleach and other household chemicals should always be kept out of a child's reach.*

▼ FIGURE 16.2

CONSERVING HEAT AND ELECTRICITY

Conserving resources is everybody's job. **How does turning off lights help the environment?**

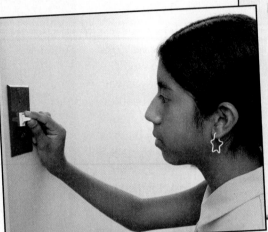

Heating and cooling. Keep doors and windows closed when the furnace or air conditioner is running. Seal cracks around doors and windows. When possible, use fans instead of air conditioners. Dress to keep yourself at a comfortable temperature. For example, in cold weather, wear a sweater. In warmer weather, wear lightweight clothing.

Lighting and appliances. Turn off lights when you leave a room. Turn off appliances, TVs, radios, and computers when they are not in use. Use fluorescent bulbs when possible. If possible, choose energy-efficient appliances. Insulate your hot-water heater. Wash clothes in cold water when you can. Dry clothes on a clothesline instead of in an electric dryer. When you cook a small amount of food, use a microwave oven. Don't preheat an oven more than necessary. Keep the oven door closed while cooking.

Conserving Energy and Water

Some natural resources, like oil from oil wells, can only be used once. Oil is a nonrenewable resource. **Nonrenewable resources** are *substances that cannot be replaced once they are used.* Other examples are the natural gas used to heat many homes and the coal used by many power plants to produce electricity.

Other resources are always being renewed. For example, the supply of freshwater is constantly being renewed through the water cycle. The water cycle is the movement of water through, around, and over the earth. Even renewable resources, however, need to be protected. There is a limited amount of freshwater. Pollution makes freshwater more expensive because polluted water has to be cleaned before it is used. Conservation is a good way to protect resources such as water. **Conservation** is *the saving of resources.* **Figure 16.2** and **Figure 16.3** can help you conserve resources at home.

G Online

Visit **glencoe.com** and complete the Interactive Study Guide for Lesson 2.

Reading Check **Explain** What is conservation?

▼ FIGURE 16.3

CONSERVING WATER

This teen is conserving water by doing a full load of laundry. **If water is a renewable resource, why do we have to conserve it?**

- **Inside** Avoid running the washing machine or dishwasher until you have a full load. Run the washer at the lowest water level that will clean that load. Fix leaky faucets. Never let water run unnecessarily. Install water-saving showerheads. Take shorter showers.

- **Outside** Turn the hose off when you are washing the car. Use the hose only for rinsing the car. Water lawns only when needed. Use soaker hoses for watering gardens. Garden with plants that conserve water.

Lesson 2 Review

📖 After You Read

Review this lesson for new terms, major headings, and Reading Checks.

What I Learned

1. *Vocabulary* What is the *Environmental Protection Agency?*

2. *Give Examples* What can you do to reduce air pollution?

3. *List* Name three ways you can help keep water clean.

4. *Explain* What is a nonrenewable resource? Give one example of a nonrenewable resource.

5. *Identify* Why is it a good idea to turn off lights when you leave a room?

Thinking Critically

6. *Analyze* If conservation is a good idea, why do you think people might still need to be reminded to conserve resources?

7. *Synthesize* Explain how purchasing an item that has less packaging than another similar item can help conserve resources and reduce waste.

Applying Health Skills

8. *Advocacy* Write and illustrate a comic book that encourages teens to conserve electricity and water. In your comic book, be sure to explain why conservation of these resources is important.

Building Health Skills

Accessing Information

Practicing Healthful Behaviors

Stress Management

Analyzing Influences

Communication Skills

Refusal Skills

Conflict Resolution

Decision Making

Goal Setting

Advocacy

What Does Accessing Information Involve?

Accessing information involves finding reliable information to make healthy choices. When looking at a source of information, ask yourself these questions:

- Is it scientific?
- Does it give more than one point of view?
- Does it agree with other sources?
- Is it trying to sell something?

Finding Facts About the Environment

Follow the Model, Practice, and Apply steps to help you master this important health skill.

❶ Model

Read how Cory uses Internet research to access valuable health information.

Cory has asthma and wanted to find out if there is a link between indoor air pollution and asthma. He started by looking on the Internet. Three sites stated that indoor air pollution has contributed to the increase in asthma cases. Two sites were for pharmaceutical companies. These sites featured ads for asthma drugs. The addresses of those Web sites ended in ".com."

A third site was sponsored by a well-known government agency and ended in ".gov." Cory decided the information was probably accurate since all three sites agreed. However, he questioned whether other information at the first two sites was reliable because they were trying to sell medicines. He had more confidence in what he found at the government's site.

② Practice

Help Brandon use accessing-information skills to determine if the Web site information provided by a furnace manufacturer is valid.

Brandon wants to find out what could be done to reduce indoor air pollution. He searched the Internet and found a Web site sponsored by a furnace manufacturer. The site suggested that replacing an old, inefficient furnace with one that was properly vented would help reduce indoor air pollution.

1. Should Brandon accept this information as valid? Why or why not?

2. Explain the steps that he could take to determine if this information is valid.

③ Apply

Apply what you have learned about accessing information to complete the activity below.

Choose an area of the environment that interests you. For example, you may choose pollution or a way to conserve resources such as energy or water. Use three reliable sources of information to find four environmental health facts that teens should know. For example, you might access the Environmental Protection Agency's (EPA) Web site or go to the library to find a book by an expert on the environment. Report your facts to the class. Explain why you think each source that you used is a reliable one.

Self-Check
- Did I find four facts about the environment? Did I use three valid sources?
- Can I tell why each source is reliable?

Building Health Skills

Managing the Packaging

Packaging can be useful when it protects a product. Packaging can also be wasteful. Unnecessary packaging uses up the earth's resources and can harm the environment when discarded.

What You Will Need

- Small bag of potato chips
- Wrapped slices of cheese
- Video game (in original packaging)
- Batteries (in original packaging)
- Graph paper and pencil

What You Will Do

1. Work in small groups to create a graph.
2. Determine the unnecessary packaging of each of the four products. Rate them on a scale from 1 to 5, with 5 being the most unnecessary. Mark the product's rating on the graph's vertical (y) axis.
3. On a scale from 1 to 5, with 5 being the highest, rate the likelihood that a product could be recycled or reused. Mark the product's rating on the horizontal (x) axis.
4. Draw a horizontal line out from the product's packaging rating. Draw a vertical line up from the product's recycling rating. Where the lines meet, write the name of the product.

Wrapping It Up

Which items are easy to rate and which are hard? What did you consider before deciding where to place the product on the graph? Where on the graph do you find the objects that are the most environment-friendly? Where are the least environment-friendly objects?

Reading Review

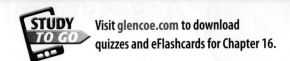
STUDY TO GO Visit glencoe.com to download quizzes and eFlashcards for Chapter 16.

FOLDABLES™ Study Organizer

Foldables™ and Other Study Aids Take out the Foldable™ that you created for Lesson 1. Find a partner and quiz each other using this study aid.

Lesson 1 How Pollution Affects Your Health

Main Idea Pollution harms the environment and your health, and is often ugly.

- Pollution is made up of dirty or harmful substances in the environment.
- Burning fossil fuels such as coal, oil, and natural gas pollutes the air.
- Gases given off during the burning of fossil fuels mix with moisture in the atmosphere to form acid rain.
- Ozone mixes with other air pollutants to form smog.
- Smog worsens respiratory conditions like asthma, bronchitis, and emphysema.
- Chemicals used on land are the primary source of water pollution.
- Water polluted with sewage contains pathogens that can cause disease.
- Landfills are huge, specially constructed pits where solid waste is buried.
- Hazardous waste includes human-made, liquid, solid, sludge, or radioactive wastes.
- Hazardous waste should never be thrown out with the regular trash.
- Biodegradable waste, like food, wood, and paper, is solid waste that can be easily broken down in the environment.

Lesson 2 Protecting the Environment

Main Idea There are many things that you can do to protect the environment.

- Walking, riding a bike, carpooling, taking public transportation, staying tobacco free, and planting trees can all help reduce air pollution.
- Reduce waste by not using plastic cups, plates, forks, knives, and spoons.
- Think of other ways to reuse objects, like grocery bags instead of throwing them away.
- Buy goods made from recycled materials.
- Picking up after pets, picking up litter, using environment-friendly products, and disposing of chemicals properly can all reduce water pollution.
- Some resources, such as fossil fuels, are nonrenewable, meaning that they can be used only once.
- Conserving energy and heat helps reduce pollution and saves natural resources.
- It is important to conserve water because it is a limited resource.

After You Read

HEALTH QUIZ

Now that you have read the chapter, look back at your answers to the Health Quiz on the chapter opener. Would you change any of them? What would your answers be now?

Reviewing Vocabulary and Main Ideas

On a sheet of paper, write the numbers 1–9. After each number, write the term from the list that best completes each statement.

- pollution
- acid rain
- ozone
- smog
- sewage
- groundwater

- landfills
- biodegradable
- hazardous wastes

Lesson 1 How Pollution Affects Your Health

1. _____ are huge, specially designed pits where waste materials are dumped and buried.

2. _____ can carry pathogens that cause disease.

3. Up in the atmosphere, _____ protects people from UV rays; closer to earth, it is part of smog.

4. Waste that is _____ can easily break down in the environment.

5. _____ include antifreeze and nail polish remover.

6. Water that is stored under the earth's surface is called _____.

7. Dirty or harmful substances in the environment are _____.

8. _____ can ruin forests and even eat away at stone.

9. The yellow-brown haze that hangs over cities is called _____.

Lesson 2 Protecting the Environment

*On a sheet of paper, write the numbers 10–15. Write **True** or **False** for each statement below. If the statement is false, change the underlined word or phrase to make it true.*

10. Riding a bike instead of getting a ride in a car can <u>reduce</u> air pollution.

11. The <u>EPA</u> is a government agency that helps reduce pollution.

12. Buying a food container that can be used many times to store food is an example of <u>recycling</u>.

13. Oil, natural gas, and coal are <u>renewable</u> resources.

14. Using fluorescent light bulbs can <u>save</u> electricity.

15. Conservation is the <u>wasting</u> of resources.

On a sheet of paper, write the numbers 16 and 17. After each number, write the letter of the answer that best completes each statement.

16. Planting trees
    a. can help clean the air.
    b. pollutes the air.
    c. reduces solid waste in the environment.

17. Burning fossil fuels
    a. creates renewable resources.
    b. eliminates hazardous waste.
    c. contributes to air pollution.

Go Online Visit **glencoe.com** and take the Online Quiz for Chapter 16.

Thinking Critically

Using complete sentences, answer the following questions on a sheet of paper.

18. Infer What do you think is meant by the saying "We all live downstream"?

19. Interpret A volcanic eruption can send tons of smoke and ash into the air. Do volcanoes pollute? Explain your answer.

Write About It

20. Persuasive Writing Write a short essay explaining why you think some products have more packaging than necessary. Include ideas as to how reducing excess packaging could help the environment.

↗ Applying Technology

A Clean Community

Use iMovie® to make a public service announcement about what people can do to improve life in their communities.

- With a group, choose one of these four topics: recycling, conserving water, conserving electricity, and reducing air pollution.
- Use a video camera to film members of your group showing how your topic helps the environment.
- Export the video to iMovie®.
- Using the editing tab, add titles over a colored screen. In a few sentences, state what your topic is and how it helps the environment.
- Make sure that you say something that will make people want to help the environment.
- Edit for proper punctuation and spelling.
- Save your project.

Standardized Test Practice

Reading

Read the passage and then answer the questions.

Landfills fill up quickly, often because people use and throw away so much plastic. Years ago, before plastics were popular, many items that people threw away would biodegrade fairly easily. Objects made of wood, paper, cotton, or wool would break down naturally over time. Plastic does not break down, so plastic wastes must be stored in a landfill. Recently, scientists have discovered a way to make a sturdy, durable plastic that biodegrades when buried in dirt. Scientists are optimistic that using biodegradable plastic will help reduce the amount of waste buried in landfills.

1. What is the main point of the passage?
   A. Life was better years ago.
   B. Wood and paper are biodegradable.
   C. Biodegradable plastic will reduce the waste in landfills.
   D. Throwing away more plastic will actually reduce the waste in landfills.

2. What does *optimistic* mean in this sentence?

Scientists are optimistic that using biodegradable plastic will help reduce the amount of waste buried in landfills.
   A. certain
   B. doubtful
   C. hopeful
   D. worried

▶ Reading: What's in It for You?

What role does reading play in your life? There are many different ways that reading could be part of what you do every day. Are you on a sports team? Perhaps you like to read the latest news about your favorite team or find out about new ways to train for your sport. Are you interested in music or art? You might be looking for information about ways to create songs or about styles of painting. Are you enrolled in an English class, a math class, or a health class? Then your assignments probably require a lot of reading.

Improving or Fine-Tuning Your Reading Skills Will:

- ◆ Improve your grades
- ◆ Allow you to read faster and more efficiently
- ◆ Improve your study skills
- ◆ Help you remember more information
- ◆ Improve your writing

▶ The Reading Process

Good reading skills build on one another, overlap, and spiral around just like a winding staircase goes around and around while leading you to a higher place. This Reading Guide will help you find and use the tools you'll need before, during, and after reading.

Strategies You Can Use

- ◆ Identify, understand, and learn new words
- ◆ Understand why you read
- ◆ Take a quick look at the whole text
- ◆ Try to predict what you are about to read
- ◆ Take breaks while you read and ask yourself questions about the text
- ◆ Take notes
- ◆ Keep thinking about what will come next
- ◆ Summarize

▶ Vocabulary Development

Vocabulary skills are the building blocks of the reading and writing processes. By learning to use a number of strategies to build your word skills, you will become a stronger reader.

Use Context to Determine Meaning

The best way to increase your vocabulary is to read widely, listen carefully, and take part in many kinds of discussions. When reading on your own, you can often figure out the meanings of new words by looking at their **context**, the other words and sentences that surround them.

> ## Tips for Using Context
>
> **Look for clues such as:**
>
> A synonym or an explanation of the unknown word in the sentence:
> *Elise's shop specialized in **millinery**, or hats for women.*
>
> A reference to what the word is or is not like:
> *An **archaeologist**, like a historian, deals with the past.*
>
> A general topic associated with the word:
> *The **cooking** teacher discussed the best way to braise meat.*
>
> A description or action associated with the word:
> *He used the **shovel** to **dig up** the garden.*

Predict a Possible Meaning

Another way to determine the meaning of a word is to take the word apart. If you understand the meaning of the **base,** or **root,** part of a word, and also know the meanings of key syllables added either to the beginning or end of the base word, you can usually figure out what the word means.

Word Origins Since Latin, Greek, and Anglo-Saxon roots are the basis for much of our English vocabulary, having some background in languages can be a useful vocabulary tool. For example, *astronomy* comes from the Greek root *astro*, which means "relating to the stars." *Stellar* also has a meaning referring to stars, but it's from Latin. Knowing root words in other languages can help you figure out meanings, word sources, and spellings in English.

Prefixes and Suffixes A prefix is a word part that can be added to the beginning of a word. For example, the prefix *semi* means "half" or "partial," so *semicircle* means "half a circle." A suffix is a word part that can be added to the end of a word. Adding a suffix often changes a word from one part of speech to another.

Using Dictionaries A dictionary gives the meaning or meanings of a word. Look at the example on the next page to see what else a dictionary can offer.

Thesauruses and Specialized Reference Books A thesaurus gives synonyms and sometimes antonyms. It is a useful tool to expand your vocabulary. Remember to check the exact meaning of words in a dictionary before you use a thesaurus. Specialized dictionaries such as *The New American Medical Dictionary* and *Health Manual* list terms that are not always included in a general dictionary. You can also use online dictionaries.

Glossaries Many textbooks have a condensed dictionary. This kind of dictionary offers an alphabetical listing of vocabulary words used in the text along with definitions.

Dictionary Entry

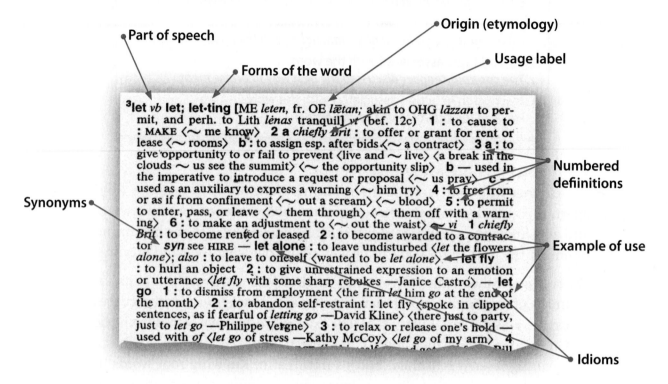

Part of speech

Forms of the word

Origin (etymology)

Usage label

Synonyms

Numbered definitions

Example of use

Idioms

³**let** *vb* **let; let·ting** [ME *leten*, fr. OE *lǣtan;* akin to OHG *lāzzan* to permit, and perh. to Lith *lénas* tranquil] *vt* (bef. 12c) **1** : to cause to : MAKE ⟨~ me know⟩ **2 a** *chiefly Brit* : to offer or grant for rent or lease ⟨~ rooms⟩ **b** : to assign esp. after bids ⟨~ a contract⟩ **3 a** : to give opportunity to or fail to prevent ⟨live and ~ live⟩ ⟨a break in the clouds ~ us see the summit⟩ ⟨~ the opportunity slip⟩ **b** — used in the imperative to introduce a request or proposal ⟨~ us pray⟩ **c** — used as an auxiliary to express a warning ⟨~ him try⟩ **4** : to free from or as if from confinement ⟨~ out a scream⟩ ⟨~ blood⟩ **5** : to permit to enter, pass, or leave ⟨~ them through⟩ ⟨~ them off with a warning⟩ **6** : to make an adjustment to ⟨~ out the waist⟩ ~ *vi* **1** *chiefly Brit* : to become rented or leased **2** : to become awarded to a contractor *syn* see HIRE — **let alone** : to leave undisturbed ⟨*let* the flowers *alone*⟩; *also* : to leave to oneself ⟨wanted to be *let alone*⟩ — **let fly** **1** : to hurl an object **2** : to give unrestrained expression to an emotion or utterance ⟨*let fly* with some sharp rebukes —Janice Castro⟩ — **let go** **1** : to dismiss from employment ⟨the firm *let* him *go* at the end of the month⟩ **2** : to abandon self-restraint : let fly ⟨spoke in clipped sentences, as if fearful of *letting go* —David Kline⟩ ⟨there just to party, just to *let go* —Philippe Vergne⟩ **3** : to relax or release one's hold — used with *of* ⟨*let go* of stress —Kathy McCoy⟩ ⟨*let go* of my arm⟩ **4**

"By permission. From *Merriam-Webster's Collegiate® Dictionary, Eleventh Edition©* 2005 by Merriam-Webster, Incorporated (www.merriam-webster.com)

Recognize Word Meanings Across Subjects Have you learned a new word in one class and then noticed it in your reading for other subjects? The word might not mean exactly the same thing in each class, but you can use the meaning you already know to help you understand what it means in another subject area. For example:

Math After you multiply the two numbers, explain how you arrived at the **product.**

Science One **product** of photosynthesis is oxygen.

Health The **product** of a balanced diet and regular exercise is a healthy body.

▶ Understanding What You Read

Reading comprehension means understanding or gaining meaning from what you have read. Using a variety of strategies can help you improve your comprehension and make reading more interesting and more fun.

Read for a Reason

To get the greatest value from what you read, you should **establish a purpose for reading.** In school, you have many reasons for reading. Some of them are to:

- Learn and understand new information
- Find specific information
- Review before a test
- Finish an assignment
- Prepare to write

As your reading skills improve, you will notice that you use different strategies to fit the different reasons for reading. If you are reading for fun, you might read quickly, but if you read to gather information or follow directions, you might read more slowly. You might also take notes, develop a graphic organizer, or reread parts of the text.

Draw on Personal Background

Drawing on your own background is also called activating prior knowledge. Before you start reading a text, ask yourself questions like these:

- What have I heard or read about this topic?
- Do I have any personal experiences that might connect to this topic?

Using a KWL Chart A KWL chart is a good device for organizing information you gather before, during, and after reading. In the first column, list what you already **know,** then list what you **want** to know in the middle column. Use the third column when you review and assess what you **learned.** You can also add more columns to record places where you found information and places where you can look for more information.

K (What I already know)	W (What I want to know)	L (What I have learned)

Adjust Your Reading Speed Your reading speed is an important factor in how well you understand what you are reading. You will need to change your speed depending on the reason you are reading.

Scanning means running your eyes quickly over the material to look for words or phrases. Scan when you need specific information.

Skimming means reading a section of text quickly to find its main idea. Skim when you want to determine what the reading is about.

Reading for detail involves careful reading while paying attention to the structure of the text and to your own understanding. Read for detail when you are learning about new ideas or when you are following directions. It is also important when you are getting ready to analyze a text.

▶ Techniques to Understand and Remember What You Read

Preview

Before beginning a selection, it is helpful to **preview** what you are about to read.

> ### Previewing Strategies
>
> **Read the title, headings, and subheadings of the selection.**
> **Look at the illustrations and notice how the text is set up.**
> **Skim the reading: Take a quick look at the whole thing.**
> **Decide what the main idea might be.**
> **Predict what the reading will be about.**

Predict

Have you ever read a mystery, decided who was the criminal, and then changed your mind as more clues were offered? You were changing your predictions based on the information you had available. Did you smile when you found out you guessed the criminal? You were checking your predictions.

As you read, take educated guesses about story events and outcomes; that is, **make predictions** before and during reading. This will help you focus your attention on the text, and it will improve your understanding.

Determine the Main Idea

When you look for the **main idea,** you are looking for the most important sentences in a text. Depending on what kind of text you are reading, the main idea can be found at the very beginning (news stories in a newspaper or magazine) or at the end (scientific research document). Ask yourself:

- What is each sentence about?
- Is there one sentence that is more important than all the others?
- What idea do details support or point out?

Taking Notes

Cornell Note-Taking System There are many methods for note taking. The **Cornell Note-Taking System** is a well-known method that can help you organize what you read. To the right is a note-taking activity based on the Cornell Note-Taking System.

Graphic organizers Using a graphic organizer will help you remember and hold on to new information. You might make a **chart** or **diagram** that helps you organize what you have read. Here are some ways to make graphic organizers:

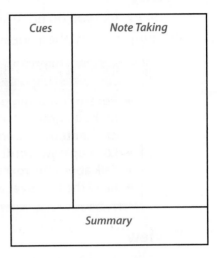

Venn diagrams When mapping out a comparison-and-contrast text structure, you can use a Venn diagram. The outer parts of the circles will show how two characters, ideas, or items contrast, or are different. The overlapping part in the middle will compare two things, or show how they are alike.

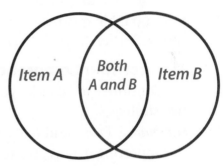

Flow charts To help you track the order of events, or cause and effect, use a flow chart. Arrange ideas or events in their logical, step-by-step order. Then draw arrows between your ideas to show how one idea or event flows into another.

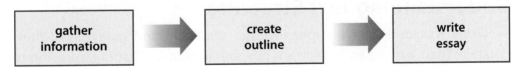

Visualize

Try to form a picture in your mind of scenes, characters, and events as you read. Use the details and descriptions the author gives you. If you can picture, or visualize, what you read, it will be more interesting and you will remember it better.

Question

Ask yourself questions about the text while you read. Ask yourself about the importance of the sentences, how they relate to one another, if you understand what you just read, and what you think is going to come next.

Clarify

If you feel you do not understand the meaning of what you read (through questioning), try these ideas:

> **What to Do When You Do Not Understand**
>
> - Reread confusing parts of the text.
> - Make diagrams that show how pieces of text, ideas, and sentences connect to each other.
> - Look up new words.
> - Talk about the text to yourself.
> - Read the text over again.

Review

Take time to stop and review what you have read. Use your note-taking tools (graphic organizers or Cornell notes charts). Also, think about what you've written in your KWL chart.

Monitor Your Comprehension

Continue to check your understanding by using the following two strategies:

Summarize Pause and tell yourself the main ideas of the text and the key supporting details. Try to answer the following questions: Who? What? When? Where? Why? How?

Paraphrase Pause, close the book, and try to retell what you have just read in your own words. It might help to pretend you are explaining the text to someone who has not read it and does not know the material.

▶ Understanding Text Structure

Good writers do not just put together sentences and paragraphs; they organize their writing with a certain purpose in mind. That organization is called text structure. When you understand and follow the way a text is set up, it is easier to remember what you are reading. There are many ways text may be structured. Watch for **signal words.** They will help you follow the text's organization (also, remember to use these ideas when you write).

Compare and Contrast

This structure shows similarities and differences between people, things, and ideas. This is often used to show that things that seem alike are really different, or vice versa.

Signal words: similarly, more, less, on the one hand / on the other hand, in contrast, but, however

Cause and Effect

Writers use the cause and effect structure to show why something takes place and to look at what happens because of certain actions.

Signal words: so, because, as a result, therefore, for the following reasons

Problem and Solution

Sometimes writers organize text around the question "how?" To do this, they state a problem and then present answers for the reader to think about.

Signal words: how, help, problem, obstruction, overcome, difficulty, need, attempt, have to, must

Sequence

Sequencing tells you in which order to think about ideas or facts. Examples of sequencing are:

Chronological order tells you the order in which events take place.
Signal words: first, next, then, finally

Spatial order describes the way things are arranged in space (to describe a room, for example).
Signal words: above, below, behind, next to

Order of importance lists things or thoughts from the most important to the least important (or the other way around).
Signal words: principal, central, main, important, fundamental

▶ Reading for Meaning

It is important to think about what you are reading to get the most information out of the text and to gain an understanding of what the text is saying. This will also help you to remember the key points and will guide you to form your own thoughts about what you've read.

Interpret

Interpreting is asking yourself, "What is the writer really saying?" and then using what you already know to answer that question.

Infer

Writers do not always say exactly everything they want you to understand. By providing clues and details, they sometimes imply certain concepts. An inference involves using your reason and background to develop ideas on your own. These ideas are based on what an author implies or suggests. What is most important when making inferences is to be sure that you have correctly based your guesses on details from the reading. If you cannot point to a place in the text to help back up your inference, you may need to go back and think about your guess again.

Draw Conclusions

A conclusion is a general statement you can make and explain with reasoning, or with details from a text. If you read a story describing a sport where five players bounce a ball and throw it through a high hoop, you may conclude that the sport is basketball.

Analyze

Persuasive nonfiction is a text that presents facts and opinions that lead to a conclusion. To understand this kind of text, you need to look at statements and examples to see if they connect to the key ideas. An informational text, like a textbook, gives information instead of opinions. To understand this kind of text, you need to notice how ideas are put together to find the key points.

Hint: Use your graphic organizers and notes charts.

Distinguish Facts and Opinions

This is one of the most important reading skills you can learn. A fact is a statement that can be shown to be true. An opinion is what the writer believes. A writer may support opinions with facts, but an opinion cannot be proven. For example:

Fact: California produces fruit and other agricultural products.

Opinion: California produces the best fruit and other agricultural products.

Evaluate

Would you take seriously an article on nuclear fission if you knew a comedy actor wrote it? If you need true and correct information, you need to find out who wrote what you are reading and why. Where did the writer get the information? Is the information one-sided? Can you show that the information is true?

▶ Reading for Research

You will need to think about what you are reading while you read in order to research a subject. You also may need to develop an interesting and fitting **question** that you can study on your own. Be sure to find the right kind of information from many different sources, including print material, and nonprint material. Then you will need to determine key ideas so that you can **organize** the information in a way that fits your readers. Finally, you should **draw conclusions** that connect to your research question. This may lead you to other areas for study.

Locate Appropriate Print and Nonprint Information

In your research, try to use many different sources. This will help you see information in different ways, and will help your project to be interesting and fairly presented.

Literature and Textbooks These texts include any book used for learning or gathering information.

Book Indices A book index, or a bibliography, is an alphabetical listing of books. Some book indices list books on certain subjects; others are more general. Other indices have an array of topics or resources.

Periodicals Magazines and journals are issued regularly, such as weekly or monthly. One way to find information in magazines is to use the *Readers' Guide to Periodical Literature*. This guide can be found in print form in most libraries.

Technical Manuals A manual is a guide or handbook intended to give instruction on how to do a task or operate something. A vehicle owner's manual might give information on how to use and take care of a car.

Reference Books Reference books include encyclopedias and almanacs, and are used to find specific pieces of information.

Electronic Encyclopedias, Databases, and the Internet There are many ways to find information using your computer. Infotrac, for instance, acts as an online reader's guide. The Internet or encyclopedias on CD-ROM can easily provide information on most subjects.

Organize and Convert Information

As you gather information from different sources, taking careful notes, you will need to think about how to **synthesize** the information. This means you will have to join the pieces of information together to make a whole text. You will also need to change it to a form that will fit your audience and will meet the requirements of the assignment.

1. First, ask yourself what you want your readers to know.
2. Then, think about a pattern of organization, a structure that will best show your key ideas. You might ask yourself the following questions:
   - When comparing items or ideas, what graphic aids can I use?
   - When showing the reasons something happened and the results of certain actions, what text structure would be best?
   - How can I briefly and clearly show important information to my readers?
   - Would an illustration or even a cartoon help to make a certain point?

Glossary

A

Abdominal thrusts Quick inward and upward pulls into the diaphragm to force an obstruction out of the airway. (page 496)

Abstinence The conscious, active choice not to participate in high-risk behaviors. (pages 27 and 190)

Abuse The physical, emotional, or mental mistreatment of another person. (page 217)

Accidental injuries Injuries caused by unexpected events. (page 473)

Acid rain Rain that is more acidic than normal rain. (page 509)

Acne Skin condition caused by active oil glands that clog hair follicles. (page 332)

Acquaintance Someone you see occasionally or know casually. (page 184)

Addiction A mental or physical need for a drug or other substance. (page 244)

Adolescence The stage of life between childhood and adulthood, usually beginning somewhere between the ages of 11 and 15. (page 364)

Adrenaline A hormone that increases the level of sugar in the blood, giving your body extra energy. (page 157)

Advertisement A message designed to influence consumers to buy a product or service. (page 341)

Advocacy Taking action in support of a cause. (page 17)

Aerobic (ah·ROH·bik) **exercise** Rhythmic, moderate-to-vigorous activity that uses large amounts of oxygen and works the heart and lungs. (page 64)

Aftershocks Smaller earthquakes, as the earth readjusts after the main earthquake. (page 490)

AIDS (acquired immunodeficiency syndrome) A disease that interferes with the body's ability to fight infection. (page 427)

Alcohol A drug created by a chemical reaction in some foods, especially fruits and grains. (page 264)

Alcohol abuse Using alcohol in ways that are unhealthy, illegal, or both. (page 270)

Alcoholism A disease in which a person has a physical and psychological need for alcohol. (page 271)

Allergens Substances that cause allergic responses. (page 441)

Allergy Extreme sensitivity to a substance. (page 441)

Alternative Another way of thinking or acting. (page 317)

Alveoli (al·VEE·oh·lye) The tiny air sacs in the lungs. (page 234)

Amphetamines (am·FE·tuh·meenz) Strong stimulant drugs that speed up the nervous system. (page 304)

Anabolic steroids (a·nuh·BAH·lik STAIR·oydz) Substances that cause muscle tissue to develop at an abnormally high rate. (page 88)

Anaerobic exercise Intense physical activity that builds muscle but does not use large amounts of oxygen. (page 64)

Angioplasty A surgical procedure in which an instrument with a tiny balloon, drill bit, or laser attached is inserted into a blocked artery to clear a blockage. (page 450)

Anorexia nervosa (a·nuh·REK·see·ah ner·VOH·sah) An eating disorder in which a person strongly fears gaining weight and starves herself or himself. (page 132)

Antibodies Specific proteins that attach to antigens, keeping them from harming the body. (page 410)

Antigens (AN·ti·genz) Substances that send the immune system into action. (page 410)

Antihistamines Medicines that reduce the production of histamines. (page 443)

Anxiety disorder Extreme fears of real or imaginary situations that get in the way of normal activities. (page 160)

Arteries Blood vessels that carry blood away from the heart to various parts of the body. (page 71)

Arteriosclerosis (ar·tir·ee·oh·skluh·ROH·sis) A group of disorders that cause a thickening and hardening of the arteries. (page 447)

Arthritis (ar·THRY·tus) A disease of the joints marked by painful swelling and stiffness. (page 461)

Assault An attack on another person in order to hurt him or her. (page 211)

Assertive Willing to stand up for yourself in a firm but positive way. (page 318)

Assertive response A response that declares your position strongly and confidently. (page 187)

Asthma Chronic inflammatory disorder of the airways that causes air passages to become narrow or blocked, making breathing difficult. (page 443)

Astigmatism (uh·STIG·muh·tiz·uhm) An eye condition in which images appear wavy or blurry. (page 337)

Atherosclerosis (a·thuh·roh·skluh·ROH·sis) A condition that occurs when fatty substances build up on the inner lining of the arteries. (page 447)

Bacteria Simple one-celled organisms. (page 403)

Battery The beating, hitting, or kicking of another person. (page 217)

Benign (bi·NYN) Not cancerous. (page 452)

Binge drinking Having several alcoholic drinks in a short period of time. (page 279)

Binge eating An eating disorder in which a person repeatedly eats too much food at one time. (page 133)

Biodegradable Easily broken down in the environment. (page 511)

Biopsy The removal of a sample of tissue from a person for examination. (page 455)

Blizzard A very heavy snowstorm with winds up to 45 miles per hour. (page 488)

Blood alcohol concentration (BAC) The amount of alcohol in the blood. (page 265)

Blood pressure The force of blood pushing against the walls of the blood vessels. (page 73)

Body composition The proportions of fat, bone, muscle, and fluid that make up body weight. (page 63)

Body image The way you see your body. (page 128)

Body language Postures, gestures, and facial expressions. (page 175)

Body Mass Index (BMI) A method for assessing your body size by taking your height and weight into account. (page 129)

Body system A group of organs that work together to carry out related tasks. (page 384)

Brain The command center, or coordinator, of the nervous system. (page 273)

Bronchi (BRAHNG·ky) Two passageways that branch from the trachea, one to each lung. (page 237)

Bronchodilators (brahng·koh·DY·lay·turhz) Medications that relax the muscles around the air passages. (page 445)

Bulimia (boo·LEE·mee·ah) **nervosa** An eating disorder in which a person repeatedly eats large amounts of food and then purges. (page 133)

Bullying A type of violence in which one person uses threats, taunts, or violence to intimidate another again and again. (page 213)

Calorie (KA·luh·ree) A unit of heat that measures the energy available in foods. (page 112)

Cancer A disease that occurs when abnormal cells multiply out of control. (page 451)

Capillaries Tiny blood vessels that carry blood to and from almost all body cells and connect arteries and veins. (page 71)

Carbohydrates The starches and sugars found in foods. (page 105)

Carbon monoxide A colorless, odorless, poisonous gas produced when tobacco burns. (page 231)

Carcinogen A substance that can cause cancer. (page 453)

Cardiopulmonary resuscitation (CPR) A first-aid procedure to restore breathing and circulation. (page 494)

Cardiovascular (kar·dee·oh·VASS·kyoo·luhr) **endurance** The measure of how well your heart and lungs work during moderate-to-vigorous physical activity or exercise. (page 62)

Cartilage A strong, flexible tissue that allows joints to move easily, cushions bones, and supports soft tissues. (page 66)

Cataract An eye condition in which the lens becomes cloudy as a person ages. (page 336)

Cell The basic unit of life. (page 384)

Central nervous system (CNS) The brain and the spinal cord. (page 272)

Character The way a person thinks, feels, and acts. (page 47)

Chemotherapy The use of powerful medicines to destroy cancer cells. (page 456)

Chest thrusts Quick presses into the middle of the breastbone to force an obstruction out of the airway. (page 497)

Chlamydia (kluh·MI·dee·uh) A bacterial STD that may affect the reproductive organs, urethra, and anus. (page 423)

Cholesterol (koh·LESS·tuh·rawl) The waxy, fat-like substance that the body uses to build cells and make other substances. (page 106)

Chromosomes Threadlike structures that carry genes. (page 383)

Chronic Present continuously on and off over a long period of time. (page 440)

Circulatory system The group of organs and tissues that act as transfer stations carrying needed materials to cells and removing their waste products. (page 71)

Cirrhosis (suh·ROH·suhs) The scarring and destruction of liver tissue. (page 269)

Club drugs Illegal drugs that are found mostly in nightclubs or at all-night dance parties called raves. (page 306)

Cold turkey Stopping all use of tobacco products immediately. (page 255)

Collaborate Work together. (page 207)

Colon (KOH·luhn) A tube five to six feet in length that plays a part in both digestion and excretion. (page 124)

Communicable disease A disease that can be spread to a person from another person, an animal, or an object. (page 402)

Communication The exchange of information through the use of words or actions. (page 174)

Comparison shopping Collecting information, comparing products, evaluating their benefits, and choosing products with the best value. (page 343)

Compromise When both sides in a conflict agree to give up something to reach a solution that satisfies everyone. (pages 186 and 207)

Conditioning Training to get into shape for physical activity or a sport. (page 90)

Confidence Belief in your ability to do what you set out to do. (page 151)

Conflict A disagreement between people with opposing viewpoints, interests, or needs. (pages 16 and 202)

Conflict-resolution skills The ability to end a disagreement or keep it from becoming a larger conflict. (page 16)

Consequences The results of actions. (page 24)

Conservation The saving of resources. (page 516)

Consumer A person who buys products and services. (page 340)

Contagious period Length of time that a particular disease can be spread from person to person. (page 414)

Cooldown Gentle exercises that let the body adjust to ending a workout. (page 81)

Criteria Standards on which to base decisions. (page 38)

Cultural background The beliefs, customs, and traditions of a specific group of people. (page 21)

Cumulative risk When one risk factor adds to another to increase danger. (page 25)

Dandruff A condition that results when too many dead skin cells flake off the outer layer of the scalp. (page 333)

Dating violence When a person uses violence in a dating relationship to control his or her partner. (page 214)

Deafness A condition in which someone has difficulty hearing sounds or has complete hearing loss. (page 338)

Decibel The unit for measuring the loudness of sound. (page 338)

Decision making The process of making a choice or solving a problem. (page 36)

Dehydration The excessive loss of water from the body. (page 88)

Depressants (di·PRE·suhnts) Drugs that slow down the body's functions and reactions, including heart and breathing rates. (page 305)

Dermis The skin's inner layer. (page 330)

Diabetes A disease that prevents the body from converting food into energy. (page 458)

Diaphragm (DY·uh·fram) A large, dome-shaped muscle below the lungs that expands and compresses the lungs, enabling breathing. (page 237)

Digestion (di·JES·chuhn) The process by which the body breaks down food into smaller pieces that can be absorbed by the blood and sent to each cell in your body. (page 122)

Digestive system The group of organs that work together to break down foods into substances that your cells can use. (page 122)

Disease Any condition that interferes with the proper functioning of the body or mind. (page 402)

Dislocation A major injury that happens when a bone is forced from its normal position within a joint. (pages 93 and 498)

Distress Stress that prevents you from doing what you need to do, or stress that causes you discomfort. (page 156)

Drug A substance other than food that changes the structure or function of the body or mind. (page 298)

Drug abuse Intentionally using drugs in a way that is unhealthful or illegal. (page 300)

Drug misuse Taking or using medicine in a way that is not intended. (page 300)

Drug possession When a person has or keeps illegal drugs. (page 315)

Drug-free zone A 1,000-yard distance around a school where anyone caught with drugs can be arrested. (page 314)

Earthquake A shifting of the earth's plates, resulting in a shaking of the earth's surface. (page 490)

Eating disorders Extreme eating behaviors that can lead to serious illness or even death. (page 132)

Electrical overload A dangerous situation in which too much electric current flows along a single circuit. (page 475)

Embryo The developing organism from two weeks until the end of the eighth week of development. (page 384)

Emotions Feelings such as love, joy, or fear. (page 153)

Empathy Identifying with and sharing another person's feelings. (page 147)

Emphysema A disease that results in the destruction of the alveoli in the lungs. (page 234)

Endocrine system The system of glands throughout the body that regulate body functions. (page 370)

Endorsement A statement of approval. (page 342)

Endurance (en·DUR·uhnce) The ability to perform difficult physical activity without getting overly tired. (page 62)

Environment All the living and nonliving things around you. (page 19)

Environmental Protection Agency (EPA) An agency of the U.S. government that is dedicated to protecting the environment. (page 513)

Enzyme (EN·zime) A substance that aids in the body's chemical reactions. (page 122)

Epidermis The outermost layer of skin. (page 330)

Epiglottis (eh·pi·GLAH·tis) A flap of tissue in the back of your mouth that keeps food out of your trachea. (page 237)

Ethical Choosing to take the right action. (page 37)

Evaluate Determine the quality of. (page 22)

Excretion (eks·KREE·shun) The process the body uses to get rid of waste. (page 125)

Excretory (EKS·kru·to·ree) **system** The group of organs that work together to remove wastes. (page 125)

Exercise Planned physical activity done regularly to build or maintain one's fitness. (page 60)

Family The basic unit of society, it includes two or more people joined by blood, marriage, adoption, or a desire to support each other. (page 178)

Fatigue Tiredness. (page 157)

Fats Nutrients that promote normal growth, give you energy, and keep your skin healthy. (page 105)

Fertilization The joining of a male sperm cell and a female egg cell to form a fertilized egg. (page 380)

Fetus The developing organism from the end of the eighth week until birth. (page 384)

Fiber A complex carbohydrate that the body cannot break down or use for energy. (page 105)

Fight-or-flight response The body's way of responding to threats. (page 157)

Fire extinguisher A device that sprays chemicals that put out fires. (page 476)

First aid The immediate care given to someone who becomes injured or ill until regular medical care can be provided. (page 493)

First-degree burn A burn in which only the outer layer of skin has burned and turned red. (page 498)

Fitness Being able to handle physical work and play each day without getting overly tired. (page 60)

Flammable Able to catch fire easily. (page 475)

Flexibility The ability to move joints fully and easily through a full range of motion. (page 63)

Fluoride A chemical that helps prevent tooth decay. (page 329)

Fossil fuels The oil, coal, and natural gas that are used to provide energy. (page 508)

Fracture A break in a bone. (pages 93 and 498)

Fraud A calculated effort to trick or fool others. (page 342)

Frequency The number of days you work out each week. (page 81)

Friendship A relationship with someone you know, trust, and regard with affection. (page 184)

Fungi (FUHN·jy) Organisms that are more complex than bacteria, but cannot make their own food. (page 403)

Gang A group of young people that comes together to take part in illegal activities. (page 212)

Generic products Products sold in plain packages at lower prices than brand-name products. (page 343)

Genes The basic units of heredity. (page 383)

Genital herpes (HER·peez) A viral STD that produces painful blisters on the genital area. (page 423)

Genital warts Growths or bumps in the genital area caused by certain types of the human papillomavirus (HPV). (page 423)

Germs Organisms that are so small they can only be seen through a microscope. (page 402)

Glaucoma (glah·COH·mah) An eye condition in which fluid pressure builds up inside the eye. (page 336)

Gonorrhea (gah·nuh·REE· uh) A bacterial STD that affects the mucous membranes of the body, particularly in the genital area. (page 424)

Groundwater Water that collects under the earth's surface. (page 510)

Gynecologist A doctor who specializes in the female reproductive system. (page 382)

Hair follicles Small sacs in the dermis from which hair grows. (page 330)

Hallucinogens Drugs that distort moods, thoughts, and senses. (page 307)

Hazardous wastes Human-made liquid, solid, sludge, or radioactive wastes that may endanger human health or the environment. (page 511)

Hazards Potential sources of danger. (page 473)

Health The combination of physical, mental/emotional, and social well-being. (page 4)

Health insurance A plan in which a person pays a set fee to an insurance company in return for the company's agreement to pay some or all medical expenses when needed. (page 354)

Health maintenance organization (HMO) A health insurance plan that contracts with selected physicians and specialists to provide medical services. (page 354)

Heart attack A serious condition that occurs when the blood supply to the heart slows or stops and the heart muscle is damaged. (page 447)

Hepatitis (hep·uh·TY·tis) A viral disease characterized by an inflammation of the liver and yellowing of the skin and the whites of the eyes. (page 415)

Hepatitis B A disease caused by the hepatitis B virus that affects the liver. (page 425)

Heredity (huh·RED·I·tee) The passing of traits from parents to their biological children. (page 18)

Histamines (HIS·tuh·meenz) The chemicals that the immune cells release to draw more blood and lymph to the area affected by the allergen. (page 442)

HIV (human immunodeficiency virus) The virus that causes AIDS. (page 427)

Homicide A violent crime that results in the death of another person. (page 211)

Hormones Chemical substances produced in certain glands that help to regulate the way your body functions. (page 370)

Hurricane A strong windstorm with driving rain that forms over the sea. (page 488)

Hygiene Cleanliness. (page 418)

Hypertension A condition in which the pressure of the blood on the walls of the blood vessels stays at a level that is higher than normal. (page 448)

Hypothermia A sudden and dangerous drop in body temperature. (page 489)

Immune (i·MYOON) **system** A combination of body defenses made up of cells, tissues, and organs that fight pathogens in the body. (page 407)

Immunity The ability to resist the pathogens that cause a particular disease. (page 412)

Infancy The first year of life after birth. (page 389)

Infection A condition that happens when pathogens enter the body, multiply, and cause harm. (page 402)

Inflammation The body's response to injury or disease, resulting in a condition of swelling, pain, heat and redness. (page 408)

Influenza A communicable disease characterized by fever, chills, fatigue, headache, muscle aches, and respiratory symptoms. (page 414)

Infomercial A long television commercial whose main purpose seems to be to present information rather than to sell a product. (page 342)

Inhalants The vapors of chemicals that are sniffed or inhaled to get a "high." (page 308)

Insulin (in·suh·lin) A protein made in the pancreas that regulates the level of glucose in the blood. (page 458)

Integrity Being true to your ethical values. (page 48)

Intensity How much energy you use when you work out. (page 81)

Interpersonal communication Sharing of thoughts and feelings with other people. (page 15)

Intoxicated (in·TAHK·suh·kay·tuhd) Being drunk. (page 265)

Joints The places where two or more bones meet. (page 66)

Kidneys Organs that remove waste material, including salts, from the blood. (page 125)

Landfills Huge, specially designed pits where waste materials are dumped and buried. (page 510)

Ligaments A type of connecting tissue that holds bones to other bones at the joint. (page 66)

Liver A digestive gland that secretes a substance called bile, which helps to digest fats. (page 124)

Long-term goal A goal that you plan to reach over an extended period of time. (page 44)

Lungs Two large organs that exchange oxygen and carbon dioxide. (page 237)

Lymphatic system A secondary circulatory system that helps the body fight pathogens and maintains its fluid balance. (page 409)

Lymphocytes (LIM·fuh·sytes) Special white blood cells in the blood and lymphatic system. (page 409)

Mainstream smoke The smoke that is inhaled and then exhaled by a smoker. (page 248)

Malignant (muh·LIG·nuht) Cancerous. (page 452)

Managed care plans Health insurance plans that emphasize preventative medicine and work to control the cost and maintain the quality of health care. (page 354)

Media literacy The ability to understand the goals of advertising and the media. (page 246)

Mediation Resolving conflicts by using another person or persons to help reach a solution that is acceptable to both sides. (page 208)

Medicine A drug that prevents or cures an illness or eases its symptoms. (page 347)

Melanin Substance that gives skin its color. (page 331)

Menstruation The flow from the body of blood, tissues, and fluids that result from the breakdown of the lining of the uterus. (page 379)

Mental and emotional disorders Illnesses that affect a person's thoughts, feelings, and behavior. (page 159)

Mental and emotional health The ability to handle the stresses and changes of everyday life in a reasonable way. (page 145)

Metabolism The process by which the body gets energy from food. (page 371)

Mind-body connection How your emotions affect your physical and overall health and how your overall health affects your emotions. (page 8)

Minerals Substances the body uses to form healthy bones and teeth, keep blood healthy, and keep the heart and other organs working properly. (page 106)

Minor A person under the age of adult rights and responsibilities. (page 281)

Mononucleosis (MAH·noh·nook·klee·OH·sis) A viral disease characterized by a severe sore throat and swelling of the lymph glands in the neck and around the throat area. (page 415)

Mood disorder A mental and emotional problem in which a person undergoes mood swings that seem extreme, inappropriate, or last a long time. (page 161)

Mood swings Frequent changes in emotional state. (page 153)

Muscle endurance The ability of a muscle to repeatedly use force over a period of time. (page 62)

Muscular system Tissues that move parts of the body and control the organs. (page 67)

MyPyramid food guidance system A guide for developing a healthful eating plan. (page 112)

Narcotics Drugs that get rid of pain and dull the senses. (page 307)

Neglect Failure to provide for the basic physical and emotional needs of a dependent. (page 217)

Negotiation The process of talking directly to the other person to resolve a conflict. (page 207)

Neurons Cells that make up the nervous system. (page 272)

Neutrality A promise not to take sides. (page 208)

Nicotine An addictive, or habit-forming, drug found in tobacco. (page 230)

Noncommunicable disease A disease that cannot be spread from person to person. (page 440)

Nonrenewable resources Substances that cannot be replaced once they are used. (page 516)

Nonverbal communication Getting messages across without using words. (page 175)

Nurture Fulfill physical, mental/emotional, and social needs. (page 179)

Nutrient dense Foods having a high amount of nutrients relative to the number of calories. (page 119)

Nutrients (NOO·tree·ents) Substances in foods that your body needs to grow, have energy, and stay healthy. (page 104)

Nutrition (noo·TRIH·shuhn) The process of taking in food and using it for energy, growth, and good health. (page 111)

Occupational Safety and Health Administration (OSHA) A branch of the U.S. Department of Labor that protects American workers. (page 513)

Ophthalmologist (ahf·thahl·MAH·luh·jist) A physician who specializes in the structure, functions, and diseases of the eye. (page 336)

Optimistic Having a positive attitude about the future. (page 150)

Optometrist (ahp·TAH·muh·trist) A health care professional who is trained to examine the eyes for vision problems and to prescribe corrective lenses. (page 336)

Organ A body part made up of different tissues joined to perform a particular function. (page 384)

Osteoarthritis (ahs·tee·oh·ar·THRY·tus) A chronic disease that is common in older adults and results from a breakdown in cartilage in the joints. (page 462)

Ovaries The female endocrine glands that release mature eggs and produce the hormones estrogen and progesterone. (page 378)

Overdose Taking more of a drug than the body can tolerate. (page 303)

Over-the-counter (OTC) Found on the shelves of local pharmacy or grocery stores. (pages 299 and 348)

Overworking Conditioning too hard or too often without enough rest between sessions. (page 90)

Ovulation The process by which the ovaries release mature eggs, usually one each menstrual cycle. (page 379)

Ozone A gas made of three oxygen atoms. (page 509)

Pancreas (PAN·kree·uhs) A gland that helps the small intestine by producing pancreatic juice, a blend of enzymes that breaks down proteins, carbohydrates, and fats. (page 124)

Passive smokers Nonsmokers who breathe in secondhand smoke. (page 248)

Pathogens Germs that cause diseases. (page 402)

Pedestrian A person who travels on foot. (page 480)

Peer pressure The influence that your peer group has on you. (page 187)

Peers People close to you in age who are a lot like you. (page 187)

Peripheral nervous system (PNS) The nerves that connect the central nervous system to all parts of the body. (page 272)

Personality A combination of your feelings, likes, dislikes, attitudes, abilities, and habits. (page 146)

Pharmacist A person trained to prepare and distribute medicines. (page 348)

Physical activity Any movement that makes your body use extra energy. (page 60)

Physical dependence An addiction in which the body develops a chemical need for a drug. (page 244)

Plaque A thin, sticky film that builds up on teeth and leads to tooth decay. (page 329)

Plasma (PLAZ·muh) The yellowish, watery part of blood. (page 74)

Pneumonia A serious inflammation of the lungs. (page 416)

Point-of-service (POS) plan A health insurance plan that combines the features of HMOs and PPOs. (page 355)

Pollen A powdery substance released by the flowers of some plants. (page 441)

Pollution Dirty or harmful substances in the environment. (page 508)

Pores Tiny openings in the skin that allow perspiration to escape. (page 330)

Positive stress Stress that can help you reach your goals. (page 156)

Preferred provider organization (PPO) A health insurance plan that allows its members to select a physician who participates in the plan for a reduced cost or to visit the physician of their choice. (page 355)

Prejudice A negative and unjustly formed opinion. (page 204)

Preschooler A child between ages three and five. (page 389)

Prescription medicine A medicine that can be obtained legally only with a doctor's written permission. (page 348)

Prevention Taking steps to avoid something. (page 26)

Primary care provider Health care professional who provides checkups and general care. (page 353)

Probation Set period of time during which a person who has been arrested must check in regularly with a court officer. (page 315)

Product placement When a company pays to show its products in media being used by celebrities. (page 246)

Proteins (PROH·teenz) The nutrient group used to build and repair cells. (page 105)

Protozoa (proh·tuh·ZOH· uh) One-celled organisms that are more complex than bacteria. (page 404)

Psychological dependence A person's belief that he or she needs a drug to feel good or function normally. (page 244)

Puberty The time when you develop physical characteristics of adults of your own gender. (page 365)

Pulmonary circulation When blood travels from the heart, through the lungs, and back to the heart. (page 72)

Radiation therapy A treatment using X rays or other forms of radiation to kill cancer cells. (page 456)

Rape Forced sexual intercourse. (page 211)

Recycle To change items in some way so that they can be used again. (page 515)

Referral Suggestion to seek help or information from another person or place. (page 165)

Refusal skills Ways to say no effectively. (pages 16, 192, and 286)

Reliable Trustworthy and dependable. (page 11)

Reproduction The process by which living organisms produce others of their own kind. (page 374)

Reproductive system Consists of the body organs and structures that make it possible to produce children. (page 374)

Rescue breathing A first-aid procedure where someone forces air into the lungs of a person who cannot breathe on his or her own. (page 494)

Resilience The ability to recover from problems or loss. (page 147)

Resources Places to get information, support, and advice. (page 165)

Respiratory system The organs that supply your blood with oxygen. (page 236)

Rheumatoid arthritis A chronic disease characterized by pain, inflammation, swelling, and stiffness of the joints. (page 462)

Risk The chance that something harmful may happen to your health and wellness. (page 23)

Risk behaviors Actions or choices that may harm you or others. (pages 24 and 190)

Risk factors Characteristics or behaviors that increase the likelihood of developing a medical disorder or disease. (page 452)

Role model A person who inspires you to think or act a certain way. (page 50)

S

Safety conscious Being aware that safety is important and being careful to act in a safe manner. (page 473)

Saliva (suh·LI·vah) A digestive juice produced by the salivary glands in your mouth. (page 122)

Saturated fats Fats that are usually solid at room temperature. (page 105)

Second-degree burn A moderately serious burn in which the burned area blisters. (page 498)

Secondhand smoke Air that has been contaminated by tobacco smoke. (page 248)

Self-concept The way you view yourself overall. (page 149)

Self-esteem How you feel about yourself. (page 150)

Semen (SEE·muhn) A mixture of sperm and fluids that protect sperm and carry them through the tubes of the male reproductive system. (page 375)

Sewage Human waste, garbage, detergents, and other household wastes washed down drains and toilets. (page 510)

Sexual abuse Sexual contact that is forced upon another person. (page 218)

Sexually transmitted diseases (STDs) Infections that are spread from person to person through sexual contact. (page 422)

Short-term goal A goal that you can achieve in a short length of time. (page 44)

Side effect A reaction to a medicine other than the one intended. (page 349)

Sidestream smoke Smoke that comes from the burning end of a cigarette, pipe, or cigar. (page 248)

Skeletal system The framework of bones and other tissues that supports the body. (page 66)

Small intestine A coiled tube from 20 to 23 feet long, in which about 90 percent of digestion takes place. (page 123)

Smog Yellow-brown haze that forms when sunlight reacts with air pollution. (page 509)

Smoke alarm A device that sounds an alarm when it senses smoke. (page 476)

Specialist Health care professional trained to treat a special category of patients or specific health problems. (page 353)

Sperm Male reproductive cells. (page 375)

Spinal cord A long bundle of neurons that sends messages to and from the brain and all parts of the body. (page 273)

Sprain An injury to the ligament connecting bones at a joint. (page 92)

Stimulant A drug that speeds up the body's functions. (page 304)

Strength The ability of your muscles to use force. (page 62)

Strep throat Sore throat caused by streptococcal bacteria. (page 416)

Stress The body's response to real or imagined dangers or other life events. (pages 13 and 156)

Stress fracture A small fracture caused by repeated strain on a bone. (page 93)

Stress management Identifying sources of stress and learning how to handle them in ways that promote good mental/emotional health. (page 13)

Stressors Sources of stress. (page 157)

Stroke A serious condition that occurs when an artery of the brain breaks or becomes blocked. (page 448)

Suicide The act of killing oneself on purpose. (page 161)

Syphilis (SIH·fuh·luhs) A bacterial STD that can affect many parts of the body. (page 424)

Systemic (sis·TEH·mik) **circulation** When oxygen-rich blood travels to all body tissues except the lungs. (page 72)

Tact The sense of what to do or say to avoid offending others. (page 176)

Tar A thick, dark liquid that forms when tobacco burns. (page 231)

Target audience A group of people for which a product is intended. (page 246)

Target heart rate The number of heartbeats per minute to aim for during moderate-to-vigorous aerobic activity to most benefit the circulatory system. (page 82)

Tartar Hardened plaque that hurts gum health. (page 329)

Tendonitis Painful swelling of a tendon caused by overuse. (page 92)

Tendons A type of connecting tissue that joins muscles to bones and muscles to muscles. (page 66)

Testes The pair of glands that produce sperm. (page 375)

Third-degree burn A very serious burn in which all the layers of skin are damaged. (page 498)

Tinnitus A ringing in the ears. (page 338)

Tissue A group of similar cells that do a particular job. (page 384)

Toddler A child between the ages of one and three. (page 389)

Tolerance The body's need for larger amounts of a drug to produce the same effect. (pages 245 and 303)

Tornado A whirling, funnel-shaped wind-storm. (page 487)

Trachea (TRAY·kee·uh) A passageway in the throat taking air into and out of your lungs. (page 237)

Trans fatty acids A kind of fat formed when hydrogen is added to vegetable oil during processing. (page 106)

Trichomoniasis (TREE·koh·moh·NI·ah·sis) An STD caused by the protozoan *Trichomonas vaginalis*. (page 424)

Tuberculosis (too·ber·kyuh·LOH·sis) A bacterial disease that usually affects the lungs. (page 416)

Tumor (TOO·mer) A group of abnormal cells that forms a mass. (page 451)

Ulcer (UHL·ser) An open sore in the stomach lining. (page 269)

Ultraviolet (UV) rays Invisible form of radiation that can enter skin cells and change their structure. (page 331)

Unsaturated fats Fats that are usually liquid at room temperature. (page 105)

Uterus A pear-shaped organ, located within the pelvis, in which the developing baby is nourished and protected. (page 378)

Vaccine (vak·SEEN) A preparation of dead or weakened pathogens that is introduced into the body to cause an immune response. (page 412)

Values The beliefs that guide the way a person lives. (page 37)

Veins Blood vessels that carry blood from all parts of the body back to the heart. (page 71)

Verbal communication Expressing feelings, thoughts, or experiences with words, either by speaking or writing. (page 175)

Violence An act of physical force resulting in injury or abuse. (page 284)

Viruses (VY·ruh·suhz) The smallest and simplest pathogens. (page 403)

Vitamins Compounds that help to regulate body processes. (page 106)

Warm-up Gentle exercises that get heart muscles ready for activity. (page 80)

Warranty A company's or a store's written agreement to repair a product or refund your money if the product does not function properly. (page 344)

Weather emergencies Dangerous situations brought on by changes in the atmosphere. (page 486)

Wellness A state of well-being or balanced health over a long period of time. (page 7)

Withdrawal Symptoms a person experiences when he or she stops using an addictive substance. (pages 244 and 287)

Youth court A program in which teens decide punishments for other teens for bullying and other problem behaviors. (page 215)

A

Abdominal thrust/presión abdominal Presión rápida, hacia adentro y arriba sobre el diafragma, para desalojar un objeto que obstruye las vías respiratorias de una persona.

Abstinence/abstinencia Opción activa y conciente de no participar en comportamientos de alto riesgo.

Abuse/abuso Maltrato físico, emocional o mental de otra persona.

Accidental injuries/heridas accidentales Daños causados por sucesos inesperados.

Acid rain/lluvia ácida Lluvia que es más ácida de lo normal.

Acne/acné Condición de la piel causada por glándulas sebáceas activas que obstruyen folículos de cabello.

Acquaintance/conocido Alguien a quien ves ocasionalmente o conoces casualmente.

Addiction/adicción Necesidad mental o física de una droga u otra substancia.

Adolescence/adolescencia Período de la vida entre la niñez y la adultez que empieza generalmente entre los 11 y los 15 años.

Adrenaline/adrenalina Hormona que aumenta el nivel de azúcar en la sangre y por lo tanto, proporciona energía adicional al cuerpo.

Advertisement/publicidad Mensaje diseñado para influenciar a los consumidores para que compren un producto o servicio.

Advocacy/promoción Actuar en apoyo de una causa.

Aerobic exercise/ejercicio aeróbico Actividad rítmica, moderada o fuerte que usa grandes cantidades de oxígeno y hace trabajar el corazón y los pulmones.

Aftershocks/réplicas sísmicas Temblores más pequeños que ocurren mientras la tierra se reajusta después de un terremoto mayor.

AIDS (acquired immunodeficiency syndrome)/sida (síndrome de inmunodeficiencia adquirida) Enfermedad mortal que interfiere con la habilidad del cuerpo para combatir infecciones.

Alcohol/alcohol Droga producida por la reacción química en algunos alimentos, especialmente frutas y granos.

Alcohol abuse/abuso de alcohol Uso del alcohol en formas que son no saludables, ilegales o ambas.

Alcoholism/alcoholismo Enfermedad que se caracteriza por la necesidad física y psicológica de consumir alcohol.

Allergens/alergenos Sustancias que causan reacciones alérgicas.

Allergy/alergia Sensibilidad extrema a una sustancia.

Alternative/alternativa Otra forma de pensar o actuar.

Alveoli/alvéolos Pequeños sacos de aire en los pulmones.

Amphetamine/anfetamina Droga fuertemente estimulante que acelera el sistema nervioso.

Anabolic steroids/esteroides anabólicos Sustancias que causan que los tejidos musculares se desarrollen rápida y anormalmente.

Anaerobic exercise/ejercicio anaeróbico Actividad física intensa que desarrolla músculos pero no usa mucho oxígeno.

Angioplasty/angioplastia Proceso quirúrgico en el cual un instrumento con un globo pequeño, un pequeño taladro, o láser es insertado en una arteria obstruida para abrirla.

Anorexia nervosa/anorexia nerviosa Trastorno de la alimentación en el cual una persona teme mucho subir de peso y se mata de hambre.

Antibodies/anticuerpos Proteínas que se pegan a los antígenos, impidiendo que éstos le hagan daño al cuerpo.

Antigens/antígenos Sustancias que provocan el funcionamiento del sistema inmunológico.

Antihistamines/antihistamínicos Medicinas que reducen la producción de histaminas.

Anxiety disorder/trastorno de ansiedad Temores extremos a situaciones reales o imaginarias que se interponen en el desarrollo de actividades normales.

Arteries/arterias Vasos sanguíneos que transportan sangre desde al corazón hacia otras partes del cuerpo.

Arteriosclerosis/arteriosclerosis Conjunto de trastornos que provoca el engrosamiento y endurecimiento de las arterias.

Arthritis/artritis Enfermedad de las articulaciones caracterizada por inflamación dolorosa y anquilosamiento.

Assault/asalto Ataque hacia otra persona con la intención de herirla.

Assertive/firme Dispuesto a defenderse de manera resuelta y positiva.

Assertive response/reacción de firmeza Reacción que establece tu posición con fuerza y confianza.

Asthma/asma Trastorno crónico inflamatorio que causa que los pasajes de aire se hagan más pequeños o que se obstruyan haciendo que la respiración se dificulte.

Astigmatism/astigmatismo Afección del ojo que causa que las imágenes se vean distorsionadas y los objetos aparezcan ondulados o borrosos.

Atherosclerosis/aterosclerosis Condición de arteriosclerosis que ocurre cuando sustancias grasosas se forman en el interior de las arterias.

Bacteria/bacterias Organismos simples de una sola célula.

Battery/lesiones Dar palizas, golpear o dar puntapiés a otra persona.

Benign/benigno No canceroso.

Binge drinking/borrachera Ingerir varias bebidas en un período de tiempo corto.

Binge eating disorder/trastorno de la alimentación compulsiva Trastorno en la alimentación por el cual una persona come repetidamente grandes cantidades de alimentos de una vez.

Biodegradable/biodegradable Que se descompone fácilmente en el medio ambiente.

Biopsy/biopsia Tomar una muestra de tejido de una persona para examinarlo.

Blizzard/ventisca Tormenta de nieve fuerte, con vientos que llegan a 45 millas por hora.

Blood alcohol concentration (BAC)/ contenido de alcohol en la sangre Cantidad de alcohol en la sangre.

Blood pressure/presión sanguínea Fuerza que ejerce la sangre contra las paredes de los vasos sanguíneos.

Body composition/composición del cuerpo Proporción de grasa, hueso, músculo y líquidos que componen el peso del cuerpo.

Body image/imagen corporal Forma en la que ves tu cuerpo.

Body language/lenguaje corporal Posturas, gestos y expresiones faciales.

Body Mass Index (BMI)/índice de masa corporal Método que evalúa el tamaño indicado de tu cuerpo utilizando tu peso y tu estatura.

Body system/sistema o aparato Grupo de órganos que trabajan juntos para ejecutar funciones relacionadas.

Brain/cerebro Centro de mando, o el coordinador, del sistema nervioso.

Bronchi/bronquios Dos pasajes que se ramifican desde la tráquea hacia los dos pulmones.

Bronchodilator/broncodilatador Medicina que relaja los músculos que están alrededor de los bronquios.

Bulimia nervosa/bulimia nerviosa Trastorno de la alimentación por el cual una persona come grandes cantidades y después se induce el vómito.

Bullying/intimidar Tipo de violencia en el cual una persona usa amenazas, burlas o actos violentos para intimidar a otra persona una y otra vez.

Calorie/caloría Unidad de calor que mide la energía que contienen los alimentos.

Cancer/cáncer Enfermedad causada por células anormales cuyo crecimiento está fuera de control.

Capillaries/vasos capilares Pequeños vasos sanguíneos que transportan sangre desde y hacia casi todas las células del cuerpo y conectan arterias y venas.

Carbohydrates/hidratos de carbono Almidones y azúcares que proporcionan energía.

Carbon monoxide/monóxido de carbono Gas incoloro, inodoro y tóxico que produce el tabaco al quemarse.

Carcinogen/carcinógeno Sustancia del medio ambiente que produce cáncer.

Cardiopulmonary resuscitation (CPR)/ resucitación cardiopulmonar Procedimiento de primeros auxilios para restaurar la respiración y la circulación de la sangre.

Cardiovascular endurance/resistencia cardiovascular Medida por la cual se define qué tan bien funcionan el corazón y los pulmones durante actividad física o ejercicio moderado o fuerte.

Cartilage/cartílago Tejido fuerte y flexible que permite que las articulaciones se muevan fácilmente, amortigua huesos y sirve de soporte para tejidos suaves.

Cataract/catarata Condición del ojo en la cual el cristalino se pone borroso a medida que la persona envejece.

Cell/célula Unidad básica de la vida.

Central nervous system (CNS)/sistema nervioso central Cerebro y médula espinal.

Character/carácter Manera en que piensas, sientes y actúas.

Chemotherapy/quimioterapia Uso de medicina poderosa para destruir células cancerosas.

Chest thrust/presión torácica Presión rápida en el centro del esternón para desalojar un objeto que obstruye la vía respiratoria de una persona.

Chlamydia/clamidia Infección de transmisión sexual bacteriana que puede afectar los órganos de reproducción, la uretra y el ano.

Cholesterol/colesterol Sustancia grasosa y cerosa que el cuerpo utiliza para crear células y otras sustancias.

Chromosomes/cromosomas Estructuras filiformes que contienen los códigos genéticos de los rasgos hereditarios.

Chronic/crónico Que está siempre presente o reaparece repetidamente durante un largo período de tiempo.

Circulatory system/aparato circulatorio Grupo de órganos y tejidos que transportan materiales necesarios hacia las células y eliminan los desperdicios.

Cirrhosis/cirrosis Cicatrización y destrucción del tejido del hígado.

Club drugs/drogas de club Drogas ilegales que normalmente son utilizadas en discotecas y otras fiestas que duran toda la noche llamadas raves.

Cold turkey/parar en seco Acto de parar inmediatamente el uso de productos que contienen tabaco.

Collaborate/colaborar Trabajar juntos.

Colon/colon Tubo que mide entre cinco y seis pies que es utilizado en el proceso de digestión y excreción.

Communicable disease/enfermedad contagiosa Enfermedad que se puede propagar de una persona a otra de un animal o de un objeto.

Communication/comunicación Intercambio de información a través del uso de palabras y acciones.

Comparison shopping/comparación de productos Recolectar información, comparar productos, evaluar sus beneficios y escoger el producto que tiene mejor valor.

Compromise/compromiso Cuando los dos lados de un conflicto concuerdan con dejar algo de lado para alcanzar una solución que satisfaga a todos.

Conditioning/acondicionamiento Entrenamiento para ponerse en forma para alguna actividad física o deporte.

Confidence/confianza Creer en tu habilidad de hacer lo que te propones hacer.

Conflict/conflicto Desacuerdo entre dos personas con puntos de vista, intereses o necesidades opuestas.

Conflict-resolution skills/habilidades de solución de conflictos Habilidad de poder resolucionar un desacuerdo o hacer que el desacuerdo no se convierta en algo más grande.

Consequences/consecuencias Resultados de los actos.

Conservation/conservación Protección de los recursos naturales.

Consumer/consumidor Persona que compra productos y servicios.

Contagious period/periodo de contagio Periodo de tiempo en que se puede transmitir una enfermedad determinada de una persona a otra.

Cool-down/recuperación Ejercicios moderados que permiten que el cuerpo se ajuste al ir finalizando el plan de ejercicios.

Criteria/criterios Principios en que se basa una decisión.

Cultural background/base cultural Creencias, costumbres y tradiciones de un grupo específico de personas.

Cumulative risk/riesgo acumulativo Cuando un factor riesgoso se suma a otro e incrementa el peligro.

Dandruff/caspa Cuando demasiadas células de piel muertas se descaman de la capa exterior del cuero cabelludo.

Dating violence/relación violenta Cuando una persona usa la violencia en una relación amorosa para poder controlar a su pareja.

Deafness/sordera Condición en la cual una persona tiene dificultad para escuchar sonidos o ha perdido completamente la capacidad de oir.

Decibel/decibel Unidad que se usa para medir el volumen del sonido.

Decision making/toma de decisiones Proceso de hacer una selección o de resolver un problema.

Dehydration/deshidratación Pérdida excesiva de agua del cuerpo.

Depressant/sedantes Drogas que disminuyem las funciones y reacciones del cuerpo, incluso el ritmo cardiaco y la respiración.

Dermis/dermis Capa interior de la piel.

Diabetes/diabetes Enfermedad que impide que el cuerpo convierta los alimentos en energía.

Diaphragm/diafragma Músculo grande en forma de cúpula debajo de los pulmones que expande y comprime los pulmones, posibilitando la respiración.

Digestion/digestión Proceso por el cual el cuerpo desintegra las comidas en pedazos más pequeños que pueden ser absorbidos por la sangre y enviados a cada célula en el cuerpo.

Digestive system/aparato digestivo Conjunto de órganos que trabajan juntos para descomponer los alimentos en sustancias que puedan usar las células.

Disease/enfermedad Toda afección que interfiere con el buen funcionamiento del cuerpo o de la mente.

Dislocation/dislocación Daño mayor que ocurre cuando un hueso es forzado fuera de lugar en la articulación.

Distress/angustia Estrés negativo. Es estrés que te impide hacer lo que necesitas hacer o estrés que causa molestia.

Drug/droga Sustancia no alimenticia que causa cambios en la estructura o en el funcionamiento del cuerpo o la mente.

Drug abuse/abuso de drogas Uso de drogas intencionalmente en una forma no saludable o ilegal.

Drug posession/posesión de drogas Cuando una persona tiene drogas ilegales.

Drug-free zone/zona libre de drogas Distancia de 1,000 yardas alrededor de una escuela en la cual cualquier persona que posea drogas puede ser arrestada.

Earthquake/terremoto Cambio de las placas terrestres que hace que tiemble la superficie terrestre.

Eating disorder/trastorno de la alimentación Conducta de alimentación extrema que puede causar enfermedades graves o la muerte.

Electrical overload/sobrecarga eléctrica Situación peligrosa en que demasiada corriente eléctrica fluye a través de un solo circuito.

Embryo/embrión Organismo en desarrollo desde las dos hasta las ocho semanas de desarrollo.

Emotions/emociones Sentimientos como el amor, la alegría o el miedo.

Empathy/empatía Identificar y compartir sentimientos de otra persona.

Emphysema/enfisema Enfermedad que resulta de la destrucción de los alvéolos de los pulmones.

Endocrine system/sistema endocrino Sistema de glándulas a través del cuerpo que regulan las funciones corporales.

Endorsement/aprobación Declaración de aceptación.

Endurance/resistencia Habilidad de desempeñar actividades físicas sin cansarse demasiado.

Environment/medio Todas las cosas vivas y no vivas que te rodean.

Environmental Protection Agency (EPA)/Agencia de Protección Ambiental Agencia del gobierno de Estados Unidos a cargo de la protección del medio ambiente.

Enzyme/enzima Sustancia que ayuda en las reacciones químicas del cuerpo.

Epidermis/epidermis Capa más externa de la piel.

Epiglottis/epiglotis Pedazo de tejido que se encuentra en la parte trasera de la boca que no deja que la comida pase a la tráquea.

Ethical/ético Escoger la acción correcta.

Eustress/estrés positivo Tensión que puede ayudarte a lograr tus metas.

Evaluate/evaluar Determinar la calidad.

Excretion/excreción Proceso mediante el cual el cuerpo se deshace de los desechos.

Excretory system/sistema excretor Grupo de órganos que trabaja en conjunto para eliminar desperdicios del cuerpo.

Exercise/ejercicio Actividad física planeada realizada regularmente para crear o mantener un buen estado físico.

Family/familia Unidad básica de la sociedad que incluye dos o mas personas unidas por sangre, matrimonio, adopción o el deseo de ser apoyo el uno del otro.

Fatigue/fatiga Cansancio.

Fats/grasas Nutrientes que promueven el crecimiento normal, dan energía y mantienen la piel saludable.

Fertilization/fertilización Unión de una espermatozoide masculino con un óvulo femenino para formar un óvulo fertilizado.

Fetus/feto Organismo en desarrollo desde el final de la octava semana hasta el nacimiento.

Fiber/fibra Carbohidratos complejos que el cuerpo no puede deshacer para usarlos como energía.

Fight-or-flight response/respuesta de combate o huida Forma del cuerpo de responder a las amenazas.

Fire extinguisher/extintor de incendios Aparato que rocía sustancias químicas que apagan fuegos.

First aid/primeros auxilios Cuidado inmediato que se da a una persona herida o enferma hasta que sea posible proporcionarle ayuda médica normal.

First-degree burn/quemadura de primer grado Quemadura en que sólo la capa exterior de la piel se quema y se enrojece.

Fitness/buen estado físico Poder resistir trabajo físico y jugar cada día sin cansarse demasiado.

Flammable/inflamable Sustancia que se enciende fácilmente.

Flexibility/flexibilidad Habilidad de mover articulaciones completa y fácilmente a través de una extensión completa de movimiento.

Fluoride/fluoruro Producto químico que ayuda a prevenir caries en los dientes.

Fossil fuel/combustible fósil Petróleo, carbón y gas natural que se usan para proporcionar energía.

Fracture/fractura Rotura de un hueso.

Fraud/fraude Esfuerzo calculado para engañar a otros.

Frequency/frecuencia Número de horas que haces ejercicios cada semana.

Friendship/amistad Relación con una persona que conoces, en la que confías y aprecias con afecto.

Fungi/hongos Organismos que son más complejos que bacterias, pero que no pueden producer su propio alimento.

Gang/pandilla Grupo de jóvenes que se juntan para participar en actividades ilegales.

Generic products/productos genéricos Productos que se venden en envases comunes y a menor precio que los de marca.

Genes/genes Unidades básicas de la herencia.

Genital herpes/herpes genital Infección de transmisión sexual, causada por un virus, que produce ampollas dolorosas en el área genital.

Genital warts/verrugas genitales Erupciones o protuberancias en el área genital causadas por ciertos tipos del virus papiloma de los seres humanos.

Germs/gérmenes Organismos tan diminutos que se ven sólo a través de un microscopio.

Glaucoma/glaucoma Afección del ojo en la cual la presión de fluido crece dentro del ojo.

Gonorrhea/gonorrea Infección de transmisión sexual causada por bacterias que afecta las membranas mucosas del cuerpo, en particular en el área genital.

Groundwater/agua subterránea Agua acumulada debajo de la superficie de la tierra.

Gynecologist/ginecólogo Médico que se especializa en el aparato reproductor femenino.

Hair follicles/folículos pilosos Saquito membranoso en la dermis donde nace el pelo.

Hallucinogen/alucinógeno Droga que altera el estado de ánimo, los pensamientos y los sentidos.

Hazard/peligro Fuente posible de peligro.

Hazardous wastes/desperdicios peligrosos Líquidos, sólidos, sedimentos, o desperdicios radiactivos producidos por humanos que ponen en peligro la salud humana o el medio ambiente.

Health/salud Combinación de bienestar físico, mental-emocional y social.

Health insurance/seguro médico Plan en el que una persona paga una cantidad fija a una compañía de seguros que acuerda cubrir parte o la totalidad de los gastos médicos.

Health maintenance organization (HMO)/ organización para el mantenimiento de la salud Plan de seguro de salud que contrata a ciertos médicos y especialistas para dar servicios médicos.

Heart attack/ataque cardiaco Afección seria que se presenta cuando el flujo de sangre al corazón disminuye o cesa, dañando el músculo cardiaco.

Hepatitis/hepatitis Enfermedad viral caracterizada por inflamación del hígado, el tono amarillo de la piel y la parte blanca del ojo.

Hepatitis B/hepatitis B Enfermedad causada por el virus de la hepatitis B que afecta el hígado.

Heredity/herencia Transferencia de características de los padres biológicos a sus hijos.

Histamines/histaminas Substancias químicas que las células inmunitarias sueltan para atraer más sangre y linfa hacia el área afectada por los alergenos.

HIV (human immunodeficiency virus)/ VIH (virus de inmunodeficiencia humana) Virus que causa el sida.

Homicide/homicidio Crimen violento que resulta en la muerte de otra persona.

Hormones/hormonas Substancias químicas, producidas por ciertas glándulas que ayudan a regular las funciones del cuerpo.

Hurricane/huracán Tormenta de vientos y lluvia torrencial que se origina en alta mar.

Hygiene/higiene Limpieza.

Hypertension/hipertensión Afección en que la presión arterial de una persona se mantiene a niveles más altos de lo normal.

Hypothermia/hipotermia Descenso rápido y peligroso de la temperatura del cuerpo.

Immune system/sistema inmunológico Combinación de las defensas del cuerpo, compuesta de células, tejidos y órganos que combaten agentes patógenos.

Immunity/inmunidad Habilidad del cuerpo de resistir los agentes patógenos que causan una enfermedad en particular.

Infancy/infancia Primer año de vida después del nacimiento.

Infection/infección Afección que se produce cuando agentes patógenos invaden el cuerpo, se multiplican y dañan las células.

Inflammation/inflamación Reacción del cuerpo a lesiones o enfermedades que resulta en hinchazón, dolor, calor y enrojecimiento.

Influenza/influenza Enfermedad viral muy contagiosa que se caracteriza por fiebres, escalofríos, dolores de cabeza, dolor muscular y síntomas respiratorios.

Infomercial/anuncio informativo Anuncio de televisión largo cuyo propósito principal parece ser proveer información acerca de un producto en vez de vender el producto.

Inhalants/inhalantes Vapores de substancias químicas que son olidos o inhalados para drogarse.

Insulin/insulina Proteína elaborada en el páncreas que regula el nivel de glucosa en la sangre.

Integrity/integridad Ser fiel a tus valores éticos.

Intensity/intensidad En cuanto al estado físico, la cantidad de energía que usas cuando haces ejercicio.

Interpersonal communication/comunicación interpersonal Compartir pensamientos y sentimientos con otra persona.

Intoxicated/embriagado Borracho.

Joint/articulación Lugar en donde se unen dos o más huesos.

Kidneys/riñones Órganos que eliminan desperdicios, incluyendo sales, de la sangre.

Landfill/terraplén sanitario Pozo enorme con diseño específico donde se arrojan y se entierran desechos.

Ligament/ligamento Tipo de tejido conjuntivo que mantiene en su lugar los huesos en las articulaciones.

Liver/hígado Glándula digestiva que secreta una sustancia llamada bilis que ayuda a digerir las grasas.

Long-term goal/meta a largo plazo Objetivo que planeas alcanzar en un largo período de tiempo.

Lungs/pulmones Dos órganos grandes que intercambian oxígeno y monóxido de carbono.

Lymphatic system/sistema linfático Aparato circulatorio secundario que le ayuda al cuerpo a defenderse de agentes patógenos y a mantener el equilibrio de los líquidos.

Lymphocytes/linfocitos Glóbulos blancos especiales en la linfa.

Mainstream smoke/humo directo Humo que el fumador aspira y exhala.

Malignant/maligno Canceroso.

Managed care plans/planes de medicina administrada Planes de seguro médico que enfatizan la medicina preventiva y el trabajo para controlar el costo y el mantenimiento del cuidado de salud de calidad.

Media literacy/conocimiento de los medios de comunicación Habilidad de entender las metas de la publicidad en los medios publicitarios.

Mediation/mediación Resolución de conflictos por medio de otra persona que ayuda a llegar a una solución aceptable para ambas partes.

Medicine/medicina Droga que previene o cura enfermedades o que alivia sus síntomas.

Melanin/melanina Sustancia que le da el color a la piel.

Menstruation/menstruación Sangre, tejidos y fluidos del cuerpo que resultan del desprendimiento del interior del útero.

Mental and emotional disorders/trastornos mentales y emocionales Enfermedades que afectan los pensamientos, sentimientos y comportamiento de una persona.

Mental and emotional health/salud mental y emocional Habilidad de hacerles frente de manera razonable al estrés y a los cambios de la vida diaria.

Metabolism/metabolismo Proceso mediante el cual el cuerpo obtiene energía de los alimentos.

Mind-body connection/conexión de la mente con el cuerpo Forma en la cual tus emociones afectan tu salud física y general y cómo tu salud general afecta tus emociones.

Minerals/minerales Sustancias que el cuerpo utiliza para formar huesos y dientes sanos, mantener la sangre saludable y mantener el corazón y otros órganos funcionando como deben.

Minor/menor Persona que es menor de la edad en que se tienen derechos y responsabilidades de adultos.

Mood disorder/trastorno del ánimo o del humor Problema emocional y mental en el cual la persona tiene cambios de humor que parecen extremos, inapropiados o que duran mucho tiempo.

Mood swings/cambios de ánimo Cambios frecuentes del estado emocional.

Muscle endurance/resistencia muscular Habilidad de un músculo de usar fuerza repetitivamente en un periodo de tiempo.

Muscular system/sistema muscular Tejidos que mueven partes del cuerpo y controlan los órganos.

MyPyramid food guidance system/pirámide alimenticia Guía para desarrollar un plan alimenticio saludable.

Narcotic/narcótico Droga que alivia el dolor y entorpece los sentidos.

Neglect/abandono Fallas en el proceso de satisfacer las necesidades físicas y emocionales de una persona considerada como dependiente.

Negotiation/negociación Proceso de hablar directamente con otra persona para solucionar un conflicto.

Neurons/neuronas Células que forman el sistema nervioso.

Neutrality/neutralidad Promesa de no tomar partido durante un conflicto entre otros.

Nicotine/nicotina Droga adictiva que forma hábito y se encuentra en el tabaco.

Noncommunicable disease/enfermedad no contagiosa Enfermedad que no se puede transmitir de una persona a otra.

Nonrenewable resources/recursos no renovables Sustancias que no se pueden reemplazar después de usarse.

Nonverbal communication/comunicación no verbal Trasmitir mensajes sin el uso de palabras.

Nurture/cuidar Satisfacer necesidades físicas, mentales, emocionales y sociales.

Nutrient dense/rico en nutrientes Tener una alta cantidad de sustancias nutritivas en comparación con la cantidad de calorías.

Nutrients/nutrientes Sustancias de los alimentos que el cuerpo necesita para desarrollarse, tener energía y mantenerse saludable.

Nutrition/nutrición Proceso de ingerir alimentos y usarlos para la energía, el desarrollo y el mantenimiento de la buena salud.

Occupational Safety and Health Administration (OSHA)/oficina de Salud y Seguridad Ocupacional Rama del Ministerio del Trabajo que protege la seguridad de los trabajadores estadounidenses.

Ophthalmologist/oftalmólogo Médico que se especializa en la estructura, funciones y enfermedades del ojo.

Optimistic/optimista Tener una actitud positiva con respecto al futuro.

Optometrist/optómetra Profesional de la salud que está preparado para examinar la vista y recetar lentes correctivas.

Organ/órgano Parte del cuerpo que comprende distintos tejidos unidos para cumplir una función particular.

Osteoarthritis/osteoartritis Enfermedad crónica, común en los ancianos, que es el resultado de la degeneración del cartílago de las articulaciones.

Ovaries/ovarios Glándulas endocrinas femeninas que sueltan huevos maduros y producen hormonas como el estrógeno y la progesterona.

Overdose/sobredosis Tomar una cantidad de droga que supera lo que el cuerpo puede tolerar.

Over-the-counter (OTC) medicine/medicamento sin receta Medicina que se puede comprar sin receta de un médico.

Overworking/ejercicio excesivo Acondicionamiento muy fuerte o muy seguido sin descanso suficiente entre sesiones.

Ovulation/ovulación Proceso en el cual los ovarios sueltan óvulos maduros, normalmente uno en cada ciclo menstrual.

Ozone/ozono Gas hecho de tres átomos de oxígeno.

Pancreas/páncreas Glándula que le ayuda al intestino delgado, a través de la producción de jugo pancreático, el cual está formado por una mezcla de varias enzimas que descomponen las proteínas, hidratos de carbono y grasas.

Passive smoker/fumador pasivo Persona que no fuma pero que inhala humo secundario.

Pathogens/gérmenes patógenos Gérmenes que causan enfermedades.

Pedestrian/peatón Persona que se traslada a pie.

Peer pressure/presión de compañeros Influencia que tu grupo de compañeros tiene sobre ti.

Peers/compañeros Personas de tu grupo de edad que se parecen a ti de muchas maneras.

Peripheral nervous system (PNS)/sistema nervioso periférico Nervios que unen el sistema nervioso central con todas partes del cuerpo.

Personality/personalidad Combinación de tus sentimientos, gustos, disgustos, actitudes, habilidades y hábitos.

Pharmacist/farmacéutico Persona capacitada para preparar y distribuir medicinas.

Physical activity/actividad física Todo movimiento que cause que el cuerpo use energía.

Physical dependence/dependencia física Adicción por la cual el cuerpo llega a tener necesidad química de una droga.

Plaque/placa bacteriana Película delgada y pegajosa que se acumula en los dientes y contribuye a las caries dentales.

Plasma/plasma Líquido amarillento, la parte líquida de la sangre.

Pneumonia/neumonía Inflamación severa de los pulmones.

Point-of-service (POS) plan/plan de lugar del servicio Plan de seguro médico que combina las características de las organizaciones para el mantenimiento de la salud y las organizaciones de proveedores preferidos.

Pollen/polen Sustancia en forma de polvo que despiden las flores de ciertas plantas.

Pollution/contaminación Sustancias sucias o dañinas en el medio ambiente.

Pores/poros Orificios pequeños en la piel que permiten el proceso de transpiración.

Positive stress/estrés positivo Estrés que te puede ayudar a alcanzar tus metas.

Preferred provider organization (PPO)/ organización médica preferida Plan de seguro de salud que permite que sus miembros seleccionen a un médico que participa en el plan o a uno de su preferencia.

Prejudice/prejuicio Opinión formada negativa e injustamente.

Preschooler/niño en edad preescolar Niño entre las edades de tres y cinco años.

Prescription medicine/medicinas bajo receta Medicina que puede ser obtenida legalmente solo con el permiso escrito de un médico.

Prevention/prevención Tomar pasos para evitar algo.

Primary care provider/profesional médico principal Profesional de la salud que proporciona exámenes médicos y cuidado general.

Probation/libertad condicional Periodo de tiempo en el cual una persona que ha sido arrestada tiene que presentarse ante un oficial de la corte regularmente.

Product placement/colocación de productos Acuerdo pagado hecho por una compañía para mostrar su producto en los medios de publicidad.

Proteins/proteínas Nutrientes que se usan para reparar las células y tejidos del cuerpo.

Protozoa/protozoarios Organismos unicelulares que tienen una estructura más compleja que las bacterias.

Psychological dependence/dependencia psicológica Cuando una persona cree que necesita una droga para sentirse bien o para trabajar normalmente.

Puberty/pubertad Etapa de la vida en la cual una persona comienza a desarrollar ciertas características físicas propias de los adultos del mismo sexo.

Pulmonary circulation/circulación pulmonar Circulación que lleva la sangre desde el corazón, a través de los pulmones y de regreso al corazón.

Radiation therapy/terapia de radiación Tratamiento que usa rayos equis u otra forma de radiación para matar células cancerosas.

Rape/violación Relaciones sexuales forzadas.

Recycle/reciclar Cambiar un objeto de alguna manera para que se pueda volver a usar.

Referral/recomendación Sugerencia de buscar ayuda o información de otra persona o lugar.

Refusal skills/habilidades de rechazo Estrategias que ayudan a decir no efectivamente.

Reliable/confiable Confiable y seguro.

Reproduction/reproducción Proceso mediante el cual los organismos vivos producen otros de su especie.

Reproductive system/aparato reproductor Órganos y estructuras corporales que hacen posible la producción de hijos.

Rescue breathing/respiración de rescate Procedimiento de primeros auxilios en el que una persona llena de aire los pulmones de una persona que no está respirando.

Resilience/capacidad de recuperación Habilidad de recuperarse de un problema o perdida.

Resources/recursos Lugares en donde puedes conseguir información, apoyo y consejos.

Respiratory system/aparato respiratorio Órganos que suministran el oxígeno en la sangre.

Rheumatoid arthritis/artritis reumatoide Enfermedad crónica caracterizada por dolor, inflamación, hinchazón y anquilosamiento de las articulaciones.

Risk/riesgo Posibilidad de que algo dañino pueda ocurrir en tu salud y bienestar.

Risk behaviors/conductas riesgosas Actos o decisiones que pueden causar lesiones o daños a ti o a otros.

Risk factor/factor de riesgo Característica o conducta que aumenta la posibilidad de llegar a tener un problema médico o enfermedad.

Role model/modelo de conducta Persona que inspira a otras a que se comporten o piensen de cierta manera.

S

Safety conscious/consciente de la seguridad Que se da cuenta de la importancia de la seguridad y actúa con cuidado.

Saliva/saliva Líquido digestivo producido por las glándulas salivales de la boca.

Saturated fats/grasas saturadas Grasas que son sólidas a la temperatura ambiente.

Second-degree burn/quemadura de segundo grado Quemadura moderadamente seria en la que se forman ampollas en el área quemada.

Secondhand smoke/humo secundario Aire que está contaminado por el humo del tabaco.

Self-concept/autoconcepto La manera en que te ves a ti mismo.

Self-esteem/autoestima Cómo te sientes sobre ti mismo.

Semen/semen Mezcla de esperma y fluidos que protege a los espermatozoides y los transporta a través de los tubos del sistema reproductivo masculino.

Sewage/aguas cloacales Basura, detergentes y otros desechos caseros que se llevan las tuberías de desagüe.

Sexual abuse/abuso sexual Contacto sexual forzado por una persona.

Sexually transmitted diseases (STDs)/enfermedades de transmisión sexual Enfermedades que se propagan de una persona a otra, a través del contacto sexual.

Short-term goal/meta a corto plazo Meta que uno puede alcanzar dentro de un breve periodo de tiempo.

Side effect/efecto secundario Reacción no deseada de una medicina.

Sidestream smoke/humo indirecto Humo que procede de un cigarrillo, pipa o cigarro encendido.

Skeletal system/sistema osteoarticular Armazón de huesos y otros tejidos que sostiene el cuerpo.

Small intestine/intestino delgado Tubo enrollado que mide entre veinte y veintitrés pies, en el cual ocurre el noventa por ciento de la digestión.

Smog/smog Neblina de color amarillo-café que se forma cuando la luz solar reacciona con la contaminación del aire.

Smoke alarm/alarma contra incendios Aparato que hace sonar una alarma cuando detecta humo.

Specialist/especialista Profesional del cuidado de la salud que está capacitado para tratar una categoría especial de pacientes o un problema de salud específico.

Sperm/espermatozoides Células reproductoras masculinas.

Spinal cord/médula espinal Largo conjunto de neuronas que transmiten mensajes entre el cerebro y todas las otras partes del cuerpo.

Sprain/torcedura Daño al ligamento que conecta huesos con articulaciones.

Stimulant/estimulante Droga que acelera las funciones del cuerpo.

Strength/fuerza Capacidad que tienen los músculos para ejercer una fuerza.

Strep throat/amigdalitis estreptocócica Dolor de garganta causado por estreptococos.

Stress/estrés La reacción del cuerpo hacia peligros reales o imaginarios u otros eventos en la vida.

Stress fracture/fractura leve Fractura pequeña causada por una torcedura repetitiva del mismo hueso.

Stress management/control del estrés Identificación de lo que causa el éstres y aprender cómo reaccionar a ello de manera que permita mantener la buena salud mental y emocional.

Stressors/factor estresante Fuentes de estrés.

Stroke/derrame cerebral Afección seria que se produce cuando una arteria en el cerebro se rompe o se obstruye.

Suicide/suicidio Matarse intencionalmente.

Syphilis/sífilis Infección de transmisión sexual, causada por una bacteria, que puede afectar muchas partes del cuerpo.

Systemic circulation/circulación sistémica Circulación que lleva sangre rica en oxígeno a todos los tejidos del cuerpo, menos a los pulmones.

Tact/tacto Sentido de qué hacer o decir para evitar ofender a otros.

Tar/alquitrán Líquido espeso y oscuro que forma el tabaco al quemarse.

Target audience/público objetivo Grupo de gente al cual es dirigido un producto específico.

Target heart rate/ritmo cardiaco meta Número de latidos del corazón, por minuto, que una persona debe tratar de alcanzar durante una actividad de intensidad moderada a vigorosa, para obtener el máximo beneficio posible para el aparato circulatorio.

Tartar/sarro Placa endurecida que daña la salud de las encías.

Tendon/tendón Tipo de tejido conjuntivo que une un músculo a otro o un músculo a un hueso.

Tendonitis/tendinitis Hinchazón dolorosa de un tendón causada por el uso excesivo.

Testes/testículos Las dos glándulas que producen los espermatozoides.

Third-degree burn/quemadura de tercer grado Quemadura muy severa en que todas las capas de la piel quedan dañadas.

Tinnitus/acúfeno Sonido constante en el oído.

Tissue/tejido Grupo de células similares que tienen una función en particular.

Toddler/niño que empieza a andar Niño entre uno y tres años.

Tolerance/tolerancia Necesidad del cuerpo de mayores cantidades de una droga para obtener el mismo efecto.

Tornado/tornado Tormenta en forma de torbellino, que gira en grandes círculos y que cae del cielo a la tierra.

Trachea/tráquea Pasaje en la garganta que lleva el aire de y hacia los pulmones.

Trans fatty acids/ácidos grasos trans Forma de grasa formada cuando el hidrógeno es adherido al aceite vegetal durante el procesamiento.

Trichomoniasis/tricomoniasis Enfermedad de transmisión sexual causada por los protozoarios *Trichomonas vaginalis*.

Tuberculosis/tuberculosis Enfermedad causada por bacterias que generalmente afecta los pulmones.

Tumor/tumor Grupo de células anormales que forma una masa.

Ulcer/úlcera Llaga abierta en el recubrimiento del estómago

Ultraviolet (UV) rays/rayos ultravioletas Forma invisible de radiación que puede penetrar células de la piel y cambia su estructura.

Unsaturated fats/grasas no saturadas Grasas que son líquidas a la temperatura del ambiente.

Uterus/útero Matriz, órgano en forma de pera en el cual se nutre un bebé en desarrollo.

Vaccine/vacuna Fórmula compuesta por gérmenes patógenos muertos o debilitados que es introducida en el cuerpo para causar una reacción inmunológica.

Values/valores Creencias que guían la forma en la cual vive una persona.

Vein/vena Tipo de vaso sanguíneo que lleva la sangre de todas partes del cuerpo de regreso al corazón.

Verbal communication/comunicación verbal Expresar sentimientos, pensamientos, o experiencias a través de palabras, ya sea hablando o escribiendo.

Violence/violencia Acto de fuerza física que resulta en un daño o abuso.

Viruses/virus Gérmenes patógenos más simples y pequeños.

Vitamins/vitaminas Compuestos que ayudan a regular los procesos del cuerpo.

Warm-up/precalentamiento Ejercicio suave que prepara a los músculos cardíacos para estar listos para actividad física moderada o fuerte.

Warranty/garantía Promesa escrita de un fabricante o una tienda de reparar un producto o devolver el dinero al comprador si el producto no funciona debidamente.

Weather emergency/emergencia meteorológica Situación peligrosa debido a cambios en la atmósfera.

Wellness/bienestar Mantener una salud equilibrada por un largo período de tiempo.

Withdrawal/síndrome de abstinencia Serie de síntomas físicos y mentales dolorosos por los cuales una persona pasa cuando deja el uso de una sustancia adictiva.

Youth court/tribunal juvenil Programa escolar especial en el cual unos adolescentes deciden el castigo para otros adolescentes por intimidación y otros problemas de comportamiento.

Index

A

Abdominal strength, 65
Abdominal thrusts, 496
Abstinence, 190–192
  behaviors supporting, 192–193
  definition of, 27
  as only sure method of birth control/disease prevention, 192
  from premarital sexual activity, 191–192, 425–426, 431
  for risk reduction, 26, 392
  from tobacco, alcohol, and drugs, 190–191
Abuse, 217–221
  of alcohol, 270
  dating violence, 214
  of drugs, 300
  effects of, 219
  emotional, 217
  finding help for, 221
  neglect, 217
  physical, 217
  risk factors for, 219
  sexual, 218
  silence about, 220
  warning signs of, 218
Acceptance (in grieving process), 154
Accessing information, 10–12
  on alcoholism, 269
  community resources, 164
  drowning prevention, 483
  drug use, 309
  evaluating information in ads, 21
  eating right, 120
  on glasses or contacts, 356–357
  on health-related products/ services, 342, 346
  juvenile rheumatoid arthritis, 461
  on medical specialists, 353
  on organizations, 50
  safe drinking water, 405
  on sexually transmitted diseases, 425, 432–433
  on tobacco use, 245, 250
Accident chain, 473–474
Accidental injuries, 473
  and drug/alcohol use, 277
  and head protection, 276
  preventing, 276, 477, 479
  responding to. See First aid
  in sports, 91–92
Accidents, 472–474
Acetaminophen, 348

Achilles tendon, 66
Acid, digestive, 123, 124
Acid rain, 509
Acne, 332
Acquaintance (definition), 184
Addiction
  to alcohol, 264
  to drugs, 301
  to tobacco, 244–245
Adolescence, 364–369, 389–390
  emotional development during, 367
  endocrine system during, 370
  and hormones, 370
  mental development during, 366
  physical development during, 365–366
  social development during, 368
Adrenal glands, 371
Adrenaline, 157
Adulthood, 390–393
Adults
  choking first aid for, 496–497
  communicating openly with, 281, 287, 317, 367
  seeking help from, 151, 155, 161, 482
  as source of information, 11
Advertising, 243, 245–247, 341–343
Advertising, evaluating information in, 21
Advocacy, 28, 48, 50, 232, 288, 457
  cancer risk reduction, 457
  breast self-examination, 381
  diabetes management, 372
  drug-free school campaign, 314
  encouraging teens to avoid alcohol, 288
  for waste management, 514–515
  helping others say no to drugs, 320–321
  physical fitness campaign, 15
AED (Automated external defibrillator), 495
Aerobic exercise, 64, 76
Affection, showing, 426
After-school programs, 216
Aftershocks (earthquakes), 490
AIDS (acquired immunodeficiency syndrome), 427–431.
  See also HIV
Air pollution, 508, 514
Airbags, 481–482

Airlines, smoking bans on, 250
Alcohol, 264–271, 278–289
  abstinence from, 27, 190–191
  and accidental injuries, 277
  addiction to, 264
  alternatives to using, 289
  benefits of avoiding, 287
  as cause of violence, 212
  dangers of, 265
  depressants and, 305
  and driving, 266
  effects of, 266–270
  forms of, 265
  getting help for problems with, 287
  harmfulness of, 279–281
  and heart failure, 449
  and high blood pressure, 449
  illegal use of, 191
  long-term effects, 268–270
  and nervous system disorders, 275
  reasons for avoiding, 287
  refusal skills for, 286–291
  risks of using, 282–285
Alcoholism, 270–271
Allergens, 441
Allergies, 349, 441–443
Allergists, 353
Alternative activities
  to alcohol use, 289
  to drug use, 317
  tobacco-free events, 254
Alveoli, 234, 238, 240
American Cancer Society, 255, 454
American Heart Association, 255
American Lung Association, 255
American Red Cross, 484
America's Promise, 50
Amino acids, 105
Amphetamines, 304
Anabolic steroids, 88
Anaerobic exercise, 64
Analyzing influences, 14, 430, 449. See also Influences
  fat information in advertisements, 449
  media messages about food, 136–137
  media messages about tobacco, 256–257
  on personality, 146
  on sexual behavior, 430
Anger, 154
Anger management, 368
Angioplasty, 450

Anorexia nervosa, 132
Antibiotics, 348
Antibodies, 410, 411
Antigens, 410–412
Antihistamines, 348, 443
Antismoking efforts, 246–247
Anus, 126
Anvil (ear), 338
Anxiety disorders, 160
Aorta, 72
Applying Technology, 33, 57, 101, 141, 171, 199, 227, 261, 295, 325, 361, 399, 437, 469, 505, 523
Appreciation, showing, 180
Arterial diseases, 446–447
Arteries, 71, 446–450, 497
Arteriosclerosis, 447
Arthritis, 461–463
Assault, 211
Assertiveness, 318
Asthma, 239, 240, 443–445
Astigmatism, 337
Atherosclerosis, 447
Atria, 72
Auditory canal, 338
Automated external defibrillator (AED), 495
Avocados, 105

B

B cells, 409–411
Bacteria, 403–405
Balance
    in health, 7
    sense of, 338
    test for, 64
Ball-and-socket joints, 67
Barbiturates, 305
Bathrooms, safety in, 477
Battery, 217
Beans, 105–106, 112–113
Behavior(s). See also Practicing healthful behaviors
    avoiding unhealthful, 154–155
    and personality, 146
    risk. See Risk behaviors
    as sign of conflict, 204
    signaling conflict escalation, 209–210
Benign tumors, 452
Better Business Bureau, 345
Bicycling, 93, 481
Bile, 124
Billboards, influence of, 22
Binge drinking, 279
Binge eating disorder, 133
Biodegradable materials, 511
Biological Scientist, 384

Biopsy, 455
Bipolar disorder, 161
Birth and infancy, 388–389
Bladder, 125
Bladder cancer, 233, 235
Bleeding, first aid for, 497
Blended families, 178
Blizzards, 488–489
Blood, 74–75
    circulation of, 72
    diseases transmitted through, 404–405
    transmission of HIV through, 428
Blood alcohol concentration (BAC), 265–266
Blood pressure, 73, 233
Blood types, 75
Blood vessels, 71, 72
    alcohol and, 268
    alcohol's effects on, 267
    factors straining, 76
    and heart disease, 446–447
    in skin, 330
    tobacco's effect on, 235
BMI. See Body Mass Index
Body composition, 63, 134
Body decoration, 331
Body image, 128–129
Body language, 175, 176, 204
Body Mass Index (BMI), 129
Body systems
    basic units of, 384
    circulatory system, 71–76
    digestive system, 122–124, 126
    endocrine system, 370–373
    excretory system, 125–126
    female reproductive system, 378–382
    immune system, 407–412
    male reproductive system, 374–377
    muscular system, 67–70
    nervous system, 272–277
    respiratory system, 236–241
    skeletal system, 66–67, 69–70
    tobacco's effects on, 234–235, 239–240
Bones, 66–67, 106, 498
Booster seat, 482
Boys & Girls Clubs of America, 50
Brain, 267, 272–277
    alcohol and, 266–267
    concussion, 94
    tobacco's effect on, 234
Brain stem, 274
Breads, 105
Breakfast, 117–118
Breast cancer, 381, 452

Breathing, 236–241
Breathing, rescue, 494, 495
Bronchi, 237, 238
Bronchioles, 238
Bronchodilators, 445
Bruises, 499
Brushing teeth, 328–329
Building blocks, for total health, 11
Building Health Skills
    accessing information, 432, 518
    advocacy, 320
    analyzing influences, 136, 256
    communication skills, 194
    conflict resolution, 222
    decision making, 96, 356
    goal setting, 52, 464
    practicing healthful behaviors, 500
    refusal skills, 290, 394
    stress management, 166
Bulimia nervosa, 133
Bullying, 213
Burns, first aid for, 498
Butter, 105, 106
Buying decisions. See Consumer choices
Bypass surgery, 450
Bystanders, 213

C

Caffeine, 89
Calcium, 106
Calories, 112–113
    daily requirements, 113
    in snack foods, 119
    and weight management, 134–135
Camping safety, 485
Cancer, 451–457
    from alcohol use, 267
    causes of, 452–453
    diagnosis of, 455
    in females, 381
    lung, 239
    in males, 376
    prevention of, 453–454, 457
    risk factors for, 452
    from secondhand smoke, 248
    from tobacco use, 230, 232, 233, 235, 240
    treatment of, 456
    types of, 452
    warning signs of, 455
Capillaries, 71, 72, 238
Carbohydrates, 105, 118
Carbon dioxide, 72, 125, 237, 238
Carbon monoxide, 231, 234, 248

Carcinogens, 453
Cardiac muscle, 67, 71
Cardiologists, 353
Cardiopulmonary resuscitation
　　(CPR), 494, 495
Cardiovascular endurance, 65
Cardiovascular system. *See*
　　Circulatory system
Career goals, 44
Careers in health
　　biological scientist, 384
　　emergency room physician, 498
　　environmental engineer, 516
　　epidemiologist, 416
　　health officer, 20
　　nurse practitioner, 44
　　nutritionist, 132
　　oncologist, 456
　　paramedic, 313
　　pathologist, 232
　　pharmacist, 354
　　physical therapist, 92
　　psychologist, 146
　　school counselor, 204
　　social worker, 186
　　substance abuse counselor, 270
Caring, 48, 49, 185
Cartilage, 66
Cataract, 336
CAUTION (signs of cancer),
　　454, 455
Cells, 384. *See also specific cell types*
Central nervous system (CNS), 272
Cereals, 106
Cerebellum, 274
Cerebral palsy, 274
Cerebrum, 274
Cervix, 379, 381
Changes
　　during adolescence, 364–369
　　emotional, 367
　　mental, 366
　　physical, 365–366
　　during pregnancy, 385
　　during puberty, 365–368
　　social, 368
Character, 47–51
　　and advocacy, 48
　　and caring, 48, 49
　　and citizenship, 48, 49, 284
　　development of, 50–51
　　exercise and responsibility, 62
　　and fairness, 48–49
　　and integrity, 48
　　and life experiences, 49–50
　　and respect, 48, 286
　　and responsibility, 48, 181
　　traits of good character, 48, 49
　　and trustworthiness, 48, 49, 185

Checkups. *See* Health screenings
Cheese, 106, 117
Chemical dependency, 244, 270.
　　See also Addiction
Chemotherapy, 456
Chest thrusts, 497
Chewing, 123
Chewing tobacco, 232
Chicken pox, 414
Childhood, 389
Children
　　choking first aid for, 496
　　growth and development
　　　of, 389
　　and vehicle safety, 482
Chlamydia, 423
Choice(s)
　　consumers' right to choose, 345
　　food, 111–120
　　health, 21–22
　　making. *See* Decision making
　　and self-esteem, 150
Choking, first aid for, 495–497
Cholesterol, 106
Chromosomes, 383–384
Chronic diseases, 440
Chyme, 124
Cigarettes, 232
Cigars, 232
Circulatory system, 71–76, 233, 235
Cirrhosis, 268, 269
Citizenship, 48, 49, 50, 284, 482
Cleanliness. *See* Hygiene
Clothing, workout, 78–79
Club drugs, 306
CNS. *See* Central nervous system
Cocaine, 304
Cochlea, 338
Codeine, 307, 313
"Cold turkey" quitting, 255
Cold weather safety, 484
Colds, 239, 240, 413, 414
Collaboration, 207
Colon, 124
Colon and rectal cancer, 452
Communicable diseases, 402–431
　　causes of, 402–406
　　chicken pox, 414
　　common colds, 413
　　definition of, 402
　　and drug use, 404
　　flu, 414
　　hepatitis, 415–416
　　HIV and AIDS, 427–430
　　and hygiene, 418–420
　　and the immune system,
　　　407–412
　　measles, 414–415
　　mononucleosis, 415

　　mumps, 415
　　pneumonia, 416
　　prescribed medicines for, 420
　　preventing spread of, 418–421,
　　　427–428
　　prevention of, 404–406,
　　　418–421
　　and sexual abstinence,
　　　425–426, 431
　　sexually transmitted diseases,
　　　422–431
　　strep throat, 416–417
　　tuberculosis, 416
Communication, 174–177, 181
　　about problems, 289
　　in writing, 177
Communication skills, 15,
　　176–177, 181. *See also* Refusal
　　skills
　　listening skills, 176
　　practicing, 194–195
　　speaking skills, 176
　　speaking up, 221
Communities
　　citizenship in, 48
　　information resources in, 11
　　safety in, 216, 482
　　violence in, 211–212
Community health, 354
　　contributing talents to, 48
　　environmental factors in, 19–20
　　media influence on, 22
　　technology influence on, 22
Comparison shopping, 343
Complex carbohydrates, 105
Composting, 511
Compromise, 186–187, 207
Concern, demonstrating, 182
Concussion, 94
Conditioning, 90
Confidence, 151
Conflict, 202–205
　　avoidance of, 205
　　common causes of, 203–204
　　definition of, 16, 202
　　and demeaning statements, 210
　　escalation of, 209–210
　　signs of, 204
Conflict resolution, 16, 206–210
　　compromise for, 207
　　mediating a conflict, 208–209
　　peer mediation for, 208
　　school programs for, 215
　　settling a disagreement, 209
　　T.A.L.K. strategy for, 207
　　through collaboration, 207
　　through negotiation, 207
Connecting neurons, 273
Connecting tissue, 66

Consequences
    advance consideration of, 391–392
    and decision making, 37
    of premarital sexual activity, 426, 431
    responsibility for, 366
    of risk behavior, 24
Conservation, 516–517
Constructive feedback, 147, 151
Consumer, definition of, 340
Consumer advocates, 345
Consumer choices, 340–346
    and advertising, 341–343
    influences on, 340–346
    responsibility in making, 343–344
    and rights of consumers, 345–346
Consumers Union, 345
Contact lenses, 337
Contact sports, 86
Contagious diseases. See Communicable diseases
Contagious period, 414
Cooking, fires caused by, 476
Cool-down exercises, 80
Coping skills, 158
Cornea, 335, 337
Coronary heart disease, 235
Cost, of food, 115
Counseling
    for abuse, 221
    for families, 182
    for mental/emotional problems, 164
Counselor, school, 221
Couples (family unit), 178
CPR. See Cardiopulmonary resuscitation
Crack, 304, 313
Cramp, muscular, 92
Creatine, 89
Crime(s)
    alcohol and, 283
    drug use and, 315
    hate, 212
    violent, 211–212
Crisis hot lines, 221
Criteria for decision making, 38
Critical thinking, 36
Cultural background, 21
Culture, 115, 341
Cumulative risks, 25
Cuticles, 333
Cyanide, 231
Cystic fibrosis (CF), 240

D

Daily Value, 109, 110
Dairy products, 105–107, 112–113, 117
Dandruff, 333
Dating violence, 214
Deafness, 338
Death(s)
    from accidents, 472
    from alcohol use, 265, 267, 279
    from cancer, 452
    coping with, 182
    from smoking-related illnesses, 230, 249
Decibels, 338
Decision making, 36–41, 96
    about personal health, 7, 21–22, 37–38
    alcohol and, 267
    alcohol's effect on, 265, 282–283
    to avoid tobacco, 252–253
    and drug use, 313
    environment-friendly products, 514
    H.E.L.P. criteria for, 38
    helping a friend, 39, 284
    influences on, 39, 41
    with peer pressure, 185
    process of, 40
    for sports safety, 93, 276
    taking medicine, 299
    and values, 37–38
    scheduling a dosage, 350
    when taking medicines, 350
Dehydration, 88, 268
Dental screenings, 126, 329
Dependence
    on alcohol, 270
    psychological vs. physical, 244
    on tobacco/alcohol/drugs, 244, 270
Depressants, 265, 305
Depression, 161, 301
Dermatologists, 353
Dermis, 330
Development. See Growth and development
Diabetes, 131, 458–460
Diaphragm, 237, 238
Dietary Guidelines for Americans, 107–108, 117
Dietary supplements, 117
Diet(s). See also Nutrition
    fad, 135
    and heart disease, 446
Digestion, 122
Digestive system, 122–124, 126, 233, 234

Disagreement, 204
Disease prevention. See also specific diseases
    for communicable diseases, 404–406, 418–421
    health department services for, 355
    immunizations for, 348
    personal hygiene for, 418–420
    wellness exams for, 352–353
Diseases
    and air pollution, 509
    alcoholism, 270–271
    arterial, 446–447
    in children of smokers, 249
    communicable. See Communicable diseases
    coping with, 182
    cultural factors in developing, 21
    definition of, 402
    and germs, 402–404
    noncommunicable. See Noncommunicable diseases
    pathogens causing, 403
    and secondhand smoke, 248
    and weight, 131
Dislocation, 93
Distress, 156
Divorce, coping with, 182
Doctors, 353
Dress codes, 214
Drinking water, 510
Driving safety, 266
Drowning prevention, 483, 484
Drug possession, 315
Drug-free school campaign, 314
Drug-free zone, 314
Drugs, 298–319, 347–350
    abstinence from, 190–191
    and accidental injuries, 277
    for AIDS treatment, 430
    alcohol, 264–271
    alternative to using, 317
    amphetamines, 304
    anabolic steroids, 88, 308
    and brain damage, 277
    as cause of violence, 212
    cocaine/crack, 304
    dangers of using, 303–309
    depressants, 305
    illegal, 191, 303–308
    marijuana, 305–306
    medicines as, 347–351
    reasons for avoiding, 316–317
    refusal skills for, 290–291, 317–319
    stimulants, 304

use/abuse of, 24, 25, 275,
299–302
Drunk driving, 266, 282–283

E

Ears, 337–338, 339
Earth Day Network, 50
Earthquakes, 490–491, 492
Eating. *See* Foods; Nutrition
Eating disorders, 132–133
Education, consumer, 345
Egg cells, 380, 383, 384
Eggs (food), 105
Ejaculation, 375
Electric shocks, prevention of,
477, 479
Electrical overload, 475
E-mail, 177
Embryo, 384
Emergencies
first aid for, 493–499
supply kits for, 491
weather, 486–490
Emergency room physicians, 498
Emotional abuse, 217
Emotional development, 367
Emotional health. *See* Mental/
emotional health
Emotional needs, 179
Emotions, 153–155, 367
and alcohol abuse, 280–281,
284–285, 289
communicating, 181
and conflict, 204
and drug use, 313
expression of, 6, 367
identifying/recognizing, 6,
153–154
managing, 6
and mind-body connection, 8
Empathy, 147
Emphysema, 234, 239, 240
Endocrine system, 370–373
Endorsements, 342
Endurance, 62, 63, 65, 76
Energy
conservation of, 516
physical, 87–88, 114, 134
Environment, 19–20, 508–517
diseases related to, 441
energy conservation, 516
and individual/community
health, 19–20
male sterility and hazards
in, 376
and personality, 146
pollution, 508–516
protection of, 513–517
social, 20

waste management, 514–515
water conservation, 517
Environmental engineers, 516
Environmental Protection Agency
(EPA), 513
Enzymes, 122–124
EPA (Environmental Protection
Agency), 513
Epidemiologist, 416
Epidermis, 330
Epididymis, 375
Epiglottis, 123, 237, 238
Epinephrine, 443
Esophagus, 123
Ethical values, 37, 146
Eustachian tube, 338
Evaluate/evaluation, 11–12, 21, 22,
25, 342
Excretion, 125
Excretory system, 125–126, 233
Exercise(s), 60. *See also* Physical
activity and fitness
aerobic, 64, 76
anaerobic, 64
warm-up/cool-down, 80–81
workouts, 81–82
Exhaling, 238
Extended families, 178
External influences, 18–20
Eye contact, 176
Eyeglasses, 337
Eyes, 334–337

F

Facilities, health care, 354
Fad diets, 135
Failures, learning from, 151
Fairness, 48, 49
Fallopian tubes, 379
Falls, preventing, 477
Families, 178–183
abuse in, 218–221
and buying decisions, 341
changes/challenges in, 181–182
and health choices, 21
and personal health, 180
risks of alcohol to, 284
and self-esteem, 150
strengthening relationships in,
180–181
stress and health of, 182
types of, 178
Family emergency plans, 491
Family members, older, 181
Family therapy, 164
Farsightedness, 337
Fatigue, 157
Fats, 105–108, 114, 116, 117, 449
Fat-soluble vitamins, 106

Fear, 154, 220
Feces, 126
Feedback, 147, 151
Feelings. *See* Emotions
Females
adolescent physical changes in,
365–366
alcohol tolerance of, 266
cancer self-exams for, 381, 454
chromosomes determining, 383
daily calorie requirements, 113
reproductive system in,
378–382
Fertilization, 380, 384
Fetal alcohol syndrome (FAS),
269–270
Fetus, 384, 385
Fever, 408
Fiber, 126
Fight-or-flight response, 157
Fights, 205. *See also* Conflict
resolution
Fingernails, 333
Fire safety, 475–478
First aid, 493–499
for bleeding, 497
for burns, 498
cardiopulmonary resuscitation,
494, 495
for choking, 496–497
First-degree burns, 498
Fish, 117
Fitness, 60, 77–83. *See also* Physical
activity and fitness
assessing progress, 83
measuring, 64–65
Fitness tests, 64–65
F.I.T.T. formula, 81–82
Flammable materials, 475
Flexibility, 63, 64
Floods, 489–490
Flossing (teeth), 329
Flu, 239, 240, 414
Fluoride, 329
Focus on the future, 42–43
Foldables
for accident chain, 471
for air pollution, 507
for alcohol, 263
for allergies and asthma, 439
for causes of conflict, 201
for changes during
adolescence, 363
for communicable diseases, 401
for decision making, 35
for drug use and abuse, 297
for fitness elements, 59
for mental/emotional
health, 143

for nutrients, 103
for personal care information, 327
for three aspects of health, 3
for tobacco effect on respiratory system, 229
for verbal and nonverbal communication, 173
Follicles, 330
Food groups, 87, 112–114
Food Guide Pyramid. *See* MyPyramid
Food pyramid. *See* MyPyramid
Foods. *See also* Nutrition
  contaminated, 405
  for healthful meals, 116–118
  influences on choices of, 114–115
  media messages about, 136–137
  nutrient dense, 119
  for nutritious snacks, 119
  safe handling of, 120–121
Formaldehyde, 231
Fossil fuels, 508, 509, 516
Fractures, 93, 498
Fraud, 342
Freedom, responsibility and, 189
Frequency, of workouts, 81
Friends, 184–187
  alcohol's effects on, 283–284
  and consumer choices, 341
  disagreements with, 209
  and food choices, 115
  and health choices, 22
  importance of, 184–185
  qualities of, 184–187
  and self-esteem, 150
Friendship (definition), 184
Frostbite, 94
Fruits, 105, 107, 112, 113
Fungi, 403
Future, focus on, 42–43

G

Gallbladder, 124
Gangs, 212
  and acts of revenge, 203
  strategies for avoiding, 212
Gastric juice, 123
Generic products, 343
Genes, 383. *See also* Heredity
Genital herpes, 423
Genital warts, 423
Germs, 402–406. *See also* Pathogens
Gestures, 176
Glands, 330, 370–371, 375
Glaucoma, 336
Gliding joints, 67

Global Response Youth Action, 50
Glucose, 458, 460
Goal setting, 42–44, 52, 79
  and achieving goals, 45
  benefits of, 42–44
  for fitness, 77, 96–97
  for heart disease prevention, 464–465
  for physical activity and fitness, 43, 64
  plan for, 44–46
  recognizing strengths/ limitations in, 43
  for self-esteem, 151
  short- and long-term goals, 44
  for weight training, 85
Gonorrhea, 424
Government
  consumer rights agencies of, 345
  health care programs of, 355
  pollution prevention by, 513
Grains, 105–108, 113
Grief, 154
Grieving, 154, 182
Groundwater, 510
Group therapy, 163, 164
Growth and development, 364–393
  during adolescence, 364–369, 389–390
  during adulthood, 390
  alcohol and, 280
  during childhood, 389
  drug use and, 312
  endocrine system influence on, 370
  of female reproductive system, 378–382
  fertilization stage of, 380
  of fetus after fertilization, 384–386
  and heredity, 383–384
  individual rates of, 365–366
  during infancy, 389
  of male reproductive system, 374–377
  during pregnancy, 384–386
  and preparation for adulthood, 391–393
Growth patterns
  individual differences in, 365–366
  and weight, 129
Guardians, communicating with, 425. *See also* Parents
Gums, 328–329
Gun safety, 479
Guns, 212
Gynecologists, 353, 382

H

Habitat for Humanity, 50
Hair, 332–333
Hair follicles, 330
Hallucinations, 275
Hallucinogens, 307
Hammer (ear), 338
Handwashing, 419, 420
Happiness, 154
Hate crimes, 212
Hazardous wastes, 511–512
Hazards, 473
HDL cholesterol, 106
Head lice, 333
Health, 4. *See also* Personal health care; specific topics
  building blocks for, 11
  and choices you make, 21–22
  community. *See* Community health
  cultures influence on, 21, 425, 430, 431
  and environment, 19–20
  and family, 21–22
  friends' influence on, 22, 184–187
  and heredity, 18–19
  influences on, 18–22
  measuring, 9
  media's influence on, 22
  mental/emotional, 6
  and mind-body connection, 8
  peer pressure's influence on, 187–188
  physical, 4–5
  and physical activity, 61
  prenatal, 385–387
  and risk behaviors, 23–27
  social, 6–7
  and wellness, 7
Health care services, 352–355. *See also* Personal health care
Health care system, tobacco's strain on, 251
Health departments (governmental), 355
Health eSpotlight
  choosing to be drug free, 297
  healthy peer relationships, 173
  making smart food choices, 103
  personal safety, 471
  taking charge of your health, 35
Health insurance, 251, 354
Health Inventories
  conflict resolution, 201
  healthy habits, 3
  physical activity, 59
  preventing disease, 439
Health maintenance organizations (HMOs), 354–355

Health officers, 20
Health Online
    acne, 332
    across the ages, 392
    creative conflict resolution, 207
    fitness that fits, 85
    healthy snacks, 119
    lending a helping hand, 161
    positive health behaviors, 7
    being proactive about the
        environment, 514
    substance abuse, 317
    tobacco, 253
    values and ethics, 37
Health Quiz
    alcohol, 263
    communicable diseases, 401
    the environment, 507
    growth/change, 363
    mental/emotional health, 143
    taking responsibility, 35
    tobacco effects, 229
Health screenings
    dental, 126, 329
    for diabetes, 460
    gynecological, 382
    for teen females, 381, 382
    for teen males, 376
    vision, 336
    wellness exams, 352–353, 421
Health skills, 10–17. See also
        specific skills
    accessing information, 11–12,
        21, 50, 120, 164, 245, 250,
        269, 309, 405, 425, 461, 483
    advocacy, 15, 234, 288, 381, 457
    analyzing influences, 14, 430,
        449
    communication skills, 15, 181
    conflict resolution, 16, 209
    decision making, 36–41, 93,
        284, 299, 350, 514
    drug-free school campaign, 314
    goal setting, 42–46, 52–53, 79
    interpersonal communication,
        15–17
    diabetes management, 372
    practicing healthful behaviors,
        12, 89, 377, 410, 420, 491
    refusal skills, 16, 193, 254, 319
    self-management, 12, 368
    stress management, 13,
        166–167, 280, 391
    tobacco, 245, 250, 254
Health triangle, 5, 9
    interrelationships in, 5–7, 62
    mind-body connection in, 8
    wellness and balance in, 7
Hearing, 337–338

Heart, 76, 82, 267, 268
Heart and lung endurance, 62, 76
Heart attack, 235, 447–448
Heart disease, 131, 233, 235, 446–449
Heart rate, 82, 233
Heart transplants, 450
Heat exhaustion, 94, 483
Heatstroke, 94, 483–484
Helmets, 87, 94
H.E.L.P. decision-making criteria,
        38, 187
Hepatitis, 415–416, 425
Heredity, 18–19, 146, 383–384, 446
Hernias, 376
Heroin, 307, 313
High blood pressure, 267, 447
Hiking safety, 485
Hinge joints, 67
Histamines, 442
HIV (human immunodeficiency
        virus), 331, 427–430. See also
        AIDS
    and drug use, 307, 308
Hives, 442
HMOs (health maintenance
        organizations), 354
Home. See also Families
    conflicts at, 204
    safety in, 477
Homicide, 211
Honesty, 152
Hormones, 157, 370, 375
Hospices, 354
Hot lines, 165, 221
Hot weather safety, 483–484
Hugh O'Brian Youth
        Leadership, 50
Human papilloma virus (HPV), 423
Hurricanes, 488
Hurt feelings, 203
Hygiene, 418–420
Hypertension, 448
Hyperthyroidism, 373
Hypothermia, 94, 489
Hypothyroidism, 373

I

"I" messages, 176
Ibuprofen, 348
Identity, 149, 368
Illegal drugs, 303–308
Illness. See Diseases
Immune system, 407–412
Immunity (to disease), 412
Immunizations, 348, 412, 421
Impulsive behaviors, 36, 38, 39,
        154
Individual differences, 365–366
Individual health

caring for. See Personal health
        care
    environmental factors
        contributing to, 9
    influences on, 14, 21–22
    media influence on, 22
    and stress, 13, 156
    technology influence on, 22
Individual sports, 86
Individual therapy, 164
Infants
    choking first aid for, 496
    fetal alcohol syndrome,
        269–270
    growth and development
        of, 389
    of smoking mothers, 249
    and vehicle safety, 482
Infections
    as cause of nervous system
        damage, 275
    definition of, 402
    ear, 337
    immune system's response
        to, 411
Infertility, 381
Inflammation, 408
Influences
    analyzing. See Analyzing
        influences
    on consumer choices, 341
    on decisions, 39–41
    on food choices, 114–115
    on health, 18–22
    internal/external, 14
Influenza, 239, 240, 414
Infomercials, 342
Information
    accessing. See Accessing
        information
    right to, 345
    sources of, 11–12
    validity of, 11–12
Ingredient lists, 108
Inguinal hernias, 376
Inhalants, 308
Inhaling, 238
Inherited traits, 18–19, 396
Injuries
    accidental, 91–92, 276–277, 473,
        477, 479
    as cause of nervous system
        damage, 273–274
    common, 92–93
    coping with, 182
    flexibility for prevention of, 63
    preventing, 27, 91–92, 335,
        477, 479
    P.R.I.C.E. formula for, 95

related to drug use, 303–308
responding to. *See* First aid
treatment of, 70
Inner ears, 338
Insulin, 372, 458–460
Insurance, 354
Integrity, 48
Intensity, of workouts, 81
Interferon, 408
Internal influences, 21–22
Internet, 11–12. *See also* Media
Interpersonal communication,
15. *See also* Communication
skills
Intestines, 124, 126
Intoxication, 265–266
Involuntary muscles, 69
Iris (eye), 335
Iron, 106

J

Job loss, 182
Joints, 63, 66, 67, 462
Journals, 155, 177
JRA (Juvenile rheumatoid
arthritis), 461, 462
Judgment, 265. *See also* Decision
making
Juvenile rheumatoid arthritis
(JRA), 461, 462

K

Kidneys, 125, 267, 268
Kitchens, safety in, 477

L

Labels
food, 109–110
medicine, 349
product, 344
Labia, 379
Land pollution, 510–512, 514–515
Landfills, 510
Language arts connections, 81,
108, 124, 307
Large intestine. *See* Colon
Laser surgery, 336
LDL cholesterol, 106
Legal issues
with alcohol, 266, 281
with anabolic steroid use, 88
in decision making, 38
with driving while intoxicated,
266, 281
with drug possession/use,
313–315
with secondhand smoke, 250
with substance possession/
use, 191

with tobacco, 242, 247
with unmarried minors and
sexual activity, 191
Lens (eye), 335
Leukemia, 452
Libraries, 11
Lice, 333
Lifecycle, 388–390
adolescence and adulthood,
389–390
aging process, 390
birth and infancy, 388–389
childhood, 389
death and dying, 390
Life experiences, 49–50
Lifestyle, 276, 421
Lifting, 70, 276
Ligaments, 66
Lighting, outdoor, 216
Limitations, 43, 151
Liquid wastes, human, 125
Listening skills, 16, 176
Liver, 124, 267, 268, 269. *See also*
Cirrhosis
Liver failure, misuse of medicines
and, 350
Long-term goals, 44, 45
Lunches, 118
Lung cancer, 233, 239, 240, 452
Lung endurance, 62, 76
Lungs, 72, 237, 238, 444, 466
Lyme disease, 406
Lymph, 409
Lymphatic system, 409
Lymphocytes, 409
Lymphoma, 452

M

Macrophages, 409, 411
Magnesium, 106
Mainstream smoke, 248
Major injuries, 93
Males
and abuse, 220
adolescent physical changes in,
365–366
cancer self-exams for, 454
chromosomes determining, 383
daily calorie requirements, 113
reproductive system in, 374–377
Malignant tumors, 452
Managed care plans, 354
Margarine, 106
Marijuana, 305–306, 311, 313
Math connections
calculating BMI, 129
calculating SPF, 94
drunk driving data, 283
personal finances, 255

sports injuries, 26
smoking costs, 255
Maturing, individual rates of,
365–366
Meals, 108, 116–118, 126
Measles, 414–415
Meats, 105–107, 112, 113, 116
Media
advertising development by,
341–342
and alcohol, 278–279
and buying decisions, 341–343
and drugs, 311
as health influence, 14, 22
and health information, 11
as influence on individual and
community health, 22
influences on food choices,
114, 115
as source of information, 11
television, 212
and tobacco, 243, 245–246,
256–257
Media literacy, 246
Media messages, 150
Media watch, 14, 212, 311
Mediation, 208–209
Medical quackery 342, 345, 346
Medical specialists, 353
Medicines, 347–351. *See also*
specific diseases
definition of, 347
misuse of, 350–351
over-the-counter, 348
prescription, 348
safe use of, 349
Melanin, 331
Memory B and T cells, 411, 412
Meningitis, 275
Menstruation, 378–380
Mental conditioning, for
sports, 89
Mental development, 366
Mental needs, 179
Mental/emotional health, 6,
143–165
anxiety disorders, 160
and avoiding unhealthful
behaviors, 154–155
benefits of physical activity to,
61–62
and drug use, 301, 313
interrelationship of physical/
social health and, 5, 7,
61–62
mood disorders, 161
and personality, 146
problems with, 160–165
and self-concept, 149

and self-esteem, 149–152
strategies for identifying
    disorders, 161
and stress management,
    156–158
and suicide, 161–162
survey of, 9
treating problems with,
    163–165
and understanding emotions,
    153–154
warning signs of problems
    with, 161
Messages
    carried by neurons, 273
    "I" messages, 176
    media, 22
Metabolism, 371, 373
Methyl ethyl ketone, 231
Middle ear, 338
Milestones, for long-term goals, 45
Milk, 105, 106, 112, 113
Mind-body connection, 8
Mineral supplements, 116–117
Minerals, 106–107
Minor injuries, 92
Minors, 281
Mirroring thoughts/feelings, 176
Mistakes, learning from, 151
Modified push-ups, 65
Mononucleosis, 415
Mood disorders, 161
Mood swings, 161, 367
Morphine, 307, 313
Motor neurons, 273
Motor skills, 265, 312
Mouth, 123, 237
Mouth cancer, 239, 240
Mouth sores, 240
Movies, tobacco in, 246
Moving, coping with, 182
Mucous membranes, 408
Multiple sclerosis, 274
Mumps, 415
Muscle cramp, 92
Muscle endurance, 62
Muscles, 63, 67–69. See also
    Physical activity and fitness
Muscular system, 67–70
MyPyramid (food pyramid),
    112–114

N

Nail care, 333
Narcotics, 307
National Weather Service (NWS),
    486, 488, 490
Natural disasters, 489–491

Nearsightedness, 337
Negative peer pressure, 187
Negative stress, 13, 156
Neglect, 217
Negotiation, 207–208
Neighborhood Watch
    programs, 216
Neighborhoods, safety in, 482
Nerve endings, 330
Nervous system, 233, 272–277
    alcohol's effect on, 280
    and mind-body connection, 8
    tobacco's effects on, 234
Neurons, 272, 273
Neutrality (conflict
    resolution), 208
Nicotine, 230–231, 233, 245, 254
NK cells, 409
Noise, 338
Noncommunicable diseases,
    440–463
    allergies, 441–443
    arthritis, 461–463
    asthma, 443–445
    cancer, 451–457
    diabetes, 458–460
    heart disease, 446–450
Nonrenewable resources, 516
Nonsmokers, 248–249
Nonverbal communication, 175
Nose, 236
Nuclear families, 178
Nurse practitioner, 44
Nurture, definition of, 179
Nutrient dense foods, 119
Nutrients, 104–107
Nutrition, 105–120, 129–135
    and circulatory system
        health, 76
    and Dietary Guidelines for
        Americans, 107–108
    and eating disorders, 132–133
    and food groups, 112–114
    and MyPyramid, 112–114
    and Nutrition Facts panels,
        109–110
    and physical activity, 134
    and planning healthful meals,
        116–118
    for skeletal/muscular fitness, 70
    for skin health, 331
    and snacks, 119
    for sports, 87–88
    and stress management, 158
    for tooth and gum health, 328
    and weight management,
        129–135
Nutrition Facts panel, 109–110

Nutritionist, 132
Nuts, 105, 117
NWS. See National Weather
    Service

O

Obsessive-compulsive disorder
    (OCD), 160, 164
Occupational Safety and Health
    Administration (OSHA), 513
Oil glands, 330
Oils, 105, 113
Olives, 105
Oncologist, 456
Online information. See Health
    online
Ophthalmologists, 336, 353
Optic nerve, 335
Optimism, 150
Optometrists, 336
Organs, 66, 384, 385. See also
    specific body systems
Orthodontists, 353
Orthopedists, 353
OSHA (Occupational Safety and
    Health Administration), 513
Osteoarthritis, 461, 462
Osteoporosis, 105
OTC medicines. See Over-the-
    counter medicines
Outdoor safety, 480–485
Outer ear, 338
Ovarian cancer, 381
Ovaries, 371, 378, 379
Overeating, 133
Overheating, 94
Over-the-counter (OTC)
    medicines, 299, 348
Overworking (overtraining), 90, 94
Ovulation, 379
Oxygen, 72, 236–238, 509
Ozone, 509

P

Pacemakers, 450
Pain, 95, 348
Pancreas, 124, 371, 459
Paramedic, 313
Parathyroid glands, 371
Parents
    communicating with, 287,
        417, 425
    and health information, 11
    as role models, 50
    seeking help from, 151, 482
Passive smokers, 248
Pasta, 105
Pathogens, 402–406

diseases caused by, 403
immune system's response
to, 411
immunity to, 412
major barriers to, 408
preventing spread of, 418–420
spread of, 404–406
Pathologist, 232
Pedestrian safety, 480
Pediatricians, 353
Peer mediation, 208
Peer pressure, 187–188
and alcohol, 279
as cause of violence, 212
and decision making, 185
and drug use, 311, 317–319
positive/negative, 187–188
as source of conflict, 203
Penis, 375
Peripheral nervous system
(PNS), 272
Personal emergency plans, 491
Personal fitness program, 77–83
Personal health. *See* Individual
health
Personal health care, 328–337
ears, 337–338
eating disorders, 132–133
enhancing/maintaining
through life span, 391–392
eyes, 334–337
hair, 332–333
making decision about, 21–22,
391–392
nails, 333
skin, 330–332
teeth and gums, 328–329
Personal identity, 368
Personal values, 37
Personality, 146
Phagocytes, 408
Pharmacist, 348, 354
Phobias, 160
Phosphorus, 106
Physical abuse, 217
Physical activity and fitness,
60–65, 77–89
balance with food, 108–109
and body composition, 64
for circulatory system
health, 76
definition of, 60
and flexibility, 63
goals of, 43, 64, 77
for heart and lung
endurance, 76
and heart disease, 446
for managing emotions, 155
and muscular endurance, 62

and nutrition, 134
and personal fitness program,
77–83
safety rules for, 91–92
for skeletal/muscular systems,
69
and strength, 62
for stress management, 158
Physical bullying, 213
Physical dependence, 244
Physical development, 365–366
Physical factors,
environmental, 20
Physical health, 4–5
behaviors damaging, 190
benefits of physical activity
to, 61
interrelationship of mental/
emotional/social health and,
5, 7, 61–62
survey of, 9
Physical needs, 179
Physical therapists, 92
Physiological changes (during
pregnancy), 386
Piercings, 331
Pipes (tobacco), 232
Pituitary gland, 371
Pivot joints, 67
Plaque, 329
Plasma, 74
Plastic surgeons, 353
Platelets, 74
PMS (premenstrual
syndrome), 382
Pneumonia, 239, 416
PNS (peripheral nervous
system), 272
Point-of-service (POS) plans, 355
Poisoning, 477
Polio, 275
Pollen, 441
Pollution, 508–516
air, 508, 514
hazardous wastes, 511–512
land, 510–512, 514–515
prevention of, 513–515
solid waste, 510–512
water, 510, 515–516
Pores, 330
POS (point-of-service) plans, 355
Positive peer pressure, 188
Positive stress, 13, 156
Positive thinking, 158
Post-traumatic stress disorder
(PTSD), 160
Posture, 69
Potassium, 107
Potatoes, 105

Poultry, 105
PPOs (preferred provider
organizations), 355
Practicing healthful behaviors
benefits of, 12
for cancer prevention,
453–454, 457
for emergency supplies, 491
for fire safety, 500–501
immune system, 410
for keeping food safe,
120–121
Preferred provider organizations
(PPOs), 355
Pregnancy
abstinence for prevention
of, 192
care during, 385–387
development of fetus during,
384–386
fertilization, 380
physiological changes during,
385, 386
related to drug/alcohol use,
308, 309
tobacco use during, 249
use of medicines during, 350
Prejudice, 204, 212
Premenstrual syndrome
(PMS), 382
Prenatal health, 385–387
Preschoolers, 389
Prescription medicines, 348
Pressure points, 497
Prevention, 26
of abuse, 221
of alcohol use, 190–191
of diseases. *See* Disease
prevention
of drug use, 190–191
of future health problems,
391–392
of injuries, 27, 91–92, 335,
352–353, 391, 477, 479
of school violence, 214, 215
of sports-related injuries, 91–92
of substance abuse, 392
of tobacco use, 190–191
P.R.I.C.E. first aid formula,
95, 499
Primary care providers, 353
Privacy, 181, 220
Probation, 315
Product labels, 344
Product placement, 246
Property (as source of
conflict), 203
Prostate cancer, 376
Prostate gland, 375

Protective sports equipment, 86,87
Proteins, 105, 118
Protozoa, 404
Psychiatrists, 353
Psychological bullying, 213
Psychological dependence, 244
Psychologists, 146
Puberty, 365–368. *See also*
    Adolescence
Public health (government health
    care), 355
Pulmonary circulation, 72
Pulse rate, 82
Pupil (eye), 335
Push-ups, 65

R
Rabies, 275, 276
Radiation therapy, 456
Rape, 211
Reading Is Fundamental, 50
Reading check
    for alcohol, 266, 268, 281, 285,
        286, 288, 289
    for character, 50
    for communicable diseases, 420
    for consumer influences, 342
    for digestive system, 124
    for drugs, 304, 348
    for environment, 508, 509, 514
    for general health, 22
    for growth and development,
        366, 368
    for help for abuse, 221
    for health skills, 44
    for noncommunicable diseases,
        441, 443, 448, 456, 462
    for personal health, 333
    for safety, 473, 474, 479,
        481, 482
    for social health, 179, 181, 183,
        186, 192
    for tobacco, 232, 243, 247, 250,
        251, 252, 254–255
Realistic goals, 43
Recreational safety, 483–485
Recycling, 515
Red blood cells, 74, 75
Red Cross, 484
Reducing waste, 515
Referrals (for mental health
    care), 165
Refusal skills, 16, 192–193
    for alcohol, 286–289
    for drugs, 290–291, 317–319
    for sexual activity, 394–395
    refusing drugs, 319
    S.T.O.P. formula for, 16,
        192–193, 286, 319

    for risk behaviors, 193
    for tobacco, 252–253, 254
    and ways of saying "no,"
        192–193
Relationships
    alcohol's effects on, 283–284
    dating violence, 214
    influence of positive/negative,
        22, 187–188
Relaxation, 158
Reproduction, 374
Reproductive cancers, 452
Reproductive systems, 374–382
    female, 378–382
    male, 375–377
Rescue breathing, 494, 495
Resiliency, 147
Resolving conflicts. *See* Conflict
    resolution
Resources, nonrenewable, 516
Respect, 48, 49, 287
    among friends, 185–186
    for dignity of others, 150
Respiratory diseases, 240
Respiratory system, 233, 234,
    236–241, 442–445
Responsibility, 48, 49, 181,
    189–190
Retina, 335
Reuse of waste, 515
Revenge (as source of
    conflict), 203
Rh factor, 75
Rheumatic fever, 417
Rheumatoid arthritis, 461, 462
Rice, 105
Richter scale, 491
Risk behaviors, 23–27
    abstinence from, 27
    avoiding, 190
    consequences of, 24
    cultural factors in, 21–22
    and cumulative risk, 25
    definition of, 24
    drug use as, 303–308
    percentage of teens
        participating in, 25
Risk factors, 25
    for abuse, 219
    for cancer, 452
Risk(s), 23, 391–392
    cumulative, 25
    of drug abuse, 310–319
    evaluating, 25
    reducing/avoiding, 26
    types of, 23–24
Role models, 50
Rules, family, 181

S
Sadness, 154
Safety, 472–499
    in cold weather, 484
    and emergency supplies kit, 491
    fire safety, 475–478
    and first aid, 493–499
    in fitness programs, 78–79
    in food handling, 120–121
    with guns, 479
    head protection, 276
    in hot weather, 483–484
    and injury prevention, 477, 479
    with medicine use, 349
    in natural disasters, 489–491
    with physical activities, 91–92
    in recreational activities,
        483–485
    right to, 345
    in schools, 214–215, 479
    with sports, 90–93
    in traffic, 480–482
    from violence, 215
    in weather emergencies,
        486–490
    in your neighborhood, 482
Safety belts, 24, 25, 482
Safety consciousness, 473
Saliva, 122, 123, 408
Salivary glands, 123
Salt, 107, 108
Saturated fats, 105–108
Scalp problems, 333
Schedule, fitness, 78
Schizophrenia, 160
School bus, 482
School counselor, 204
Schools
    conflicts at, 204
    risks of alcohol, 282
    risks of drugs, 314
    safety precautions in, 479
    violence prevention in, 214–215
    weapons rules in, 215, 479
    youth court, 215
Science connections
    alcohol, 265
    body decoration, 331
    building bones, 105
    caffeine, 304
    calcium in diet, 105
    depression, 366
    dietary supplements, 117
    epinephrine, 443
    finding a cure, 274
    vision correction, 336
    heart activity and strength, 75
    heart of the matter, 75

schizophrenia, 160
scoliosis, 69
stress chemicals, 13
trans fats, 449
finding a cure, 274
vision correction, 336
West Nile virus, 404
why teens need more sleep, 5
Sclera, 335
Scooters, 481
Screenings. *See* Health screenings
Scrotum, 375
Seafood, 106
Seat belts. *See* Safety belts
Second-degree burns, 498
Secondhand smoke, 248–249
Security systems, school, 215
Self-assessment, 9
Self-concept, 149
Self-confidence, 149, 151
Self-esteem, 149–152
Self-examinations
    cancer, 454
    for females, 381
    for males, 377
Self-management skills, 12. *See also* Practicing healthful behaviors
Semen, 375
Semicircular canals, 338
Sensory neurons, 273
Separation (of parents), 182
Serving sizes, food, 113, 116
Sewage, 510
Sexual abuse, 218
Sexual activity
    abstinence from, 27, 191–192, 425–426, 431
    alcohol and, 267, 283
    disease transmission through, 405
    and HIV, 427–428
    illegal, between unmarried minors, 191
    refusal skills for, 394–395
Sexually transmitted diseases (STDs), 422–431
    abstinence for prevention of, 192
    reducing risk of, 392
    related to drug/alcohol use, 283, 307, 308
    and sterility, 376, 381
Sexually transmitted infections (STIs), 422
Sharing, 181
Shock (in grieving process), 154
Shopping, 343–344
Short-term goals, 44, 45
Sibling, new, 182

Side effects (medicines), 349
Sidestream smoke, 248
Sight, 334–337
Simple carbohydrates, 105
Single-parent families, 178
Skateboarding, 481
Skating, 481
Skeletal muscles, 67–68
Skeletal system, 66–67, 69–70
Skin, 330–332, 408
Skin cancer, 452, 454
Skipping meals, 117
Sleep, 158
Small intestine, 123–124
Small-claims courts, 345
smart shopping, 14
Smog, 509
Smoke alarms, 476
Smoke-free environments, 249–250
Smokeless tobacco, 232, 233, 240
Smoking. *See also* Tobacco
    and circulatory system health, 76
    fires caused by, 476
    legal restriction of, 250
Smooth muscles, 67
Snacks, 119
Snuff, 232
Social development, 368
Social health, 6–7, 174–193
    and abstinence, 190–192
    acting responsibly for, 189–190
    benefits of physical activity to, 62
    communication skills for, 174–177
    and drug use, 302
    effective refusal skills for, 192–193
    and families, 178–183
    and friends, 184–187
    interrelationship of mental/emotional/physical health and, 5, 7, 61–62
    and peer pressure, 187–188
    survey of, 9
Social studies connections, 133, 154, 175, 414
Social workers, 186
Society, hidden costs of smoking to, 251
Sodium, 107–108
Sodium chloride, 106–107
Solid wastes
    in environment, 510–512
    human, 124–126
Sound levels, 338
Speaking skills, 16, 176
Specialists, 353

Sperm cells, 375, 380, 383
SPF rating, 94
Spinal cord, 273
Spinal cord injuries, 273–274
Sports, 85–95
    and anabolic steroids, 88
    individual, 86
    injuries, 91–95
    mental conditioning, 89
    nutrition for, 87–88
    preventing injuries in, 91–92
    protective equipment for, 87
    safety in, 90–92
    team, 86
    tobacco advertising at events, 246
Sprains, 92, 499
Stairs, safety on, 477
Standardized test practice, 33, 57, 101, 141, 171, 199, 227, 261, 295, 325, 361, 399, 437, 469, 505, 523
Starches, 105
STDs. *See* Sexually transmitted diseases
Sterility, 376, 381
Steroids, anabolic, 88, 308
Stimulants, 89, 304
Stirrup (ear), 338
STIs (sexually transmitted infections), 422
Stomach, 123, 267
Stomach acid, 408
Stomach ulcers, 233, 267
S.T.O.P. refusal model, 16, 192–193, 286, 319
Storms, 486, 488–490
Strategies. *See also* Decision making
    for abuse prevention, 221
    for abuse prevention/intervention, 221
    for avoiding gangs, 212
    for avoiding violence, 214
    for circulatory system health, 76
    for conflict resolution, 206–209
    for coping with family changes/challenges, 182
    for digestive/excretory system health, 126
    for environmental protection, 513–519
    for good health, 107–109
    of healthy families, 180–183
    for identifying mental/emotional disorders, 161
    for managing emotions, 154–155
    prevention as, 26

for reaching fitness goals, 78
for reaching goals, 44–46
for risk reduction, 26
for self-esteem and self-confidence, 151
for skeletal/muscular system health, 69–70
Strength training. *See* Weight training
Strength(s)
  exercises for, 63
  focusing on, 151
  in goal setting, 42
  physical, 62
  test for, 64
Strep throat, 416–417
Stress, 13, 156–158
  and family health, 182
  how to avoid, 157
  managing. *See* Stress management
Stress fracture, 93
Stress management, 13, 158, 391
  alternatives to alcohol, 281
  and asthma, 445
  dealing with emotions, 280
  and heart disease, 449
  learning, 166–167
  reducing, 391
  managing anger, 368
Stressors, 157
Stretching exercises, 80
Strokes, 233, 235, 267, 448
Students Against Destructive Decisions (SADD), 50, 283
Substance abuse counselors, 270
Substance use/abuse, 303–308. *See also* Drugs
  and commitment to abstinence, 190–192
  legal issues with, 191
  prevention of, 392
Sudden Infant Death Syndrome, 249
Sugars, 105, 108, 114, 116
Suicide, 161–162
Sun exposure
  and cancer, 453
  and ozone layer, 509
  and skin health, 331
  when playing sports, 94
Sunscreen, 94, 331
Supplements, vitamin and mineral, 116–117
Support, within family, 180
Support groups, 255, 269
Surface water, 510
Surgery
  for cancer, 456

eye, 336
  for heart disease, 450
Swallowing, 123
Syphilis, 424
Systemic circulation, 72
Systems, body. *See* Body systems

T
T cells, 409, 410, 411, 427, 428
Tact, 176
T.A.L.K. strategy, 207, 209
Talking (stress management), 158
Target audience, 246
Target heart rate, 82
Tartar, 329
Tattoos, 331
Teachers, help from, 205
Team sports, 86
Tears, 408
Technology, health influences of, 22
Teeth and gums, 123, 126, 328–329
Television, 22, 212
Tendonitis, 92
Tendons, 66
Territory (as source of conflict), 203
Testes (testicles), 371, 375
Testicular cancer, 376
Testosterone, 375
Therapy, 163–164
Thinking
  abilities during teen years, 389–390
  critical, 36
  positive, 158
Third-degree burns, 498
Thunderstorms, 489
Thyroid diseases, 373
Thyroid gland, 371, 373
Ticks, 406
Time
  family, 180
  management of, 157
  of workouts, 81
Tinnitus, 338
Tissues, 384, 385
Tobacco, 230–235, 242–251
  abstinence from, 27, 190–191
  addiction to, 244–245
  and air pollution, 514
  avoiding, 252–255
  benefits of not using, 253
  effects of, 233–235
  forms of, 232
  and heart disease, 449
  hidden costs of, 251

illegal use of, 191
  nonsmokers and effects of, 248–250
  quitting use of, 254–255
  reasons for using, 242–243
  substances in, 230–231
Toddlers, 389
Toenails, 333
Tolerance, 245
Tooth decay, 108, 233, 329
Tornadoes, 487–488
Toxic shock syndrome (TSS), 381
Trachea, 123, 237
Traffic safety, 480–482
Tranquilizers, 305
Trans fats, 449
Trans-fatty acids, 106
Trustworthiness, 48, 49, 185
TSS (toxic shock syndrome), 381
Tuberculosis, 239, 416
Tumors, 451–452

U
Ulcers, 267, 269
Ultraviolet (UV) rays, 331, 334
Umbilical cord, 385
Unintentional injuries. *See* Accidental injuries
Unsaturated fats, 105
Ureters, 125
Urethra, 125, 375
Urine, 125
Urologists, 353
U.S. Department of Agriculture (USDA), 107, 112
Uterus, 378, 379, 381
UV rays. *See* Ultraviolet rays
Uvula, 123

V
Vaccines, 275, 348, 412, 416, 430
Vagina, 379
Vaginitis, 381
Values, 37–40, 179, 187, 203
Vegetable oils, 105
Vegetables, 106, 107, 112, 113, 117
Vehicular safety, 482
Veins, 71, 72
Ventricles, 72
Verbal bullying, 213
Verbal communication, 175
Victims, of abuse, 220
Villi, 123–124
Violence, 211–216
  and acts of revenge, 203
  alcohol and, 284–285
  bullying, 213
  causes of, 211–212

in communities, 216
consequences of, 211, 213,
217–220
and dating, 214
and nonviolent ways to respond,
194, 196, 206–209, 210, 222,
223, 224, 227, 368
prevention of, 214–216
protection from, 214, 215, 482
in schools, 214–215
in society, 211
Viruses
cold, 413
definition of, 403
HIV, 427–430
spread of, 404
Vision, 334–337
Vitamin supplements, 116–117
Vitamins, 106, 118, 330
Vocational goals, 44. *See also*
Careers
Voluntary muscles, 68

W

Warm-up exercises, 80
Warning labels, 250
Warranties, 344
Waste management, 514–515
Wastes
biodegradable, 511
hazardous, 511–512
human, 124–126
Water
conservation of, 516, 517
contaminated, 405

hot weather safety, 483–484
in human body, 125
as a nutrient, 107, 126
pollution of, 510, 515–516
when playing sports, 88, 94
Water safety, 484
Water-soluble vitamins, 106
Weapons, 211, 479
Weather emergencies, 486–490
Weight
and alcohol tolerance, 266
and diabetes, 459, 460
and fad diets, 135
healthy, 129
and heart disease, 449
management of, 129–135
Weight training, 84–85
Wellness, 7, 129
Wellness exams, 352–353
West Nile virus, 404, 406
What Teens Think, 6, 48, 78, 114,
150, 185, 207, 246, 279, 301,
342, 389, 404, 447, 477, 510
White blood cells, 74
Withdrawal, 244, 254, 287
Working out. *See* Exercise(s);
Fitness
Writing skills
for alcohol, 264, 278, 282, 286
for abuse prevention, 217
for body systems, 122
for character, 47
for communicable diseases,
402, 407, 413, 418, 422, 427
for conflict resolution, 206

for consumer choices, 340
for drugs, 303, 310, 316
for environment, 508, 513
for food and nutrition, 104,
111, 116, 128
for general health, 4, 18
for goal setting, 42
for growth and development,
364, 370, 374, 383, 385
for health care, 352
for health decisions, 10, 36
for health skills, 36
for mental/emotional health,
144, 153, 156, 159, 163
for nervous system, 272
for noncommunicable diseases,
440, 446, 451, 458
for personal health, 328, 334
for physical activity and fitness,
60, 66, 71, 77, 84, 91
for respiratory system, 236
for risk behavior, 23
for safety, 472, 475, 480,
486, 493
for social health, 174, 178,
184, 189
for tobacco, 230, 242, 252
Written communication, 177

X

Xrays, 455

Y

Youth court, 215
Youth Volunteer Corps, 50

Photo Credits